Expositions of the Psalms

Augustinian Heritage Institute, Inc.

THE WORKS OF SAINT AUGUSTINE
A Translation for the 21st Century

Part III – Books
Volume 17:
Expositions of the Psalms
51-72

THE WORKS OF SAINT AUGUSTINE
A Translation for the 21st Century

Expositions of the Psalms
51-72

III/17

translation and notes by
Maria Boulding, O.S.B.

editor
John E. Rotelle, O.S.A.

New City Press
Hyde Park, New York

Published in the United States by New City Press
202 Comforter Blvd., Hyde Park, New York 12538
©2001 Augustinian Heritage Institute

Cover picture (paperback): From the choir books of the Augustinian Monastery of Lecceto, Italy:
A group of faithful giving praise to God. Artist: Pellegrino di Mariano. 15th Century, Siena, Biblioteca
Comunale.

Library of Congress Cataloging-in-Publication Data:

Augustine, Saint, Bishop of Hippo.
    The works of Saint Augustine.
    "Augustinian Heritage Institute"
    Includes bibliographical references and indexes.
    Contents: — pt. 3, v .15. Expositions of the Psalms, 1-32
—pt. 3, v. 1. Sermons on the Old Testament, 1-19.
— pt. 3, v. 2. Sermons on the Old Testament, 20-50 — [et al.] — pt. 3,
v. 10 Sermons on various subjects, 341-400.
    1. Theology — Early Church, ca. 30-600. I. Hill,
Edmund. II. Rotelle, John E.   III. Augustinian
Heritage Institute.   IV. Title.
BR65.A5E53   1990   270.2   89-28878
ISBN 1-56548-055-4 (series)
ISBN 1-56548-156-9 (pt. 3, v. 17)
ISBN 1-56548-155-0 (pt. 3, v. 17: pbk.)

2nd printing November 2012
3rd printing January 2013

We are indebted to Brepols Publishers, Turnholt, Belgium,for their use of the Latin critical text of *Enarrationes
in Psalmos I-CL*, ed. D. Eligius Dekkers, O.S.B. et Johannes Fraipont, *Corpus Christianorum Latinorum*
XXXVIII-XL (Turnholt, 1946) 1-2196.

Nihil Obstat: John E. Rotelle, O.S.A., S.T.L., Censor Deputatus
Imprimatur: + Patrick Sheridan, D.D., Vicar General
                Archdiocese of New York, July 22, 1999

The *Nihil Obstat* and *Imprimatur* are official declarations that a book or pamphlet is free of doctrinal or moral
error.No implication is contained therein that those who have granted the *Nihil Obstat* and *Imprimatur* agree
with the contents, opinions or statements expressed.

Printed in the United States of America

Contents

Verses 20-22. Persevering refusal of the truth — 73; Verse 22. But heretics have their usefulness — 74; God's word seems hard, but it is tender to believers — 76; Verse 23. The power of the gentle words — 77; Verse 24. Donatists are bound for the pit as perpetrators of violence and deceit — 78

Verse 1. The people who objected to a title — 81; The title, concluded: the winepress — 83; Verse 2. The trampling process — 84; Verses 3-4. "The height of the day" — 85; Health, insensibility and immortality are three different states — 86; Verse 5. Yours, because God gave; yours only if you confess the gift — 88; Verse 6. Like Master, like servant — 89; Verse 7. The enemies that lurk within the Church — 89; Verse 8. Salvation is free — 93; Verse 9. Proclaiming the life you have, but not for yourself — 94; Verse 10. Walk behind, and be corrected — 95; God, but my God too — 96; Chaste love is disinterested love — 97; Verses 11-12. Sacrifice from within — 99; Verse 13. The light of the living — 100

Introduction: Christ's command and example of love; head and body — 103; Verse 1. The Jews, imitating Saul, persecuted the true David — 104; How Christ, like David, hid in a cave — 106; Verse 2. The whole Christ prays, and teaches us to pray — 107; Verse 3. God is most high, yet near — 108; Verse 4. Prophecy fulfilled: Christ is raised, and the Jews carry the scriptures for us — 109; Christ is mercy and truth — 110; Verse 5. Christ's willing sleep; Jewish responsibility — 111; Verse 6. Christ's glory pervades the earth — 113; Verse 7. Sinners always entrap themselves — 114; Verse 8. The prepared heart — 116; Verse 9. One risen flesh, two melodies — 117; Verses 10-12. Mercy as high as heaven, truth down to the clouds — 118

Verses 1-2. Do not treat others as you would not wish to be treated — 120; An illustration: what if you stand to gain dishonestly? — 121; The Lord's judgment on hypocrisy — 123; Verse 3. The chains of sin — 125; Verse 4. You are still in the womb of the Church — 126; The aborted Donatists — 127; Verses 5-6. Scriptural imagery comes from various sources; read with discernment — 128; Willful deafness; the Sanhedrin and Stephen — 130; Willful deafness: the Donatists — 130; Learn from the snake's tactics — 131; Verse 7. Convicted out of their own mouths — 133; The inconsistency of the Donatists with regard to the law — 135; Verse 8. Do not be intimidated by the torrent of impiety — 138; Verse 9. Sin is its own punishment — 139; Conquer bodily desires before they grow too strong — 141; Verse 10. The bramble, the fire, and the thorns — 142; Verse 11. How to wash your hands in the blood of sinners — 144; Verse 12. The just rejoice even in this life — 145; Conclusion: building on rock — 146

Verse 1. The uncorrupted title — 148; The whole Christ speaks in the psalms — 149; Saul attempts to kill David, and the Jews to kill faith in the resurrection — 150; Verses 2-3. The cry of the persecuted Christ — 151; Verse 4. The self-styled strong and the humbly weak

expounding the psalm, Augustine appended the following remarks about an astrologer whom he pointed out among the people — 227

blush over me" — 376; Verse 8. The right kind of shamelessness — 377; Verses 9-10. Christ's own people did not recognize him — 378; Verses 11-13. Fasting, sackcloth and derision — 379; Verse 14. Turn to God by prayer — 381; Verses 15-16. You may be mud-bound in body while free in spirit. Crying to God from the pit — 381

Exposition of Psalm 51

A Sermon to the People[1]

Introduction: the background to the psalm, Saul and David

1. We have undertaken to speak to you, dearest friends,[2] about a psalm that is short, certainly; but its title may give us a little trouble. Bear with us patiently while we disentangle it as best we can, and as the Lord enables us; for these questions must not be passed over too lightly, especially since some of our brethren have decided not only to take in what we say with their ears and hearts, but also to commit it to writing. So we have to think of readers as well as hearers.

A particular historical event gave rise to this psalm, an event which is related in the Book of the Kingdoms[3] in a passage which we selected to be read out to you. Saul was chosen as king by the Lord, but not with a view to permanence; he was granted to the people at the request of their hard, stubborn hearts,[4] and granted to them not because he was good for them but to teach them a lesson, as sacred scripture indicates when it says of God, *He raises a hypocrite to royal rank, because of the people's perversity* (Jb 34:30). Saul was a man of this character, so he kept on persecuting David.[5] But in David God was foreshadowing a reign of eternal salvation, and he had chosen David to abide for ever in his posterity. Our King, the King of the ages, with whom we shall reign eternally, was descended from David according to the flesh.[6] Now since God had chosen David, chosen him in advance and predestined him to be king, it was not God's will that David should take possession of his kingdom until he had freed him from his persecutors. Such was the divine decision, so that in this respect David might prefigure us, the body of which Christ is the head. Think about it: if even our head willed to reign in heaven only after he had completed his travail on earth, and willed only by way of suffering to raise to glory the body he had received below, what business have the members to hope that they will be more fortunate than their head? *If they have called the master of the household Beelzebub, how much more his servants?* (Mt 10:25). Let us not hope for an easier[7]

---

1. Possibly preached in the winter of 412-413, at Carthage.
2. *Caritati vestrae.*
3. In our usage, 1 Samuel.
4. See 1 Sm 8:7.
5. See 1 Sm 19-30.
6. See Rom 1:3.
7. Variant: "a better."

path; let us go where he went first, let us follow where he led. If we stray from the path he traced, we are lost.

So you see what was foreshadowed in David, and you see what was foreshadowed in Saul: a bad kingdom in Saul, a good kingdom in David; death in Saul and life in David. The only thing that really persecutes us is death: death, over which we shall triumph in the end, demanding, *Where is your strife, O death? Where, O death, is your sting?* (1 Cor 15:55). What do I mean by saying that our only persecutor is death? I mean that if we were not mortal, the enemy would have no power against us. Can he do anything to hurt the angels? But death, our fiercest persecutor, will be done away with eventually even in us, if we are found to be just, as it has already been done away with in our head. Its struggle against us will be over in the end, when we rise from the dead. For in dying Christ became death's slayer, and death died in him rather than he in death.

2. Now let us consider the name itself, for it is fraught with mysterious meaning. "Saul" is interpreted "request," and that implies desire for something. It can hardly be doubted that we brought death on ourselves, for death was born from human sin. It is true to say, then, that human beings themselves desired death, and so death's name is "Request." Scripture tells us, *God did not make death, and he takes no pleasure in the destruction of the living. God created all things to be, and endowed all the nations of the world with the capacity to be healed.* And then, as though you had asked where death could have come from, it continues, *But by deeds and words the godless invited death, and believing it to be their friend, they were submerged* (Wis 1:13.14.16). They sank by desiring it, and rushed toward death thinking it to be their friend, just as the people thought they were getting a friend when they begged for a king who turned out to be their enemy. They wheedled a king from the Lord, and they were given Saul. But it would be truer to say that having with deeds and words invited death they were delivered into death's hands, and in getting Saul they found death. This is why the 17th psalm bears the title, *On the day when the Lord whisked David to safety from the hand of all his enemies, and from the hand of Saul* (Ps 17(18):1). It first says, *all his enemies* and then, *from the hand of Saul*, because death will be the last enemy to be destroyed.[8] Why does it say, *and from the hand of Saul*? Because Christ has plucked us from hell and freed us from the clutches of death.

The title, continued. David, kingly and priestly, is betrayed by Doeg

3. While the holy man David was on the run from Saul's persecution, he fled to a place where he thought he would be safe. He passed by the house of a priest named Ahimelech, and accepted loaves from him. In so doing he acted in the

---

8. See 1 Cor 15:26.

role not of a king only, but of a priest too, because he ate the Bread of the Presence which *it was unlawful for anyone other than the priests to eat,* as the Lord reminds us in the gospel (Mt 12:4). Saul, when later he began to hunt him, was angry with his retainers because none of them was willing to betray David. The story has just been read from the Book of the Kingdoms. But there was a man present that day named Doeg, who was an Edomite and the principal herdsman in Saul's service; he too had come to Ahimelech the priest. He was present again when Saul raged against his followers because none of them would betray David. Doeg revealed where he had seen him. Saul immediately sent for the priest and all his family to be brought before him, and ordered that they be killed. Not one of Saul's entourage dared raise a hand against the priests of the Lord, even under orders from the king. But this Doeg, who had betrayed David's whereabouts, was like Judas; he did not recoil from his evil purpose but persisted in bringing forth fruit from that same root even to the end, the kind of fruit typical of a rotten tree. So at the king's order Doeg slew the priest and all his family, and afterwards the city of the priests was demolished.[9]

We have seen, then, that this man Doeg was the enemy of both David the king and Ahimelech the priest.[10] Doeg was a single person, but he represents a whole class of people. Similarly David embodies both king and priest,[11] like one man with a dual personality, though the human race is one. So too at the present time and in our world let us recognize these two groups of people, so that what we sing, or hear sung, may profit us. Let us recognize Doeg still with us today, as we recognize the kingly and priestly body today, and so we shall recognize the body that is opposed to king and priest still.[12]

David and Doeg, the two opposing kingdoms

4. Notice from the outset how mysteriously significant their names are. Doeg is said to mean "Movement," and Edomite means "Earthly." Already you can see what kind of people this "Movement," this Doeg, symbolizes: the kind that does not remain stable for ever, but is destined to be moved elsewhere. As for "Earthly": why expect any fruit from an earthly person? But the heavenly humans will last for ever. [13]

---

9. See 1 Sm 21:1-9; 22:7-19.
10. A crucial point in the argument he is about to build up; see following note.
11. *David et corpus ipsum regis et sacerdotis.* Augustine contrasts two "bodies" throughout this sermon: the body of Christ and the "body" of the worldly-minded. They correspond to the two opposed cities, or kingdoms, a theme dear to Augustine.
12. Opposed, that is, to the body of Christ, royal and priestly by participation in him.
13. The editors of the Latin text by changing one letter and punctuating differently extract the meaning, "Why expect heavenly fruit from an earthly person? A human being will. . . ."

So, to put it briefly and succinctly, there is an earthly kingdom in this world today, but there is also a heavenly kingdom. Each of them has its pilgrim citizens, both the earthly kingdom and the heavenly, the kingdom that is to be uprooted and the kingdom that is to be planted for eternity. For the present the citizens of both are thoroughly mixed together in this world: the body of the earthly kingdom is intermingled with the body of the heavenly. The heavenly kingdom groans as the citizens of the earthly kingdom surround it; and from time to time the earthly kingdom presses the citizens of the heavenly kingdom into service, as the heavenly kingdom for its part also commandeers the citizens of the earthly kingdom. We must not pass over this fact in silence; we will demonstrate both points to you from the divine scriptures. Daniel and the three young men in Babylon were made responsible for the king's business;[14] and Joseph in Egypt was given a position second only to that of the king and empowered to administer the affairs of state[15]—that very state from which God's people would later be rescued. Joseph was, in a sense, giving enforced service to the state, as were the three young men and Daniel. It is obvious, therefore, that the earthly kingdom had taken citizens of the heavenly kingdom into its employment, for its own purposes and to serve that earthly kingdom, but not to further its evil practices. But now what about the kingdom of heaven: how does it take the citizens of the earthly kingdom into temporary employment in this world? Well, did the apostle not speak of people who were spreading the gospel from murky motives, preaching about the kingdom of heaven, but on the lookout all the time for earthly rewards? They were seeking their own ends even while proclaiming Christ. Yet even these men were enlisted as mercenaries for the service of the kingdom of heaven, as you know, and the apostle was glad of it. *There are some people*, he says, *who proclaim Christ not from pure motives but out of jealousy and in a quarrelsome spirit, thinking to stir up trouble for me in my imprisonment. But what does it matter? Whether in sincerity or through opportunism, let Christ be preached. I rejoice over this, and will continue to rejoice* (Phil 1:17-19). Christ too showed up such people when he said, "*The scribes and Pharisees have taken their place in the chair of Moses; do what they tell you, but do not imitate what they do, for they talk, but do not act accordingly* (Mt 23:2-3). What they say belongs to David, what they do, to Doeg. Listen to me through them, but beware of imitating them." These two categories of people coexist on earth today, and of them our psalm sings.

---

14. See Dn 2:49.
15. See Gn 41:40-44.

Verses 1-2. The hidden meaning of the title

5. The psalm carries this title: *To the end, understanding for David, when Doeg the Edomite came and told Saul, "David came into Abimelech's house."* Yet we read that it was to the house of Ahimelech that he came. We might quite reasonably assume that the variations in the title are due to the similarity of the two names, and dismiss them as a discrepancy that affects only one syllable, or rather one letter. Yet when we examined the codices of the psalms we found Abimelech more often than Ahimelech. Moreover in another place you find a very well-known psalm offering not a variant but a different name altogether: I am referring to the title of that other psalm which runs, *When he altered his behavior in the presence of Abimelech*,[16] whereas David altered his behavior in the presence of King Achis, not King Abimelech, and forsook him, and went away. The change of name alerts us to the mystery. Without it, you might simply concentrate on an historical episode and ignore the sacred veils that conceal the meaning. The name we are examining in that other psalm, Abimelech, is said to mean "my father's kingdom." Now in what sense did David leave his father's kingdom? Surely it refers to Christ's leaving the kingdom of the Jews and moving over to the Gentiles? Perhaps this is why, when the prophetic spirit wished to assign a title to our present psalm, the name chosen was not Ahimelech but Abimelech, because it was when David came to "his father's kingdom" that he was betrayed. And in the same way when our Lord Jesus Christ came to the kingdom of the Jews, that kingdom which had been founded by his Father, but of which Christ said to the Jews, *The kingdom of God will be taken away from you, and given to a nation that brings forth the fruit of it, righteousness* (Mt 21:43), then it was that he was betrayed to death; and "death" is what the name "Saul" signifies.

But David was not killed, any more than was Isaac, who also prefigured our Lord's passion. However, the prefiguration was not achieved without bloodshed, in the one case by the slaying of a ram,[17] and in the other by that of the priest Ahimelech. It would not have been opportune for those people to be killed for whom resurrection was not yet opportune; Jesus preferred to signify their resurrection by delivering their lives from mortal peril, even at the cost of shed blood. In this way the resurrection was symbolized in them, but the reality of it was reserved for our true Lord. Much more could be said on this subject, if we had undertaken to treat in this sermon of the mysteries latent in the events.[18]

---

16. See Ps 33(34).
17. See Gn 22:13.
18. The editors of the Latin text amend the last sentences as follows: ". . .opportune, but only that their lives should be delivered from mortal peril. However, the shedding of blood was a more powerful symbol of the resurrection, which was thus prefigured in them. But since the resurrection was reserved for our Lord, many more things could be said on this subject, if we. . . ."

The mingling of good and evil, and their ultimate sifting

6. We have finished dealing with the title—rather too elaborately and long-windedly perhaps, but as the Lord enabled us—so now let us listen to what is said about the two categories of people. Think carefully about these two kinds: the one composed of those who labor, the other of those amid whom the laboring goes on; the one that thinks about the earth, the other that reflects on the things of heaven; the one consisting of people who sink their hearts to the depths, the other of people who unite their hearts with the angels; the one composed of those who trust in the earthly resources with which this world abounds, the other of people who set their hopes on the heavenly rewards promised by a God who does not deceive.[19] But these two groups of people are mixed together. We find a citizen of Jerusalem, a citizen of the kingdom of God, entrusted with secular administration. He may wear the purple, or be an officer of state, or a magistrate, or a proconsul, or a general. He discharges civic duties, but he keeps his heart raised above them if he is a Christian, a believer, a Godfearing person, one who sets little store by the circumstances in which he finds himself and puts his hope in those he has not attained yet. The holy woman Esther was of this type. Though the wife of a king, she put herself in danger to plead for her compatriots. When she prayed to God, in whose presence there can be no dishonesty, she confessed that her royal finery was no better than a soiled rag in his eyes.[20]

We should not despair of the citizens of the heavenly kingdom, therefore, when we see them transacting the business of Babylon[21] or dealing with earthly matters in this earthly political arena; on the other hand, nor should we too hastily congratulate all those whom we see handling heavenly business. Pestiferous people are sometimes found seated in the chair of Moses, and concerning them we are warned, *Do what they tell you, but do not imitate what they do, for they talk, but do not act accordingly* (Mt 23:3). The former lift up their hearts to heaven from the midst of earthly things; the latter talk of heavenly things but drag their hearts in the mud. The time for winnowing will come, when the two kinds will be sifted out with the utmost care, so that never a grain will be dropped into the heap of straw set aside for burning, nor a wisp of chaff find its way into the heap of grain to be stored in the barn.[22]

---

19. Here the editors of the Latin text insert the following variant, some of which occurs further on: "We must not despair of good people who undertake the administration of earthly business; nor, on the other hand, should we too hastily congratulate those who are seen to deal with heavenly matters. It often happens that people involved in secular business keep their hearts raised up all the time, while those who are for ever proclaiming heavenly realities are dragging their hearts along the ground."

20. See Est 14:16.

21. The type of the earthly city: see Exposition 2 of Psalm 26, 18, and Exposition of Psalm 44, 25, and notes there.

22. See Mt 3:12.

Well then, as long as the two kinds are mixed together, let us hear our own voice in this psalm: the voice of heaven's citizens, that is; for it must be our aim to tolerate bad people here, rather than be tolerated ourselves by the good. Let us unite ourselves to heaven's citizens with our ears and tongues and hearts and works. If we do that, the speaker in this psalm is ourselves, and we are speaking the very words we hear. So now let us deal with the evil body first, the body of the earthly kingdom.

Verse 3. The power to build is greater than the power to destroy

7. *Why does he boast of his malice, this one who is powerful?* Listen, brothers and sisters, to the boasting of malevolence, the boasting of bad people. What do they boast of? *Why does he boast of his malice, this one who is powerful?* That is to say, what does a person powerful in malice have to boast about? It is a fine thing to be powerful, as long as it is in goodness, not in malice. Is there anything great about boasting of malice? Few people have the ability to build a house, but any fool can destroy one. Few have the power to sow seed, cultivate the crop, wait until it matures, and then enjoy the fruit on which the labor was expended; but anyone can set fire to the whole crop with a single spark. To beget or bear a child,[23] to feed the child once born, to bring up a boy or girl to young adulthood—this is a mighty task; but anyone at all can kill the youngster in a single moment. Destruction is very easy.

Let anyone who boasts, boast in the Lord (1 Cor 1:31), let anyone minded to boast, boast of goodness. Yet you boast that you are powerful in wickedness. What are you going to do, then, you powerful person, you with your loud-mouthed boasting? You are going to kill someone, are you? But a scorpion can do that, one short bout of fever can do that, and so can a poisonous toadstool. Is all your power reduced to this—equality with a poisonous toadstool?

What about the good citizens of Jerusalem, who boast not of malice but of goodness? This is how they conduct themselves. First of all they glory not in themselves but in the Lord. Then, they take great care over whatever they do in the way of building up, and they make things that are strong enough to last. If they have to do anything destructive, it is only in order to discipline people who are making progress, not to oppress the innocent.[24] When the earthly body is compared with power like this, surely it can hear the challenge, *Why does he boast of his malice, this one who is powerful?*

---

23. *Suscipere infantem*: the phrase can be used of either parent.
24. A possible reference to criticisms leveled by outsiders and heretics against Christian magistrates.

Verse 4. The malicious person's inner torment; the razor's work

8. *All day long your tongue is engaged with injustice.* When the psalm says, *all day long*, it implies without wearying, without respite, without ceasing. And when you are not performing evil deeds, you think about them, so that when there is nothing bad on your hands you at least make sure that evil is not absent from your heart. Either you are doing something malignant or, when you have no opportunity to do it, you speak evil by uttering maledictions or, when you cannot even do that, you desire evil and devise it. And you do this *all day long*, without a break.

We expect such a person to incur punishment. But is he not already a punishment to himself, and no light one either? You may threaten him, but when you do so, to what kind of fate do you want to consign him? Leave him to himself. If you wanted to be very severe, you would cast him to the wild beasts, but he is worse than the beasts to himself. A wild animal would only savage his body; but he cannot refrain from injuring his own heart. He is raging against himself inside, and are you looking to rain blows on him outside? No, pray to God for him, that he may be delivered from himself.

However, in this psalm, brothers and sisters, there is neither prayer for the wicked nor prayer against the wicked; there is simply a prophecy of what will happen to the wicked. You must not think that the psalm is saying anything out of spite; what is said is uttered in the spirit of prophecy.

9. So what is the outcome? All your power, all your planning of iniquity throughout the day, all the malice you revolve on your tongue without ceasing—what has it achieved? What effect has it had? *You worked your guile like a sharp razor.* This is what the wicked do to the saints—just shave off their hair! Why do I say that?

Well now, if there are any citizens of Jerusalem listening, persons of such caliber that they can hear their Lord, their King, as he bids them, *Do not be afraid of those who kill the body, but cannot kill the soul* (Mt 10:28), and that question too that was read out in the gospel just now, *What advantage is it to anyone to gain even the whole world, and suffer the ruin of his own soul?* (Mt 16:26)—if there are any such, I say, they make light of all the good things of this present life, and even of life itself. What harm can Doeg's razor do to those who while on earth meditate on the kingdom of heaven, and will one day be in the kingdom of heaven, having God with them and abiding for ever with God? What will that razor do? It will shave off the hair and leave a bald scalp. And this relates a person to Christ, who was crucified at a place called Calvary.[25] It makes us the children of Korah, a name which is said to mean "baldness." Hair symbolizes a

---

25. This play on "Calvary," the "place of the skull," as derived from *calvitium* (baldness), and on the "children of Korah," is found also in Augustine's Expositions of Psalms 41,2; 43,1; 44,1; 46,2; 68,9.

superfluity of temporal goods. This is not to say that God had no purpose in creating hair for the human body; no, he gave it to us as an adornment. However, since we feel nothing when hair is cut off, those who cling to God in their hearts regard earthly things as though they were no more than hair.

Still, hair can sometimes be put to good use, as when you break your bread to the hungry, when you take a homeless person into your house, and when on seeing a person naked you clothe him.[26] The martyrs used their hair for our benefit, making what the razor could cut off or shave serve a good purpose, for they went the whole way in imitating the Lord by pouring out their blood for the Church, hearkening to that admonition in scripture, that as Christ *laid down his life for us, we too must lay down our lives for our brothers and sisters* (1 Jn 3:16). Another example of how something good can be done even with our hair is provided by the sinful woman who wept over our Lord's feet, and then dried with her hair those feet her tears had washed.[27] What does that suggest? That when you feel sorry for people, you should also help them in practical ways if you can. When you are moved to pity, it is as though you were shedding tears; but when you give help, you are drying them with your hair. And if this is true of anyone and everyone, how much more does it apply to our Lord's feet? Who are the Lord's feet? The holy evangelists, of whom it was said, *How beautiful are the feet of those who announce peace and bring good news!* (Is 52:7; Rom 10:15). Let Doeg whet his tongue like a razor, let him sharpen his trickery as much as he can. All he will cut off is temporal superfluity. He will never shave off the necessary things, the eternal things, will he?

Verses 5-6. Kindness and justice cannot be kept under

10. *You loved malice above kindness.* Kindness was there in front of you, and you should have set your love on it. It was not as though you would have been forced to go to great expense, or to make a journey overseas to fetch what you loved from afar. Kindness is there in front of you, and so is iniquity. Compare the two, and choose. But perhaps you have the kind of eyes that can see malice, but no eyes to see kindness. Woe to the unjust heart! What is even worse, such a person turns away deliberately, in order not to see what he or she has the ability to see. Remember what scripture says elsewhere of people like this: *He has refused to understand, and so act well.* Notice that it does not say, "He could not," but, "He would not." He refused to understand, and so do the right thing; he closed his eyes against the light that was available. And how does that passage continue? *He plotted iniquity in his bedroom* (Ps 35:4-5(36:3-4)), which means in the private, inner place of his heart. This is the kind of obstacle in the path of the Edomite Doeg,

---

26. See Is 58:7.
27. See Lk 7:38.

that malicious body of people, the earthly movement that will not last, that does not belong to heaven. *You loved malice above kindness.* Do you want proof that an evil person can see both, malice and kindness, yet chooses malice and turns away from kindness? Here it is. Why do such people complain when suffering unjustly? Why do they, in that situation, exaggerate the injustice as much as possible while commending kindness, and denounce the offender who in treating them so badly has put malice above kindness? Let such people be their own criterion; let them judge their own behavior by their experience. If they will only obey scripture's injunction, *You shall love your neighbor as yourself* (Mk 12:31; Mt 22:39), and *Whatever good you want people to do for you, do the same yourselves for them* (Mt 7:12), they will have within themselves evidence that they must not treat others as they would not wish to be treated themselves.[28] *You have loved malice above kindness.* Unjustly, perversely, in a way that violates right order, you want to float water on top of oil; but the water will sink and the oil will rise to the surface. You want to hide light beneath darkness; but darkness will flee and light will abide. You want to put earth above heaven; but earth will fall by its own weight to its true place. And you yourself will sink by loving malice above kindness, for malice will never tread down kindness. *You have loved malice above kindness, and unjust talk better than saying what is just.* Before you is justice, before you injustice; you have one tongue, and you can turn it whichever way you choose. Why, then, turn it toward injustice rather than to what is right? Is it not foolish to withhold bitter food from your stomach, yet give iniquitous food to your malicious tongue? As you are finicky about what you eat, be equally fastidious about what you say. You give preference to injustice over justice, and to malice over kindness; you give the preference, but what can be uppermost, except kindness and justice? When you take your stand on things which must necessarily sink to the bottom, you do not exalt them above the good, but sink down yourself with them into the foul depths.

11. This is why the psalm contines, *You have loved all abysmal words.* Avoid drowning, if you can! You are trying to escape from a shipwreck, yet you hug a leaden weight! If you don't want to go down with it, grab a plank, let yourself be borne up by wood, allow the cross to see you safe. But no, you are Doeg the Edomite, you are "earthly movement," so what do you do? *You have loved all abysmal words, and a tongue full of guile.* The guileful tongue came first, and the sinking words followed. What is this guileful tongue? A guileful tongue is the servant of liars; it is the tool of those who have one thing in their hearts and something different on their lips. But their subversion leads to their submersion.

---

28. See Tb 4:16.

Verse 7. Be rooted in charity

12. *Therefore God will destroy you in the end,* even though at present you seem to be flourishing like grass in the field before the summer heat comes. For all flesh is grass, and human grandeur is like the flower in the meadow. The grass withers and the flower wilts, but the word of the Lord abides for ever.[29] Be careful where you take hold; fix your root in what abides eternally. If you entwine your roots in the grass or the flower in the meadow, *God will destroy you in the end,* because the grass will wither and the flower will wilt. Even if he does not destroy you now, he will ultimately, when the time comes for winnowing and the pile of straw is separated from the heap of grain. The grain is destined for the barn, isn't it, and the straw for the fire?[30] This whole crowd embodied in Doeg will be standing to the left when the Lord says, *Depart from me into the eternal fire which was prepared for the devil and his angels* (Mt 25:41). *God will destroy you in the end; he will pluck you up and turn you out of your tent.* The Edomite, Doeg, is evidently in the tent now, but a servant does not keep his place in the household for ever.[31] Yet even a servant like this effects some good, if not by his own actions, at least through the words of God, for though he is seeking his own ends in the Church[32] he is at least speaking about Christ. But *he will turn you out of your tent,* for the Lord says, *I tell you truly, they have had their reward* (Mt 6:2), *and uproot you from the land of the living.* So the land of the living is the place where we must strike root. That is where our roots must be fixed. Now a root is hidden. The fruits of a tree can be seen, but not its root. Our root is our charity, and our fruits are our deeds. What matters is that your deeds spring from charity, and that your root is in the land of the living. That fellow Doeg will be uprooted; he will have no staying power at all, because he has not plunged his root deep enough. He is like those seeds that fall on rock; they try to put down roots, but wilt and die as soon as the sun rises, because they have no moisture.[33]

But what about people who plunge their roots deeper: what do they hear from the apostle? *I bend my knees on your behalf to the Father of our Lord Jesus Christ, so that you may be rooted in love and built up on love.* And because your root is already there, he continues, *And so you may come to grasp what is the height and breadth and length and depth, and have a knowledge that surpasses knowing of Christ's charity, that you may be filled unto all the fullness of God* (Eph 3:14.17.18-19). A root so powerful, so simple, so productive, so deeply

29. See Is 40:6-8.
30. See Mt 3:12.
31. See Jn 8:35.
32. See Phil 2:21.
33. See Mt 13:5.

grounded for budding[34] is worthy to bear such fruit. But the other kind of root is torn out of the land of the living.

Verse 8. A time to fear and a time to laugh

13. *The righteous will see, and be afraid, and they will laugh at him.* When will they be afraid? And when will they laugh? Let us try to understand, and distinguish between two periods of time, one for salutary fear and the other for laughter. As long as we are in this world, we should not laugh, lest we have occasion to weep later. We read of the fate reserved for Doeg at the end, and because we read and understand, we see it, and we are afraid. This is what the psalm says: *the righteous will see, and be afraid.*

But as long as we see what will happen to evildoers in the end, why should we be afraid? Because the apostle warned us, *Work out your own salvation in fear and trembling* (Phil 2:12), and because a psalm told us, *Serve the Lord in fear, and rejoice before him with trembling* (Ps 2:11). But why in fear? Because *anyone who thinks he stands must take care not to fall* (1 Cor 10:12). Why with trembling? Because the apostle tells us in another place, *My brothers and sisters, if someone is involved in some wrongdoing, you who are spiritual must instruct such a person in a spirit of gentleness, taking heed to yourself, lest you be tempted as well* (Gal 6:1). Accordingly those who are righteous today because they are living by faith see this fellow Doeg and what will happen to him, but they see it in such a way that they are still fearful on their own account; for they know what they are today, but not what they will be tomorrow. For the present, therefore, *the righteous will see, and be afraid.*

But when will they laugh? When iniquity has passed away, when it has flown by, as the time of uncertainty has already in large measure flown by, when the darkness of this world has been dispelled. In this darkness we are walking now with only the scriptures for our light, and so we are fearful as in the night. We walk by the illumination of prophecy, of which the apostle Peter speaks: *We have the trusty message of the prophets to rely on, and you will do well to attend to it, for it is like a lantern burning in a dark place until day breaks and the morning star rises in your hearts* (2 Pet 1:19). As long as we walk by lamplight, we cannot but live fearfully. But when our day dawns—the day of Christ's manifestation, of which the apostle says, *When Christ appears, Christ who is your life, then you too will appear with him in glory* (Col 3:4)—then the righteous will laugh at Doeg. For there will be no occasion for works of mercy then, as there is now, when on seeing someone living a bad life you have the urge to work with

---

34. *Tam germinans, in germina tam alte fundata.* Variants: *tam germana, tam alte fundata*, "so genuine, so deeply rooted"; *tam germinans in germine, tam alta et fundata et profunda*, "so budding in its shoot, so tall and well established and deep."

him and set him on a better course. At this present stage an unrighteous person may turn round and become righteous, just as a righteous one may go wrong and become unrighteous. This is why you must neither be presumptuous about your own case nor despair of his; but if you are kind, if you do not love malice above kindness, you must do all in your power to correct a person who is going astray and set on an evil course, and put him or her onto the right track. At the end, though, it will be a different matter, because when the time for judgment comes there will be no opportunity for correction, but only for condemnation. Repentance then there will be, but unfruitful repentance, because it will come too late. Do you want your repentance to be fruitful? Make sure not to repent too late, then; correct yourself today. You are guilty, and God is the judge: correct the guilty party and you will rejoice to face the judge. He encourages you today so that he will not need to judge you tomorrow; he who will one day be your judge is today your advocate.

So then, brothers and sisters, the time for laughter is saved up for the future. The Book of Wisdom hinted at that future derision of the wicked by the righteous, for through her own disciples, in whose souls she has made her dwelling, Wisdom will say, *I called, and you refused to listen; I spoke to you, and no one took notice. You have despised all my counsel and ignored my reproofs; so I will laugh heartily over your disaster* (Prv 1:24.26, LXX). This is what the righteous will do on that day, when they look at Doeg. For the present, then, let us see and be afraid, lest we become what we denounce in him. If we were like that, let us amend ourselves. By being afraid now, we may hope to laugh later.

Verse 9. The true riches, the true poverty

14. What will they be saying, those who laugh later? The psalm tells us: *They will laugh at him, and say, Look at the person who would not take God as helper.* Here you have the earthly "body." The maxim of the greedy, the grasping, those who oppress innocent people, is this: "You are as great as your possessions." This is the watchword of those who appropriate the goods of others, and hang on to things lent to them. What kind of a maxim is it, "You are as great as your possessions"? It means that the more money you have and the more you can acquire, the more powerful you will be. *Look at the person who would not take God as helper, but trusted in the amplitude of his riches.*

But a poor person who is also bad has no business to be complacent, and say, "I don't belong to that body." This poor person has heard the prophet declaring that the unrighteous has *trusted in the amplitude of his riches*, so he looks at his own rags, and glances at some rich person who happens to be standing beside him in the assembly of God's people, and observes how much more ornately that rich person is dressed. So the poor man says in his heart, "The psalm must mean

him. It can't mean me, can it?" Don't be too sure. Don't think yourself exonerated unless you have seen, and felt fear, so that you may laugh later on. What
credit is it to you that you lack resources, if you are aflame with desire? Our Lord
Jesus Christ watched a rich man walk away saddened, one to whom he had
offered the invitation, *Go and sell all you possess and give the money to the
poor: you will have treasure in heaven. Then come, follow me* (Mt 19:21). He
had just indicated the apparently hopeless situation of the rich by saying that it
was easier for a camel to pass through the eye of a needle than for a rich man to
enter the kingdom of heaven. And how did the disciples immediately react?
They were dismayed, and questioned among themselves, *Who can be saved,
then?* (Mt 19:25). When they asked that question, *Who can be saved?* were they
considering only the few rich people they knew, and forgetting the enormous
number of the poor? Should they not have been saying to each other, "Well,
perhaps it is difficult, even impossible, for the rich to get into heaven, just as it is
impossible for a camel to squeeze through a needle's eye, but at least let all the
poor get in. It's only the rich who need be shut out." Isn't that what they might
have said? "After all, how many rich people are there? Yet the poor are past
counting. We shan't be examining people's clothes in the kingdom of heaven.
The dazzling glory of righteousness is what will count as everyone's vesture.
That means that the poor will be on a level with the angels of God. They will be
arrayed in the robes of immortality, and will shine like the sun in their Father's
kingdom.[35] So why should we worry about a handful of rich people, or go to any
trouble about them?"

But that was not the way the apostles understood it. When the Lord said, *It is
easier for a camel to squeeze through the eye of a needle than for a rich person to
enter the kingdom of heaven* (Mt 19:24), and they inquired among themselves,
Who can be saved, then? what were they taking into account? Not resources, but
desires. They saw that those same people, though poor, still harbored avarice.

So now, listen to me, and I will show you that what is condemned in a rich
person is not money, but avarice. Look at that well-to-do person standing near
you. Perhaps he or she has money, but no avarice, while you have avarice but no
money! A certain poor man was covered with sores, deeply distressed, licked by
dogs, destitute, without food and perhaps even without clothing, and he was
carried away into Abraham's embrace.[36] (So you are well off now, you pauper.
You don't want ulcers, do you? Your inheritance is good health.) Now Lazarus
deserved his happiness not by his poverty but by his piety. You see who was
carried off; but don't you see where he was carried to? Who was it who was
carried away by angels? A poor man, distressed and covered with sores. And
where was he carried to? Into Abraham's arms. But wait, if you read the scrip-

---

35. See Mt 13:43.
36. See Lk 16:22.

tures you will find that Abraham was a rich man.[37] He had plenty of gold, silver, livestock and servants, and into his embrace the poor man, Lazarus, was transported. This shows that it is not riches that make a person guilty.[38] A poor man rests in the embrace of a rich man—or would it be truer to say that both are rich in God, both poor in greed?

15. What, then, does scripture condemn in this man Doeg? It did not say, "Look at a man who was rich," but, *Look at the person who would not take God as helper, but trusted in the amplitude of his riches.* Such a person is not censured for having wealth, but for trusting in it and not trusting in God. This is why he is condemned, and punished, and turned out of his tent as an "earthly movement," like the dust which the wind sweeps away from the face of the earth;[39] this is why his root is torn out of the land of the living. Very different are the rich of whom the apostle Paul says, *Instruct the rich of this world not to be high-minded* (like Doeg), *nor to put their trust in unreliable wealth* (as did the one who *trusted in the amplitude of his riches*), *but in the living God* (unlike Doeg, who *would not take God as helper*). So what orders does Paul give concerning them? *Let them be rich in good works, give readily, and share what they have* (1 Tm 6:17-18). And if they have given readily, if they have shared what they have with the have-nots, what are their prospects? Will they get through the eye of the needle? Most certainly they will, for there was One who went through it first, One on whom no one could have laid the burden of his passion, as a camel is loaded, if he had not first lowered himself to the ground.[40] He told us himself that *what is impossible for human beings is easy for God* (Mt 19:26).

Let this Doeg be condemned, and let the righteous be fearful now because of him, and laugh over him later. He is justly condemned, because *he would not take God as helper*, whereas you, who may have money, put your trust not in your money but in God. *He trusted in the amplitude of his riches*, and became like those folk of whom the popular verdict runs, "It's a lucky people that has all this," namely, the good things of this earth. But to such a popular saying the one who laughs at Doeg immediately retorts, *Blessed*, rather, *is the people whose God is the Lord* (Ps 143(144):15). A psalm enumerates those good things in which a nation is declared to be blessed; but they who declared it spoke as foreigners, like that fellow Doeg, who was an Edomite, an earthling. *Their mouths spoke empty words, and their right hand is a hand that deals unjustly. "Their sons are like well-set saplings, their daughters are gathered round them*

---

37. See Gn 13:2.
38. Variant: "earn punishment."
39. See Ps 1:4.
40. An unusual and daring image for Christ, perhaps to be associated with the metaphor of earthly life subject to sin as a desert; see the Exposition of Psalm 62, sections 3 and 8.

like the pillars of the temple, their storerooms are full to overflowing, their oxen are sturdy and their ewes fruitful, increasing at every lambing-time. Never is their hedge broken down, nor is there rioting in their streets" (Ps 143(144):11-14). To all appearances they enjoy great happiness amid their earthly peace. But that earthly fellow is also named "earthly movement," unstable like the dust swept away by the wind from the face of the earth. So what is it ultimately that is censured in such folk? Not the fact of possessing wealth, because good people have wealth too. What then? Note the answer carefully, for you must not disparage the rich indiscriminately, nor must you think yourself secure just because you are hard up. If we may not rely on riches, much less may we rely on poverty; our only reliance is on the living God. What is the hallmark of the worldly-minded? The fact that *they call people who have these things blessed.* They are thereby known as foreigners, *whose mouths have spoken empty words, and whose right hand is a hand that deals unjustly.* And what of you? *Blessed is the people whose God is the Lord.*

Verse 10. Disinterested love

16. He has been condemned, then, he who *trusted in the amplitude of his riches, and grew strong in his stupidity*—stupidity, yes, for what could be more stupid than to set a higher value on a coin than on God? They stand condemned, those who declared, *People who have these things are blessed*; so what of you, who retorted, *Blessed is the people whose God is the Lord?* How do you see your own case? What are your hopes for yourself?

As for me (listen, the other body is speaking now)—*As for me, I am like a fruitful olive tree in God's house.* This is not a single individual speaking, but the fruitful olive from which proud branches were cut out so that the humble oleaster might be grafted in.[41] *Like a fruitful olive tree in God's house I have put my trust in the mercy of God.* In what did those others put theirs? *In the amplitude of their riches*; that is why their root will be pulled up from the land of the living. But *as for me,* because *I am like a fruitful olive tree in God's house,* whose root absorbs nourishment and is not pulled up, *I have put my trust in the mercy of God.*

But does that mean with a view to the present life? This is a mistake people make sometimes. They do worship God, to be sure, and to this extent they are not like Doeg; but although they rely on God, it is with an eye to temporal well-being, so that they say to themselves, "I worship my God, because he will make me rich in this world, and will give me children, and a wife." It is true that only God gives such gifts, but he does not want us to choose him as our love for the sake of them. He often gives them to the wicked too, so that the good may

---

41. See Rom 11:17.

learn to seek something else from him. So in what sense do you profess, *I have put my trust in the mercy of God*? To gain temporal advantages? Rather it must be *for ever, and for unending ages*. The psalmist first said, *for ever*, and then reinforced it by adding, *and for unending ages*, to show by the reiteration how firmly established he was in love for the kingdom of heaven and in the hope of eternal happiness.

Verse 11. God's mercy alone does the work

17. *I will confess to you for ever, because this is your doing.* What is your doing? You have condemned Doeg and crowned David. *I will confess to you for ever, because this is your doing.* That is a great confession: *this is your doing.* What have you done? Surely all that the psalm has related, so that I, like a fruitful olive tree in God's house, may put my trust in the mercy of God for ever, and for unending ages. It is your doing, for the ungodly cannot justify themselves. Who is it who justifies you? Scripture speaks of God's grace *to the one who believes in him who justifies the impious* (Rom 4:5), and demands, *What have you that you did not receive? And if you did receive it, why boast as though you had not* (1 Cor 4:7), as though you had it in your own right? "Far be it from me to boast like that," says the person who opposes Doeg, who puts up with Doeg on earth until he is turned out of his tent and uprooted from the land of the living. "I will not boast as though it were not a gift; only in God will I glory. *And I will confess to you because this is your doing*, because you have done it not out of any merits of mine, but out of your mercy. For what have I done? *I was originally a persecutor and a blasphemer, and acted unjustly*, remember. But what did you do? *You granted me mercy, because I acted in ignorance* (1 Tm 1:13). *I will confess to you for ever, because this is your doing.*"

The delightful name of God

18. *And I will look to your name, for it is delightful.* The world is bitter, but your name is delightful. Some delicious things there are in this world, but they are scattered among bitter experiences. Your name is all-surpassing, not only in its greatness, but in its delighfulness too.[42] The wicked have told me tales about their pleasures, but none compare with your law, O Lord.[43] If it had not been sweet and delightful to the martyrs, they could not have borne such bitter sufferings with equanimity. The bitterness was obvious to all, but it was no easy matter for anyone to taste the sweetness. God's name is delightful to those who love

---

42. The Latin editors amend to "Your name surpasses both the bitterness and the delightfulness."
43. See Ps 118(119):85.

him more than any other delight. *I will look to your name, for it is delightful.* To whom can you demonstrate the delight of it? Give me someone with a palate sensitive enough to taste its sweetness. You may commend honey with all your might, you may exaggerate its delicious sweetness with the most expressive words you can find, but if you are talking to someone who does not know what honey is and has never tasted it, he will not know what you are talking about.

That is why another psalm invites you to experience it. What does it say? *Taste and see how sweet the Lord is* (Ps 33:9(34:8)). You declare it delightful, and yet are unwilling to taste it? What are you calling delightful? If you have tasted it, the fact will be apparent in the fruit you bring forth, not merely in your words. You must not be like that fig tree that bore leaves only, and deserved to wither away under the Lord's curse.[44] *Taste and see how sweet the Lord is*, says the psalm. *Taste and see*: only when you taste will you see. How can one prove it to someone who refuses to taste? Though you praise the delightfulness of God's name as fulsomely as you can, all you say is just words. Taste is something different. The impious too hear these expressions of praise, but only the saints taste how sweet that name is.

The psalmist experiences the sweetness of God's name, and longs to explain it, longs to demonstrate it, but finds no one to whom he can speak. To the saints he need not prove it, because they already taste it for themselves and they know. The wicked cannot discern what they refuse to taste. So what is the psalmist to do about this delightful name of God? He holds himself aloof from the crowds of unbelievers, and says, *I will look to your name, because it is delightful in the eyes of your saints.* Your name is delightful, but not in the eyes of the impious. I know how sweet it is, but only to those who have tasted it.

---

44. See Mt 21:19.

Exposition of Psalm 52

A Sermon[1]

Verse 1. Pain and parturition. Pragmatic atheism

1. We have undertaken to study this psalm with you, insofar as the Lord brings ideas to our mind, for a brother is ordering us to bend our will to the task, and praying that we may have the strength.[2] If I leave out anything in my hurry, he whose mercy grants even to us the ability to say whatever we can say will himself make up the deficiency in you.

The title of the psalm is *To the end, for Maeleth, understanding for David himself.* As we have learned from the interpretation of Hebrew names, *for Maeleth* seems to mean "for one who labors to give birth," or "for someone in pain." The faithful know who is laboring to give birth, and who is in pain in this world, because they themselves are part of the one concerned. It is Christ who is in travail here, Christ who suffers pain here; the head is on high, but his members are below. If he were not laboring and in pain, he would hardly have asked, *Saul, Saul, why are you persecuting me?* (Acts 9:4). While Saul was a persecutor, Christ was in labor with him, but later he made the converted Paul undergo the same birthpangs himself; for once Paul had been enlightened[3] and engrafted into those members he had formerly persecuted, he became pregnant with the same charity, and was accustomed to address his converts as *my little children, with whom I am in travail over again, until Christ be formed in you* (Gal 4:19).

This psalm is sung, then, for the members of Christ, for his body which is the Church,[4] for one single person, for that unified organism whose head is on high. This person groans, and brings forth laboriously, and is in pain. Why is this, and among whom is the Church in pain? It has heard and understood the answer in the prophetic words of its head: *with iniquity increasing mightily, the love of many will grow cold* (Mt 24:12). But if that is the case, and, with the spread of iniquity, the love of many will grow cold, who will be left to give birth? The next

---

1. Possibly preached at Thagaste in Eastertide, 414
2. *Iubet frater ut velimus et orat ut possimus* is the best reading, and prompts the Maurists' suggestion that a pressing request from a fellow bishop had occasioned the sermon; but the editors of the Latin text amend to *Iubete, fratres, ut velimus, et orate...*: "Order us to bend our will to the task, brethren, and pray. . . ."
3. *Illuminatus*, often used for baptism.
4. See Col 1:24.

31

verse tells us: *whoever perseveres to the end will be saved* (Mt 24:13). But then what would persevering amount to, if it were not amid troubles and trials and upsets and scandals that we had to persevere? No one is commanded to be brave amid good fortune. But since this is what scripture says about the sufferer, and this psalm is sung about the sufferer, let us see what the endurance involves. On behalf of this laboring person the psalm rebukes those amid whom the groaning and the pain are endured, but at the psalm's end comfort is expressly offered to this one who grieves in parturition. Listen, then, and let us identify those among whom we labor to give birth in our groaning—if we are the body of Christ, that is, if we live under that head, if we are counted among his members.

2. *The imprudent one has said in his heart, "God does not exist."* These are the sort of people in whose company Christ's body suffers and groans. But if they are like this, it seems there are not many whom we must bring to birth. Very few indeed, as far as we can discern. It may be quite difficult to come across anyone who says in his or her heart, *God does not exist*; but they are few only in this sense, that they dare not utter their denial among the many, and so they think it in their hearts. So it is not much that we are commanded to put up with, is it, if we detect scarcely anyone who *says in his heart, God does not exist*? They are a rare species!

Perhaps we should understand it differently, though. Then we may find that what we thought must occur in only a few cases, or in a tiny handful, or in scarcely any at all, is really to be diagnosed in many people. Let those who lead wicked lives step forward. Let us examine the deeds of the infamous, criminals, the profligate—there are plenty of these. They cultivate their sins with daily care, and so habituated do they become to their ill-doing that they lose all sense of shame. So numerous are they that Christ's body, living among them, hardly dares to denounce what it must refuse to countenance. It finds that it has more than enough to do to keep its own innocence intact, and to avoid doing what it dare not condemn, because so commonly done. Or if Christ's body has dared to utter any condemnation, the free voice of those who lead good lives is easily shouted down by the protests of evildoers. Now these are the people who *say in their hearts, "God does not exist."* I can convict them. How? Because such people imagine that their deeds are acceptable to God. Notice that the psalm does not declare, "Some people say. . ." but *the imprudent has said in his heart, "God does not exist."* These ill-living people do believe in God, to the extent that they suppose what they do is acceptable to God. But if you, a prudent person, take note of what is said—*the imprudent has said in his heart, "God does not exist"*—if you understand this and investigate it, you will see that anyone who thinks evil deeds pleasing to God does not really believe him to be God. For if he is God, he is just; and if he is just, injustice displeases him, iniquity displeases him. And so if you think iniquity pleasing to him, you are denying God; for if he is a God to whom iniquity is offensive, but he does not seem to you to be a God offended by iniquity, and there is no other God but the God who is offended by iniquity, it follows that when you say, "God looks favorably on my iniquities," you are saying nothing else but, *God does not exist.*

Verse 2. Denial of Christ's godhead, by denying his coming as judge

3. We may compare this attitude with what Christ our Lord met with, even he, our head. When he appeared on earth in the form of a servant, his crucifiers said, "This is not God."[5] Since he was the Son of God, he certainly was God; but they had become corrupt and hateful, so what did they say? "This is not God. Come, let's kill him; this is not God." You can hear them saying that in the Book of Wisdom, but before we listen to it, observe how they had become so corrupt that they could say in their hearts, "This is not God." The first verse of the psalm told us that *the imprudent one has said in his heart, "God does not exist,"* and then, as though to assign the reason why the imprudent could say this, it adds, *They have become corrupt and hateful in their iniquities.* Listen to how corruption progresses. To begin with they talked among themselves without thinking straight. Their corruption began with wrongheaded notions, and then proceeded to depraved conduct, and thence again to the most heinous sins. This is how it escalates. What was it that they said among themselves when they were not thinking straight? *Our life is short and wearisome* (Wis 2:1). From a wrong-headed conviction like this follows the attitude which the apostle mentions: *Let us eat and drink, for tomorrow we shall die* (1 Cor 15:32). But in the Book of Wisdom their licentiousness is more fully described: *Let us garland ourselves with roses before they fade, and let us leave signs of our merrymaking everywhere.* And after this ample indication of their revelry, what follows? *Let's kill that poor, righteous man* (Wis 2:8-10). And this is tantamount to denying that the poor, righteous Christ is God. Their first words seemed harmless enough: *Let us garland ourselves with roses before they fade.* What could be prettier, more delicate? Would you ever expect the cross to arise from such delicacy, or the sword? Don't be surprised, though. The roots of thorn-bushes are delicate and soft, no one will be pricked by handling them; but from them spring the thorns that wound. So too these wanton revelers *have become corrupt and hateful in their iniquities. The imprudent one has said in his heart, "God does not exist. If he is the Son of God, let him come down from the cross"* (Mt 27:40). This is the same as saying plainly, "He is not God."

---

5. The Latin of Augustine's psalter has *Non est Deus*. This has been taken to mean "there is no God," or "God does not exist;" but in the present paragraph the meaning shifts to "Christ is not God."

4. But in what sense does the body of Christ groan among such people? The apostles, and Christ's other disciples who lived at that time, groaned among them indeed; but what trouble do they cause us? How can we be said to suffer birthpangs among them? We can, because there are still those who say, "Christ is not God." Those pagans who still survive take this line; and so indeed do the Jews, who are dispersed everywhere as a sign of their shame; and so too do many heretics. The Arians said, "Christ is not God";[6] the Eunomians said, "Christ is not God."[7] Furthermore, brothers and sisters, those people we were talking about just now, the ones who lead sinful lives, are saying nothing else but, "Christ is not God." How is that? When we remind them that Christ will come as judge, according to the teaching of the scriptures which cannot deceive us, they prefer to bend their ears to the serpent who whispers, *No, you will not die* (Gn 3:4). This is what he said in paradise, contradicting the all-truthful God who had laid a command on our first parents and told them that if they disobeyed, *you will certainly die* (Gn 2:17). Those people are therefore quite wrong who tell themselves, "When Christ comes he will grant forgiveness to everyone." So he is a liar, is he, who told us that he will separate the wicked from the just, placing the wicked at his left and the just at his right? He will say then, *Come, you whom my Father has blessed; take possession of the kingdom prepared for you since the world was made*; but to the wicked he will say, *Depart from me, you accursed, into the eternal fire which was prepared for the devil and his angels* (Mt 25:34.41). How then can you maintain that he will grant forgiveness to everyone? How can you think that no one will be condemned? If you are right, Christ must be lying; and if that is what you assert, you are saying, *He is not God*. Is it not more likely that you are the liar? You are a human being, and he is God; God is truthful, whereas no human is trustworthy.[8]

But what about you, body of Christ? For this in-between time keep clear of them in your heart and in your way of life; take care not to imitate them, or get used to them, or assent to their views, or approve of their doings. Rather you should rebuke them. Why pay any respect to people who talk like this? *They have become corrupt and hateful in their iniquities, and not one of them does anything good.*

---

6. See note on Arius of Alexandria at Exposition of Psalm 35, 9.
7. Eunomius was an Arian bishop in Mysia, who died around 395. He held that the Son is not generated within the Godhead, but created by the Father to be the creator of all else. The Son's first creature was the Holy Spirit. Eunomius's writings evoked replies from Saint Basil and Saint Gregory of Nyssa.
8. See Ps 115(116):11.

Verse 3. Does God need to find out?

5. *God has looked down from heaven upon the children of men,*[9] *to see if there is anyone who understands and seeks God.* What does this mean? All those who say, *"God does not exist,"* have become corrupt and hateful in their pleasures, we are told. But was God unaware of what they had become? Could their inner thoughts have been revealed to us, if God's word had not revealed them? So if God knew all about them, what does the psalm mean by saying that he *looked down from heaven upon the children of men, to see if there is anyone who understands and seeks God?* Such an action is necessary for one who is trying to find out about something, not for one who knows; yet *God looked down from heaven upon the children of men, to see if there is anyone who understands and seeks God.* And it goes on in the same vein, as though he had found out what he was investigating by looking down from heaven: *but they have all turned aside, and all alike have become useless. There is not one who will act rightly, not a single one.*

Two questions arise, both fairly difficult. If God looked down from heaven to see whether there is anyone who understands and seeks God, the thought may occur to some imprudent person that God does not know everything. That is one problem: what is the other? If there is no one who does anything good, not even a single one, who is laboriously giving birth among the wicked?

The answer to the first difficulty is as follows. Scripture often speaks as though what a creature does by God's gift, God himself does. So, for instance, when you take pity on the poor, and do so by God's gift, God is said to be taking pity on them. When you know who you are, and know yourself through God's illumination of you, so that you are moved to confess, *You, Lord, will light my lamp; my God, you will enlighten my darkness* (Ps 17:29(18:28)), then what you have come to know through God's gift and God's working, he knows. If this were not so, what could that other text mean, *the Lord your God tests you, in order to know if you love him* (Dt 13:3)? What does *in order to know* mean? That he may cause you to know, through his gift.

The same holds for our text here: *God looked down from heaven upon the children of men, to see if there is anyone who understands and seeks God.* May he be at hand to help us, and as he has by his gift caused us to conceive an idea in our heart, so may he now help us to bring it to birth. The apostle says, *We have not received the spirit of this world, but the Spirit which is of God, that we may know what gifts have been bestowed on us by God* (1 Cor 2:12). So it comes about that through this Spirit, by whom we recognize the gifts given us by God, we also distinguish between ourselves and others to whom they have not been

---

9. *Super filios hominum.* The translation "children of men," rather than "human race" or similar, is necessary here, because Augustine goes on to make a point of the contrast between them and the children of God; see section 6.

given; we know them in contradistinction from ourselves. If we understand that we could not have possessed anything good, except by his gift from whom all good things derive, we see equally well that people to whom God has not given these gifts cannot have anything good. This power of discernment comes to us from the Spirit of God, and by the very fact that we see the difference, God sees it, because it is God who makes us see it. This is why in the same passage the apostle also says, *The Spirit searches all things, even the depth of God* (1 Cor 2:10). He does not mean that the Spirit, who knows everything, needs to search; he means that the Spirit who is given to you causes you to search those depths; and what you do through his gift, he is said to do, because you would not be doing it without him. This is why God is said to do something when you do it.

Now the gift of the Spirit makes us children of God, and those to whom the Spirit of God has been given *look down upon the children of men, to see if there is anyone who understands and seeks God*; but since they do so by the gift of God, by the Spirit of God, God is said to look out and see. But why does the psalm say, *from heaven*, if it is human beings doing it? Because the apostle tells us, *We have citizens' rights in heaven* (Phil 3:20). Where is your lookout post, from where do you try to see? From what vantage point do you look out in your effort to understand? From your heart, surely. But if your heart is your lookout post, Christian, be sure you have your heart on high. If your heart is on high, you are looking out *from heaven* on the earth. And because you do so by God's gift, *God has looked down from heaven on the children of men*. This is the best we can do, with our limited ability, to solve the first of our two problems.

Verse 4. God shares our humanity, to make us sharers in his divinity

6. Now what is it that we observe when we look out? What does God observe when he looks out? What does he observe, he who gives us the power? Listen, the psalm tells us: he sees that *they have all turned aside, and all alike have become useless. There is not one who will act rightly, not a single one.* What was that other question I raised a few minutes ago? If *there is not one who will act rightly, not a single one*, there is nobody left to groan when surrounded by evildoers, is there?

"But wait," says the Lord, "do not jump to conclusions. I have given human beings the power to behave well, but they do so by my enabling, not from any goodness of their own. Of themselves they are bad. When they act wrongly they are children of men; when well, they are my children." This is what God brings about. He transforms children of men into children of God, because he made the Son of God become the Son of Man. Look what our participation in him means: we have been promised a share in his divinity,[10] but he would be deceiving us if he had not first become a sharer in our mortality. The Son of God was made a

---

10. See 2 Pt 1:4.

sharer in our mortal nature so that mortals might become sharers in his godhead. Having promised to communicate his goodness to you, he first communicated with you in your badness; he who promised you divinity first showed you charity. Therefore if you take away people's status as children of God, all that is left is that they are children of men, and then *there is not one who will act rightly, not a single one*.

Verse 5. God's people devoured by predators

7. *Will they never know, all those sinners who devour my people, eating it like bread?* He asks, *Will they never know?* Will the truth not dawn on them? Speak to them, warn them, tell them in your capacity as the one who gives birth in pain, for it is your people that is being devoured, eaten like bread; it is God's people being devoured like this. To be sure, scripture has said that *there is not one who will act rightly, not a single one*, but we must interpret that according to the principle we have discussed already. This people that is being eaten, the people that is enduring the wicked, that is groaning and giving birth among the wicked, is the company of those who have already been transformed from children of men into children of God, and for that very reason are being devoured. Another psalm reproachfully charges the persecutor, *You have frustrated the plan of the poor person because the Lord is his hope* (Ps 13(14):6), for the reason why God's people is condemned and falls prey to persecution is often nothing else but the fact that it is God's people. "I will seize him and strip him of his goods," says the wicked man. "If he is a Christian, what retaliation can he envisage against me?" But the psalmist speaks up for this wronged person, as he speaks also for the one who is giving birth, and he threatens the devouring persecutor: *Will they never know, all those sinners?* Anyone who colluded with a thief he might chance to see, and continually threw in his lot with adulterers, anyone who would sit down to slander a brother, and put a stumbling-block in the way of his mother's son, such a person has been saying in his heart, *God does not exist*. On this ground sentence is pronounced against him or her in another psalm: "*All this you did, and I was silent, but you were wrong to think that I will be like you*, for if I were like you, I would not be God." And how does it continue? *I will rebuke you, and bring you face to face with yourself* (Ps 49(50):18-21). And that is just what is foretold here too: *I will rebuke you, and bring you face to face with yourself*. You are not willing now to recognize how unpleasant you are, but later you will recognize it to your grief. God will not fail to make their sinfulness evident to the wicked. Were he not certain to do so, how could scripture represent them as wailing, *What good has our pride done us, and what benefit has come to us from our vaunted wealth?* (Wis 5:8). Then they will know indeed, those who refuse to know now.

Will they never know, all those sinners who devour my people, eating it like bread? Why does the psalmist add those last words, *eating it like bread*? The persecutors devour my people as though they were bread. I think he specifies this because with other things we eat we can vary the menu, choosing now this food, now that: we do not always eat cabbage, or always meat, or always fruit; but bread we eat all the time. So what does this mean: *they devour my people, eating it like bread*? It means uninterruptedly; they never stop *devouring my people, eating it like bread.*

Verses 6-7. Loving God for himself alone, and fearing nothing else

8. *They have not invoked God.* Here consolation is being offered to the mourner, and particularly the consolation that this reminder[11] affords, lest we be tempted to imitate the wicked in their evildoing, seeing how they often prosper. What has been promised to you is being saved up for you. Their hope is here at hand for them, yours is in the future; but theirs is unstable, yours certain; theirs false, yours real. Why? Because *they have not invoked God.* "But," you object, "don't such people invoke God every day?" No, they don't. Give me your full attention, and with God's help I will try to explain this point. God wants to be worshiped gratis, he wants to be loved gratis; this is what chaste love means. He wants to be loved, not because he gives us something besides himself, but because he gives us himself. Therefore anyone who invokes God in order to get rich is not invoking God, for what we invoke is what we want to come to us. What does "invoke" mean, if not to call something or someone into oneself?[12] Invoking means calling into ourselves. Now if you say, "Please, God, give me wealth," you do not want God to come to you; you want wealth to come to you. What you are invoking is what you want to come your way. If you invoked God, he himself would come to you, and he would be your wealth. But as it is, you want full coffers and an empty soul.[13] What God fills is not your coffers but your heart.[14] What use are material riches to you if you are oppressed by inner poverty? Clearly then, those who invoke God for worldly gain, earthly goods, temporal life or happiness in this world are not truly invoking God.

9. What does the next line have to say about them? *They were filled with fear where there was no need to fear.* Is there anything to be afraid of in losing riches? There is no need to fear that, yet people do fear it, whereas to lose wisdom is indeed a disaster to be feared, yet people are not afraid of it. Listen now, get this point clear in your mind, and take the measure of such folk. Suppose a purse full of money is entrusted to someone's keeping. He is unwilling to return it, he

---

11. *Ex commemoratione*; but some codices have *ex comparatione*, "the comparison."
12. The point is more obvious in Latin: *invocare*, to "call in."
13. *Conscientia*, but wider in meaning than the English "conscience."
14. *Pectus*, "breast."

counts it as his own, he thinks there is no possibility of its being demanded back. He regards it as his property and evades repayment. Let such a person see what it is that he fears to lose, and what he does not care to keep. Money and faith[15] are balanced against each other. Which is the more valuable, which would represent the more serious loss? Yet you are prepared to lose your faith in order to hang onto your gold. You are crippled by the more serious loss even while you celebrate your gain! You were *filled with fear, where there was no need to fear.* Give back the money—indeed, don't just give it back, throw it away, rather than lose your faith. You were reluctant to hand back the money, but unperturbed about losing your faith! Look at the martyrs: they not only refrained from taking other people's property, but made light of their own, rather than lose their faith. They thought nothing of losing their money when they were proscribed: they lost their lives as well when they suffered; they forfeited their life in order to find it in life eternal.[16] They were afraid, certainly, but only of what was truly fearful.

How different were those others, the ones who said of Christ, "This is not God." *They were filled with fear where there was no need to fear.* Their cry was, *If we leave him alone like this, the Romans will come, and sweep away our land and our nationhood* (Jn 1:48). What stupidity, what crass lack of good sense, in the heart that says, "This is not God"! That heart was afraid of losing a patch of earth, and it lost heaven; it was afraid the Romans would come and take away a land and nationhood, but could they take away its God? What can be done now? What else but confess that it has disastrously lost what it sought to keep, and lost it precisely by trying to keep it? It has lost both territory and nationhood by killing Christ. You chose to put Christ to death rather than lose your land, so in the end you lost land and nationhood and Christ as well. What was this fear that drove them to kill Christ; why were they afraid? *Because God has ground to pieces the bones of those who curry favor with men.* Anxious to please human beings, they feared to lose their land. Christ was not afraid of that, Christ of whom they said, "This is not God." He chose rather to offend people like them; he chose to offend children of men, not children of God. Their bones were ground to pieces, therefore, whereas no one broke Christ's bones. *They were put to shame, because God spurned them.* Yes indeed, brothers and sisters, on their part the shame is overwhelming. In that very place where they crucified our Lord in order not to lose their land and their nationhood there are no Jews now. *God spurned them,* yet by spurning[17] them he also warned them to turn about. Let them acknowledge[18] Christ now, and confess, "He is God," even he of whom

---

15. "Faith" in the following lines means fidelity, a good conscience, "faith working through charity."
16. See Mt 10:39.
17. Variant: "by breaking."
18. A few codices unite these two sentences as follows: "...he also warned them where they should turn, and how they should acknowledge..."

they asserted, "This is not God." Let them reclaim their ancestral birthright, return to the inheritance of Abraham, Isaac, and Jacob, and along with the patriarchs possess eternal life, even if temporal life has been lost. Why? Because children of men have been turned into children of God. But as long as they remain what they are, and refuse to change, *there is not one who will act rightly, not a single one; they have been put to shame, because God spurned them.*

Yet now at last he seems to turn to them and ask, *Who will send out of Zion salvation to Israel?* What fools you are! Who is this, whom you are shouting at, insulting, buffeting, smearing with spittle, crowning with thorns, and hoisting onto a cross? *Who will send out of Zion salvation to Israel?* Who else but he of whom you said, "This is not God"? *When God overturns the captivity of his people . . .* and no one overturns the captivity of his people except the one who consented to be a captive in your hands; but who will understand this? *When God overturns the captivity of his people, then Jacob will dance for joy, and Israel rejoice.* The true Jacob, the true Israel, that younger son to whom the elder has become a servant,[19] will dance for joy, because he will understand.[20]

---

19. See Gn 25:23.
20. The Church, that is, represented by the younger son.

Exposition of Psalm 53

A Sermon to the People[1]

Verses 1-2. The importance of the title; the Ziphites

1. The title of this psalm is somewhat long, but all the more useful for that, if we understand it rightly. Since the psalm itself is short, and we shall not need to delay too long over it, let us compensate by spending more time on the title, for from this title every verse that is sung derives its meaning. Anyone who has taken careful note of the sign on the front of a house will enter without hesitation, and once inside will not go astray. So too plain indications are given on the doorpost of this psalm to save us from taking the wrong turning inside.

The title runs like this: *Unto the end, in hymns, understanding for David himself, when the Ziphites came to Saul and told him, "Do you not realize that David is hiding among us?"* We are well aware that Saul was a persecutor of the holy man David; and we remember pointing out to you, dearly beloved,[2] that Saul represents the kind of temporal sovereignty which promotes not life, but death.[3] Moreover you must know that David prefigured Christ, or the body of Christ. Or rather you should remind yourselves of this, for you know it already.

So then, what is this about Ziphites? Ziph was a village, and its inhabitants were called Ziphites. David had gone into hiding in their territory when Saul was trying to find him and kill him. The Ziphites learned of this, and betrayed him to the persecuting king, saying, *David is hiding among us, isn't he?* (1 Sm 23:19). But their treachery brought them no advantage, nor did it harm David at all. Obviously they bore him ill-will, but even after receiving the information Saul was unable to capture David. In a cave in that region Saul fell into David's power and could have been killed, but David spared him, holding back from what he had the power to do,[4] whereas Saul was intent on doing something that was not in his power. Let any who have been Ziphites take the matter to heart; but let us for our part see what the psalm has to offer us, taking its cue from them.

---

1. Possibly preached at Carthage in the winter of 412-413.
2. *Vestrae caritati.*
3. See his Exposition of Psalm 51, sections 1-2.
4. See 1 Sm 24:4.

Gaining friends through astute use of riches

2. Well now, if we inquire what the name "Ziphites" means, we find that it signifies "those who flourish" or "flower." So some flourishing persons were enemies to holy David; flourishing people were hostile to the hidden one. If we wish to understand the psalm, we must look for them in the human race today. Let us first track down David in his hiding-place, and then we shall find his flourishing foes. This is where you will find the hidden David: to the members of Christ the apostle says, *You are dead, and your life is hidden with Christ in God.* And when will these hidden members come to flourish? *When Christ appears, Christ who is your life*, the apostle continues, *then you too will appear with him in glory* (Col 3:3-4). When the members of Christ reach their flowering stage, the Ziphites will be withering with drought, for mark to what kind of blooms a prophet compares their prosperity: *All flesh is but grass, and all human glory like the flower of grass.* And what fate awaits it? *The grass is dried up and the flower is fallen.* Where will David be then? Look at the sequel: *but the word of the Lord abides for ever* (Is 40:6.8). There are two kinds of people, then. You must distinguish between them, and choose which you want to be; for what is the point of your knowing this, if you hang back from making your choice? At present the power to choose lies ready to your hand, but a time will come when you no longer have the choice, the time when God will no longer put off passing sentence.

Who, then, are these flourishing Ziphites? No one else, surely, but the body of Doeg the Edomite, about whom we spoke to you only a few days ago, beloved.[5] Of him it was said, *Look at the person who would not take God as helper, but trusted in the amplitude of his riches, and grew strong in his stupidity* (Ps 51:9(52:8)). These are the flourishing children of this world, who in the gospel we have just heard were said to be more astute in their own fashion than the children of light. Astute, because they give the impression of provident foresight, but for a future they cannot be sure they will see. You heard about the steward's dealings with his master's property: how he feathered his own nest at his master's expense by generous discounts to the debtors, so that when he was dismissed from his job he might find a welcome with them.[6] So although he had defrauded his employer, the master nevertheless commended his intention,[7] taking less notice of his own loss than of the servant's acumen. How much more eager should we be to use sinful mammon to gain ourselves friends, when our Lord Jesus Christ himself urges us to do so! "Mammon" means "riches." Our riches are where our eternal home is, in heaven. The only people who call the

---

5. *Caritati vestrae.* See his Exposition of Psalm 51, especially section 4.

6. See Lk 16:1-9.

7. *Cor*, his "heart," the directing force of his actions.

money of this temporal world riches are they who cannot flourish except in this temporal world, and have no desire to use it to gain friends for eternity, because they do not recognize true riches. Only iniquity that blooms briefly like grass regards them as riches.[8] Such are the Ziphites, David's enemies who flourish in this world.

Why do the wicked seem to prosper?

3. Even the children of light are weak, and sometimes when they observe such flourishing persons their feet begin to slide under them. They see the wicked prosperous and fortunate, and they say in their hearts, "What good is my innocent life doing me? What do I get out of serving God, keeping his commandments, ill-treating no one, seizing no one else's property, doing no one down, and giving alms as I am able? All these things I do, yet they flourish while I have a hard time." What? Do you too want to be a Ziphite? They flourish in this world, but they are due to wither on judgment day, and after withering in that drought they will be thrown into eternal fire. Is that your ambition for yourself? Do you not know what he promised, he who came to you,[9] and what he exemplified in himself? If the prosperity of the Ziphites were truly something desirable, would not your Lord himself have flourished even in this world? Do you think he lacked the power to flourish? But he preferred to remain hidden among the Ziphites. To Pontius Pilate, who was like the very bloom of Ziphites and, suspicious about Christ's kingly power, was interrogating him, he replied, *Mine is not a kingship of this world* (Jn 18:36). This is why he remained hidden. All good people lie hidden here, because what they hold dear is within, in their hearts, where faith and hope and charity reside, where they have their treasure. Are these precious things visible in this world? They lie hidden, just as the reward they will gain lies hidden. In what sense is worldly distinction a splendid thing? It renders someone illustrious for a time, but does it last? It is like the grass in winter, that stays green only until summer comes.

Our minds must not follow the example of one we hear about in another psalm. There someone confesses that he stumbled and almost fell, that his feet slithered as he tried to walk in the way of God, because he observed a kind of happiness and prosperity in sinful people. But afterwards he understood what God was holding in reserve for the wicked at the end, and what it was that he who cannot deceive was promising to the just after their labors. Full of thankfulness at this insight he cried, *How good God is to Israel, to those of straightforward hearts!* Why do you say this, psalmist? *My feet had all but slipped*, he admits. And why was that? *Because I*

---

8. *Has ergo divitias sola iniquitas putat.* The editors of the Latin text amend *sola* to *solas*: "Iniquity deems only those things riches."
9. Variants: "he who came from God"; "he who will come to you."

envied sinners, seeing the peace that sinners enjoy. But his feet were steadied after he had come to understand what must happen in the end. It was a serious problem to him, as he says a little further on in the same psalm: *"It is too hard for me*. A baffling question arose in my mind as to why some people act wrongly on earth, yet seem to flourish, while many who act well lead such hard lives on this earth. Since this has been a major problem in my eyes, and difficult to unravel, *it is too hard for me until I enter God's holy place, and understand what the final outcome must be"* (Ps 72 (73): 1-3. 16-17). What is this final outcome? What else, but what we know to have been already foretold in the gospel? *When the Son of Man comes in his majesty, all nations will assemble before him. He will separate them from one another, as a shepherd separates sheep from goats; then he will station the sheep at his right hand, and the goats at his left* (Mt 25:31-33). So you see, the Ziphites are already set apart, and the next stage for this separated group is fire. What will become of the flowering of those standing at the Lord's left? They will be groaning then, won't they? They will be in anguish with a repentance that comes too late, asking, *What good has our pride done us*, or what benefit has come to us from our vaunted wealth? *All these things have passed away like a shadow* (Wis 5:8-9). O you Ziphites, when you find yourselves at Christ's left it will be too late to feel remorse over the way you flourished in that shadow. Why did you not recognize David, whose hiding-place in your midst you betrayed? If you had corrected yourselves then, your sorrow would not have been sterile. You see, brothers and sisters, there is fruitful sorrow and sterile sorrow. Your sorrow is fruitful if you accuse yourself now, and repudiate your evil conduct, and bear down heavily on what you have repudiated, and rid yourself of those things you have been hard on, and having rid yourself of them allow yourself to be changed, stripping off the old nature and putting on the new, choosing to be despised with Christ rather than to flourish with the Ziphites.

But what if some worldly distinction happens to come your way while you are holding onto your true good in secret, hiding among the Ziphites and clinging to the promise of reward that is also secret? Do not give yourself airs about it, for if you make it an excuse for exalting yourself you will tumble into the flowering Ziphites. Remember how a certain holy woman, Esther, bore herself. She was of the Jewish race but was the wife of a foreign king. At a time when her compatriots were in danger it fell to her to plead with the king on their behalf. She set herself to pray, and in her prayer she confessed that all her royal insignia were of no more value to her than a dirty rag.[10] If women are capable of that, can men not do the same? And if a Jewish woman could do it, can the Christian Church not do it too? What I would like to commend to you, beloved,[11] are the words, *If riches are plentiful, do not set your hearts on them* (Ps

---

10. See Est 14:16.
11. *Caritati vestrae*.

61:11(62:10)). Though they abound, and worldly prosperity dogs your steps, do not trust yourself to the sea, even if it smiles at you. If riches are plentiful, if you are awash with wealth, tread it underfoot and let yourself be suspended above it by your God. If you keep it all below you, and hang from him, then when the riches are taken away you will not fall. Otherwise a bad thought may come into your mind, a thought in no way Christian, about which another psalm warns us. After speaking there about the flourishing Ziphites, that psalm continues, *Exceedingly deep are your designs.* I repeat, scripture declares, *Exceedingly deep are your designs. The thoughtless man will not recognize these things, nor the fool understand.* What will he not understand? That *though sinners spring up like grass, and all those who commit iniquity seem to have fair prospects, they are destined to perish for ever* (Ps 91:6-8(92:5-7)). The flowering of the wicked entranced them, and they said to themselves, "Look how the wicked bloom! I think God must love bad people." And bewitched by the ephemeral flowering of sinners, they turn to sin themselves, only to perish. Their ruin will be no short-lived phenomenon, like the prosperity of those others, but will last *for ever.* Why? Because *the thoughtless man will not recognize these things, nor the fool understand,* for want of going into God's holy place to gain understanding of the final outcome.

Such understanding may be rather difficult to attain, however; so our psalm began by referring to David hiding among the Ziphites, so as not to be seduced by their prosperity, preferring to accept a lowly status among them, and enjoy unseen glory in the presence of God. Accordingly, what does the title ascribe to him? *Unto the end, in hymns.* That means in songs of praise—what kind of praise? *The Lord gave, and the Lord has taken away. This has happened as the Lord willed: may the Lord's name be blessed* (Jb 1:21). Did you think he had withered away from drought, having lost all he had? By no means. Only the leaves had fallen; the root was alive. Now we can see why the title says, *Unto the end, in hymns, understanding for David himself.* What does it mean by *understanding for David himself?* The *understanding* it has in mind is opposed to that of *the thoughtless man,* who *will not recognize these things,* the fool who does not understand. This is the kind of understanding David was showing *when the Ziphites came to Saul and told him, "Do you not realize that David is hiding among us?"* Let him stay hidden among you; heaven preserve him from flowering like you! Listen now to his voice.

Verse 3. Christ, savior through weakness, will judge in power

4. *O God, save me by your name, and judge me in your power.* This must be the prayer of the Church hiding among the Ziphites. Let the body of Christians say it, the body whose good way of life is cherished in secret, as it secretly hopes

that its merits will be rewarded: *O God, save me by your name, and judge me in your power.* You came to us in humble guise, O Christ, you were scorned and scourged and crucified and killed; but on the third day you rose again, on the fortieth day you ascended into heaven, you are enthroned at the right hand of the Father and now no one sees you. From heaven you sent your Spirit. Those who were worthy received him and, filled with your love, they preached throughout the world and among all nations the glorious tale of your humility. Today I see your name illustrious in our human race, yet you were proclaimed as the one who was made weak for us. The very teacher of the Gentiles professed that he knew nothing among us save Christ Jesus, and him crucified,[12] so that we might choose Christ's despised lowliness rather than renown among the flourishing Ziphites. Indeed, what does Paul say of Christ? *Though he died in weakness, he is alive by the power of God* (2 Cor 13:4). He came to die in weakness, but he will come again to judge in the power of God. Yet it is on account of the weakness of the cross that his name has become glorious. Anyone who refuses to believe in that name which has been glorified through weakness will be terrified by the advent of the judge in power. May he save us by his name, and then judge us in his power; may he not sift us out and place us at his left hand when he comes in strength, this Christ once weak. But who dare make so bold a prayer, who dare say to God, *Judge me?* Do not people use that as a curse to hurl at others, "May God be your judge"? A curse it is indeed if God judges you in his power without having first saved you by his name; but if his saving name has priority, his subsequent judgment in power will be your salvation. Do not fear: that judgment will mean for you not punishment but discernment; and that is what another psalm prays for: *Judge me, O God, and distinguish my cause from that of an unholy people* (Ps 42(43):1). What is meant, then, by *Judge me?* It means, "Mark me out from the Ziphites among whom I lie hidden. I have held out while they bloomed; let my time of flowering come now. They bloomed for a brief spell, and then their grass dried and their blossom wilted; but what will my flowering be?" Of us it is said, *Planted in the Lord's house, they will flourish in the courts of our God* (Ps 91:14(92:13)). Flowers there will be for us, unfading flowers like the foliage of that tree planted by the waters, of which another psalm says, *Its leaves will not fall off* (Ps 1:3). *O God, save me by your name, and judge me in your power.*

Verse 4. God hears our prayers, but does not always give us what we want

5. *O God, hear my prayer, let the words I speak reach your ears.* May they find their way to your ears, these words that I address to you, because I am not looking to win from you prosperity like that of the Ziphites. *Let the words I speak*

---

12. See 1 Cor 2:2.

reach your ears—your ears, I mean; may you receive my words, for even if my prayer is audible to the Ziphites they will not take it in, because they have no understanding. They wallow in temporal goods, and have no idea how to long for the good things of eternity. Let my prayer reach you. My longing for the joys you will lavish upon us in eternity has wrung this prayer from me and launched it on its way to you. I am directing it to your ears. Help it to speed true; do not let it falter and fall limply short of its mark.

But even if the good things for which I plead do not come to me now, I am quite sure they will later. Scripture tells of someone who in a sinful state besought God, and found his prayer refused, but for his own good. Worldly desires had prompted his petition. When he saw himself beset by temporal troubles, he hoped that they would pass, and that the ephemeral bloom of the grass would return. So he prayed, *My God, my God, why have you forsaken me?* We hear in this the voice of Christ himself, but he is speaking on behalf of his members. This is *the tale of my sins*, he says; *I have cried to you all day, and you have not listened; and in the night, but you will not collude with my foolishness* (Ps 21:2-3(22:1-2)). He means, "Even during the night I have cried to you, and you did not listen; yet your refusal to listen was not to compound my foolishness but rather to teach me wisdom, so that I might come to understand what I ought to be asking of you. Until then I had been asking for things that would perhaps have harmed me if I had received them." You pray for riches, human creature, yet how many have been ruined by their riches! How do you know that it will be good for you to have wealth? Plenty of people have been much safer when they were poor and obscure; once they grew rich and began to be illustrious they fell prey to the powerful, did they not? How much better it would have been for them to remain hidden and unknown; once rich they were hunted not for what they were but for what they had.

As far as temporal benefits are concerned, brothers and sisters, we advise you, we exhort you in the Lord's name, to ask not for some definite gift but simply for what God knows will be expedient for you. You have no idea yourselves what this expedient gift may be. Sometimes what you think will be advantageous to you may turn out to be a hindrance, whereas what you consider to be an obstacle in your path may really be for your good. Remember that you are ill, so do not dictate to the doctor what remedies he is to apply. If even Paul, the teacher of the Gentiles, confesses that *we do not know how to pray as we ought* (Rom 8:26), how much less do we ourselves know? Paul believed that he was making a prudent prayer when he begged to be relieved of a sting of the flesh, a messenger of Satan that buffeted him to ensure that he would not get above himself because of the magnificence of his revelations; but what answer did he receive from the Lord? Was his wish granted? No, it was refused, so that he might be given what would profit him. What did he hear the Lord say? *Three times I begged the Lord to take it away from me*, he tells us, *but he said to me, "My grace is sufficient for you, for my power finds complete scope in weakness* (2 Cor 12:8-9). I have applied a remedy to your wound, and I know when to put it on and when to take it off."

Let the patient not take himself out of the doctor's hands, nor let him presume to give the doctor advice. The pains last only for a time. If troubles are your lot, then if you sincerely worship God you can be sure that he knows what is best for each of us. If prosperity falls to you, be all the more careful that it does not corrode your mind, and estrange it from the One who gave you prosperity. What does our understanding psalmist say? *O God, hear my prayer; let the words I speak reach your ears.*

Verse 5. The apparent riches of the "foreigners"

6. *Because foreigners have risen up against me.* Who are these foreigners? David was a Judean, was he not, a man from the tribe of Judah? And the town of Ziph belonged to the tribe of Judah; it was in Judean territory. How could its inhabitants be called foreigners, then?

Foreigners they were, not by their city or their tribe or their kindred, but by the nature of their flowering. If you want to recognize these foreigners, look at the description in another psalm of people called "alien children": *Their mouths spoke empty words, and their right hand is a hand that deals unjustly.* It goes on to describe the prosperity of the Ziphites: *Their sons in youth are like well-set saplings; their daughters are adorned and gathered round them like the pillars of the temple; their store rooms are full to overflowing; their ewes are fruitful, increasing at every lambing-time, and their oxen sturdy. Never is their hedge broken down, there are no miscarriages, nor is there rioting in their streets.* Look at the Ziphites, these people with their brief flowering! Popular opinion *calls those who have these things blessed*, but they are more justly called "foreigners." What is your opinion, you who are hiding among the Ziphites? *Blessed is the people whose God is the Lord* (Ps 143(144):11-15). Quite right: from that conviction springs your prayer, the prayer you direct to the Lord's ears, as the psalmist begs, *Let the words I speak reach your ears, because foreigners have risen up against me.*

7. *And the powerful have sought my life.* My brothers and sisters, those who pin their hopes to this world have found a new method of attacking the race of the saints, the company of those whose hopes are withheld from the world. The two kinds of people are mingled together, yes; and live together, certainly; but they are absolutely opposed to one another. The one type attaches all its hope to secular realities and temporal happiness, the other places its hope firmly in the Lord its God. The Ziphites seem peaceable, but you must not put too much reli-

ance on their friendliness; it lasts only as long as it is not tested. When some test occurs—say when one of them is reproved[13] about his or her worldly prosperity—then I do not say merely that such a person will quarrel with the bishop: he or she will not be willing to come near the Church at all, lest any of the blossom gets brushed off. Why do I say this, brothers and sisters? You all like to hear me saying it in the name of Christ; you understand what I am saying and you shout your approval. You certainly would not be applauding if you did not understand. But this understanding of yours must bear fruit, and whether it is fruitful or not only testing will show. You are reckoned as our people, and the trial must not suddenly show you up as foreigners. The Church must not say of you, *Foreigners have risen up against me, and the powerful have sought my life.* Nor must these words be found to apply to you: *They have not set God before their eyes.* How is anyone who has eyes for this world alone going to set God before his eyes? All his thought is to pile coin upon coin, increase his crops, fill his warehouses, and say to his soul, "Enjoy yourself, feast, and eat all you want." Will such a person keep in sight the one who says to a boastful, gaudily flowering Ziphite, *You fool* (and you are a fool because you have no understanding, you are thoughtless and lack prudence): *your life will be taken from you this very night; and then who will own what you have prepared?* (Lk 12:20). No, of course not. *They have not set God before their eyes.*

Verses 6-7. God's hidden help

8. *For lo, God is helping me*, though the Ziphites among whom I am hiding do not know it. If they too were to set God before their eyes, they would discover how God helps me. All the saints are helped by God, but within themselves, where no one sees. Just as the wicked endure fierce inner torment from their consciences, so do God-fearing persons find in their consciences immense joy, for, as the apostle claims, *Our boast is this: the witness of our own conscience* (2 Cor 1:12). Such people take pride in this, but within themselves, not in the showy outward prosperity of the Ziphites. Accordingly they testify here, *"Lo, God is helping me.* However far away in the future the fulfillment of his promises may be, his help is comforting and close at hand for me today. Already today my heart's joy tells me how little cause the impious have to complain, *Who has anything good to show us?* For I know that *the light of your countenance has set its seal upon us, O Lord; you have given joy to my heart* (Ps 4:6-7). To my heart, not to my vineyard, not to my flock, not to my wine-vat, not to my table, but *to my heart*, for *lo, God is helping me."* And how does he help you? *The Lord upholds my life.*

---

13. Or possibly "when someone's bluff is called": *ut arguatur aliquis.*

9. *Deflect misfortunes onto my enemies.* However vigorous they are, however flourishing, they are destined for the fire. *Scatter them by your strength.* What if they flourish at present, what if they spring up like grass? You must not be a thoughtless person or a fool, to be dazzled by their prosperity and so perish along with them for ever.[14] No, pray to the Lord: *Deflect misfortunes onto my enemies.* If you are within the body, the body of the true David, he will scatter them by his strength. Sinners flower in the world's favor, but perish by God's strength. Their flowering is not like their perdition: they flower for a brief spell and then perish for ever, flower amid illusory good fortune and perish in real torments. *Scatter them by your strength*, those whom you bore with in your weakness.

Verse 8. Sacrifice to God and love God for himself alone

10. *Of my own free will I will offer sacrifice to you.* Can anyone understand what this treasure of the heart is, if people have never tasted it for themselves, but only listened to someone else telling them about it? What does this line mean: *of my own free will I will offer sacrifice to you*? All the same, I am going to tell you. Let any who are capable take it in as best they can; and let those who are not capable believe me, and pray that comprehension may be given them. Even if many are incapable, have we the right to omit this verse, and not draw your attention to it? I assure you, beloved ones,[15] God's love itself is enough inducement to me to say something about it, and I thank him that you are listening attentively. If I noticed that you were too weary to listen, I would remain silent about this verse, though reluctantly. But even then, insofar as God enabled me, I would not be silent in my heart. So then, let my tongue bring to birth what my heart has conceived; let what is cradled in my mind be proclaimed by my voice; and let us explain to the best of our ability what the psalm means by *of my own free will I will offer sacrifice to you.*

What sacrifice is implied here, brothers and sisters? What can I worthily offer to the Lord in response to his mercy? Shall I look for victims in a flock of sheep, shall I pick out a ram, or select a bull from the herds, or at least bring incense from the land of the Sabeans? What am I to do? What shall I offer?

What else but the gift of which another psalm speaks: *by a sacrifice of praise I shall be honored* (Ps 49(50):23). But why does our psalm say, *Of my own free will*? Because what I praise I love freely, gratis. I praise God, and find joy in the very act of praising him; I delight to praise him, and never will it be an occasion of shame for me. Very different is the way a charioteer, or a gladiator, or some actor is praised by his fans at rubbishy shows; there the fans incite others to join

---

14. See Ps 91:7-8(92:6-7).
15. *Caritati vestrae.*

them in praising their champion, and egg each other on until all of them are yelling together; and then often enough there are red faces all round when their hero is defeated. With our God it is a different matter. Let him be praised with our free will and loved with charity; and let the love we give, the praise we offer, be offered gratis. What is gratuitous praise? It is the praise offered to him for his own sake and not with a view to anything else; for if you praise God in the hope that he will give you something, you are not loving God gratis. You would be ashamed, wouldn't you, if your wife loved you only for your money, and then, if some accident reduced you to poverty, she began to think of adultery? Since, then, you want your spouse to love you gratis, are you prepared to love God with an eye to something other than God? What reward do you expect to get from God, you greedy suppliant? It is not the earth that he is holding in reserve for you, but himself, who made heaven and earth. *Of my own free will I will offer sacrifice to you.* Do not sacrifice under duress. If you praise God with some other thing as your objective, you are praising him under duress, for if the thing you really love were within your reach, you would not be praising him. Get clear in your minds what I am saying: suppose, for example, you praise God in the hope that he will give you lots of money. If you could get plenty of money from some other source, and not from God, would you be praising him? You wouldn't, would you? So if it is for the sake of money that you are praising God, you are offering sacrifice to him not of your own free will but under duress, because you are in love with something other than God.

This is why scripture says, *Of my own free will I will offer sacrifice to you.* Leave all those other things aside, and attend to him. Even the things he has given are good only because the Giver is good. He does give them, certainly he does; these temporal gifts are from him, and to some people he gives them for their profit, to others for their ruin, according to the lofty, deep wisdom of his decrees. The apostle gazed terrified into the abyss of those judgments, and exclaimed, *Oh how deep are the riches of God's wisdom and knowledge, how unfathomable his decisions and inscrutable his ways! Who shall understand his ways, or comprehend his designs?* (Rom 11:33-34). He knows when to give, to whom to give, when to take away, and from whom to take away. Make sure, then, that you beg from him in this present life what will profit you in the future; beg for what will help you for eternity. But love God for himself alone, love him disinterestedly, for you cannot possibly think of anything he could give you better than himself. Or if you can, ask for that! *Of my own free will I will offer sacrifice to you.* Why *of my own free will?* Because gratis. And what does "gratis" mean? *I will praise your name, O Lord, because it is good*, for no other reason than because it is good. Does the psalmist say, "I will praise your name, O Lord, because you give me productive estates, because you give me gold and silver, because you give me a huge fortune, lots of money and a position of honor"? No. Why, then? *Because it is good.* I can find nothing better than your name; therefore *I will praise your name, O Lord, because it is good.*

Verse 9. The vantage point of the heart

11. *Because you have pulled me free from all my tribulation.* This is how I came to understand that your name is good; for if I had been in a state to know it before tribulations came upon me, perhaps I would not have needed them. But tribulation was sent to me as a warning, and the warning prompted me to praise you. I would not have understood my position if I had not been warned of my weakness; and so you pulled me free from all my troubles.

And my eye looked down on my foes, my glance fell upon those Ziphites. I passed beyond their prosperity as I sailed up to the high place of my heart, and there I reached you. From there I looked down on them and saw that *all flesh is but grass, and all human glory like the flower of grass* (Is 40:6). So too another passage says, *I saw the godless exalting himself very high, overtopping the cedars of Lebanon. But I passed further on, and look! He was not there.* Why was he not there? Because you have passed him by. How did you pass him by? By hearkening to the invitation, "Lift up your hearts,"[16] to good purpose. You refused to dally on earth, where you could only rot away; you lifted up your soul to God, and soared above the very cedars of Lebanon; from that height you looked down, and *he was not there.* You searched, but *his place was not to be seen* (Ps 36(37):35-36). No longer is this too hard for you to understand, for you have entered the sanctuary of God, and understood what the final outcome must be.[17]

Accordingly the psalm ends like this: *My eye looked down on my foes.* Do the same in your own minds, brothers and sisters: raise up your hearts, sharpen the keen edge of your intelligence, learn to love God gratis, learn to sit lightly to this present world, learn to offer a sacrifice of praise of your own free will, so that you may soar above the fleeting blossoms of the grass and look down on your foes.

---

16. See note at Exposition of Psalm 10, 3.
17. See Ps 72(73):16-17.

Exposition of Psalm 54

A Sermon to the People

The title: Christ our end and our perfection

1. The title of this psalm is *Unto the end, in hymns, understanding for David himself.* We need only remind you briefly what this "end" is, because you know already. *Christ is the end of the law, bringing justification to everyone who believes* (Rom 10:4). Our intention therefore must be directed to the end, directed to Christ. Why is he called "the end"? Because whatever we do is referred to him, and when we have reached him we shall have nothing further to seek. We speak of "an end" in the sense of something being exhausted, but also of "an end" meaning the completion of something. When we say, "The food we were eating has come to an end," we mean something quite different from "the weaving of that tunic is finished." In both cases we speak of something being ended or finished, but in the one instance it means that the food no longer exists, in the other that a garment has reached its perfection. So, in the case of ourselves, our "end" must mean our perfection, and our perfection is Christ. We are made perfect in him because he is our head and we are his members; and he is called the end of the law because without him no one perfectly keeps the law. Many of the psalms have this superscription, *Unto the end,* and when you hear it you must not think of something being consumed, but of something consummated.

2. *In hymns,* the title continues; that means with songs of praise. Whether we are troubled and hemmed in by difficulties, or glad and dancing for joy, God is to be praised, because he schools us through tribulations and comforts us with joy. God's praise should never depart from the heart and mouth of a Christian. We must not praise him when things go well with us and curse him when they go wrong; rather we must obey the injunction of another psalm: *I will bless the Lord at all times; his praise shall be in my mouth always* (Ps 33(34):1). When you feel happy, acknowledge the Father who is caressing you; when you are distressed, acknowledge the Father who is chastening you. Whether through caresses or through chastisement he is educating his child, for whom he is preparing an inheritance.

The title, concluded: Understanding for David, who prefigures Christ, head and members

3. What does this imply: *understanding for David himself?* As we know, David was a holy prophet, a king of Israel, and the son of Jesse. But when our Lord Jesus Christ came for our salvation, he was from David's seed, according to the flesh,[1] and so he is often figuratively called by the name "David." And David himself figuratively stands for Christ, in virtue of being Christ's carnal ancestor. In one respect Christ is the son of David, and in a different respect he is David's Lord: son of David according to the flesh, but Lord of David in his divinity. If all things were made through him,[2] then certainly David himself was made through him—David, whose descendant Christ was when he came to humankind. This is made clear when the Jews, questioned by our Lord as to whose son the Messiah would be, replied, *David's.* But he could see that they had remained at the level of the flesh and lost sight of the Messiah's divinity, so he corrected them by posing a further question: *Then how is it that David in the Spirit calls him "Lord," saying, The Lord said to my Lord, "Sit at my right hand, until I make your enemies into your footstool"? If David in the Spirit calls him "Lord," how can he be David's son?* (Mt 22:42-45). He is putting the question to them, not denying his sonship: "You have heard that the Messiah is David's Lord, so tell me how he is David's son; you have heard that he is David's son, so tell me how he is his Lord." The Catholic faith has the answer to this dilemma. How is he Lord? Because *in the beginning was the Word, and the Word was with God; he was God.* And how is he David's son? Because *the Word was made flesh, and dwelt among us* (Jn 1:1.14).

So David represents Christ. But as we have often reminded you, dearest friends,[3] Christ is both head and body, and we must not think ourselves alien to Christ, since we are his members. Nor must we think of ourselves as separate from him, because *they will be two in one flesh. This is a great mystery*, says the apostle, *but I am referring it to Christ and the Church* (Eph 5:31-32). Since, then, the whole Christ consists of head and body, we must understand that we too are included in David when in the psalm's title we hear of *understanding for David himself.* Christ's members must have this understanding, and Christ must understand in the persons of his members, and the members of Christ must understand in Christ, because head and members form one Christ. The head was in heaven when he insistently asked, *Why are you persecuting me?* (Acts 9:4). Through hope we are with him in heaven, and through charity he is with us on earth. This is why our psalm can speak about *understanding for David himself.*

---

1. See Rom 1:3.
2. See Jn 1:3.
3. *Caritatem vestram.*

Let us take it to heart when we hear it, and let the Church understand, for it is our business to make the greatest possible effort to assess the evil situation we are in and from what evil we wish to be delivered, mindful of the Lord's prayer, which ends with our petition, *Deliver us from evil.*

Amid the manifold troubles of this world, our psalm about understanding utters its lament. Anyone who lacks understanding will not join in this lament. But we must remember, beloved,[4] that we have been made in the image of God, and that this image is to be found only in our understanding. We are outdone by[5] the beasts in many respects, but in that faculty where human beings know themselves to be made in God's image, there especially do they know that they have been granted something greater than anything given to the animals. When humans consider all their endowments, they find that they are most specifically distinguished from the animals by their possession of understanding. This is why certain people are rebuked by their Creator for belittling that faculty in themselves which is most properly human and is his most special gift to them: *Do not be like a horse or a mule, devoid of understanding*, he tells them (Ps 31(32):9). And in another passage he says, *Human beings failed to understand how they were honored; they were no better than the foolish beasts, and became like them* (Ps 48:13(49:12)).

Let us recognize our dignity, then, and try to understand. If we understand we shall see that where we live now is a place not for gladness but for groaning, not yet a place for exultation but still a place for lamentation. Even if a certain exultation is habitually present in our hearts, it is the joy of hope, not of fulfillment. We rejoice over God's promise, because we know that he who promises does not deceive us. But as far as the present time is concerned, listen to what a bad situation and what straits we are in. If you are keeping to the path, what you hear will find an echo in your own experience. Anyone who is not yet walking the way of dedication to God will be amazed that David's members have so much to groan over, for such a person has no experience of like troubles in himself. As long as he does not share the pain he is not there: he does not feel what the body feels because he is outside the body. Let him be incorporated, and he will feel the same. Let the body speak, then, and let us listen. Let us listen, and make these words our own.

Verses 2-3. The wicked put good people to the proof

4. *Hear my appeal, O God, and do not disdain my prayer; pay heed to me and hear me.* These are the words of someone who is anxious, apprehensive, beset by

---

4. *Carissimi.*
5. *Superamur.* But the editors of the Latin text amend to *non separamur*, "we are not divided from."

tribulation. He is suffering acutely as he prays, and longing to be delivered from his trouble. It is for us to find out what his plight is and, when he begins to tell us, to realize that we are in it too, so that as we share his tribulation we may unite our prayer with his. *I am deeply saddened in my ordeal, and very distressed.* Where is he deeply saddened? Where distressed? *In my ordeal,* he says. He is about to identify[6] the wicked people he is enduring, and he has called this endurance of them his ordeal. You must not think that bad people are in this world uselessly, or that God cannot employ them for good purposes. Every bad person is either allowed to live so that he or she may be corrected, or else allowed to live so that through him or her a good person may be put to the proof. Would that those who are a trial to us now might be converted, and then tried along with us! However, as long as they remain the sort of people who put us through our paces we must not hate them, because we never know whether any one of them will persist in his evil way to the very end. It often happens that when you think you have been hating an enemy, you have unwittingly hated a brother or sister. It is the devil and his angels who are plainly indicated to us by holy scripture as destined for eternal fire. In their case alone may we despair of correction. Against them we wage hidden warfare, a struggle for which the apostle forearms us, saying, *It is not against flesh and blood that you have to struggle*—against human beings we can see, that is—*but against principalities and powers and the rulers of this world of darkness* (Eph 6:12). Possibly you might have thought that when he said *this world* he meant that they were rulers of heaven and earth; so to guard against this misconception he specified, *this world of darkness.* He thereby indicated the lovers of this world, the world of the godless and the unjust, that *world* of which the gospel says, *The world did not know him* (Jn 1:10). This world did not know the light; for although the light shone in the darkness, the darkness was never able to master it. This darkness which could not master the light even when present is called "the world." It follows, then, that this is the darkness of which the devil and his angels are rulers. Concerning these rulers we have scripture's definite statement that there is absolutely no hope of conversion for any one of them; but the case is different for the darkness over which they rule, for we are uncertain whether those who once were darkness may not become light. After all, the apostle says to some who have become believers, *You were darkness once, but now you are light in the Lord* (Eph 5:8). Darkness when left to yourselves, but light in the Lord.

Well then, brothers and sisters, all bad people, while they are bad, put the good to the proof. I will make the point briefly: listen and grasp what I am saying. If you are good, you can have no enemy except a bad person. But observe the standard of goodness that is placarded up before you: you must imitate the good-

---

6. Variant: "has identified."

ness of your Father, who *causes his sun to rise over the good and the wicked, and sends rain upon just and unjust alike* (Mt 5:45). It is not as though you were the only one to have an enemy, and God had none. You have as your enemy someone who was created just like you; but God's enemy is someone he has himself created. We often find scripture calling bad and unjust people enemies of God, yet he spares them—he against whom no enemy could have any grudge, he to whom every enemy is ungrateful, since it is from God that the enemy holds whatever good he has. Even in any trouble he has to undergo, this enemy is the recipient of God's mercy, because he is sent the trouble only to save him from getting proud. He is subjected to it so that he may be brought low and acknowledge the Most High. But what about you? What have you given to that enemy of yours whom you find insufferable? If that person is God's enemy, and yet God has given him so much, causing *his sun to rise over the good and the wicked, and sending rain on just and unjust alike*, can you not keep just one thing for your enemy, you who have no power to make the sun rise or to send rain on the earth? Can you not allow the peace promised on earth to people of good will[7] to be yours?

Moreover, a ruling principle of love has been established for you, that you must imitate your Father by loving your enemy, for Christ commands, *Love your enemies* (Lk 6:27.35); and how are you going to get any training in observing it if you never have to put up with an enemy? So you see, he or she is doing you some good. And let the fact that God spares the wicked do you good as well; let it inspire you to show mercy, for though you are good now you may perhaps have been bad in earlier days, so if God did not spare bad people you would not have emerged to give him thanks today. May he who has spared even you be merciful to others as well. The road to a devout life must not be barred after you have traveled along it.

Verse 4. The storm all around

5. Now what about the speaker in this psalm, the one beset by bad people and feeling sorely tried by their hostility? What is his prayer, what does he say? *I am deeply saddened in my ordeal, and very distressed.* He stretched his love so far that he could love even his enemies, but now weariness has overtaken him. There are so many enemies, a great crowd is barking furiously all round him, and he has succumbed through human weakness. He saw that a wicked, diabolical suggestion was beginning to force an entry into his heart, persuading him to grant admission to[8] hatred for his enemies. He is struggling against the hatred, trying to make his love perfect, and as he wrestles and fights he is distressed. His

---

7. See Lk 2:14.
8. *Inducat.* Some codices have *induat*, "to put on," like a garment or arms.

voice is heard in another psalm too: *My eye was inflamed by anger.* And how does the psalm continue there? *I have grown old among all my enemies* (Ps 6:8(7)). He began to sink beneath the waves, like Peter, as the storm overwhelmed him; for the people who can tread underfoot the waves of this world are the ones who love their enemies. Christ walked on the sea without fear, because love for his enemies could not be torn out of his heart by any means whatever. Even when hanging on the cross he kept saying, *Father, forgive them, for they do not know what they are doing* (Lk 23:34). But Peter too wanted to walk on the water. Christ did so as head, Peter as body, for Christ had said, *Upon this rock I will build my Church* (Mt 16:18). He was commanded to walk, and walk he did, but by the grace of the one who gave the order, not by his own strength. When he felt the power of the wind, he was afraid, and began to sink, very worried when tested like this. What was this powerful wind? I was distressed, says the psalmist, *by the shouting of the enemy and the trouble caused by a sinner.* Just as Peter cried out from the waves, *Lord, I'm sinking, save me!* (Mt 14:30) so too had the psalmist cried out long before, *Hear my appeal, O God, and do not disdain my prayer; pay heed to me and hear me.* Why? What is the matter? What are you groaning about? *"I am deeply saddened in my ordeal, and very distressed.* You have put me among the wicked to test me, I know, but I have not the strength to withstand their onslaught. Give me tranquillity, for I am very upset; stretch out your hand to me, for I am sinking. *I am deeply saddened in my ordeal, and very distressed by the shouting of an enemy and the trouble caused by a sinner, for they have brought down iniquity upon me, and cast a shadow over me with their anger."*

You have heard about the waves and the winds. They buffeted him and he seemed to be brought low, but he kept on praying. The din of their insults raged all round him, but he continued to invoke in his heart someone they could not see.

Snatching victory from the jaws of defeat

6. When a Christian has to suffer anything like this, he or she must not be too ready to make an angry attack on the tormentor, or hope to subdue the wind. We should turn to prayer, so as not to lose our love. In any case, why be afraid of what a human enemy can do? What can he do? He can say nasty things, and hurl abuse at you, and make plenty of savage uproar; but how does that hurt you? Our Lord tells us, *Rejoice and dance for joy, because your reward is great in heaven* (Mt 5:12; Lk 6:23). As the enemy redoubles his ranting on earth, you are doubling your profits in heaven. But suppose he becomes yet more ferocious, and has power to inflict more harm that that? You are still completely safe, for you have been told, *Do not be afraid of those who kill the body, but cannot kill the soul* (Mt 10:28). What have you to fear, then, when you have to tolerate an

enemy? Do not let the love that is in you be disturbed, the love you bear that enemy.

Now this enemy is a human being, a creature of flesh and blood, and what he attacks in you is something visible. The world of flesh and blood is attacking you, this dark world, but behind it stands another enemy, a hidden one, the ruler of this dark world. He attacks what is hidden in you; he is bent on destroying your interior treasures. Keep both these enemies in sight: the one overt, the other secret; the overt human foe, and the hidden foe, the devil. Your human adversary is the same as you are in respect of human nature; in respect of faith and love he or she is not yet what you are, but may still become so. Two enemies, then. Observe the one, and apprehend the other with your mind; love the one, and shun the other. The enemy you can see wants to humiliate in you whatever it is that gives you the advantage over him. If he is inferior to you in wealth, for instance, he wants to reduce you to poverty; if he is your inferior in rank, he wants to bring you down; if his strength is not equal to yours, he wants to weaken you. He is trying to spoil or steal whatever in you makes him feel inferior. The invisible enemy likewise wants to take away from you what sets you above him. As a human being you may be superior to other humans in your human good fortune, but you are superior to the devil by your love for your enemy. Just as that other human person strives to take from you, or curtail, or subvert your happiness because it surpasses his, so does the devil try to get the better of you, a human being, by stealing from you that very thing by which you get the better of him. Take great care, then, to preserve in your heart love for your enemy, because with that you overcome the devil. Let man or woman rage to their utmost, let them steal from you whatever they can; if the one who rages openly is loved, the one who rages in secret is vanquished.

Verse 5. Avoid hatred; it kills

7. But the psalmist went on praying, deeply distressed and saddened, as though his eye was inflamed by anger. If anger against a brother or sister becomes hardened, it is hatred. Anger inflames the eye, but hatred blinds it; anger is a splinter, hatred a beam. Perhaps at some time or other you felt hatred for someone you rebuked for being angry? There was hatred in you, anger in the person you corrected, and you deserved to hear the Lord's command, *Take the beam out of your own eye first, then you will see clearly to take the splinter out of your brother's* (Mt 7:5). Here is an illustration to help you understand the vast difference between anger and hatred: parents are angry with their children every day, but are there any parents who hate their children? I have yet to see them. This disturbed, saddened psalmist went on praying and struggling against all the insults of those who abused him, but not in order to get the better of them by trading insults. All he wanted was to avoid hating any of them. That is why he

prays, that is why he pleads when confronted *by the shouting of the enemy and the trouble caused by a sinner, for they have brought down iniquity upon me, and cast a shadow over me with their anger. My heart is deeply disturbed within me.* This is the same lament that he made elsewhere: *my eye is inflamed by anger* (Ps 6:8(7)). And if his eye is inflamed, what is the consequence? *The fear of death fell upon me.* Love is our life, and if love is life, hatred is death. When a person begins to fear that he may hate the one he used to love, he is afraid of death; and the death he fears is one more dreadful and more interior, because it is a death that slays not the body but the soul. Think about it: you were faced with a fellow human who was furious with you; but what harm could he or she do you, in view of the security the Lord gave you against such enemies? He bade you, *Do not be afraid of those who kill the body* (Mt 10:28). In his rage the enemy may kill the body, but by hating him you have killed the soul; and whereas he has killed the body of another, you have killed your own soul. This is what is meant by *the fear of death fell upon me.*

Verses 6-7. The longing to flee from troublemakers

8. *Fear and trembling came upon me, and darkness covered me. And I said. . . .* Anyone who hates a brother or sister is in darkness still, for if love is light, hatred is darkness.[9] Now what is he saying to himself, this man beset by weakness and distressed amid his trials? *Who will give me wings, as though to a dove?*[10] *Then I will fly away and find rest.* He was either hoping for death or longing for solitude. "As long as it is indicated to me, or rather enjoined upon me, that I must love my enemies," he says, "their continually mounting insults are like a shadow falling across me; they trouble my eyes, distort my vision, thrust at my heart and kill my soul. I wish I could get away, and so avoid piling sins upon sins, but I am too weak for that.[11] At least I would like to withdraw for a little while from human society, so that my wound may not be constantly aggravated. Then when it had healed I could return to the fray."

This does happen, brothers and sisters. A desire for solitude does often arise in the mind of a servant of God from no other cause than a host of troubles and difficulties, so that he or she exclaims, *Who will give me wings, as though to a dove?* Is the speaker complaining of being wingless, or is it rather that his wings are tied? If he has none, let them be given him; if they are bound, let them be

---

9. See 1 Jn 2:9-11.

10. *Quis dabit mihi pennas sicut columbae?*, usually taken to mean "wings of a dove"; but *columbae* could be either genitive or dative, and Augustine apparently understands it as dative, since further on in this paragraph he says, "not as to a raven" (*corvo*, unambiguously dative).

11. So most manuscripts. A few have "sins upon sins, because I am weak, and so. . .," which makes better sense.

loosened; for anyone who frees a bird's wings from entanglements is giving the bird its wings, or at any rate giving them back. The bird did not really own them as long as it was unable to use them for flying. Tied wings are nothing but a burden. So the psalmist cries out, *Who will give me wings, as though to a dove? Then I will fly away and find rest.* Where will he find rest? As I have pointed out already, this can be taken in either of two senses: death or solitude. It may mean what the apostle meant when he longed *to die and to be with Christ, for that is much the best* (Phil 1:23). However strong he was, however great, however valiant of heart, however invincible as a soldier of Christ, Paul was distressed by his trials, as we read: *Let no one give me any further trouble* (Gal 6:17). He seemed to be echoing the complaint in another psalm: *Disgust possessed me at the sinners who abandon your law* (Ps 118(119):53). One may often strive to correct perverse, depraved people for whom one is responsible, yet on whom all human effort and vigilance seem wasted. If one cannot correct them, there is nothing for it but to endure them. But what if such an incorrigible person is one of your own, not merely because you are fellow-members of the human race, but even, as may often be the case, because you are bound together in the fellowship of the Church? He or she is within; so what are you going to do about it? Where will you go to get away? What place can you find to withdraw to, in order to suffer this no longer? No, stay here, talk to them, exhort them, be kind to them, threaten them, bring them to a better mind.

"But I have done all that. I have poured out all the strength I could command, wrung it all out of myself, but I can see that I have made no progress at all. All that effort has been spent, and nothing but grief is left to me. How can my heart find any rest from such people, unless I beg, *Who will give me wings?*"

But give them to him *as though to a dove.* Do not give him the wings you would give to a raven,[12] because though a dove certainly does seek to fly away from perplexities, it does not let go of love. A dove is considered to be the symbol of love, and its moaning is a loveable sound. No creature is as much given to moaning as a dove; it moans all day long and at night, evidently thinking the place where it lives to be one appropriate to moaning.

So then, this is the voice of a lover, and what has he to say? "I cannot bear all this abuse. People hiss at me, they are beside themselves with savagery, they are incandescent with rage, their anger is like a dark cloud over me. I can do nothing to help them, so I want to get some rest elsewhere, distant from them in body, but not in love,[13] simply so that the love that is in me may not be agitated any more. If

---

12. *Sicut columbae tamen, non sicut corvo.* See note 10 above.
13. *Amore,* the general word for love, often but not always carrying carnal overtones. Within the present sentence, as throughout this Exposition, Augustine uses *dilectio,* a word conveying the love of deliberate choice, but it is not clear that any difference of meaning is implied in the present context.

I cannot do them any good through my instruction or in conversation with them, perhaps I shall be of more use by praying for them."

People say this, but often they are so tied down that flight is impossible. They may be held fast not by glue but by their office. If it is the responsibility of their position that binds them, and they cannot abandon it, they have to say, *"I longed to die and to be with Christ, for that is much the best; but it is necessary for you that I remain in the flesh"* (Phil 1:23-24). This dove was tied by affection, not greed for profit; it was rendered unable to fly not by any lack of merit but by its determination to discharge its duty. All the same, we must have this desire in our hearts. Only the person who has begun to walk in the narrow way[14] feels the pangs of this desire; and obviously we must feel them if we realize that the Church is never free from persecutions, even in this age when it seems to enjoy peace from the kind of persecution our martyrs endured. Persecutions are never lacking, because that saying of scripture is true, *all who want to live devoted to God in Christ will suffer persecution* (2 Tm 3:12). If you do not experience persecution, you cannot be wanting to live a life devoted to God in Christ. And what does it mean, to live this devoted life in Christ? It means that you must in your heart of hearts experience the anguish the apostle felt: *Is anyone weak, and I am not weak too? Is anyone tripped up, without my being afire with indignation?* (2 Cor 11:29). The weaknesses of others, the stumbling-blocks set in other people's paths—these were the persecutions Paul suffered. And are they absent today? No, there are plenty of them for those who have to worry about these things. When one of us is viewed from a distance, an observer may say, "Everything seems to go well with him." Either the speaker tastes the bitterness of his own life but is incapable of tasting that of others, or else he has no bitterness to taste in his own, and so no sympathy for another who is not merely tasting it but obliged to swallow it in large doses. Let such an observer undertake to live devoted to God in Christ, and he will experience the truth of what is said here. Then he will begin to long for wings, long to travel far off and flee and stay in the desert.

Verse 8. *You can never escape from troublesome companions*

9. Why do you suppose the desert places have been filled with God's servants, my brothers and sisters?[15] If life among other people had suited them well, would they have withdrawn from others? Look what they are doing—they too! They flee as far away as they can, and live in the desert. But is each of them

---

14. See Mt 7:14.
15. The monastic movement had become significant during the fourth century. The *Life of Antony*, attributed to Saint Athanasius and translated into Latin by Evagrius, had influenced many, including Augustine; see his *Confessions* VIII,6,15.

solitary there? By no means. Charity obliges them to stay with many companions, and among these multitudes are some who are a trial to them. In any large gathering of people there will inevitably be some bad ones. God knows that we need to be tested, so he mixes in among us some who will not persevere in the right way, and some spurious ones who have not even begun to walk in the path in which they ought to persevere. God knows that learning to bear with bad people is a necessity for us, and that we thereby make progress in goodness ourselves. Let us love our enemies, and correct them, punish them, excommunicate them, even cast them out from our society, provided we do so in love. Remember the apostle's advice: *If anyone disobeys our command conveyed in this letter, take note of such a one, and avoid his company.* He warns you, though, that anger must not creep in to inflame your eye in this situation: *But do not regard him as an enemy. Correct him as a brother, so that he may be ashamed* (2 Thes 3:14,15). The apostle prescribes separation from such a person, but does not cut off love from him. If that eye of yours is healthy, you are alive yourself. To lose love is the death of you. The psalmist was afraid of losing love when he lamented, *"The fear of death fell upon me,* and so, to save me from losing this life that is love, *who will give me wings, as though to a dove? Then I will fly away and find rest."*

But where will you go? Where will your flight take you? Where will you find rest? *Lo, I fled far away, and stayed in the desert.* But what desert? Wherever you are, others will gather there too; they will seek the desert along with you, and they will have an impact on your life. You cannot avoid the society of your brothers and sisters. And there will be some bad characters impinging on you as well, for some trials are still owing to you. *Lo, I fled away, and stayed in the desert.* What desert? Do you mean, perhaps, the inner place of your own soul,[16] where no other human being gains entry, where no one is with you, where there is only yourself and God? Well and good; but if "desert" means a geographical place, how are you going to stop people congregating there? You cannot separate yourself from the human race as long as you live the life of humankind. Console yourself, rather, by keeping your gaze fixed on our Lord and King, our Ruler and Creator, who became also a creature among us. Remember that he included among his twelve one who would be a cause of suffering to him.

Verse 9. Christ stills the storm

10. *Lo, I fled away, and stayed in the desert.* Perhaps the speaker sought refuge in his own soul, as I have already suggested, and there found some measure of solitude where he could rest. Yet charity itself disturbs him there. He

---

16. Literally "conscience."

is alone in his soul, but not alone as far as charity is concerned. In his innermost soul he was finding consolation, but tribulations continued to pester him without. Tranquil in himself, but on tenterhooks about others, and still distressed as a result, he says, *I was waiting for him who would save me from faintheartedness in the storm.* You are in the sea, and a storm is raging; there is no hope for you except to shout, *Lord, I'm sinking!* (Mt 14:30). May he who walks fearlessly upon the waves stretch out a hand to you, and lift you up in your terror, and grant you safety and stability in himself. May he speak to you interiorly and bid you, "Keep your eyes on me and on what I endured. Can it be that when you suffer a treacherous brother or sister, or the enemy's onslaughts from without, you are suffering anything I did not undergo? The Jews raged against me outwardly, and from within my own circle a disciple plotted to betray me."

So the tempest roars, but he saves us *from faintheartedness in the storm.* Perhaps your boat is rocking because he is asleep in you. When a rough sea was battering the boat in which the disciples were sailing, Christ was asleep; eventually they realized that the man who slept on board with them was the ruler and creator of the winds, so they approached him and woke him up. He gave orders to the gale, and there was a mighty calm.[17] Your heart is very likely to be turbulent if you have forgotten about him in whom your faith rests; you will find your troubles unendurable if you do not keep in mind what Christ suffered for you. If you do not keep Christ in mind, it is as though for you he is asleep. Awaken Christ and remember your faith. He sleeps in you when you forget his sufferings;[18] he is awake in you when you are mindful of his sufferings. When you contemplate with all your heart what he endured for you, will you too not bear your pain calmly, perhaps even gladly, since your experience of suffering likens you in some degree to your king? As with this in mind you begin to find comfort and joy, he arises, he gives orders to the gale, and tranquillity reigns. *I was waiting for him who would save me from faintheartedness in the storm.*

Verse 10. Pride issues in mutual unintelligibility;
the Spirit restores unanimity

11. *Engulf them, Lord, and confuse their languages.* The psalmist is thinking of those who harass him and cast a shadow over him, and this is his wish. But notice this, brothers and sisters: it is not prompted by anger. If people have wickedly exalted themselves, it is good for them to sink; if they have conspired in wickedness, it is for their good that they lose their comprehension of each other's languages. Let them reach a common mind for good purposes, and then let their tongues chime in harmony. But if *with common purpose all my enemies*

---

17. See Mk 4:36-40; Mt 8:23-26; Lk 8:22-25.
18. Some witnesses add here, "and if you deny that he is the true Son of God."

kept whispering against me, as another psalm complains (Ps 40:8(41:7)), they had better relinquish this common purpose and find their languages diversified, so that they cannot understand each other. *Engulf them, Lord, and confuse their languages.* Why does he pray, *Engulf them*? Because they have lifted themselves up. And why, *Confuse their languages*? Because they have conspired in wickedness. Remember the tower that certain proud people built after the flood. What was their intention? "Let us construct a high tower," they said. "We don't want to perish in another flood."[19] They thought their pride could protect them, so they built their high tower; but the Lord fragmented their speech. They began to find each other unintelligible, and that was the origin of all the different languages. Until that time there had been only one tongue; and one tongue was expedient for people who were of one mind, one single language was right for humble people. But when that unanimity degenerated into a conspiracy of pride God dealt mercifully with them by estranging their tongues, to make it impossible for them to form a dangerous unity by understanding each other. Through proud persons human languages were diversified, and through the humble apostles languages were harmonized; the spirit of pride fragmented language, and the Holy Spirit gathered dispersed languages into one. When the Holy Spirit came upon the disciples they spoke in the tongues of all who heard, and were understood by all.[20] The fragmented languages were reunited. If there are still pagans on the rampage today, it is just as well that they speak different languages. If they aspire to one common language, let them come to the Church, for here, though we differ in our natural tongues,[21] there is but one language spoken by the faith of our hearts. *Engulf them, Lord, and confuse their languages.*

The glory of the cross

12. *For I have seen iniquity and denial in the city.* He had good reason to seek the desert, for all he saw in the city was iniquity and denial. There is a certain city full of unrest; it is the same as the city that built the tower, the one that was thrown into confusion and is called Babylon.[22] It was scattered among innumerable peoples,[23] and from there the Church has been called out into the desert of a good conscience, for it had met with denial in the city. "Christ has come," says the Church. "And who is Christ?" demands the objector. "The Son of God." "So God has a Son?" "Yes, he was born of a virgin, he suffered, and he rose again." But your contradictions continue: "How could that happen?" Have regard at

---

19. See Gn 11:4.
20. See Acts 2:4.
21. *In diversitate linguarum carnis.*
22. As often in Augustine, the type of the earthly city set over against the city of God. See Exposition 2 of Psalm 26, 18; Exposition of Psalm 44, 25, and notes at both places.
23. See Gn 11:9.

least to the glory of his cross. That cross, once the butt of his enemies' ridicule, is now worn on the foreheads of kings. Its effect has demonstrated its power:[24] it has conquered the world, but by wood, not steel. The wood of the cross seemed to Christ's enemies an object of ridicule, and they stood before that tree wagging their heads, and saying, *If he is the Son of God, let him come down from the cross* (Mt 27:40). He kept on stretching out his hands to a people who refused to believe, a people that denied him.[25] If a person who lives by faith is just,[26] one who has no faith is iniquitous; so when the psalm here speaks of *iniquity* I take it to mean perfidious denial. Our Lord constantly saw iniquity and denial in the city, and he kept on stretching out his hands to a people that refused to believe and went on denying him. Yet he was waiting for them still, for he prayed, *Father, forgive them, for they do not know what they are doing* (Lk 23:34). The remnants of that city persist in their rage even today; still they deny him. But from the foreheads of us all he still stretches out his hands to the unbelieving, denying remnants. *For I have seen iniquity and denial in the city.*

Verse 11. The city of pride

13. *Day and night iniquity will march round it upon its ramparts, and there will be labor.* On its ramparts, as though attached to its cornices, which represent its noble folk. "If that nobleman were a Christian, no one would remain pagan," people say. "No one would still be a pagan, if he were a Christian." Yes, they say that often: "If he became a Christian, would anyone remain a pagan?" So as long as such noble persons do not become Christians, they are like the ramparts of the city that does not believe, the city of denial. How long will those ramparts stand? Not for ever. As the ark was carried round the walls of Jericho, so too the time will come for this city of unbelief and denial when its walls will crumble at the seventh circuit of the ark.[27] But until this happens the psalmist is distressed in his ordeal. He finds the remnants of the argumentative, denying folk burdensome, and he yearns for wings to carry him in flight, yearns for the peace of the desert. Yet he must stand fast amid the objectors, bear the threats, drink in the insults, and wait for the one who will save him from faintheartedness and storm. He must keep his gaze fixed on the head, on whom his life[28] is modeled, and he must find tranquillity in hope, even if he is still harassed in reality. *Day and night iniquity will march round it upon its ramparts, and there will be labor within it, and*

---

24. Reading *effectus probavit virtutem*; but most codices have *effectis proba virtutem*: perhaps "verify its power by things accomplished."
25. See Is 65:2; Rom 10:21.
26. See Hb 2:4; Rom 1:17.
27. See Jos 6:3.
28. Variant: "his way."

injustice. Because iniquity is there, labor will be there; because injustice is there, inevitably labor will be too. If only they would listen to him who stretches out his hands inviting them, *Come to me, all you who labor!* You shout, you deny, you jeer; how different is he who says to you, *"Come to me, all you who labor* in your pride, and you will rest in my humility. *Learn from me, for I meek and humble of heart, and you shall find rest for your souls"* (Mt 11:28-29). Why are they laboring? Because they are not meek and humble of heart. God became humble; let men and women blush for being proud.

Verse 12. Debts, financial and spiritual

14. *Usury and deceit are never lacking in its streets.* Usury and deceit, evil though they are, are not even hidden; they are publicly rampant. When someone does a bad thing at home, at least he is ashamed of his evil deed, but here *usury and deceit* are flaunted even in the streets. Moneylending ranks as a profession, and is reckoned a technical skill. Its practitioners form a corporation, one allegedly necessary to the state, and as a profession moneylending is taxed. This is how something that should at least be hidden is instead paraded in the street.

There is an even worse kind of usury, however, and that is the refusal to forgive someone who is in your debt. Then your eye is inflamed indeed when you reach that line in the prayer, *Forgive us our debts.* What are you to do, when you want to pray, and you get to that line? You have been rudely spoken to, perhaps, and you want the offender to be committed for torture in return! At all events you should not demand more than you paid out, you unjust lender. Someone punched you, did he, and you want him killed? That is wicked usury. How are you going to find your way into prayer? Or, if you give up prayer, how do you propose to wend your way to the Lord? Consider your situation. You will say, *Our Father, who art in heaven, hallowed be thy name. Thy kingdom come. Thy will be done, on earth as it is in heaven.* So far, so good. You continue, *Give us this day our daily bread.* And then—here it comes—*Forgive us our debts, as we forgive those who are in debt to us* (Mt 6:9-12). Wicked, usurious attitudes may be commonplace in the city of pride, but they must not come within our walls; here we beat our breasts. So what are you going to do, when you and this verse meet here head-on? One skilled in heavenly law composed the prayer for you; the expert who knew what goes on in heaven tells you, "On no other condition will your request be granted. *Truly I tell you, if you forgive other people for their offenses, you will be forgiven; but if you do not forgive the offenses of others, neither will your Father forgive you"* (Mt 6:14-15). Who says this? One who understands the cause you stand there pleading. You must see this: he himself has undertaken to be your advocate. He who is your legal expert, he who is the Father's assessor, he who is your very judge—he has told you, "On no other condition will your plea be granted."[29] So what are you going to do? You will not get what you want if you do not say this prayer, nor will you get what you want if you say it insincerely. Either you must say it, and make your actions conform to your words, or you will not deserve to gain what you ask. Any who fail to meet the condition are compromised by their vile usury. Those who still worship idols, or have recourse to them, can continue in usury if they like, but not you, people of God, not you, Christ's people, not you, the body that belongs to that head. Remember the peace that binds you together, remember the promise that is your life. What good will it do you, if you insist on inflicting injuries in return for those you have received? Does revenge make you feel better? Or will you enjoy someone else's misfortune? A bad person has harmed you: very well, forgive him, or there will be two bad people. *Usury and deceit are never lacking in its streets.*

Verses 13-15. Treachery on the part of familiar friends

15. In view of this you longed for solitude and wished for wings. You grumble, you cannot bear it—all this argument and iniquity in the city. Take your rest, then, with those who live with you inside the Church, and do not seek solitude. However, you need to listen to what the psalm says even of them: *If an enemy had slandered me . . .*, he says. Earlier he had been very distressed in his ordeal by the shouting of an enemy and the trouble caused by a sinner, but at that time he was perhaps still living in the proud city that erected the tower. The tower was sunk,[30] you remember, so as to fragment their languages. But now listen to how he groans within the Church on account of the dangers that threaten from treacherous brethren: *If an enemy had slandered me, I could have borne it; or if someone who hated me had talked arrogantly against me*—that is, if he had insulted me in his pride, and given himself airs while belittling me, and threatened me with any damage he could do to me—*I could surely have hidden from him.* Where would you have hidden, to escape from this enemy outside? Among those inside the Church, of course. But now consider. There may be no possibility open to you except to seek solitude, for the psalm continues, *But it was you, a like-minded person, my guide and my familiar companion.* Time was, when you gave me good advice, when you went ahead of me and gave me salutary counsel. We were at one in God's house. *You were to me a like-minded person, my guide and my familiar companion, who were wont to eat delicious food with*

---

29. In his *Homilies on the Gospel of John* 7,11, Augustine elaborates this idea. If we wish to win our case in court, we must first approach a legal expert, to ensure that it is properly presented.

30. *Submersa*, alluding to verse 9. The editors of the CCL text unnecessarily amend to *subversa*, "overthrown."

me. What delicious food is meant? Not all of you who are present know what it is.[31] But let those who do know not think it sour,[32] but say to those who do not know, *Taste and see how sweet the Lord is* (Ps 33:9(34:8)).

You were wont to eat delicious food with me. In the house of God we walked together in harmony. How, then, did the dissension arise? It looks as though someone who used to be inside became an outsider. That person walked with me in God's house in agreement, but then set up a rival house in opposition to the house of God.[33] Why did you leave this house, where we walked in concord? Why is it left deserted, this house where together we ate sweet food?

Verse 16. The revolt of Korah, Dathan, and Abiram prefigured the Donatist schism

16. *May death fall upon them, and may they go down alive into the underworld.* By this figure of speech he reflects upon the primal outbreak of schism, reminding us how among the ancient race of Israel a few proud persons separated themselves from the rest and wished to offer sacrifice apart. A novel kind of death overtook them, for the earth opened and swallowed them up.[34] *May death fall upon them, and may they go down alive into the underworld.* What does the word *alive* suggest? It means that they know they are perishing, yet they perish all the same.

Listen now to an illustration of how ruin can overtake living persons, how they can be sucked down into a cleft of the earth by the earthly desires that devour them. Suppose you say to someone, "What's the matter, brother? We are brothers and sisters, we call upon the one God, we believe in the one Christ, we listen to the same gospel, we sing the same psalm, we respond with the one 'Amen,' we ring out the one 'Alleluia,' we celebrate the one Easter. So why are you outside, and I inside?" This often drives him into a corner and, seeing the truth of what you say, he replies, "It's the fault of our forebears—God will have to settle the account with them!" So even as he perishes, he is alive. You go further, and admonish him: "Isn't the disaster of separation bad enough? Must you compound it by repeating baptism? Acknowledge in me the reality you have yourself; and even if you hate me, be kind to the Christ in me." This pernicious practice is often the most grievous point of all to them, and they will admit, "Yes, it's true; this does happen. How we wish it did not! But what can we do about the statutes our ancestors handed down to us?" *May they go down alive into the*

---

31. A reference to the catechumens, to whom the mystery of the eucharist had not yet been proposed.
32. Reading *amaricent* with most witnesses. One has *amaricentur*, "become sour."
33. The Donatists, presumably, of whom he speaks in the next paragraph, or heretics and schismatics in general.
34. See Nm 16:1-33.

underworld. If you were already dead as you descended there, you would not know what you were doing. But as it is, you know that what you are doing is wrong, but still you do it; so you are alive as you go down there, aren't you?

Now why did the yawning earth swallow those leaders in particular, while fire from heaven consumed the other people who had taken their part?[35] The psalm which recalls their punishment began with the ordinary people and concluded with the leaders. *May death fall upon them*: this phrase refers to the people on whom fire fell from heaven; and then the psalm immediately adds, *May they go down alive into the underworld*, referring to the leaders who were swallowed up by the earth. This must be the right way to read it, because how could those of whom it had been said, *May death fall upon them*, be described as going down alive? If death had already overtaken them, they could hardly descend alive. No, we must take it that the psalm begins with the minor characters and ends with the important ones. *May death fall upon* those who consented and followed; but what of the leaders, the people of substance? *May they go down alive into the underworld*, because they are well versed in the scriptures, and from their daily reading they know clearly that the Catholic Church is so widely diffused throughout the world that all gainsaying of it is absurd. They know perfectly well that no justification whatever can be alleged for their schism. And therefore they go down to the underworld alive, for they know that the wrong they do is wrong indeed.

As for the lesser folk, the fire of God's anger consumed them. Aflame with zeal for controversy, they were unwilling to abandon their wicked leaders; so fire fell upon them, the fire of destruction upon the fire of dissension.[36]

May death fall upon them, and may they go down alive into the underworld, for there is wickedness in their lodgings and in their midst. It says, *In their lodgings,* to indicate places where they stay temporarily before moving on; for they will not be here always, even though they fight so hard in their time-bound vehemence. Wickedness is *in their lodgings,* and wickedness is *in their midst,* for nothing is so central to them as their hearts.

Verse 17. The unity among the many

17. *I cried out to the Lord.* The body of Christ, the unity of Christ, is crying out in its anguish, its weariness, its affliction, in the distress of its ordeal. It is one single person, a unity grounded in an individual body, and in the distress of its soul it cries from the bounds of the earth: *from the ends of the earth I have called to you, as my*

---

35. See Nm 16:31-35.
36. These remarks demonstrate Augustine's sympathy for the simple and innocent among the Donatists, whose schismatic status was merely inherited, as opposed to the deliberate stance of the well-informed.

soul grew faint (Ps 60:3(61:2)). It is one, but the oneness is a unity made from many; it is one, but not because of confinement to any one place, for this is one person crying out from the ends of the earth. How could one individual cry out from the ends of the earth, unless that individual were one formed from many?

I cried out to the Lord. Yes, do just that: you cry out to the Lord, not to Donatus. Don't let him be your lord in place of our true Lord, he who refused to be your fellow-servant under our Lord. *I cried out to the Lord, and the Lord hearkened to me.*

Verse 18. *Evening, morning, and high noon*

18. *At evening, in the morning and at midday I will tell my tale, and proclaim it, and he will hear my voice.* Your job is to preach the good news. Do not be silent about what you have received. *At evening* tell of what is past, *in the morning* of what is still to come, and *at midday* of what is everlasting. So when the psalm says, *At evening,* it refers to a story that is to be told; when it says, *In the morning,* it thinks of an announcement; and when speaking of *midday* it looks to the effective hearing of its prayer. It puts *midday* as a finale, a high noon from which there is no sinking towards sunset. At noon the light is at its highest, like the splendor of wisdom and the ardor of love.

At evening, in the morning, and at midday. At evening the Lord was on the cross, in the morning he arose, at midday he ascended. At evening, then, my tale is of a dying man's patience, in the morning I proclaim the life of him who rises from the dead, and I will pray that at midday he who is seated at the Father's right hand may hear me. He who intercedes for us[37] will hear my voice. What security this is, what comfort, what an encouragement in the face of faintheartedness and storm! What strength against malicious people, against sadness both outside and within, and among those who were once inside but are now out!

Verse 19. *Few are truly "with us"*

19. When you see turbulent, proud self-seekers within this very congregation, my brothers and sisters, when you see within these four walls arrogant folk who instead of harboring a chaste, quiet zeal for God take too much on themselves, when you see them all ready to foment dissension but lacking only the opportunity, you know that they are the chaff in the Lord's threshing-floor. The wind of pride has blown a few of them away from us, but the main bulk of the chaff will not fly away until the Lord comes to winnow his crop at the end.[38]

---

37. See Rom 8:34.
38. See Mt 3:12.

What are we to do meanwhile? We must sing with the psalmist, pray with him, lament with him, and yet say in all confidence, *God will redeem my soul in peace*. Despite those who do not love peace, *he will redeem my soul in peace*, for with those who hate peace I dealt peaceably.[39]

He will redeem my soul in peace from those who draw near to me. Those who are far away from me present no difficulty: I am unlikely to be taken in by someone who says, "Come and worship the idol," for such a person is very far away from me. But when I inquire of someone, "Are you a Christian?" and the other says, "Yes, I am," then he or she is a very close adversary, one near at hand. *He will redeem my soul in peace from those who draw near to me, for in many respects they were with me.* Why did I say, *They draw near to me*? Precisely because *in many respects they were with me*. Two different explanations of this verse suggest themselves.

Here is the first. *In many respects they were with me.* We had a common baptism, so they were with me in that. We were both accustomed to read the gospel; they were with me in that. We both customarily celebrated the festivals of the martyrs; in that too they were with me. We always observed the solemnity of Easter, and they were with me in that also. But they are not with me in all respects: they are not with me in their schism, nor with me in their heresy. In many matters they are with me, but in a few they are not; and because of those few in which they are not with me, the many others in which they are with me do them no good. To make this point clear, brothers and sisters, look at the many items Paul listed, while insisting that there was only one that mattered, and that if this one was missing, all the rest were pointless: *if I speak with human tongue or angel's tongue . . . if I have the gift of prophecy, and have cognizance of all mysteries and all knowledge; if I have such perfect faith that I can move mountains . . . if I distribute all my resources to feed the poor, and deliver my body to be burnt* (1 Cor 13:1-3) . . . what a lot of things he has enumerated! But one thing is lacking among these many things: one thing only, charity. The others are many in number, but charity exceeds them in weight. So too today: in all the sacraments they are with me, but in this one thing, charity, they are not. *In many respects they were with me.*

Here is the second possible interpretation of the verse. It could mean *among the many they were with me.*[40] The people who have cut themselves off from me were formerly with me, but they were not among the few—only among the many. Throughout the whole wide world there are only a few grains, but many husks. What is the psalm suggesting? As husks, as chaff, they were with me,

---

39. See Ps 119:7(120:6-7).
40. *In multis erant mecum.* The Latin can mean "many things," "many people," "many respects," etc. The translation has been altered in the present paragraph to reflect Augustine's different interpretation.

certainly, but not with me as grain. The chaff is very near the grain; it emerges from the one seed, and strikes root in the one field, and is nourished by the same rain; it is subjected to the same reaper and undergoes the same threshing. It awaits the same sifting, but it does not find its way into the one barn. Only *among the many were they with me.*

Verses 20-22. Persevering refusal of the truth

20. *God will hear me and will humble them, God who exists before all ages.* Presumptuously they trust in some leader or other, an upstart of yesterday, but *God will humble them, God who exists before all ages.* This can be said of him because although Christ was born in time from the Virgin Mary, nonetheless before all ages, in the beginning, was the Word, and the Word was with God, and the Word was God.[41] *He will humble them, God who exists before all ages,* asserts the psalmist, *for with them there is no change,* "with them, I mean, who will not alter their course." He knew there would be some who would persist in their wickedness, and would die still persisting in it. We all know people like this: they will not change. Those who die in this state, in their perversity, in their schism, do not alter their course. But God will humble them, he will lay them low in condemnation because they reared up in dissension. There is no alteration in them, because they change not for the better but for the worse, and this holds not only for the present world, but even for the resurrection, because *though we shall all indeed rise again, we shall not all be changed.*[42] Why not? Because with such people *there is no change, and they have not feared God.* There is but one remedy, brothers and sisters: let them fear God and cut loose from Donatus. To a Donatist you say, "You are heading for perdition in your heresy, in your schism. God must necessarily punish such sins. You will be damned; don't deceive yourself with words. Don't follow a blind guide, for if one blind person leads another, both fall into the ditch."[43] "What do I care?" he replies. "As I lived yesterday, so do I live today. What my parents were, I am too." "Then you do not fear God." Where there is fear of God, anyone must realize that all these things we read about are true, and that the faith of Christ cannot err. How can such a person remain in heresy[44] in the face of such overwhelming evidence in favor of the holy Catholic Church? God has spread it throughout the world; he promised it

---

41. See Jn 1:1.
42. 1 Cor 15:51. In the original Greek the sense of this verse is "We shall not all die, but we shall all be changed:" Paul was thinking of the prospect for those who would be still alive at the Lord's second coming. But the Old Latin which Augustine was using, like the Vulgate, understood it differently.
43. See Mt 15:4; Lk 6:39.
44. The editors of the CCL text reorganize these two sentences to make them part of the address to the heretic: "You must fear God. Realize that . . .err. How can you remain in heresy?"

before diffusing it, announced it in advance, and then displayed it as he had promised. Let those who do not fear God be wary and watchful, then. *He stretches out his hand to requite them.*

21. *They have defiled his covenant.* Read the promise that announced this covenant they have defiled: *In your seed all nations shall be blessed* (Gn 12:3; 26:4). But *they have defiled his covenant.* What have you to say in contradiction to these words, spoken by the author of the covenant? "Africa alone has been worthy of this grace through Saint Donatus," you say. "The Church of Christ has survived only in him." The Church of Donatus you mean: go on, say it! Why bother to add the name of Christ—Christ to whom the promise referred, *in your seed all nations shall be blessed*? Do you want to follow Donatus? Bypass Christ, then, and off you go!

Look what follows. *They have defiled his covenant.* What covenant is this? The apostle answers: *To Abraham were the promises made, and to his seed.* He argues, *Brethren, even a human will and testament once proved cannot be nullified or overruled by anyone. To Abraham were the promises made, and to his seed. Scripture does not say, "To his descendants," as though indicating many, but as to one only: "And to your seed," which is Christ* (Gal 3:15-16). What then was the covenant promised in this seed, in Christ? *In your seed all nations shall be blessed.* It follows then, you Donatist, that because you have let slip the unity of all nations and clung to a part only, you have defiled his covenant. The fate that falls upon you—extermination and banishment from your inheritance—proceeds from God's anger. *They have defiled his covenant, and they have been banished by the wrath of his countenance.* What plainer language can you expect, brothers and sisters? Could heretics be more clearly indicated? *They have been banished by the wrath of his countenance.*

Verse 22. But heretics have their usefulness

22. *His heart has come near.* Whose heart is meant? God's surely, by whose anger they were banished. In what sense has *his heart come near*? In enabling us to understand his will. Thanks to heretics, the Catholic faith has been clearly enunciated, and in reaction to people with wrong opinions, those with right opinions have been tested and approved. Many truths were contained in the scriptures in an obscure way; and the heretics, after being cut off, rocked God's Church with their questions. But this served to lay open hidden truths, and so God's will came to be understood better. This is why in another psalm it is said that *a batch of bulls is among the cows of the peoples, so that those who have been proved sound by silver may be pressed out* (Ps 67:31(68:30)), in the sense, "may stand out clearly," or "may become visible."[45] In the silversmith's craft

---

45. *Excludantur.*

those who press out the form from the undifferentiated lump are called *exclusores*.[46] Among God's people there were many individuals capable of explaining the scriptures with excellent discernment, but they were unknown. There was no occasion for them to put forward a solution to difficult questions as long as nobody arose to make false claims. Was any complete account of the Trinity offered, before the Arians began to bay at it?[47] Was there any satisfactory treatment of penitential practice, before the Novatianists challenged it?[48] In the same way we had no complete teaching on baptism until the "rebaptizers" had put themselves outside the Church.[49] The things that needed to be said about the unity of Christ's body in this connection were not said with anything like the same clarity until the Donatist schism began to press hard on our weaker brothers and sisters. Others in our ranks, who were well able to discuss and find out the truth of the matter, were then prompted to bring obscure points of teaching into the open in their sermons and disputations, and thus save from ruin

---

46. Augustine uses the word in this sense in his Exposition of Psalm 67, 39, and in *The Spirit and the Letter*, 17. The root idea is that of separation ordered to the emergence of significant form or meaning.

47. On Arius, see note at Exposition of Psalm 35, 9. The principal point of his heresy was the effort to safeguard the unity of God by denying eternity and divinity in the full sense to the Second Person of the Trinity. The Son was held to have been created out of nothing by the Father as the first of his creatures, through whom the Father then created all else. Divinity was subsequently bestowed upon him in view of his righteousness. The heresy was influential in the 320s and spread widely. At the prompting of the Emperor Constantine a council was held at Nicea in A.D. 325 which condemned the Arian heresy, largely thanks to the leadership of Saint Athanasius, then still a deacon. This council coined the non-scriptural term *homoousios* ("of the same nature") to express the relationship of Son to Father, and the word became the touchstone of orthodoxy during the fierce controversies of the following decades. One of the bishops condemned at Nicea for Arian views was the influential Church historian Eusebius of Nicomedia. Others rallied to him and Arianism lived on, splitting eventually into three wings: (1) the extreme Anomoeans (proponents of "dissimilarity"); (2) the middle party of Homoeans (acknowledging "similarity" between Father and Son, but anxious to avoid the doctrinal precision of the homoousios); (3) the Semi-Arians, who were very close to the orthodox position, and eventually rallied to the orthodox ranks after the councils of Seleucia and Ariminum in 359 had seemed to mark the triumph of Arianism. Political influence, especially in the eastern half of the Empire, had contributed to this short-lived triumph; but Athanasius had stood firm throughout in spite of being repeatedly exiled from his see at Alexandria, and the faith of Nicea was reasserted by a council at Alexandria in 362. After Athanasius' death in 373 the orthodox faith was defended and expounded by the three great Cappadocian fathers, Basil, Gregory of Nazianzus, and Gregory of Nyssa.

48. Novatian was an orthodox Roman theologian, who at first espoused Saint Cyprian's relatively lenient policy on the treatment of those Christians who had apostatized and denied the faith during the persecution of Decius (A.D. 249-250). Later, after the election of Saint Cornelius as pope (251), and the confirmation of this policy, Novatian joined the rigorist party which opposed the readmission of repentant apostates. Novatian led a schism and was consecrated as a rival Bishop of Rome. A rigorist Novatianist church lingered on until Augustine's day. The importance of the schism was that it forced the Church to clarify its practice with regard to the forgiveness of sins in this crucial area.

49. The Donatist practice of repeating baptism in the case of any Catholic who transferred to their sect was a sore subject. Augustine frequently points out the illogicality of the Donatist position.

the weaker ones who were worried by the objections of the wicked. In this way our opponents were banished by the wrath of God's countenance, whereas his heart drew near to us so that we might understand.

In the light of these facts you must interpret the saying of the other psalm, *a batch of bulls* (of proud folk, pushing with their horns, that means) *is among the cows of the peoples.* Who are being called *cows?* Souls easily led astray.[50] But why does this occur? So that *those who have been proved sound by silver may be pressed out.* That is to say, so that those who were formerly hidden may appear openly. But why *by silver?* This means by God's word, for another psalm says, *The words of the Lord are pure words, silver tried by fire for the earth, purified seven times* (Ps 11:7(12:6)). This may seem an obscure interpretation, but look how the apostle presses it out[51] into the light: *Heresies there must be,* he says, *so that those who have been proved sound may be clearly identified among you* (1 Cor 11:19). What does *proved sound* mean? To be *proved sound by silver* means to be proved by God's word. And what is meant by *may be clearly identified?* The same thing as *may be pressed out.* And how does that come about? Because of the heretics. Why do I say, "Because of the heretics"? Because of that *batch of bulls among the cows of the peoples.* This is how the schismatics *have been banished by the wrath of his countenance,* while to us *his heart has come near.*

God's word seems hard, but it is tender to believers

23. *God's words are smoother than oil, but they are javelins.* Some of the sayings in scripture used to seem hard while they were still obscure; but once explained they are gentle and tender. The first heresy among Christ's disciples arose from the apparent hardness of something he had said. He had warned them, *No one can have life except by eating my flesh and drinking my blood;*[52] but they did not understand, and said to each other, *This is a hard saying; who could listen to it?* Complaining how hard it was, they withdrew from his company, and he was left with the twelve. When these pointed out to him that the ones who had left had been scandalized by his words, he asked them, *Do you want to go away too?* And Peter answered, *You have the word of eternal life. To whom should we go?* (Jn 6:61.68.69).

Take this to heart, we beg you. Be like little children and learn childlike piety. Did Peter understand then the mystery concealed in that saying of the Lord? No, he did not yet understand it, but in his childlike docility he believed. If some saying is hard, then, and not yet intelligible, let it be hard to the unbeliever, but

---

50. Augustine elaborates on this idea when commenting on that psalm; see Exposition of Psalm 67, 39.
51. *Excludat.*
52. See Jn 6:54.

tender to you because of your piety. When eventually it is made plain it will seem to you like oil, soaking right into your bones.

Verse 23. The power of the gentle words

24. Now it seems as though Peter has something further to say to us.[53] After those others had been, as he thought, scandalized by the hardness of the Lord's words, he asserted, *You have the word of eternal life. To whom should we go?* But now he adds, *Cast your care upon the Lord, and he will nourish you.* You are but a child, and you do not yet understand the mysteries concealed in these words. Bread is withheld from you, perhaps, and you still need milk as your food.[54] Do not disdain the breast, for it will bring you to the stage of being able to eat the food you cannot manage yet. Remember how many hard sayings have been softened, on the occasion of the heretics' departure. God's hard sayings have become softer than oil, yet they are javelins too. They have armed the preachers of the gospel: these very words are shot into the heart of any and every hearer by preachers who press home the message in season and out of season.[55] By this preaching, by these arrow-sharp words, human hearts are struck and brought to love peace. The sayings were hard, and they have become tender; in so doing they have lost nothing of their strength, but have turned into javelins. *God's words are smoother than oil, but they*, yes, these very words which seem gentle, *they are javelins*.

But as for you, perhaps you are not yet grown up enough to be armed with these javelins, and the obscure, hard points in the saying have not yet become luminous to you? Then *cast your care upon the Lord, and he will nourish you.* Cast yourself upon the Lord. And, given that you want to cast yourself upon the Lord, make sure that no one else usurps the Lord's place. *Cast your care upon the Lord.* There was a certain mighty warrior for Christ who refused to let the cares of the little ones be cast upon himself; listen to what he says: *Was Paul crucified for you, or were you baptized in Paul's name?* (1 Cor 1:13). What else was he urging, if not *Cast your care upon the Lord, and he will nourish you*? But today it happens that some little one wants to cast his or her care upon the Lord, and some fellow comes along and says, "I'll take you on." He is like someone who meets a ship in distress and says, "I'll look after you." You must answer, "It's the harbor I'm making for, not the reef." *Cast your care upon the Lord, and he will nourish you.* You will see that the harbor does indeed welcome you, for God *will not allow the righteous one to waver for ever.* You seem to waver on the sea of this world, but the harbor is there for you. Just make sure that you do not

---

53. In the following lines Augustine seems to be thinking of 1 Pt 5:7; 2:2.
54. See 1 Cor 3:2.
55. See 2 Tm 4:2.

break loose from the anchor[56] before you reach harbor. An anchored ship does toss about, but she is not driven far from the shore, nor will she be subject to turbulence for ever, even though she must suffer it for a time now. Some words we heard earlier refer to this present wavering: *I am deeply saddened in my ordeal, and very distressed. I was waiting for him who would save me from faint-heartedness in the storm.* It is a storm-tossed person who speaks here, but one that will not waver for ever. He is lashed to the anchor, and the anchor is his hope. God *will not allow the righteous one to waver for ever.*

Verse 24. Donatists are bound for the pit as perpetrators of violence and deceit

25. Now what about the schismatics? *You will consign them to the pit of corruption, O God.* The pit of corruption is the same thing as the engulfing darkness. The psalm declares that *you will consign them to the pit of corruption* because when one blind person guides another, both fall into the ditch.[57] When God is said to lead them into the pit of corruption, it implies not that he is the author of their guilt, but that he is the judge of their iniquities. God has delivered them to the lusts of their own hearts[58] because they loved darkness rather than light, and blindness, not vision. The Lord Jesus has shed his light on the entire world, and these people should be singing in unison with the whole world, because *no one can hide from his heat* (Ps 18:7(19:6)). Yet they have crossed over from the whole to a part, from the body to a wound, from live belonging to amputation; so what else can their fate be, but to go down to the pit of decay?

26. *Men of blood and deceit.* The psalm calls them *men of blood* because they kill; but if only it were corporal and not spiritual death that they meted out! When blood flows from a body we see it and shudder, but does anyone see the heart that bleeds when baptism is repeated? It takes a different kind of eyes to see those deaths. Not that the Circumcellions, armed and widespread as they are, hold their hand from visible killings;[59] and if we have visible killings in mind, they certainly are *men of blood.* If you are a peaceable person, and not bloodthirsty, look at that armed ruffian. If only he carried nothing worse than a cudgel! But no, he carries a sling,[60] he carries an axe, and stones, and a lance. Armed with these weapons the Circumcellions wander wherever they can, thirsting for the blood of the innocent, so even with regard to these visible murders they are *men of*

---

56. See Heb 6:19.
57. See Mt 15:14; Lk 6:39.
58. See Rom 1:24.
59. On the Circumcellions, see note at Exposition of Psalm 10, 5.
60. *Fundibalum,* literally a slinging or hurling machine, but this would hardly be portable. *Funda,* from which it is derived, usually means a sling, but can also mean the missile launched from it, the stone; hence *fundibalum* could mean the leather strap which holds and fires the stone.

blood. Yet we must still say, "If only these were all their killings, and they did not slaughter souls too!"

Just in case the *men of blood and deceit*[61] accuse us of misunderstanding this phrase, *men of blood,* by referring it to slayers of souls, let me remind them that they themselves so characterized their own Maximianists.[62] In the course of their condemnation of the Maximianists the Donatists included the following words in the decree of their own council: *Their feet are swift to shed the blood* of the messengers.[63] *Chagrin and unhappiness beset their ways, and they know not the path to peace.*[64] The Donatists made this accusation against the Maximianists, but I put this question to them: when did the Maximianists shed blood in a physical sense? (Not that they would have refrained from doing so had their numbers permitted. But they were too much afraid, being so few, so it was more a case of their suffering violence at the hands of others than of doing anything of the kind themselves.) So now I question any Donatist: in your council you applied to the Maximianists the words, *their feet are swift to shed blood.* Very well: show me one person on whom the Maximianists laid a finger? "No," you say, "that's not the point. Those who have cut themselves off from our united fellowship, and kill souls by leading them astray, shed blood not carnally but spiritually." Exactly! You have explained the matter very clearly. Now let your explanation show up to you what you have done yourself. *Men of blood and deceit:* your deceit lies in your trickery, your pretense, your misleading of others. What are we to say of people who *have been banished by the wrath of his countenance?* That these are the *men of blood and deceit.*

27. But what does scripture say will happen to them? *They will not see even half their days.* What does that mean—*they will not see even half their days?* It means that they will not advance as far as they expect to; before the time they hope for is up, they will perish. They are like the partridge of which scripture says, *Halfway through his days they will leave him, and he will be reckoned as a fool at the end.*[65] They do advance, but only for a time, for what does the apostle say? *People of ill-will and seducers go from bad to worse, in error themselves*

---

61. The main Donatist party, as opposed to the Circumcellions.

62. On this schism within a schism, see note at Exposition of Psalm 35, 9, and Augustine's extensive treatment of the Acts of the Maximianist Council of Cebarsussa in his Exposition 2 of Psalm 36, 19-23.

63. *Annuntiatorum,* "of the announcers." This last word is not present in the decree of the Donatist Council of Bagai (A.D. 394) as quoted by Augustine in his *Answer to Cresconius* 4,4,5. On the council, see Note at Exposition of Psalm 21, 31.

64. Ps 13(14):3. The Greek text of this psalm, from which the African Psalter used by Augustine and his opponents derived, contains extra words not found in the Hebrew. It is quoted by Paul with the extra words at Rom 3:10-18.

65. See Jer 17:11. Part of the verse is omitted here, which leaves the comparison obscure. The image given by Jeremiah is that of a partridge hatching eggs not her own, like a person who amasses riches but will have to leave them at his premature death.

and leading others into error (2 Tm 3:13). If one blind person leads another, both fall into the ditch.[66] They fall into *the pit of corruption* deservedly. But notice what the apostle says: *They go from bad to worse*, but not for very long; for just before this he says, *They will not last* (which means, *they will not see even half their days*), and he goes on to tell us why not: *for their lunacy will be obvious to everyone, as was that of the opponents of Moses* (2 Tm 3:9). *Men of blood and deceit will not see even half their days. But I will hope in you, O Lord.* With good reason they will not see even half their days, for they have put their trust in human resources. But I have passed beyond the days of time to the day of eternity. Why? Because I have hoped in you, O Lord.

---

66. See Mt 15:14; Lk 6:39.

Exposition of Psalm 55

A Sermon[1]

Verse 1. The people who objected to a title

1. When we are about to enter a house, we look at the name written up over it, to find out who owns it and who lives there, for we need to make sure we are not rushing rudely in where we have no right to go, or, on the other hand, hanging back from some place we ought to enter. This is what we must do in the case of the present psalm. Just as on a property we might read, "This estate belongs to So-and-So," what we find inscribed on the lintel as we approach this psalm is the title, *Unto the end, for a people that moved far away from the saints over the writing of a title, for David himself when the allophyli[2] captured him in Gath.* So let us try to identify the *people that moved far away from the saints over the writing of a title.* It refers to a certain David whom you well know how to recognize in a spiritual sense. It is none other than the one of whom scripture says, *Christ is the end of the law, bringing justification to everyone who believes* (Rom 10:4). Accordingly when you hear the words, *to the end*, direct your mind to Christ; otherwise you may be held up on the way and never reach the end. You may have halted to shelter under something, but, whatever it is, as long as you have not yet reached Christ, the divine word has only one piece of advice for you: "Come nearer; you are not yet in a place of security." There is indeed a place where we can find completely sure footing; there is a rock on which our house can be built in safety, where it will have no fear of the storms that may beat upon it. Rivers crash against that house, but it does not collapse, because it is founded on rock.[3] And *that rock is Christ* (1 Cor 10:4). Christ is called "David" in a figurative sense, because scripture says that Christ *was made for God from David's line, according to the flesh* (Rom 1:3).

2. Well now, who is this people who *moved far away from the saints over the writing of a title?* It is the mention of a title that gives us the clue to the identity of the people. At the time of the Lord's passion, when he was about to be crucified,

---

1. Preached at Carthage in the Basilica Restituta, possibly during the winter 412-413.
2. "People of another race," a common way of designating the Philistines in the Septuagint, almost synonymous with "Gentiles" or "the heathen." Augustine's use of it here is therefore ironic, since he applies it precisely to the Jewish establishment who opposed Christ's claims as a threat to their national identity.
3. See Mt 7:25.

a certain title was penned, and it was inscribed in Hebrew, Greek, and Latin, as though in these three languages the title was being authenticated by three witnesses, for the evidence of two or three witnesses is required to establish any charge.[4] On reading this title the Jews were indignant, and said to Pilate, *Do not put "The King of the Jews;" put "He said, I am the King of the Jews."* Write, "He said so," they demanded, not that he was what he said he was. But another psalm rightly warns, *Do not tamper with the title that has been inscribed* (Ps 56(57):1); and Pilate therefore retorted, *What I have written, I have written* (Jn 19:21-22), which was tantamount to telling them, "Even if you espouse falsehood, I am not going to distort the truth." But the Jews continued to be angry and persisted in their blasphemy, protesting, *We have no king but Caesar* (Jn 19:15), and so they moved far away from the saints by taking offense at the title. Let all those who acknowledge Christ as their king, and desire to have him ruling over them, draw near to the saints and bind themselves inseparably to the holy people. But let those others move further off from the saints, those who by disputing the title have rejected God as king and chosen a mere man as their king instead. Any race that finds its full satisfaction in human sovereignty, and refuses to have the Lord reign over it, is far removed from the saints. What it has rejected is a subjection to God's lordship that would have enabled his subjects themselves to exercise dominion over their wayward desires.

Do not suppose, brothers and sisters, that such a refusal is to be observed in the Jews alone. They stood as a kind of primordial example, so that their conduct might show up plainly what we must all avoid. They openly refused to have Christ as their king, and chose Caesar instead. Caesar is indeed sovereign, but only as a human being over other human beings to regulate human affairs. There is another king for the things of God. There is a king with responsibility for temporal life, but another for the life of eternity; an earthly king, but a heavenly king too: an earthly king who is subject to the heavenly king, and a heavenly king who is sovereign over all. They sinned, therefore, not in acknowledging Caesar as their king, but in rejecting the kingship of Christ. So too today many people refuse to have Christ as their king, even though he is enthroned in heaven and his reign is universal. And these are the very people who harass us.

Against people of this sort the present psalm gives us strength. It is necessary for us to go on bearing with them to the very end; we should not have to put up with them if it were not for our good. Every trial we undergo is designed to prove us, and all such probation is fruitful. We are for the most part an unknown quantity to ourselves; we do not know what we can bear and what we cannot. Sometimes we think we can carry something, though it is really beyond our strength, and at other times we feel hopeless about carrying something that is within our

---

4. See Dt 19:15.

powers. So the trial comes, and it puts us to the question, and we discover ourselves. What we are had been hidden from us, but not from him who made us. Think of Peter. He presumed on interior strength that was not yet there, and promised that he would stand by the Lord Jesus Christ even to death. Peter was ignorant of his own capacity, but the Lord knew it. He who fashioned Peter told him that he was not equal to the ordeal. Peter's creator knew what strength he meant to give to the man he had made, but he had not given him sufficient strength yet. Peter, not having yet received it, knew nothing of that strength; but the trial came upon him; he denied Christ, he wept, and then he received it.[5] We do not know what we should ask for before we have it, nor how to be thankful when we do receive it, and therefore we are in constant need of being trained through trials and tribulations while we are in this world. But the only people who can provide these trials for us are those who move far away from the saints. You must understand this to mean distance of heart, brothers and sisters, not bodily distance. It often happens that someone who is on a journey, and far away from you, is closely knit to you because he or she loves the same things as you do; again it often happens that someone at your side is united to you by loving the same things as you do. But it also happens that someone close beside you is very distant from you, because he or she loves the world, whereas you love God.

The title, concluded: the winepress

3. What then is the meaning of another statement, still part of the title, that *the allophyli captured him in Gath*? Gath was a city of the allophyli—the foreigners, that is, a people certainly far removed from the saints. The very fact that they are foreigners implies distance, not propinquity. All who reject Christ as their king make themselves foreigners. How is that? Well, remember that vine, the vine of God's own planting. When it had become sour, what did it hear God saying? *How could you have turned so sour, you alien vine?* (Jer 2:21). God does not say, "My vine," because if you were mine, you would be sweet. If you are sour, you cannot be mine, and if you are not mine, you are alien.

Now *the allophyli captured him*, David, *in Gath*. We certainly do read that David, the son of Jesse and later King of Israel, went abroad to the allophyli when he was being hunted by Saul,[6] and that he stayed in that city and with its king, but we do not read that he was held prisoner there. Clearly the David who is meant is Jesus Christ, who was born of David's line. Him the allophyli held in Gath, and hold him they still do. I will explain why. We have remarked that Gath was a city, and if we investigate its name, we find that it means "winepress." As head, Christ is the Savior of his body. He was born of a virgin, he was crucified,

---

5. See Lk 22:33-34.56-62.
6. See 1 Sm 21:10-15.

and he gave us a guarantee of our own resurrection in the resurrection of his own flesh. He sits at the Father's right hand and intercedes for us; but he is here too, in his body, the Church. Because the body is joined to its head, the head cries out on behalf of the body, *Saul, Saul, why are you persecuting me?* (Acts 9:4). The body is likewise present in the head, as the apostle shows: *he has raised us up with Christ, and made us sit with him in the heavenly places* (Eph 2:6). Both are true: that we are enthroned there, and that he is in travail here. We are enthroned there through hope, and he is here with us through his charity. This union makes us one person with him; it makes us two in one flesh, the Bridegroom with the bride. That is why the Lord says, *They are two no longer, but one flesh* (Mt 19:6).

But in what sense is he held prisoner in Gath? His body, his Church, is held in the winepress. It is under pressure. But the pressure exerted in a winepress is productive. The cluster of grapes feels no pressure while on the vine; it looks quite unharmed there, but nothing flows out of it. Then it is put into the winepress, trampled, crushed; to all appearances the grapes are being injured, but that injury is not sterile. On the contrary: the grapes would remain sterile if they suffered no injury.

Verse 2. The trampling process

4. Whatever pressure the saints may endure,[7] let them turn their thoughts to this psalm and recognize themselves in it; let those who suffer what is described here make the words the expression of their own prayer. If anyone stands clear of the suffering, I put that person under no obligation to join in with the psalm. But let any such person take care that in wishing to avoid the suffering, he or she does not move far away from the saints.

Well now, each of us must think about our enemy. If we are Christians, our enemy is the world. When we prepare to listen to what this psalm has to say we must not think of private quarrels; rather let us remind ourselves that our wrestling is not against flesh and blood, but against principalities and powers and wicked spirits[8]—against the devil and his angels, no less. When we suffer from troublesome human beings, it is the devil who is stirring them up and inciting them, and using them as his tools. We have to keep two enemies in sight: one we can see, and another we cannot see. We see the human foe but do not see the devil; we must love the human enemy but beware of the devil. Let us pray for our human adversary but pray against the devil, and say to God, *Have pity on me, Lord, because a man has trampled on me.* Do not be afraid because you are trampled on; just be full of wine, for you were made to be a cluster of grapes[9] so that

---

7. The editors of the CCL text amend to "Whoever the saints may be who are under pressure..."
8. See Eph 6:12.
9. Or perhaps "a grape"; *uva* can have either meaning. But a little later he uses *botrus* for Christ.

you could be trampled. *Have pity on me, Lord, because a man has trampled on me; he has troubled me with his assaults all day long*, this person who has moved far away from the saints. But why should we not think that this is a reference to the devil in person? Because the psalm says, *a man*? That proves nothing, for the gospel says, *Some hostile man has done this*,[10] and do you think the gospel made a mistake there? The devil can be figuratively called a man, but cannot be a man. So we can take it either way: when the psalmist said, *A man has trampled on me*, he may have meant the devil, or he may have been thinking of a whole people, or any individual within it, far removed from the saints. It is through enemies of this latter type that the devil harasses God's people, the people that holds fast to the saints, holds fast to the Holy One, the King. It was the title over this King that aroused them to indignation and revulsion, and drove them far away. So whichever foe he envisages, let the psalmist pray, *Have pity on me, Lord, because a man has trampled on me*, and then he will not lose courage under the trampling, but remember whom he is invoking and by whose example he has been made strong. The first grape[11] to be put under pressure was Christ. When in his passion that grape was pressed out, there flowed forth the wine that filled the most excellent, intoxicating chalice.[12] Let Christ's body contemplate its head, and say too, *Have pity on me, Lord, because a man has trampled on me; he has troubled me with his assaults all day long.* All day long, the psalm says, all the time. Let no one think, "There were tribulations in our fathers' days, but not in ours." If you consider yourself to be free from tribulations, you have not yet begun to be a Christian. What would become of the apostle's assertion, *All who want to live devoted to God in Christ suffer persecution* (2 Tm 3:12)? If you suffer no persecution at all for Christ, ask yourself whether you have yet begun to live devoted to God in Christ. Once you have begun to, you will find you have stepped into the winepress; and then you must be ready for the pressing. You don't want to be found so shriveled that nothing will flow out, surely?

Verses 3-4. "The height of the day"

5. *My enemies have trampled on me all day long.* They are far removed from the saints, those enemies of mine. The phrase, *all day long*, has been used already. But what about the next one, *from the height of the day*—what does that mean? Something too high for us to understand, perhaps, above our heads. Yet it is no wonder that the psalm speaks of the height of the day, for perhaps the reason why those people moved far away from the saints is that they could not reach that high point of the "Day" of which the apostles are the twelve brilliant

---

10. Mt 13:28. The Latin is *inimicus homo hoc fecit*, "an enemy-man has done this."
11. *Botrus.*
12. See Ps 22(23):5.

hours.[13] Thus it was that they went wrong about the "Day" and crucified Christ as though he had been no more than human. Why were they so shrouded in darkness as to wander far from the saints? The Day was shining there on high, but hidden from them, for they did not recognize him; if they had, they would never have crucified the Lord of glory.[14] They were repelled by this high Day, and distanced themselves from the saints, and so they turned into enemies who would trouble and trample the grapes in the winepress.

Another interpretation is possible, though. *From the height of the day my enemies have trampled me all day long*—all the time, that is. But *from the height of the day* means "out of ephemeral pride." While they are trampling they are in a high position, for those being trampled are the lowly, and those who do the trampling are on top. But do not worry about their superior position; it is nothing but the height of the day, a superiority that is fleeting, not eternal.

Health, insensibility and immortality are three different states

6. *The many foes who attack me will be struck with fear.* But when? When that day which has seen them so lofty has passed away. They are uplifted for a time only, and once their spell of exaltation is over they will be struck with fear. *But as for me, I will hope in you, O Lord.* Notice that he does not say, "As for me, I will not be afraid," but, *the many foes who attack me will be struck with fear.* When the day of judgment dawns, all the tribes of the earth will mourn; but when the sign of the Son of Man appears in heaven,[15] then all the saints will be secure. What they have been hoping for, what they have longed for, what they were praying for, will happen. But for those others no further opportunity for repentance will be left, because at the time when repentance could have been productive they hardened their hearts against the Lord's admonition. Will they be able to build a wall against the Lord when he comes to judge?

Now take note of the reverent attitude of the psalmist and, if you belong to Christ's body, imitate it yourself. After predicting that *the many foes who attack me will be struck with fear*, he did not point out the contrast by saying, "Not I, though," lest by ascribing fearlessness to himself as something of his own, he might find himself too on those temporal heights, and through temporal pride lose his entitlement to eternal rest. No, he preferred to show you the reason why he expected to be free from fear: *But as for me, I will hope in you, O Lord.* He emphasized not his confidence, but the ground of his confidence. "If I am to be unafraid, it is possible that my fearlessness may be due to hardness of heart; for

---

13. The "Day" is Christ.
14. See 1 Cor 2:8.
15. See Mt 24:30; Rv 1:7.

there are many people who are afraid of nothing because their pride is so extreme."

Let me have your attention, beloved friends.[16] Bodily health is one thing, bodily insensitivity is another, and bodily immortality something else again. The only perfect health is immortality; but the health we have in this life can also be called health in a qualified way. When we are not ill, we can be called healthy; and the doctor pronounces us healthy when he has looked us over. When someone falls ill, that health is impaired; when he recovers, he is restored to health. Observe these three bodily states, and examine them with care: health, insensibility, immortality. A healthy body has no disease, but when it is hit or hurt, it feels pain. An unconscious body feels no pain. It has lost all awareness of pain, and the worse its condition, the less it feels. An immortal body feels no pain either, for all decay has been swallowed up, what was perishable has put on imperishability, and its mortal nature has been clothed with immortality.[17] So then, no pain in an immortal body, and no pain in an insensible body. But that does not mean that an insensible person can think that he is already immortal. The health of a person in pain is nearer to immortality than is the numbness of one who cannot feel anything. Suppose you come across someone who is so swollen with pride that he has convinced himself that he is afraid of nothing. Do you consider him braver than the man who lamented over *fighting without, and fears within* (2 Cor 7:5)? Do you even think him braver than our head, our Lord and God, who said, *My soul is sorrowful to the point of death* (Mt 26:38; Mk 15:34)? No, he is not braver, and you should not admire his insensitivity. He has not put on immortality, but only stripped off all feeling. For yourself, have a soul that is not devoid of sensitivity, for scripture has condemned the insensitive;[18] and from your healthy but painful experience ask, *Is anyone weak, and I am not weak too? Is anyone tripped up, without my being afire with indignation?* (2 Cor 11:29). Just imagine: if some scandal, or the ruin of some weak person, had left Paul unmoved, if he had been stiff and immune to pain, would he have seemed a greater man? Far from it! That would have been callousness, not tranquillity.

It will be a different matter, brothers and sisters, when we have arrived at that place, that throne, that blessed state, that heavenly homeland, where our souls will be fully confident, filled with peace and everlasting felicity. No pain will there be then, for no cause for pain will exist. As the psalmist says, *the many foes who attack me will be struck with fear.* Even those crass folk who fear nothing now will be afraid one day, because the terror that overtakes them will be enough to crack and shatter that hard shell. *The many foes who attack me will be struck with fear; but as for me, I will hope in you, O Lord.*

---

16. *Caritas vestra.*
17. See 1 Cor 15:53-55.
18. See Rom 1:31.

Verse 5. Yours, because God gave; yours only if you confess the gift

7. *In God I will seek praise for my words;*[19] *in God I have hoped;*[20] *I will not fear anything flesh may do to me.* Why not? "Because I will hope in God." But why? "Because it is in God that I will seek praise for my words." If you seek praise for your words in yourself, I do not counsel you not to be afraid, because you cannot be anything but afraid. Either you will know that your words are lies, and yours because they are lies; or, if they are truthful, but you do not think you received them from God, and suppose that you are speaking them as from yourself, then the words will be true but you will be a liar. However, if you are convinced that you have no power to say anything in accord with the wisdom of God and the true faith unless you have received it from him—remember, scripture demands, *What have you that you did not receive?* (1 Cor 4:7)—then indeed you are seeking praise for your own words, but doing so in God. And then you will be praised in God yourself, by God's own words. Indeed you will, because if you honor what is in you by God's gift, then you who have been made by God will be honored in God. But if you pay honor to God's gift in you as though it were something of your own, not God's, you will be wandering far away from the Holy One, just as that unbelieving people drew far away from the saints.

In God I will seek praise for my words, then. If they are *in God*, in what sense are they *my words*? Both are true: that they are in God, and that they are mine. In God, because they derive from him; mine, because I received them. He who gave them wanted them to be mine; and they became mine when I, knowing they are truly his, loved him who gave them to me. Were this not the way of it, how could we pray, *Give us today our daily bread*? How is it *our bread*, when at the same time we ask God to give it? When you beg him for it you will not go hungry, and by calling it yours you will not be ungrateful; for if you cannot call it yours you have not truly received it, but, on the other hand, if you call it your own in the sense that it derives from yourself, you lose what you have received, because you have proved ungrateful to him from whom you received it. Therefore *in God I will seek praise for my words*, because in God is the font of true words, the font that is himself. But they are *my words* too, because in my thirst I approached the fountain and drank there.

---

19. In the Hebrew this verse means "In God I will praise his word" (or, "in God, whose word I will praise...,"); that is, the confidence expressed by the psalmist in face of adversity is grounded in God's "word" or promise of assistance. The same sense is implied in verse 11 below, although there the pronoun "his" is not expressed. In the Septuagint, however, the sense is altered: the word of God ("his word") becomes "my words;" and this is carried over into the Latin version Augustine was using: *in Deo laudabo sermones meos*, which is scarcely intelligible. In the translation here offered the phrase has been rendered somewhat loosely, to reflect the meaning Augustine attaches to it in the following paragraphs.

20. Variant: "I will hope."

In God I will seek praise for my words; in God I have hoped; I will not fear anything flesh may do to me. But are you not that speaker who not long since was praying, *Have pity on me, Lord, because a man has trampled on me; he has troubled me with his assaults all day long?* How then can you now be declaring, *I will not fear what flesh may do to me?* What will it do? You have answered the question yourself a moment ago: *he has trampled on me, and troubled me.* Will he do you no harm, if he does that?

The psalmist turned his gaze to the wine that trickled from the trampling, and answered, "Yes, he has trodden on me; yes, he has given me trouble. But what will he be doing to me thereby? I was only a cluster of grapes, but now I shall become wine. *In God I have hoped. I will not fear anything flesh may do to me.*"

Verse 6. Like Master, like servant

8. *All day long they treated my words with loathing.* Yes, that is how it goes, as you know. Speak the truth, preach the truth, proclaim Christ to pagans, proclaim the Church to heretics, proclaim salvation to all—and they contradict, they treat my words with loathing. But when they do so, whom are they loathing, do you think? Him, surely, in whom *I will seek praise for my words.* Yet *all day long they treat my words with loathing.* At least let them be content with that; let them go no further in their censure and rejection. Let it not go further! Why do I say that? Because when they reject the words, when they abhor those words that spring from the fountain of truth, what may they do to the one through whom the words are spoken? What else, but treat him as the next line suggests: *All their plans were devised against me, to do me harm?* If they loathe the bread, are they likely to respect the little dish in which it is served? *All their plans were devised against me, to do me harm.* If they treated the Lord like this, the body must not shrink from following the head's example; rather must head and body be undivided. Your Lord was despised, and is it your ambition to be honored by those folk who have departed so far from the saints? You have no business to be arrogating to yourself privileges the head did not enjoy before you. A disciple is not greater than the teacher, nor a servant than the master. If they called the head of the household Beelzebub, how much more his staff?[21] *All their plans were devised against me, to do me harm.*

Verse 7. The enemies that lurk within the Church

9. *They will take up residence, and hide.* To take up residence[22] implies being a displaced person; those who live in a land not their own are called resident

---

21. See Mt 10:24-25.
22. *Incolo* corresponds to the Greek "~-""*Τῖμε̈* , used in the Septuagint of resident aliens who did not have citizens' rights.

aliens.[23] But everyone is on the move in this life. During our earthly journey we are wrapped around with flesh, through which our heart cannot be seen. This is why the apostle says, *Pass no judgment prematurely, before the coming of the Lord, for he will light up the dark, hidden places, and reveal the purposes of our hearts, and then there will be commendation from God for each one* (1 Cor 4:5). Until this comes about we each carry our own heart along in the journey of our bodily life, and every heart is shut against every other. Those enemies whose plans were devised to harm the psalmist are therefore said to *take up residence and hide*. They are travelers, carrying flesh, and so they cover up their deceit in their hearts; there they hide all the wickedness they are devising. How can they do that? Because their life is a time of travel, and of sojourning as aliens. Let them hide it, though, for the time being; what they are hiding will be brought to light, and they themselves will not remain hidden.

This notion of hiddenness suggests an alternative interpretation, which you may find more persuasive. From the ranks of those who have moved far away from the saints certain impostors worm their way into the Church, and the trouble they make for Christ's body is all the worse in that they are not shunned as complete strangers would be. The more serious danger they represent was pointed out by the apostle when he was enumerating all he had to endure: *I have been in danger from rivers, in danger from robbers, in danger from my own people and in danger from the Gentiles, endangered in the city and endangered in the wilderness, in danger at sea, and in danger* (notice this) *from false brethren* (2 Cor 11:26). These last are especially dangerous. Another psalm says of them, *They kept coming in to have a look* (Ps 40:7(41:6)). They make a habit of coming in to have a look, and no one says to them, "You can't come in here." Such a person comes in like one of your own, and is not avoided like a stranger. These are the ones who *take up residence, and hide*. They come into the great house, but with no intention of staying there for good, so they are no more than resident aliens. Our Lord wanted us to regard these sinners as slaves in the house: this is the sense of his teaching in the gospel: *Whoever commits sin is the slave of sin;* he says, *but a slave does not stay in the house permanently, whereas a son stays for ever* (Jn 8:34-35). Anyone who enters the house as a son will stay there for good: he or she is no resident alien. But anyone who comes in as a slave, as a sly sinner trying to make a favorable impression, or looking for something to steal, or something to denounce or decry—a person like that enters the house only as an alien, not intending to live there permanently.

This does not mean that we should be afraid of them, my brothers and sisters. *In God I have hoped; I will not fear anything flesh may do to me.* Resident aliens they may be, infiltrators they may be, pose they may, hide they may; but they are

---

23. *Incolae.*

still flesh. You must hope in the Lord, and then there will be nothing flesh can do to you. "But he brings trouble down on me, and tramples on me!" Never mind, the grapes are being pressed; now watch for the wine. Your tribulation will not be useless. Someone else will see you, and follow your lead, just as you learned to put up with your enemy by contemplating your head, the primordial grape. The traitor Judas "came in to see" him, and sojourned in his company, and hid there. You need not fear them, then, those who come in under false pretenses and reside among us, and hide. The ancestor of all such people was Judas; he lived with our Lord, though the Lord knew what he was. Judas, the traitor, habitually resided there, concealing himself, yet his heart lay wide open to the Lord of all things. In full awareness the Lord chose this particular man, in order to give comfort to you, who are not aware whom you ought to avoid. He could perfectly well have excluded Judas, for he knew what Judas was, as he made clear to his disciples when he said, *Have I not chosen all twelve of you? Yet one of you is a devil* (Jn 6:71). Does that mean a devil was one of his elect? If not, how was it that he chose twelve, and not eleven? Yes, that man was chosen, but for a different purpose. The eleven were chosen with a view to their probation; the one was chosen to be the means of their testing. How otherwise could the Lord give an example to you, who do not know the bad people you ought to avoid, the deceitful impostors you should steer clear of, the resident aliens who conceal themselves? How else, except by reminding you, "I too had one like that in my company; I trod that path before you, I endured it. I willingly put up with it in full awareness, so as to encourage you, who have no such awareness. What the traitor did to me, he will do to you as well. He will bring groundless accusations against you to maximize his power, to create havoc, and to ensure that false-hood[24] may prevail. But will any such schemes prevail against you, that did not prevail against me first? Against me they certainly did prevail, but they did not snatch heaven away from me."

It is true: even after his burial the Lord's flesh had to tolerate lying witnesses. It was not enough for him to endure them during his trial; he had to endure them even in the grave. They were bribed to lie, so they said, "While we were asleep, his disciples came and removed him."[25] So blind were the Jews that they believed a preposterous statement: they believed witnesses who had been asleep! Either it was untrue that they had fallen asleep, in which case they were liars and lacked credibility, or it was true that they had slept, in which case they could not have known what had happened. *They will take up residence, and hide.* Well, let them; what can they achieve? *In God I have hoped; I will not fear anything flesh may do to me.*

---

24. Variant: "false witnesses."
25. See Mt 28:13.

10. *They will keep watch on my heel.* Yes, they reside among us, concealing themselves, in order to pounce when someone falls. They keep their eyes glued to our heels to watch for any lapse, all ready to grip our feet and bring us down, or to stick out their own foot and trip us, or in one way or another find some charge to bring against us. And which of us so walks as never to stumble? If in no other way, we offend with the tongue; indeed, it is written that *if anyone has not sinned with his tongue, he is a perfect man* (Jas 3:2) and who would dare to say or think he is perfect? Inevitably, then, each of us will slip up through our tongue. But those who come in as resident aliens, and hide themselves, are like poachers watching all our words. They seek to lay snares and entangle us in their calumnies; but before they have succeeded in enmeshing others they become enmeshed, so that they are caught and killed themselves before they have caught and destroyed anyone else. How so? Because the quarry hastens back to his or her own heart, and from there hastens back to God, and has the wit to say, *"I will seek praise for my words in God.* If I have said anything good, anything true, what I have said belongs to God,[26] and as from God I said it. If I have perhaps said anything else that I should not have said, I said it as a mere human being, though I said it under God." He who confirms us when we walk aright, and threatens us when we go wrong, forgives us when we admit our fault; he curbs our tongue and calls back to him the one who falls. The righteous person will fall and get up again seven times a day, whereas the godless will grow weaker in evildoing.[27] No one among us should fear those cunning persecutors, the trappers of words, the people who almost count our syllables, yet themselves break the commandments. A person of this type studies you carefully to find grounds of accusation, but does not listen to you in order to come through you to faith in Christ. Listen, you sly fellow, to those words you are so keen to criticize; they may have some salutary lesson for you. "What," says this censorious person, "can someone who committed such a fault with his tongue have anything salutary to say to me?" Well, this he may usefully teach you, perhaps: to be not a trapper of words, but a collector of the commandments. *They will keep watch on my heel.*

11. *Even so my soul stood fast.* "I am relating what my soul withstood": an experienced sufferer was speaking here. *They will take up residence and hide, but even so* against them *my soul stood fast.* Let my soul indeed stand fast against all comers: those who bay[28] without and those who hide within. Temptation comes[29] from outside, sweeping in like a river, but let it find you on a rock, and

---

26. *Dei dixi.* Compare his Exposition of Psalm 49, 23: "If you hear good words, you are hearing God, no matter through whom you hear them."
27. See Prv 24:16.
28. *Latrantes.* Some codices have *latrones,* "robbers."
29. The editors of the CCL text punctuate differently, to produce the meaning, ". . . who bay without and those who hide within. Let it stand fast against those who come from outside, for temptation comes . . ."

hurl itself against you but not topple you, for your house is built rock-solid.[30] If the enemy is within, he will reside there temporarily and hide. Very well, let him be close to you, but only as chaff. Let the trampling oxen enter, let the threshing-sledge of temptation move in. You will be purified, but the chaff will be pounded to dust.

Verse 8. Salvation is free

12. *Even so my soul stood fast. You will save them for nothing.* The Lord has taught us to pray even for these, however. They *will take up residence, and hide*, yes; they are deceitful, admittedly; they are impostors and infiltrators, to be sure; but you must pray for them, and not say, "Is God ever going to straighten out someone like that, such a bad and perverted person?" Do not give up hope. Keep your eyes on the One to whom you make the plea, not the one for whom you make it. You see the gravity of the disease, but do you not see the power of the physician? *They will take up residence, and hide; but even so my soul stood fast.* Stand fast, and pray. What is the result? *You will save them for nothing.* You will save them, Lord, as though it cost you nothing, as though no effort on your part were required. Human resources offered no hope for them at all, but you cure them with a word; you expend no labor in curing them, though we are amazed as we look on.

Another interpretation of this verse is possible: *You will save them for nothing* means that you will save them without any preceding merits on their part. *I was originally a blasphemer*, says the apostle, *and a persecutor, and harmed people* (1 Tm 1:13). He used to obtain letters from the priests authorizing him to bind Christians wherever he might find them, and throw them into prison.[31] But in order to bind and arrest them he would first insinuate himself and hide. No merits had stood to this man's credit in advance, therefore, only deeds which should have earned him damnation. He had contributed nothing good, but he was saved. *You will save them for nothing.* They will not bring you he-goats, rams or bulls; they will offer no gifts or perfumes[32] in your temple; they pour out no libation from a good conscience. Everything inside them is in a dreadful state, all black and abominable; yet though they bring you nothing that could win them salvation, *you will save them for nothing*, by your grace, given freely.[33] What had the robber brought with him to the cross? He went from murder[34] to judgment,

---

30. See Mt 7:25.
31. See Acts 9:2.
32. Variant: "jewels."
33. *Gratis data gratia tua*, a very Augustinian theme and a phrase that became technical.
34. *De fauce*, literally "from [cutting someone's] throat." So some codices, probably correctly. In his *Homilies on the Gospel of John* 7,12, Augustine says, *Latro qui procedit ad faucem occidere hominem* (perhaps "goes for the jugular"). But a few codices read *de falce*. The *falx* was a sickle or similar agricultural tool, and by extension a curved sword or the scythes fixed to chariot wheels.

from judgment to the tree, from the tree to paradise.[35] He believed, and therefore he spoke.[36] But who gave him this faith, if not the One who hung beside him? *You will save them for nothing.*

13. *In your anger you will lead the peoples along.* You are angry yet you lead them, you are enraged yet you save, you terrify them yet you call them. What does it mean, *in your anger you will lead the peoples along*? You fill everything with troubles, so that people may not be led astray by pleasures and wrong-headed security, but may have recourse to you when they find themselves in difficulties. It seems like anger on your part, but it is a father's anger. A father is angry with a son who ignores his orders; in his anger he slaps his son, beats him, takes him by the ear, or drags him along by the hand, and leads him to school. *In your anger you will lead the peoples along.* What a lot of people have entered the Lord's house, what crowds have packed into it, brought here by his anger, because they were frightened by those troubles, and that was how they came to faith! Tribulation shakes us violently, but for the very purpose that a vessel filled with wickedness may be emptied out completely, and so filled with grace. *In your anger you will lead the peoples along.*

Verse 9. Proclaiming the life you have, but not for yourself

14. *I have made my life known to you.* You caused me to live, and for this reason I tell forth my life to you. But was God ignorant about the life he had given? No? Then what are you telling him about? Do you want to inform God? No, of course you don't. So why say, "I have made it known to you"? Does the psalmist imply, perhaps, "I have told forth my life to you because that serves your purposes"? How is God served thereby? God is served because he makes gains when someone acts like this. I have told the story of my life to God, because God endowed me with life. This is how Paul sketched his life-story: *I was originally a blasphemer and a persecutor and harmed people,* he began; but now let him tell the rest: *but I received mercy* (1 Tm 1:13). He told the story of his life not for his own benefit but for God's, because he told it in such a way as to bring people to believe in God; and so not Paul but God would be the gainer. This is clear from what Paul says elsewhere: *To this end Christ died and rose again, that they who are alive may live not for themselves, but for him who died for all* (2 Cor 5:15). So if you are alive, and your life is not something of your own (since he granted you the power to live), proclaim your life. Proclaim it not to yourself but to him, not seeking your own advantage. Live not for yourself, but for him who died for us all. Contrast what the apostle says about certain depraved char-

---

35. See Lk 23:43.
36. See Ps 115(116):10.

acters: *They all seek their own ends, not those of Jesus Christ* (Phil 2:21). If your motive in telling forth your life is to gain some advantage for yourself, and not for other people, you are proclaiming it to yourself, not to God. But if you tell your story in such a way as to invite others to receive the life you received, then you are telling forth your life to him who gave it to you, and your reward will be the more generous because you have proved yourself not ungrateful for what you received.

I have made my life known to you, O God; you have kept my tears in your sight. You heard me when I pleaded with you, *just as you promised*; for as you had promised, so you heard me. You said you would hear anyone who wept in your presence: I believed that, I wept, and I was heard. I have found you to be merciful in promising and faithful in keeping your word, *just as you promised*.

Verse 10. Walk behind, and be corrected

15. *Let my enemies be turned back.* This is for their good; the psalmist is not wishing misfortune upon them. They aspire to the front place, and that means they are unwilling to be corrected. Imagine this situation: you admonish your enemy, you tell him to lead a better life and amend his ways; he responds with scorn and rejects your advice. "Look who's warning me! Look who's giving me instructions on how to conduct my life!" He wants to forge ahead of you, and if he does so he will not be corrected. He fails to notice that the words you speak are not your own; he fails to see that you are telling forth your life to God, not to yourself. Because he rushes ahead he cannot be corrected; it would be better for him to be turned back, and to follow the one he wanted to precede. The Lord was one day speaking to his disciples about his impending passion. Peter was appalled, and protested, *Far be it from you, Lord; this will not happen*, though just before this he had confessed, *You are the Christ, the Son of the living God.* He confessed Christ to be God, but feared his death as a man. Yet the Lord had come in the human condition so that he could suffer, for in no way could we have been saved, had we not been redeemed by his blood. A moment earlier the Lord had commended Peter's confession, saying to him, *It is not flesh and blood that revealed this to you, but my Father, who is in heaven. Therefore I tell you that you are Peter, and upon this rock I will build my Church, and the gates of the underworld will not overcome it; and I will give to you the keys of the kingdom of heaven.* Look how Peter had carried through his truthful, reverent, fully confident confession, acknowledging that *You are the Christ, the Son of the living God.* Yet as soon as the Lord began to speak about his passion, Peter was afraid that Christ would perish by death, whereas in fact it was we who would have perished if Christ had not died. So Peter protested, *Far be it from you, Lord; this will not happen.* And the Lord, who had just now said to Peter, *Blessed are you,*

and upon this rock I will build my Church, now said to him, *Get behind me, Satan; you are a stumbling-block to me*. How could he now call Peter "Satan," when a moment earlier he had called him "blessed," and "rock"? *You have no taste for the things of God, but only for human things* (Mt 16:16-19. 22-23), said the Lord, yet only moments before it had indeed been to the things of God that Peter's spiritual taste was sensitive, for *it is not flesh and blood that revealed this to you, but my Father, who is in heaven*. As long as Peter was seeking praise for his words in God, he was no Satan but Peter, the rock-like Peter; but when he spoke from himself, out of human weakness and merely natural love for a human being, he was addressed as "Satan," because his attitude would have been an obstacle to his own salvation and that of everyone else. Why? Because he was trying to run ahead of the Lord, and to give earthly counsel to his heavenly leader. *Far be it from you, Lord; this will not happen*. Listen to what you are saying, Peter: *Far be it*, and *Lord*. If he is the Lord, he is acting in power; if he is the teacher, he knows what he must do, and knows what to teach. But you are trying to lead the leader, teach the teacher, give orders to the Lord, and make choices for God. You are getting much too far in front, so *get behind*.

And was this not the most profitable outcome for the enemies in the psalm? *Let my enemies be turned back*, but do not let them remain stuck there. They need to be turned back and taught not to rush ahead, but turned back so that they may follow, not that they may remain stationary in the rear. *Let my enemies be turned back*.

God, but my God too

16. *On whatever day I call upon you, lo, I know that you are my God*. That is the all-important thing to know! He does not say, "I know that you are God," but *that you are my God*. He is yours when he comes to your help, yours when you are not alienated from him. This is why it is said in another psalm, *Blessed is the people whose God is the Lord*. Why specify that he is *their* God? Is there anyone whose God he is not? Obviously he is the God of everyone, but he is most properly called the God of those who love him, hold fast to him, possess him, and worship him. These are the ones who belong to his household as his strong family, redeemed by the strong blood of his only Son. What magnificent generosity God has shown us, that we should be his, and he ours!

But those other folk of alien race who have gone far away from the saints are foreigners. Look what is said of them in another psalm: *Rescue me, and deliver me from the hands of foreigners, whose mouths have spoken empty words, and whose right hand is a hand that deals unjustly*. And notice too how high and mighty they appear to be, though their exalted fortunes are nothing but "the height of the day," temporal pride. *Their sons are like well-set saplings, their daughters are adorned and gathered round them like the pillars of the temple.* This is a description of happiness in the present world, where wayward mortals, who set great store by temporal happiness, do not bother to seek the true happiness that lasts forever. Consequently they are deemed foreigners, not children of God: *Their sons are like well-set saplings, their daughters are adorned and gathered round them like the pillars of the temple, their storerooms are full to overflowing, their oxen are sturdy and their ewes fruitful, increasing at every lambing-time. Never is their hedge broken down or their property invaded, nor is there rioting in their streets.* And what conclusion is drawn from all this? *People who have these things are called blessed.* Who said so? The foreigners, *whose mouths have spoken empty words.* But you, what do you say? *Blessed is the people whose God is the Lord* (Ps 143(144):11-15).

Yes, that's it. The psalm has finally swept aside all the things that God gives, and given you God himself. Remember, brothers and sisters, that all these things the foreigners have reeled off are gifts of God. But he gives them to foreigners, to bad people, to blasphemers, just as he also makes his sun rise over good and bad alike, and his rain fall on just and unjust equally.[37] To the good he sometimes gives these blessings, and sometimes he withholds them; to bad people he sometimes gives them, and sometimes not. But for the good he is reserving his very self, whereas for the bad he reserves everlasting fire. So there is a bad thing that he does not give to good people, and a good thing that he does not give to bad people; but in between there are many other things, both good and bad, that he gives to both the good and the wicked.

Chaste love is disinterested love

17. Let us love God purely and chastely, brothers and sisters. It is no chaste heart that worships God with an eye to the reward. What am I saying? That we shall gain no reward for worshiping God? On the contrary. A reward we shall have, but it will be nothing less than the very God we worship. He himself will be our recompense, for we shall see him as he is.[38] Fix your minds on the reward that is awaiting you. What does our Lord Jesus Christ promise to his lovers? *Anyone who cherishes my commandments and keeps them, that is the one who loves me; and whoever loves me will be loved by my Father, and I will love him.* What will you give to such a lover? *I will show myself to him* (Jn 14:23,21). If you do not love God, that may seem a paltry payment. But if you are in love, if you are yearning for him, if you worship him freely who redeemed you freely (for you had no prior merits to induce him to purchase you), if after reviewing all his

37. See Mt 5:45.
38. See 1 Jn 3:2.

kindness to you you long for him, and feel your heart restless with desire for him, then do not seek anything else, because he himself is enough for you. However greedy you are, God is enough for you. In your greed you aspired to own the whole earth, did you? Have heaven as well, because he who made heaven and earth is greater still.

Let me give you an illustration, brothers and sisters. If you think about human marriage you get an idea of what a chaste heart is with regard to God. It is earthly marriage we are talking about, but all the same, a husband does not truly love his wife if he loves her only for the sake of the dowry she brings him, and a wife does not chastely love her husband if she loves him only for the gifts he has given her, or because his gifts have been lavish. He is her husband while he is rich, but still her husband if he has become poor.[39] How many husbands have there been who, when they fell foul of the law, found themselves loved more fondly by their chaste wives? How often has conjugal fidelity been proved chaste by the calamities that overtook the husbands, as wives have not only refused to desert them, but have proved more loyal than ever, to show that nothing other than their husbands was dear to them? If then in human marriage a husband is loved chastely when he is cherished with disinterested love, and a wife is loved chastely when she too is loved gratis, how is God to be loved, he the true and faithful husband of our souls, the spouse who makes us fruitful with the new life of eternity, and will not have us barren?

Let us set our love on him in this way, and let nothing but himself be loved. Then what we have sung will be true in us, for it is our voice that testifies in the psalm, *On whatever day I call upon you, lo, I know that you are my God.* Calling upon God means calling upon him without seeking reward. Exactly that; because what does scripture say of certain people? That *they have not invoked the Lord.* They pretended to themselves that they were invoking the Lord, and they offered him their petitions concerning legacies, or increasing their income, or prolonging their earthly life, or other temporal issues; yet what is scripture's verdict? *They have not invoked the Lord.* And how does it reinforce the point? *They quaked with fear where there was nothing to fear* (Ps 13:5(14:4-5)). What does it mean by *where there was nothing to fear*? They were afraid their money might be stolen, afraid of some loss in their household, even afraid that they might see fewer years than they hoped in this life. Yes indeed, they were fearful where there was no reason to be afraid. The attitude of the Jews was similar: *If we leave him alone like this, the Romans will come, and sweep away our land and our nationhood* (Jn 11:48). *They quaked with fear where there was nothing to fear.* But as for me, *I know that you are my God.* This is a great treasure for the

---

39. *Et dives maritus, et pauper factus maritus est.* By repeating the verb *donavit* at the end of the preceding sentence, the editors of the CCL text slightly alter the meaning: "Her husband gave her gifts while he was rich, but when he has become poor he is still her husband."

heart, a great light for the inner eye, a great and unshakable security! *Lo, I know that you are my God.*

Verses 11-12. Sacrifice from within

18. *In God I will commend a word; in the Lord I will praise a promise;*[40] *in God I have hoped; I will not fear what anyone may do to me.* This is a repetition of what was said earlier.

19. *The good things I have vowed to give you, and the praise I will render you, are within me, O God.* Make your vows to the Lord your God, and carry them out.[41] What are you to vow, what duly offer? The animals that were customarily sacrificed on altars in days of old? No, nothing of that kind. What you must vow and what you must duly offer is within you. From the coffer of your heart bring forth the incense of praise, and from the store of a good conscience the sacrifice of faith. And whatever you bring, set it alight with charity. Within yourself are the offerings you must present in praise of God. In praise of whom? Of God: for what has he done for you? *You have saved my soul from death.* This is the life which the psalmist proclaims in God's hearing: *O God, I have made my life known to you;* for what was I before? Dead. Of myself I was dead; but thanks to your power, what am I now? Alive! Therefore *the good things I have vowed to give you, and the praise I will render you, are within me, O God.* I love my God, and no one can snatch him away from me. Nor can anyone take from me what I must give to him, because it is locked away in my heart. The psalmist was fully justified in that confidence he showed earlier: *What can any mortal do to me?* Mortals may rage. Let them be permitted to rage, let them be allowed to succeed in their efforts; what will they steal? Gold, silver, livestock, slaves, maidservants, lands, houses—let them take the lot! Will they be able to take the sacrifices that are within me, the sacrifices I will offer to God in praise? The tempter was permitted to put holy Job to the test, and in a single attack he took away everything. He seized all the property Job had, robbed him of his inheritance and slew his heirs. And all this came upon him not little by little, but as a troop of misfortunes, in one blow, one onslaught, as all the bad news was announced to him at once. Everything had been taken away and Job remained alone; but inside himself he had those sacrifices of praise that he could offer to God. Yes, there within him, for the thieving devil had not broken into the treasury of his breast, and it was full of sacrificial gifts. Listen to what he had there, and what he brought forth: *the Lord gave, and the Lord has taken away. This has happened as the Lord willed: may the Lord's name be blessed* (Jb 1:21). How precious are

---

40. See note on verse 5 above.
41. See Ps 75:12(76:11).

those inner riches that no thief can touch! God himself had given what was now being given back to him; he had himself endowed Job with the means of offering him the kind of sacrifice he desired.

What God seeks from you is praise. Your confession[42] is what God demands of you. Are you going to give him something from your crops? Fine; but he sent the rain that enabled you to grow them. Or will you give him some of your savings? But he set you up in business. What are you going to give him that you did not first receive from him? What have you that you did not receive?[43] Will you give him treasures from your heart? He gave you faith, and hope, and charity; this is what you must present, this you must offer in sacrifice. An enemy can take away all those other things against your will, but this he cannot take without your consent. Those other things anyone may lose unwillingly: one who wants to possess gold may lose the gold; one who wants to own a house may lose that house. But no one loses faith, except by throwing it away.

Verse 13. The light of the living

20. *The good things I have vowed to give you, and the praise I will render you, are within me, O God. For you have saved my soul from death, my eyes from tears, and my feet from stumbling, that I may be pleasing to God in the light of the living.* Not pleasing to the foreigners, though, who are far distant from the saints, for they do not enjoy the light of the living, and so are unable to see what pleases God. The light of the living is the light of the immortals, the light of the saints. A person who is not in darkness pleases God in the light of the living. We may observe someone from the outside, and all his or her possessions, but no one knows what that person is really like; only God knows. Sometimes even the devil is ignorant about it, and will not find out unless he puts that person to the test, as he did in the case of the holy man about whom I have just reminded you. God knew what Job was made of, and bore witness to him; but the devil did not know, which is why he asked, *Job hardly worships the Lord for nothing, does he?* (Jb 1:9). Look at the lengths to which the enemy had gone in his provocation, for what he pointed to was true perfection! Consider what the enemy was trying to allege against him. The devil saw someone who was serving God, obedient in all respects, conducting himself well in all things. And because this man was rich, and his household so abundantly blessed, the enemy accuses him of worshiping God for that very reason: because God has given him all this. *Job hardly worships the Lord for nothing, does he?* It would mean, you see, that Job was in the true light, the light of the living, if he worshiped God gratis. And it was

---

42. As usually in Augustine, "confession" in the sense of thanksgiving, acknowledgement of God's greatness and grace, as well as confession of sin.
43. See 1 Cor 4:7.

true: God saw the freely offered worship of himself in the heart of his servant. Job's heart was pleasing in the Lord's sight, in the light of the living; but from the devil it was hidden, because the devil was in darkness. God gave the devil free rein, not so that God himself might find out what he knew already, but to show it to us, for our instruction and imitation. If the tempter had not been given leave, would we have seen in Job what we ought to imitate, and to what we should aspire? No. The tempter was therefore let loose, and took all Job's goods away. Job remained alone, stripped of his possessions, stripped of his household servants, bereaved of his children, but full of God. Admittedly his wife was left, but do you think that was mercy on the devil's part, to leave him his wife? Not so; he knew who had deceived Adam. The devil left her in place as his ally, not as a comfort to her husband.

Job was left, then, full of God, and the offerings of praise that he would present were within him. To prove that he worshiped God disinterestedly, and not because he had received so much, to prove that he was of the same mind when all these things had been taken from him, Job said, *The Lord gave, and the Lord has taken away. This has happened as the Lord willed: may the Lord's name be blessed.* He was a mass of wounds from top to toe, but inwardly he was whole. Out of the light of the living, out of the light that was in his heart, he replied to the woman who tempted him, *You have spoken like the silly woman you are* (Jb 2:10), like one who lacks the light of the living; for wisdom is the light of the living, and silly talk is the darkness of fools. *You have spoken like the silly woman you are*: you see my flesh, but you do not see the light in my heart. She would have been able to love her husband all the more tenderly if she had been aware of his inward beauty, if she had looked within to see how fair he was in God's sight, for there within him were the gifts he would offer to praise God. What a precious inheritance that was, and one immune to the devil's attacks! How inviolate was that treasure he already possessed! Yet on account of it he hoped to possess still more as he progressed from strength to strength.[44]

Well then, brothers and sisters, let all this be a powerful incentive for us to love God without looking for rewards, to hope in him always, and to fear neither human foe nor the devil. Neither the one nor the other can do anything except by God's permission, and they are given permission for nothing except what will be to our profit. Let us tolerate bad people and be good ourselves, because we too were bad once. God will save them for nothing, all those of whom we so presumptuously despair. Let us then despair of no one, but pray for all those who are a trial to us, and never forsake God. Let him be our patrimony, let him be our hope, let him be our salvation. Here below he gives us comfort, hereafter he will reward us, and everywhere he is the author and giver of life. No other life is this

---

44. Or "from many virtues to one single virtue," as Augustine takes it in his Exposition of Psalm 83, 11.

than the life of which it was said, *I am the way, and the truth, and the life* (Jn 14:6). So may we be pleasing in the sight of the Lord, both here in the light of faith, and there in the light of vision, the light of the living.

Exposition of Psalm 56

A Sermon to the People

Introduction: Christ's command and example of love; head and body

1. My brothers and sisters, we have just heard in the gospel how dearly our Lord and Savior loves us. As God he is intimate with the Father, as man he is intimate with us. He is from our race, yet now enthroned at the right hand of the Father, and you have heard how much he loves us. He spoke of the measure of his charity, and required the same measure of us, telling us of his commandment: that we love one another. Perhaps we might have been doubtful and perplexed as to how much we should love one another, and what the perfect charity might be that pleases God, for perfect charity is that charity which cannot be surpassed. So to dispel our doubts he put the standard into words himself, and taught us. *No one can have greater charity than this*, he said, *to lay down one's life for one's friends* (Jn 15:12). He acted himself in accordance with what he taught, the apostles acted as they had learned from him, and then they preached to us that we must do the same. Let us do likewise; for though if we think of him as our Creator we are not what he is, we are what he is with regard to what he became for our sake. If he alone had achieved it, perhaps no one among us would aspire to imitate him, for though human, he was human in such a way that he was also God. But human he was, and so servants have imitated their Master, and disciples have imitated their Teacher, and our predecessors in his family have done it, people who though they were our ancestors are yet our fellow-servants. Moreover, God would not have commanded us to do likewise if he had judged it impossible for human beings to love like that. When you take your weakness into account, do you feel yourself collapsing under the weight of this commandment? Draw strength from his example, then. Or do you find even his example overwhelming? Be confident: he who gave you the example is at hand, to give you help as well.

Let us listen to him in this psalm. Most opportunely, and by the Lord's disposition, it happens that the gospel chimes in with the psalm, for while the gospel reminds us of the love of Christ, who laid down his life for us so that we might lay down ours for our brothers and sisters, the psalm shows us how he laid down his life, for it sings about his passion. So the conformity and harmony between gospel and psalm are evident.

Now the whole Christ consists of head and body. You are certainly aware of this. The head is our Savior himself, who suffered under Pontius Pilate and now, after rising from the dead, is seated at the Father's right hand. His body is the Church: not this or that local church, but the Church that extends throughout the world. It is made up not only of people alive today, for those who have gone before us belong to the Church too, and so do those who will come after us, even to the end of time. All the faithful are Christ's members, and the Church is thus made up of all who believe. The head of the Church is enthroned in heaven, from where he rules and guides his body; and though the body is still debarred from the vision of him, it is linked to him by charity.

Since, then, the whole Christ consists of the head and his body, we must be alert to the accents of the head in all the psalms in such a way that we catch the voices of the body too. He would not have us speaking apart from him, any more than he wants to be apart from us, for he said, *Lo, I am with you even to the end of the ages* (Mt 28:20). If he is with us, he speaks in us, speaks about our concerns, and speaks through us, because we also speak in him; and only because we speak in him do we speak the truth.[1] If we attempt to speak in our own persons and of ourselves, we shall linger in lies.

Verse 1. The Jews, imitating Saul, persecuted the true David

2. The psalm sings of our Lord's passion, so let us look at the title it bears: *To the end.* The "end" is Christ.[2] Why is he called "the end"? Not because he consumes anything, but because he consummates it. To consume a thing means to destroy it; to consummate means to bring it to perfection. When we say a thing is "finished," we derive the phrase from the notion of "the end."[3] But we say it in two different senses: "the bread is finished," and "the tunic is finished." The bread is finished up, all eaten; the tunic is finished when the weaver has completed the job. The bread comes to an end in the sense of being used up, but the weaving of the tunic is ended when it has been brought to perfection.

Now Christ is the end of all our striving, because however hard we try, we are made perfect only in him and by him. Our perfection is to reach him. But when you reach him you will look for nothing further, for he is your end. When you are on a journey, your end is the place you are making for, and when you reach it, there you will stay. Similarly the end of your endeavor, of your enterprise, of your striving and your intention, is he to whom you are making your way; and when you reach him, you will desire nothing further, because you could never

---

1. This sentence epitomizes Augustine's teaching on the psalms.
2. See Rom 10:4.
3. More obvious in Latin: *finitum* ("finished") from *finis* ("end").

have anything better. Christ has set us an example of how to live our lives here, and he will give us our reward in the life to come.

3. *For the end, as a title for David himself that is not to be tampered with, when he fled into a cave from Saul's pursuit.* On referring to sacred scripture we find that David, King of Israel (from whom the Davidic Psalter takes its name), was indeed pursued by King Saul. Many of you are familiar with the story, because you have had the scriptures in your hands, or have listened to them. David was persecuted by Saul. But David was very moderate, and Saul very fierce, David gentle and Saul jealous, the one long-suffering and the other cruel, the one kind and the other ungrateful. David treated Saul with such leniency that when he had him in his power he laid no hand upon him, nor harmed him at all.[4] David was given by the Lord God an opportunity to kill Saul if he chose, but he preferred to spare him. Yet not even by such kindness was Saul persuaded to give up his persecution. So we have found that in those days, when Saul was persecuting David, there was a king already repudiated pursuing one who was destined to be king in the future, and that David fled from Saul into a cave.

What has this to do with Christ? If the events of that time prefigured what was to come, we can find Christ in this story, and very clearly indeed; for I do not see how the words, *a title that is not to be tampered with,* can apply to David. There was no title written for David which Saul attempted to falsify. But we do see that in our Lord's passion a title was inscribed: *King of the Jews,* a title calculated to rebuke the effrontery of those who did not keep their hands off their king. In them Saul was present, and in Christ, David. As the gospel that derives from the apostles testifies, and as we know, as we confess, Christ was *from David's line, according to the flesh* (Rom 1:3), but only according to the flesh, for in his divinity he is far above David, above heaven and earth, above all things visible and invisible; for everything was made through him, and apart from him nothing was made.[5] Yet when he came to us he deigned to become man from the lineage of David, for the Virgin Mary, who bore Christ, was of David's line, and so Christ was born into David's tribe.

Well then, a title was inscribed: *King of the Jews.* As we have said, Saul represented the Jewish people, as David stood for Christ. And there it was, the title, *King of the Jews.* The Jews were incensed at it, for they were ashamed to acknowledge as their king someone they had the power to crucify. They did not foresee that the cross to which they nailed him would one day adorn the brows of kings. In their indignation at the title they went to the judge, Pilate, to whom they had delivered Christ for crucifixion; and they said to him, *Do not put "The King of the Jews"; put "He said, I am the King of the Jews"* (Jn 19:21). And because under the guidance of the Holy Spirit scripture had long ago sung, *For the end, as*

4. See 1 Sm 24.
5. See Jn 1:3.

a title that is not to be tampered with, Pilate answered, *"What I have written, I have written*. How dare you prompt me to lie? I do not distort the truth."

How Christ, like David, hid in a cave

4. Now that we have heard what that phrase means, *a title that is not to be tampered with*, let us pass on to the next: *when David fled into a cave from Saul's pursuit*. What does that signify? The David of the Old Testament certainly did this, but we did not find in him any connection with the writing of a title; now, conversely, let us see whether flight into a cave has any relevance to the new David. That cave which the old David used to cover himself prefigured something. Why did he cover himself? In order to remain hidden; he did not want to be found. But what does being covered by a cave suggest? Being covered by earth. If a person takes refuge in a cave, he is covered over completely by the earth, and so cannot be seen. Jesus went about carrying earth, since the flesh he wore had been taken from the earth, and he was concealed by it so that his godhead might not be discovered by the Jews; for if they had known it, they would never have crucified the Lord of glory.[6] How was it that they did not discover the Lord of glory? Because he had covered himself with a cave. What I mean is this: he displayed before their eyes the weakness of his flesh, but kept the majesty of his godhead covered over by his body, as though hidden in the earth. Consequently they failed to realize that he was God, and crucified him as a man. He was not capable of dying, except in his humanity, or of being crucified, except in his humanity, or of being held prisoner, except in his humanity. He exposed the earth in him to those who sought him with evil intent, and kept his life for those who seek him in the right way. His flesh, then, was his means of fleeing from Saul into a cave. You can take the idea further, if you like, and say that the Lord fled from Saul into a cave in the sense that he underwent his passion and hid himself from the Jews even to the point of dying. The Jews unleashed their utmost savagery against him, yet they still went on thinking, until the moment of his death, that he might be set free, and prove by some miracle that he was indeed the Son of God. These events had been foretold in the Book of Wisdom: *Let us condemn him to the most shameful of deaths, for his claims will be taken care of, according to his own account. If he truly is the Son of God, he will deliver him from the hands of his adversaries* (Wis 2:20.18). Since, therefore, he was hanging on the cross and not being rescued, they concluded that he was not God's Son. They insulted him as he hung there, shaking their heads and saying, *If you are the Son of God, come down from the cross! He saved others, but he can't save himself.*[7] And as they said it, the prophecy in the Book of Wisdom

---

6. See 1 Cor 2:8.
7. See Mt 27:40.42.

came true: *So they thought, but they were mistaken, for their malice completely blinded them* (Wis 2:21). Would it have been a great feat to come down from the cross, for someone who so easily rose from the grave?

Why was it his will to suffer even to the point of death? This was another way in which he fled from Saul into a cave. A cave, you see, can be thought of as a place underground. Now it is well known to us all that his body was laid in a tomb that had been hewn out of rock; and this tomb was therefore a kind of cave, and there he took refuge from Saul. The Jews persecuted him to the very moment when he was laid in that cave. How do I prove that their persecution went on as long as that, even to his burial? Well, consider: even after he was dead, but still hanging on the cross, they wounded his body;[8] but when he had been wrapped with due care in burial cloths and placed in the cave, the Jews could inflict no further outrage on his flesh. Then the Lord arose from that cave where he had taken refuge from Saul; he arose unhurt, untouched by decay, and, while concealing himself from those impious people whom Saul had foreshadowed, he showed himself to his own members. The limbs of the Risen One were handled by those who were themselves limbs of his body, and they believed.[9] And so Saul achieved nothing.

We have spent enough time discussing the title, as the Lord graciously enabled us. Now let us listen to the psalm.

Verse 2. The whole Christ prays, and teaches us to pray

5. *Have mercy on me, O God, have mercy, for my soul trusts in you.* Christ is praying in his passion, *Have mercy on me, O God.* God is saying to God, *Have mercy on me.* He who, together with the Father, has mercy on you is crying out in you, *Have mercy on me.* Something in him that belongs to you is crying out, *Have mercy on me*, something that he took from you; for he clothed himself in flesh to set you free. Now this same flesh is pleading, *Have mercy on me, O God, have mercy*; the whole man is pleading, the man who is soul and flesh, for the Word assumed our entire humanity, the Word became a complete man. True, the evangelist expresses it by saying, *The Word was made flesh, and dwelt among us* (Jn 1:14), but you must not take this to mean that he had no human soul. This is far from the truth. In the language of scripture, "flesh" means "human being." So scripture says elsewhere, *All flesh will see the salvation of God* (Is 40:5; Lk 3:6). This does not mean that flesh alone will see it, and the soul will have no place, does it? Again, the Lord himself, referring to the human race, says, *As you have given him power over all flesh* (Jn 17:2). Surely he did not mean that his power

---

8. See Jn 19:34.
9. See Lk 24:39; Jn 20:27-28.

extended over flesh only, and not, much more importantly, over souls? Was it not his primary reason for coming, to set souls free? So in the case of our Lord himself, the soul was there and the flesh was there; a whole man was there. This whole man was one with the Word, and the Word was one with this human being; the man and the Word together were one single human being, and the Word and the man together were one God. Let him say, then, *Have mercy on me, O God, have mercy,* and let us not take fright when we hear the voice of one who both pleads for mercy and grants it. He pleads for it precisely because he also grants it, for he became man because he is merciful. He was born not by any necessity of his condition, but to set us free from our condition of necessity. *Have mercy on me, O God, have mercy on me, for my soul trusts in you.* You hear your Teacher praying, so learn to pray. He prayed for this very reason, to teach us to pray, just as he suffered to teach us to suffer, and rose from the dead to teach us to hope for resurrection.

6. *And beneath the shadow of your wings I will hope, until iniquity shall pass away.* This is certainly the whole Christ speaking; here is our voice too. Iniquity has not passed away yet; no indeed, iniquity is still at the boiling-point. The Lord himself indicated that in the last days iniquity will be very widespread: *with iniquity increasing mightily, the love of many will grow cold, but whoever perseveres to the end will be saved* (Mt 24:12-13). But who will persevere to the end, until iniquity has passed away? Only the one who is within Christ's body, who is among the members of Christ, and has learned from the body's head the long-suffering that perseveres. You as an individual pass away, and at once your personal temptations have passed away with you. If you have led a holy life, you go away into another life, into which other holy people have entered already. Into that life the martyrs entered, and if you become a martyr you pass into that other life too. But does this mean that because you have passed beyond this life, iniquity has gone away as well? Clearly not. Other bad people are born all the time, just as other bad people die. And just as other bad people are being born and other bad people are always dying, so too other righteous people are taking leave of us and others being born. Until the end of time there will always be iniquity causing affliction and righteousness enduring it. *And beneath the shadow of your wings I will hope, until iniquity shall pass away.* This means: "You, Lord, will protect me, so that I do not get scorched under the sun of iniquity. You will provide shade for me."

Verse 3. God is most high, yet near

7. *I will cry to God Most High.* If he is most high, how can he hear your crying? "My confidence is born from experience," the psalmist replies, "because I am praying to *God, who has dealt kindly with me.* If he dealt kindly

with me before I sought him, will he not hear me now that I am crying out to him?" The Lord God dealt kindly with us by sending us our Savior Jesus Christ, to die for our misdeeds and rise for our justification.[10] And for what kind of people did God will his Son to die? For the godless. The godless were not seeking God, but God sought them. He is "most high" indeed, but in such a way that our wretchedness and our groans are not far from him, for the Lord is close to those who have bruised their hearts.[11] *I will cry to God Most High, to God who has dealt kindly with me.*

Verse 4. Prophecy fulfilled: Christ is raised, and the Jews carry the scriptures for us

8. *He sent from heaven and saved me.* It is quite obvious that the man Jesus, this very flesh, this very Son of God, has been saved already insofar as he partakes of our nature. The Father did send from heaven and save him; the Father sent from heaven and saved him from the dead. But you need to keep in mind that the Lord also raised himself. Both truths are stated in scripture—that the Father raised him and that he raised himself. Affirming that the Father raised Christ, the apostle says, *He was made obedient to the point of death, even death on a cross, which is why God raised him high and gave him a name above every other name* (Phil 2:8-9). You have there a statement that the Father raised and exalted his Son. Now listen to another, showing that the Son also raised up his own flesh. Using the imagery of the temple he said to the Jews, *Dismantle this temple, and in three days I will raise it up again*; and the evangelist explained to us what he meant: *He was speaking of the temple of his body* (Jn 2:19.21). But now he speaks in the person of one praying, of a human being, of a being of flesh, and he says, God *sent from heaven, and saved me.*

9. *Those who trampled on me he has consigned to disgrace.* He has reduced to disgrace those who trampled on Christ, insulted him after his death, and crucified him as a mere man because they did not understand that he was God. This has happened already, hasn't it? We are not being asked to believe in something future; we only need to observe what is already accomplished. The Jews raged against Christ, and persecuted him in their pride—but where? In the city of Jerusalem. In the stronghold of that kingdom about which they were so conceited, there they raised their arrogant heads against him. But after the Lord's passion they were uprooted, and they lost the kingdom where they had refused to acknowledge Christ as king. Consider how completely they have been consigned to disgrace: they have been scattered throughout all nations, with no stability anywhere, and nowhere any secure home.

---

10. See Rom 4:25.
11. See Ps 33:19(34:18).

But the Jews survive still, and for a special purpose: so that they may carry our books, to their own confusion. When we want to prove to the pagans that Christ's coming was prophesied, we produce these scriptures. But possibly pagans obstinately opposed to the faith might have alleged that we Christians had composed them, fabricating prophecies to buttress the gospel we preach. They might have thought that we were trying to pass off our message by pretending that it had been foreshadowed in prophecy. But we can convince them of their error by pointing out that all those scriptures which long ago spoke of Christ are the property of the Jews. Yes, the Jews recognize these very writings. We take books from our enemies to confute other enemies!

In what sort of disgrace do the Jews find themselves? A Jew carries the book which is the foundation of faith for a Christian. Jews act as book-bearers for us, like the slaves who are accustomed to walk behind their masters carrying their books, so that while the slaves sink under the weight, the masters make great strides through reading.[12] Such is the shameful position to which the Jews have been reduced, and the prophecy uttered so long ago has been fulfilled: *those who trampled on me he has consigned to disgrace*. What a disgrace it is indeed for them, brothers and sisters, that they can read this verse like blind people looking into their own mirror! In that holy scripture which they are carrying the Jews are reflected in the same way as a blind person's face is reflected: it is seen by others, but the blind man cannot see himself. *Those who trampled on me he has consigned to disgrace*.

Christ is mercy and truth

10. Perhaps when the psalm said, *He sent from heaven and saved me*, you wondered, "What did he send from heaven? Whom did he send from heaven? Did he send an angel to save Christ, a servant to save the Lord?" No. All the angels form part of the creation that is at Christ's service. Angels could be sent to obey, they could be sent to render services, but not to help Christ. Admittedly it is written that angels ministered to him,[13] but not like merciful beings ministering to one in need: rather as subjects to the Omnipotent. What, then, did he *send from heaven* to save me? In the next line we hear what he sent from heaven: *He sent his mercy and his truth*. To what purpose? *And he rescued my soul from amid the lion-cubs*. The psalm says, *He sent* from heaven *his mercy and his truth*; and Christ himself declared, *I am the truth* (Jn 14:6). Truth was sent here to rescue my soul from amid the lion-cubs, and mercy too was sent. So we find that

---

12. *Illi portando deficiant, illi legendo proficiant.* Possibly the image of the *paedagogus* referred to in Gal 3:24 is also in Augustine's mind. Compare his Exposition of Psalm 40, 14. A *librarius* (his word here) was more often either a copyist, scribe, secretary, or a bookseller.
13. See Mt 4:11; Mk 1:13; Lk 22:43.

Christ is both mercy and truth: mercy that suffers with us, and truth that requites us. This is connected with what I said a moment ago about Christ raising himself from the dead. If Truth raised Christ, and if Truth delivered Christ's soul from amid the lion-cubs, then as he was merciful in dying for us, so was he true in rising to justify us. He had said that he would rise again, and Truth cannot lie. Because he was Truth and spoke truly, he displayed real scars, as he had received real wounds. The disciples touched these scars, handled them and assured themselves of their reality. The one who put his fingers into the pierced side exclaimed, *My Lord and my God!* (Jn 20:28), confessing that Christ had in mercy died for him, and in truth had risen and shown himself to him.

He sent from heaven *his mercy and his truth, and rescued my soul from amid the lion-cubs*. Who are these lion-cubs? They are the little people who were cruelly deceived and wickedly seduced by the Jewish leaders;[14] the leaders were lions, and the common people lion-cubs. But they all roared, and all killed. In the succeeding verses of the psalm we shall hear about the slaughter they wrought.

Verse 5. Christ's willing sleep; Jewish responsibility

11. *He rescued my soul from amid the lion-cubs*, says the psalm. Why do you say, *He rescued my soul*? What had you endured, that you needed to be rescued? *Though disturbed, I lay down to sleep*. This is Christ's way of indicating his death. We read that the Old Testament David fled into a cave, but not that he slept in it; so one David was in the cave, but it is the other David who says here, *Though disturbed, I lay down to sleep*. It must be a special kind of disturbance that is meant, for it seems he was not subject to disturbance, even though they were disturbing him. He described himself as "disturbed" with reference only to the belief of his furious enemies, not from any consciousness of having yielded to them. They thought they had disturbed him, they thought they had won; but he, *though disturbed, lay down to sleep*. This "disturbed" man was so placid that he slept when he wanted to. No one who is genuinely disturbed can sleep. All who suffer disturbance are either awakened from sleep, or prevented from sinking into it. Yet this man was "disturbed," and fell asleep. Great was the humility of this "disturbed" man, and great the power of the sleeper. What power enabled him to sleep? That power of which he testified, *I have the power to lay down my life, and I have the power to take it up again. No one takes it away from me; but I lay it down of my own accord, that I may take it up again* (Jn 10:18.17). They disturbed him, but he lay down to sleep.

In this respect Adam was a type of Christ. God sent a deep sleep upon Adam, in order to fashion a wife for him from his side.[15] Was God unable to make a wife

---

14. Variant: "by the chief priests."
15. See Gn 2:21.

for the first man by taking her from his side while he was awake? Surely not. Or was it that God wanted Adam to be asleep so that he would not feel it when one of his ribs was pulled out? But who sleeps so soundly as not to be aroused if a bone is torn out? If God had power to remove a rib from a sleeping man without causing pain, he could have done so equally well when the man was awake. So why did he want to do it while Adam slept? Because in Christ's case, a bride was made for him as he slept on the cross, and made from his side. With a lance his side was struck as he hung there, and out flowed the sacraments of the Church.[16]

Though disturbed, I lay down to sleep, he says. He made the same point in another psalm, where he said, *I rested and fell asleep*; he there indicated his power. He could perfectly well have said, *I slept*, without the personal pronoun, as he does in our present psalm; so why did he say, *I slept*, with the emphatic pronoun included?[17] Clearly he meant to imply, "I slept because I chose to do so. They did not put me to sleep by force, against my will. I slept voluntarily in accordance with my claim *I have the power to lay down my life, and I have the power to take it up again*." That is why he goes on to say, in the earlier psalm, *I rested and fell asleep, and I arose because the Lord will uphold me* (Ps 3:6(5)).

12. *Though disturbed, I lay down to sleep*. What was disturbing him? Who were causing the disturbance? Let us see how he brands the Jews with the stigma of a bad conscience, though they meant to hold themselves not guilty of killing the Lord. Their motive in delivering him to the judge was to make it look as though they had not killed him themselves, as the gospel makes plain. Pilate, who sat as judge at the time, had said to them, *Take him, and try him according to your own law*; but they replied, *It is not lawful for us to put anyone to death* (Jn 18:31). So it was unlawful for you to kill anyone, but lawful to hand him over to be killed? Who is really killing him, anyway? The man who yielded on hearing the uproar, or the one who by raising the uproar extorted the death sentence? Let the Lord give his own evidence as to who killed him. Was it Pilate, who killed him reluctantly? Because he was so unwilling he even had Jesus scourged, clothed him in a ridiculous garment, and after the scourging brought him out into full view before them, in the hope that they would be sated by the punishment of flogging and not insist on his being put to death. For the same reason, when he saw that they were not relenting, he went so far as to wash his hands, as we read in the gospel, and protested, *I am innocent of the blood of this just man* (Mt 27:24). Make up your mind whether he was truly innocent, even though he only

---

16. See Jn 19:34. This imagery became commonplace in the Fathers, and was further developed in the middle ages with reference to the devotion to the Sacred Heart; see especially Bonaventure: *Lignum Vitae* 29-30.

17. Some paraphrase has been used in the translation to convey the contrast Augustine is pointing out between *dormivi* in the psalm he is commenting on, and *ego dormivi* in Psalm 3.

gave way in response to their clamor. But even if he was not, much more guilty were they who tried to force him by their shouting to kill Christ.

Let us question the Lord himself and listen to what he has to say, and to whom he attributed his death. He has told us, *Though disturbed, I lay down to sleep.* So let us press him further. If you were disturbed, yet lay down to sleep, who persecuted you? Who put you to death? Was it Pilate, who handed you over to his soldiers to hang you up on the tree and fasten you with nails? No? Listen, he says, and I will tell you who it was: simply *human beings.*[18] Those, he tells us, those are the persecutors I had to endure. But how did they put him to death, if they carried no weapon? They unsheathed no sword, launched no frontal attack on him; so how did they kill him? *Their teeth are weapons and arrows, their tongue a sharp sword.* Ignore the weaponless hands and watch the armed mouth, for that is where the sword is wielded that slew Christ; so too from Christ's own mouth proceeded the sword with which the Jews would in their turn be slain. He has a sharp, two-edged sword[19] and when he rose from the dead he smote them, and severed from their company those he meant to make his faithful followers. They had an evil sword, he a good sword; they had wicked arrows, he good arrows; for truly he does have his store of good arrows, which are his good words. He shoots them into every believing heart, that he may win its love. Quite different are their arrows, and their sword. *The teeth of human beings are weapons and arrows, their tongue a sharp sword.* The tongue of these people is a sharp sword,[20] and their teeth are offensive weapons and arrows. When did they strike at him? When they shouted, *Crucify, crucify!* (Jn 19:6).

Verse 6. Christ's glory pervades the earth

13. And what did they achieve against you, Lord? Let the prophet dance for joy now. All the preceding verses were spoken by the Lord—and by the prophet, of course, but only because the Lord was speaking in him. And equally, now that the prophet begins to speak as from himself, the Lord still speaks through him, inasmuch as the Lord dictates to him the truth he speaks. You have good reason, then, brothers and sisters, to listen to the prophet when he speaks in his own name. Moved by the Spirit,[21] this prophet beheld the Lord humiliated, buffeted, scourged, punched, slapped, spat on, crowned with thorns and hung on the tree. He beheld the executioners behaving savagely and Christ enduring it; he saw in

---

18. *Filii hominum*, literally "sons of men." In other contexts, such as his Exposition of Psalm 8, 10-11; Exposition of Psalm 35, 12-14, Augustine makes a special point of this expression, associating it with Christ's own title, "Son of Man." But in the present context he does not insist on this.
19. See Rv 1:16.
20. *Machaera*, a single-edged sword. In the lines above he has been using *gladius*.
21. Or "in spirit."

the Spirit[22] them triumphing and him apparently defeated. He saw too that after all his humiliation and their savagery Christ rose again, and that all the furious Jews had done had come to nothing. The prophet was transported with joy, as though he saw it all happening, and he cried, "*Be lifted up above the heavens, O God. A man you were on the cross, but God above the heavens. Let them remain on earth to rant, but you be in heaven to judge.*" Where are they who rampaged? Where are those teeth of theirs, teeth that were *weapons and arrows*? Is it not true of them that *the wounds they inflict are like those from the arrows of mere children* (Ps 63:8(64:7))? This is what a psalm says of them elsewhere, intending to suggest how futile was their fury, and how uselessly they had worked themselves into their rage. *The wounds they inflicted were like those from the arrows of mere children,* for they were powerless against Christ, who was crucified for an hour or two, but then rose again and is seated in heaven. How do young children fashion arrows for themselves? Out of reeds. And what sort of arrows are they, what force do they have? What kind of bow launches them? Is that a real shot? Does it wound anyone?

Be lifted up above the heavens, O God, and may your glory pervade the whole earth. Why, O God, are you exalted above the heavens? Think about this, brothers and sisters: we do not see him as God exalted above the heavens, but we believe him to be so, whereas we not only believe that his glory spreads over the earth, for we see that it does. I put it to you, then: consider what madness afflicts the heretics who have severed themselves from the bonded unity of Christ's Church. Clinging to a part and thereby losing the whole, they refuse to be in communion with the entire world, where Christ's glory is diffused. We Catholics, on the contrary, are present all over the earth, because we are in communion with the whole of it, wherever Christ's glory is deployed. We see now that what was sung in the psalm has been perfectly realized. Our God has been exalted above the heavens, and his glory shines over all the earth. How mad you are, you heretic! What you cannot see, you believe, in company with me; but what you can see, you deny. Along with me you believe Christ to be exalted above the heavens, though we cannot see this; yet you deny that his glory irradiates the whole earth, which we do see! *Be lifted up above the heavens, O God, and may your glory pervade the whole earth.*

Verse 7. Sinners always entrap themselves

14. Now the psalm takes up the Lord's own words again. The Lord himself begins to teach us, as though he were speaking directly to us, even while the psalmist goes on joyfully shouting, *Be lifted up above the heavens, O God, and*

---

22. Or "in spirit."

may your glory pervade the whole earth! Yes, the Lord in person encourages us, as though demanding of us, "What were they able to effect against me, those persecutors of mine?" But why is he talking to us? Because the persecutors attack us in the same way. But though they have made similar attempts on us, they achieve nothing. Consider, then, beloved,[23] how the Lord addresses us and spurs us on by his own example. *They set a snare[24] for my feet, and bent my soul down.* They almost thought to dethrone him from heaven, and thrust him into the depths: *they dug a pit in front of me, but fell into it themselves.* Am I the one they harmed, or did they harm themselves? See him exalted above the heavens as God, and see his glory shining over all the earth. Christ's kingdom is plain to see, but where is the kingdom of the Jews? What they ought not to have done, they did; now the justice they ought to suffer is done to them. They *dug a pit, and fell into it themselves.* Their persecution of Christ did him no ultimate harm, but ultimately harmed them.

Do not suppose that this happened to them alone, brothers and sisters. Anyone at all who digs a pit for a brother or sister must of necessity fall into it. Give me your close attention now, and look at the matter with Christian eyes. Do not be taken in by appearances. Perhaps when I say this, someone comes into your mind, someone who tried to trick a brother or sister, and meant to contrive a hidden snare. He laid it, it worked, and his brother fell into the trap. The victim was despoiled and wronged, perhaps unjustly imprisoned through perjured testimony or some malicious accusation. It looks as though this unhappy person is the oppressed and the other the oppressor, as though he is conquered and the other his conqueror. So you will think we are talking nonsense when we say that whoever has dug a pit for his brother or sister will fall into it himself. But I have a question to put to you as Christians, because as Christians you can read the answer from our own experience. The pagans persecuted the martyrs. The martyrs were arrested, bound, thrown into prison, exposed to the beasts. Others were executed with the sword, others again burnt to death. Now, does this mean that the persecutors were victorious, and the martyrs vanquished? Far from it! Look hard, and you will see the glory of the martyrs before God; look for the pit that the pagans dug, and you will find it in their torn consciences, for that is where the hole gapes, where the godless come to grief—in their bad consciences. Can you suppose that someone who has lost the light of Christ and been struck blind has not fallen into a pit? If such a one had not fallen into it he would see where he is putting his feet. But in fact he does not know where he is going. If someone is on his way, and then falls into a hole, he has lost his way. So you see, all evildoers lose their way, and become entangled in their crimes.

---

23. *Caritas vestra.*
24. Literally "mousetrap."

All the same, perhaps your enemy has thrown you into a robber's clutches, or into the hands of some villain, of some judge he has bribed; you are in a tight spot. But he is delighted; he is crowing over you. Do not look at the case with pagan eyes. I have said this already, and say it again: do not look at it as a pagan would, but with Christian eyes. You see him jumping for joy, yes, and his very jumping is the trap that will get him. Better the grief of someone suffering wrong than the joy of someone doing wrong. The joy of someone who does wrong is itself a snare, and anyone who falls into it loses the power of sight. Are you sorry for yourself because you have lost your coat, and not sorry for the person who has lost integrity?[25] Which of you has sustained the graver loss? He kills, and you are killed; does that mean that he is alive, and you are dead? Heaven forbid! Where is your faith, your Christian faith?[26] Where are those who die—for a while? Let them hearken to their Lord: *Any who believe in me, though they die, shall yet live* (Jn 11:25). It follows that one who does not believe, though he lives, is dead. *They dug a pit in front of me, and fell into it themselves.* This is what happens to all bad people, unavoidably.

Verse 8. The prepared heart

15. With hearts prepared, good people embrace the will of God with patience, and in patience they even glory in their sufferings, crying, *My heart is ready, O God, my heart is ready. I will sing and play the psaltery.* What has my enemy achieved against me? He prepared a trap, but my heart was prepared too. He has prepared a snare to cheat me, and shall I not prepare my heart to endure it steadfastly? He has prepared a trap to afflict me; shall I not prepare my heart to bear it? He will fall into it himself, but I will sing and play the psaltery. Listen to how fully prepared the apostle's heart was as he imitated his Lord: *We even glory in our sufferings,* he says, *knowing that suffering fosters endurance, and endurance constancy, and constancy hope; but hope does not disappoint us, because the love of God has been poured out into our hearts through the Holy Spirit who has been given us* (Rom 5:3-5). Paul was beset by harsh conditions, in chains, in prison, beaten, enduring hunger and thirst, cold and in need of clothing, desolate amid all his labors and afflictions, yet he kept saying, *We glory in our sufferings.* How could he say it? Only because his heart was prepared. Accordingly he sang and played psalms: *My heart is ready, O God, my heart is ready. I will sing and play the psaltery.*

---

25. *Fidem*; but he means "good faith," "honesty."
26. Or perhaps, "What becomes of Christians who keep faith?"

Verse 9. One risen flesh, two melodies

16. *Arise, O my glory!* The man who fled from Saul into a cave is speaking. *Arise, O my glory!* May Jesus be glorified after his passion. *Arise, psaltery and lyre!* What is he calling out to, what does he command to arise? I find two instruments mentioned here, yet I perceive Christ's body to be one. It was one single flesh that rose; yet in a sense two instruments did rise. The psaltery is one kind of musical instrument, the lyre another.[27] Whatever is made to accompany singing, and is a bodily object a singer can use, is called a musical instrument.[28] But these instruments differ from each other; and insofar as the Lord enables me, I want to suggest to you how psaltery and lyre differ, why they are distinct, and why the summons, *Arise!* is addressed to both.[29] We have already pointed out that the Lord's flesh arose single and undivided, yet two instruments are addressed: *Arise, psaltery and lyre!* The psaltery, as you know, is an instrument which is held in the hands of the player. It has strings stretched across it. But the wooden, concave sounding-chamber which lends resonance to the strings, the vaulted piece which resounds to the touch because it is filled with air, is in a psaltery located in the upper part. A lyre, on the contrary, has its concave, wooden sounding-chamber at the bottom.[30] This means that in a psaltery the strings derive their resonance from above, whereas in the lyre they derive it from the lower part. This is the difference between a psaltery and a lyre.

What, then, do these instruments symbolize for us? The Lord Christ, our God, arouses both his psaltery and his lyre, and prophesies, *I will arise at dawn.* You do not need to be told that this is a reference to our Lord's resurrection. We have read about it in the gospel; notice this allusion to the time at which he rose. How long was Christ being sought[31] through the shadows? He shone forth; let him be acknowledged; he arose at dawn. But still, what is the psaltery? What is the lyre? The Lord used his flesh for two kinds of operations: miracles and sufferings. The miracles came from above, the sufferings from below. The miracles he performed were divine, but he worked them through his body, he wrought them through his flesh. So when the flesh performs divine works, it is a psaltery; but

27. Some liberty has been taken in the translation here. Augustine refers to both psaltery and lyre as types of "organ," and goes on to say that it is not only the large instrument inflated with bellows that can be called an "organ," but any other musical instrument too. Since this is alien to our usage, a phrase has been omitted.
28. *Organum.* The reference to "a bodily object" prepares the following development on the flesh of Christ.
29. The verb, "arise," is singular throughout, even when psaltery and lyre are jointly addressed; the point is important for Augustine's interpretation.
30. This difference was a favorite theme for Augustine. Compare his Exposition 2 of Psalm 32, 5; Exposition of Psalm 42, 5; Exposition 2 of Psalm 70, 11; Exposition of Psalm 80, 5.
31. So the codices. The editors of the CCL text change the indicative to a subjunctive: "How long should Christ be sought . . . ?"

when the flesh suffers human pain it is a lyre. Let the psaltery give forth its melody: let the blind see the light of day, the deaf hear, the paralytics feel their muscles toned up, the lame walk, the sick spring from their beds, the dead arise. All this is the sound of the psaltery. But the lyre must give its voice too: let Christ hunger, thirst, sleep, and be arrested, scourged, mocked, crucified, and buried. In his flesh you hear some music sounding from above, and some from below; yet it was one flesh only that arose, and in that one flesh we catch the notes of both psaltery and lyre. These two types of action fill the gospel. And so is he preached among the nations, for both the miracles and the sufferings of the Lord are proclaimed.

Verses 10-12. Mercy as high as heaven, truth down to the clouds

17. Both psaltery and lyre arose[32] at dawn, and now give praise to the Lord. What does the psalm say next? *I will praise you among the peoples, Lord, and sing psalms to you among the Gentiles; for your mercy is magnified even to the heavens, and your truth reaches to the clouds.* The heavens are above the clouds, and the clouds below the heavens, yet the clouds belong to that region of the sky which is quite near to us. They thicken at that height which is so close to us that sometimes the clouds envelop our mountains. The higher region of heaven is above this; there is the home of Angels, Thrones, Sovereignties, Authorities, and Powers.[33] In view of this it would seem that the psalm ought to have said, "Your truth is magnified even to the heavens, and your mercy reaches down to the clouds." Yes, surely it should have put it that way round? In heaven the angels praise God, contemplating the very form of truth in totally unclouded vision, with no trace of falsehood to distort it. They see him, love him, praise him, and never tire. There is the place of truth. But our miserable state here is the appropriate place for mercy, for it is to the miserable that mercy must be shown. There is no need for it above, where no one is miserable. I make this point to explain why I suggested that it would have been more fitting to say, "Your truth is magnified even to the heavens, and your mercy reaches down to the clouds."

But we understand "clouds" to be the preachers of truth, mere mortals carrying this murky flesh, we might say, but clouds nonetheless from which the Lord flashes the lightning of his miracles and thunders his commandments. Moreover these are the clouds Isaiah mentions when, speaking in the Lord's name, he rebukes a wicked, barren, thorn-choked vineyard, threatening, *I will forbid my clouds to send rain upon it* (Is 5:6); which is to say, "I will give orders to my apostles to abandon the Jews and offer them the gospel no more, but to evangelize in the good soil of the Gentiles, which will produce not thorns, but

---

32. Singlar verb.
33. See Col 1:16.

grapes." We know that those who preach the truth—the prophets, the apostles, and all who duly offer the word of truth—are God's clouds. There is light concealed within them, just as the clouds have an inner luminosity whence they produce lightning. Mortal preachers are clouds.

What, then, is the meaning of this verse, Lord: *your mercy is magnified even to the heavens, and your truth to the clouds*? Truth resides predominantly in the angels, but you have granted it to humans too, and brought it down as far as the clouds. Angels, on the contrary,[34] do not seem to need mercy. But you deal mercifully with miserable mortals; you grant them mercy by giving them a share in the resurrection, and so you make them equal to the angels. This is how your mercy reaches even up to the heavens.

Glory be to our Lord, and to his mercy, and to his truth, because in his mercy he has not ceased to bless us through his grace, nor yet deprived us of his truth. Truth first came to us clad in flesh, and through his flesh healed the inner eye of our hearts, so that we might one day have the strength to see him face to face.[35] Let us give thanks to him, and in harmony with the psalm say these last lines, which occurred earlier as well: *Be lifted up above the heavens, O God, and may your glory pervade the whole earth*. The prophet said that to God many, many years ago; we see now that it has come true, so let us say it with him.

---

34. *Rursus*, with all the codices; but the editors of the CCL text read *sursum*, "above."
35. See 1 Cor 13:12.

Exposition of Psalm 57

A Sermon to the People[1]

Verses 1-2. Do not treat others as you would not wish to be treated

1. It would be better for us to be listening to the words we have just sung, rather than shouting them; for truth itself is shouting them to all of us, as though the whole human race had been convoked to an assembly. *If you truly speak about justice, men and women,[2] judge rightly in your own case.* Any rogue can talk about justice glibly enough, can't he? Anyone at all when questioned about what is just can easily give the right answer, as long as he or she is not an interested party! And this is not surprising, for by the hand of our Fashioner truth has written in our very hearts the precept, *Do not do to another what you would not want anyone to do to you* (Tb 4:16). Even before the law was given no one was allowed to be ignorant of it, for even those to whom the law had not been revealed were held liable to judgment by this standard. But to take away from human beings any grounds for complaining that they had not been provided for, a law written on tablets was given. It stated what was already written in their hearts, for they had not hitherto lacked a written law; they had simply been unwilling to read it. Now it was held before their eyes so that they would be forced to see it in their consciences, and as God's voice admonished them from outside, they were thrust inward to confront their own inner truth. As scripture says, *An inquiry will be instituted in the thoughts of a godless person* (Wis 1:9), and where there is an inquiry, we must infer that there is a law. Because men and women were so avid for external things that they had become estranged from themselves, a written law was given. This did not imply that its provisions were not already inscribed in human hearts; but you, mortal, were a deserter from your heart, and so you are arrested by him who is present everywhere, and you are called back within yourself. What appeal does the written law make to those who have abandoned the law engraved in their hearts? *Return to your hearts, you transgressors* (Is 46:8).

After all, who taught you to resent it if another man makes approaches to your wife? Who taught you to hope that you will not be robbed? Who taught you to be

---

1. Possibly preached in September 403, at Carthage in the Basilica Restituta.
2. *Filii hominum.*

indignant if you suffer some injury? Plenty of other examples can be given, relating to public or private issues. There are many such points on which, if people are questioned, they will unhesitatingly reply that they do not want to suffer such treatment. Come now, tell me: if you do not want to be treated like that, do you think you are the only person who matters? You live as a member of human society, don't you? Someone created along with you is your companion, and all your companions have been made in the image of God, though some of them may by earthly lusts deface the form he gave them. Well then, *do not do to another what you would not want anyone to do to you.* You judge something to be bad from the fact that you do not want to have it done to you; and it is the secret inner law, written in your very heart, that has taught you to view it so. When you behaved toward someone else like that, he or she cried out under your ill-treatment; and when you endure the same at the hands of another, are you not driven back to your own heart? Is theft a good thing? No? I ask you: is adultery a good thing? Everyone shouts, "No!" Is homicide good? They all shout their detestation of it. Is it good to covet your neighbor's property? The unanimous reply is, "No!" If you are not yet persuaded on this subject, imagine that someone comes trying to get his hands on your things. I hope you enjoy it! Then come back and give me your answer. Clearly, then, everyone questioned about such actions will attest that they are not good.

The same principle holds for kind actions; it applies not only to refraining from hurting others, but also to generosity in giving. Suppose you interrogate a starving person: "You are hungry; someone else has bread and to spare, well beyond his own requirements. He knows you are in need, but he gives you nothing. Do you find that outrageous, when you are hungry? Yes? Then you must find it equally outrageous, when you are well fed, and refuse someone else who is starving." Or again, suppose a traveler arrives in your region. He has no roof over his head, yet no one takes him in. He protests that this is an inhuman city, that he could more easily have found a place to stay among savages. He is keenly aware of the injustice, because he is the victim of it. You perhaps are insensitive to it; but you should imagine yourself in the same situation, on a journey, and ask yourself how you would resent it if someone refused to give you what you are unwilling to give to that traveler in your own country.

I put it to you, all of you: are these things true? "Yes, they are true," you say. Is this a just appraisal? "Yes," you say, "just it is."

An illustration: what if you stand to gain dishonestly?

2. But listen to the psalm: *If you truly speak about justice, men and women, judge rightly in your own case.* Do not let justice be on your lips only; let it regulate your actions. If your actions contradict your words, you are speaking well, but judging badly, for how can your judgment be at variance with your conduct?

If you are asked which is better, gold or honesty,[3] you will not be so perverse, so far adrift from truth, as to reply that gold is preferable. So you rank honesty above gold if you are questioned, and you have spoken justly. But did you hear what the psalm said? *If you truly speak about justice, men and women, judge rightly in your own case.* How am I to prove to you that your judgment in your own case is at odds with your statement?

I have it on record that you have said honesty is of higher value than gold. Now, suppose a friend turns up and entrusts some gold to your keeping, with no witnesses present. As far as human beings are concerned, he and you are the only ones who know about it; but there is a Witness, one who is not seen but sees. Your friend has entrusted the money to you in secret, in your private room, far away from anyone who could corroborate; but the Witness who is present is not confined within the walls of your bedroom. He is within the secret chambers of your consciences, yours and your friend's. So your friend has entrusted the gold to you and gone away, without telling any of his family what he has done, because he expects to come back and retrieve what he deposited. But human affairs are uncertain, and he dies, leaving a son as his heir. The son does not know how much money his father had, nor with whom he deposited it. Now return to your heart, you transgressor, return to your heart! There you find inscribed the law, *do not do to another what you would not want anyone to do to you.* Imagine that you were the one who had entrusted your gold to a friend without telling any of your relatives, and that you had died, leaving a son. What would you have wanted your friend to give him?

Answer me, give me your judgment on the case. The judge's tribunal is within your mind. There God takes his seat; there your conscience serves as counsel for the prosecution, and there stands the torturer waiting, the torturer whose name is Fear. A transaction between human beings is in question, and you belong to human society. Ask yourself, then, what you would wish your friend to give to your son. I know what answer your thoughts will give you; so judge as you hear. Judge: the verdict will be forthcoming.[4] The voice of truth is not silent; it does not shout from the lips, but makes itself heard in the heart. Open your ear to it, and in your heart stand beside your friend's son. Perhaps you see him as a needy wanderer, who does not know how much money his father had, where he put it, or to whom he entrusted it. Now think of your own son. Imagine that the dead friend you are prepared to disregard is alive; then think of yourself as dead, so that you may live!

---

3. *Fides*, here and throughout this section; but clearly he means "good faith" or "faith expressing itself in righteous action," "honesty."

4. *Iudica, vox erit,* so most codices. A few omit *vox erit,* and one gives *iuridica vox erit:* "this will be the judicial verdict."

But avarice is prompting you differently; avarice is giving you orders against God's will. God tells you one thing, avarice something different. Our Creator gave a command in paradise, and the seducing serpent a command directly opposed to it. Remember your original fall: because of it you are subject to death, because of it you are condemned to toil, because of it you earn your living by the sweat of your brow, because of it the earth brings forth thorns and thistles for you.[5] Learn from experience what you are reluctant to learn from the commandment. Greed overcomes you, does it? Why is truth not more powerful? And what has become of the profession you used to make? Here are you, intending to deny that you ever had the money, minded to conceal it absolutely from your friend's heir. Not long since I put to you the question: Which is better, gold or honesty? Why do you say one thing, and do something different? Have you no respect for the psalm's injunction, *If you truly speak about justice, men and women, judge rightly in your own case*? You told me that honesty is more valuable, but by your judgment you have rated gold more highly. You have not judged as you spoke; you spoke truly but judged falsely. That means that when you were speaking justly, you were not speaking the truth, for *if you truly speak about justice, men and women, judge rightly in your own case*. When you gave me the right answer concerning justice, you were not confessing the truth but speaking out of embarrassment.

The Lord's judgment on hypocrisy

3. But now, please, let us get to work on the psalm. Its voice is sweet and familiar to the Church's ears, for it is the voice of our Lord Jesus Christ, and the voice of his body, the voice of the Church as it struggles along its pilgrim way on earth, living in peril amid those who curse and those who flatter. You will have no fear of a threatener, if you do not love a flatterer. The psalmist whose voice we hear observed the scene, and saw that everyone spoke justly; for who dare speak otherwise? No one wants to be thought unjust. As though listening to them all, and observing the lips of all, he insistently cried to them, *If you truly speak about justice*, if your profession of justice is no falsehood, if what blares from your lips is not at variance with what is concealed in your hearts, then, *men and women, judge rightly in your own case*. Listen, each of you, to our Lord's voice in the gospel, the same voice that we hear in this psalm. *"You hypocrites*, said the Lord to the Pharisees, *how can you, who are evil, utter good things? Either make a tree good, and its fruit good with it, or make the tree bad and its fruit bad too* (Mt 12:34.33). Why attempt to whiten yourself, mud wall that you are? I know what is inside you; your outer coating does not deceive me. I know what you flaunt

---

5. See Gn 3:17-19.

outwardly, and what you cover within." *For he did not need anyone to tell him what was inside a person*, says the evangelist. *He knew himself what a person had within* (Jn 2:25). He who had made men and women knew what was in them; he had become human to seek out human beings. Consider, then: these two sayings match, don't they? *You hypocrites, how can you, who are evil, utter good things?* and *If you truly speak about justice, men and women, judge rightly in your own case.* You spoke justly, didn't you, when you said, *Teacher, we know that you are just, and do not truckle to anyone* (Mt 22:16)? But "Why did you cover up guile in your hearts?" he asks them. "Why do you show Caesar's image to your Creator, while effacing the Creator's image in your hearts? Have I not heard what you are going to say, while being well aware of how you will judge? Did you not crucify him whom you had called just? *If you truly speak about justice, judge rightly in your own case.* Why should I give you a hearing when you say, *We know that you are just*, when I foresee your judicial sentence, *Crucify him! Crucify him!* (Jn 19:6)?"

If you truly speak about justice, men and women, judge rightly in your own case. What were you doing, when you vented your cruelty against God who was man, and killed your king? You killed him, though he was to rise again, but your killing did not mean he would not be your king. On the label over the Lord's cross were written the words, *The King of the Jews*, in the three languages, Hebrew, Greek, and Latin. If a human judge had the wit to say of the title, *What I have written, I have written* (Jn 19:22), could God not say, "What I have written, I have written"? Most certainly he is your king. Living, he is your king; slain, he is still your king. Now he has risen, and in heaven he is your king. But he will come again, and then woe betide you, for he is your king. Go on, then, go on speaking about justice but refusing to judge rightly, men and women; if you are unwilling to judge rightly, rightly will you be judged. Your king is alive; he dies no more, nor will death ever have dominion over him again.[6] He is coming, so *return to your hearts, you transgressors* (Is 46:8). He will come indeed, so correct yourselves before he comes, forestall him by coming into his presence confessing.[7] Yes, come he will, and he is your king. Remember the title over his cross. Even if you no longer see it in writing, it is valid still; it cannot now be read on earth, but it is preserved in heaven. Do you suppose that title has been falsified? What does the title of this psalm say?[8] *For the end, as a title for David himself that is not to be tampered with.* That title written over the cross is inviolable. Christ is your king because Christ is the universal king: *the kingship is the Lord's, and he will hold sway over the nations* (Ps 21:29(22:28)). If, then, he is

6. See Rom 6:9.
7. See Ps 94(95):2.
8. See Augustine's commentary on the warning not to tamper with the title, in his Exposition of Psalm 55, 2; Exposition of Psalm 56, 3.

your king, listen: before he comes, he says to you, "I am still speaking, not judging as yet. I shout my warnings to you like this, because I do not want to strike you with my judgments." So then, men and women, *If you truly speak about justice, judge rightly in your own case.*

Verse 3. The chains of sin

4. What are you doing about it now? Why am I saying all this to you? *Because in your hearts you commit sins on earth.* In your heart only? No; listen to the consequences. The hands follow the heart's lead; the hands are servants to the heart. The thought is entertained and the deed is done; or, if it is not done, we refrain because we lack the power, not the will. Whatever you want to do, but are unable to do, God counts as done. *In your hearts you commit sins on earth.* And what follows? *Your hands link sin to sin.* What does *link* suggest? A sin springs from another sin, sin urges us to further sin, sin is committed for the sake of sin. Here is an example. Someone steals. That is a sin. But he was seen doing it, so he seeks to kill the person who saw him, and so sin is linked to sin. Now by some mysterious judgment of God he has been allowed to kill his intended victim, but he is aware that the murder is known, so he looks to kill someone else too. He has added a third link. While he is laying his plans he consults an astrologer,[9] perhaps in order not to be found out, or not to be convicted of the crime; so that means a fourth sin has been added. Perhaps the astrologer foretells hard and painful consequences, so the criminal has recourse to a diviner[10] to avert the omen.[11] But the diviner says he cannot free him from the curse, so off goes the client to look for a magician.[12] These sins are all linked to each other, and are getting past counting. *Your hands link sin to sin.* As long as you continue to forge the links, you are binding one sin to another. Disentangle yourself from your sins. "But I can't," you protest. Then cry to God, *Who will deliver me from this death-ridden body, wretch that I am?* (Rom 7:24). God's grace will come to you, and give you a pleasure in righteousness that will replace the pleasure you took in iniquity. Then, as a released prisoner, you will cry out to God, *You have burst my bonds* (Ps 115(116):16) — and what can that mean, if not "You have forgiven my sins"? Bonds they are indeed, for listen to the testimony of scripture: *Each one of us is bound by the fine hairs of our own sins* (Prv 5:22). Your sins are not only chains, but fine hairs that twist themselves round you in the end; this is what

---

9. *Mathematicum.* See a note on the evolution of this term at Exposition 2 of Psalm 33, 25.
10. *Aruspicem.* The *aruspex* or *haruspex* was originally an Etruscan functionary, one who foretold future events by inspecting the entrails of sacrificed animals.
11. *Ut expietur.*
12. *Maleficum.* The *maleficus* could be a practitioner of black magic, though the term was more loosely used.

you were doing to yourself when you linked sin to sin. *Woe to those who drag out their sins into a long cord*, cries Isaiah (Is 5:18). *Woe to those who drag out their sins into a long cord*: what else can that mean, but "Woe to those whose hands link sin to sin"? And because it is true that each one is bound by his own sins, and each felled by his own sins, the Lord drove the traders out of the temple with a whip made of little cords.[13] Yet you are not willing to have your bonds broken now, because you do not feel them as bonds. They are even attractive to you; they give you pleasure. But you will feel them in the end, when the Lord will order concerning you, *Bind his hands and feet, and throw him into the darkness outside, where there will be weeping and gnashing of teeth* (Mt 22:13). You shudder, you are terrified, you beat your breast, you declare that sins are evil and righteousness is good, do you? Very well: *if you truly speak about justice, men and women, judge rightly in your own case*. Let your words be proved true in your life, let your profession be verified in your actions. Do not link sin to sin, for the chain you forge will be used to fetter you. But they do not listen, or at any rate not all of them do; and those who do not listen are known in advance by God.

Verse 4. You are still in the womb of the Church

5. *Sinners have been alienated even from the womb, they have gone astray even from the belly, they have spoken falsehoods.* When they speak sinfully they speak falsehoods, because sin is deceitful; but when they speak about justice they still speak falsehoods, because they profess one thing with their mouths, but conceal something different in their hearts. *Sinners have been alienated even from the womb*: what does that signify? Let us examine the statement carefully. Perhaps it means that God knew human beings as sinners in advance, even in the wombs of their mothers. Otherwise how could it have happened that while Rebecca was pregnant, and carrying twins in her womb, she was told, *I have loved*[14] *Jacob, but hated Esau* (Mal 1:2-3; Rom 9:13)? It was prophesied further that *the elder shall serve the younger* (Gn 25:23). God's mysterious decision operated there. It is *from the womb*, from the very origin of their existence, that *sinners have been alienated*. Alienated from what? From the truth. Alienated from their homeland, from a life of blessedness.

Or could it mean that they have been alienated from the womb itself? But what sinners were so alienated, from the very womb? Who would ever be born, if they had not been kept safely in the womb? Who would be alive today to hear these things (though without profit), unless they had been born first?

---

13. See Jn 2:15.
14. *Dilexi*, the love that implies free choice.

But I think there is a womb from which sinners are alienated: that womb in which charity was agonizing in labor pains, causing the apostle to say to some of his converts, *My little children, I am in travail with you over again, until Christ be formed in you* (Gal 4:19). Wait then, let yourself be formed. Do not arrogate to yourself a decision you are perhaps not competent to make. Carnal you still may be, but you have been conceived, and by the very fact of receiving the name of Christ you have been sacramentally born within the bowels of your mother. It is not only from their mother's bowels that new humans are born; they are born within the mother's bowels too: born within first, in order to be born outside later. That is why it was said to Mary,[15] *What is born in her is of the Holy Spirit* (Mt 1:20). What was in her had not yet been born from her, but had already been born in her. Similarly, little ones are born within the bowels of the Church, and it is desirable for them to emerge fully formed; they must not be aborted. Let your mother bring you to birth, do not force her to miscarry. If you are prepared to be patient until you are fully formed, until the truth you are taught is firmly set in you, your mother's womb must hold you close. If you hammer impatiently on its walls your mother will thrust you out. That will be painful for her, but your loss will be greater than hers.

The aborted Donatists

6. *Sinners have been alienated even from the womb, they have gone astray even from the belly, they have spoken falsehoods.* Are we to understand that they have gone astray from the belly because they spoke falsehoods? No; better to take it, I think, that they have spoken falsehoods because they have gone astray from the belly, for truth abides in the belly of the Church. It is inevitable that anyone who breaks out of the Church's womb should speak falsehoods. I repeat, it is inevitable that anyone who either refuses to be conceived there, or having been once conceived is aborted from that womb, should speak falsehoods. This is why heretics raise their clamor against the gospel. Let us confine our consideration to these abortions that we deplore.[16] We read out to them, "Christ said, *It was necessary for Christ to suffer, and to rise from the dead on the third day*" (Lk 24:46), and we go on to tell them, "In this saying I recognize our head, and I recognize our bridegroom. Come, and together with me acknowledge the bride; for look what scripture says immediately after this: *and for repentance and forgiveness of sins to be preached in his name throughout all nations, beginning from Jerusalem* (Lk 24:47). Come to us, then, come to us! Or, rather, look at the Church extending *throughout all nations, beginning from Jerusalem*. So I need not say, 'Come here,' for the Church comes to you."

---

15. Variant: "concerning Mary."
16. The Donatists, as his following remarks make clear.

But they grow too deaf to hear the gospel, and will not allow us to read them the words of God. How ironic: they boast of having saved those words from the fire, but try to delete them with their tongues![17] Instead they speak words that are their own, and therefore empty. "That fellow handed over the books," they say, "and that other one too." Yes, all right; I will say the same: "That fellow handed them over, and so did that other," and I am speaking the truth. But what has that to do with me? You can't find the names of those you accuse in the gospel, can you? Nor can I read out to you from the gospel the names of those I mentioned. Let our documents[18] be moved out of the way and God's book take center stage. Listen to what Christ says, listen to Truth speaking: *And for repentance and forgiveness of sins to be preached in his name throughout all nations, beginning from Jerusalem.* "No," they reply, "listen to what we have to say. We don't want to hear what the gospel says." *Sinners have been alienated even from the womb, they have gone astray even from the belly, they have spoken falsehoods.* Let us speak the truth, because we have heard the truth, the truth that the Lord speaks, not what humans tell us. A human being can lie, but it is not possible for Truth to lie. From the womb of truth I recognize Christ, who is Truth itself, and from the words of Truth I recognize the Church, which participates in the Truth. Let no one who has strayed away from that matrix in the bowels of the Church speak falsehoods to me; I would wish to find out first what he wants to teach me. I see him as alienated from the womb, astray even from the belly; so what am I likely to hear from him, except falsehoods? *They have gone astray even from the belly, they have spoken falsehoods.*

Verses 5-6. Scriptural imagery comes from various sources; read with discernment

7. *Their fury is like the venom of a snake.* You are about to hear something very remarkable. *Their fury is like the venom of a snake.* He seems to hear us asking, "What? What did you say?" So he goes on, *Like that of a deaf asp.*[19] Why deaf? Because it *blocks its ears for fear of hearing the voice of the charmer, the voice of the medicine endowed with healing power by a wise man.* Yes, we have heard of this phenomenon: people who know about it from careful research attest it, but the Spirit of God knows far more about it than any human scholar. It is not set down here without purpose; what we have heard reported about the asp

---

17. An allusion to the Donatists' claim that their ancestors had refused to hand over the sacred scriptures to be burnt during the persecution, whereas the Catholics were descendants of the *traditores* who had done so.

18. *Chartae*, leaves of papyrus, or what was written on them, hence documents, here with the meaning "foundation documents," historical records seeking to legitimize the Donatist schism.

19. A small venomous snake, native to North Africa and Arabia.

must be true. When the asp begins to fall under the influence of a Marsic charmer[20] who is trying to lure it out into the open with special chants (as is the way with many magical practices), the snake reacts in a particular fashion, which I will describe. But before we go into that, brothers and sisters, there is something to be said, in case the imagery worries anyone. It is not the case that when scripture takes similes from various sources, the things used as an image are necessarily commended. For instance, no praise was implied for the conduct of the unjust judge who was reluctant to give the widow a hearing, because he had no reverence for God nor respect for his fellows; yet the Lord used him as an illustration.[21] Nor did he praise the lazy man who eventually gave his friend three loaves, not for friendship's sake, but only because he was wearied by the persistence of the one who was asking; yet the Lord used him too as a parable.[22] Even from episodes that do not merit approval, examples can, with necessary qualifications, be drawn. And in case you might think that the activities of the Marsians are approved, because you have heard about them in God's scripture, you should reflect that the same would hold for the theatrical shows of which the apostle said, *I do not deal blows like someone merely flailing the air* (1 Cor 9:26), for to engage in boxing is to take part in a complete combat.[23] Does this mean that because a parable was derived from such shows, we ought to be fans of them? Or does the apostle's comparison, *Everyone who enters the contest undertakes strict abstinence* (1 Cor 9:25), imply that a Christian should enjoy these empty, ridiculous athletic events?[24] You must carefully distinguish between the image which is used for purposes of comparison, and the reality which is forbidden you.

So then, we are given here a parable about a Marsian who sings his charms to lure the asp from its dark lair. He aims to draw it out into the daylight, but the asp prefers to coil itself up in its own darkness, where it can hide. So, we are told, since it does not want to emerge, yet feels those sounds compelling it to come, it refuses to listen. It presses one ear to the ground, and plugs the other with its tail. So it muffles the sounds as best it can, and does not come out to the charmer. The Spirit of God uses this snake as an image of people who do not hear God's word: that is, people who are not merely disobedient to the word, but are firmly resolved not even to hear it in order to obey.

---

20. The Marsians were a people who lived in Latium, near what is now Lake Fucino. Originally they had been a distinct nation, but they demanded Roman citizenship in the Social War, and afterward disappeared as a distinct entity. Marsic magicians were famous as wizards and snake-charmers; reputedly they had learned these arts from the founder of their tribe, Marsus, son of Circe. They were also credited with skill in curing snake-bite. A local deity of healing, Angitia, was worshiped in their territory.
21. See Lk 18:2-5.
22. See Lk 11:5-8.
23. *Pancratium*, a form of gymnastic contest which included boxing and wrestling.
24. On Augustine's vehement opposition to "shows," see a note at Exposition of Psalm 39, 8.

Willful deafness; the Sanhedrin and Stephen

8. This is what happened in the early days of the faith. The martyr Stephen was preaching the truth; it was as though he was singing charms to darkened minds to draw them forth into the light. But when he came to mention Christ, about whom they wished to hear nothing, what happened? What does scripture tell of them? It says, *They blocked their ears* (Acts 7:57). And the account of Stephen's passion describes their next move. They were not deaf, but they made themselves deaf. The ears of their hearts were not open, but so violently was the word rushing in through their fleshly ears, so hard was it hammering at the ears of their hearts, that they blocked even their fleshly ears and reached for the stones.[25] They were deaf asps, harder than the stones they hurled at their charmer. They did not hear the charmer's voice, or the *medicine endowed with healing power by a wise man.* What medicine is this, endowed with healing power by a wise man? Perhaps the psalm means a medicine specially mixed. Or perhaps we should seek some significance in this, that to something that is already a medicine, some fresh healing power is imparted. There were medicines in the prophets, and medicines in the law; all these precepts were medicines, but healing virtue had not yet been instilled into them. It was the coming of the Lord that endowed the medicines with healing power; but that was what Stephen's opponents could not bear. They were not being cured by the medicine as it stood, and so that medicine was fortified with healing power by the Lord's coming. Stephen's incantations offered them this fortified medicine, but they refused to listen; they blocked their ears against him who had given the medicine its new power. Yes, this they did, for it was when Christ was named that they stopped their ears. Their fury was like the fury of a snake. Why block your ears? Wait, listen—and then be savage if you still can. But savagery was all they intended, so they refused to listen. If they had listened, perhaps their savagery would have abated. Their fury was like the fury of a snake.

Willful deafness: the Donatists

9. We have to put up with the same kind of people. At first they considered themselves standard-bearers of the faith. God did not give up, he did not fall silent. Truth was preached in his Church, and in that maternal womb their lies were shown up. Plainly the Church shone out; the city set on a mountain-top was made manifest, the city that cannot remain hidden, the light set on a lampstand that illumines everyone in the house.[26] It became unmistakable, for where is the Church ever obscured? Where is Christ's truth ever hidden? Christ, surely, is

---

25. See Acts 7:59.
26. See Mt 5:14-15.

that mountain which grew out of a small stone to fill the whole surface of the earth.[27] Our adversaries are convicted by it, and have nothing to allege against the Church. What is left for them to say? "Why do you look for us? Why do you want us? Get away, leave us alone"—that is all they say to us. But to their own adherents they say, "No one must talk to the Catholics, no one may join them or listen to them." So their fury is the fury of snakes, like that of the *deaf asp which blocks its ears for fear of hearing the voice of the charmer, the voice of the medicine endowed with healing power by a wise man.* The snake will not hear the voice of the medicine, so says the psalm. And this gives us a clue, I think, to the kind of medicine that is in question, since it is a medicine with a voice. Can medicine have a voice? Yes, there is one that does. We have this medicine in our keeping: listen to its voice, don't be deaf asps. *If you truly speak about justice, men and women, judge rightly in your own case.* This is the voice of the medicine endowed by a wise man with healing power, for Christ came to bring the law and the prophets to their fulfillment[28] and to strengthen truth itself. His twofold precept sums up the whole law and the prophets.

Learn from the snake's tactics

10. Should we perhaps seek some lesson from the method the asp allegedly employs to shut its ears? It presses one ear to the ground, and blocks the other with its tail. What does that suggest? Obviously the tail represents the hinder part, and hence the things that are behind us, the past on which we must turn our backs in order to press forward to what is promised to us. So we must take no pleasure in our past life. But neither must we in the things of the present. The apostle warns us on both points. *What fruit did you reap then from those things of which you are now ashamed?* he asks (Rom 6:21), calling us back from past experiences that we may perhaps remember with pleasure, and even with some desire to repeat them. But what of the present? How does he command us to sit lightly to that as well? *We keep our eyes not on things that are seen, but on those which are not seen,* he says, *not on temporal things, but on those that are eternal; for things which are seen are temporal, but things unseen are eternal* (2 Cor 4:18). Again, with reference to our present life he says, *If our hope in Christ is a matter for this present life only, we are in a more wretched state than all the rest of humankind* (1 Cor 15:19). So forget the past and all those circumstances in which you lived a bad life; and set little store by present realities which support your temporal life, lest these present things fetter you and prevent you from attaining what lies in the future. If you find your satisfaction in this present life,

---

27. See Dn 2:35.
28. See Mt 5:17.

you are pressing your ear to the ground; if you seek satisfaction in your past experiences, even as they slide away beneath you, you have blocked your other ear with your tail.

Once you have heard the voice of that medicine endowed by a wise man with healing virtue, you must make your way into the light, leaving the darkness behind. Then, walking in the light and leaping for joy, you must say, *I forget what lies behind and strain to what lies ahead* (Phil 3:13) — and notice that the apostle did not say, "I forget what lies behind and find the present satisfactory." By saying, *I forget what lies behind* he made sure that he did not block one ear with his tail; and by saying, *I strain to what lies ahead*, he ensured that not even present circumstances would deafen him. He is fit to hear, therefore, fit to preach. His tongue is ready to rejoice as he preaches the truth in this new life, after casting off his old garment. On this point too the serpent's craftiness is worth noting, and indeed our Lord exhorts us to imitate it: *Be as crafty as snakes* (Mt 10:16), he says. What does he mean by *crafty as snakes*? Be like the snake, present all your members to the enemy who strikes at you, as long as you keep your head unhurt. And *the head of every man is Christ* (1 Cor 11:3).[29]

All the same, there is a weight on you, like a heavy skin, the burdensome decrepitude of your old nature. Hearken, then, to the apostle who tells you, *Strip off the old self, and be clothed in the new* (Col 3:9-10). "And how am I to strip off my old self?" you ask. Imitate the snake's cunning. What does a snake do to rid itself of its old garment? It squeezes itself through a narrow aperture. "And where am I to find such a narrow aperture?" you inquire. Listen: *How narrow and confined is the way that leads to life, and how few they are who walk in it!* (Mt 7:14). Do you dread that road, are you unwilling to walk along it, because so few are there? But that is the place where you will get rid of your old garment; you cannot do it anywhere else. On the other hand, if you really want to be hampered by your old self, to be weighed down and burdened by it, avoid the narrow way, because if you are laden with the weight of your old sin and your old life, you will not be able to squeeze through. Since the corruptible body is a load on the soul,[30] we must ensure that at least carnal desires do not weigh us down, or, better still, that the cravings of the flesh are stripped off altogether. And how can they be stripped off, unless you go by the narrow path, unless you are as crafty as the snake?

---

29. In the context of the Pauline argument, definitely "man" here, not "person."
30. See Wis 9:15.

Verse 7. Convicted out of their own mouths

11. *God smashed the teeth in their mouths*. Whose teeth? The teeth of those whose fury is like a snake's, like that of a deaf asp which blocks its ears for fear of hearing the voice of the charmer, the voice of the medicine endowed with healing power by a wise man. What did our Lord do to them? *He smashed the teeth in their mouths*. This really happened. It happened at the beginning, and it still happens now. But would it not have been sufficient, brothers and sisters, to say simply, *God smashed their teeth*? Why add, *in their mouths*?

The Pharisees obstinately refused to hear the law, and refused to hear the teachings of the truth from Christ; they were like snakes, like asps. They were pleased with their past sins, and unwilling to let go of their present life—unwilling, I mean, to exchange earthly joys for the joys of heaven. They were blocking one ear by their enjoyment of the past, and the other with their enjoyment of the present; they were determined not to hear. What else but this does their anxiety suggest, when they said, *If we leave him alone like this, the Romans will come, and sweep away our land and our nationhood* (Jn 11:48)? Obviously they were afraid of losing their land, for they had clapped an ear against the ground, refusing to listen to words endowed by a wise man with healing power. Moreover they were denounced for being misers and lovers of money: their whole way of life, both past and present, was described by the Lord in the gospel. Anyone who reads the gospel carefully will find out how they blocked both ears.

Now give me your attention, beloved ones.[31] What did the Lord do? *He smashed the teeth in their mouths*. What does *in their mouths* imply? He acted in such a way as to make them pronounce their own refutation; he forced them to give the verdict against themselves out of their own mouths. They were trying to find grounds of accusation against him in the matter of the tribute. He said neither, "It is right to pay it," nor "It is not right to pay it." Certainly he wanted to smash those teeth with which they were snapping at him and trying to bite, but he wanted it to happen in their own mouths. If he had said, "Tribute ought to be paid to Caesar," they would have accused him of belittling the Jewish nation by reducing it to tributary status; in fact they had been humbled for their sins and obliged to pay tribute, as their own law had foretold they would. "If he orders us to pay the tribute, we've got him as a renegade who insults our nation," they said. "But if he answers, 'No, do not pay it,' we've got him on the charge of undermining our loyalty to Caesar." They set this double noose in an attempt to catch the Lord. But whom were they attacking? One who well knew how to smash the teeth in their mouths. *Show me the coin*, he said. *"Why are you putting me to the test, you hypocrites?* (Mt 22:19.18). Are you genuinely perplexed about the

---

31. *Caritas vestra.*

rights and wrongs of the tribute? Do you really want to act justly? Are you looking for just counsel? *If you truly speak about justice, men and women, judge rightly in your own case.* But in this instance you are speaking in one way and thinking quite differently, so you are hypocrites. *Why are you putting me to the test?* I am going to smash your teeth in your own mouths, so *show me the coin.*" And they gave him one. He did not say, "This belongs to Caesar," but asked them, "Whose is it?" so as to smash their teeth in their mouths. When he asked them whose image and whose inscription the coin bore, they answered, "Caesar's." Now, watch the Lord smashing the teeth in their mouths: "You have given the right answer. The teeth are already broken in your mouths. *Render to Caesar what is Caesar's, and to God what is God's* (Mt 22:21). Caesar demands his image — give it to him! God demands his image — give it to him! Caesar must not go short of his coin from you, and God must not go short of his coin in you." They had no reply to make. They had been sent to find grounds of accusation against him, and they returned saying that no one could answer him at all. Why not? Because the teeth in their mouths had been smashed.

12. The same thing happened in another argument. *By what authority are you doing these things? But I have a question to put to you—just one. Answer me* (Mk 11:28.29). And the question he put to them was about John: where did John's baptism come from? From heaven or from some human source? This ensured that whatever reply they gave, it would tell against them. They were reluctant to answer, "From a human source," because they were afraid people might stone them, since John was popularly believed to be a prophet. Even less were they prepared to answer, "From heaven," because that would be to acknowledge Christ himself, for John had proclaimed him as the Messiah. They were in a tight spot, boxed in on both sides; so these questioners who had come prepared to accuse him were forced to proclaim themselves ignorant. *We do not know*, they said (Mk 11:33). They were preparing their charge when they asked, *By what authority are you doing these things?* If he had said, "Because I am the Messiah," they could have seized him as an arrogant, pretentious blasphemer. But he did not choose to say, "I am the Messiah." Instead he asked them about John, who had attested that Jesus was the Messiah. They dared not cast any slur on John, fearing that the people might kill them if they did; but neither did they dare to admit, "John spoke the truth," because then Christ could have said, "Believe him, then." They were dumb, they confessed that they did not know. So they no longer had the power to bite, did they? Why not? I can see you know the answer already! The teeth had been smashed in their mouths!

13. On another occasion a Pharisee who had invited the Lord to dinner found fault with him because a notoriously sinful woman had come close to his feet. The Pharisee murmured against him, *If this man were a prophet, he would know who this woman is, who has approached his feet* (Lk 7:39). But you are not a

prophet yourself, are you, so how do you know he is ignorant about the woman at his feet? Presumably the Pharisee entertained suspicions about him because the Lord was not being careful about Jewish ritual purity, which was observed outwardly in bodily matters but kept well away from the heart. But the Lord, who knew the woman's sins, also heard the thoughts of his host; and how he replied, you know. To put it briefly, he wanted to smash the Pharisee's teeth in his mouth. He put the case to him like this: *There was a certain creditor to whom two people were in debt. One owed him five hundred denarii, the other fifty. Since neither had the means to pay, he let them both off. Which of them will love him more?* (Lk 7:41-42). The Lord asked the question to evoke a response from the other, and, sure enough, he responded in a way that would smash the teeth in his mouth. Covered with shame, he gave his reply, and was shut out from that mercy to which the woman was granted access. She had burst into the house of a stranger, but she had approached a God who was no stranger. *The Lord smashed the teeth in their mouths.*

14. *The Lord shattered the jawbones of the lions*, not of the asps only. How do they compare with the asps? The aim of the asps is to inject their venom stealthily, to spatter it about and hiss. But the Gentiles raged quite openly, roaring like lions. *Why have the nations raged, and the peoples devised futile schemes?* (Ps 2:1). When the questioners sneaked up to the Lord, asking, *Is it lawful to pay tribute to Caesar, or not?* (Mt 22:17), they were asps, snakes; and their teeth were smashed in their mouths. But later they shouted, *Crucify him! Crucify him!* not with snakes' tongues but with the savagery of lions. Nonetheless *the Lord shattered the jawbones of the lions* too. It is perhaps significant that the psalm did not add the words, "in their mouths," in the case of the lions. Those who attempted to ensnare Christ with their captious debates were overcome willy-nilly by their own replies; but would those who raged openly be confuted by debate? No; yet their jawbones too were shattered: the crucified Christ rose again, ascended into heaven, and was glorified. He is worshiped now by all nations, worshiped by the kings of all the earth. Let the Jews rampage now, if they can. But they do not rampage, for *the Lord has shattered the jawbones of the lions.*

The inconsistency of the Donatists with regard to the law

15. We have an instructive example of the same thing in our experience with the heretics, for we find that they too are snakes, deaf because they have blocked their ears, determined not to listen to the medicine endowed with potency by a wise man. And in their case also the Lord has smashed their teeth.

Remember how they used to rage against us, complaining that we were persecutors because we kept them out of the basilicas. Well now, question them:

Should heretics be excluded from the basilicas, or should they not? Let them answer that one. Suppose they reply, "No, they should not." In that case, the Maximianists can reclaim their basilicas.[32] If they want to prevent the Maximianists reclaiming those basilicas, the Donatists must reply, "Yes, heretics should be excluded." But in that case, what becomes of the charge you leveled against us? Your teeth have been smashed in your mouths, haven't they?

"What have kings to do with us?" they ask. "What do emperors matter to us? You are basing your argument on imperial authority." Yes, but I will counter that with a similar point: why do you have recourse to proconsuls sent by emperors? Why do you appeal to the law, when emperors have legislated against you? Emperors who belonged to our communion have passed laws against all heretics;[33] and they certainly regard all who are not of our communion as heretics, which obviously includes you. If the laws are just, they are valid against you as heretics; if they are unjust, why should they have any validity against persons you deem heretics?

Brothers and sisters, try to concentrate for a few minutes, and to understand what we are saying. The Donatists invoked the law against the Maximianists, attempting to expel them as schismatics, condemned as such by the Donatists, from places they had held since ancient times, places to which they had succeeded after the death of bishops who had preceded them. In their attempt to expel the Maximianists from these sees, the Donatists appealed to the laws of the state, took their case to the magistrates, and professed themselves to be Catholics, in order to exclude their opponents as heretics. Now tell me, you Donatist: why do you call yourself a Catholic in order to get a heretic ejected, rather than really being a Catholic, so as not to be excluded as a heretic yourself? You are temporarily a "Catholic," only to bolster your case and oust a heretic.

The judge had no power to make a decision except in accordance with his laws. They claimed to be Catholics, and they were given a hearing. They declared their adversaries to be heretics, and when the judge demanded proof of this, they read out the decree of the Council of Bagai,[34] which condemned the Maximianists. This decree was inserted into the proconsular Acts. It had thus

---

32. On the Maximianist schism within Donatism see Augustine's Exposition 2 of Psalm 21, 31, and Exposition 2 of Psalm 36, 19-23, and notes in both places. Augustine often exploited the Maximianist schism to expose the inconsistency of the Donatist position, sometimes with regard to the non-repetition of baptism, but here in connection with the status of heretical sects under the imperial law.

33. Perhaps a reference to the decrees of the Emperor Constans in 347 and 348, or the anti-heresy laws of the Emperor Theodosius in 392. In 405, after hearing a report from two Catholic bishops on the activities of the Donatists, the Emperor Honorius issued an Edict of Union, whereby the Donatists were formally assimilated to other heretical sects. But it is not certain whether the present sermon is later than this Edict.

34. Held in April 394. It sought to rehabilitate Primian, the Donatist Bishop of Carthage, whose violent and brutal conduct had been condemned by the Maximianist Council of Cebarsussa the previous year.

been established that the Maximianists, being condemned as heretics, had no right to possess the basilicas, and the proconsul announced his decision in conformity with the law. But what law? The law passed against heretics.

But it follows, you Donatist, that if it is a law against heretics, it is a law against you. "Why against me?" he objects. "I am no heretic." But if you are not a heretic, you are implying that those laws are unsound, because they were enacted by emperors who certainly do not belong to your communion, and they brand as heretics all who do not belong to their communion. However, let us set aside the question of whether those laws are right or not, if that is still a question. I want to argue on your own terms. By your reckoning, are those laws sound or faulty? If they are sound, they are to be trusted and obeyed; if they are faulty, why do you take advantage of them? You said to the proconsul, "I am a Catholic. Expel that heretic." The proconsul sought proof that your opponent was a heretic; you produced your conciliar decree and demonstrated that you had condemned him. The proconsul may have been lazy,[35] or may not have understood; but in any case he acted as a judge must, in accordance with the law. So you persuaded the judge to a line of conduct you have no intention of following yourself, for if the judge made use of an imperial law at your suggestion, why do you not make use of it for your own correction? Face the truth: he ejected the man you call a heretic in accordance with the law passed by the emperor, his master; why do you not want him to eject you as well by the same law?

Let us run through your actions once more. The basilicas formerly held by the Maximianists are now in your possession. The Maximianists have been turned out of them. The appointment of the proconsuls is a public matter, and the conciliar Acts are made available.[36] The magistrate's assistants are approved, the cities are in turmoil, and people are thrust out of their places. Why? "Because they are heretics," you say. By what law are they expelled? Answer me, and let us see whether your teeth are not smashed in your mouth. Is the law a bad one? Then it should have no force against anyone you call a heretic. Is it a good one? Then it should have force against you.

They have nothing to say in reply, because *God has smashed the teeth in their mouths.* Unable to slither in like asps with their slippery lies, they take to rampaging like lions with open violence. Armed bands of Cirmcumcellions[37]

---

35. *Connivens*: "may have connived," "may have winked at it," etc. But a few codices have *conhibens* or *cohibens*, perhaps "attempting to contain the trouble."

36. This could be understood differently, as an interjection by the Donatist after Augustine's previous sentence, referring to the situation after the ruling, perhaps as "Quite right too! The orders of the proconsuls stand firm, and the conciliar decrees are extant." But the chronological pattern in these sentences suggests that he is still thinking of the stage of preparation for the hearing.

37. On these terrorists see note at Exposition of Psalm 10, 5.

rush savagely into action, wreaking as much havoc as they can, yes, as much as ever they can. But *the Lord has shattered the jawbones of the lions* too.

Verse 8. Do not be intimidated by the torrent of impiety

16. *They will be scorned like water that flows away.* You should not be intimidated by rivers that are reputed to be powerful torrents, my brothers and sisters. They are full of winter rain, but don't worry; after a short time their force abates. The water rushes down and roars for a while, but it will soon subside; it cannot continue in spate for long. There have been plenty of heresies that have died away. They flowed between their banks as long as any force remained in them; but then the water level dropped, the river-beds dried, and their memory scarcely survives today. People do not recall that they ever existed. *They will be scorned like water that runs away.* But the same is true of the whole world. It goes on its noisy course for a while and tries to drag along anyone it can catch. All the unbelievers, all the proud folk, crash against the rocks of their pride with a din like that of water rushing toward a confluence, but they must not frighten you. They are only swollen winter rivers that cannot flow all the year round; they will inevitably dwindle toward their proper place, which means the end of them.

Yet the Lord himself drank from this torrent of the world. Here it was that he suffered, from this same torrent he drank, but he drank by the wayside, as he passed it, for he did not stand in the way of sinners.[38] What does scripture say of him? *He will drink from the torrent beside the way, and therefore he will raise his head* (Ps 109(110):7). This means: because he died, he was glorified; because he suffered, he rose again. Had he been unwilling to drink from the torrent on the way, he would not have died; if he had not died, he would not have risen from the dead, and would not have been glorified. But in fact *he will drink from the torrent beside the way, and therefore he will raise his head.* Our head is raised up already; let his members follow him.

The impious *will be scorned like water that flows away. God bends his bow, until they lose their power.* God's threats do not fade away, and God's threats are his bow. His bow is bent, but he does not yet launch his arrows. *He bends his bow, until they lose their power.* Even at the bending of it many have been terrified and have lost their strength.[39] One who thus lost his power, for example, was the man who asked, *What do you want me to do?* when he heard the Lord say, *I am Jesus the Nazarene, whom you are persecuting* (Acts 9:6.5). The One who was calling from heaven was bending his bow. Many who were his enemies were weakened like this, and converted, and thereafter refrained from rearing

---

38. See Ps 1:1.
39. Some codices add "and have been converted."

their proud heads against that perpetually tensed bow. He too was weakened, the man who warned us not to fear being weak, by declaring, *When I am weak, then I am strong* (2 Cor 12:10). When he prayed to be relieved of the sting in his flesh, what answer did he get? *My power finds complete scope in your weakness* (2 Cor 12:9). God goes on bending his bow, until they lose their strength.

Verse 9. Sin is its own punishment

17. *They will be disposed of like melted wax.* I know what you were about to say: "But not all of them are reduced to weakness and so led to faith, as I have been. Many stick to their evil ways and their wickedness." But not even on their account should you be worried, for *they will be disposed of like melted wax.* They will not stand their ground against you, they will not last; they will perish in the fire kindled by their own lusts. There is a hidden punishment implied here, and the psalm will be discussing it from this point to the end. Only a few verses remain, so keep up your concentration.

There is a punishment reserved for the future: the fire of hell, eternal fire. This future punishment is of two kinds. It may be that fire in the underworld in which the rich man was burning, the man who craved for a drop of water to be trickled onto his tongue from the finger of a poor man he used to despise, the pauper who had lain at his gate. *I am in agony in this flame*, he cried (Lk 16:24). The other kind is the fire that will burn at the end of time, concerning which the people relegated to the Lord's left hand will hear, *Depart from me, you accursed, into the eternal fire which was prepared for the devil and his angels* (Mt 25:41). These punishments will be enforced when it is time to depart from this life, or at the end of time when the dead rise again.[40]

But what of the present? Is there no punishment here; does God allow sins to go entirely unpunished until that day? No; there is a secret punishment here, and this is what we shall now discuss. The Spirit of God wishes to draw our attention to it. Let us understand what it is, and beware of it, and avoid it, and so not fall into those very terrible torments hereafter. Now perhaps someone is going to object, "Yes, there certainly are painful things in this life, things like imprisonment, exile, torture, death, many kinds of pain and trouble. These are the common lot, and they are dispensed by God's judgment. For many they serve as probation, while for many others they are a punishment. Yet sometimes we see good people afflicted by these calamities, while bad people are exempt." Yes, and that was what made a psalmist totter, even though he later gave thanks: *How good God is to Israel, to those of straightforward hearts! Yet my feet had all but slipped, because I envied sinners, seeing the peace that sinners enjoy* (Ps

---

40. A theological tension expressed later as "particular judgment" and "general judgment."

72(73):1-3). He had seen bad people happy, and he was tempted by the idea of being bad himself; he could see how wicked people dominated, and how things went well with them, how they had plenty of all those temporal good things which he himself as a child used to beg from the Lord. So he teetered, until he came to see what must truly be hoped for or dreaded at the end. Later in the same psalm he said, *I tried to solve the problem, but it is too hard for me until I enter God's holy place, and understand what the final outcome must be* (Ps 72(73):16-17). Evidently what we are meant to understand here is not the punishments of the underworld, nor the punishments of eternal fire after the resurrection, nor those punishments which while we are still in this world fall upon just and unjust indiscriminately, and often more severely on the just than on the unjust. The Spirit of God is directing our attention rather to some kind of punishment that operates in the present life. Focus your minds on this, and listen, for although what I am going to tell you is something you know already, it will be easier for you to take it in when it is demonstrated in a psalm which looked obscure until it was explained. I am bringing out for inspection things you already know, but when I bring them out from a place where you had not yet seen them, it will make previously known truths seem to you delightfully new. Listen, then, to the punishment of the impious: *They will be disposed of like melted wax,* says the psalm. I have told you that this happens to them through their inordinate cravings. Evil craving is a burning force, even a fire. Now if fire consumes a garment, will adulterous lust not consume the soul? Speaking of adultery merely contemplated, scripture says, *If someone wraps up fire in his bosom, will his clothes not be singed?* (Prv 6:27). If you carry live coals next to your chest, they will burn holes in your tunic; and if you carry adultery in your mind, will your soul remain unharmed?[41]

18. Few people see these punishments, which is why the Spirit of God emphasizes them more particularly. Listen to what the apostle has to say: *God delivered them to the lusts of their own hearts* (Rom 1:24). This is the fire before which they melt like wax. Being loosened from charity, they no longer have the stability it gave them; and hence as they pursue their impure cravings they are as though dissolved and fluid. What makes them fluid? What dissolves them? The fire of their lusts. *God delivered them to the lusts of their own hearts, to do things that should not be done. They became full of every iniquity* (Rom 1:24. 28-29). The apostle gives a list of many things which are sins, and calls them punishments for sins. He says that the primary punishment is pride, or rather that pride is not a punishment, but the primordial sin. Pride is the first sin, and the last punishment is eternal fire or the fire of hell — last, because it is the punishment of the damned. Between that first sin and this ultimate punishment there are

---

41. See Prv 6:28-29.

other things which are both sins and punishments. The apostle enumerates many actions which are detestable sins, yet he calls them punishments. *Accordingly, he says, God delivered them to the lusts of their own hearts, to act impurely, to do things that should not be done.* And lest any sinners might think that the deeds they at present enjoy are the only thing they will suffer in the way of punishment, and that they need not fear what will befall them in the end, he mentions the ultimate punishment: *Though they had known the justice of God, they did not understand that those who do such things deserve death; and not only those who do them, but also people who consent to those who behave so* (Rom 1:32). *Those who do such things deserve death* — what things are these? Those very things which he had listed as punishments; for he said, *God delivered them to the lusts of their own hearts, to do things that should not be done.* To be an adulterer is already a punishment; to be a liar, a miser, a cheat, a murderer—these are already punishments. Punishments for what sin, then? For the original apostasy, for that sin of pride: *the starting-point of human pride is rebellion against God,* and *the starting-point of all sin is pride* (Sir 10:14.15). That is why the apostle named it as the first sin: *Though they had known God, they did not glorify him as God, or give him thanks. Their thoughts wandered into futility and their stupid hearts were darkened* (Rom 1:21). This darkening of the heart is already their punishment. What brought it on them? *Believing themselves to be wise, they sank into folly* (Rom 1:22). By claiming that what they had received from God derived from themselves, or, if they knew they had received it from him, by not glorifying him for giving it, they were *believing themselves to be wise.* And their punishment followed immediately: *they sank into folly, and their hearts were darkened. Believing themselves to be wise, they sank into folly.* Is that a light punishment? Even if we confine our discussion to this darkening of the heart, is spiritual blindness a light penalty? If someone who committed theft all of a sudden lost an eye, everyone would say that God had been watching, and had punished the thief. But a sinner has lost the eye of his heart, and people think he has been spared! *They will be disposed of like melting wax.*

Conquer bodily desires before they grow too strong

19. *Fire fell upon them from above, and they could not see the sun.* He is describing the punishment of darkening, you see. *Fire fell upon them from above*: the fire of pride, thick with smoke, the fire of desire, the fire of anger. How powerful is the fire? So powerful that no one on whom it falls will see the sun. That is why scripture commands, *Do not let the sun set on your wrath* (Eph 4:26). Beware of this fire of evil desire, brothers and sisters, unless you want to be melted like wax, and leak away from God's presence; for otherwise this fire will fall upon you, and you will not see the sun. What "sun" is meant? Not this

visible sun, obviously, not the sun that animals and even flies see along with you, and good people and bad people equally, because God causes his sun to rise over good and bad alike.[42] No, there is another sun, that of which the wicked will one day admit, *The sun never rose for us; all these things have passed away like a shadow. No doubt of it, we strayed from the path of truth. On us the light of righteousness did not shine, nor did the sun rise for us* (Wis 5:6,9). And why not? Because *fire fell upon them from above, and they could not see the sun.* The desire of the flesh was too strong for them.

Where does this desire come from? Give me your careful attention. You are born from the same stock as the enemy you must overcome. Do not go looking for other foes to fight; vanquish the one you were born with. You came into the stadium of this life in its company; get to grips with the adversary who entered the lists with you. If you cannot prevail against it, why challenge the hordes of other desires? Carnal pleasure is born with every human being, my brothers and sisters. Any well-instructed person attacks this enemy on sight, and wrestles, and soon wins; for we are strong enough to take on opponents not fully grown. But if anyone neglects to conquer that carnal desire with which he or she was born from sinful stock, and instead arouses and evokes many other lusts, that person will have great difficulty in getting the better of them. Anyone so divided against himself is burnt up by his own fire. Do not delude yourself that the only punishments are those laid up for the future: take stock of those that are present. *Fire fell upon them from above, and they could not see the sun.*

Verse 10. The bramble, the fire, and the thorns

20. *Before the bramble*[43] *brings forth your thorns, he will swallow them up as though they were alive, as though in his anger.* What is this bramble? It is a kind of prickly bush, and its thorns are said to be very dense. At first it is a young green stalk,[44] and at that stage it is soft and pretty. But it will thrust out its spikes later. In the same way our sins are delightful at first, and do not seem to prick us. The bramble is still a tender green stalk, yet it is an incipient thorn-bush. *Before the bramble brings forth thorns* means "before the unmistakable torments due to your wicked indulgence and pleasures emerge." All those who are enamored of something they cannot get should question themselves. Let them see if they are not tortured by desire; and then, if they gain what they illicitly desire, let them see if they are not racked by fear. They must see that they are getting their

---

42. See Mt 5:45.
43. *Rhamnos* or *rhamnus*, a Latinized form of a Greek name for several kinds of thorny shrubs. Pliny refers to it (*Nat.* 24, 124). Perhaps to be identified as the Christ's thorn, *paliurus spina Christi.*
44. *Herba.*

punishment here, before the time comes for our bodily resurrection, when the opportunity for us to change will have passed, for *though we shall all indeed rise again, we shall not all be changed* (1 Cor 15:51). Then they will suffer a corruption of their flesh which will cause them pain but not kill them, for if it killed them their sufferings would be ended. That is when the thorns of the bramble will be evident in them, in every kind of chagrin and piercing pain.

What kind of thorns are they destined to feel, those who will be saying of the righteous, *These are the people we once held in derision* (Wis 5:3)? They will endure the thorns of remorse, but a remorse that comes too late and is fruitless; the bramble will be barren. Repentance in this present time is a medicinal pain; repentance at that future time is penal. You do not want to suffer those thorns, do you? Then make sure you are punctured here by the thorns of repentance, and imitate the psalmist who said, *I was reduced to bitterness when the thorn stuck fast in me. I perceived my sin, and did not cloak my unrighteousness. I said, I will declare my unrighteousness against myself to the Lord, and you have forgiven the impiety of my heart* (Ps 31(32):4-5). Get on with it now, let the thorn of compunction stab you now. Let not the fate befall you that scripture speaks of in connection with certain loathsome people: *They were torn apart, yet suffered no compunction* (Ps 34(35):16). Observe these people, who *were torn apart, yet suffered no compunction.* You can see some like that, people torn away, and you see how little compunction they feel. Look at them: they are outside the Church, yet they do not regret it in such a way as to return to the body from which they tore themselves. Their bramble will bring forth its thorns later. They refuse to undergo medicinal compunction now, so they will suffer the penal sort later. Yet even now, before the bramble brings forth its thorns, a fire has fallen upon them that prevents them from seeing the sun; it swallows them up even while they are still living, under the sentence of God's wrath. This is the fire of sinful desires, of worthless honors, of pride and avarice; and where does it drive them? Toward a refusal[45] to recognize the truth, lest they should seem to be defeated, lest truth itself should triumph over them. What can be more glorious, brothers and sisters, than to be overpowered and conquered by the truth? Let yourself be willingly overcome by the truth, otherwise it will defeat you one day against your will.

The fire of sinful cravings fell from above and prevented them from seeing the sun. It has devoured the bramble before any thorns appeared; that is to say, it conceals the wickedness of their life before that life has brought forth the torments due to it, which will be plainly seen at the end. But it is by a decree of God's anger that this fire obscures the bramble, for it is no small punishment that they are unable to see the sun now, and do not believe that the thorns of punishment will emerge later from their wicked lives to hurt them. "You are the

---

45. A variant supported by a few codices, PL, and the CCL editors, yields the sense ". . . avarice, and whatever drives them toward a refusal. . . ."

bramble," this psalm is telling them, "and under God's anger fire is devouring you even now, while you still tarry in this life, before the bramble that is your very selves produces in the future the spikes of your punishment. It devours you now in the sense that it seems to envelop the bramble and hide it from sight." The words could be ordered more clearly like this, or so I think: *fire fell upon them from above, and they could not see the sun.* This fire *came as though in anger, and devoured the bramble, that is, yourselves, as though you were alive, before it could produce your thorns.* To put it briefly, he found you, you yourselves, to be a bramble; and even before your death the fire devours you; this happens even before the bramble brings forth thorns after death, when you rise again to receive punishment.

Why did the psalm say, *As though they were alive,* rather than just "alive"? Surely because the life of the impious is a sham, no true life. They do not truly live; they only think they live. And again, why did it not say, "in anger," but *as though in his anger*? Obviously because God is entirely tranquil when he acts thus. This too scripture tells us: *You judge in tranquillity, O Lord of might* (Wis 12:18). Even when he threatens he does not get angry, nor is he disturbed; but because he punishes and avenges ill-doing, he is "as though angry." And those who refuse to be corrected are "as though alive," but not really alive; for the punishment of the first sin, and of the others they have added to it, remains upon them, and we call this the anger of God, since it proceeds from God's judgment. This is why the Lord says of one who refuses to believe, *The anger of God remains upon him* (Jn 3:36). As mortals we are born under the sign of God's anger; as the apostle says, *By nature we too were children of wrath, like the rest* (Eph 2:3). What is meant by being *children of wrath by nature,* if not that we carry with us the punishment of the first sin? But if we turn around, the wrath is turned away, and grace is bestowed. If you refuse to turn round, you add to the legacy you were born with, and then you will be devoured even in this present life, as though by God's anger.

Verse 11. How to wash your hands in the blood of sinners

21. Think about that punishment, and be glad that you do not share it, all you who are making progress, all you who understand the truth and love it, all you who would rather have truth winning the victory in you than be victorious yourselves. To you I say this, you who do not shut your ears against the truth, either by wallowing in present pleasures or by remembering those that are past, lest you be like the dog that returns to its vomit.[46] All of you who live so, look at the punishment of those who live otherwise, and rejoice. The pains of hell have not

---

46. See 2 Pt 2:22.

come into operation yet, nor is the eternal fire yet at hand; all the same, let anyone who is growing in God compare himself or herself even now with the godless, compare a blind heart with a heart illumined: compare the two! They are as different as is a person with bodily sight from one who is blind. Yet bodily sight is not everything. Did Tobit enjoy the use of his bodily eyes? No, he did not, and his son did, yet the blind man showed the way of life to the one with sight.[47]

So then, when you see the punishment others suffer, be glad it does not fall on you. This is in accord with scripture's word here: *the righteous will rejoice to see vengeance done*. It cannot mean the future vengeance, for look what follows: *they will wash their hands in the blood of a sinner*. Whatever does that suggest? Your attention is needed, beloved.[48] It can hardly mean that when murderers are executed, the innocent should go along and dabble their hands there, can it? Of course not. What does it mean, then, that *in the blood of a sinner the righteous will wash their hands*?

It means that when a just person sees a sinner punished, he or she profits thereby; the death of one is powerfully life-giving for the other. If people are dying within themselves, blood is flowing out of them in a spiritual sense; and when you see them suffering such vengeance, you must wash your hands in that blood, and live more cleanly yourself thereafter. And why will such a person need to wash his hands, if he is just? What dirt will he have on his hands, if he is just? Well remember that the one who lives by faith is just.[49] Scripture calls believers "just," and so from the time you came to believe, you began to qualify as a just person, for then your sins were forgiven. It may be true that in your subsequent life there are some sins, the kind that inevitably seep in, like sea-water into a ship's bilge. Nonetheless you have come to believe; and you see a person who is wholly turned away from God being done to death in his blindness, unable to see the sun for the fire that has fallen upon him. Then because you aspire to see in direct vision Christ whom you already see by faith, and because it is the one who lives by faith that is just, you are the one to learn a lesson from the dying unbeliever, and purge yourself of sins. In this way you will, in a sense, wash your hands in a sinner's blood. *The just will wash their hands in the blood of a sinner.*

Verse 12. The just rejoice even in this life

22. *And everyone will say, "If the just are so rewarded. . . ."* Even before the promised happiness comes our way, before eternal life is given to us, before the

---

47. See Tb 4:2-23.
48. *Caritas vestra.*
49. See Hb 2:4; Rom 1:17.

godless are cast into everlasting fire, even here in this life the just are rewarded. What is their reward? They are even now *rejoicing in hope, patient in anguish* (Rom 12:12). How are the just rewarded? *We even glory in our sufferings, knowing that suffering fosters endurance, and endurance constancy, and constancy hope; but hope does not disappoint us, because the love of God has been poured out into our hearts through the Holy Spirit who has been given us* (Rom 5:3-5). If a drunkard is merry, shall the just not be merry too, the just whose reward is charity? The former is wretched even in his drunken state, the just person is happy even when hungry and thirsty. One is glutted with immoderate drinking, the other is fed by hope. Let the just look on the punishment of sinners, and on their own joy, and think on God. If God has given them such joy now, joy in their faith, in their hope, in charity, in the truth of his scriptures, what kind of joy is he preparing for them at the end? If he feeds them like this on the journey, how will he feast them in their homeland? *Everyone will say, "If the just are so rewarded. . . ."* Let all who see this believe, let them see it and understand.

The righteous will rejoice to see vengeance done. If such a person lacks eyes to see the vengeance, he or she will be saddened, and will not be corrected by it. But any who see it will see how great is the difference between an eye of the heart shrouded in darkness, and an eye of the heart illumined, between the cool refreshment of chastity and the flame of lust, between security born of hope and the fear that follows villainy. When they see this, they must mark the difference between their own lives and those others, and wash their hands in sinners' blood. Let them profit from the contrast, and say, *If the just are so rewarded, God is already judging sinners on earth*: not yet in the life to come, not yet in everlasting fire, not yet in hell, but here on earth. Look at the rich man in the gospel: he is still wearing his purple and fine linen, still banqueting magnificently every day. Not yet has the bramble sprouted its thorns, not yet is he moaning, *I am in agony in this flame* (Lk 16:24). But already the blindness of the mind is upon him, already his spiritual eye has been put out. If a physically blind person were to sit down at a sumptuous banquet, you would feel sorry for him; but if someone is inwardly blind, and cannot see the bread that is Christ, is he or she fortunate? Only someone equally blind would say so. *If, then, the just are so rewarded, God is already judging sinners on earth.*

Conclusion: building on rock

23. Forgive us if the sermon we have preached has been rather long. We beg you in the name of Christ to think over what you have heard and allow it to bear fruit. Just as preaching the truth is worthless if the heart is out of tune with the tongue, so listening to the truth is useless if the hearer does not build on rock. The one who builds on rock is the one who hears and acts accordingly; anyone who

hears but does not so act is building on sand.[50] The person who neither hears nor acts is not building at all. But just as the one who builds on sand is preparing ruin for himself, so will the one who has done no building at all be swept away, homeless, when the river rises. There is nothing for it but to build, and to build on rock: that is, to hear and to act in accordance with what you hear.

Let no outsider demand, "Why should I go to church? Look at those people who go to church every day: they do not act in accordance with what they hear." Perhaps not, but at least they are doing something by going to hear, and through this effort they may eventually manage to hear and act! But what about you? Aren't you moving even further away from acting as you should, by running away from even hearing? "But I am not building on sand," replies our objector. Then the river will find you exposed. Will it hold back for that reason, and forbear to carry you away? Will the rain leave you alive because you are without shelter? Will the winds spare you, and not sweep you off, because you are undefended? I do not think so. "All right then, I will come along and hear you." Good, but when you hear, act on it. If you hear, but do not act, you will have built, certainly, but only on sand. So then, if we have neglected to build, we are exposed to the elements. If we live in a building founded on sand, we are buried when it collapses. It only remains for us to build on rock, and act in accordance with what we have heard.

---

50. See Mt 7:24-27.

Exposition 1 of Psalm 58

First Sermon[1]

Verse 1. The uncorrupted title

1. It is customary for scripture to announce the mysterious content of the psalms in their titles, to adorn the façade[2] of a psalm with sublime indications of the sacred truths it contains. In this way when we are about to enter we can read the notice on the doorpost, as it were, and find out what goes on within, whose house this is, and who is the owner of the property. The title of the present psalm is concerned with a title, for its inscription runs, *To the end, as a title written for David himself that is not to be tampered with.* This is why I said that it is a title about a title. The gospel tells us what this written title was that the psalm forbids anyone to tamper with; for when the Lord was crucified, a title was inscribed by Pilate and affixed to his cross. It said, *The King of the Jews*, in three languages: Hebrew, Greek, and Latin, the three noblest languages in the whole world. Now, it is evident that if he who was crucified was King of the Jews, and if the Jews crucified their own king, they did not so much destroy him by doing so as make him king of the Gentiles. Admittedly they did their best to rid themselves of Christ, but they succeeded from their own point of view, not ours. He died for us, and redeemed us with his blood.

All the same, the title has not been falsified, because he is indeed king, not of the Gentiles only, but even of the Jews. How is that? Could they subvert his lordship over them simply by denying it? No; he is their king, for he is the king who bears an iron scepter, which he uses both to rule and to break his foes. *I have been established by him as king over Zion, his holy mountain, preaching the Lord's decree. The Lord said to me, You are my Son, today have I begotten you. Ask of me, and I will give you the nations as your heritage, and the ends of the earth for your possession. You will rule them with an iron rod, and you will dash them to pieces like a potter's vessel* (Ps 2:6-9). Whom will he rule? And whom will he dash to pieces? He will rule those who obey him, but shatter those who resist.

The words, *not to be tampered with*, are both very apt and prophetic. The Jews at that time complained to Pilate: *Do not put "The King of the Jews"; put*

---

1. Tentatively assigned to the winter of 412-413, at Carthage. Pelagianism had begun to be an issue for Augustine; see section 19.
2. Or "deck the brow," but the imagery of the house seems to favor taking *frons* metaphorically.

148

"He said, I am the King of the Jews," they urged, "for that title confirms his sovereignty over us." But Pilate replied, *What I have written, I have written* (Jn 19:21.22); and so the prophetic warning contained in the psalm's title was vindicated: *Not to be tampered with.*

The whole Christ speaks in the psalms

2. This is not the only psalm that has a warning written up over it, to the effect that the title is not to be interfered with. Some other psalms begin with the same indication,[3] and in all of them the Lord's passion is foretold. So we should understand that the Lord's passion is meant here too, and be ready for Christ to speak to us, Christ who is both head and body. We must always, or nearly always, hear Christ's voice speaking from a psalm in such a way that when we contemplate our head, the one mediator between God and humankind, himself human, Christ Jesus,[4] we do not contemplate him in isolation. In respect of his godhead he is the Word who was in the beginning, God with God, the Word who was made flesh and dwelt among us;[5] in respect of his humanity he was flesh from the stock of Abraham, born from David's seed of the virgin Mary. But when we hear Christ speaking we should not think of him, our head, in isolation. We must think of him as head and body, one whole perfect man, for to us the apostle Paul says, *You are Christ's body, and his limbs* (1 Cor 12:27). And of Christ himself the same apostle declares that he is the Church's head.[6] But if he is the head, and we are the body, the whole Christ consists of head and body. Sometimes you come across words that are unsuitable to the head, and unless you make the necessary adjustment and understand them of his body, you will be baffled. Or again you will find words that do not fit the body, yet Christ is speaking in them. But there is no need for anyone to be misled, for the listener will hasten to apply to the head what is obviously unsuited to the body. After all, when Christ was hanging on the cross he cried out in the person of his body, *My God, my God, look upon me, why have you forsaken me?* (Ps 21:2(22:1)). God had not forsaken Christ, any more than he had been abandoned by Christ. Do you really suppose that the Son came to us in such wise that he deserted the Father, or that the Father banished him in sending him? But humankind had been forsaken by God; that is to say, sinful Adam, who had been accustomed to rejoice in God's presence, had been frightened off by his consciousness of sin and fled from that joy;[7] so it is true that God did abandon him, because he first forsook God. Thus when Christ had taken

---

3. See Psalms 56 and 57 (57 and 58), and Augustine's commentary in his Exposition of Psalm 56, 3.
4. See 1 Tm 2:5.
5. See Jn 1:1.14.
6. See Eph 1:22; Col 1:18.
7. See Gn 3:8.

flesh from Adam, he spoke these words in the person of that flesh, because our old humanity was nailed to the cross with him.[8]

Saul attempts to kill David, and the Jews to kill faith in the resurrection

3. Now let us listen to what comes next. *When Saul sent men to invest David's house and kill him.* This phrase also refers to the passion of the Lord, but not to his cross. Christ was crucified, he died, and he was buried. We could say that his sepulcher was like a house, and that the kingdom of the Jews intended to invest it when guards were stationed at the tomb.[9] It is true that in the Books of the Kingdoms[10] there is a whole story about Saul sending men to surround David's house and kill him; but when we are discussing the title of our psalm we need only consider that element of the story that the psalmist took from it. Perhaps all he meant to indicate to us was that a force was sent to surround the house and kill David. But if David prefigured Christ, in what sense was the "house" besieged so that Christ might be killed? He was laid in the tomb only after he had been killed on the cross.

Clearly we must refer this passage to Christ's body. In that perspective to kill Christ means to suppress the name of Christ so that no one would believe in him, and to do so by propagating the lies of the guards, who were bribed to say that while they were asleep, Christ's disciples had come and removed him.[11] That really is an attempt to "kill Christ": to snuff out the news of his resurrection, so that lies should win the day over the gospel. But just as Saul did not succeed in killing David, neither did the kingdom of the Jews succeed in passing off the testimony of sleeping guards as more credible than that of vigilant apostles. What were the guards instructed to say? "We will give you money," said the Jewish leaders, "as much money as you want. Then you are to say that while you were asleep, his disciples came and stole him away." Just look what kind of witnesses they adduced, those enemies of Christ whom Saul had prefigured! Witnesses to lies, as against the truth of Christ and his resurrection. Go on, then, unbelievers, interrogate your slumbering witnesses, and let them tell you what happened at the tomb. If they were asleep, how could they know? If they were awake, why did they not arrest the thieves? Let the next verses tell you why not.

---

8. See Rom 6:6.
9. See Mt 27:66.
10. 1 Sm 19:11-17 in our usage.
11. See Mt 28:13.

Verses 2-3. The cry of the persecuted Christ

4. *Rescue me from my enemies, O my God, and redeem me from those who rise up against me.* This was the experience of Christ in his flesh, and our experience too. Our enemies are the devil and his angels who constantly, daily, rise up against us and try to dupe us in our weakness and fragility. They are relentless in their attempts to ensnare us by their tricks, promptings, temptations, and any traps they can devise, as long as we live on earth. But let our voice be wide awake to God[12] and cry out in the members of Christ, subordinate to their head in heaven, *Rescue me from my enemies, O my God, and redeem me from those who rise up against me.*

5. *Rescue me from those who work iniquity, and save me from men of blood.* Men of blood they were indeed, who slew the just man in whom they had found no fault; men of blood they were, for when a foreigner washed his hands and sought to release Christ, they shouted, *Crucify him! Crucify him!* Men of blood they were, for when the crime of shedding Christ's blood was laid to their charge, they offered it to their descendants to drink: *His blood be upon us, and upon our children!* (Mt 27:25).

Yet men of blood have not ceased to rise up against Christ's body, for even after his resurrection and ascension the Church suffered persecutions. Indeed, they broke out first of all at the instigation of the Jews, that people from whom the apostles sprang. At the very outset Stephen was stoned,[13] and received what his name signified, for "Stephen" means "crown." Stoned in humility, he was crowned in sublimity. Then among the Gentiles pagan kingdoms rose up; this was before the prophecy had been fulfilled in them that *all the kings of the earth will worship him, and all nations will serve him* (Ps 71(72):11). The savage force of that kingdom[14] was unleashed against the witnesses of Christ. A great and mighty flood of martyrs' blood was poured out; but through its shedding the crop of the Church sprouted all the more vigorously,[15] and filled the whole world, as we see it does today. From these men of blood Christ is rescued: not the head only, but the body too. Christ is delivered from men of blood, from those of former days, those of today, and those who will persecute in the future. The Christ who is rescued is the Christ of earlier days, and the Christ of today, and the Christ who will be, for Christ is the whole body of Christ. All who are good

---

12. A terse and vivid expression of Augustine's understanding of prayer: *vox nostra vigilet ad Deum.*

13. See Acts 7:58.

14. Singular here: either he means the Roman Empire of the early days, or, more probably, he thinks of all persecuting pagan powers as a single kingdom ruled by Satan. The type of this is Babylon, the city of wickedness opposed to the city of God; see Exposition 2 of Psalm 26, 18; Exposition of Psalm 44, 25; Exposition of Psalm 54, 12, and notes.

15. An echo of Tertullian's famous boast, *Semen est sanguis Christianorum* (*Apol.* 50).

Christians now, and those who preceded us, and those who will come after us—all these are the whole Christ who is rescued from men of blood, and so the truth of this verse is vindicated: *save me from men of blood.*

Verse 4. The self-styled strong and the humbly weak

6. *For see, they have hunted my soul.* They were powerful enough to hold me, powerful enough to kill me, *they hunted my soul.* Then what has become of the triumphant cry, *You have burst my bonds* (Ps 115(116):16)? What has become of the shout, *The trap is broken, and we have escaped* (Ps 123(124):7)? What of the thanks we offer to God who *did not leave us like prey between their teeth* (Ps 123(124):6)? They hunted me, to be sure, but he who guards Israel does not leave me in the hunters' hands.

See, they have hunted my soul; the strong pounced upon me. We must certainly not pass over this mention of "the strong" in silence; careful investigation is needed to find out the identity of these strong insurgents. Against whom are they strong? Obviously against the weak, the feeble, those devoid of strength. Yet for all that, the weak win praise and the strong are condemned. If you want to know who the strong are, remember that the first to be called strong by the Lord was the devil. *No one can get into a strong man's house and carry off his implements, unless he has tied up the strong man first* (Mt 12:29). So said the Lord, and therefore he bound the strong one with the chains of his own dominion, and carried off his implements, and turned them into implements for his own use. All sinful people had been the devil's implements, but on becoming believers they were transformed into tools at Christ's disposal. To them the apostle said, *You were darkness once, but now you are light in the Lord* (Eph 5:8), the Lord *who made his riches known toward the vessels of his mercy* (Rom 9:23).[16] These can be understood as "the strong."

But among human beings there are some others who are strong with a strength altogether objectionable and worthy of censure, full of self-confidence, but only on the grounds of their temporal prosperity. Don't you think the rich man we heard about in the gospel just now was strong, the one whose lands were doing so well, and yielding him plentiful harvests? He was concerned about the abundance, and toyed with plans for rebuilding. He would dismantle his old barns, build new and larger ones, and when they were ready say to his soul, *You have plenty of good things, my soul. Feast, have a good time, eat your fill* (Lk 12:19). But what sort of strong man do you observe here? *Look at the person who*

---

16. "Vessels" here is the same word as "implements" just above. The Latin *vasa* means first "containers" or "vessels," then any kind of tools, equipment, kit.

would not take God as helper, but trusted in the amplitude of his riches! Yes, look how he grew strong! He *grew strong in his stupidity* (Ps 51:9(52:7)).

7. Then again there are other strong people who base their self-assurance not on wealth, nor on their robust physique, nor on any superior rank or temporal power, but on their own righteousness.[17] This type of strong person is especially to be feared, avoided, and kept out of your company. These, as I was saying, are people who pride themselves not on physical qualities, nor on their wealth, nor on their pedigree, nor on their rank; after all, anyone can see that these are merely temporal advantages—fleeting, perishable, here today and gone tomorrow. No, the ground of their pride is their own righteousness. Strength of this kind has hindered the Jews from entering through the eye of the needle,[18] for relying on themselves as righteous and considering themselves to be in good health, they refused the medicine and even killed the physician. These self-styled strong who disdained to be weak were not the ones whom the Lord came to call. *It is not the healthy who need the physician, but the sick,* he said. *I did not come to call the righteous, but sinners to repentance* (Mt 9:12; Lk 5:32). These "strong" people were the ones who taunted Christ's disciples because their master was entering the houses of weak and sickly folk, and sharing meals with them. *Why does your master eat with tax collectors and sinners?* (Mt 9:11). O you strong ones, who need no physician! Strength like this is the mark of fatuity, not fitness,[19] for no one is stronger than madmen. They are more powerful than sane persons, and the stronger they are, the nearer looms their death. God grant that we may never imitate strong people of this type. There is a real danger that some may want to imitate them. But the Teacher of humility became a sharer in our infirmity to enable us to share in his divinity; he came down to us both to teach us the way and to become the way,[20] and he graciously willed to make his own humility above all a lesson to us. This is why he did not disdain to be baptized by his servant for our sake. He meant to teach us to confess our sins, to become weak in order to be strong, and to make our own the words of the apostle, *When I am weak, then I am strong* (2 Cor 12:10). With this in view, the Lord refrained from displaying his own strength.

However, those who aspired to be strong—those, I mean, who laid claim to righteousness while presuming on their own resources—tripped over the stumbling-block.[21] The Lamb looked like a goat to them, and because they killed him as a goat they lost their chance of being redeemed by the Lamb. These were the "strong" who made their onslaught against Christ, vaunting their righteousness.

---

17. This paragraph is ostensibly directed against the Jews, but the Pelagians may be in Augustine's sights also.
18. See Mt 19:24.
19. *Non sanitatis est, sed insaniae.*
20. See Jn 14:6.
21. See Rom 9:32.

Listen now to these strong people. Certain citizens of Jerusalem were dispatched by them to seize Christ, but they dared not do so; he who was genuinely strong would be seized only when he chose to be. So the authorities asked them, *Why were you unable to arrest him? They replied, "No one ever spoke as he did."* But these strong men demanded, *Has anyone from the Pharisees believed in him, or any of the scribes? Anyone at all, apart from this rabble that is ignorant of the law?* (Jn 7:45-46, 48-49). They thought themselves superior to the crowd of weaklings running after the doctor; and on what grounds? Because they were strong themselves, and, what was worse, they even won the crowd over to their own way of thinking, and killed the man who would have been the healer of them all. Nonetheless from his death itself he compounded a medicine for the sick out of his blood. *The strong pounced upon me.*

Be wary above all of strong people of this type. If human beings cannot presume on their own righteousness, ask yourselves whether they have a leg to stand on. If a person who has relied on righteousness itself, as something of his own, falls so low, think where others must lie who take their stand on riches, or bodily vigor, or noble birth, or worldly dignity. *The strong pounced upon me.* We know someone else who belonged to the company of these "strong" people: the man who boasted of his prowess, *O God, I thank you that I am not like other people: frauds, cheats, adulterers; or like that tax collector there. I fast twice a week, and give tithes from everything I own.* Just listen to that strong man vaunting his powers! Then observe the weak man standing far off, yet drawing near to God by his humility: *the tax collector stood a long way off, and dared not even raise his eyes to heaven, but beat his breast, saying, Lord, be merciful to me, a sinner. Truly I tell you, that tax collector went down to his house at rights with God, rather than the Pharisee.* Now see wherein righteousness lies: *for anyone who exalts himself will be humbled, but the one who humbles himself will be exalted* (Lk 18:11-14).

The strong who pounced upon him were the proud who, knowing nothing of God's righteousness and wishing to set up a righteousness of their own, would not submit to the righteousness of God.[22]

Verses 5-6. The so-called strong persecute the sinless Christ

8. How does he continue? *No iniquity, no sin of mine, Lord.* "The strong, confident in their own righteousness, have pounced upon me; yes, they have attacked indeed, but have found no sin in me." Clearly it was only under the guise of righteousness that these people could have persecuted Christ by making him out to be a sinner. But let them see that their strength derives from their

---

22. See Rom 10:3.

raging fever, not from robust health; let them see how strong they are, who under pretense of righteousness loosed their savagery against one they represented as a sinner. *No iniquity, no sin of mine, Lord. I ran without iniquity, and steered a straight course.* That was why those strong people could not follow me, and why they thought me a sinner: because they could not see my footprints.

9. *I ran without iniquity, and steered a straight course; rise up and come to meet me, and see.* It is to God that he says, *I ran without iniquity, and steered a straight course; rise up and come to meet me, and see.* This is puzzling, isn't it? Surely he does not mean that God cannot see unless he comes to meet him? It would be as though you were walking along a road, and could not be seen by someone else because the other person was too far away; and you shouted to that other person, "Come and meet me, and see how I am walking, because when you look at me from such a distance you cannot watch my steps." Is he implying that God likewise needed to come and meet him in order to check that he was steering his straight course without any iniquity, and running without sin? Probably not; the words, *rise up and come to meet me,* could equally well be taken to mean, "Help me." He added, *and see*; and this must mean, "Make it to be seen that I am running, cause it to be seen that I steer a straight course." It is the same idiom that was used when God said to Abraham, *Now I know that you fear God* (Gn 22:12). If God says, *Now I know,* what else can he mean but "Now I have caused you to know"? Before temptation comes to search us, we do not know ourselves. Peter was ignorant about himself when he made his presumptuous declaration, and in his denial he learned what kind of strength he had. From his wavering he came to understand that his estimate of himself had been wide of the mark; he wept,[23] and by his tears he deserved to know what he had been, and to become what he had not been.[24] It was the same with Abraham: through being put to the test he was made known to himself, and he heard God's word to him, *Now I know*; that is, "Now I have caused you to know." We use the same figure of speech ourselves when we speak of "a happy day," meaning a day that makes us happy; or we call some event, "a sorry business," because we are made sorrowful by experiencing it.[25] Similarly we speak of God seeing something when we mean that he makes us see it. So the psalmist begs him, *Rise up and come to meet me, and see.* What does *and see* suggest? "Help me," he means. Help me in the matter of those who attack me, that they may truly see the course I run, and follow me. Let what is straight not seem to them crooked, let them not regard as twisted what holds to

---

23. See Mt 26:35.69-75.
24. This could simply mean "become strong, which he had not been earlier." But it could also be an allusion to Jn 21:15-17, where Peter's triple denial is atoned for by a triple declaration of love, as Augustine points out in his *Homilies on the Gospel of John*, CXXIII, 5. Thus Peter became "what he had not been" when designated shepherd of the whole flock.
25. A free translation. What Augustine actually says is that "we call bitterness (or a bitter drink) sad because it makes us sad." But in English we do not, so an equivalent is offered.

the rule of truth. *For I ran without iniquity, and steered a straight course; rise up and come to meet me, and see.*

The image of the mother-hen; Christ's dignity and weakness

10. I am prompted by the sublime dignity of our head to say something further here. He became weak even to the point of dying; he assumed our weak flesh in order to gather the chicks of Jerusalem under his wings, like a hen that is weakened with her babies. We have never seen this phenomenon in any other bird, not even in those species which nest before our eyes, like the house sparrows, or the swallows which are our annual visitors, or the storks, or various other species of birds which build their nests in full view, and sit on their eggs, and feed their young, or even the pigeons that we see every day. We are unaware of any other bird that becomes so weak with its young; we have watched no others, seen no others, like this. How does the hen reduce herself to weakness? What I am talking about is a familiar sight, something that takes place daily as we watch. We know how her voice becomes hoarse, how she makes her whole body a fluffy muddle. Her wings droop, the feathers are relaxed, and she looks almost ill over her chicks. This is maternal love, expressing itself as weakness. For what other reason did our Lord liken himself to a hen in scripture? *Jerusalem, Jerusalem, how often I wanted to gather your children to myself, as a hen gathers her chicks under her wings, but you would have none of it!* (Mt 23:37). But the Gentiles he did gather, as a hen her chicks, he who became weak for our sake by taking flesh from our race, and being crucified, despised, slapped, scourged, hung on the tree and wounded with a lance. All this is the mark of a mother's weakness, not of lost majesty. This was the state to which Christ was reduced, and this is why he was despised, why he became a stone to trip people and a rock to stumble over, and why many did trip over him.[26] Because he was so weakened, and yet had assumed flesh without sin, we confess that he participated in our weakness, but not in our iniquity, to the end that by sharing weakness with us he might destroy our iniquity.

Accordingly he proclaims, *I ran without iniquity, and steered a straight course.* Does it mean that he is not to be acknowledged in his godhead? Is he to be considered only in respect of what he was made into for us, and not in respect of the power by which he made us? By no means. His divinity is certainly to be considered. It is essential to loving reverence on your part to know who suffered for you, as well as what he suffered. It is not as though some unimportant little person did all that for you, who are so high and mighty. No, he who is most high did it for you who are weak. And did what? He became little, for *he humbled*

---

26. See Rom 9:32; 1 Pt 2:8.

himself, and was made obedient to the point of death. And who is this, who
humbled himself? Listen to the rest: *being in the form of God he deemed it no
robbery to be God's equal.* Yet, equal to God though he was, *he emptied himself
and took on the form of a slave, bearing the human likeness, sharing the human
lot* (Phil 2:6-8). He emptied himself in such a way that he assumed a nature that
had not been his before, but he did not lose what he had always been. In what
sense, then, did he empty himself? By appearing to you in that humble guise, by
not revealing to you the dignity he had with the Father, by offering to you now
only his weakness, and reserving the sight of his glory for you later, when you
are purified.

He who is equal to the Father reduced himself to this, yet even in such weakness he is to be recognized, not in vision but by faith. What we cannot yet see, we
must at least believe in, in the hope that by believing what we do not see, we may
deserve to see it. With good reason did the risen Christ say to Mary Magdalene,
to whom he graciously appeared before all others, *Do not cling to me; I have not
yet ascended to the Father* (Jn 20:17). But why did he say that? Shortly afterward
other women clung to him, for he met them as they came away from the tomb,
and they worshiped him, clasping his feet.[27] The disciples even handled his
scars.[28] What can his command mean, then, *Do not cling to me; I have not yet
ascended to the Father*? What else but this: "Do not think that what you see is all
there is of me, or your eyes will be as restricted as your sense of touch. I appear
lowly to you, for *I have not yet ascended to the Father*; but when I descended to
you I did not leave him. Nor have I ascended to him in such a way as to abandon
you." He came down without forsaking the Father, and he ascended without
forsaking us.

But what does he mean, that he ascended to the Father? He ascends when he
makes himself known to us as the Father's equal. We ascend by making progress
until we have the capacity to see this, to understand it, in some degree to take it
in. This is why he deferred tactile contact, but did not forbid it, or fend it off, or
refuse it. *I have not yet ascended to the Father*, he said.

From highest heaven he sets out, says another psalm, *and reaches even to
heaven's height as he returns* (Ps 18:7(19:6)). *Highest heaven* signifies that the
Father is the most sublime reality among all spiritual beings. That is his point of
departure. His return journey is to heaven's height. Only of one who is God's
equal can it be said that he reaches that uttermost point. Think how it is when we
compare two things of unequal length. We lay them side by side, the short one
beside the long, to see how they match; and if we find them unequal, we usually
say something like, "It doesn't reach"; or if they are equal, we say, "Yes, it

---

27. See Mt 28:9.
28. See Lk 24:39; Jn 20:27.

reaches to the end."[29] We can therefore say of the Son, *He reaches even to heaven's height*, because he is equal to the Father.

This is how he wanted to become known to those who believe in him, and this is why he said, *Do not cling to me.* In saying with the psalm, *Rise up and come to meet me*, he was asking for this grace to be granted by the Father to his faithful ones: "Make them realize that I am equal to you." But why *and see*? What does *and see* mean? "Make them see that I am equal to you. How long is Philip to go on saying to me, *Show us the Father, and that is enough for us*? How long am I to go on replying to him, *Have I been all this time with you, and yet you have not known the Father? Whoever has seen me, Philip, has seen*[30] *the Father. Do you not believe that I am in the Father, and that the Father is in me?* (Jn 14:8-11). And perhaps he still does not believe me to be your equal. *Rise up and come to meet me, and see.* Make me be seen, make yourself seen, make men and women know our equality. Do not let the Jews think they have crucified a mere human being." There would of course have been in him no possibility of crucifixion, if he had not been human, but all the same they did not truly know the man they crucified. If they had, they would never have crucified the Lord of glory.[31] "May those who believe in me come to know me as the Lord of glory. *Rise up and come to meet me, and see.*"

The Church of all nations

11. *And do you, Lord God of hosts, God of Israel, ...* God of Israel you are, but you are thought to be God of Israel alone. You are thought to be the God only of the one nation that worships you, while all the Gentiles worship their idols. *Do you, God of Israel, set yourself to visit all nations.* Let that prophecy be fulfilled in which Isaiah addresses your Church in your name. To your Church he speaks, to your holy city, to that barren woman whose children are multiplying: *Many are the children of the forsaken one, more than of her who has a husband.* And to her the summons is sent, *Rejoice, you barren woman, you who are childless, break out and cry aloud, you who bear no children; for many are the children of the forsaken one, more than of her who has a husband*, more than those of the Jewish race which has a husband and was given the law. Your children outnumber those of the nation that had a king it could see. Your king is hidden, and by that invisible bridegroom you bear many children. To the Church are the words addressed, *Many are the children of the forsaken one, more than of her*

---

29. Augustine is playing with the words *occurro, occursus*, which he found in his Latin version of both the present psalm and Psalm 18(19). The root meaning is "meet, come to meet, confront, reach, be in the path of."
30. Variant: "sees" in both clauses.
31. See 1 Cor 2:8.

who has a husband; and the prophet continues, *Widen your encampment and stretch out your tent;*[32] *do not hold back. Lengthen your guy-ropes and drive your pegs in firmly; spread further and further, to right and to left.* Hold the good people at your right, hold the bad at your left, until the winnowing fork comes into play.[33] But claim all the Gentiles as your possession. Let both good and bad be invited to the wedding, and the wedding feast be filled with guests,[34] for the servants' job is to invite people, the Lord's prerogative to sort them out. *Spread further and further, to right and to left. Your descendants will inherit the nations, and will people deserted cities* — deserted they have been by God, deserted by the prophets, deserted by the apostles and deserted by the gospel, but they are populated by demons. *Your descendants will people the deserted cities. You have nothing to fear, for you will prevail; you need feel no shame that you were once abhorred.* So although you are forced to say, *The strong pounced upon me*, you need not be ashamed. Though in former days the Christian name was outlawed, and it was a stigma and a disgrace to be a Christian,[35] *you need feel no shame that you were once abhorred, for you will forget your confusion for ever, and no longer be mindful of the stigma of your widowhood. For I am the Lord, and I create you. The Lord is his name, and he who has rescued you will be called the Lord God of Israel and the God of all the earth* (Is 54:1-5). *Do you, Lord God of hosts, God of Israel, set yourself to visit all nations.* This I pray, *set yourself to visit all nations.*

Justice and mercy; sin must be punished

12. *Show no mercy to any who deal unjustly.* This certainly strikes fear into us. Who would not be frightened by it? Is there anyone who does not tremble on looking into his or her own conscience? Your conscience may know itself as devout, but it would be amazing if you were not conscious of unjust dealing as well, for everyone who sins deals unjustly,[36] and if you, Lord, keep a record of our iniquities, who, Lord, will withstand it?[37]

Yet God did show mercy to Paul, who earlier as Saul was dealing unjustly, for what good had Paul done to deserve God? Was he not hounding God's saints to their deaths? Was he not provided with letters from the chief priests, authorizing him to arrest and punish Christians wherever he might find them? Was it not while engaged in such business, on his way to seize them, breathing and panting

---

32. *Aulas*, "courts." Variant: *aulaeas*, "curtains, hangings."
33. See Mt 3:12.
34. See Mt 22:9-10.
35. Compare Tertullian: *Ad Nationes* 1,7; *Apol.* 2-4.
36. See 1 Jn 3:4.
37. See Ps 129(130):3.

slaughter, that he was addressed by a noble voice from heaven, as scripture testifies? Was he not thrown down and raised up again, blinded and illuminated, killed and brought to life, ruined and restored? And how had he deserved it? It is not for us to say; let us listen to his own account: *I was originally a persecutor and a blasphemer, and acted unjustly; but I received mercy* (1 Tm 1:13).

Clearly the petition, *show no mercy to any who deal unjustly*, can be understood in two different ways. It may mean that God leaves no sins whatever unpunished; or it may mean that God shows no mercy whatever to those who are guilty of a particular type of injustice. We must briefly enlarge on these two meanings, beloved,[38] insofar as time permits.

13. According to the first interpretation, the verse means this: every violation of justice, slight or grave, must necessarily be punished, either by the repenting sinner or by an avenging God. Those who repent are punishing themselves. Let us punish our own sins, brothers and sisters, if we seek the mercy of God. God cannot show mercy to any who deal unjustly, in the sense of regarding sins with leniency or not rooting them out. So the choice is yours: either you punish them, or God does. You don't want him to punish them? Very well, punish them yourself. What you have done cannot go unpunished, but it is better that it be punished by you, better that you do what another psalm recommends: *Let us forestall him by coming into his presence confessing* (Ps 94(95):2). What does that mean—let us forestall him with our confession? Before the Lord takes notice and punishes your sin, you get in first with your confession and punish it. Don't let him find anything to punish. When you punish your unjust conduct, you restore justice.[39] And therefore God will show mercy to you, because he finds you already upholding justice. In what sense are you then behaving justly? You hate in yourself what God also hates; and so you begin to be pleasing to God, when you punish whatever in yourself is displeasing to God. He cannot leave sin unpunished; the psalm is right to say, *Show no mercy to any who deal unjustly.*

Don't try to blame God for your sins

14. Now let us examine the other possible interpretation of this plea. There is a special kind of unjust dealing which excludes the perpetrator from God's mercy. Are you wondering what it is? It is the act of defending one's sins. Anyone who defends his or her sins is committing a grave injustice by defending what is hateful to God. And look how perverse, how unjust, such an attitude is. If the sinner has done anything good, he claims the credit; if he has done anything

---

38. *Caritati vestrae.*
39. *Cum tu punis iniquitatem, facis aequitatem.* We could translate, "When you punish your law-breaking, you re-establish the rule of law."

bad, he attributes it to God. People who act like this defend their sins by holding God responsible, which makes matters worse. How can they do that? Well, certainly no one would dare to say, "Adultery is a good thing, homicide is good, fraud and perjury are good." Obviously no one will take that line, if only because people who commit these sins make such a fuss when the same treatment is handed out to them. You cannot possibly find anyone whose mind is so perverted, or who is such an outcast from human society and from our common sharing in the blood of Adam, as to maintain that adultery, fraud, robbery, perjury—all those things I mentioned—are good. How then can they defend such deeds? "If God had not willed it, I would not have done that," they say. "What do you expect me to do about it, if that is my destiny?" So you want to discover your fate, and you have recourse to the stars. But inquire who made the stars and set them in their courses: God did. So when you defend your sin like that, you are blaming God for it. The guilty party is exonerated so that the Judge may be convicted. God evidently cannot show mercy to a person who commits injustice like this. *Show no mercy to any who deal unjustly.* "Pursue them," the psalmist implies; "punish them, stab them with remorse, bring them round before their own faces, these people who try to put themselves behind themselves,[40] and make them ashamed of themselves, that they may rejoice in you. *Show no mercy to any who deal unjustly.*"

Verse 7. The hungry dogs are fed

15. *Let them be converted in the evening.* The psalm is speaking of some who formerly dealt unjustly, who were formerly darkness; and it says they are converted in the evening. What does *in the evening* suggest? Eventually. What does *in the evening* suggest? Late in the day; for they ought to have recognized their healer before they crucified Christ. Instead of that, it was only after he had been crucified, had risen again and had ascended into heaven, only after he had sent his Holy Spirit, only after all those gathered in one house had been filled with the Spirit and begun to speak in the tongues of all nations—only then were Christ's crucifiers afraid, and pierced in their consciences. Only then did they beg the apostles for salutary advice; and they were told, *Repent, and let every one of you be baptized in the name of the Lord Jesus Christ, that your sins may be forgiven* (Acts 2:38). After you have killed Christ, after you have poured out his blood, your sins are forgiven. Christ willed so to die as to redeem with his blood even those who shed it. You shed it in fury, now drink it in faith.

There is sound reason for saying, *Let them be converted in the evening, and feel hungry like dogs.* The Jews called Gentiles "dogs," as unclean creatures. Our Lord himself used the same expression. A Canaanite woman was shouting

---

40. See Jer 2:27. A favorite image with Augustine; compare *Confessions* II,3,6.

after him—a Canaanite, not a Jewess—trying to steer his mercy toward her daughter, who was in need of healing. The Lord foresaw the whole outcome and knew all he would do, but he wished to make an example of her faith, so he deferred his act of kindness and kept her in suspense. How did he do that? *I was not sent except for the lost sheep of the house of Israel*, he said. If the Israelites are sheep, what are the Gentiles? *It is not good to give the children's bread to the dogs.* He called the Gentiles dogs, signifying that they were unclean. How did this hungry woman react? She did not bridle at his reply, but humbly accepted the reproof, and thereby merited the reward. However, we should not really call our Lord's answer a reproof. If a slave said something like that to his master, it would be insulting, but when a master speaks so to slave, it should rather be called gracious condescension.[41] So she says, *Quite right, Lord.* What does she mean by *quite right?* "You are speaking the truth, the undeniable truth; a dog I am. *But even dogs eat from the crumbs that fall from their masters' tables.*" And swiftly came the Lord's reply: *O woman, great is your faith* (Mt 15:24-28). Not long since she was called a dog; now she is addressed as "woman." How was a dog so quickly transformed into a woman? By confessing humbly, and not rejecting what the Lord had said.

So the Gentiles are dogs, and like all dogs they are hungry. The Jews would do well to acknowledge that they are sinners, and *be converted*, even though it be *in the evening*, and feel hungry like dogs. The man who claimed, *I fast twice a week*, was unhealthily full. But the tax collector was a dog, and famished, so in his hunger for the goodies the Lord was going to give him he kept saying, *Be merciful to me, a sinner* (Lk 18:12-13). Let the Jews too *be converted in the evening, and feel hungry like dogs.* Let them long for the grace of God and understand that they are sinners. Let those strong folk become weak, those plutocrats become paupers, those self-styled righteous recognize that they are sinners, those lions turn into dogs. *Let them be converted in the evening, and feel hungry like dogs, and they will make their way around the city.* To what city is the psalm referring? It means this world, for in several places scripture calls the world "the city that lies around us."[42] This was the phrase used among the Jews, because the world had crowded around the Jewish nation, which therefore called it "the city that lies around us." Once the Jews have been turned into hungry dogs they will make their way around that city. How? By preaching the gospel. Saul had been a wolf,[43] but became a dog at evening, because he was converted late in the day.

---

41. An indication of the value placed on slaves. The Roman Empire numbered them in millions.
42. The LXX has "ἐ̃ῖ ̃ῖ̃τ̃ἰῳῖ at Ps 30:22; 59:11; 107:11, which in Augustine's Latin becomes *civitas circumstantiae.* Compare his comments on the phrase in Exposition 4 of Psalm 30, 9.
43. King Saul, and his New Testament namesake Saul-Paul, were of the tribe of Benjamin, called a "raging wolf" in Gn 49:27.

He ate from his Lord's crumbs, and then by the grace of the same Lord he ran his course, making his way around the city.

Verses 8-9. Impatient preachers

16. *Lo, they will speak with their mouths, and on their lips will be a sword.* This is the two-edged sword to which the apostle refers: *the sword of the Spirit, which is the word of God* (Eph 6:17). Why two-edged? Why else, but because it smites from both Testaments? This was the sword to be used for slaying those animals about which the command was issued to Peter: *Slaughter and eat* (Acts 10:13). *On their lips will be a sword; but who hears us?* That is what their mouths will be saying: *Who hears us?* This is their exasperated cry about people who are slow to believe. Not long ago they were themselves refusing to believe, but now they are impatient over unbelievers. Yes, brothers and sisters, it still does happen like that. You find someone very sluggish before becoming a Christian; every day you implore him, but he is converted only with great difficulty. Let him be once converted, though, and here he is wanting everyone else to turn Christian, and amazed because not all have yet done so. It has slipped his mind that it was only in the evening that he was converted himself; but now that he has grown hungry like a dog, he also has a sword on his lips, and he demands, *Who hears us?* What is implied by *Who hears us?* A prophet lamented, *Who has believed our report, and to whom has the arm of the Lord been revealed?* (Is 53:1). *Who hears us?* The Jews do not believe, so the preachers have turned to the Gentiles with the good news. Most Jews did not believe in earlier days either, yet through those Jews who did believe, the gospel made its way around the city. But still its preachers complained, *Who hears us?*

17. *And you, Lord, will laugh at them.* You were asking, *Who hears us?* All nations will be Christians one day, yet you ask, *Who hears us?* And why does the psalmist say to God, *You will laugh at them*? Because, as he goes on to say, *You will make light of all the nations*, they will seem to you of no importance, so very easy will it be for you to bring all nations to believe in you.

Verse 10. God, our support

18. *I will guard my strength as yours.* Those strong people I spoke about came to grief because they did not guard their strength as yours; they rushed upon me with full force, but put their reliance on themselves. Not I, though; *I will guard my strength as yours*; for if I withdraw from you, I fall, but if I come near to you, I grow stronger. Consider how it is with the human soul, brothers and sisters. It has no light of its own, no power of its own. The only beauty the soul has consists of power and wisdom, but it is not wise of itself, nor strong of itself, nor is it the

source of its own light, or its own power. There is another source and wellspring of strength, there is a root of wisdom; there is a country of immutable truth, if I may so express it. When the soul departs from that country it is darkened, but it is illuminated as it approaches. *Draw near to him and receive his light* (Ps 33:6(34:5)), for by moving away you are darkened. *I will guard my strength as yours,* then; I will not leave you, nor will I rely on myself. *I will guard my strength as yours, because you are my support,*[44] *O God.* Where was I, and where am I now? From what depth did you take me up? For what sins did you forgive me? Where was I lying prostrate, and how did you make me stand tall? I ought to remember all this, for in another psalm it is said, *My father and mother have abandoned me, but the Lord has taken me up* (Ps 26(27):10). So *I will guard my strength as yours, because you are my support, O God.*

Verse 11. Prevenient mercy

19. *He is my God, because his mercy will forestall me.* This is a clarification of what the psalmist has just said, *I will guard my strength as yours,* for I will place no reliance whatever on myself. What good did I contribute, that you should have mercy on me and justify me? What did you find in me? Only sins. The only thing in me that belonged to you was the nature you created; all the rest was evildoing of my own, which you blotted out. I did not take the initiative by standing up to meet you; you came to me to arouse me. *His mercy will forestall me.* Before ever I do anything good, *his mercy will forestall me.* What has the miserable Pelagius to say to this?

Verse 12. Vessels of wrath, vessels of mercy

20. *My God has given me proof of it, by his dealings with my enemies.* What is the psalmist telling us here? "God's treatment of my enemies has shown me how great his mercy has been in my own case." Let the one who was gathered up compare himself or herself with those who were left behind, the one chosen with those who were rejected. Let the vessel of mercy compare itself with the vessels of wrath, and reflect that from the same lump of clay God made *one vessel for honorable use, and another for lowly purposes.* What is the implication of the psalmist's words, *God has given me proof of it, by his dealings with my enemies*? The apostle tells us, *God willed to show his anger, and give proof of his power, by producing*[45] *with the utmost patience vessels of wrath, made for destruction.*

---

44. Or "you take me up," *susceptor meus es.* See a note on the overtones of the verb *suscipere* and its derivatives at Exposition of Psalm 3, 3; Exposition of Psalm 45, 11; Exposition of Psalm 83, 9.

45. *Adtulit,* in Augustine's Latin version. The Greek, followed by the Vulgate, has the sense, "tolerating."

But why? Only to *make his riches known toward the vessels of his mercy* (Rom 9:21-23). If, then, he produced vessels of wrath in order to demonstrate by means of them his riches towards the vessels of mercy, it is supremely right to say, *His mercy will forestall me; my God has given me proof of it, by his dealings with my enemies.* This means, by his dealings with others to whom he did not show mercy, he has demonstrated to me how great his mercy has been toward me. If a debtor did not hang, another whose debt had been forgiven would be less grateful.[46] *My God has given me proof of it by his dealings with my enemies.*

The non-assimilation of the Jewish people

21. But now, what about those enemies? *Do not kill them, let them never forget your law.* He is praying for his enemies, and so fulfilling the commandment.[47] What is the meaning of that earlier prayer, *Show no mercy to any who deal unjustly,* in the face of this fresh one, *Do not kill them, let them never forget your law*? In what sense does God withhold mercy from all who deal unjustly, and in what sense does he at the same time hold back from killing them, lest they forget his law?

Clearly the psalmist said this with reference to his enemies. What is implied? Do his enemies deal justly? Hardly: if those who are hostile to him deal justly, it must mean that the speaker himself deals unjustly. But no, he deals justly, and obviously he and anyone else who deals justly will promptly have to endure injustice from those at odds with him. So we must conclude that those who are at enmity with a just person deal unjustly. How is it, then, that he could say a little while earlier, *Show no mercy to any who deal unjustly,* yet now say of his enemies (unjust, as we have seen), *Do not kill them, let them never forget your law*? Perhaps the former petition means, "Withhold pity from them, so that you may kill their sins," and the second plea, "Do not kill those people whose sins you kill." What is it, to be killed? It is to forget the law of the Lord. That is true death, that is to sink into the depths of sin. This can be understood in connection with the Jews. How does this prayer apply to them: *Do not kill them, let them never forget your law*? Do not slay those enemies of mine who slew me. Let the Jewish race survive. It has been conquered by the Romans, to be sure; its city has been destroyed, certainly; the Jews are debarred from their own city, yes; but there are still Jews. So many provinces have been subjugated by the Romans, and who can tell any longer which nation is which, now that they are all within the Roman Empire? They have all become Romans, and all are called Romans. Yet the Jews remain distinct, marked with their sign; they have not been so

---

46. Or "if a debtor were not kept in suspense, he would be less grateful to the one through whom his debt had been remitted."

47. See Mt 5:44.

conquered as to be absorbed by their conquerors. It was on Cain, and, significantly, after he had slain his brother, that God put a mark, to prevent anyone killing him.[48] This is the sign that the Jews bear today. They preserve tenaciously the remnants of their law; they practice circumcision, observe the Sabbath, slaughter the paschal lamb, and eat unleavened bread. The Jews abide; they have not been killed, for they are necessary to Gentile believers. Why? So that God may give us proof of his mercy by his dealings with our enemies. *My God has given me proof of it by his dealings with my enemies.* In the branches lopped off for their pride he has demonstrated his mercy to the wild olive engrafted in their place.[49] Look where they lie, those who were so proud, and look where you, who used to lie there, have now been grafted in. Do not be proud, lest you deserve to be lopped off. *O my God, do not kill them, let them never forget your law.*

Verses 12-14. A hasty conclusion

22. *Scatter them by your power.* This has already happened: the Jews have been scattered among all nations, witnesses to their own iniquity and our truth. They hold the books in which Christ was foretold, and we hold Christ. Now it sometimes happens that some pagan is skeptical when we recount to him the prophecies about Christ; he is dumbfounded by the evidence they provide, and so great is his amazement that he thinks we must have forged them. Then it is from the books belonging to the Jews that we prove that these things were foretold long ago. So you see, we confute our enemies by means of other enemies. *Scatter them by your power:* take their power away from them, rob them of their strength. *And lead them, O Lord, my protector. The sins of their mouths, the utterance of their lips; and let them be caught in their pride. And their consummations will be announced as a result of their cursing and lies, in the anger of consummation, and they will be no more.* These verses are obscure, and I am not sure I can explain them properly. You are already tired out by listening, so if you do not mind, beloved,[50] we will postpone the rest until tomorrow. The Lord will help us to discharge our debt to you, because it is in his name rather than our own that we make you this promise.

---

48. See Gn 4:15.
49. See Rom 11:17-21.
50. *Caritati vestrae.*

Exposition 2 of Psalm 58

The Second Sermon

Verse 10. Our hearts must be productive

1. Yesterday's sermon went on for rather a long time, yet still left me in your debt for today. But since the Lord has willed it so, the time has come to discharge the debt. You must be as eager to demand your rights as we are assiduous in paying what we owe. What I mean is that whatever the Lord grants and we pass on to you (for he is the Lord, we only servants), you must receive in such a way that your listening bears fruit in your lives. If a field has been cultivated but bears no crop, or is so ungrateful as to yield the farmer only thorns instead of the anticipated harvest, its produce is fit for the fire, not the barn.

However, just as you are used to seeing the Lord our God visit our earth with his regular rains, so too does he graciously visit our hearts with his word, cultivating them as his field. And so he looks for our hearts to produce crops, for he knows what he has sown there, and how much rain he has sent. Without him we are nothing, for before we came into existence we were nothing at all, and once we do exist, any one of us who wants to exist independently of him is nothing but a sinner. Moreover the verse in our psalm which declares, *I will guard my strength as yours,* points us toward a further truth: whatever we achieve we lose, unless we guard it as the Lord's, for otherwise we shall be moving away from him. If we have been far away, we must try to draw closer and closer, advancing toward him not on foot, nor by traveling in some vehicle, nor on swift steeds, nor by taking wings, but by the purity of our desires and the probity[1] of our holy conduct.

Verses 11-14. The Jews have preserved their identity

2. Now let us look at what is left of this psalm. We broke off at the point where the psalmist had begun to speak to God about his enemies, praying, *Do not kill them, let them never forget your law.* Even though he had called them enemies, he begged God that they should not be killed and forget his law. Now it is not to be thought that simply to hold onto the law in one's mind, and not forget it, is already perfection, or a sure title to reward, or that it gives us the right to be care-

---

1. Variant: "acceptability."

free about possible punishment. Not at all, for there are some people who retain the law in their memories but do not fulfill it in their lives, whereas those who carry it out in their lives cannot possibly let it slip out of their memories. If any man or woman puts God's commandments into practice, and by habitually living in the light of them acts on what the heart retains, such a person by his life-style is constantly reminding himself of the law that has been written into our hearts by God. He or she is constantly working to ensure that it is not erased, and keeps God's law faithfully. Such a person will not be reckoned an enemy.

How does this apply to the Jews? They seem to be the enemies whom the psalm has in view. They hold to God's law, certainly, and that is why the psalm prays concerning them, *Do not kill them, let them never forget your law*. The psalmist prayed that the Jewish nation might survive, and that through its survival the multitude of Christians might increase. And undoubtedly they do survive throughout all nations; they are still Jews, and have not lost their iden-tity. That people has not made such concessions to the code of the Romans as to lose its Jewish character. It is subject to the Romans, but in such a way as to hold onto its own laws, which are the laws of God. But what has happened among them? The Lord makes pointed accusations: *You tithe mint and cumin, but you have neglected the weightier matters of the law—mercy and justice. You strain out a gnat and gulp down a camel* (Mt 23:23.24). Truly this is how things are with them. They retain the law, they retain the prophets. They read it all, they chant it all; but they fail to see him who is the light of the prophets, Christ Jesus. Not only do they fail to see him now, enthroned in heaven, but they failed to see him when he was walking humbly among them, and they incurred guilt by shed-ding his blood—but not all of them. This is what I want to emphasize to you today, beloved ones:[2] not all of them were guilty. Many Jews were converted to the one they had killed, and by believing in him they earned pardon from the very blood that had been shed. They provided an example for all men and women, who learn thereby not to doubt that all sins can be forgiven them, since those who confessed were forgiven even for the sin of murdering Christ.[3]

Providential mercy for Gentile and Jew alike

You are my support, O God. He is my God, because his mercy will forestall me. His mercy has taken the initiative, forestalling any good merits of mine. If he finds nothing good in me, he himself makes me good; he justifies the one who has turned back to him, as he also calls to conversion the one who is still turned away. *My God has given me proof of this by his dealings with my enemies*, he

---

2. *Caritati vestrae.*

3. This is the main theme of the present sermon: God used the most heinous of crimes to bring its perpetrators to humble confession and openness to his mercy.

continues. He has demonstrated to me how much he loves me, and how generously he lavishes on me his goodness, by the contrasting fortunes of my
enemies; for since the vessels of wrath and the vessels of mercy are made from
the same lump of clay,[4] the vessels of mercy can learn how bountiful God has
been with his goodness in their regard, by comparing their lot with that of the
vessels of wrath.

But the psalm begs, *Do not kill them, let them never forget your law*, and this
refers to the Jews. What will you do with them, then? *Scatter them by your
power*. Show them how strong you are, unlike those who, presuming on their
own power, failed to acknowledge your truth. Your power is not like that of the
strong enemies, of whom the psalmist complained, *The strong pounced upon
me*; your power is effective to scatter them. *And lead them, O Lord, my
protector*; this means, "Yes, scatter them, but do not abandon them, *lest they
ever forget your law*. And by that same providence protect me too, so that in their
dispersion I may have a proof of your mercy."

*Some obscure lines: pride and malice were frustrated by Christ's
resurrection*

3. The next words are, *the sins of their mouths, the utterance of their lips*.
What is this phrase connected to, where does it belong? The text just says, *The
sins of their mouths, the utterance of their lips*, but gives us no indication of what
these phrases should be linked with. *The sins of their mouths, the utterance of
their lips; and let them be caught in their pride. And their consummations will be
announced as a result of their cursing and lies, in the anger of consummation,
and they will be no more*. We observed yesterday that all this is obscure, which is
why we deferred the explanation until your minds were fresh. So now, since you
cannot claim that you are already tired out with listening, lift up your hearts and
prepare to help me with your attention; otherwise our discourse may not succeed
in making clear to you what is, after all, an obscure and puzzling passage. Moreover you must contribute something yourselves, to supplement from your own
intelligence the shortcomings of my explanation. Now the phrase we are
discussing stands all by itself in the middle, so it is difficult to see where we
should attach it: *the sins of their mouths, the utterance of their lips*. We had better
go back to an earlier line: *Do not kill them, let them never forget your law*. He
said this — *do not kill them, let them never forget your law* — about people
whom he had called his enemies; so he added two further petitions: *Scatter them
by your power, and lead them, O Lord, my protector*. And then he immediately
added, *The sins of their mouths, the utterance of their lips*. He must have meant,

---

4. See Rom 9:21.

"Kill that utterance, but don't kill them." *Do not kill them, let them never forget your law*, but there is something in them that you must kill in order to answer the prayer made earlier in the psalm: *Show no mercy to any who deal unjustly.* So *scatter them*, but also *lead them*; do not abandon them when you scatter them, because if you do not forsake them altogether there is something you can do in them, as long as they are not killed off. What are you going to kill? *The sins of their mouths, the utterance of their lips.* What will you kill in them? Kill that shout of theirs, *Crucify him! Crucify him!* but not the people who shouted. They sought to get rid of Christ, to destroy him, to make away with him; but you, by raising up the Christ they wanted to destroy, kill *the sins of their mouths, the utterance of their lips.* Indeed this is what has happened. They are terrified to find that the man for whose death they clamored is alive; and they are taken aback to see that he whom they despised on earth is worshiped in heaven by all nations. And so the sins of their mouths and the utterance of their lips are put to death.

4. *And let them be caught in their pride.* What does that suggest — *let them be caught in their pride*? It means that their assaults came to nothing. The Lord appeared to yield to them, so that in their own eyes they seemed to have gained their ends, and defeated him. They were able to crucify a man; weakness was able to triumph and power to be killed. So they seemed to themselves to be something, like strong people, powerful people, conquerors; like the lion poised to spring on its prey, like fat bulls, as scripture has it in another text: *fat bulls besieged me* (Ps 21:13(22:12)). But what did they achieve against Christ? They did not slay life; all they slew was death. Death was snuffed out in him as he died, and life rises from the dead in him as he lives [5] (for he raised himself by his own power, for there was also in him something incapable of dying). What, then, did they achieve? Listen to scripture's answer. They destroyed the temple. But what did Christ do? Within three days he raised it up.[6] By this means the words of their mouths and the utterance of their lips were put to death.

But what happened to those who were converted? *Let them be caught in their pride.* They were informed that he had risen, this man they had killed. They believed him to be risen, because they beheld him raised up to heaven, and realized that from there he had sent the Holy Spirit to fill those who believed in him. So they came to see that their condemnation of him, and all their efforts, had come to nothing. Their action was nullified, but their sin remained real. They had been caught in their pride, since their sentence had been shown up as invalid, yet the sin still lay upon those who had passed it; and so they saw themselves burdened by their iniquity. One course remained open to them: to confess their

---

5. Three good codices have "by him who is alive," apparently reinforcing the point made in the parentheses that follow.
6. See Jn 2:19.

sin that he might pardon them, he who had surrendered himself into their sinful hands. Slain by dead men, he would give life to the dead, and thus he would forgive them his death. They were caught in their pride.

The obscure lines, continued: pride is the most dangerous obstacle

5. *Their consummations will be announced as a result of their cursing and lies, in the anger of consummation, and they will be no more.* We have a difficulty here too in deciding where to attach the words, *they will be no more.* What will they *be no more*? Let us begin from the line we have just considered: when they have been caught in their pride, *their consummations will be announced, as a result of their cursing and lies.* What are "consummations"? Perfections; because to be consummated is to be made perfect. To be consummated is not the same as to be consumed. A thing which is brought to an end in the sense of being made perfect is said to be consummated, but a thing that comes to an end in the sense that it no longer exists is said to be consumed. Now pride was the block that stopped men and women becoming perfect; nothing is so great an obstacle to perfection.

You must pay careful attention for a little while to what I am saying, beloved.[7] Think about a very dangerous evil, one you must avoid at all costs. How serious do you really think it is? How long must I go on hammering home this message about the evil of pride? The devil earned his punishment by this alone. To be sure, he is the lord of all sins;[8] certainly it is he who seduces us into all the sins we commit. But he is not accused of adultery, or drunkenness, or fornication, or seizing anyone's property; he fell by pride alone. However, pride has a companion. Its name is envy, and so every proud person is of necessity envious too. By reason of this vice, which inevitably follows pride, the one who had fallen envied the one who still stood, and set himself to seduce men and women, for he feared they might otherwise be exalted to the status from which he had been thrown down. That is why he takes care to entice us to real sins, for we have a judge in whose court the devil cannot make groundless accusations. If our case were to be heard by a mere human judge, one who could be deceived by false allegations, the devil would not bother to tempt us to sin, because he would be able to wrong the innocent simply by deceiving the judge, and drag those unfortunate victims over to his own side, where they would share his condemnation. But in fact he knows that we have the kind of judge who cannot be hoodwinked, and is too just to be biased. The devil therefore makes a point of haling before him persons who are so guilty that the judge, being just, has no option but to

---

7. *Caritas vestra.*
8. Or "of all sinners."

condemn them. Out of envy he exerts himself to induce us to sin, because envy is the necessary concomitant to pride.

Pride, then, is the evil thing that stands in the way of our perfection. People may boast of their riches, and boast of their beauty or their bodily strength, but all these assets are mortal, and it is ridiculous to boast of mortal advantages. Even during their lifetime people are often forsaken by such things, and at any rate must forsake them when they die. Pride is the fountainhead of vices. When a person has begun to make progress, he or she is tempted by pride, and so may lose all that has been gained. When we are doing wrong, we are in danger of falling into all the other vices, but it is when we are acting rightly that we have most to fear from pride. It is hardly surprising that the apostle was so humble that he confessed, *When I am weak, then I am strong.* What sort of medicine did he tell us had been prescribed for him by the doctor who knew his patient's need? What remedy had the doctor applied to the swelling, to keep the apostle from being tempted to this vice? *To make sure that I would not grow conceited over these great revelations*, he tells us, *a sting of the flesh was sent to me, a messenger of Satan to buffet me. Three times I begged the Lord to take it away from me, but he said to me, "My grace is sufficient for you, for my power finds complete scope in weakness"* (2 Cor 12:7-10). Now we can see what being consummated entails. The apostle himself, the teacher of the Gentiles, the man who became a father to believers through the gospel, was given a sting of the flesh to buffet him. Would any of us have dared to suggest this, if he had not chosen to admit it? If out of some mistaken notion of doing him honor we were to deny that Paul underwent this, we should be making him out to be a liar. But he is a truthful person, and truth he has told, so we have to believe that a messenger of Satan was assigned to him, to keep him from growing conceited over his mighty revelations. How deadly, then, is the snake of pride!

Now what happened to the people in the psalm? They were caught in their pride, because they put Christ to death, but because of the very heinousness of their sin they were all the more humbled, and through this deeper humility they deserved to be raised up. *Let them be caught in their pride. And their consummations will be announced as a result of their cursing and lies.* This must mean that they will be made all the more perfect for having been intercepted in cursing and lies. What prevented them from being made perfect was pride. But then their crime, and their confession of it, swept away their pride; through the mercy of God forgiveness blotted out their crime, and so as a result of their cursing and lies their consummation was announced. To each sinful man or woman it was said, "You have seen what you are, you have experienced what you are. You have gone astray and become blind, you have sinned and fallen, and now you recognize your weakness. Beg help from the physician, do not pretend to be healthy. Where did your delirium show itself? You killed the doctor, didn't you?

You lacked the strength to get rid of him entirely, but you did all that lay in your power: you killed him." *And their consummations will be announced, as a result of their cursing and lies.* What you did, you Jews, was to pronounce a curse, for scripture says that *accursed is anyone who is hanged upon a tree* (Dt 21:23; Gal 3:13). You crucified Christ, reckoning him accursed. Then go on, add lies to the cursing: you set guards at his tomb, and bribed them to lie.[9] But see, Christ is risen! Where is the curse of the cross you laid on him? What has become of the lies of the guards you bribed?

The essential lesson from the obscure lines: where sin abounded, grace triumphed the more

6. *Their consummations will be announced, as a result of their cursing and lies, in the anger of consummation, and they will be no more.* Whatever does this mean—*in the anger of consummation their consummations will be announced?* There is an anger that consummates, and a different anger that consumes. When God vindicates, it is always anger; but sometimes he vindicates in order to make someone perfect, while in other instances he vindicates only to condemn. How would he vindicate to perfect someone? *He whips every child whom he accepts* (Heb 12:6). And how does he vindicate with a view to condemnation? *Depart from me into the eternal fire which was prepared for the devil and his angels* (Mt 25:41): this is the anger that consumes, not the anger that consummates. But *their consummations will be announced in the anger of consummation.* This is a way of saying that the apostles will preach the good news that *where sin abounded, grace abounded all the more* (Rom 5:20), and that human weakness has contributed to the humiliation that has proved to be our medicine.

As they ponder these truths, recognizing and confessing their iniquities, *they will be no more.* What or where will they *be no more?* In their pride. Just before this the psalmist had said, *Let them be caught in their pride.* Then he added, *And their consummations will be announced, as a result of their cursing and lies, in the anger of consummation, and they will be no more*—no more in their pride, evidently, that pride in which they were caught.

7. *And they shall know that God will hold sway over Jacob, and the ends of the earth.* They considered themselves righteous before this, because the Jewish nation had received the law and kept God's commandments. Now they are made to understand that they did not really keep them, because in these very commandments of God they did not discern Christ, for blindness had fallen upon part of Israel.[10] The Jews now see that they have no right to scorn the Gentiles,

---

9. See Mt 28:12-14.
10. See Rom 11:25.

whom they used to dub dogs and sinners, for as the Jews have been found on the same footing with regard to iniquity, so too will they be on the same footing as the Gentiles in the attainment of salvation. *Not from the Jews alone were they called*, says the apostle, *but also from the Gentiles* (Rom 9:24). This is why *the stone rejected by the builders has become the headstone of the corner* (Ps 117(118):22), so that he could unite the two in himself; for a cornerstone ties two walls together. The Jews considered themselves very high and mighty, and thought the Gentiles weak people, sinners, slaves of demons and idol-worshipers; and yet iniquity was found in both. The Jews too were shown up as sinners, for Paul testified that *there is no one who does good, not even a single one* (Rom 3:12). But they have laid aside their pride now and ceased to begrudge the Gentiles salvation, because they have acknowledged their own weakness, a weakness to match that of the Gentiles. United in the cornerstone, Jews and Gentiles together have come to worship the Lord. *And they shall know that God will hold sway over Jacob, and the ends of the earth.* He will be Lord not only of the Jews, but of the ends of the earth as well, and they would not have known this if they had still been in their pride. If they still considered themselves righteous they would still be in their pride; but once they had ceased to think themselves righteous, *their consummations* were announced to them *as a result of their cursing and lies, in the anger of consummation.* They had been caught out in their pride, and in the curse they laid upon Christ by killing him as they did. But look what our Lord Jesus Christ did: he died at the hands of the Jews, and redeemed the great throng of Gentiles. His blood was poured out among the Jews, and for the Jews it availed to salvation; but it availed also for the salvation of all who would be converted. The Jews came to recognize who it was that they had put to death, and so deserved to win from him forgiveness for the terrible sin they had committed by killing him.

Verses 15-16. A sinner who is humbled makes rapid progress

8. What else does the psalm say of them? The same as it had said earlier: *Let them be converted in the evening*, converted rather late, after they have killed our Lord Jesus Christ. *Let them be converted in the evening, and feel hungry like dogs.* Like dogs, notice. Not like sheep or calves, but like dogs, like Gentiles, like sinners who used to reckon themselves righteous but have come to acknowledge their sin. Another psalm says of them, *Thereafter they made haste*, just as here the psalm speaks of *evening*. That earlier psalm said, *Their infirmities have been multiplied, but thereafter they made haste* (Ps 15:4(16:3)). Why did they *make haste thereafter*? Because *their infirmities were multiplied*; for if they had still believed themselves to be healthy they never would have made haste. So the earlier statement, *their infirmities were multiplied*, corresponds to what is said

here, *let them be caught in their pride, and their consummations will be announced, as a result of their cursing and lies, in the anger of consummation.* And again, the earlier declaration that *thereafter they made haste* is echoed here by the promise, *and they will be no more* in their pride. *They shall know that God will hold sway over Jacob, and the ends of the earth,* and *they will be converted in the evening.* So it is a good thing for a sinner to be humbled. No one is more difficult to cure than a person who thinks himself well. *And they will make their way around the city.* We explained yesterday about this city: it is "the city that lies around us" from the Jewish point of view, and therefore the city of all the nations.

9. *They will be dispersed in order to eat*; that is, to win others, who by believing will be assimilated into the body to which the preachers belong. *But if they are not satisfied, they will complain.* Their grievances were mentioned earlier, when we heard them lamenting, *Who hears us?* But, says the psalmist, *you, Lord, will laugh at them* when they complain, *Who hears us?* Why will he laugh? Because *you will make light of all the nations.* So too here: *if they are not satisfied, they will complain.*

Verse 17. In the morning the whole Church will rejoice

10. Let us finish the psalm now. Listen to the corner-Church shouting for joy as it is filled with gladness over both its walls.[11] The Jews used to be proud, but they have been humbled; the Gentiles were without hope, but they have been raised up. Let them come to the corner, let them meet there, let them run to that union, let them find there the kiss of peace. Let them come from their diversity, but in no spirit of adversity; let them come from the circumcised, and from the uncircumcised. The walls were formerly far apart, but that was before they came to the corner; let them hold fast to the corner now. And what must the Church say, this whole Church built from both walls? *I will sing of your power, and in the morning I will shout for joy over your mercy.* In the morning when all our trials will be over and done with, in the morning when the night of this world has passed away, in the morning when we tremble no more at the traps set by robbers and by the devil and his angels, in the morning when we walk no longer by the lamp of prophecy but contemplate the Word of God himself, the true Sun—then *in the morning I will shout for joy over your mercy.* With ample reason does another psalm promise, *In the morning I will stand before you, and contemplate* (Ps 5:5(3)); and rightly too did our Lord's resurrection take place at first light, to fulfill the prophecy in yet another psalm, *weeping will linger in the evening, but toward morning there will be rejoicing* (Ps 29:6(30:5)). In the evening the disci-

---

11. See Eph 2:14-22.

ples mourned over their dead Lord, Jesus Christ; but at first light they rejoiced as he rose. *In the morning I will shout for joy over your mercy.*

Verses 17-18. O God, my mercy: this says it all

11. *Because you have become my support and my refuge in my day of trouble. O my helper, I will sing psalms to you, for you, O God, are my support.* What was I without your aid? How hopelessly sick would I have remained, if you had not healed me? Where would I have lain, if you had not passed by? I was imperiled by a grievous wound, a wound that called for an omnipotent doctor. No malady is beyond the healing power of an almighty doctor, nor is there any patient whom he will not accept. You need only want to be healed, and put yourself in his hands. Even if you do not want to be cured, he addresses himself to your wound so that you can be. When you run away from him he calls you back; he almost compels the fleeing patient to return to him; he allures us. In all his treatment of us he demonstrates the truth of that earlier saying, *his mercy will forestall me.*

Think about that: he will forestall me. If you brought anything along first, if you deserved God's mercy by any prior good of your own, he did not forestall you. When can you even begin to understand that God has the initiative, unless you take to heart the apostle's words, *What have you that you did not receive? And if you did receive it, why boast as though you had not?* (1 Cor 4:7). That means the same as our verse here, *his mercy will forestall me.*

Finally the psalmist reviews all the good things we can possibly have, the good things inherent in nature, in providential dispensations, in our conversion[12] itself; the gifts of faith, hope, and charity, the gifts of honorable conduct, of righteousness and of reverence for God; and he sees it all as having no being whatever except as given by God. And so he cries out in conclusion, *My God, my mercy!* Filled as he was with these good gifts of God, what else could he call his God, except "his mercy"? And what a name this is, a name for everyone to shelter under, to escape from despair! *My God, my mercy,* he says. Why does he say, *My mercy?* If you call God "my salvation," I understand that you do so because he grants salvation; if you call him "my refuge," I understand that you mean you run to him for refuge; if you call him "my strength," I understand you to do so because he gives you strength. But why do you call him, "my mercy"? All that I am, absolutely everything that I am, comes from your mercy. Oh, so I first deserved you, did I, by invoking you? But what did I do to bring myself into existence? What did I do to confer existence on myself so that I could invoke you? If I did anything to bring about my own existence, I must have existed before I existed! But that is absurd: I was nothing whatever before I existed, and

---

12. Reading *conversione.* Variant: *conversatione,* "in the way we live our life."

so I had no merit at all in your sight that could have been rewarded by my existing. You made me exist; and did you not also make me good? You gave me existence; is it possible that someone else granted me the gift of being good?[13] If that were so; if you gave me existence, but someone else gave me goodness, that other giver who gave me goodness is better than the one who gave me existence. But obviously no one is better than you, no one is more powerful than you, no one is more generous in mercy than you. From God I received the gift of being, and from him I received the gift of being good. *My God, my mercy.*

13. It appears that he is thinking here of the goodness inherent in anything that exists, the goodness that the Creator saw in all that he had made, rather than of the gift of justification.

Exposition of Psalm 59

A Sermon to the People[1]

Verses 1-2. The title: David's victories, and their symbolism for Christians

1. This psalm has a fairly long title, but we should not be daunted by that, because the psalm itself is quite short. Let us be just as attentive as we should be if we had listened to a somewhat longer psalm. We speak in the Church of God, in Christ's name, for the benefit of those already well nourished, and for those still in need of nourishment; but what we have to say must not always be presented to you as unfamiliar material, for you are no strangers to the distinctive flavor of the scriptures, as the world is. You have heard these things often, and if you chew over them appreciatively in the mouth of your thought, never allowing them to be buried in forgetfulness in your stomach, this recollection and remembering on your part will be a great help to us. We shall not need to explain things at length, as though disentangling them for ignorant people, because we shall be able to take it for granted that you understand already. And we certainly remember that you have often heard us make this point: that you can scarcely find any other voice in the psalms than that of Christ and the Church, or of Christ alone, or of the Church alone—the Church which is ourselves, or at any rate of which we form a part. It follows that when we recognize our own voice we can hardly remain unmoved, and our joy is all the more intense as we feel ourselves to be present there.

Now King David was a single individual, but he represented more than one individual. He stood for the Church, which is made up of many and reaches to the ends of the earth. When he does prefigure one individual, he stands for the Mediator between God and humankind, the man Christ Jesus.[2] This is why certain victorious exploits of David are mentioned in this psalm, or rather in its title, deeds which he bravely performed in overcoming enemies, and reducing them to vassalage. This was when after the death of his persecutor, Saul, David publicly assumed Saul's sovereignty over Israel. David had, of course, been king even before he was hounded by Saul, but at that stage his royal status was known only to God. Later his royalty was manifested publicly, and he took over the kingship in open and solemn fashion; then it was that he defeated the enemies

---

1. Possibly preached in the winter of 412-413, at Carthage.
2. See 1 Tm 2:5.

enumerated in the title here. Thus the psalm was given the following superscription: *Unto the end, for those who will be changed into an inscribed title, into teaching, for David himself, when he burnt Mesopotamia of Syria,*[3] *and the Syrians of Zobah,*[4] *and Joab turned round and smote Edom, twelve thousand men, in the Valley of the Salt-pits.*[5] We read of these events in the Books of the Kingdoms, which tell us how all those listed here were defeated by David, namely Mesopotamia of Syria, the Syrians of Zobah, Joab,[6] and Edom. These things happened. How they happened is described there; the scriptures tell the story, and anyone who wishes may read it. However, the spirit[7] of prophecy in the titles of the psalms usually stands back a little from the straightforward narrative of events, and says something which is not to be found in the history. This is to warn us that titles of this sort are not provided to instruct us about historical episodes, but to prefigure future events. So, for instance, the title of another psalm states that David altered his behavior in the presence of Abimelech, and forsook him, and went away,[8] whereas the story in the Books of the Kingdoms has him doing this not in the presence of Abimelech, but in the presence of King Achis.[9] The same holds for the title of the present psalm, where we find something that points us toward something else. In the narrative of King David's wars and doughty deeds, by which all those enemies we have mentioned were subdued, we find no mention of his having burned anything. Yet here, in the title of the psalm, we find it emphatically stated that he burned Mesopotamia of Syria, and the Syrians of Zobah, though the history says nothing about it. We must begin, then, by discussing these events with reference to their value as signs of what was to come, and coax these obscure, shadowy allusions into the light of the Word.

2. *Unto the end*: you know what that means, for *Christ is the end of the law* (Rom 10:4). You also know who these people are who are changed. Who else can they be, than those who pass over from the old life into the new? Obviously it is not some deterioration that is meant here; that would be absurd. The title is not

---

3. Aram Naharaim, the land "between the two rivers" in Mesopotamia and northern Syria, inhabited by various Aramean groups. Haran, where Abraham had lived before his migration to Canaan, was there; see Gn 24:10.
4. More Aramean peoples, dominated by the small kingdom of Zobah in Anti-Lebanon.
5. These exploits are summarized in 2 Sm 8:3-14; 10:6ff.
6. If this is David's famous general it is surprising to find him mentioned among the enemies defeated in David's campaigns. Some older commentators therefore took Joab to be the name of some other defeated people. But could it have been a slip, either by Augustine or by a stenographer, for Moab? Moab is mentioned among the subjugated peoples in 2 Sm 8, and appears later in the psalm. Such a slip of tongue or pen would have been facilitated by the mention of Joab in the title. On the other hand, he interprets the name Joab as "the enemy" in the following section.
7. Or Spirit.
8. See Ps 33(34).
9. See 1 Sm 21:10-15.

speaking of Adam's change from righteousness to iniquity, or from comfort to toil; it is referring to the change that has come about in those to whom scripture says, *You were darkness once, but now you are light in the Lord* (Eph 5:8).

Now these people are changed *into an inscribed title*, and you know what that inscription was. A title was fixed above the Lord's cross; it ran, *This is the King of the Jews* (Lk 23:38). Those who pass over from the devil's realm into Christ's kingdom are changed into what this inscribed title indicates, and a good change it is. But they are changed *into teaching*, as the psalm goes on to state; for after saying that the psalm is *for those who will be changed into an inscribed title*, it adds, *into teaching, for David himself.* This suggests that they are changed not for their own sakes, but for the sake of David himself, and changed into teaching. Christ is not a king who will reign in a worldly way; he openly asserted that *mine is not a kingship of this world* (Jn 18:36). Let us then pass over into his teaching, if we wish to be changed into the full implications of that inscribed title. The change will not be for our own sake, but "for David himself," because they who are alive will consequently live no longer for themselves, but for him who for their sake died and rose again.[10] And when did Christ bring about this change in us? Surely when he carried through the task he had set himself: *I have come to set fire to the earth* (Lk 12:49). Obviously if Christ came to send fire into the world it was for the world's salvation and well-being, not in the sense that he will one day consign the world to fire. But in what sense will he *set fire to the earth*?

If this was what he came to do, we need to inquire next what is meant by Mesopotamia, that was set alight, and what the Syrians of Zobah may be. Let us examine the interpretations given of these names in the Hebrew tongue, which was the original language of the scriptures. Interpreters tell us that Mesopotamia signifies "an exalted vocation," and indeed we see today that the whole world has been exalted by its vocation. Syria means "sublime." But the city that was formerly sublime has been burned and humiliated. And just as the formerly exalted one has been humiliated, so too will the humiliated one be exalted. Zobah is understood to mean "old and useless." So thanks be to Christ for burning it. When old scrub is burned off, new green shoots take its place; and the new growth comes on faster, more abundantly, and more vigorously when the fire that burned off the old material has done its work first. We have no reason to be afraid of Christ's fire; it devours only grass; for all flesh is but grass, and all human glory no more than the grass' transient bloom.[11] These he has burned away with his fire.

And Joab turned round. Joab is said to mean "the enemy." The enemy was turned round. You can take that any way you like. If it was an enemy turned back

---

10. See 2 Cor 5:15.
11. See Is 40:6.

and routed, it refers to the devil; if it was an enemy converted to the faith, it means a Christian. Routed? How? From the Christian heart: as Christ declared, *Now has the ruler of this world been cast out.*[12] But what if the reference is to a Christian converted to the Lord—how is such a person an enemy turned round? Because one who was formerly an enemy has turned into a faithful disciple. *He smote Edom.* Edom is said to mean "earthly," and that earthly one needed to be smitten. Why should one who ought to be living as a heavenly citizen go on living as an earthling? Our earthly life has been slain; let us live as heavenly people. If we have borne the image of the earthly man, let us now bear the image of the man from heaven.[13] Watch the former being killed off: *Put to death your members that belong to the earth* (Col 3:5).

But when Joab smote Edom, he smote *twelve thousand men in the Valley of the Salt-pits.* Twelve thousand is a perfect number, akin to the perfect number of the twelve apostles. It was not a matter of chance that they were twelve in number, but because the word was to be sent forth throughout the world. Christ is the Word of God, and Christ is in the clouds, that is to say, in the preachers of truth. Now the world is comprised of four cardinal points. The four directions are well known to everyone, and often mentioned in scripture, which also calls them the four winds:[14] east, west, north and south. The word was sent out in these four directions, so that all should be summoned in the Trinity. But three times four makes twelve. This is why twelve thousand earthlings were smitten. The whole world was smitten, for from the whole world has come the Church, God's elect, slain as far as earthly life is concerned. But why *in the Valley of the Salt-pits*? A valley suggests lowliness, and salt-pits represent savor. Many people are brought low, but uselessly and stupidly; they are old and useless in their humiliation. A person may endure distress for the sake of money, or to win worldly honors, or to acquire the good things of this life. Such a one is going to endure distress in any case, and be brought low; so why not do it for God's sake? Why not for Christ? Why not undergo it to make sure the salt retains its flavor? You were warned, weren't you, that *you are the salt of the earth*? And that *once salt has become insipid, it is no good for anything, except to be thrown away* (Mt 5:13)? The best thing, then, is to be brought low, but to keep your saltiness.[15] Are not heretics brought low nowadays? Have not laws been passed against them even by human authorities—passed against heretics who in any case fall under divine law? Those divine laws had already condemned them, but now they are humiliated, routed, and subjected to persecution, yet all this for a life unseasoned

---

12. The Greek has *shall be cast out* at Jn 12:31, to which Augustine is clearly referring; he is perhaps conflating the text with Jn 16:33, *I have overcome the world.*
13. See 1 Cor 15:49.
14. Compare Ez 37:9.
15. *Sapienter.* The play is on the root meaning of *sapientia*, wisdom, a faculty of taste for the things of God.

by wisdom, for their insipidity, for their uselessness. The salt has lost its flavor now, and so it has been thrown out; let everyone trample on it.

We have listened to the title of the psalm; let us listen now to the text of it.

Verses 3-4. Sinners testify to anger and mercy, demolition and rebuilding

3. *O God, you have repulsed us and ruined us.* This can't be David speaking, can it, the man who smote and burned and defeated his enemies? Clearly the speakers here must be the people to whom he did all this. Those who had been bad were smitten and repulsed, but then they were given new life and they found their way back to lead a good life for the future. The David who wrought this slaughter was our strong-armed Christ,[16] whom the original David prefigured. Christ effected this slaughter with his own sword and his own fire, for he brought both into this world. You find in the gospel, *I have come to set fire to the earth,* and you also find, *I have come to bring not peace, but a sword* (Lk 12:49; Mt 10:34). He brought fire to burn up Mesopotamia of Syria and the Syrians of Zobah; and he brought a sword to smite Edom. The slaughter was wrought for the sake of those who are being changed into the inscribed title, for David himself. Let us listen to their testimony; they were struck down to salutary effect, so now that they are on their feet again, let them speak. Let them speak, for they have changed for the better, changed to match that inscription in the title, transformed into his teaching to become the property of David himself. Let them declare, *O God, you have repulsed us and ruined us; you were angry, but then you had mercy on us.* You ruined us in order to build us up; you dismantled our shoddy buildings and demolished our useless old lives, to build us up into new people, in a building job that will last for ever. We have good reason to say that *you were angry, but then you had mercy on us.* You could not have treated us mercifully without having first been angry. You tore us down in your anger, but your anger was directed against our old dilapidation; it was our old selves that you meant to demolish. But you had mercy on us with a view to making us new, for the sake of those who are being transformed into what the inscribed title implied; for if our outer nature is in process of demolition, our inner selves are being renewed from day to day.[17]

4. *You shook the earth, and threw it into confusion.* How was the earth thrown into confusion? By being made aware of its sins. "Where shall we go? Whither flee from the sword that flashes, *Repent, for the kingdom of heaven is near?*" (Mt

---

16. Augustine believed that the name David meant "strong of hand"; see, for instance, his Exposition of Psalm 17, 1.
17. See 2 Cor 4:16.

3:2). *You shook the earth, and threw it into confusion. Heal its breaches, for it quaked.* It does not deserve to be healed unless it has shuddered first, but you speak, you preach, you deliver menaces from God, you are not silent about the coming judgment, you warn us about God's commandment. You never cease from admonishing us, so if anyone who hears is not afraid, if anyone is unmoved, such a person is unworthy of healing. Others who hear are shaken, and stimulated, and beat their breasts, and pour out their tears. *Heal its breaches, for it quaked.*

Verses 5-6. The usefulness of suffering to the converted

5. So now our earthly nature has received the death-blow, our old selves have been burned away, humankind changed for the better, and light bestowed on those who had been in darkness. The next development is indicated in another part of scripture: *My son, when you enter God's service, stand fast in righteousness and reverence, and prepare your soul for trials* (Sir 2:1). Your first work is so to loathe yourself that you do battle against your sins, so that you may be changed into something better; your second task, in virtue of being changed, is to endure the tribulations and trials of this world, and to persevere through them to the end. The psalm speaks of these and reminds us about them by adding, *You have meted out harsh treatment to your people.* Notice that they are now "your people," because since David's victory they owe allegiance to him. *You have meted out harsh treatment to your people.* What was this? The persecutions which Christ's Church suffered, in which so many martyrs' blood was shed. *You have meted out harsh treatment to your people; you have made us drink a pungent wine.* Why does it speak of pungency? Because this is no fatal dose, not a draught to kill, but a medicine that smarts. *You have made us drink a pungent wine.*

6. What was the purpose of this? *You have given a sign to those who fear you, so that they may flee before your bow.* What the psalm is saying is that through temporal troubles you signaled to your own people that they must shun the anger which issues in eternal fire. The apostle Peter announces, *It is time for judgment to take place, beginning from the house of the Lord.* Peter was exhorting the martyrs to endurance, while the world would rage against them, while persecutors would spread carnage, while the blood of the faithful would be spilled on every side, while Christians would be enduring many hardships in chains, in prisons, and under torture. And lest Christians should faint under such trials, this is how he addressed them: *It is time for judgment to take place, beginning from the house of the Lord; and if it originates with us, what will be the outcome for*

those who do not believe in the gospel of God? What will become of the wicked and the sinner if the righteous will scarcely be saved? (1 Pt 4:17-18).

What will happen, then, at that future judgment? So far the bow is only threatening; it is not yet operative.[18] Now think how a bow works. The arrow is to be shot forward, isn't it? But the string is stretched backward, in the opposite direction, and the further backward the string is drawn, the greater will be the arrow's impetus forward. How does this apply to what I have been saying? The longer the judgment is deferred, the greater will be the force of its coming. We should therefore thank God for temporal troubles, because through them he has given his people a signal *to flee before his bow*. His faithful people are kept on their toes by temporal tribulations, that they may be found worthy to escape the sentence of eternal fire that will overtake all who do not believe these admonitions. *You have given a sign to those who fear you, warning them to flee before your bow.*

Verses 6-7. Prayer for salvation is always answered

7. That your beloved may be set free. Save me with your right hand, and listen to me. Save me with your right hand, Lord; so save me that I may stand at your right hand. *Save me with your right hand*: I am not asking for temporal well-being; as far as that is concerned, may your will be done. We have absolutely no idea what is good for us in this present time, for we do not know how to pray as we ought.[19] But *save me with your right hand*. In this present life I may have to undergo some troubles, but once all this night of tribulations has passed, let me be found among the sheep at your right hand, not with the goats at your left. *Save me with your right hand, and listen to me.* Now I am pleading for what you wish to grant; I am not crying out all day in those sinful words of mine that you refuse to hear, nor all night, so that you would refuse to listen to me and to collude with my foolishness.[20] If you seem not to hear, it is only as a reminder to me, only to add piquancy from the Valley of the Salt-pits, that I may learn what I ought to ask for in my trouble. But what I am begging for now is life eternal, so listen to me; I am pleading for your right hand.

You must try to understand this, beloved friends.[21] There is many a faithful person who has God's word at heart, fears the judgment to come, and lives with

---

18. *Adhuc in comminatione est, nondum in praesentatione.* Lewis and Short quote this phrase as an example of the use of the post-classical word *praesentatio*; but they wrongly assume the subject to be *iudicium*, and so make it mean "a showing," "representation," "placing before." But the subject is *arcus*, bow, and the meaning nearer to that of the adjective *praesentaneus* found in Seneca, Pliny, and Suetonius: "immediately operative" or "prompt in effect."

19. See Rom 8:26.

20. See Ps 21:2-3(22:1-2).

21. *Caritas vestra.*

integrity lest the holy name of his Lord be brought into disrepute on his account. Such a person offers many a prayer concerning this world, and the prayer goes unheard. Yet if he or she prays to attain eternal life, that prayer is heard, always. Is there anyone who, when ill, does not pray to be cured? Yet perhaps it is for his own good that he remain ill. It may happen that your prayer on this matter is not heard; but though you are not heard with respect to your wishes, you are heard with respect to your true welfare. It is quite different when you pray that God will give you eternal life, that God will give you the kingdom of heaven, that he will give you a place to stand at the right hand of his Son when he comes to judge the earth. In that case, be entirely confident. You will get what you ask. If you do not get it at once, that is because the time has not come yet. You are heard, though you do not know it; your petition is being taken care of, though you do not know where or how. The answer is present in the root, though the fruit does not show yet. *Save me with your right hand, and listen to me.*

Verse 8. Christ's burden has wings

8. *God has spoken in his holy one.*[22] Why be afraid that what God has guaranteed may not happen? Suppose you had a friend, a weighty and wise person, how could you doubt him like that? The friend has made certain assertions, and what he has said must necessarily come to pass; he is a solidly dependable man, not given to levity or easily dislodged from his opinion. If he has promised, it is as good as done. All the same, he is only human, and it may happen that he wants to carry out what he has promised, but lacks the power. You need have no fear on this score where God is concerned. That he is truthful, everyone agrees; that he is omnipotent, everyone agrees. So he cannot cheat you, and he has the means to fulfill his promise. Why fear to be deceived? You would do better to watch that you do not deceive yourself, and that you hold on to the end, when he will give what he has promised. *God has spoken in his holy one.* Who is his *holy one*? Scripture tells us that *God was in Christ, reconciling the world to himself* (2 Cor 5:19). He was in that Holy One of whom you heard it said elsewhere, *Your way, O God, is in your Holy One* (Ps 76:14(77:13)).

God has spoken in his holy one. I will rejoice and divide Shechem. Because God has said so, this will happen: the Church is speaking here. It does not tell us the words God spoke; but because *God has spoken in his holy one*, nothing can happen except what God has said. The following events are therefore bound to occur: *I will rejoice, and divide Shechem, and measure out the Valley of Shelters.* Shechem means "shoulders." The story has it that when Jacob returned with all his family from the country of his father-in-law, he buried at Shechem the

---

22. Or "in his holy place," but Augustine refers it to Christ.

idols they had brought from Syria.[23] He had sojourned there for a long time, but now at last he was on his way back; he built shelters there for his sheep and herds, and called the place, "Shelters."[24] And this, says the Church, is what I will divide.

What does it mean, then—*I will divide Shechem*? If it refers to the story about the burial of the idols, it means the Gentiles: "I am dividing the Gentiles." Why "dividing"? Because not all have faith.[25] But how are they "divided"? Because some will believe, and others will not; but, all the same, those who believe must not be fearful, though surrounded by unbelievers. At present they are marked off from the others by their faith; later they will be separated at the judgment: sheep to the right, goats to the left. Now we have come to understand in what sense the Church divides Shechem.

But if we are to take into account also the interpretation of the name Shechem, "shoulders," what are we to make of "dividing the shoulders"? Shoulders are differentiated among themselves by the fact that some are weighed down by a load of sins, while others bear the burden of Christ. It was these willing shoulders that Christ was looking for when he said, *My yoke is kindly and my burden light* (Mt 11:30). Every other burden oppresses you and feels heavy, but Christ's burden lifts you up; any other burden is a crushing weight, but Christ's burden has wings. Think of it this way: suppose you tried to relieve a bird of its load by removing its wings. The more you lightened its load, the more surely would it be kept on the ground. This creature you wanted to relieve lies there immobilized; it cannot fly, because you have taken its burden away from it. Give it back the burden, and off it flies. Christ's burden is like that. Let all carry it; let them not hang back. They must pay no attention to people who are unwilling to carry it. Let those who are willing shoulder it, and they will discover how light it is, how delightful, how pleasant, how effective in dragging them up to heaven and whisking them away from the earth. *I will divide Shechem, and measure out the Valley of Shelters*. Since the sheep that were to be sheltered belonged to Jacob, the Valley of Shelters may be understood as the Jewish people. They too are divided, because those who believed passed over away from there, while the rest stood aloof.

Verse 9. The Church's fertility derives from its head's strength

9. *Gilead is mine*. We have read these names in God's scriptures. Gilead has its own meaning, and one fraught with mystery, for it is interpreted "heap of witness." And what a heap of witness there was in the martyrs! *Gilead is mine*.

---

23. From Paddan-Aram. See Gn 35:4 for the burying episode.
24. Succoth; see Gn 33:17.
25. See 2 Th 3:2.

That accumulation of witness belongs to me, says the Church; the true martyrs are mine. Others may die for their useless, decrepit, unsalted cause,[26] but do they form part of the heap of witness? By no means, for *even if I deliver my body to be burned, yet have no love, it profits me nothing* (1 Cor 13:3). On one occasion the Lord admonished us to live in peace, but immediately prefixed a reminder about salt: *Keep salt within you, and keep peace between you,* he said (Mk 9:49).

Gilead is mine, then; but Gilead, the heap of witness, was obviously built up by suffering. At that period the Church was a contemptible object in the eyes of the public. It was flung as a reproach at the widowed Church that she belonged to Christ, that she wore the sign of the cross on her forehead; for the cross was not then an honorable sign, but a disgrace. But it was precisely at that time, when the cross was no honor but an accusation, that the heap of witness was built. Through that heap of witness the charity of Christ was spread abroad, and through the spread of Christ's charity the Gentiles were overwhelmed.

The psalm continues, *And Manasseh is mine.* That name signifies "forgotten." It was said to the Church, *You will forget your confusion for ever, and no longer be mindful of the stigma of your widowhood* (Is 54:4). Confusion was the Church's lot in that earlier age, but she has forgotten it now, for she is no longer mindful of the confusion and stigma of her widowed state. At the time when it was a shameful thing in the eyes of men and women to be a Christian, the heap of witness was formed. But no one remembers now the confusion of those days when to be a follower of Christ was ignominious. No one recalls that now. Everyone has forgotten, for now *Manasseh is mine.*

And the strength of my head is Ephraim. The name Ephraim is interpreted as "fruitfulness." So the Church is claiming, "Fruitfulness is mine, and my fruitfulness is the strength of my head, for my head is Christ." How can Christ's strength be understood as fruitfulness? If a grain did not fall into the earth, it would not be multiplied; it would remain one only. But Christ fell into the earth in his passion, and fruitfulness followed in his resurrection. *The strength of my head is Ephraim.* He hung on the cross, despised by all; but inwardly he was the grain with power to draw all things after him.[27] Within any grain you examine, a vast number of seeds is latent. It looks like some poor, despicable thing, but concealed within it lies the power to change other matter into itself and to produce a harvest. So too was power concealed in Christ's cross; all that showed was weakness. Yet a mighty grain this was! Certainly he was weak as he hung there; certainly those passers-by wagged their heads at him, taunting him with, *If he is the Son of God, let him come down from the cross.*[28] But now observe his strength, for *the weakness of God is stronger than mortals* (1 Cor 1:25). The

---

26. The Donatist martyrs.
27. See Jn 12:24.32.
28. See Mt 27:30.

fruitfulness that derived from that was necessarily enormous; and this fruitfulness is mine, says the Church.

Verse 10. Moab is the boiling pot; Edom is to be subdued

10. *Judah is my king, Moab the pot that gives me hope.* The psalm declares that *Judah is my king*; who, then, is Judah? The one who sprang from the tribe of Judah. And who was Judah? The one among his sons to whom Jacob promised, *Judah, your brothers will praise you* (Gn 49:8). *Judah is my king.* Why should I be afraid of anything, when Judah, my king, tells me, *Do not be afraid of those who kill the body* (Mt 10:28)? *Judah is my king, Moab the pot that gives me hope.* Why a pot? Because it suggests tribulation.[29] But then why does it *give me hope*? Because Judah, my king, went through that tribulation first. Where he went first, do you fear to follow? Where did he precede you? Through tribulations, through constricting circumstances, through insults. That was a hedged-in path, but only until he traversed it. He has passed that way now, so you must follow, for the path has been opened by his passage. Elsewhere he says, *I am all alone*, but only *until my passover* (Ps 140(141):10). It is a lonely grain at first, but only until its passover is accomplished. Once it has passed over, the fruitfulness will follow. *Judah is my king.*

Now because *Judah is my king, Moab is the pot that gives me hope.* Moab is to be understood as belonging to the Gentiles, for that nation was born from a sinful union. The tribe stemmed from the daughters of Lot, who slept with their father while he was drunk, thus abusing their father.[30] It would have been better for them to remain childless than to become mothers by such means. But they prefigured people who make wrong use of the law. (Take no notice of the fact that the noun "law" is feminine in Latin. In Greek it is masculine; but in any case, whether feminine or masculine gender is required by our mode of speech, it is not grammar that determines reality. Law has a masculine character because it rules, rather than being ruled.) Now, what does the apostle Paul say? *The law is a good thing, if one makes lawful use of it* (1 Tm 1:8). Those daughters of Lot did not make lawful use of their father; and, similarly, as good works are born when anyone makes good use of the law, so are evil deeds brought to birth when

---

29. *Olla*, a pot, more especially a cooking pot or cauldron. Hence the imagery of heat, or a frying pan, seems to be in Augustine's mind.

30. See Gn 19:31-38. Lot and his two daughters, refugees from the destruction of Sodom, lived in a cave. Despairing of finding husbands, the daughters made their father drunk, slept with him, and became pregnant. This was supposed to have been the origin of the Moabites, the story offering a fanciful etymology of the name Moab as derived from *me-ab*, "from [the/my] father." Whatever the origin of the story, Israelite detestation of incest gave it a polemical slant, with which Augustine's interpretation here is in accord: wrongful use of the girls' father symbolizes wrongful use of the law.

anyone makes bad use of it. Those girls who abused their father were like people who misuse the law; and so they became ancestors of the Moabites,[31] who represent bad deeds. And that is where the Church's tribulations come from; there is the bubbling pot. A prophetic text speaks of *a boiling pot tilting from the north* (Jer 1:13), which can mean nothing else than from the region where the devil holds sway, for he boasted, *I will set my throne in the north*.[32] It is not surprising, then, that the worst harassments raised against the Church come from those who misuse the law. What should we infer from this? That the Church will fade away? That because of this cooking pot—the prevalence of scandals, I mean—the Church will not last out until the end?

But did not Judah, the Church's king, foretell this? Did he not say to it, *With iniquity overflowing mightily, the love of many will grow cold* (Mt 24:12)? So as the pot boils, charity grows cold! What is this, O charity? Should you not be heating up, to outdo the heat of the pot? Are you not aware that when your king was speaking about this very thing—the overflow of scandals—you were promised that *whoever perseveres to the end will be saved* (Mt 24:13)? Persevere to the end, then, against a potful of scandals. The pot of iniquity is boiling up, but the flame of charity is hotter. Never admit defeat, persevere to the end. Why are you afraid of the Moabites, those bad deeds perpetrated by people who abuse the law? How can you be afraid? Did not Judah, your king, go ahead of you in enduring just such people? Do you not know that it was the Jews, the abusers of the law, who killed Christ? Be full of hope, then, and follow in the path where your king went before you. Proclaim that *Judah is my king*. And because *Judah is my king*, what has Moab become? *Moab is the pot that gives me hope*, not the pot that destroys me. Look how for the apostle this pot is a sign of hope amid tribulations: *We even glory in our sufferings*, he declares. The pot is there, certainly, but see if he does not point out how it signifies hope: *for we know that suffering fosters endurance, and endurance constancy, and constancy hope*. If suffering fosters endurance, and endurance fosters constancy, and constancy fosters hope, then the boiling pot leads us to hope, and there is good reason to say that *Moab is the pot that gives me hope*. But *hope does not disappoint us*. How can that be? Can you match the pot's heat? Of course you can, *because the love of God has been poured out into our hearts through the Holy Spirit who has been given us* (Rom 5:3-5).

---

31. According to the story, only one of them did. The other, thanks to another ingenious etymology, was held to have been the ancestor of the Ammonites.
32. Is 14:13. The taunt-song in Is 14:4-21 was aimed at a fallen tyrant, perhaps a Babylonian ruler, but was traditionally applied to Satan by the Christian fathers, particularly because of the name "Daystar, son of Dawn" (in Latin, Lucifer). The mountain "in the north" was an idea probably derived from Phoenician mythology, where the Mountain of Assembly was the traditional abode of the gods; but the north also suggested the region of cold, away from the sun, and hence estrangement from God who is light and life.

11. *Over Edom I will reach with my sandal.* The Church is speaking. I will reach even to Edom, it says. Let persecutions rage, let the world boil over with scandals; *I will reach with my sandal* even as far as Edom, even to people who live in an earthbound way (for Edom is said to mean "earthly"), yes even to them, for *over Edom I will reach with my sandal.* Whose sandal is this? The sandal of the gospel, clearly, for scripture exclaims, *How beautiful are the feet of those who announce peace and bring good news!* (Is 52:7; Rom 10:15). And again we are warned to have *our feet shod ready to preach the gospel of peace* (Eph 6:15). It is obvious that, since *suffering fosters endurance, and endurance constancy, and constancy hope*, the pot will not overwhelm me, *because the love of God has been poured out into our hearts through the Holy Spirit who has been given us.* Let us not grow weary of preaching the gospel, nor ever flag in proclaiming the Lord. All the way to Edom *I will reach with my sandal.* Yes, for even the earthly-minded play their part, do they not? Entangled in earthly desires they may be, but still they worship Christ. We see today, brothers and sisters, how many earthbound people commit fraud for the sake of gain, and perjury to further their fraud; we see how many are driven by their fears to consult sooth-sayers and astrologers.[33] Yet all these people worship Christ, and come under his sandal; for by this time he has stretched out with his sandal all the way to Edom. *The Allophyli[34] too are subjected to me.* Who are these *Allophyli*? People of foreign stock, who do not belong to my own race. They have been *subjected*, because many of them worship Christ, even if they are not destined to reign with him.[35] *The Allophyli too are subjected to me.*

Verses 11-12. Persecution and seeming abandonment further the Church's mission

12. *Who will lead me into the city that lies around us?* What is this city that lies around us?[36] I mentioned it before, as you will remember, when it occurred in another psalm, which said, *They will make their way around the city* (Ps 58(59):15); for the city that lies around us is the encompassing throng of Gentiles. At the heart of these Gentile hordes was the one Jewish race which paid homage to the one God, whereas the mass of the nations all around addressed their petitions to idols and served demons. The mystical name of these Gentile peoples was "the city that lies around us," because the Gentiles had spread all round, and encircled the people who paid cult to the one God. *Who will lead me into the city that lies around us?* Who indeed, if not God? The question means,

---

33. *Mathematicos*: see note at Exposition of Psalm 33, 5.
34. In the Old Testament perspective, the Philistines: see note at Exposition of Psalm 55, 1.
35. Augustine remained pessimistic throughout his life about the number of the elect.
36. *Civitas circumstantiae*: see notes at Exposition 1 of Psalm 58, 15; Exposition 4 of Psalm 30, 9.

"How will he lead me there through those clouds, concerning which it is said elsewhere, *Your thunder echoes as though in a wheel* (Ps 76:19(77:18))?" This "wheel" is the same thing as the city that lies around; it is called a wheel in that other psalm, but the same round world is meant. *Who will lead me into the city that lies around us? Who will lead me even into Edom?* This is a way of saying, "I want to reign over the earthly-minded too,[37] so that even those who are not my kin, and have no ambition to better themselves through me, may venerate me."

13. *Who will lead me even into Edom? Is it not you, O God, you who repulsed us? You, O God, who will not march out with our forces again?* Is it not you, who repulsed us, who will also lead us? But how did you repulse us? You *ruined us.* And why did you ruin us? Because *you were angry, but then you had mercy on us.* You who repulsed us will lead us; you yourself, who will not march out again with our forces, O God, you will lead us. What can it mean, then, by saying, *You will not march out with our forces again?* The world will vent its fury against us, the world will trample on us, the blood of martyrs will be shed to produce a heap of witness, and the rampaging pagans will demand, *Where is their God?* (Ps 78(79):10). But in this extremity *you will not march out again with our forces, O God*; you will not show yourself in opposition to them, you will not display your power, that mighty power which you deployed in David, in Moses, in Joshua son of Nun, when Gentile nations gave way before their strength, when after great slaughter and widespread devastation you led your people into the land you had promised them. Yet in our time of need you will not act so, *you will not march out with our forces again, O God*; but you will work within us. What does the statement, *you will not march out*, suggest? You will not allow yourself to be seen. When the martyrs were led away in chains, when they were shut up in prison, when they were dragged out for their captors to make sport of, when they were exposed[38] to the beasts, when they were felled with the sword, when they were scorched in the fire, were they not despised as people abandoned, bereft of any helper? But how was God working within them all the while? How was he comforting them in their inmost souls? How was he holding out the hope of eternal life as sweet consolation to them? How was he standing by them in their hearts? For there, in their hearts, each one was at home, silently. It is a good home for a person who is good, though a bad home for a bad person. Can we suppose, then, that because God was not marching out with their forces, he was deserting them? Could we not more justly say that by not marching out with their forces, he led the Church all the way into Edom, led the Church into the city that lay round about? Indeed, yes; for if the Church had essayed warlike tactics and resorted to the sword, it would have seemed to be fighting for the present life.

---

37. Variant: " . . . over even an earthly kingdom."
38. A well-supported variant is *subrigebantur*, "they were stood up."

But because it paid little heed to the present life, it became a heap of witness to the life that shall be.

Verses 13-14. The prospect of final triumph

14. So then, O God, since you will not march out with our forces, *grant us the help that will pluck us out of our troubles, for human aid is useless.* Let those who have no salt[39] go out and seek from their cronies a temporal salvation that is merely old and useless.[40] *Grant us help*: precisely where people thought you had abandoned us, come to our aid. *Grant us the help that will pluck us out of our troubles, for human aid is useless.*

15. *In God we shall fight bravely, and he it is who will reduce our enemies*[41] *to nothing.* We shall fight bravely, but not with the sword, not with horses, not with cuirass or shield, not with the might of an army, not in outward show at all. Where then? Within, where we are not observed. Within—but what does that mean? *In God we shall fight bravely.* We shall look like contemptible fighters, trampled on and not to be reckoned with, but *God it is who will reduce our enemies to nothing.* And this is what happened to our enemies in the long run. The martyrs were trampled underfoot, to be sure; but by suffering patiently, enduring it all, and persevering to the end, they fought bravely in God. And he fulfilled the promise that follows: he reduced their enemies to nothing. Where are the martyrs' enemies now? Well, of course, those who once furiously pursued them with stones are now drunkenly pursuing them with goblets![42]

---

39. An allusion to the saltiness and wisdom of section 2 above.
40. See his interpretation of Zobah in section 2.
41. Variant: "those who harass us."
42. A satirical reference to the custom of celebrating feasts at the tombs of the martyrs. Ambrose had condemned it at Milan, as Augustine relates in his *Confessions* VI,2,2, partly because of its association with pagan practices, and partly because it often led to excess and drunkenness. It was probably more entrenched in Africa, but efforts were made to stamp it out there too. See also Augustine's comments in Exposition 2 of Psalm 32, 5, and note there.

Exposition of Psalm 60

A Sermon to the People

Verse 1. Introduction: the title, prayer of the whole Christ

1. Dearly beloved, this psalm that we have undertaken to study with you is a short one, and we hope that the Lord will help us to speak about it in a way that is concise, yet still does it justice. Insofar as I have the assistance of him who commands me to speak, I will not shirk my full duty to those who are eager to hear, but will try not to make things difficult for others of slower understanding. I will neither be long winded to please a few, nor burdensome to those who have business to attend to.

The title of the psalm need not detain us. It reads, *To the end, for David himself, among the hymns.* If it is *among the hymns*, it is obviously a song of praise. *To the end* means that it looks toward Christ, for *Christ is the end of the law, bringing justification to everyone who believes* (Rom 10:4). We must take the remaining phrase, *for David himself*, to refer to no one else but him who came from David's line, to be human among human beings and make humans equal to angels. But if we are among his members and find ourselves part of his body (which we dare to presume, since we have his word for it) we must recognize the voice that speaks in this psalm as our own voice, not as something alien. But when I say "our voice," I do not mean only the voice of us who are here today. It is the voice of all of us who are dispersed throughout the world, all of us from east to west. To make it clear to you that it is our own voice, the psalm speaks as though one single person is praying; but it is not a lone individual, it is a unity, speaking as one. In Christ we all form one human person, whose head is in heaven and whose limbs are toiling on earth. Listen now to what they say, and you will see how hard they are toiling.

Verses 2-3. The one Church, the one Christ, prays and is tempted

2. *O God, hear my plea, give heed to my prayer.* Who is saying this? It sounds like a single person. But look at the next phrase, and you will see whether it can be only one: *From the ends of the earth I have called to you, as my heart was wrung with pain.* It cannot be one alone, then; yet it is one, because Christ is one, and all of us are his members. How can a single individual call from the ends of the earth? One person can, though, because what is shouting is the heritage

193

promised to the Son in another psalm: *ask of me, and I will give you the nations as your heritage, and the ends of the earth for your possession* (Ps 2:8). This possession of Christ, this heritage of Christ, this body of Christ, this one Church of Christ, this unity that we are—this is what shouts from the ends of the earth. And what is it crying out? What I have just recited to you: *O God, hear my plea, give heed to my prayer. From the ends of the earth I have called to you.* Yes, this is what I have been shouting to you, and *from the ends of the earth* my cry has come. I have shouted it, from every place on earth.

3. But why have I cried out so? *My heart was wrung with pain.* This praying person is clearly present throughout the Gentiles all around the world, and that is a great glory; but still our praying person is beset by grave temptation. During this earthly pilgrimage our life cannot be free from temptation, for none of us comes to know ourselves except through the experience of temptation, nor can we be crowned until we have come through victorious, nor be victorious until we have been in battle, nor fight our battles unless we have an enemy and temptations to overcome. The praying person who cries from the ends of the earth is therefore wrung with pain, but not deserted. Christ willed to prefigure us, who are his body, in that body of his in which he died and rose again, and ascended into heaven, so that where the head has gone in advance, the members may confidently expect to follow him. This is why he identified us with himself[1] when he willed to be tempted by Satan.[2] In the gospel story read just now we heard about the Lord Jesus Christ being tempted by the devil in the wilderness. Yes, Christ certainly was tempted by the devil, but in Christ's person you were being tempted, for Christ accepted flesh from you and gave you salvation from himself; he accepted death from you and gave you life from himself; he accepted insults from you and gave you honors from himself; and this is why he accepted temptation on your behalf, to give you victory in his own person. Because we were tempted in him, we vanquish the devil in him. Are you so preoccupied with the fact that he was tempted, that you hardly notice his victory? In him recognize yourself being put to the proof by temptation, and then recognize yourself winning the fight in him. Christ had the power to fend off the devil from his own person; but if he had not been tempted, he would not have provided a lesson for you, who were bound to be tempted. We need not be surprised, then, if this one praying person who cries out from the ends of the earth is beset by temptations.

---

1. *Nos transfiguravit in se*, Augustine's central conviction about the Church and Christ, one which commands his whole understanding of the psalms and their viability as Christian prayer. The phrase includes the ideas of incorporation, take-over into Christ's personality, identification, and exemplary causality. See the *Introduction*, and also Exposition 2 of Psalm 32, 2, and note there.
2. See Mt 4:1-11; Lk 4:1-13. Augustine's reference in the following sentence to the gospel of the temptation having just been read has suggested to some commentators that the present sermon was delivered in Lent; but the flexibility of the liturgy at that date must be borne in mind.

But not defeated. Why not? *You have lifted me up onto a rock.* Here again we have a clue as to who this is, who shouts from the ends of the earth. We remember the gospel promise: *Upon this rock I will build my Church* (Mt 16:18). This Church, this Church which he willed to be built on rock, this Church it is who is crying from the ends of the earth. But if the Church was to be built on a rock, someone had to be the rock; and who was it? Listen to Paul; he will tell you: *That rock was Christ* (1 Cor 10:4). On him we have been built. This is why the rock who is our foundation was the first to feel the force of the winds and rivers and rain[3] when Christ was tempted by the devil. Now you see how strong is the foundation on which he willed to provide you with sure standing. This is how we know that our voice does not clamor in vain, but finds a hearing. We stand firm in unshakeable hope because *you have lifted me up onto a rock.*

Verses 3-4. Christ, mortal and risen, is our hope and our strong tower

4. *You have guided me, because you have become my hope.* Only inasmuch as he has become our hope does he guide us. As our leader he guides us; he leads us along in himself because he is our way, and he leads us finally to himself because he is our homeland. He is our guide, then; but how? Because he has become our hope. But how has he become our hope? Precisely in the way I have just been pointing out to you: by being tempted, by suffering, by rising again. That is how he has become our hope; for what do we say to ourselves when we read about these happenings? "God surely won't damn us in the end, since it was for us that he sent his Son to be tempted, to be crucified, to die, and to rise again. God cannot despise us, if he did not spare even his own Son, but delivered him up for the sake of us all."[4] That is how he has become our hope. In him you see mirrored both your labors and your reward: your labors in his passion, and your reward in his resurrection. That is how he has become our hope, for we have two lives, one in which we find ourselves now, and another for which we hope. The life we live now is well known to us, but of the life we await in hope we are ignorant. Hold out in this life you have now, and you will come to possess the life you do not have yet. What does holding out imply? Not being worsted by the tempter. Christ has made himself a pattern for the life you live now by his labors, his temptations, his sufferings, and his death; and in his resurrection he is the pattern for the life you will live later. Without him, all that we would have known of human life is that we are born, and we die; we would not have known that anyone could rise from the dead and live for ever. But he took upon himself the human lot you know, and gave you proof of what you did not know. This is why he has become our hope in distress and in temptation. Listen to the apostle's encourage-

---

3. See Mt 7:24-25.
4. See Rom 8:32.

ment: *We even glory in our sufferings, knowing that suffering fosters endurance, and endurance constancy, and constancy hope; but hope does not disappoint us, because the love of God has been poured out into our hearts through the Holy Spirit who has been given us* (Rom 5:3-5). By giving us the Holy Spirit he has become our hope, and also enabled us to march on toward our hope, for if we had no hope we could not keep marching. The apostle makes this clear: *If someone sees what he hopes for, why should he hope for it? But if we hope for what we do not see, we wait for it in patience.* And he affirms, *In hope we have been saved* (Rom 8:24-25).

5. *You have guided me, because you have become my hope, an impregnable tower against the enemy.* "My heart is wrung with pain," laments this unity which is crying out from the ends of the earth. "I am struggling amid temptations and obstacles; the pagans hate me because they have been defeated; heretics under the cloak of the Christian name try to ensnare me; even within the Church the good grain is harshly treated by the straw. Under all this pressure my heart is wrung, so I will cry out from the ends of the earth. Yet he who has lifted me up onto a rock to lead me to himself does not forsake me. In spite of all the trouble the devil stirs up against me, plotting all the time and in every place, seizing every opportunity, Christ is nonetheless an impregnable tower for me. When I flee to it I shall be out of range of the enemy's shots; but, more than that, I shall be able safely to fire at him with any weapons I choose."

Yes, Christ is a tower. For us he has become the tower that confronts the enemy, as he is also the rock on which the Church is built. Are you afraid of being shot by the enemy? Then flee to the tower. The devil's missiles will never reach you there, and in the tower you can take up your position, armed and immovable. But how are you to flee to the tower? It is important that no one, when buffeted by temptation, should look for the tower in a material sense, and then, not finding it, grow weary or yield to the tempter. The tower is there, in front of you. Remember Christ, and enter the tower. How are you to remember Christ, and make your way into it? I will tell you how. Whatever you suffer, call to mind that he suffered first, and reflect on the goal he set before him in his suffering: to die and rise again. You must set before yourself in hope the same goal that you have seen in Christ; and if you do so you will have entered the tower by refusing the enemy's allurements. Only if you consent to the enemy will the attacking darts find their mark in you. Your job is rather to launch against him the weapons that will wound and vanquish him. What weapons are they? The words of God, your faith, this same hope that inspires you, and your good works. I am not suggesting that you be idle in the tower. You are not to go there to take a rest, and content yourself with being out of the foe's firing line. No, get busy and work hard there. Do not let your hands fall slack, for your good actions are swords with power to slay the enemy.

Verse 5. Perpetual pilgrim

6. *I will be a lodger*[5] *in your tent for ever.* Clearly the person crying out here is the one we have been talking about, for none of us individually will be a lodger here for ever, will we? We live here for a few days, and then move on, for we are no more than temporary lodgers here; only in heaven shall we be dwelling in our own home. You are a lodger here, for you will certainly hear the voice of the Lord commanding you, "Move on." No one will tell you to move house once you are in your eternal home in heaven. But here, a lodger you are. This is why it is admitted in another psalm, *I am no more than a lodger in your house, and a pilgrim, like all my forebears* (Ps 38:13(39:12)). So on this earth we are only lodgers, but there beyond the Lord will give us dwelling places that abide, for he told us, *Many are the abiding habitations in my Father's house* (Jn 14:2). He will not award those abiding habitations to mere lodgers, but to qualified citizens who will dwell there for ever.

It is a different matter for the Church, my brothers and sisters, because it is not for a short time only that the Church will be here on this earth. It will be here until the end of time, and that is why the Church says, *I will be a lodger in your tent for ever.* "Let the enemy rage as he will, let him attack me and lay traps for me, let him be endlessly inventive in stirring up scandals, and wring my heart with pain. No matter; *I will be a lodger in your tent for ever.*" The Church will not be overcome; it will not be rooted out, nor will it give way, whatever the trials may be, until this world comes to an end, and we are welcomed into that eternal home to which Christ will lead us—Christ, who has become our hope. *I will be a lodger in your tent for ever.*

Perhaps we might say to the Church, then, "If you are going to be a lodger here for such a long time, you will be greatly harassed[6] on earth amid these powerful temptations. If you could expect to be here for a few days only, it would be easier for you, because then you could look forward to a speedy ending to the tempter's plots." Oh, so you want these trials to be very brief, do you? But how would the Church gather in all its children, if it did not endure to the very end? Don't be so mean-minded with regard to the others who will come after you. Don't try to chop down the bridge of mercy after you have crossed over yourself; let it remain in place for ever. In any case, what about the temptations which must necessarily multiply as scandals increase, according to Christ's own prediction? He told us, *With iniquity increasing mightily, the love of many will grow cold* (Mt 24:12). The Church which cries out from the ends of the earth

---

5. *Inquilinus,* one who sojourns in a place not his own. See Exposition of Psalm 38, 21.

6. *Laboraturus,* masculine, where we might have expected a feminine participle, since he is addressing the Church. Probably *inquilinus* has attracted it into the masculine, but Augustine may be thinking of the "one man" spoken of in section 1 above.

must be among those of whom the Lord goes on to say, *Whoever perseveres to the end will be saved* (Mt 24:13). And how will you persevere? What sort of strength can you command amid such grave offenses, such powerful temptations, such fierce fights? With what resources will you win the victory against a foe you cannot see? Not your own, surely? If this lodger has to remain here for ever, what hope is there of holding out?

I shall be covered by the shade of your wings, says the Church to God. This is why we are free from anxiety amid such unrelenting trials, until this world ends and the world of eternity opens its arms to us: we are covered by the shade of his wings. It is hot in this world, but under God's wings there is ample shade. *I shall be covered by the shade of your wings*.

Verse 6. The inheritance is promised

7. *For you, O God, have heard my prayer.* What prayer would that be? The prayer, obviously, with which the psalm began, when it begged, *O God, hear my plea, give heed to my prayer. From the ends of the earth I have called to you.* I have been shouting my prayer to you from the ends of the earth, and it is because *you have heard my prayer* that I know *I shall be covered by the shade of your wings.* This is a reminder to us, brothers and sisters, that we must not give up praying as long as the time of temptation lasts.

You have granted an inheritance to those who fear your name. Let us persevere in holy fear of the name of God. Our eternal Father does not let us down. Do children not work hard in the expectation of succeeding to their parents' estate, knowing that they will come into their inheritance once their parents are dead? But we are not working hard to receive an inheritance from our Father as though he could die and leave it to us; rather let us live with him for ever, enjoying it in his company![7] *You have granted an inheritance to those who fear your name.*

Verse 7. The days of eternity

8. *You will add days upon days to the years of the king.* This is the king of whom we are members, for Christ is our king. He is both our head and our King. On him you have conferred days upon days, O God: not merely the days of this present age, which will come to an end, but over and above them further days that will never end. Another psalm declares, *I will dwell in the Lord's house through length of days* (Ps 22(23):6). Why does it say, *Through length of days*? Surely because the days of our present life are so short. Anything that comes to

---

7. This sentence could also be understood as a question: "Do we not work hard to receive an inheritance, though it is not one to which we shall succeed on our Father's death, but rather that we may live with him for ever, enjoying it in his company?"

an end is short, but the life of our king spans days upon further days. Not only does Christ reign in his Church during the fleeting days of this present world, but the saints will reign with him through days that will know no end. In eternity there is one day, and there are many days. I have already demonstrated to you that the days of eternity are many by quoting the other psalm: *through length of days*. But you can see that eternity is also one single day from the declaration, *You are my Son, today have I begotten you* (Ps 2:7). The word *today* indicates a single day; but this is not the kind of day which is squeezed between yesterday and tomorrow; it does not begin where yesterday ended, nor does it end when tomorrow dawns. After all, God's time is also referred to as "years" in another psalm: *you are the selfsame, and your years will not fail* (Ps 101:28(102:27)). So years, and days, and a single day, all mean the same thing. You can use which-ever phrase you like about eternity. And the reason why you can choose freely which way to express it is that whatever you say will fall short of the reality. Yet you must say something, to give yourself a basis on which to think about what cannot be put into words.

You will add days upon days to the years of the king, until the day of a genera-tion and of a generation. This is an allusion to the present generation and the generation of the future. The present generation is symbolized by the moon, which at first is new-born, then waxes, and comes to the full, grows old, and dies; our mortal generations do the same. The future generation is the time of our rebirth and resurrection, when we shall abide for ever with God. We shall not be like the moon then, for the Lord used a different comparison: *then the righteous will shine like the sun in their Father's kingdom* (Mt 13:43). The moon is used in scripture as an image of the mutability of our mortal condition; and that is why the man who fell among robbers is pictured as going down from Jerusalem to Jericho,[8] for the Hebrew name for that town, Jericho, is said to mean "the moon." The traveler was thus descending from immortality to mortality, and it is not surprising that he was injured by robbers on his journey and left half dead, for he represents Adam, from whom the whole human race derives. Accordingly when our psalm says, *You will add days upon days to the years of the king, until the day of a generation*, I take it to mean the generation of our mortality. But why is the word repeated: *and of a generation*? What generation can this be? Listen to the next verse and you will see.

Verses 8-9. Seek God's merciful love and truth, but seek them in his cause

9. *He will remain for ever in God's presence.* How, and why? *Who will seek his steadfast love and his truth, in his cause?* In another place a psalm testifies,

---

8. See Lk 10:30-35.

All the Lord's ways are steadfast love and truth for those who seek his testament and his testimonies (Ps 24(25):10). It would take a mighty sermon to expound the Lord's steadfast love and truth, but we promised to be brief. So put your minds to a brief explanation of what is meant by steadfast love and truth, because it is no small matter that is comprised in that statement, *All the Lord's ways are steadfast love and truth.* God is said to act in steadfast love or mercy because he looked not to what we deserved but to his own goodness, in order to forgive all our sins and promise us eternal life; but he acts in truth too, in that he does not deceive us but delivers what he promised. We must recognize merciful love and truth here, but recognize it so effectively that we imitate it ourselves: as God has given proof of his merciful love and truth in our regard, mercifully forgiving our sins and truthfully keeping his promises, so too we must deal mercifully and truthfully with others. We have an obligation to show merciful love to the sick, to the needy, even to our enemies; but we must deal truthfully by not sinning, and especially by not piling sin upon sin. If we make great promises to ourselves about the scope of God's mercy, there can creep into our minds a tendency to represent God as unjust, and to imagine that even if we continue in our sinful ways, and make no attempt to repudiate our sins, Christ will come and assign us a place in the company of those servants who obey him. Can that be just, for him to put you in the place reserved for those who have turned away from their sins—you who are obstinately set in yours? Do you aim at the supreme injustice of making God unjust too? Why try to bend God to your will? You must align yourself with his. And who does that? Only the person who will be numbered among those of whom it is said, *Whoever perseveres to the end will be saved* (Mt 24:13).

Notice too what is said of this kind of person: *Who will seek* Christ's *steadfast love and his truth, in his cause?* Why is this phrase added, *in his cause*? It would have been sufficient to ask, "Who will seek it?" Why add, *in his cause*? It must be because many people study the sacred books to learn about God's steadfast love and truth, but, having learned, live for themselves, not for God. They pursue their own agenda, not that of Jesus Christ;[9] they preach about his merciful love and his truth, but they do not practice merciful love or truth themselves. Yet they have come to know God's mercy and truth; they could not preach it if they had not. But a person who loves God, and loves Christ, will preach God's merciful love and truth, but will seek it in God's cause and not for his own profit. He will not seek to derive some temporal gain for himself from preaching, but will seek the profit of Christ's members. By truthfully dispensing what he has come to understand, he serves Christ's faithful, so that each one of us who lives may live

---

9. See Phil 2:21.

not for ourselves but for him who died for us all.[10] *Who will seek his steadfast love and his truth, in his cause?*

10. *So will I sing psalms to your name, O God, for ages unending, that I may render thanks to you from day unto day.* If you sing psalms to God's name, do not confine yourself to a limited spell of it. Do you aspire to sing psalms for unending ages? Do you hope to go on singing them for ever? Then render thanks to him from day to day. What does that expression mean, render thanks to him from day to day? It means from this temporal day unto that eternal day. Persevere in offering your thanks to him throughout this present day, until you come to that day of eternity—which is the same as saying, *Whoever perseveres to the end will be saved.*

---

10. See 2 Cor 5:15.

Exposition of Psalm 61

A Sermon to the People[1]

Verse 1. The leaping psalmist reappears

1. All the utterances of God are to us a delight. The sweetness that we find in his word is to us an inducement to speak, and to you an incentive to listen, so that with the help of him who grants us such exquisite enjoyment, our land may yield its fruit.[2] I can see that you do not find it tedious to listen, for the palate of your hearts is a discerning one, which rejects nothing that is good for you, but seizes it eagerly and assimilates it to your profit. I congratulate you on your good taste. Insofar as the Lord enables us, therefore, we propose to speak to you today about the psalm we have just sung. Its title is, *To the end: Idithun's song for David himself.* I recall that the meaning of "Idithun" was suggested to you on an earlier occasion.[3] According to the interpretation of the Hebrew name, as it has been passed on to us, "Idithun" signifies "One who leaps over them." So the singer is jumping over certain people, and then viewing them from above. We must inquire how far he has leapt, over whom he has leapt, and where he has now come to rest after his leaping. We need to ask what that spiritual, secure place is from which he can survey things below him. He does not look down in such a way as to risk falling; but having leapt himself he tries to move[4] lazier folk to follow him, and he means to extol the place he has attained by his leaping. His leap has landed him into a position where he is above something, but also below something else; and he is intent on telling us what this thing above him is, the thing that makes him feel safe, so that his leaping over other things may be deemed not pride but progress.

Verses 2-3. Raised above others, but subject to God

2. From the fortified stronghold where he has taken his stand the psalmist asks, *Shall not my soul surrender itself to God?* He had heard the warning, *Anyone who exalts himself will be humbled, but the one who humbles himself*

---

1. Possibly preached in September 416, at Carthage; but some commentators prefer an earlier date.
2. See Ps 84:13(85:12).
3. See his Exposition of Psalm 38, 1.
4. Variant: "advise."

will be exalted (Lk 18:14), and he was wary lest his leaping might make him proud. He felt no superiority with regard to the people below him, but deep humility in relation to the One above him. This is why, when some jealous people who resented his advancement began to threaten him, he replied to them, "*Shall not my soul surrender itself to God?* Why try to trip me as I leap? You want either to throw me down with your accusations, or to turn my head with your seductive flattery. But do you think I am so preoccupied with the thought of what is below me that I forget who is above me? *Shall not my soul surrender itself to God?* However near I draw to him, however high I soar, however far I leap over others, I shall be below God, not a rival to God. Only when he who is above all things holds me below himself, will I mount above all other things without anxiety. *Shall not my soul surrender itself to God? For my salvation comes from him. He is my very God, my savior, my protector, and I shall waver no more.* I know who is above me, I know who he is who grants his mercy to those who know him, I know under whose wings I must hope; so *I shall waver no more.* You are doing your best," he says to those ill-wishers, all the while leaping over those to whom he is talking. "You are doing your best to make me waver, but I pray *Let not the foot of pride come near me.*"

This is how the prayer uttered in another psalm is answered, the prayer that continues, *nor the hand of sinners dislodge me* (Ps 35:12(36:11)), for the assertion in our present psalm that *I shall waver no more* means the same thing. That earlier psalm's prayer, *let not the hand of sinners dislodge me*, is echoed here by *I shall waver no more*; and the earlier petition, *let not the foot of pride come near me*, finds its counterpart here in the question, *Shall not my soul surrender itself to God?*

3. The speaker is looking out from his lofty aerie; he is fortified and safe, for the Lord has become his refuge. God himself has become for him a fortified stronghold. He considers the people he has leapt over, and, looking down on them, he speaks as though from a high tower. This image was used elsewhere to describe his situation, for another psalm called God *an impregnable tower against the enemy* (Ps 60:4(61:3)). The speaker looks at the people below, and asks them, "*How long will you pile your loads on one man?* By your accusations, by hurling insults, by trying to ambush him and persecuting him, you load burdens on a person. You load on him all that a human being can bear; and if indeed he can bear it, it is only because he is submissive to the one who made human beings. *How long will you pile your loads on one man?* If it is only my human condition that is your target, go on, *kill me, all of you.* Go ahead, pile on the burdens, do your worst. *Kill me, all of you. Press on me as on a leaning wall or a shaky fence*: keep at it, push hard, and you will bring it crashing down. And then, you think, what becomes of my boast, *I shall waver no more*? But why is it that I can claim, *I shall waver no more*? Only because *he is my very God, my*

savior, my protector. Human yourselves, you have power to load burdens onto a human being, but can you load anything onto God, who protects that human sufferer?"

Verse 4. Filling up the measure of Christ's sufferings

4. *Kill me, all of you.* How could there be enough room in a single human body for that person to be killed by all? There is, though, because we must understand this person as ourselves, as the person of our Church, the one person that is Christ's body. Jesus Christ is one man consisting of head and body, the Savior of the body and the body's members, two in one flesh.[5] They are two in one voice as well, and two in one passion; and when iniquity has finally passed away, they will be two in one rest. The sufferings of Christ are therefore not undergone by Christ alone; yet in another sense we can say that the sufferings of Christ are endured nowhere else but in Christ. If you think of Christ as consisting of head and body, Christ's sufferings are always undergone in Christ and nowhere else; but if by Christ you mean the head alone, his sufferings are not confined to his own person. If it were true that Christ's sufferings were undergone by Christ alone—by the head alone, I mean—how could a certain member of Christ, the apostle Paul, say that he was suffering *that I may fill up what is lacking to the sufferings of Christ in my own flesh* (Col 1:24)?

If you are numbered among the members of Christ, whoever you are, mortal sufferer who hear these words (and whoever you are who do not hear them, for that matter; though in fact you do hear them if you are a member of Christ), then whatever you may suffer at the hands of those who are not Christ's members was lacking to the sufferings of Christ. This statement that it "was lacking" means that you are filling up the appointed measure: not that you are causing it to spill over, but that you are suffering just so much as was necessarily to be contributed from your passion to the universal passion of Christ. He suffered as our head, and he suffers in his members, which means in us. We each pay what we owe into this commonwealth of ours, according to our limited means; we contribute our quota of suffering from the resources allotted to us. There will be no final balancing of accounts in the matter of suffering until this world ends.

How long will you pile your loads on one man? Whatever the prophets suffered, from the shedding of the blood of righteous Abel to the blood of Zechariah,[6] was suffering loaded onto this one man, because some of Christ's members preceded his coming in the flesh. At the birth of a child it once happened that a hand came out first, before the head appeared,[7] yet the hand was

---

5. See Gn 2:24; Eph 5:31.
6. See Mt 23:35.
7. See Gn 38:27.

obviously connected to the head. Never doubt, brothers and sisters, that all the righteous people who have endured persecution from the wicked were already members of Christ. This is just as true in the case of those who lived before the advent of the Lord, those who were sent to foretell his coming. They too had their place among Christ's members. It is unthinkable that anyone who belongs to that city which has Christ for its king should not also have a place among his members. That holy city is the heavenly Jerusalem, unique and undivided; and this one city has one king. The king of the city is Christ, for *Zion, my mother, a man will say*. He addresses her as *mother*, but it is *a man* who so speaks. *Zion, my mother, a man will say; he was made man in her, and the Most High himself established her* (Ps 86(87):5). He, the Most High who founded her, is the king of that city, and he himself was made in her the humblest of men. Before his coming in the flesh he sent ahead of him certain of his members; and after they had foretold his advent he came himself, organically connected to them. Recall that episode during the birth of a child of which we spoke: the hand came forth before the head, but it belonged to the head and was under the head's command.

Now when the apostle was extolling the dignity of the elder people, and mourning the natural branches that had been broken off,[8] he spoke about Christ: *Theirs is the adoption, and the covenants, and the establishment of the law*, he says. *The patriarchs belong to them; and from them Christ was born according to the flesh, he who is sovereign over all, God, blessed for ever* (Rom 9:4-5). The statement that *from them Christ was born according to the flesh* implies the same as *he was made man in her*, in *Zion*; and in saying that Christ is *sovereign over all, God, blessed for ever*, the apostle acknowledges that *the Most High himself established her*. In saying, *From them Christ was born according to the flesh*, he recognizes Christ to be the son of David; but by confessing that Christ is *sovereign over all, God, blessed for ever*, he points to him as David's Lord.

The entire city is speaking, therefore: all of it from the murdered, righteous Abel to the slaughtered Zechariah, and then further still, from the blood of John,[9] through the blood of the apostles, on through the blood of the martyrs, to the blood-shedding of all Christ's faithful. One single city is speaking, one person is saying, "*How long will you pile your loads on one man? Kill me, all of you*. But let us see if you destroy this person, let us see if you can stamp him out, let us see if you can banish his name from the earth. Let us see whether you are not after all the people who devise futile schemes,[10] asking, *When will he die, and his name disappear?* (Ps 40:6(41:5)). Press upon me, push me *like a leaning wall or a shaky fence*, but remember what I told you earlier: *God is my protector, and I*

---

8. See Rom 11:17-21.
9. The Baptist.
10. See Ps 2:1.

shall waver no more. I was pushed at like a heap of sand to make me topple, but the Lord held me up."[11]

Verse 5. Persecution succeeded by honor: the Old Testament Joseph

5. *Yet they thought to refuse me honor.* The persecutors are defeated and forced to yield even as they go about their murderous work, for by the blood of the slain they are only multiplying believers,[12] and they are obliged to admit defeat when they can kill no more.[13] *Yet they thought to refuse me honor.* Since no one can now be put to death for being a Christian, they bend their efforts to dishonoring us; for the hearts of the impious are wrung with misery by the honor in which Christians are held. A reversal of fortunes has come to Christians like that which befell Joseph, by whom they were spiritually prefigured. He was sold by his brothers, then carried off from his homeland into a Gentile country (Egypt, in his case), and humiliated in prison because he was falsely believed guilty on a trumped-up charge. He experienced the anguish of which another psalm says, *A sword entered his soul* (Ps 104(105):18). And after all this he is honored. No longer is he helpless in the hands of brothers who sell him; now he is handing out grain to these same brothers in their hunger.[14] These wicked fellows have been defeated by his humility and his chastity, his probity, his trials and his sufferings; now they see him raised to high rank, yet they would refuse him honor if they could. Their thoughts are running on the lines indicated by another psalm-verse: *the sinner will see* (for he can hardly fail to see, since a city set on a mountain cannot remain hidden[15]), *the sinner will be enraged at the sight; he will gnash his teeth and pine away* (Ps 111(112):10). The venomous hatred of those who rage and fume lies hidden in their hearts and is belied by their demeanor; this is why our psalm mentions their thoughts only: *they thought to refuse me honor;* for they dare not put their thoughts into words.

We must hope that good may come to them, even though they hope for evil. *Judge them, O God, let them fall away from their thoughts.*[16] For what can be better for them, what more advantageous, than that they fall away from the place where they have taken their wicked stance, be corrected, and be in a position to say, *You have set my feet upon a rock* (Ps 39:3(40:2))?

---

11. See Ps 117(118):13.
12. See note at Exposition 2 of Psalm 58, 5.
13. Here, as often in these Expositions, Augustine alludes to the vast change that came over the Church when persecution ceased in Constantine's reign.
14. See Gn 37; 39-41.
15. See Mt 5:14.
16. Ps 5:11(10). In his Exposition of Psalm 5, 13, Augustine considered this benign interpretation of the verse, but rejected it as incompatible with the phrase that immediately follows: "Drive them out." He therefore took it to mean "Let them fall by their own thoughts," but acquitted the speaker of malice by asserting that this was a prophecy, not a petition.

The two cities

6. *Yet they thought to refuse me honor.* Is it all against one, or one against all, or all against all, or one against one? Well, by saying, *You pile loads on one man*, he does, of course, seem to indicate one person as the target, and by saying, *Kill me, all of you*, he must mean that all are massed against that one. However, all those enemies are really pitted against all of us, because as Christians, though we are many, we are all incorporated into one. But what about all those diverse errors that are inimical to Christ: must we think of them as simply plural, to be referred to as "all," and in no other way? Can we not speak of them too as a single individual? Yes, we can. I am not afraid to call them one person, as it were. There is one city, and over against it another one city, one people and another one people, a king and a king. What am I talking about—one city and another one city? Babylon is one,[17] and Jerusalem is one. Whatever mystical names may be applied to it elsewhere, it remains one city set over against another one city. One has the devil for its king, but Christ is king of the other.

A passage in the gospel comes to my mind. I find it disturbing, and I think you will too. A crowd of people had been invited to a wedding banquet. There were both good and bad among them, and all the places at table were filled, because the servants had been sent out and had invited both good and bad people, in accordance with their instructions. The king went in to meet the guests, and found a man there who was not suitably attired for a wedding. The king questioned him. You know what he asked: *My friend, how is it that you came in here without wedding clothes? But he had nothing to say* (Mt 22:12). Then the king ordered that he be bound hand and foot, and thrown out into the darkness. So this man, whoever he was, just one man out of the great crowd of guests, was picked up, removed from the banquet, and consigned to punishment. But clearly the Lord wanted us to understand this one person as representative of very many others when the king ordered him to be thrown out, and sent to well-deserved punishment, because the warning swiftly follows, *for many are invited, but only a few are chosen* (Mt 22:14). What does that mean? You called the people together in crowds, Lord, and a great multitude came. You announced the news and spoke the message, and they were multiplied, in numbers beyond reckoning.[18] The wedding banquet had its full complement of guests. One single person, one only, was ejected; yet you say, *Many are invited, but only a few are chosen*. Would it not be more accurate to say, "All were invited, many are chosen, but one is excluded"?

---

17. On Babylon, see Exposition 2 of Psalm 26, 18; Exp. of Psalm 44, 25; Exp. of Psalm 54, 12; Exp.1 of Psalm 58, 5, and notes in these places.
18. See Ps 39:6(40:5).

If he had said, "Many are invited, most are chosen, but a few have been rejected," we might more easily have taken these "few" to mean just the one man. But in fact the Lord tells us that one single person was thrown out, and adds, *Many are invited, but only a few are chosen.* Who are the chosen ones? Those who remained at the banquet, evidently. One was expelled, and the chosen stayed on. But then, if only one out of the whole crowd was ejected, how can the chosen ones be called "few"? Only, I think, because in the one who was thrown out, many are included.

All those who have no taste but for the things of this earth, all who prize earthly happiness above God, and all who seek their own ends, not those of Jesus Christ,[19] belong to that city whose mystical name is Babylon, the city that has the devil as its king. But all whose taste is schooled to the things above, who ponder the realities of heaven,[20] who live with circumspection in this world, taking care not to offend God, who are wary of committing sin, but if they do sin are not ashamed to confess it, all who are humble, gentle, holy, just, devout and good—all these belong to the one city whose king is Christ. The former has priority as to time, but no priority in nobility or honor. This is the elder, and that other city is younger. The one began with Cain, the other with Abel. They are two bodies, active under their respective rulers and citizens of their respective cities. They are opposed to one another and will be so until the end of time, until those who are now commingled are separated. Then some will be placed at Christ's right hand, and others at his left. To those at his right he will say, *Come, you who are blessed by my Father; take possession of the kingdom prepared for you since the world was made*; but to the others, *Depart from me, you accursed, into the eternal fire which was prepared for the devil and his angels* (Mt 25:34.41). Christ, as king of his own city, as victor over all, issues the invitation, *Come, you who are blessed by my Father; take possession of the kingdom prepared for you since the world was made.* But to those stationed at his left he speaks as to the city of the wicked: *Depart*, he says, *into the eternal fire.* And does he separate their king from them? No, for he adds, *which was prepared for the devil and his angels.*

The building of the new Jerusalem

7. Concentrate now, brothers and sisters; concentrate, I beg you, for I want to say a little more to you about this sweet city. I love talking about it. *Glorious things are spoken of you, city of God* (Ps 86:4(87:3)), and *if ever I forget you, Jerusalem, let my right hand forget me* (Ps 136(137):5). One homeland we have,

---

19. See Phil 2:21.
20. See Col 3:2.

one homeland most dear to us, one only homeland; and compared with that whatever we have now is nothing but a journey.

So I am going to tell you something you know already, something to which you will give your assent. I am going to remind you of a truth already familiar to you; I am not teaching you anything you have not heard before. Well then, the apostle tells us that *it is not the spiritual that comes first. The animal body comes first, and what is spiritual afterward* (1 Cor 15:46). So you can see why the wicked city is the elder, for Cain was the first-born, and Abel was born later.[21] All the same, in their case too the prophecy was verified, that *the elder shall serve the younger* (Gn 25:23). Now we read that Cain built a city.[22] Before any other cities existed, at the very beginning of human history, Cain built a city. Obviously you must infer that from these two brothers, and from their descendants, many other people had been born by this time, so that there were sufficient numbers to justify calling them a city. Cain, then, built a city where no city had existed before. Much later Jerusalem also was built: Jerusalem, God's kingdom, the holy city, the city of God; it was established to be a sign or figure, foreshadowing what was to come.

You must be alert to the profound mystery concealed in these events, and keep in mind what I said to you earlier: *it is not the spiritual that comes first. The animal body comes first, and what is spiritual afterward.* That is why Cain was the first to build his city, and why he built it where no city had been before. When the time came for Jerusalem to be built, it was not established on a site where no city had previously existed; there had been a city there called Jebus,[23] from which the Jebusites derived their name. That place was captured, decisively defeated and subjugated; and a new city was built there, a new one after the destruction of the old. This new city was called Jerusalem, the vision of peace, the city of God.

No single one of us born from Adam immediately belongs to Jerusalem. We each carry with us the side-shoots of iniquity and the punishment due to sin, and we are liable to death. So in a sense we still belong to the old city. But if we are predestined to belong to the people of God, the old self will be destroyed and the new person will be built. This is why Cain built his city where none had previously existed, as we have seen. Each one of us begins from mortality and a bad nature, so that we may become good later, *for as through one man's disobedience many were accounted sinners, so through the obedience of one man many shall be accounted righteous* (Rom 5:19). And *all of us die in Adam* (1 Cor 15:22), as each one of us is born from Adam. Each of us must therefore make our passage over to Jerusalem; then the old self will be destroyed and the new built.

---

21. See Gn 4:1-2.
22. See Gn 4:17.
23. See Jos 18:28.

Elsewhere the apostle commands us, *Strip off the old self, and be clothed in the new* (Col 3:9-10), as though envisaging the defeat of the Jebusites to make way for Jerusalem to be built. To those who are already built into Jerusalem, and are sparkling with the radiance of grace, it is said, *You were darkness once, but now you are light in the Lord* (Eph 5:8). From the beginning of history the wicked city lives on, and the good city is continuously being formed by the conversion of bad people.

Interchange and mingling between the two cities

8. During the present age these two cities are mingled together, but they will be separated at the end. They are in conflict with each other, one fighting on behalf of iniquity, the other for justice; one for what is worthless, the other for truth. This mixing together in the present age sometimes brings it about that certain persons who belong to the city of Babylon are in charge of affairs that concern Jerusalem, or, again, that some who belong to Jerusalem administer the business of Babylon. That sounds like a puzzling statement that I have proposed to you, doesn't it? Be patient, though, and I will clarify it by examples. As the apostle writes, all the things that occurred in the experience of the earlier people *happened to them with symbolic import, for they are written down as a rebuke to us, upon whom the climax of the ages has come* (1 Cor 10:11). Consider that elder people, then, the people created to be a sign of the later people, and see in them the point I am trying to make.

There were bad[24] kings who reigned in Jerusalem. This is a well-known fact; they are listed and named. They were therefore sinful citizens of Babylon, yet they were administering the affairs of Jerusalem. All of them were destined to be cut off from Jerusalem at the end, for they belong nowhere but in the devil's domain. On the other hand, we find citizens of Jerusalem wielding authority over some part of Babylonian business. Nebuchadnezzar, impressed by the miracle he had witnessed, appointed the three youths to be ministers in his kingdom,[25] and gave them authority over his own satraps. So citizens of Jerusalem were in charge of Babylonian affairs.

Now reflect on how the same things happen in the Church, even in our own day, fulfilling the prophetic type. What about all those concerning whom we are warned, *Do what they tell you, but do not imitate what they do* (Mt 23:3)? They are all citizens of Babylon, but they control the public affairs of the city of Jerusalem. This is incontestable, because if they had no such authority over Jerusalem's business, how could we be commanded, *Do what they tell you*? And how could it be said of them, *They have taken their place in the chair of Moses* (Mt

---

24. Variant: "great."
25. See Dn 3:97.

23:2)? But then, if they are citizens of Jerusalem, destined to reign for ever with Christ, how can it be said, *Do not imitate what they do*? That must imply that they are to hear one day, *Depart from me, all you who act unjustly* (Mt 7:23; Lk 13:27).

You can see, then, that citizens of the bad city have some control over the affairs of the good city; but now let us see whether the converse is true. Do the citizens of the good city take charge of any business belonging to the bad city? Keep in mind that every earthly state will undoubtedly perish. Its sovereignty will pass away at the coming of the Lord's reign, that reign about which we pray, *Your kingdom come*, and of which it has been foretold that *his kingdom will have no end* (Lk 1:33). In spite of this, every earthly state makes use of some of our citizens to administer its affairs. How many of the faithful are there among its citizens, among its loyal subjects and its magistrates, its judges, generals, governors and even kings? All these are just and good, and all they have at heart are the surpassingly glorious things that have been spoken about the city of God.[26] They are like villains in a state doomed to pass away, and for the time being they are under orders from the teachers in the holy city to serve their masters conscientiously, *whether the king, as one who holds supreme authority, or the officials appointed by him*[27] *to punish evildoers but to commend those who behave well* (1 Pt 2:13-14). Or, if they are slaves, they are directed to be submissive to their masters, even if this means Christians submitting to pagans, and a better person keeping faith with someone less good, in the knowledge that he or she will have to be in servitude for a time, but will enjoy dominion for eternity. Matters are arranged like this until iniquity passes away.[28] Slaves are directed to put up with unjust and cantankerous masters: we are told that the citizens of Jerusalem must bear with the citizens of Babylon, and indeed offer them more generous compliance than they would if they were citizens of Babylon themselves, for in this way they fulfill the injunction, *if anyone obliges you to go a mile, go freely with him two miles more*.[29]

To all this scattered city, spread widely, mixed together, the psalm speaks: *How long will you pile your loads on one man? Kill me, all of you* — all of you, whether you are outside, like thorns in the hedges or woodland trees that bear no fruit, or inside like weeds amid the crop or chaff in the wheat. All of you, however numerous you are, who are separated or inextricably mingled, to be borne with or to be fended off, *kill me, all of you. Press on me as on a leaning*

---

26. See Ps 86(87):3.
27. Variant: "by God."
28. See Ps 56:2(57:1).
29. Mt 5:41. In arguing against Donatists Augustine had frequently insisted that there are weeds among the wheat while the Church is still in historical time. Here he shows that there is also a good deal of wheat among the weeds.

wall or a shaky fence. Yet they thought to refuse me honor. They did not say so, but they thought to do it. *They thought to refuse me honor.*

The Lord's thirst

9. *I ran thirstily*, for they kept requiting my good deeds with evil.[30] They kept on killing, kept on refusing and thrusting me away, yet all the while I was thirsting for them. They thought to refuse me honor, but I was constantly thirsting to suck them into my body. Don't be surprised by that expression, dear friends, for what else do we do when we drink? We draw some moisture that was outside us into our bodily frame, we introduce it into our body. That was what Moses did with the head of the golden calf. This calf's head represented the body of godless people, who are like a calf munching grass, since they are in quest of earthly things, and *all flesh is grass* (Is 40:6). Well then, as I said, the calf's head represented the body of the godless. Moses was furious. He threw it into the fire, pounded it into fragments, scattered it into water and gave this to the people to drink.[31] The prophet's anger became the instrument of a prophecy, for that body of the godless is cast into the fire of tribulations and ground to pieces by the word of God. What I mean is this: the impious are dissociating themselves little by little from the body to which they belonged, and as time passes it is getting worn out, like an old garment. Each one of them who becomes a Christian is separated from that people, chipped away from the block. Conspiring together, they hate; broken apart,[32] they believe. All men and women were meant to be sucked in through baptism to the city of Jerusalem, of which the Israelite people were the type: what could be plainer than that? For no other reason did Moses scatter the pieces into water, so that it could be drunk.

Accordingly Christ's thirst persists to the end; he is running, and he is thirsty. He has already drunk many people, but his thirst will never be slaked. That is why he begged the Samaritan, *I am thirsty, woman: give me a drink.*[33] The Samaritan woman at the well perceived the Lord's thirst, and her own thirst was satisfied by the one who thirsted; she initially became aware of him as a thirsty man, so that he might drink her as she came to believe.[34] And on the cross he cried, *I am thirsty* (Jn 19:28), though they had no intention of giving him what he longed for. He was thirsting for them, but all they gave him was vinegar; not the new wine with which new wineskins were to be filled,[35] but old wine, not mature

---

30. See Ps 34(35):12.
31. See Ex 32:20.
32. Variant: "piecemeal."
33. See Jn 4:7.
34. *Sensit prior illa sitientem, ut biberet ille credentem.*
35. See Mk 2:22.

but sour.[36] Those old men and women are rightly called stale, vinegary wine, those of whom another psalm said, *With them there is no change* (Ps 54:20(55:19)). But with the Jebusites turned out, the way was clear for Jerusalem to be built.[37]

The thirst of Christ's body

10. But the body that belongs to this head is running thirstily too, even to the end of time. The body might be challenged: "Why thirstily? What more can you want, body of Christ, Church of Christ? You are held in high honor, you are so exalted and enjoy a status of such dignity even in this world, how can you still be dissatisfied? The prophecy that *all the kings of the earth will worship him, and all nations will serve him* (Ps 71(72):11) is being fulfilled in your own experience. How can you still be thirsty? What are you thirsting for? Are you not satisfied with all these peoples?"

"But what kind of peoples are you talking about?" the Church might reply. *With their mouths they were blessing, but cursing in their hearts all the while.* As the Lord warned, *Many are invited, but only a few are chosen* (Mt 22:14). Recall the case of the woman who suffered from a hemorrhage. She touched the hem of the Lord's garment and was healed; but the Lord was interested to find out who had touched him, because he had felt power flowing out of him to heal the woman. So he demanded, *Who touched me?* The disciples were astounded. *The crowds are pressing round you*, they said, *and you ask, "Who touched me?"* (Mk 5:31). But he insisted, *Somebody touched me* (Lk 7:46). It seemed that he was distinguishing between people: "Only one person really touched me, though the crowds are pressing round me." The people who throng our churches at the festivals of Jerusalem fill the theaters on Babylon's high days; yet they serve, honor and pay homage to Christ. This is true of those who are signed with Christ's sacraments while hating Christ's commandments, and true also of others who are not even signed with his sacraments—true even of pagans, even of Jews. They honor, praise and proclaim him, but only *with their mouths* are they blessing. "I am not concerned with lip-service," says the Church, "for he who teaches me knows that they are *cursing in their hearts all the while.*" Where they saw a chance of denying me honor, there they cursed.

Verses 6-7. Only in God is patient endurance possible for us

11. Now what about you, Idithun, body of Christ, you who leap over them? How do you get on amid all these things? What? Will you sink under them? Can

---

36. *Vinum vetus, sed male vetus.*
37. See 2 Sm 5:6.

you not hold out to the end? Aren't you listening to the promise and the warning, *Whoever perseveres to the end will be saved*, although *with iniquity increasing mightily, the love of many will grow cold* (Mt 24:13.12)? What has become of that agility of yours that sent you leaping over them? And what of your claim that your life is lived in heaven?[38] These people stick fast in earthly things; they are earthbound and have no sensitivity to anything but the earth. They are earth themselves, snakes' food. What are you doing amid all this?

In spite of it all, replies this hard-pressed one, even though they do indeed behave so, even though their thoughts are so hostile, even though they attack me, even though they pushed me hard when I was almost falling, even though when I am standing upright they still think to deny me honor, even though they utter blessings with their lips but curses in their hearts, even though they ambush me where they can and slander me wherever they have opportunity, *all the same, my soul will surrender itself to God.* Who could command the strength to endure so much—the open warfare and the subtle trickery? Who could find the strength to endure it all amid both blatant enemies and treacherous brethren? Who could stand it? Any man or woman? And if any human being could bear so much, would such endurance ever come from his own resources? No. But I have not so leapt across as to be exalted and risk a speedy fall: *to God will my soul be subject, for my patience comes from him.* What patience can there be in the face of such obstacles but that of which scripture speaks: *if we hope for what we do not see, we wait for it in patience* (Rom 8:25)? My pain is near at hand, but my rest will come later; my time of trial is coming, but my purification will be as surely effected. Does gold gleam brightly in the refiner's furnace? No, not yet. It will be bright in the necklace, it will gleam when it finds its place in the jewel; but for the present it must endure the furnace, for only so will it be purged of its impurities and attain its brightness. So we need the furnace. There is the straw, there is the gold, and there is the fire, and as the refiner blows into the furnace the straw burns and the gold is purified. The one is reduced to ashes, the other emerges freed from its dross. For me, the furnace is this world, bad people are the straw, the troubles I undergo are the fire, and God is the refiner. As the refiner wills, I act; wherever the refiner places me, I endure. I am commanded to suffer it, and he well knows how to assay me. Even if the straw is set on fire to burn me, even if it seems likely to consume me, it is the straw that is turned to ashes; I emerge freed from my impurities. Why? Because *to God will my soul be subject, for my patience comes from him.*

12. What is he to you, then, he from whom your patience derives? *He is my God and my salvation; he is my refuge, and I shall never leave him.* Because *he is my God*, he calls me; because *he is my salvation*, he justifies me; and because *he*

---

38. See Phil 3:20.

is my refuge, he glorifies me.[39] Here on earth I am called and justified, and there beyond I shall be glorified. From that place to which I shall be raised in glory, *I shall never leave him.* Not always shall I be on pilgrimage, for I must eventually depart from here, but I shall go to a place whence there will be no departing. On earth I am no more than a lodger[40] in your house, like all my forebears.[41] I shall have to move on and lose my tenure, but from my heavenly home I shall never depart.

Verse 8. Justification, salvation, and glory

13. *In God is my salvation and my glory.* I shall be saved in God, and I shall be glorious in God. It is not a case of being saved and no more, of being barely saved. I shall be glorious too: saved, because being changed from an impious to a just person, I have been justified by him; but glorious too, because I am not merely justified, but also honored. Scripture says, *Those whom he predestined, he also called*; but what then? Having called them, what else did he do? *Those whom he called, he also justified; and those whom he justified, he glorified as well* (Rom 8:30). Justification is the requirement for being saved, glorification means that we are to be honored. This latter point needs no proof; obviously glorification implies being honored. However, we need to seek some teaching from the Lord to show us that justification is necessary for salvation.

The gospel provides it. Certain persons considered themselves just, and rebuked the Lord for welcoming sinners to a feast, and sharing meals with tax collectors and sinners. The critics were proud folk, important people in the world's eyes and very high and mighty; they were ostentatious about the good health they believed themselves to possess, though they really had no such health at all. What reply did the Lord give them? *It is not the healthy who need the physician, but the sick* (Mt 9:12). Now whom is he calling healthy? And whom sick? He makes it explicit by continuing, *I did not come to call the righteous, but sinners to repentance* (Lk 5:32). So by "healthy" he meant the just—not that the Pharisees were just, but they thought they were. And thinking so, they adopted a haughty attitude, and begrudged the sick their doctor. And being even more gravely ill themselves, they killed the doctor.

All the same, the Lord called just people healthy, and sinners sick. "So it is by his gift that I was justified," says our leaper, "and by his gift that I shall be glorified. *In God is my salvation and my glory.* He is *my salvation*, because it is only through him that I am saved, and *my glory*, because thanks to him I shall be honored."

---

39. See Rom 8:30.
40. *Inquilinus*; see note at Exposition of Psalm 38, 21.
41. See Ps 38:13(39:12).

Yes, that will come later, but what about now? *"He is the God who helps me; my hope is in God* until I attain perfect justification and salvation, for *in hope we have been saved. But if hope is seen, it is hope no longer* (Rom 8:24). In him I hope, until I attain that state of glory where the just will shine like the sun in their Father's kingdom.[42]

"But still, what about the present? What about my struggle amid temptations, iniquities, scandals, overt opposition and deceitful flattery, among people who have blessings on their lips but curses in their hearts, among those who think to refuse me honor? What about my life here? It is *God who helps me*; he supports those who are locked in the fight." And against whom are you fighting? *"It is not against flesh and blood that we have to struggle, but against principalities and powers* (Eph 6:12). In this contest *God* it is *who helps me; my hope is in God."* He is our hope as long as the promise remains to be fulfilled, and we go on believing in what we do not see; but when the fulfillment has come, he will be our salvation and our glory. Even now, while these things are deferred, we are not abandoned, for *God* it is *who helps me; my hope is in God.*

Verses 9-10. Hope in God, and love your enemies

14. *Hope in him, you whole assembly of the people.* Take Idithun as your model. Leap over your enemies, leap over all those who offer you resistance, or block your path, or hate you: leap over all of them. *Hope in him, you whole assembly of the people. Pour out your hearts in his presence.* Do not give ground before those who taunt you with "Where is your God?" Another psalm lamented, *My tears have been bread to me day and night, as every day I hear the taunt, Where is your God?* And how did that person respond? *I reflected on these things, and poured out my soul above myself* (Ps 41:4-5(42:3-4)). I called to mind the derision I had heard, *Where is your God?* I remembered it, *and poured out my soul above myself.* In search of my God I poured out my soul above myself, seeking to reach him, for I did not want to remain confined within myself. You must do likewise: *hope in him, you whole assembly of the people. Pour out your hearts in his presence,* pleading, confessing, and full of hope. Do not keep your hearts shut up inside your hearts, but *pour out your hearts in his presence.* What you pour out is not lost. He is *my refuge.* If he makes himself your refuge, why are you afraid to pour out your hearts? Cast your care upon the Lord[43] and hope in him. *Pour out your hearts in his presence, for God is our ally.* Why are you frightened amid whisperers, talebearers, people hateful to God?[44] They oppose you openly where they can, and where they cannot they secretly lay

42. See Mt 13:43.
43. See Ps 54:23(55:22).
44. See Rom 1:29-30.

traps; they pretend to speak to you fair, while their real intention is hostile. But why be frightened of them? *God is our ally.* Are they challenging God? Are they stronger than he is? *God is our ally,* have no fear. *If God is for us, who can stand against us?* (Rom 8:31). *Pour out your hearts in his presence,* leaping over to him, for *God is our ally.*

15. So there you are in your stronghold, secure in your impregnable tower against enemy attacks, but you must have pity on those who used to terrify you. Your duty is to run thirstily. From your fortified position look down on them and say, "*How futile mortals are, what liars the children of men!* How long will you be heavy-hearted, human creatures? Empty-minded people, lying folk, why love emptiness, human creatures, why chase falsehood?"[45] Say this with real compassion, meaning what you say. If you have truly leapt across, if you love your enemies, if your ambition is to destroy only in order to build anew, if you love him who executes judgment among the nations and rebuilds their ruins,[46] this must be your attitude. Do not hate them, do not repay evil with evil.

What liars the children of men are, with their scales![47] *Intent on deception, in their empty pursuits they are as one.* Numerous they are, certainly, yet that man who was thrown out from the concourse of guests at the banquet was a sole individual. So how can the psalmist speak of them as many? Because they all conspire, they all pursue temporal gods, and all these carnally-minded folk seek carnal things, hoping to get one day whatever it is they want. Accordingly they are at one and agreed with regard to their empty desires, however divided in their variegated opinions. Their errors are certainly diverse and assume many forms; and no kingdom divided against itself can stand firm.[48] Nonetheless one frivolous and lying intent is common to them all, being the mark of that king with whom it will be thrown into eternal fire.[49] *In their empty pursuits they are as one.*

Verse 11. Justice is the only power that lasts

16. But look how Idithun is thirsting for these very people; look how thirstily he is running. Being so thirsty for them he turns to them and pleads, "*Do not set your hope on iniquity.* My own hope is in God. *Do not set your hope on iniquity.* If you are unwilling to go the whole way and leap across, at least *do not set your hope on iniquity.* I have leapt across, and so my hope is in God; and is there any iniquity in God?"[50] *Do not set your hope on iniquity.*

---

45. See Ps 4:3(2).
46. See Ps 109(110):6.
47. This could mean "... the children of men are, when weighed in the balance," but shortly after this Augustine refers it to deceitful dealings with falsified scales.
48. See Mk 3:24.
49. See Mt 25:41.
50. See Rom 9:14.

But they insist, "Let's do this, let's do that, let's think up a plan about so-and-so, let's set the trap this way," because in their obsession with emptiness they are as one. For them you must thirst. The people who scheme against you are forsaken by those whom you drink.[51] *Do not set your hope on iniquity.* Iniquity is empty, is nothing. The only powerful reality is justice. Truth may be obscured for a while, but it cannot be defeated. Iniquity may flourish for a while, but it cannot persist.

Do not set your hope on iniquity, or your desires on robbery. You are not rich, so you think of robbing someone? But what will you acquire, and what will you lose? It's a very damaging gain! You win some money, and you lose justice. *Do not set your desires on robbery.* "But I'm poor, I haven't got much!" So you want to seize something by force? You see what you are grabbing; don't you see who is robbing you? Don't you know that the enemy is prowling round like a ravening lion, looking for someone to pounce on?[52] The booty you plan to seize is the bait in a mousetrap; as you grab it you are grabbed. So don't set your desires on robbery, poor though you are; set your desire on God, who gives us everything to enjoy in abundance.[53] He who made you will feed you. Do you suppose that he who nourishes a brigand will not nourish an innocent person? He who makes his sun rise for the good and the wicked, and sends his rain upon just and unjust alike,[54] will certainly feed you. If he feeds those destined for damnation, will he not care for those who are to be delivered? Do not set your desires on robbery.

What I have been saying applies to a poor person, who perhaps may be tempted to rob out of necessity. Now let a rich person step forward. "I am under no necessity to rob anyone," he says. "I need nothing, I've got it all." But there is a lesson for you too: *if riches flow in abundance, do not set your heart on them.* The other man had no wealth; this one has plenty; the former must not seek to steal what he does not have, nor the latter set his heart on what he has. *If riches flow in abundance*: that means, if they overflow, like water gushing from a spring, *do not set your heart on them*: do not rely on your own resources, do not attach yourself to your riches. This phrase at least ought to put you on your guard: *if riches flow in abundance.* Do you not see that if you attach yourself to your wealth, you are liable to flow away with them? You are rich, and so you no longer covet anything, having so much. All right, listen now: *Instruct the rich of this world not to be high-minded.* And what does that same text say about not attaching your heart? *nor to put their trust in unreliable wealth* (1 Tm 6:17).

---

51. Variant: "you must thirst for those who think otherwise; they are the relatives of those whom you drink."
52. See 1 Pt 5:8.
53. See 1 Tm 6:17.
54. See Mt 5:45.

Take note, then: *if riches flow in abundance, do not set your heart on them.* Do not put your trust in wealth, do not be presumptuous, do not set your hope on it, lest of you it should be said, *Look at the person who would not take God as helper, but trusted in the amplitude of his riches, and grew strong in his stupidity* (Ps 51:9(52:8)).

So then, you empty-minded people, you lying folk, do not rob others, nor, if riches flow in abundance, set your hearts on them. Do not love emptiness, do not chase falsehood. That person is blessed whose God is the Lord, and who has had no regard for empty things and lying foolishness.[55] When you are minded to deceive someone, and want to defraud people, what do you use for your deception? Misleading scales. That is what the psalm alleges: *what liars the children of men are, with their scales!*, for by employing falsified scales they hoodwink others. With your fraudulent calculation you trick everyone who is watching, but do you not see that there is Someone else who is weighing things up, Someone who is judging you in the matter of your weights? The client for whom you are weighing the goods does not see your deception, but there is Someone who does see, and weighs you along with your weights.[56]

"In short," says Idithun, "do not be greedy for fraud or robbery, and do not set your hope on what you have. I have warned you, and pointed out the consequences."

Verses 12-13. How can God be said to have spoken only once?

17. What comes next? *Only once has God spoken, but these two things have I heard: that power belongs to God, and to you, O Lord, mercy; for you will requite each of us according to our deeds.* This is what Idithun said. He shouted from the lofty place to which he had leapt; he heard something there, and told us what it was. But I am somewhat troubled by what he has told us, brothers and sisters, and I would ask you to give me your full attention while I share my worry with you, or any relief I may find. After all, we have with the Lord's help reached the end of the psalm, so after the discussion we are about to undertake now there will be none of it left to be explained. Try your hardest along with me, then, and let us see if we can understand this part. If I cannot myself, but one of you is able to understand it where I am baffled, I shall be happy, not jealous.

It is extremely difficult to work out how the psalm can first state, *Only once has God spoken*, and then, when he has spoken once only, to continue, *these two things have I heard.* If the psalmist had said, "Only once has God spoken, and I heard this one thing," he would have disposed of part of our inquiry, because then we would have needed only to ask what it was that God spoke only once.

---

55. See Ps 39:5(40:4).
56. Or "you and your client."

But, as it is, we are obliged to ask both what God spoke only once, and also what were the two things the psalmist heard in that one speaking.

18. *Only once has God spoken.* What are you saying, Idithun? Is it really you, you who have leapt across, who are telling us, *only once has God spoken*? If I look up another scriptural passage, it tells me, *God spoke at sundry times and in various ways to our fathers through the prophets* (Heb 1:1), so what can it mean to say, *only once has God spoken*? Moreover is he not the God who in the earliest moments of the human race spoke to Adam? Did he not speak also to Cain, to Noah, to Abraham, to Isaac, to Jacob, to all the prophets, and to Moses? Yes, Moses—one man, yet how many times did God speak to him? So God spoke not once, but often, to this single individual. In the end God spoke to his Son on earth: *You are my beloved Son* (Mk 1:11). Then again God spoke to the apostles, and spoke to all the saints, even if not in a voice resounding from a cloud, at any rate in their hearts, where he resides as their teacher. Why else should a psalm declare, *I will listen to what the Lord God speaks within me, for he will speak peace to his people* (Ps 84:9(85:8))? What is the meaning, then, of your assertion that *only once has God spoken*?

This man had leapt a very long way to arrive at that place where God spoke only once. There you are, beloved friends: I have given you the short answer to our query. Here on earth, among human beings, God has indeed spoken frequently to us, in many ways, in many places, using many a created medium. But within himself God has spoken only once, because God begot one Word. And that is where Idithun's leap took him. He had leapt with the penetrating gaze of his mind, with his strong, bold, supremely confident keen-sightedness; he had leapt over the earth and all it contains, beyond the air and all the clouds from which God spoke much and often, and to so many people. He had leapt with the sharp gaze of his faith even beyond the angels, for this leaper was not content with earthly things, but like a soaring eagle was carried beyond all the cloud that enshrouds the entire earth, that cloud of which Wisdom testifies, *Like a cloud I covered all the land* (Sir 24:6). So as he leapt beyond all created things, seeking God, he attained to a limpid reality; he poured out his soul above himself,[57] he reached the very Beginning, the Word who is God-with-God. He found the unique Word of the unique Father, and he knew then that God did indeed speak only once. He beheld the Word through whom all things were created,[58] in whom all things exist at once, neither diversified, nor separated, nor unequal; for God was not ignorant of the creation he wrought through the Word, and if he already knew what he was making, whatever came to be must have been in God before it existed. If it was not, how could he have known the thing he was making? You cannot maintain that God made things previously unknown to him. God

---

57. See Ps 41:5(42:4).
58. See Jn 1:1-3.

undoubtedly knew what he made. But how did he know it before he made it, when things are not knowable unless they are made?

This impossibility of knowing things before they are created is an impossibility only for those who are themselves created—for you, that is, for you, a human being created in your lowly condition and assigned to your lowly place. Before all these things came to be they were known to him by whom they were made; he made what he knew. In the Word, in that Word through whom God made all things, all things were before they came to be. Once made, all things are there still, but the mode of their being is not the same here as there. With us, they exist in their own nature, in the particular nature given them at their creation; in the Word they exist in the archetypal principle of their createdness.[59] Who could ever explain this? We can but try. Go with Idithun, and see.

What were the "two things" I heard?

19. I have told you as best I can how God can be said to have spoken only once. Now let us see how Idithun heard two things, for this is what he says: *these two things have I heard*. It was not necessarily the case that he heard two things only, but this is what he says, *these two things have I heard*, so he must have heard two special things about which we needed to be told. No doubt he heard many others as well, but there is no need for us to hear about them. After all, the Lord himself said, *I have many things to tell you, but at present you are not able to bear them* (Jn 16:12).

Now what is implied when he says, *These two things have I heard*? He means, "These two things I am about to say to you I am not saying from myself; I am telling you only what I have heard." *Only once has God spoken* because he has one Word, God-only-begotten. In that Word are all things, because all things were made through the Word. God has one Word, in whom all the riches of wisdom and knowledge are hidden.[60] Because God has only one Word, it can be said that *only once has God spoken*. But these two things I am going to tell you I *heard* there, says Idithun; I am not speaking as of myself, I am not telling you something out of my own head. This is the point that the phrase, *I have heard*, is making. *The bridegroom's friend stands and hears him* (Jn 3:29) in order to speak the truth. He hears him, lest by speaking from himself he may speak falsehood;[61] and lest you might challenge him, "Who are you, to tell me this? By what authority do you speak so to me?" "I heard these two things," he asserts, "and I

---

59. Though he is expounding John's Prologue, Augustine is echoing the Platonic and Neoplatonic doctrine of pre-existent forms. The archetypes or exemplary causes of created beings are present in the Word.

60. See Col 2:3.

61. See Jn 8:44.

am speaking to you precisely because these were the two things I heard, even though I also acknowledge that God spoke only once." Do not disregard this hearer; he is telling you two things that you need to know. He is the person who by leaping beyond all creation attained to the sole-begotten Word of God, where he could learn that God spoke only once.

20. Let him tell us now what these two things are, for they are realities that intimately concern us. *That power belongs to God, and to you, O Lord, mercy*: are these the two things—power and mercy? They certainly are. Understand them to mean God's power and God's mercy, and almost all of scripture is summed up in these. From them and on their account came the prophets, from them the patriarchs, from them the law. From them came our Lord Jesus Christ himself, from them the apostles. From them and on their account came the whole announcement of the message, and the celebration of God's word in the Church: all because of these two things, because of God's power and mercy. Stand in awe of his power, and love his mercy. Do not be so recklessly confident of his mercy that you make light of his power, nor so fearful of his power that you despair of his mercy. In God is power, in God is mercy. One he humbles, another he uplifts:[62] one he humbles by his power, another he lifts up by his mercy. *God willed to show his anger, and give proof of his power, by producing with the utmost patience vessels of wrath, made for destruction.* There you have his power. What of his mercy? But *he wished to make his riches known toward the vessels of his mercy*, scripture continues. So the damnation of the wicked is an aspect of his power; and who has any right to ask him, "What have you done?" *Who are you, a mere mortal, to answer back to God?* (Rom 9:22.23.20). You must be fearful and tremble before his power, but hope for his mercy. The devil is a power of a kind, yet though he often wants to harm us he is not always able, because he is only a power subordinate to the Power. If the devil were able to do as much damage as he wants to, not a single just person would remain, nor would any one of the faithful be found on earth. Making use of his instruments[63] he presses hard on any leaning wall, but he presses only within the limits of the power he receives. The Lord will uphold the wall to ensure that it does not topple, for he who grants power to the tempter bestows mercy on the tempted too. Only in due measure is the devil permitted to tempt us: *you will measure out to us our due portion of weeping to drink*, says scripture.[64] Do not be afraid of what the tempter does, as he deploys the power allowed him, for you have a most merciful Savior. The devil is permitted to tempt you only to the extent that will profit you, so that you may be educated and put to the test. By this means you,

---

62. See Ps 74:8(75:7).
63. *Vasa*, the "vessels of wrath" referred to in the text from Romans just quoted.
64. Ps 79:6(80:5). When commenting on this verse in his Exposition of Psalm 79, 6, Augustine relates it to 1 Cor 10:13, as he also does in the present context.

who formerly did not truly know yourself, are enabled to find yourself. Where else can we be secure, on what else can we rely, but on the power and mercy of God, according to the apostle's teaching? *God is faithful,* says the apostle, *and he does not allow you to be tempted more fiercely than you can bear* (1 Cor 10:13).

God is powerful and inscrutable, but never unjust

21. We know, then, that *power belongs to God,* and scripture affirms that *there is no power except from God* (Rom 13:1). Do not grumble, "Who gave the devil so much power? I wish he wouldn't. Is God acting fairly in giving the devil power?" You can murmur unjustly, but God cannot lose his justice. *Is there iniquity in God? Absolutely not* (Rom 9:14). Plant that firmly in your heart, and do not let the enemy shake it loose from your thoughts. It is quite possible for God to do something for which you do not know the reason, but quite impossible that he should do anything inequitably, since in him there is no iniquity. Yet you are charging God with iniquity! (I am arguing on your terms: bear with me for a moment.) You would be in a position to denounce iniquity only if you had your eyes on justice. No one can bring a charge of injustice unless he or she has a clear view of justice as the standard against which injustice is to be discerned. So how can you know that this is unjust, without knowing what is just? What if this action you deem unjust is really just?

"Nonsense," you say. "It is unjust." And you loudly assert your opinion as though you had seeing eyes,[65] and could perceive this dispensation to be unjust by comparison with some norm of justice; as though you could assess what you perceive as crooked and check that it does not correspond with your straight ruler. You behave like a craftsman, competent to distinguish the just from the unjust. But I have a few questions for you: where do you see this standard of justice, against which you measure what you are denouncing as unjust? Where does that mysterious quality come from, which besprinkles your soul—your soul which is in many respects so clouded? Whence comes that mysterious reality which illumines your mind? From where does your just standard derive? Does it have a spring of its own? Does the standard of justice originate from you? Can you endow yourself with justice? No one can give himself what he does not have. It follows, then, that since you are unjust, you cannot be just except by turning toward a justice that abides; if you depart from it, you are unjust, but if you draw near to it, you are just. When you turn your back on it, it does not dwindle; if you approach it, it does not increase.

---

65. Variant: "believing eyes."

Where is this justice? Look for it on earth. No good; seeking justice is not like seeking gold or precious stones. Look for it in the sea, look in the clouds, look in the stars. Look among the angels, and indeed you will find it in them, but only because they too drink from the primordial spring. The justice of the angels is present in all of them, but is received from One. Take heed, then, pass beyond them and go to that place where God spoke only once. You will find the font of justice where you find the font of life: *with you is the font of life*, says another psalm (Ps 35:10(36:9)). If you aspire to judge what is just, and what unjust, on the strength of the scanty dew that dampens you, can there be injustice in God, the fountain of justice from which flows to you what discernment of justice you have (though all the while you are very undiscerning in many matters)? God possesses the very source of justice. Do not look for iniquity where shines the unshadowed light.

Obviously the reason for his actions may elude you. If you cannot understand the reason, put that down to your ignorance, and consider who you are. Take note of these two things: *that power belongs to God, and to you, O Lord, mercy*. And remember the warning, *seek not what is above you, and do not scrutinize loftier matters; but let your mind run constantly on what the Lord has entrusted to you* (Sir 3:22). The things the Lord has entrusted to you include these two: *that power belongs to God, and to you, O Lord, mercy*. Do not be afraid of the enemy; he does only what the power granted to him permits. Fear only him who holds supreme power; fear him who does whatever he wills, him who does nothing unjustly. Whatever he does is just. We were thinking, were we, that something or other was unfair? From the very fact that God did it, be sure that it is just.

God works all things together for good

22. "All right," you say. "So if someone kills an innocent person, does the killer act justly or wickedly?" Wickedly, of course. "Then why does God allow it?" Before we go into that, consider whether there is any unpaid debt of justice in your own account: *Break your bread for the hungry, and take the person with no shelter into your home. If you see anyone naked, clothe him* (Is 58:7). This is what justice means for you, for this is the commandment the Lord has entrusted to you: *Wash yourselves, make yourselves clean, get rid of the wickedness of your hearts and take it out of my sight; learn to do good, deal justly with the orphan and the widow. Then come, and let us argue it out, says the Lord* (Is 1:16-18). You want to begin the argument before you have done what is needed to qualify you; you are not yet competent to argue why God has allowed the deed. I cannot tell you what God's plan is, you poor thing; but this much I will say: whoever killed an innocent person acted unjustly, and could not have done the deed if God had not allowed it; but although the killer acted unjustly, God did

not act unjustly in allowing it. Let the reason for the deed lie hidden in that person whose fate has aroused you, whose innocence has moved you to ask your question. It would be easy enough for me to counter you by saying, "He would not have been killed if he had done no harm." Yet you believe him to have been innocent. I could still stick to my earlier line and say that you have not seen into his heart, you did not investigate his actions or examine his thoughts; so you are not sufficiently well informed to say to me, "He was killed unjustly." Yes, it would have been all too easy for me to take that line, except that a certain just man confutes me. He was undoubtedly just, incontrovertibly just. Though he was without sin, he was slain by sinners and betrayed by a sinner. Christ our Lord himself confutes me, he of whom we cannot say that he committed any iniquity at all, for he was making repayment where he had never robbed.[66]

And what am I to say about Christ? "It is about him that I want to talk to you," you say. And I to you.[67] If you frame your question about Christ, I can answer it in terms of Christ, for in that case we do know God's plan, though we should not have known it if he had not himself revealed it. When you discover that plan of God whereby he allowed his innocent Son to be killed by unjust ruffians, and you find this to be a plan that commends itself to you—indeed, you find it to be a plan that could not possibly fail to commend itself to you if you are just your-self—then you may believe that in other instances also God acts in accordance with his plan, even if it is hidden from you. That is the truth, brothers and sisters: the blood of a just man was needed to cancel the written bond that stood against us sinners;[68] the example of his patience was needed, and the example of his humility; the sign of the cross was needed to subdue the devil and his angels. We needed the passion of our Lord, for by the Lord's passion the world was redeemed.

How much good was wrought by the Lord's passion! And yet the passion of this just man would never have happened if wicked men had not slain the Lord. Does that mean that the good which has come to us from the Lord's passion is to be credited to Christ's wicked murderers? Certainly not. They willed it, and God allowed it. They would have been guilty even if they had gone no further than willing it; but God would not have allowed it, if it had not been just. Imagine a situation in which they wanted to kill him, but lacked the power to do it. Everyone will agree that they would still have been wicked, still murderers, for *the Lord questions the righteous and the ungodly* (Ps 10:6(11:5)), and *an inquiry will be instituted in the thoughts of a godless person* (Wis 1:9). God discerns what each of us has willed to do, not merely what we have effected. Suppose, then, that they had wanted to do it, but been unable to, and had not killed him,

---

66. See Ps 68:5(69:4).
67. Or perhaps, "Come on, I am asking you a question." "Yes, and I am answering you. If you...."
68. See Col 2:14.

they would have been just as guilty, but the benefit of Christ's passion would not have flowed to you. The wicked man entertained his wicked design to his own condemnation, but he was permitted to act on it for your benefit; the evil will is to be attributed to the iniquity of the perpetrator, but the permission for him to carry it out is to be attributed to the power of God. The human agent unjustly willed it, but God justly permitted it. Think what this means, brothers and sisters. Judas, the malevolent betrayer of Christ, and all persecutors of Christ, all malevolent people, all the impious, all the unjust—all of them deserve condemnation; and yet the Father *did not spare even his own Son, but delivered him up for us all* (Rom 8:32). Mark the difference, if you can; draw the distinction, if you can. Render your vows of thankfulness to God, those vows which your lips have uttered as the fruit of your discernment;[69] discern what part the unjust played, and what the Just One. The former willed it, the latter allowed it; the one unjustly willed it, the other justly allowed it. Let the unjust volition be condemned, and the just permission be glorified. What evil touched Christ, in consequence of his being killed? They are evil, the people who willed to do it, but evil did not infect the one to whom they did it. His mortal flesh was killed, but by its death it slew death, gave us an example of patience, and modeled in advance our resurrection.

How immense are the good results achieved by the Just One from the bad deeds of the unjust! This is the great deed of God:[70] that the good you effect has been given to you by God, and from the bad things you do he himself contrives good. Do not be baffled, then. What God permits, he permits by his own judgment. When he permits, he permits by measure, and number, and weight.[71] In him there is no injustice. All you have to do is to belong to him and rest your hope in him; let him be your helper and your salvation; let your fortified place and your impregnable tower be in him. May he be your refuge, and not allow you to be tempted beyond your strength, but along with the temptation himself ordain the outcome so that you may stand fast.[72] The degree of temptation which he allows you to suffer is the sign of his power, but may his tempering of it to the measure of your endurance be the work of his mercy, for *power belongs to God, and to you, O Lord, mercy; for you will requite each of us according to our deeds.*

---

69. See Ps 65(66):13-14.
70. Variant: "the reign of God."
71. An echo of Wis 11:21, a favorite text with Augustine, one which suggested to him a trinitarian pattern in the ordering of creation. "Weight" in particular evoked for him the Spirit of love. See note at Exposition 2 of Psalm 29, 10; and *The Confessions* XIII, 9, 10.
72. See 1 Cor 10:13.

After expounding the psalm, Augustine appended the following remarks about an astrologer[73] whom he pointed out among the people

23. The thirsty Church is longing to drink this man too, the man you see here. You are well aware of how many there are intermingled with Christians, who bless with their mouths but curse in their hearts all the while.[74] This man was once a Christian and a believer; now he returns to us as a penitent. Terrified by the Lord's power, he turns back to the Lord's mercy. While he was a believer he was seduced by the enemy, and then for a long time he was an astrologer. Seduced himself, he seduced others; deceived, he was a deceiver. He beguiled others, tricked others, and told many lies against God, who has given to human beings the power to do what is good and refuse what is evil. This man was accustomed to say that adultery is not the act of anyone's free will, but of Venus; that homicide is not anyone's free act, but the work of Mars; that it is not God who makes a person just, but Jove. Many another gravely sacrilegious statement did he make. How much money do you think he took from Christians?[75] How many Christians purchased falsehood from him, although we were admonishing them, *How long will you be heavy-hearted, human creatures? Why love emptiness and chase falsehood?* (Ps 4:3(2)).

But now we have it on his own trustworthy testimony that he has come to abhor falsehood, and to realize that he, who enticed so many, had been himself enticed by the devil. So he is coming back to God in repentance. In our judgment, brothers and sisters, this can have happened only under the pressure of great fear in his heart, for how otherwise can we account for it? If an astrologer were converted from paganism it would be a matter of high rejoicing, to be sure; but it might be suspected that his conversion was partly motivated by ambition for the clerical state in the Church. This man, however, is a penitent; he is seeking nothing but mercy. We must therefore commend him to your eyes and your hearts. With your hearts, love the person you see; with your eyes, take care of him. Look at him, make sure you will know him again, and wherever he goes, point him out to our brothers and sisters who are not here today. This watchfulness is a mercy, for without it the old seducer might drag his heart back again,[76] and assault him. Make yourselves his guardians: do not allow his manner of life or the course he takes to be concealed from you, so that through your guarantee we may be assured that he has truly been converted to the Lord. If he is entrusted to you like this, to be observed and kindly cared for, his reputation will be secure.

---

73. *Mathematicus* see note at Exposition 2 of Psalm 29, 10.
74. See verse 5 above.
75. The implication is that the man's Christian clients were equally guilty. Compare Augustine's strictures in his Exposition 2 of Psalm 31, 16.
76. Variant: "return to his heart."

In the Acts of the Apostles it is recorded, as you know, that many abandoned characters—practitioners of such arts and adherents of vile doctrines—brought all their books to the apostles. So great a number of books were burnt that the author of Acts thought it his business to estimate the value of them, and state it in monetary terms.[77] This event redounded to God's glory, proving that not even depraved characters of this kind were despaired of by him who knows how[78] to seek what was lost.[79] This man too was lost; but now he has been sought, and found, and brought home. He brings with him his books to be burnt, those books through which he would have incurred burning himself. Once they have been thrown into the fire, he will pass into a place of cool refreshment.

However, brothers and sisters, you ought to know that he initially knocked at the Church's door some time ago, before Easter; for it was then, before Easter, that he began to seek healing from Christ's Church. In view of the wiles in which he had been adept, however, it seemed advisable to suspect lying and deception. So he was put off for a time in case he was merely trying his luck, but then admitted, after some delay, lest the trial he was undergoing expose him to over-much danger.[80] Pray for him through[81] Christ. Begin at once: offer today's prayer for him to the Lord our God. We know with certainty that your prayer will blot out all his acts of impiety.

The Lord be with you.

---

77. See Acts 19:19.
78. Variant: "came."
79. See Lk 15:24.32.
80. *Dilatus est ne tentaret . . . ne periculosius tentaretur.* He might be "trying" the Church, so the Church "tried" him, but not for too long.
81. Variant: "to."

Exposition of Psalm 62

A Sermon to the People

Introduction: many prophecies are already fulfilled; we must believe that the rest will be

1. A few things must be briefly explained for the sake of those who perhaps are not yet well instructed in the name of Christ, for he who shed his blood for everyone gathers believers from every quarter. Our explanation will be willingly received by those of you who know about these things already, and will give those who do not know an opportunity to learn.

The psalms we sing were composed and written as the Spirit of God dictated, long before our Lord Jesus Christ was born of the virgin Mary. David[1] was king of the Jewish people. This one nation, alone among the nations, worshiped the one God who made heaven and earth, the sea and all things within them, both visible creatures and those that are invisible. The other nations paid homage either to idols that they had made with their own hands, or to God's creation rather than to the Creator himself: that is, to the sun, or the moon, or the stars, or the sea, or mountains or trees. God made all these, and he wishes us to praise him for them; but he does not want us to worship them instead of him. Among the Jewish people, however, David was king, and it was from his stock that our Lord Jesus Christ was born of the virgin Mary, because she who bore Christ was a descendant of David.[2] Now when these psalms were composed, it was prophesied in them that many years later Christ would come. Those prophets who lived before Christ was born predicted everything that would come to pass in our days. We read them today and see it for ourselves, and we are filled with joy that he who is our hope was foretold by those holy men who, in the Spirit, foresaw what was to take place in the future, without themselves beholding the fulfillment. We, for our part, read about it now, and listen to the reader declaiming it, and discuss these events. Just as we find them foretold in the scriptures, even so do we see them happening throughout the world.

Surely each one of us finds joy in this? And does it not strengthen our hope in the coming of what has not come yet, when we see that so much has been fulfilled already? I am sure it does, brothers and sisters, for you see how the

---

1. Like his contemporaries, Augustine assumes that David was directly the author of all the psalms.
2. See Lk 1:27.32; Rom 1:3.

whole world, all the earth, all nations, all countries, are rallying to the name of Christ, and believing in him. You cannot fail to see how the foolish practices of the pagans are being abolished everywhere; you must be aware of this, since it is quite obvious. It is not as though we were reading about this to you out of a book, but your eyes found no supporting evidence, is it? Yet all that you see taking place before your eyes was written about an immensely long time ago, written in these books which we are reading now as we watch the prophecies being fulfilled.

Now, other things were written there too, things which have not yet come to pass, and especially that our Lord Jesus Christ, who once came to be judged, will come again to judge. At his first coming he came in humility, at his second coming he will come in majesty. As he came once to give us an example of patience, so he will come again to judge all men and women according to their deserts—all of them, both good and bad. Clearly then, though this second advent has not taken place yet, we must believe that it will. We can be certain that our hope will not be disappointed, that Christ will come to judge the living and the dead. Only a small part of the prophecies still remains unverified; so let us believe that this too will be fulfilled, since we see already that so many things, still future at the time they were foretold, are fully realized now. It would be a foolish person who refused credence to the few remaining prophecies, when so many other things, not yet in existence when they were predicted, are now plain to see.

Head and members are one, in suffering, in glory, in the psalm

2. This psalm is spoken in the person of our Lord Jesus Christ, and that means head and members. He, the one man who was born from Mary, and suffered, and was buried, and rose again, and ascended into heaven, and now sits at the Father's right hand to intercede for us — he is our head. If he is the head, we are the limbs. The whole Church, spread abroad everywhere, is his body, and of that body he is the head. It is not only believers alive today who constitute his body: those who preceded us, and those who will come after us, even to the end of time—all these belong to his body. He, the head of the body, has ascended into heaven.

So that is firmly established: he is the head, we are the body. Accordingly, when we hear his voice, we must hearken to it as coming from both head and body; for whatever he suffered, we too suffered in him, and whatever we suffer, he too suffers in us. Think of an analogy: if your head suffers some injury, can your hand be unaffected? Or if your hand is hurt, can your head be free from pain? Or if your foot is painful, can your head be unconcerned? When any one of our members suffers, all the other members hasten to help the one that is in pain. This solidarity meant that when Christ suffered, we suffered in him; and it follows that now that he has ascended into heaven, and is seated at the Father's right hand, he still undergoes in the person of his Church whatever it may suffer amid the troubles of this world, whether temptations, or hardship, or oppression (for all these are the necessary means of our instruction, and through them the Church is purified, as gold is by fire).

A question asked by the apostle is enough to prove that we suffered in him: *if you died with Christ, why do you still determine the way you live by the standards of the world?* (Col 2:20). And again Paul teaches that *our old humanity has been nailed to the cross with Christ, that our sinful self may be nullified* (Rom 6:6). But if we died in him, we have also risen in him, and this too the apostle affirms: *If you have risen with Christ, have a taste for the things that are on high; seek what is above, where Christ is seated at the right hand of God* (Col 3:1-2). We died in him, then, and in him we have risen from the dead; but he also dies in us, and rises again in us, for he is himself the unity that binds head and body. From this we can be certain that his voice is our voice too, and our voice his. Now let us listen to the psalm, and be sensitive to Christ speaking in it.

Verse 1. The title. Desert and thirst

3. The title of the psalm is *For David himself, when he was in the desert of Edom.* The name "Edom" stands for the present world. The Edomites were a wandering tribe, and in their territory idols were worshiped. Nothing good is suggested by the mention of Edom here; and if the sense of it is pejorative, we can fairly take Edom to represent our life in this world, where we have to struggle very hard and are subject to sore distress. This life is a desert where our thirst is intense. In the psalm you will hear the voice of someone suffering thirst now.

But if we are conscious of how thirsty we are, we should look forward with equal intensity to drinking. Anyone who is thirsty in this world will drink to the full in the world to come. For this we have the Lord's promise: *Blessed are those who hunger and thirst for righteousness, for they shall be satisfied* (Mt 5:6). We should not be too fond of plentiful nourishment in this world. This is the place for thirst; we shall be fully satisfied elsewhere. But even now God sprinkles upon us the dew of his word to keep us from fainting in this desert. He does not let us become completely parched, lest we have to keep on clamoring for water;[3] but

---

3. *Ut non sit de nobis repetitio,* an obscure phrase. *Repetitio* could mean a repeated demand, like that of the Israelites in the desert; this sense is tentatively offered in the present translation. Other possibilities are (1) *repetitio* = a reclaiming, a demanding back, and seeking again: "lest a [too severe] account be demanded of us"; (2) *repetitio* = a returning, a going back, as the Israelites were tempted to return to Egypt: "lest we be tempted to turn back." The phrase seems to have puzzled some copyists: one manuscript reads *ut nunc sit nobis appetitio,* which looks like a smoothing out of the difficulty: "that we may experience the longing/appetite now."

he wills us to be so thirsty that we long to drink. He therefore provides for us by sprinkling on us some measure of his grace. Yet we are athirst still. And what does our soul then say to God?

Verse 2. Sleep and vigil

4. *O God, my God, from early light I keep watch for you*. What does keeping watch entail? Not sleeping, obviously. And what is sleeping? There is a sleep of the soul, and a sleep of the body. Bodily sleep is something we all need, because if we do not get our sleep we flag, and the whole body weakens. Our frail body cannot for any length of time support the soul that is wakeful and on the stretch in its proper activities.[4] If the soul continues for a long time in the operations proper to it, the frail, earthly body cannot contain it or sustain it in its unrelenting activity; and then the body fails and collapses. This is why God has endowed the body with the gift of sleep, during which our bodily members are restored, so that they will be strong enough once more to support the vigilant soul.

What we must beware of, however, is that the soul itself may fall asleep; for the sleep of the soul is dangerous. Bodily sleep is good, for it is the means whereby the health of the body is maintained; but the sleep of the soul is forgetfulness of its God. Whenever a soul forgets its God, it drops off to sleep. The apostle had good reason to speak as he did to certain persons who had forgotten God, and were indulging like sleepers in the absurdity of idol-worship (for the devotees of idols are like people who see nonsensical visions in their dreams; once the soul wakes up, it remembers who made it, and stops paying cult to something it made itself). To people of this type the apostle says, *Arise, sleeper, rise from the dead: Christ will enlighten you* (Eph 5:14). Was Paul trying to awaken someone who had gone to sleep in the physical sense? No, clearly not; he was arousing a slumbering soul when he urged it to let itself be enlightened by Christ.

This same kind of wakefulness is intended by the psalmist, who prays, *O God, my God, from early light I keep watch for you*. You could not possibly stay awake if you were confined within yourself: you need the rising of your light to arouse you from sleep. Christ illumines our souls and enables them to keep watch; but if he withdraws his light, they fall asleep. In another psalm the plea is made, *Enlighten my eyes, lest I ever fall into the sleep of death* (Ps 12:4(13:3)). If souls turn away from him and go to sleep, the light is still there, still available to them, but they cannot see it because they are asleep. It is like when someone is asleep in the bodily sense during the daytime: the sun is up already, and the day is growing hot, but for the sleeper it might as well be night still, because he is not

---

4. Compare Wis 9:15, often cited by Augustine, and influenced, as he was himself, by Platonic and Neoplatonic views on the relation of soul to body.

awake to see the daylight that is already at full strength. Similarly Christ is there, fully present, for some people, and the truth has already been preached to them, but their souls are still fast asleep. To such as these you must speak, if you are awake yourselves. Say to them every day, *Arise, sleeper, rise from the dead: Christ will enlighten you.* Your life and conduct must keep such faithful watch in Christ that others, especially somnolent pagans, may be aware of it, and be aroused by the wake-up call of your vigils, and shake off their sleepiness, and begin to join you in saying, *O God, my God, from early light I keep watch for you.*

The thirst of soul and body for eternal life

5. *My soul is athirst for you.* The scene is the Edomite desert. Look how thirsty the speaker is. But what a good thing it is that he can declare, *My soul is athirst for you*; for there are others who thirst, but not for God. Everyone intent on getting something for himself or herself is aflame with desire, and this desire is the soul's thirst. Think how powerful are the desires in human hearts. One person covets gold, another silver, another possessions, another ancestral lands, another plenty of ready money, another vast herds, another a spacious house, another a wife, another high rank, and another children. You are familiar with these desires, and you know how powerful they can be in the hearts of men and women. Everyone burns with desire, but there are precious few who can say to God, *My soul is athirst for you.* People thirst for the world, not understanding that they are in the desert of Edom, where their souls are meant to be thirsting for God. Let us declare it, though: *My soul is athirst for you.* We can all say it in this singular form, because in the heartfelt charity of Christ we are all one soul. Let this one soul feel its thirst in Edom.

6. *My soul is athirst for you, and for you my flesh thirsts too, in how many ways!* It is not enough to say that my soul thirsts for you; even my flesh is thirsty. But while it is quite straightforward to say that the soul thirsts for God, how can our flesh be athirst for God? When the flesh suffers thirst, what it wants is water; but when the soul thirsts, it thirsts for the fountain of wisdom. From that fountain our souls will be inebriated, as another psalm foretells: *They will be inebriated by the rich abundance of your house, and you will give them the full torrent of your delights to drink* (Ps 35:9(36:8)). We must thirst for wisdom and justice. We shall not slake that thirst, nor be fully satisfied, until this life is over and we reach what God has promised. God has pledged us equality with the angels,[5] and the angels are not thirsty, as we are now; they are not hungry, as we are; for they enjoy the total satisfaction of truth, light, and immortal wisdom. Therefore they

---

5. See Lk 20:36.

are happy. Unbounded happiness is theirs, because they are within that heavenly city, Jerusalem, from which we are still far distant on our pilgrimage. But they keep an eye on us as we plod along, and pity us, and at the Lord's command they help us, so that we may eventually reach home in that country which is ours as well as theirs, where we shall find our satisfaction at last in drinking with them from the Lord's fountain of eternal truth.

Let our soul be thirsty now, certainly. But for what is our flesh thirsting—thirsting even in manifold ways, as the psalm cries out? *And for you my flesh thirsts too, in how many ways!* it says. Why is this? Because even for our flesh there is the promise of resurrection. As beatitude is promised to our soul, even so is resurrection promised to our flesh. We are promised a resurrection of the flesh such that—wait a minute,[6] listen, and take this lesson in, and hold onto it. For what do Christians hope? Why are we Christians? We are not Christians in order to pray for some earthly prosperity, which even robbers and other criminals often enjoy. We are Christians for the sake of a different felicity, which we shall receive when our life in this world has wholly passed away. The resurrection even of our flesh is promised to us, such that this very flesh we carry now shall rise again in the end. This should not seem to you beyond belief. If when we did not exist God made us, is it any great task for him to remake us who formerly did exist? Do not deem it incredible, simply because you see the dead decompose, and return to ashes and dust. Or suppose some dead human body is burned, or torn to pieces by dogs, do you think the person cannot rise again after that? All those limbs which are mangled, or reduced to cinders and rotting away, are whole in God's sight. They return to the elements of the world, from which they originally came when we were created; we do not see them anymore, but God knows whence to draw them forth,[7] just as he knew whence to draw us forth before ever we came to be. A resurrection of our flesh is promised us such that although the flesh that will rise again is the same flesh that we bear now, it will not be subject to the corruptibility inherent in its mortal state. So frail, so corruptible are we now that if we do not eat, we grow faint and hungry; if we do not drink, we faint with thirst; if we keep vigil for a long time, we faint with weariness and fall asleep; if we sleep too long, we weaken, and need to be energetic again; if we spend too much time eating and drinking, then even though our intention was to refresh ourselves with food and drink, we shall scarcely survive what was meant to revive[8] us; if we stand for a long time, we get tired, and have

---

6. He breaks off in mid-sentence to remind them about Christian hope, and returns to his interrupted thought a few lines further on.

7. In his account of his mother's instructions before her death, Augustine represents her as saying something similar to his friends. They "asked whether she was not afraid to leave her body so far from her own city. 'Nothing is far from God,' she replied. 'There is no danger that at the end of the world he will not know where to find me and raise me up' " (*Confessions* IX, 11, 28).

8. *Ipsa . . . refectio defectio est.*

to sit down; but if we sit for a long time, we find that tiring as well, and have to stand up.

Furthermore, notice that there is no stable condition in our fleshly life. Infancy flies away into childhood; you look for the infant state, and it is not there, for it has been supplanted by childhood. Then childhood fades away into adolescence; you look for childhood, and it has vanished. Then the adolescent turns into a youth; you search for the adolescent, but he is there no longer. The young man grows old; you look for the youth, but he is not to be found. Then the old man dies; you seek the old man, but you do not find him. No age, no stage of our life stands still; everywhere there is fatigue, weariness, and decay.

When we reflect on the resurrection God promises, and on what manner of hope it instills in us, then even amid the manifold disintegration of our failing lives we thirst for that ultimate indefectibility, and our flesh thirsts for God with a many-sided longing. Here in Edom, in this desert, the more its labors are multiplied, the more multifarious becomes its thirst. As its weariness takes many, many forms, so does its thirst for that incorruptible state beyond all weariness.[9]

7. However, the flesh of a good and faithful Christian ought to thirst for God in very many ways even in this world, brothers and sisters, because if our flesh is in need of bread, or water, or wine, or cash, or a horse, we should ask God for what we need, not the demons, or the idols, or any other powers in this world. Some people there are who, when suffering from hunger, abandon God and address themselves to Mercury,[10] or they ask Jove to give them what they need, or the goddess they call "The Heavenly One,"[11] or some similar demons. The flesh of people like this does not thirst for God. Those who do thirst for God must thirst in every possible respect, which means in both soul and flesh. God gives to the soul his own bread as its proper food, which is the word of truth; and he also gives to the flesh whatever it needs, for God made both soul and flesh. Yet you go running to demons for the needs of your flesh! Surely you do not think that, while God made your soul, the demons made your flesh? No: God who created your soul created your flesh too; and he who made both, himself nourishes both. Let each of the components in us thirst for God, and after our multifarious labor may our thirst be quenched in utter simplicity.

---

9. The experience of weakness and need is itself the raw material of prayer. Augustine is in one of his most effective pastoral modes. He does not quote Rom 8:26-27, but the thought is similar.

10. Mercury, a Roman god who shared many features with the Greek god Hermes, was the son of Jove/Jupiter and Maia. He was regarded as the messenger of the gods, and as interesting himself in merchants and trading.

11. *Caelestis*, a female divinity venerated especially at Carthage. Tertullian recounts in his *Apology* that each nation had its particular god, and states that "Africa had its Caelestis" (*Apol.* 24). Earlier he mentions that Caelestis was the rain-promiser (see *Apol.* 23). Augustine admits that as a young man he had sometimes taken pleasure in the games celebrated in honor of the virgin Caelestis and Berecynthia, mother of the gods, which included many obscene elements: see *The City of God* II, 4.

Verse 3. The way and the water in our desert

8. But where do we experience this thirst? Where is our soul parched, and our flesh athirst in unnumbered ways, athirst for no one else but you, O Lord, who are our God? Where are we athirst? *In a desert land, where there is neither way nor water.* When we have said that, we have described this world; this is Edom, this is the Edomite desert from which the psalm took its title. *In a desert land —* but that is not to say much, for all it means is that no humans live there. So the psalm strengthens its description: *a land where there is neither way nor water.* If only there were a way through our desert! If only a person who had stumbled into it could at least know how to find the way out! But the traveler can see neither any human company nor any way to escape from the desert. So he wanders. If only there were water, at least, so that the wanderer could refresh himself, since there is no way out! But no, this is a pitiless desert, horrible and terrifying.

Nevertheless God has taken pity on us, and given us a way in the desert: our Lord Jesus Christ is himself the way.[12] And that is not all. He has provided strengthening companionship for us in the desert by sending us preachers of his word. Moreover he has given us water in the desert, filling his preachers with the Holy Spirit, to be in them a spring of water leaping up to eternal life.[13] All these things we truly have here, but they are not provided by the desert. That is why the psalm first reminded you of the hard facts about the desert, so that after taking stock of your bad situation you would attribute any comfort you may find, whether in companionship, or a way, or water, not to the desert but to him who has been graciously present with you in your desert.

Being seen by God, in order to see his power and glory

9. *This is why I appeared before you in the holy place: to see your power and your glory.* My soul came to know how thirsty it was for you, and my body to know how manifold was its thirst for you in this desert, this land devoid of way and water; and *therefore I appeared before you in the holy place, to see your power and your glory.* Unless we have first experienced our thirst in this desert, in this bad situation where we are, we shall never reach that good which is God. But, says the psalm, *I appeared before you in the holy place.* Simply to be in the holy place is already a great solace; but what does *I appeared before you* mean? I appeared there that you might see me, and you saw me so that I might see you. *I appeared before you to see* — this is what it says. It does not say, "I appeared before you that you might see," but *I appeared before you, to see your power and your glory.* This is what the apostle has in mind when he says, *Now you have*

---

12. See Jn 14:6.
13. See Jn 4:14.

come to know God—and, more important, you are known by God (Gal 4:9). So too here: first you appeared before God, so that God could appear to you.

To see your power and your glory. If while we are in this desert, this wilderness of a place, we seek from the desert itself what we need for our well-being, we shall never see the power of the Lord or the glory of the Lord. We shall linger here to die of thirst; we shall find neither the way, nor any comfort, nor the water that could sustain us in the wilderness. But if we stand up and say to God with every yearning that is in us, *My soul is athirst for you, and for you my flesh thirsts too, in how many ways*; if we take care to have recourse to none other than God for even the things needed by our flesh; if we make sure that we long for that resurrection of our flesh that God has promised us—if we lift our eyes and our hearts like this, we shall find no little consolation.

10. It is plain to see, brothers and sisters, that during this period when our flesh has not yet attained its risen state, but is still mortal, still so fragile, it enjoys the comforts on which our life depends: bread, water, fruit, wine, oil, and so forth. If all these comforts and supports were not available to us we would certainly not have the strength to hold out. And our flesh has all this sustenance even now, when it has not yet received the perfect health that awaits it, in which it will suffer no constriction, no penury. In the same way our soul, while here in the flesh and beset with the trials and dangers of the world, is still weak; but the soul too has the comforting support of the word, the support of prayer, the support of teaching.[14] These are the soul's comforts, as material supports are the solace of our flesh. But when our flesh has risen from the dead, it will have its proper place and state of incorruptibility, which will render those supports unnecessary; and in a similar way our soul will have its proper food, which is the very Word of God through whom all things were made.[15] Yet let us thank God because he has not left us forlorn even here in the wilderness, but gives us whatever we need for our flesh, and gives our soul too everything it needs. Sometimes it may happen that he trains us by letting us feel the pinch, but that is because he wants us to love him all the more, and to save us from becoming decadent through excess, and forgetting him. At times he withdraws from us some of the things we need, and diminishes us, so that we may know that he is both Father and Lord, not only when he caresses us but also when he chastises. He is preparing for us a very great inheritance that can never be spoiled. If you intend to bequeath to your son your sole vat of wine, or your only granary, or some other item you have at home, you educate him so that he will not waste it. You whip him and train him to live in a disciplined way, in order to ensure that he squan-

---

14. *Disputationis*, properly "of debate/discussion/argument"; but since these procedures were the common means of education, the word came to mean "preaching" or "teaching" in late Latin, and this meaning clearly fits the context here.

15. See Jn 1:3.

ders none of your property. Yet he will have to leave it behind one day, just as you will. Can you demur, then, if our Father chastises us even with the whips of needs and troubles, when he is planning to give us an inheritance that can never pass away? The inheritance God will give us is himself. We are to possess him, and be possessed by him, for all eternity.

11. Let us, then, appear in the holy place before God, so that he may appear to us. Let us appear before him in the holy place of our desire, so that he may appear to us in the power and glory of the Son of God. Many there are to whom he has not appeared; let them enter the holy place, that he may appear to them too. The reason why they do not appear before him is that many people think Christ to have been no more than human, because our preaching tells of his human birth, his crucifixion and his death, of how he walked about on earth, and ate, and drank, and did other things characteristic of human life. Consequently they think that he was no different from all the rest of our race. But when the gospel was read just now you heard how he asserted his majesty: *I and the Father are one* (Jn 10:30). Think how that high Majesty, that infinite Son equal to the Father, came down and took flesh to succour our weakness! Think how tenderly we were loved, before ever we began to love God! And if before we loved God we were so dearly loved by him that he made his coequal Son human for our sake, what must he be reserving for us now that we have come to love him?

If many people think it a trifling matter that the Son of God was seen on earth, it is because they are not in the holy place, and therefore his power and his glory do not appear to them. Since their hearts have not yet been sanctified, they have no place where they can understand his strength, his nobility, and therefore no place where they may give thanks to God, who for their sake sent so noble a Son to such a birth, and such suffering. And so they cannot see his glory or his power.

Verse 4. The many lives we choose, and the one life we are given

12. *Because your mercy is better than all possible lives.* Human lives are many and diverse, but God promises one life. This he gives us not in recognition of our merits, but out of his own mercy. What good have we done to deserve it? What good deeds on our part forestalled him, to persuade him to grant us his grace? Did he find any righteous acts to our credit that he could crown, rather than misdeeds that needed his forgiveness? By no means; indeed, if he had willed to punish those misdeeds instead of pardoning them, he would not have been unjust, for what is more just than the punishment of a sinner? Since it is just that a sinner be punished, it was only in his mercy that he decided not to punish us sinners but to justify us, to make sinners into just men and women, to change the ungodly into godly persons. This is why we can say that *his mercy is better than all possible lives.* Lives? What lives are meant by this? The different lives that people have chosen, I think. One chooses for himself a life of business, another

chooses a farmer's life, another that of a banker, another a soldier's life. One person chooses one kind of life, another chooses differently. All these lives are diverse, but *your mercy is better than all the lives* open to us. What you give to people you have straightened out is better than anything they choose for themselves while crooked. You grant us one life, a life to be preferred to all the lives we have, whatever we may have managed to choose for ourselves in this world.

Because your mercy is better than all possible lives, my lips will praise you. My lips would not be praising you if your mercy had not taken the initiative with me. Thanks to your own gift I praise you, through your own mercy I praise you. I could not praise God if he had not given me the power to praise him. *Because your mercy is better than all possible lives, my lips will praise you.*

Verse 5. Christ's uplifted hands, and ours

13. *In this way I will bless you in my life, and in your name I will lift up my hands.* The psalm declares, *In this way I will bless you in my life.* In this life which you have given me, not in that life which I, along with everyone else, chose in the world's way out of all the possible lives; no, I mean in this life which you gave me through your mercy in order that I might praise you. *In this way I will bless you in my life*: what does that phrase signify — *in this way*? It means, in such a way that I attribute this life of mine, in which I praise you, to your mercy and not to any merits of my own.

And in your name I will lift up my hands. Lift up your hands in prayer. Our Lord lifted up his hands for us on the cross; his hands were stretched wide for us. His hands were stretched out for us on the cross so that our hands might be stretched out to good works, for his cross endowed us with mercy. Consider this: he lifted up his hands, and offered himself as a sacrifice to God for our sake, and by that sacrifice all our sins were cancelled. Let us in our turn lift our hands to God in supplication, and if our hands are also well exercised in good works, our uplifted hands will not be rebuffed. What are we doing when we lift our hands? Is there any command given to us about praying to God with hands upraised? Yes; the apostle commands it: you should be *lifting up pure hands, free from anger and dissension*, he says (1 Tm 2:8). So when you raise your hands to God in prayer, have a thought for worthy conduct too. As your hands are uplifted to entreat God for what you want, you must take care that those same hands are active in good works, and then you will not be ashamed to raise them to God. *In your name I will lift up my hands.* These are the prayers that befit us here in Edom, in this desert, in the land where there is no water and no way, but where Christ is for us the way, though not a way that belongs to this earth. *In your name I will lift up my hands.*

Verse 6. Ask above all for the gift of God himself

14. And what am I to say when I lift my hands in your name? What shall I ask for? Consider carefully what you should ask for when you raise your hands, brothers and sisters, since it is from the Almighty that you are begging. Ask him for something really important, not for the kind of things requested by people who have not yet come to believe. Look at the sort of benefits that are given even to the godless. Are you inclined to ask your God for money? Does he not give that even to wicked people who do not believe in him? Is it for any great boon that you are asking, then, if he gives it to the wicked as well? But don't let it upset you that he gives it to them equally, because the gifts he gives to bad people are such trumpery things that they are suitable gifts for the purpose. You should estimate the real worth of such things from the fact that they can be given even to scoundrels. To be sure, all earthly gifts are from God, but you must realize that those he gives to bad people as well as to you are not to be regarded as the most valuable. He has something different in store for us.

Let us give a little thought to the gifts he confers on rogues, and try to understand from them what he holds in reserve for good people. The things he gives to the wicked are quite obvious. He gives them daylight;[16] both good and bad see it. He gives the rain that falls on the earth, and think of the wealth of good things that spring up as a result! But rain is a gift conferred on bad people as well as good, as the gospel reminds us; the Father *causes his sun to rise over the good and the wicked, and sends rain upon just and unjust alike* (Mt 5:45). We must indeed ask the Lord for all the produce that comes from rain and sun, because it is necessary for us; but don't let us ask him for this and no more, because these gifts are distributed to both good people and bad.

Well then, what should we ask for when we lift up our hands? The psalm has told us, insofar as it could. What do I mean by saying, "insofar as it could"? I mean insofar as human speech could convey it to human ears. The reality is expressed by human lips, and with the help of comparisons, so that all the weak may grasp it, and all our little ones. What request did the speaker make, then? *In your name I will lift up my hands*, he said—but to receive what? *May my soul be filled as with a rich and sumptuous feast.*

Do you suppose that this soul was hungering for some kind of carnal luxury, my brothers and sisters? No. He had no overwhelming desire to have fattened rams or pigs slaughtered, or to find himself in some banqueting hall where he would be faced with choice viands, from which he could eat his fill. If we think that, we are the kind of people who deserve to hear it.[17] No, we must understand the verse spiritually. Our soul aspires to a certain rich feast, for there is abundant

---

16. Augustine loved light; it is typical of him to head the list with this gift.
17. Variant: "who are unworthy to hear these things."

satisfaction in wisdom. When souls are insufficiently nourished with this wisdom they droop, and become so thin and feeble that they soon lack the strength to act well. Why do they so soon fall away from all their good works? Because they lack the rich fare that would satisfy them. When the apostle wished to urge everyone to behave generously, he spoke in terms of a well-nourished soul: *God loves a cheerful*[18] *giver*, he said (2 Cor 9:7). But how can a soul be well nourished, if the Lord does not lavish his gift on it?

Yet however richly endowed such a soul may be here on earth, what will it be in the world to come, where God feeds us? As long as we are still on pilgrimage here, what we shall be cannot be told. And perhaps even here, when we lift up our hands, we long for that ultimate satiety; we long for that state where we shall be so totally satisfied with God's lavish gifts that all our needs will vanish utterly, and we shall desire nothing; because whatever we desire here, whatever seems to us most worthy of our love here, will be available to us in its entirety.

Already our parents are dead, but God is alive. Here we cannot keep our parents always, but there we shall always have our one, living Father, when we possess our fatherland. Whatever homeland we love on earth, we cannot stay there for ever; of necessity others will be born, and the children of today's citizens are born only to oust their parents. Any child who is born is implicitly saying to his or her parent, "What are you doing here?" Those who are born, the rising generation, must exclude their predecessors; it cannot be otherwise. But there we shall all live together, and no one will succeed anyone else because no one will depart.[19] What a homeland that will be!

But perhaps your ambition here is to amass wealth? God himself will be wealth for you. Or perhaps you fancy a fine fountain? What can be more splendid than wisdom, what more sparkling? Whatever may be the object of your love here, he who made all lovable things will himself be there for you in place of them all. *May my soul be filled as with a rich and sumptuous feast, and my exultant lips will praise your name.* As I lift up my hands in your name in this desert, *may my soul be filled as with a rich and sumptuous feast, and my exultant lips will praise your name.* Now is the time for prayer, as long as our thirst plagues us; but when thirst has passed away, prayer will pass away too, and praise will take its place. *And my exultant lips will praise you.*

Verses 7-8. Remembering God, and working in the light

15. *If I remembered you upon my bed, I was mindful of you at daybreak, because you became my helper.* By his "bed" he meant a time of quiet repose. When anyone enjoys quiet rest, he or she should remember God, and take care

---

18. *Hilarem*, lively, sprightly.
19. *Non ibi erit successor quia nullus decessor.*

that a time of calm repose does not lead to laxity and forgetfulness of God. If we remember God in our time of quiet rest, we are mindful of him also when we are busy. "Daybreak" here signifies activity, because everyone who has work to do begins at daybreak. What does the speaker tell us? *If I remembered you upon my bed, I was mindful of you at daybreak also.* The converse is also true: if I did not remember you upon my bed, I was not mindful of you at daybreak either. If a person does not think about God while at leisure, how can such a one think about God at busy times? But anyone who remembers him while at rest is mindful of him also amid activity, so as not to succumb to fatigue in the work. This is why the psalm continues, *I was mindful of you at daybreak, because you became my helper.* This is certainly apposite, because if God does not help us in our good works, we cannot carry them through.

The work we do must be worthy, though. When we work as Christ teaches, we are working as though in daylight. Anyone who performs evil works operates by night, not at daybreak, as the apostle points out: *Those who get drunk, get drunk at night, and those who sleep, sleep at night; but as for us who belong to the day, let us be sober* (1 Thes 5:7-8). He exhorts us to conduct ourselves honorably as though by the light of day: *Let us walk honorably as in daylight* (Rom 13:13), he says, and elsewhere, *You are children of light and children of the day; we do not belong to the night or to the darkness* (1 Thes 5:5). Who are the children of night, the children of darkness? Those who carry out all sorts of wicked deeds. They are so closely akin to night that they fear to let their deeds be seen. It is true, of course, that some people do bad things in full view of everyone, but they do so only because such bad deeds are committed by many others. The misdeeds performed by only a few are performed in secret. The perpetrators of evil deeds in public do carry them out in the light of the sun, admittedly, but in the darkness of their hearts.

No one really acts at daybreak, therefore, except the person who works in Christ. The one who while at leisure remembers Christ is also mindful of him in every kind of activity, and being helped by Christ in the performance of good works is saved from fainting through weakness. *If I remembered you upon my bed, I was mindful of you at daybreak, because you became my helper.*

16. *And under the shelter of your wings I shall rejoice.* I shall act well with greater cheerfulness because your wings cover me. Since I am but a chick, a hawk may seize me if you do not protect me. In a gospel passage our Lord himself says to Jerusalem, the city where he was crucified, *Jerusalem, Jerusalem, how often I wanted to gather your children to myself, as a hen gathers her chicks under her wings, but you would have none of it!* (Mt 23:37). We are puny creatures; may God protect us in the shade of his wings. What about when we have grown up? It will be good for us if he protects us then too, so that we may always remain like small, young things under him who is greater; for he always

will be greater, however big we grow. No one should say, "Let him protect me, as long as I am a little child," implying that sooner or later we may attain such a stature that we can look after ourselves. Without God's protection you are nothing. Let us desire to be under his protection always; we shall always be great in him if we take care always to be small under him. *Under the shelter of your wings I shall rejoice.*

Verse 9. Glued behind God

17. *My soul is glued behind you.* Look at this person consumed with desire, look how thirsty he is, and how firmly he sticks to God! Let this sentiment be planted in you too. If it is springing up already, water it plentifully to promote its growth; let it grow to such vigor that you too may say with your whole heart, *My soul is glued behind you.* Where are we to find the strong glue? The glue is charity. Have charity in you, and it will glue your soul into place, following God. Not with God, but behind God, so that he goes ahead and you follow. If one of us wants to walk in front of God, it means that we want to live by our own decisions, rather than follow God's commandments. Peter was rebuffed for this very thing, when he wanted to give advice to Christ, who was intent on suffering for us.[20] Peter was still weak, and did not yet realize how greatly the human race would benefit from the shedding of Christ's blood. But the Lord had come to redeem us and to give his blood as our ransom, and so he began to foretell his passion. Peter was terrified at the prospect of the Lord's death, because he saw the situation through carnal eyes and was hampered by merely carnal affection for our Lord; and so he wanted the Lord to go on living on earth always, in the same form that he beheld him then. He protested, *Far be it from you, Lord. This will not happen.* But the Lord answered, *Get behind me, Satan; you have no taste for the things of God, but only for human things* (Mt 16:22.23). Why does he say, *only for human things?* "You want to rush ahead of me, but *get behind me,* and follow me." Once Peter had begun to follow Christ, he would be in a position to say, *My soul is glued behind you.*

And your right hand upholds me. There is good reason to add this further affirmation. *My soul is glued behind you, and your right hand upholds me.* Christ says this in us. In the humanity he assumed for us, and offered for us, he makes that declaration. But the Church also says it in Christ, says it in our head, because the Church also has suffered fierce persecutions on earth, and indeed suffers them even today in its individual members. Isn't anyone who belongs to Christ battered by manifold temptations? The devil and his angels interfere with

---

20. This meditation on Peter's presumption is habitual with Augustine; compare Exposition 1 of Psalm 34, 8; Exposition of Psalm 39, 5.

Christians every day, trying to pervert them with some kind of greed, or some sly suggestion: whether a promise of gain or the fear of loss, whether a promise of life or the terror of death, whether the hostility of some powerful person or some other powerful man's blandishments. The devil is constantly watchful for ways to bring us down. We live amid persecution because we have relentless enemies in the devil and his angels; but let us not be afraid. The devil and his minions are like predatory hawks, but we are sheltered beneath the hen's wings and no hawk can reach us, for the hen who shelters us is powerful. Our Lord Jesus Christ became weak for us, but he is mighty in himself; he is the very Wisdom of God. Thus the Church too can say, *My soul is glued behind you, and your right hand upholds me.*

Verses 10-11. The persecutors bring disaster on themselves

18. *But they have sought my life in vain.* What did they do to me, those enemies who sought my life, to destroy it? If only they would seek my soul in order to believe in company with me![21] But in fact they only sought my life to destroy me. What do they think to achieve? They will certainly not melt the glue that fastens my soul behind you, for *who shall part us from the love of Christ? Shall tribulation, or distress, or persecution, or hunger, or nakedness, or the sword?* (Rom 8:35). *Your right hand upholds me.* Thanks to that glue, and your most powerful right hand, *they have sought my life in vain.* In these seekers we can identify all those who have ever persecuted the Church, or want to do so; but we should understand it to refer most directly to the Jews, who sought Christ's life with the intention of destroying it, both in the head himself whom they crucified, and in his disciples whom they persecuted subsequently. *They have sought my life,* but *they shall go down to the depths of the earth.* The Jews feared to lose the earth; that was why they crucified Christ. But they descended into the depths of the earth. What are these *depths of the earth*? Earthly lusts. It is better for us to walk upon the earth in our fleshly condition than to go down under the earth through disordered desires. Everyone who is greedy for earthly goods to the detriment of his salvation is below the earth, because such a person has valued the earth more highly than himself; he has put the earth above him and himself below it.

Now the Jews were afraid of losing the earth. What did they say about the Lord Jesus Christ, when they saw vast crowds following him, impressed by the miracles he worked? *If we leave him alive, the Romans will come, and sweep away our land and our nationhood* (Jn 11:48). They feared to lose the earth, and

---

21. *Anima* can mean either "soul" or "life," which makes the ambiguity possible. Augustine plays on the same ambiguity with reference to enemies seeking Christ's life or soul in his Exposition of Psalm 37, 18, and Exposition of Psalm 39, 24. This time it is the Church's life/soul.

they went under the earth; what they feared happened to them. They wanted to kill Christ in order not to lose the earth, and they lost the earth by killing Christ. After they had killed him Christ's prophecy regarding them was verified: *the kingdom of God will be taken away from you, and given to a nation that brings forth righteousness* (Mt 21:43); for terrible and calamitous persecutions befell them. The Roman emperors and Gentile kings defeated them, and they were thrust out from the city where they had crucified Christ. In that place no Jew is to be found now, but it is full of Christians singing praise. It is emptied of Christ's enemies, but filled with people praising Christ. Look at the outcome: their land was taken from them by the Romans because they killed Christ, though they killed Christ in order that the Romans should not take their land away. *They shall go down to the depths of the earth.*

19. *They shall be delivered to the power of the sword.* This did indeed happen to them for all to see, for they were conquered as their enemies overran them. *They shall become the prey of foxes.* The rulers of this world, who held power at the time when Judea was conquered, are called foxes in this psalm. Pay close attention, so that you may understand that these are the people indicated by the term, "foxes." Our Lord himself called King Herod a fox: *Go and tell that fox*, he said (Lk 13:32). Think about it, give your minds to it, my brothers and sisters. They refused to have Christ as their king, and they became the prey of foxes. When the governor Pilate, who was procurator of Judea, was about to kill Christ at the insistence of the Jews, he asked them, *Am I to crucify your king?* Christ was called King of the Jews, and their king he truly was; but they rejected him, and shouted, *We have no king but Caesar* (Jn 19:15). They rejected the Lamb and chose a fox, so they deserved to become the prey of foxes.

Verse 12. The King's triumph

20. *The king in truth*: this qualification is added because they chose a fox and rejected their king.[22] *The king in truth*, the true king, is he over whom his title was written when he suffered. Pilate set up the inscription over his head: *King of the Jews*. It was written in Hebrew, Greek, and Latin, so that every passer-by might read in it the glory of the King and the shame of the Jews who had spurned their true King and chosen the fox, Caesar. *The king in truth will be joyful in God.* His killers became the prey of foxes, but *the king in truth will be joyful in God.* They believed that they had defeated him when they crucified him, but at the very moment when he was crucified he paid out the price of the whole world's ransom. *The king in truth will be joyful in God, and everyone who makes a vow in*

---

22. The Latin is *rex vero*, which would more naturally mean "but the king." Augustine uses the ambiguity to make his point about Christ's kingship.

him will be praised. Why should anyone *who makes a vow in him* be praised? Because anyone who does so has chosen Christ, not a fox; and this can only be because at the very time when the Jews hurled insults at Christ, he paid the price of our redemption. We are therefore the property of him who purchased us, and overcame the world for us, not by armed force but by a derided cross.

The king in truth will be joyful in God, and everyone who makes a vow in him will be praised. Who makes a vow in him? Every one of us, when we promise our life to him, when we make our vow and keep it, when we become Christians. This is what is meant by *everyone who makes a vow in him will be praised.*

For their mouths have been stopped, those who spoke unjustly. What flagrant injustice did the Jews speak! What monstrous things did others say too, not the Jews only, but all those who in defense of their idols persecuted Christians! By letting loose their savagery they thought they could put an end to Christians, but when they thought to see them finished, the Christians grew more numerous, and it was the persecutors who were finished instead. *Their mouths have been stopped, those who spoke unjustly.* No one dares to speak against Christ in public nowadays. Everyone reveres him now. *Their mouths have been stopped, those who spoke unjustly.* When the Lamb was weak, even foxes made bold to oppose the Lamb. But he has conquered now, he who is the Lion from the tribe of Judah,[23] and the foxes have fallen silent, *for their mouths have been stopped, those who spoke unjustly.*

---

23. See Rv 5:5.

Exposition of Psalm 63

A Sermon to the People

Verse 1. Introduction: the suffering of the martyrs, and of Christ their leader

1. Today is a festal celebration in honor of the passion of our holy martyrs. Let us rejoice in commemorating them, and as we remember what they suffered, let us understand where they fixed their gaze; for they could never have endured such dreadful agony in their flesh if they had not been flooded with immense peace in their minds. You listened to a long discourse yesterday, beloved,[1] but all the same we could not refuse you on today's festival the service we owe you.

It is primarily the Lord's passion[2] that is called to mind in this psalm, but we should recognize in it not his voice only, but ours too. Why? Because, in the first place, the martyrs could not have been so brave unless they had kept in view the Lord who suffered first, nor could they have endured torments like his unless they hoped for a resurrection like that of which he gave us advance proof in himself. Furthermore you well know, holy brethren,[3] that our Lord Jesus Christ is our head, and that all who cleave to him are members of the body that belongs to that head. You are very familiar with his voice, because he speaks not only in his own person as the head, but also as from his body. Hence the words we hear from him are signs pointing to the Lord Jesus Christ himself, proclaiming him who has now ascended into heaven; but they also signify and proclaim his members, who are destined to follow him there. No one should object that we today do not experience the stress of such suffering. You have often heard me telling you that while in the days of the martyrs the whole Church was under attack at once, nowadays it is put to the test in the persons of its members singly. The devil has been bound, certainly, to restrain him from doing as much harm as he can or as much as he wants to; but he is still permitted to assail us insofar as that will further our progress. It is not good for us to be altogether free from temptations. We do not ask God that we be not tempted, only that we be not led into temptation.

---

1. *Caritas vestra.*
2. The occasion of the sermon is the festival of martyrs, as Augustine says in this opening section and again in section 15; but typically he focuses on the Lord in his suffering and glory as the exemplar of the martyrs.
3. *Sanctitas vestra*

Verse 2. Deliverance from fear

2. Let us join our voices with the psalm, then, and pray, *O God, hear my prayer in my distress; deliver my soul from fear of the enemy.* Enemies loosed their fury against the martyrs, and what prayer did Christ's persecuted members raise? They prayed to be delivered from their enemies, that the persecutors should not succeed in killing them. So it looks as though the prayer was not heard, doesn't it? They were killed, and it seems that God abandoned those heartbroken servants of his, and spurned those who hoped in him. Was that what happened? Far from it! *Who has ever called upon the Lord, and been deserted? Who ever hoped in him, only to be forsaken?*[4] They were heard indeed, but they were killed; and yet they were delivered from their enemies. Other people were so frightened that they gave way, and so stayed alive, but these were swallowed up by the enemies. The slain were delivered, but the living were swallowed.

Another psalm rejoices and gives thanks about a deliverance of this kind, reflecting that *perhaps they might have swallowed us alive* (Ps 123(124):3). The ones who were swallowed were of two kinds. Many were swallowed alive, but many others were swallowed dead. The ones who were swallowed dead were people who dismissed the Christian faith as meaningless. But others knew that the gospel preached to them was the truth; they knew that Christ is the Son of God, and believed it, and held onto their faith inwardly, though they yielded under torture and offered sacrifice to idols. These were swallowed alive. The former group were swallowed because they were dead. The latter died because swallowed; for once swallowed they could not remain alive, even though they had been alive at the time of being swallowed.

With this in mind the martyrs raise their voice in prayer: *"Deliver my soul from fear of the enemy.* I do not mean, stop the enemy from killing me, but preserve me from being afraid of this murderer." This is the servant praying in the psalm for the strength to obey that command of the Master, of which we were reminded just now in the gospel. What did the Lord command us? *Do not be afraid of those who kill the body, but cannot kill the soul. Fear him rather who has the power to kill both soul and body in hell* (Mt 10:28). And he reinforced it: *Yes, I tell you, him you must fear* (Lk 12:5). Who are the killers of the body? Our enemies. And what was the Lord telling us? Not to be afraid of them. It is quite right, then, that we should pray to him to grant us the strength to obey his order. *Deliver my soul from fear of the enemy.* Free me from that fear, and subject me to fear of yourself. Let me not be afraid of anyone who wants to kill my body. But instill in me fear of him who has power to destroy both body and soul in hell. I do not ask to be immune to fear; all I want is to be a free person where fear of the enemy is in question, but a servant subject to fear of my Lord.

---

4. See Sir 2:12.11.

Verse 3. The plans of the malicious

3. *You have protected me from the conspiracy of the malicious, from the multitude of those who deal unjustly.* Let us contemplate our head in these lines. Many martyrs suffered similarly, but nowhere does the reality shine out more clearly than in the head of the martyrs, and in him we may better understand what they experienced. He was protected from the crowd of malicious enemies because God was protecting himself; that is to say, God's Son made man protected his own flesh. He is both Son of Man and Son of God: Son of God in virtue of his divine nature,[5] and Son of Man in the servant's form that he assumed.[6] He therefore possessed the power to lay down his life and take it up anew.[7] What could his enemies achieve against him? They killed his body, but they did not kill his soul. Think carefully about this. It would not have been enough for the Lord to exhort the martyrs in words only; he had to back up his words with his example. You know what the conspiracy of the malicious Jews was, and who were the multitude of those who dealt unjustly. What injustice did they plan? They purposed to kill the Lord Jesus Christ. *I have done such great good works in your sight,* he said to them. *For which of them do you want to kill me?* (Jn 10:32). He patiently supported all their sick people, he cured all the infirm among them, he proclaimed the kingdom of heaven; but he did not pass over their vices in silence. It was those vices that should have offended them, not the physician by whom they might have been cured. Yet they were ungrateful for all the healings he had performed, and were like maddened patients with raging fever, hitting out deliriously against the doctor who had come to cure them. So they devised a plan to do away with him. They almost seemed to be setting up an experiment: was he simply a human being who could die, or was he something more than human, who would not allow himself to die? We recognize their attitude in the Wisdom of Solomon: *Let us condemn him to the most shameful of deaths. Let us put him to the question, for his claims will be taken care of, according to his own account. If he truly is the Son of God, let God deliver him* (Wis 2:20.19.18).[8] Let us see what happened.

---

5. "On account of the form of God."

6. See Phil 2:6-7.

7. See Jn 10:18.

8. The style of the citation may indicate that this sermon belongs to an early period in Augustine's life, possibly to the time before he was a bishop. From the time of writing *Teaching Christianity* (396) he was not accustomed to attribute the Book of Wisdom to Solomon. Compare *Teaching Christianity* II, 8 (13).

Verse 4. Killing with sharp tongues

4. *They whetted their tongues like swords.* Another psalm makes the same accusation: *the teeth of human beings are weapons and arrows, their tongue a sharp sword* (Ps 56:5(57:4)); and so too here, *they whetted their tongues like swords.* The Jews have no right to say, "We did not put Christ to death," for they handed him over to the judge, Pilate, for no other purpose than to make it look as though they were not guilty of killing him. When Pilate objected, *Take him, and execute him yourselves*, they replied, *It is not lawful for us to put anyone to death* (Jn 18:31). They intended to shrug off the responsibility for their wicked crime onto a human judge; but could they hoodwink the divine Judge? Pilate carried the business through, and by doing so he became in some measure a collaborator; but compared with them he was far less guilty. He kept on doing his best to rescue Christ from their clutches. That was his motive in bringing Christ out before them after the scourging. It was not in any vindictive spirit that he ordered him to be scourged, but in the hope of allaying their rage, so that at least when they beheld him scourged they might be inclined to leniency, and cease to demand his death. So he tried this.[9] But when they insisted he washed his hands, as you know, and disowned the deed, claiming that he was innocent of Christ's death.[10] All the same, he did it. But if the man who did it almost against his will is guilty, are they innocent who forced him to? By no means. Pilate pronounced sentence on Christ and ordered him to be crucified, so in that sense Pilate killed him; but you too killed him, you Jews.[11] What weapon did you employ? The sword of the tongue, for you whetted your tongues; and when did you strike him? When you shouted, *Crucify him! Crucify him!* (Lk 23:21).

5. In this connection something occurs to me that I should not pass over in silence, in case anyone is worried while reading the sacred books. One evangelist says the Lord was crucified at the sixth hour,[12] and another that he was crucified at the third hour;[13] so unless we understand the reason for the discrepancy we may be puzzled. Pilate is said to have taken his seat at the tribunal at the beginning of the sixth hour, and certainly it was the sixth hour when the Lord was hoisted onto the tree. But the other evangelist was concentrating on the mind of the Jews. They wished to appear altogether innocent of the Lord's death, but this other evangelist showed up their guilt by the way he told his story, stating that the Lord was crucified at the third hour. When we take into account all the circumstances narrated, and how much effort could have gone into ensuring that the Lord would be crucified, during that time when he was in Pilate's presence,

---

9. See Jn 19:1-5.
10. See Mt 27:24.
11. Compare Acts 3:14-15.
12. See Jn 19:14.
13. See Mk 15:25.

we find that it could easily have been at the third hour that they shouted, *Crucify him! Crucify him!* They more truly killed him when they shouted like that. The agents of the ruling power crucified him at the sixth hour, but the violators of the law raised their shout at the third hour. What the former carried out with their hands at the sixth hour, the latter secured with their tongues at the third hour.[14] The people who raged with their shouting were more guilty than those who carried it out in their obedience. This was the point of the Jews' cunning, this was what they sought most insistently: to say, "Let us kill him," and at the same time, "Let us not kill him; let us dispatch him in such a way that we are not judged to have killed him." *They whetted their tongues like swords.*

Verse 5. Ambushing the immaculate Lamb

6. *They bent their bow, that bitter weapon.* By *bow* is meant trickery. Anyone who fights hand to hand with a sword fights openly; but anyone who launches an arrow employs covert means to strike the blow, for he has inflicted a wound with his arrow before his enemy can see him coming to attack and wound. But from whom are the treacherous devices of the human heart hidden? From our Lord Jesus Christ? No, for the evangelist testifies concerning him, *He did not need anyone to tell him what was inside a person. He knew himself what a person had within* (Jn 2:25). Nonetheless let us listen to them and observe them, as though the Lord were really ignorant of their plans. *They bent their bow, that bitter weapon, to shoot the undefiled one stealthily.* The statement that *they bent their bow* is echoed in the word *stealthily*, because it means that they resorted to trickery and ambush. You know what underhand methods they employed: how they bribed one of his close disciples to betray the Lord to them, and how they suborned lying witnesses. By these traps and stratagems they set themselves *to shoot the undefiled one stealthily*. What monstrous iniquity! The arrow is shot from their hiding place and it strikes the immaculate One, who has not enough defilement in him even for the arrow to find its mark. He is the stainless Lamb, wholly undefiled, eternally undefiled, not because his stains have been expunged, but because he never contracted any. He has made many others stainless by forgiving their sins, but he himself is stainless because in him there was never any sin. The Jews sought *to shoot the undefiled one stealthily*.

---

14. Augustine discusses more fully this discrepancy regarding the time in *Agreement among the Evangelists* III, 13, 40-42.

Verse 6. Sin, the deadly enemy within the gates

7. *They will loose their arrows at him suddenly, recklessly.* What stubbornness of heart this was, to seek to kill a man who was wont to raise the dead! *Suddenly*, it says, implying that they attacked with guile, as though unexpectedly, in a way he could not have foreseen. The Lord certainly bore himself among them like one who knew nothing, but they had no idea about what he really knew or did not know. Or, rather, they were ignorant of the fact that there was nothing at all that he did not know, that he knew everything, and that he had come precisely to allow them to do what they thought they were doing by their own power. *They will loose their arrows at him suddenly, recklessly.*

8. *They reaffirmed their wicked demand to their own ruin.* Yes, they *reaffirmed* their malice. Amazing miracles had been wrought, but they were unmoved, they only persisted in their wicked attitude. Christ was handed over to the judge. The judge trembled, but those who had delivered the prisoner to him did not tremble. Authority is terrified, but cruelty is not. He wants to wash his hands, but they stain their tongues. How? By their insistent reaffirmation of *their wicked demand, to their own ruin.* What strenuous efforts Pilate made! How hard he tried to dissuade them! What did he say? What did he do? Yet still *they reaffirmed their wicked demand: Crucify him! Crucify him!* This repetition was their way of reaffirming the line they had taken. Let us listen to their reaffirmation: *Am I to crucify your king? They answered, We have no king but Caesar* (Jn 19:15). So did they reaffirm their wicked demand. Pilate was offering them the Son of God as their king, but they harked back to a merely human ruler; they deserved to have him, and to lose Christ. And that is not all: listen to how they went on reaffirming their wicked demand. *I find no guilt in him that warrants the death penalty,* declared the judge.[15] But they, determined to reaffirm their wicked demand, replied, *His blood be upon us, and upon our children!* (Mt 27:25). *They reaffirmed their wicked demand,* but to their own ruin, not the Lord's. How could it be otherwise, when they had cried, *His blood be upon us, and upon our children?* What they reaffirmed, they reaffirmed to their own ruin, in the way that another psalm describes: *they dug a pit in front of me, but fell into it themselves* (Ps 56:7(57:6)). Death did not kill the Lord; he killed death. But iniquity did kill them, because they refused to kill iniquity.

9. This is important, brothers and sisters. Either you slay iniquity, or iniquity will slay you. But do not try to slay iniquity as though it were some foe outside yourself. Examine yourself, identify the enemy inside you that fights against you. Make sure that this enemy of yours, this iniquity, does not get the better of you because it has not been killed. Make no mistake; it originates within your-

---

15. See Lk 23:14.22.

self; it is your own soul that rebels against you, not some alien thing. With one side of yourself you cling loyally to God, with another side of you you are pleasurably attached to the world;[16] and the side of you that is attached to the world fights against the mind that cleaves to God. Let it go on clinging and cleaving to him, let it not weaken, let it not slacken at all, for it has a powerful ally. If it perseveres in the fight it will conquer the element in itself which rebels against it. Sin does indeed reside in your body, but it must not reign there. *Do not let sin reign in your mortal body, so as to persuade you to yield to its cravings*, says scripture (Rom 6:12). There is something in you that puts pressure on you, and makes evil seem attractive. But provided you do not yield, you prevent this thing that is in you from reigning by your refusal to obey it; and the eventual result will be that what is there now will be there no more. And when can we expect that? When death is finally swallowed up into victory, and our corruptible nature has clothed itself in incorruptibility.[17] In that risen nature there will be nothing to offer you any resistance, and you will be pleasurably attached to nothing else but God. The reason for the Jews' hatred of our Lord was that they were attached to their sovereignty. Some of them were apprehensive lest that earthly power be taken away from them, and their attachment to it was their motive for opposing the Lord. If they had opposed their own sinful attachment instead, they would have conquered their hatred of him, instead of being vanquished by it. Then the Lord would have been a savior to them, for he had come to heal. But no, they allowed their fever free rein, and opposed only the doctor. Whatever the fever drove them to, they did, and whatever contrary instructions the physician gave, they ignored. It was they who were killed, therefore, not the Lord, for in the Lord death was slain, whereas in them iniquity lived on. But with iniquity alive in them, they died.

10. *They plotted to conceal traps; they said, "Who will see them?"* They thought their traps were hidden from him whom they sought to kill; they thought to hide them from God. Now suppose Christ had been a man like others, and ignorant of what was being planned in his regard: would God too have been ignorant? Foolish human heart, why do you ask yourself, "Who sees me?" when he who made you sees you? *They said, "Who will see them?"* God saw them all the time, and Christ too saw them, for Christ is God. But why did he appear to them to be unseeing? Listen to what follows.

---

16. As often in Augustine, and in some New Testament texts, the "world" here envisaged is not the world God so loved as to send his Son to redeem it, but the principle of worldliness which fights against God, who in Christ works to reconcile the world to himself. See also note on Exposition of Psalm 76, 7.
17. See 1 Cor 15:54.

Verse 7. Feigned innocence is doubly guilty

11. *They probed iniquity minutely, but they failed as they searched out intricate schemes.* These schemes were bitterly cruel devices. "Let him not be betrayed by us, but by one of his own disciples; let him be put to death not by us, but by the judge. Let us contrive the whole thing, yet look as though we had had no part in it." But what about those raucous shouts, *Crucify him, crucify him?* You are so blind that you have gone deaf too! Feigned innocence is no innocence; feigned equity is no equity but rather a double iniquity: the iniquitous act itself and the dishonest pretense. They *failed as they searched out intricate schemes.* The more craftily they believed themselves to be laying their plans, the more they failed, because they were plunging into the murky depths of their malevolent counsels, further and further from the honest light of truth. Justice has a light of its own, which floods and illumines the soul that abides in it; but if the soul turns away from the light of justice, then the more it seeks to contrive anything incompatible with justice, the further it is thrust away from the light, and submerged in dark places.

In probing iniquity, therefore, in directing their plots against the Just One, they were moving away from justice, and the further they receded from justice, the more they failed in their intricate schemes. And what a mighty show of innocence they put up! When Judas suffered remorse at having betrayed Christ, and threw back at them the money they had paid him, they scrupled to put it into the official coffers. They said, *This is blood money; we must not put it into the treasure chest* (Mt 27:6). What was this treasure chest? God's coffer, in which were collected all the alms offered to relieve the needs of his servants. But it is your own hearts, men and women, that are God's treasury; there must his riches be guarded, there must be kept God's coin, that soul of yours stamped with the image of your Emperor. And if this is true, what was that pretense of innocence worth, when they scrupled to put blood money into the coffer, but steeped their own consciences in that very blood?

12. But what happened to them? *They failed as they searched out intricate schemes.* How was that? Because they deceived themselves, asking, *Who will see them?* They thought no one could see. That was what they told themselves, what they fancied: that no one could see them. There you discover what happens to an evil soul: it withdraws from the light of truth, and supposes that because it does not see God, it is not seen by God either. So those scoundrels withdrew, and went off into darkness, where they could not see God; and then said, "Who sees us?" He whom they were intent on crucifying saw them, but as their scheme foundered they could see neither the Son nor the Father.

But if Christ saw all along, why did he allow himself to be arrested by them, and killed by them? If he saw, why did he will their schemes to prevail against him? Why? Because he was human for the sake of human beings, and he was

God concealed in that manhood, and he had come to give an example of fortitude to us who do not know such things. That was why he, who knew everything, endured it.[18]

Verse 8. The secret of the "deep heart"

13. So then, what comes next? *A man will approach, with a deep heart;*[19] *and God will be exalted.* The Jews asked arrogantly, "Who will see us?" But *they failed as they searched out intricate schemes*, failed in their malicious plans. A man approached those schemes, one who allowed himself to be seized as a man. He could not have been taken prisoner had he not been human, or seen, unless human, or flogged, unless human, or crucified, unless human. And had he not been human, he could not have died. He faced all those sufferings which would have had no effect at all on him, had he not been human. But if he had not been human, human beings would not have been set free.

He drew near as man, but deep was his heart. A secret heart was his, one that presented a human nature to human observers, but kept its godhead hidden within. It concealed that form of God in which he is equal to the Father, and offered outwardly the form of a servant in which he is less than the Father. He stated both these truths himself, but one refers to the form of God, the other to the form of a servant. In the form of God he said, *I and the Father are one* (Jn 10:30); but in the form of a servant he said, *The Father is greater than I* (Jn 14:28). How was it that he could claim, when speaking in the form of God, that *the Father and I are one*? Because *being in the form of God he deemed it no robbery to be God's equal.* But in that case, how could he say, *The Father is greater than I*? Because he was speaking in the form of a servant, because *he emptied himself and took on the form of a slave* (Phil 2:6-7). A man drew near, and deep was his heart, and God was exalted. He was put to death as a man, and God was exalted. He was slain in his human weakness, but he rose again and ascended in his divine power.[20] *A man will approach, with a deep heart,* a secret heart, a heart hidden from sight, revealing neither what it knew nor what it was. The Jews assumed that what met their eyes was all there was to him, so they killed this man with the deep heart; but in that divine heart God is exalted, for Christ was exalted by the power of his own majesty. And whither did he ascend in his exaltation? To the place he had never left in his humbled state.[21]

---

18. Or, ". . . why he, who did know, endured it all."
19. The Vulgate here has "to a deep heart." The Hebrew is corrupt and unintelligible, but it seems likely that the original reference was to the heart of the schemers. However, the Septuagint and Augustine's Latin version had "and a deep heart," which he interprets as a reference to Christ's hidden divinity.
20. See 2 Cor 13:4.
21. That is, his glory with the Father.

14. *A man will approach, with a deep heart; and God will be exalted.* Now consider the humanity of his heart, brothers and sisters. Of what human being are we speaking? *"Zion my mother," a man will say, he who was made man in her; and the Most High himself established her* (Ps 86(87):5). He was made man in that city which he had himself founded—he, the Most High. So he approached, a man indeed, though deep of heart. Contemplate his humanity in that deep heart; and in that same heart also discern if you can, to the utmost that you can, God himself. He approached as a man, but he was also God. He was about to suffer because he willed it,[22] and he was to give an example to the weak. His murderers could inflict no suffering on him as God, but on his humanity, on his flesh, they could wreak their savagery. So how does the psalm proceed? *The wounds they inflicted were like those from the arrows of mere children.* What has become of that savagery? Where is the leonine ferocity of the people who roared, *Crucify him, crucify him*? What has become of the ambushes of the stealthy archers? Were not *the wounds they inflicted like those from the arrows of mere children*? You know how children fashion arrows for themselves out of reeds.[23] What do they hit, and how much force is there behind them? What strength in those hands, and what threat in the weapon? What kind of menace is that, from such weaklings? *The wounds they inflicted were like those from the arrows of mere children.*

Verse 9. Discomfiture of the schemers

15. *And their tongues were reduced to weakness over them.*[24] Now let them whet their tongues like swords, and strengthen their malicious demand to their own ruin. They did indeed strengthen it against themselves, because *their tongues were reduced to weakness over them.* Their plotting could not be strong against God, could it? No, and as another psalm has it, *iniquity lied to itself* (Ps 26(27):12). *Their tongues were reduced to weakness over them,* for the Lord who had been killed rose again. His enemies walked past his cross, or stood around watching him. As a psalm had foretold long ages before, *they dug holes in my hands and my feet, and numbered all my bones. They looked on and watched me* (Ps 21:17.18(22:16.17)). Then they shook their heads, saying, *If he is the Son of God, let him come down from the cross.* They were trying to find out somehow whether he truly was the Son of God; and apparently discovered that he was not, because even when they jeered at him he did not come down. If he had, that would have proved that he was the Son of God, they supposed.[25] But

---

22. See Is 53:7; Jn 10:18.
23. Or "little canes." Compare the Exposition of Psalm 56, 13.
24. "Them" = the apostles, as he makes clear later in this section.
25. See Mt 27:40-43.

what does he look like to you, this man who did not come down from the cross, but rose from the grave?

What did they achieve, then? Even if the Lord had not risen from the dead, would they have achieved anything more than the persecutors of the martyrs achieved? After all, the martyrs have not risen yet; nonetheless their persecutors have been unsuccessful, for here we are, celebrating the birthdays[26] of people not yet risen! What has become of the fury of those who ranted? *The wounds they inflicted were like those from the arrows of mere children, and their tongues were reduced to weakness over them.* Where did those intricate schemes lead them, what was the outcome of the minute probing in which they failed, if even after the Lord was dead and buried, they needed to post guards at his tomb? They petitioned Pilate in these terms: *That charlatan* (they called the Lord Jesus Christ by that name, so his servants need not take it hard when they are called charlatans). *That charlatan said while he was still alive, "I shall rise again after three days." Give orders, therefore, that the grave be guarded until the third day. Otherwise his disciples may possibly come and steal him, and then tell the people, "He has risen from the dead." That would make the situation even more misleading than it was before. Pilate replied, "You have a guard. Go and guard it as you know how." They departed and secured the grave, sealing the stone and setting guards* (Mt 27:63-66). They posted guards, military guards, at the grave. But there was a mighty earthquake and the Lord arose. Such amazing things happened around the tomb that even the soldiers, who had been stationed there as guards, became witnesses—or they would have been, had they been willing to tell the truth. But the avarice that had seduced a disciple who was Christ's companion also captivated the military guard at his tomb. *We will pay you to say that his disciples came while you were asleep, and took him away,* the priests told them.[27] How truly did they fail as they searched out their intricate schemes! What are you alleging, you ill-starred tricksters? Are you so estranged from the light of good sense and duty, so deeply sunk in deception, that you can tell the guards, "Say that while you were asleep his disciples came and removed him"? You adduce sleeping witnesses! You must be asleep yourself, if you search out unsuccessful schemes like this. If they were asleep, can they have seen anything? And if they saw nothing, what use are they as witnesses?

But *they failed as they searched out intricate schemes*, they fell away from God's light, they failed even in the implementation of their own plans, for they were able to effect nothing of what they wanted. Clearly, they failed. But why did things turn out like that? Because a man drew near, a man of deep heart, and

---

26. *Natalitia*, that is, their death-days, their birthdays into heaven. "The days of [the saints'] departure out of the world are to the Church of Christ as the birth and coronation days of kings and emperors" (Richard Hooker (c. 1554-1600), *The Laws of Ecclesiastical Polity*).
27. See Mt 28:12-13.

God was exalted. A little later, Christ's resurrection was public knowledge; and the Holy Spirit came and filled certain timorous disciples with such boldness that they no longer feared death, but dared to proclaim what they had seen. Thus was God exalted in his majesty, he who to succour our weakness had humbly submitted himself to judgment. Heavenly trumpeters shouted that he who had first come to be judged would come a second time to judge. Faced with such marvels, *all who saw these men were deeply disturbed.* When God was thus exalted and Christ proclaimed, the Jews were seen for what they were by certain of their fellow-Jews; they were seen to have failed in the intricate schemes they had devised. As certain Jews beheld stupendous miracles being wrought in the name of a crucified man, one killed by their own hands, they distanced themselves in their hearts from those of their compatriots who clung obstinately to their impiety. They recoiled from such contumacy, and sought advice about their own salvation: *What shall we do?* they asked the apostles (Acts 2:37). *All who saw these men were deeply disturbed,* obviously. They understood that the tongues of Christ's enemies had been *reduced to weakness over them,* and realized too that those enemies had in all respects failed in all the wicked plans they had devised. Disturbed indeed they were.

Verse 10. Fear of God; fearlessness in face of human threats

16. *And every human person was afraid.* Those who were not afraid were not truly human. *Every human person was afraid:* everyone, that is, who used his or her reason to understand what had been done. Those who were not afraid were rather to be called cattle, or wild, savage beasts. That people is like a ravening, roaring lion even today. But every human person was afraid, and this meant all who were willing to believe, and trembled at the prospect of judgment to come.

Every human person was afraid; and they[28] *proclaimed the works of God.* The same one who earlier prayed, *O God, deliver my soul from fear of the enemy,* is the one of whom now it is said, *Every human person was afraid.* He[29] or she was delivered from fear of the enemy, but subjected to fear of God, no longer afraid of those who kill the body, but fearing him alone who has power to cast both body and soul into hell.[30] This is verified especially in the apostles who proclaimed the Lord; for Peter was afraid at first, afraid of the enemy, because his soul was not yet delivered from this fear. When a servant-girl questioned him as to whether he was one of the disciples, he denied the Lord three times.[31] But the Lord rose from the dead and consolidated that pillar. Now Peter preaches

---

28. The apostles.
29. Especially Peter, as appears a few lines further on.
30. See Mt 10:28.
31. See Mk 14:66-72.

both fearlessly and fearfully, for he is freed from fear of those who kill the body, but he fears the One who has power to cast both body and soul into hell fire. *Every human person was afraid, and they proclaimed the works of God.* The chief priests heard about the apostles' preaching of God's works, and haled them before their tribunal. There they warned them not to preach in the name of Jesus.[32] But they replied, *Tell us whom we ought rather to obey—God, or human authorities?*[33] What could the priests answer? Men rather than God? Undoubtedly there was only one answer they could give: we must obey God first. But the apostles knew what God was commanding, and scorned the threats of the priests. Once *every human person had become afraid*, no other human being could strike terror into them, and so *they proclaimed the works of God.*

If a human being is afraid,[34] no other human can frighten him or her; for each human person should fear only him by whom all humans were made. Fear what is above all humans, and then no human will terrify you. Fear everlasting death, and you will not care about losing your present life. Long for pure, unfading joy, for the peace that can never be diminished, and you will make light of anyone who promises you temporal gains; indeed you will make light of the whole world. Love, then, and fear too: love what God promises, and fear what God threatens, and then you will neither be bribed by human promises nor frightened by human menaces.

Every human person was afraid; and they proclaimed the works of God, and understood what he had done. What does that phrase mean: *they understood what he had done?* Does it mean what you were doing, Lord Jesus Christ, when you kept silence, and were led to the slaughter like a sheep that is dumb before its shearer? What you were doing when we esteemed you as a man afflicted and beset with sorrow, familiar with the burden of infirmity? Does it mean what you were doing when you concealed your beauty, you who were fair of form beyond all the children of men?[35] Does it mean what you were doing when you seemed to have no beauty or comeliness,[36] when on the cross you bore with those who railed at you, saying, *If he is the Son of God, let him come down from the cross?* And, in truth, was there anyone among your servants, or any of those you loved, who did not cry out in their hearts, "Oh yes, if only he could come down now, and confound all these mockers"?

But that was not the way of it. He had to die for us who were condemned to death, and rise again for us who will live for ever. Those who wanted him to come down from the cross did not understand that, not at the time. But when he

32. See Acts 5:40.
33. See Acts 5:29.
34. Of God.
35. See Ps 44:3(45:2).
36. See Is 53:2-4.7.

rose again, and ascended in glory to heaven, they understood what the Lord had done. *They proclaimed the works of God, and understood what he had done.*

Verse 11. The joy of Christ's resurrection

17. *The just one will be joyful in the Lord.* No just person is sad any longer. The disciples were sad when the Lord was crucified: they went away mourning and in profound grief, thinking that their hope was gone. He rose again, and even when he appeared to them he found them sorrowful. He held fast the eyes of two of them as they walked along a road, so that they should not recognize him. He found them groaning and sighing, and he continued to restrain their eyes while he explained the scriptures, showing them through these very texts that as it had happened, so it had to be. He showed how the scriptures had foretold that the Lord must rise after the third day. And how could he have risen from the dead on the third day, if he had come down from the cross? O you who walk your way so sadly, would you not have been transported with joy if you had seen the Lord come down from the cross in response to the insults of the Jews? You would have exulted if he had stopped their mouths like that. But you must await the doctor's decision. By refusing to come down, by consenting to be killed, he is mixing[37] the antidote. And now he has risen from the dead; now listen, for he is speaking. He is delaying your recognition of him, so that when you recognize him it will be with all the more joy. Later he opened their eyes at the breaking of bread. They recognize him,[38] they rejoice, and they exclaim, *The just one will be joyful in the Lord.*

The news is told to one of more obstinate disposition: "The Lord has appeared, the Lord is risen!" But he is still sad, for he does not believe it. *Unless I put my hand into the scars of the nails, I will not believe* (Jn 20:25). And the body is offered to him, he is invited to touch; he stretches out his hand, and feels it, and cries, *My Lord and my God!* (Jn 20:28). *The just one will be joyful in the Lord.* With good reason were those just men and women joyful in the Lord, for they saw, and touched, and believed. But what of the just people of today, who neither see nor touch him? Are they not joyful in the Lord? They certainly are, for what did the Lord say to Thomas? *Because you have seen, you have believed; blessed are those who have not seen, yet have believed* (Jn 20:29).

Let us all be joyful in the Lord, then. Let all of us be one single just person in virtue of our faith,[39] and be members of the one body under the one head. Let us be joyful in the Lord, not in ourselves, for we are not our own good gift to ourselves: he who made us is our good. And he is our good to make us joyful. Let

---

37. Literally "grinding," as in a mortar.
38. See Lk 24:13-35.
39. See Rom 1:17; Hb 2:4.

none of us be joyful in ourselves, let none of us trust in ourselves or despair of ourselves; nor let any of us put our trust in any other human being. Every other person must be brought in as a participant in our hope, but not as the donor of it.

Uprightness of heart

18. *The just one will be joyful in the Lord, and will hope in him; and all the upright of heart will be commended.* The Lord is risen, he has ascended into heaven, he has given us proof of a life other than this one. He has demonstrated that his secret designs, whereby he lay hidden in that deep heart of his, were not foolish after all, because his blood was poured out to be the price of all the redeemed. Because all these things have been manifested now, and all preached[40] now, and because all of them have commanded belief, *the just one will be joyful in the Lord* everywhere under heaven; *the just one will be joyful in the Lord and will hope in him; and all the upright of heart will be commended.* Who are the upright of heart? Well, brothers and sisters, we are for ever telling you this, for it is something you need to know. Who are the right-hearted people? They are the ones who attribute whatever they have to suffer in this life not to senseless chance, but to the plan of God that works for their healing. Nor are they so confident of their own righteousness as to think that they are suffering unjustly, or that God is unjust because someone else who sins more gravely does not suffer more. You must see this point, brothers and sisters; it is one we make often. When you feel badly about something—perhaps some bodily pain, or some loss of income, or bereavement when someone you love dies—do not look askance at people whom you know to be more sinful than you are. Perhaps you would not go so far as to claim to be righteous yourself, but at any rate you know they are worse. You see them prospering in their wicked ways, and not being punished; so God's dispensation seems unfair to you, and you may grumble, "What if I am a sinner? So I am chastised for it. All right; but then why is that fellow not chastised? I know how disgraceful his behavior is. However bad my record is, have I committed as much wickedness as he has? I'm sure I haven't!"

Your heart is twisted, I tell you. How good God is to Israel, but to those who are right of heart. Your feet had all but slipped, so envious are you of sinners, as you observe the peace sinners enjoy.[41] Let God heal them and you. He who knows the wound knows what he is about. "But that other fellow isn't undergoing surgery!" No, but perhaps his case is hopeless? What if you are undergoing it precisely because yours is not? Suffer with an upright heart whatever you have to suffer; God knows what to give you and what to take away from you. If he bestows gifts on you, let it comfort you but not corrupt you; if he takes

---

40. Variant: "foretold."
41. See Ps 72(73):1-3.

things away, let it train you in fortitude and not provoke you to blasphemy. If you do blaspheme, you are being angry with God, and pleased with yourself; and that means you have a twisted, crooked heart. Worse still, you want to align God's heart with yours, to make him do what you want, whereas you ought to do what he wants. How can that be? Do you really want to bend God's eternally straight heart to fit in with the distortion of your own? Would it not be a much better idea to correct your heart by the rectitude of God? And did your Lord not teach you this, the Lord about whose passion we were reading? Was he not carrying your weakness when he said, *My soul is sorrowful to the point of death* (Mt 26:38)? Did he not take you over and identify you with himself[42] when he repeatedly prayed, *Father, if it is possible, let this cup pass from me* (Mt 26:39)? There were not two hearts, at odds with one another, in Father and Son; but in his capacity as the servant, Christ bore your heart within his own, to instruct it by his own example. But now tribulation has caught up with you and found in you a different heart, a heart that wants the trial to pass you by. This is not what God wills. God does not yield to your heart, you must yield to the heart of God. Listen to Christ's voice: *yet not what I will, but what you will be done, Father.*

Now is the time to change your heart

19. We know, then, that *all the upright of heart will be commended.* What conclusion should we draw? If *all the upright of heart will be commended,* all the crooked of heart will be condemned. Two possibilities are offered to you now; make your choice while there is time. If you are upright of heart you will be at Christ's right hand and you will be commended. How? *Come, you who are blessed by my Father, take possession of the kingdom prepared for you since the creation of the world* (Mt 25:34). But not if you are a person of crooked heart. If you have whispered against God, if you have derided his providence, if you have said in your mind, "Clearly God takes no interest in human affairs. If he did interest himself in them, would that brigand have so much, while I am in need, innocent though I am?" then you have become crooked of heart. That final judgment will come, and then all the reasons will be apparent for all God's decisions. But if you have refused to correct your heart in conformity with God's rectitude in this life, and to prepare yourself to stand at his right hand, where *all the upright of heart will be commended,* you will find yourself at his left. And there you will hear on that day, *Depart from me into the eternal fire which was prepared for the devil and his angels* (Mt 25:41). And will there be any opportunity then to rectify your heart?

---

42. *Nonne teipsum in se figurabat.* Augustine's strong Christology, which underpins his understanding of the psalms. See the Introduction.

Rectify your hearts now, brothers and sisters, correct them now. Who is preventing you? The psalm is sung, the gospel is read, the reader makes his proclamation, the teacher's message resounds. The Lord is patient: you sin, and he pardons you; you sin again, and he pardons you again; and still you go on sinning. How long is God patient? You will find that God is just too.

"We scare others because we are afraid ourselves; teach us not to be afraid, and we will scare others no more."[43] But it is better that God teach us to fear, than that some human being teach us not to; for when *all human persons were afraid, they proclaimed the works of God.* May God assign us a place among those who were afraid, and proclaimed his works.

And it is because we, for our part, are filled with this fear that we proclaim the message to you, brothers and sisters. We see your eagerness to listen to the word, we hear your insistent demands for it, and we mark your devotion. The earth is plentifully watered; may it bring forth grain, not thorns, for a barn is ready for the grain, but a fire for the thorns. You know how to deal with your field; surely God knows how to deal with his servant? The rain that falls on a fertile field is wholesome, and the rain that falls on a thorn-choked field is equally wholesome. Does a farmer who has grown thorns blame the rain for it? On the contrary: that rain will be the accuser at God's judgment seat; it will say, "I was wholesome, and I watered everyone." Take care, then, what kind of crop you bring forth, and be aware of what awaits you. If you bring forth grain, hope for a place in the barn; if you bring forth thorns, expect the fire.

But it is not time yet for either the barn or the fire. Let us make our preparations now, and there will be no need to be afraid. In Christ's name we, who are speaking, are alive; and you, to whom we speak, are alive. It is not true then, is it, that we have no place, no time, for hearkening to this advice and correcting ourselves, and changing our bad lives into good ones? Can't you do it this very day, if you want to? Can't you do it this moment, if you want to? What do you need to go and buy first? What medicaments[44] will you seek? To what Far Indies will you sail? What ship fit out in readiness? No, change your heart now, even while I am speaking. Now you have done what you are so often, so insistently, so loudly bidden to do; what will earn you everlasting punishment if you omit it.

---

43. This sentence sits oddly. Its relevance to the argument is not obvious; and the imperative "teach us" is plural, though the verbs in the preceding sentence have been singular. Possibly he is quoting a proverb or common saying.

44. Variants abound: older editions preferred *emplastra*, "plasters," but also a term used of the insertion of a graft into the bark of a tree. Others read *semplasia* or *symplasia*, perhaps "compounds." Others again read *templa Asiae*, "temples of Asia" in line with the question that follows.

Exposition of Psalm 64

A Sermon to the People

Verse 1. Jeremiah, Ezekiel, and the exile

1. In the title assigned to this psalm we can recognize the voice of prophecy. It runs, *To the end, a psalm of David. The song of Jeremiah and Ezekiel concerning the exiled people, when they were beginning to go forth.* It is not everybody who is familiar with the story of what happened to our ancestors at the time of their exile in Babylon; but those who pay careful attention to the holy scriptures, whether by listening or by reading for themselves, know about these events. The Israelite people was taken captive, and led away from the city of Jerusalem to servitude in Babylon.[1] Holy Jeremiah prophesied, however, that the people would return from captivity after seventy years,[2] and would rebuild the city of Jerusalem, over the ruin of which he had lamented.[3] At this time there were also prophets active among the exiled people in Babylon, and one of these was Ezekiel. The people were awaiting the completion of the seventy-year period forecast by Jeremiah. When the time had expired, the temple, which had been destroyed, was restored, and the majority of the people returned from captivity.

The apostle warned us, however, that *all these things happened to them, but with symbolic import, for they are written down as a rebuke to us, upon whom the climax of the ages has come* (1 Cor 10:11); and therefore it is our business to understand first of all in what sense we are captives, and then to know our liberation. We must know what Babylon is, this city by which we are enslaved, and also be aware of Jerusalem, whither we long to return.

These are two cities: they are literally cities, real cities. Jerusalem is no longer inhabited by Jews, however. After the Lord was crucified a terrible punishment was visited upon the Jews, and they were uprooted from that place where they had shamefully misused their freedom by raging deliriously against their healer. They were scattered throughout all nations, and their country was given to Christians. The Lord's prophecy concerning them was fulfilled: *the kingdom of God will be taken away from you, and given to a nation that brings forth the fruit of it, righteousness* (Mt 21:43). When the Jewish leaders in Jerusalem saw great

---

1. For the first deportation in 597 B.C. see 2 Kgs 24:10-16; for the second, in 587 or 586 B.C., see 2 Kgs 25:8-12; Jer 39:8-10; 52:12-27.
2. See Jer 25:11; 29:10, a round number which is reflected also in Dn 9.
3. The Book of Lamentations was traditionally ascribed to Jeremiah.

crowds flocking after the Lord, impressed by his preaching of the kingdom of heaven and the miracles he worked, they said, *If we leave him alone like this, everyone will believe in him, and then the Romans will come, and sweep away our land and our nationhood* (Jn 11:48). In order not to lose their land they killed the Lord, and then they lost it because they had killed him.

This Jerusalem was an earthly city, but it stood as a sign of a heavenly, eternal city, and when the heavenly city it foreshadowed came to be proclaimed more openly, the shadow was done away with. That is why there is no temple there now, for the temple was built to be a sign of the body of the Lord in the future.[4] We possess the light, and the shadow has faded away. Yet we are still subject to a kind of captivity, for scripture testifies, *As long as we are in the body we are on pilgrimage and away from the Lord* (2 Cor 5:6).

Babylon and Jerusalem

2. Consider now the names of these two cities, Babylon and Jerusalem. Babylon signifies "confusion," and Jerusalem "vision of peace." You need to study the city of confusion now, in order to understand the vision of peace; you must endure the one, and yearn for the other. How can these two cities be distinguished? We cannot separate them from one another, can we? No, they are intermingled, and they continue like that from the very beginning of the human race until the end of the world. Jerusalem began to exist with Abel, and Babylon with Cain, for it was from Cain's time that city buildings were put up. Jerusalem was situated in the territory of the Jebusites, which was why its earlier name was Jebus;[5] the Jebusites were turned out of the place when God's people was freed from Egypt and brought into the promised land.[6] But Babylon was established in the innermost part of the Persian country, and exercised dominion over other nations for a long time.[7]

---

4. See Jn 2:19-21.

5. See Jos 18:28. The name is attested from 2000 B.C.

6. There are divergent traditions on this matter within the Old Testament. The Book of Joshua presents the conquest of the promised land by the incoming Hebrew tribes as a unified campaign under Joshua's command. It included the defeat of the Jebusite ruler of Jerusalem; see Jos 10:23-26; 12:10. Augustine accepts this version of events in the present sermon. The Book of Judges remembers the Israelite displacement of the Canaanite tribes as a much slower process, with many setbacks and no unified command, and often accomplished by peaceful penetration rather than by military means. For this tradition, many important towns did not become Israelite until long after Joshua's time; and this was true in particular of Jerusalem, captured by David according to the account in 2 Sm 5:6-9; 1 Chr 11:4-7.

7. That is, during the heyday of the Neo-Babylonian Empire, 620-539 B.C., after the defeat of the Assyrian Empire. During this period Nebuchadnezzar besieged Jerusalem twice, destroyed it and deported the flower of the Israelite inhabitants. But Babylon itself fell to Cyrus, King of the Persians, in 539, and became a satrapy of the Persian Empire. On the mystical significance of Babylon, type of the city of wickedness for Augustine, compare Exposition 2 of Psalm 26, 18; Exposition of Psalm 44, 25; Exposition 1 of Psalm 58, 5; Exposition 1 of Psalm 61, 6, and notes.

These two cities were therefore founded at ascertainable times; but their purpose was to represent two cities that had existed from the earliest ages and are to remain in the world until the end of time, when they will be separated. How, then, are we to discern them now, while they are mingled together? The Lord will make the difference plain at the end, by placing some people at his right hand, and others at his left. Jerusalem will be at his right, but at his left will be Babylon. Jerusalem will hear the invitation, *Come, you whom my Father has blessed; take possession of the kingdom prepared for you since the world was made.* Babylon will hear the dismissal, *Depart from me into the eternal fire which was prepared for the devil and his angels* (Mt 25:34. 41). Nonetheless we can, insofar as the Lord enables us, make a suggestion about how to tell them apart even in this present age—about how the devout, faithful citizens of Jerusalem may be distinguished from the citizens of Babylon. Two loves create the two cities: love of God creates Jerusalem; love of the world creates Babylon.[8] All of us must therefore ask ourselves what we love, and we shall discover to which city we belong. If we find that we are citizens of Babylon we must root out greed and plant charity; but if we find ourselves to be citizens of Jerusalem, we must bear our captivity and look forward to our freedom. There were plenty of people who had been citizens of their holy mother, Jerusalem, but were corrupted by the lusts of Babylon and detained there; and so, corrupted as they were, they became Babylon's citizens. There are many such people today, and there will be many more on earth after our time. But the Lord who founded Jerusalem knows whom he has predestined to be her citizens. Though they may still be under the dominion of the devil, he knows them as destined to be redeemed by the blood of Christ; he knows them even before they know themselves.[9]

This, then, is the drama of which our psalm sings. Two prophets are mentioned in its title, Jeremiah and Ezekiel, who were captives themselves at the time, and sang when the people *were beginning to go forth*. The person who is

---

8. The heart of Augustine's thought on the symbolism of the two cities, developed further in *The City of God.* "Two loves have created the two cities: love of self even to contempt of God creates the earthly city; love of God even to contempt of self creates the heavenly city" (*City of God* XIV, 28).

9. In two different periods of his life Augustine had to grapple with religious groups who believed that a sharp demarcation was discernible even in the present life between the perfect/elect/pure on the one hand, and ordinary people on the other. In the case of the Manichees this division was all of a piece with their dualistic theosophy; in that of the Donatists it was part of an erroneous idea of the Church, and all the more dangerous for that. Augustine fought hard and long against the Donatist notion that the Church in this world is a society of the pure; he stressed frequently, as in the present sermon, that the Lord had described it as a field growing both wheat and weeds mixed together, or a net holding a mixed catch of fish. Such a view excluded complacency and false security, and left room only for humble hope in God's mercy. Augustine did not, of course, simply identify the true citizens of Jerusalem with members of the visible Church; he emphasizes that their identity is known at present only to God, and will be revealed at the end.

beginning to go forth is the one who is beginning to love. Many go forth in a hidden way, for the feet on which they go forth are the affections of their hearts. Now, it is suggested that they go forth from Babylon; and what does "Babylon" signify? That's right, "confusion." It happens like this: such people were at first confused with the rest because they were immersed in the same lusts, but then they began to be distinguished from the others by their charity. So now they are distinct, not confused. In body they are still mingled among the others, but they are distinguished by holy desire. Inasmuch as they are still part of the other crowd by their bodily existence, they have not yet gone forth, but they have begun to go forth through their hearts' desire.

Let us listen now, brothers and sisters, let us listen, and sing, and long for the city of which we are citizens. What joys are unfolded before us in song? Can love of our own city be revived in us, if through being abroad so long we have forgotten it? Yes, it can, for our Father has sent us letters. God has provided the scriptures for us, so that by these letters from him our longing to return home may be aroused.[10] We had become so attached to our exile that we had turned our faces toward our enemies, and our backs to our fatherland. So listen, what is sung to us here?

Verse 2. The song of Jerusalem and the perfect sacrifice

3. *A hymn to you in Zion is fitting, O God.* Zion is our homeland, for Zion and Jerusalem are the same; but you ought to appreciate the significance of this alternative name. As "Jerusalem" is interpreted as "vision of peace," so "Zion" means "watching" or "watching-post," that is, vision and contemplation. Some great vision is promised to us, nothing else but God himself, who founded that city. A beautiful and dignified city she is, but how much more beautiful is her Founder! *A hymn to you is fitting, O God,* says the psalm; but where is it fitting? Only *in Zion;* it would be unfitting in Babylon. As soon as any one of us has begun to be made new, we already sing with our heart in Jerusalem, for the

---

10. Christians are to remember that they are pilgrims, he emphasizes, people whose true home and true citizenship are elsewhere. There may have been a contemporary point here. In 410 the Visigoths sacked Rome, and the shock-waves reverberated throughout the Empire. One consequence of the event was that some citizens, of Rome, still attached to the old religion, tended to blame Christianity for the disaster: the old gods were taking revenge. Possibly some Roman Christians may also have been dismayed that Christ had not saved the city any more than the old gods had. A wave of refugees from the stricken city reached North Africa. They were probably in the main well-to-do, owners of property there to which they could retreat. If the tentative assignment of the present sermon to A.D. 412 is correct, Augustine's hearers may have been familiar with the sight of discontented exiles, disdainful of the conditions of their status in a foreign land, and thinking wistfully of a great city far away that was their true *patria*. That such pagans or disaffected Christians should provide a model for the Christian attitude Augustine is inculcating is an irony that would not have escaped him.

apostle tells us, *We have citizens' rights in heaven* (Phil 3:20), and he also reminds us that *though we live in the flesh, our weapons are not those of the flesh* (2 Cor 10:3). Through our desire we are in Jerusalem already; we have already cast our hope ahead of us like an anchor into that country, to safeguard us from shipwreck when the weather here is rough.[11] When a ship is riding at anchor we rightly consider her to have made landfall already, for although she is still tossed by the waves she has in a real sense been led out of the force of the winds and storms by her grip on the earth. In the same way our hope is fastened in the city of Jerusalem, safeguarding us against the perils of our voyage, and preventing us from being dashed on the rocks.

Accordingly anyone who sings in this hope is singing there, in Zion, and has the right to say, *A hymn to you in Zion is fitting, O God.* It stresses *in Zion*, not in Babylon. But you are in Babylon at present, surely? "Yes," replies this person, this lover, this citizen of Jerusalem. "Yes, I am in Babylon as to my body, but not in my heart. Both these things are true of me: that I am here in Babylon bodily, but not in heart, and that I am not in that place whence my song springs; for I sing not from my flesh, but from my heart." The song of the flesh is audible even to the citizens of Babylon, but only the founder of Jerusalem can hear the song of the heart. With this in mind the apostle exhorted Jerusalem's citizens to sing canticles of love and to arouse their longing to return to that most fair city, to that vision of peace: *Sing hymns and psalms in your hearts to the Lord*, he tells them (Eph 5:19). What does he mean by *sing in your hearts*? Do not let your songs be inspired by the place where you are now, by Babylon; but sing from where your hearts are, sing as from your habitation on high. And so *a hymn to you in Zion is fitting, O God.* In Zion it becomes you, not in Babylon; for those who sing in Babylon are Babylon's citizens, and even if they sing one of God's hymns, their rendering of it is unseemly. Listen to scripture's warning on this point: *Praise is not seemly in a sinner's mouth* (Sir 15:9). But *a hymn to you in Zion is fitting, O God.*

4. *And to you will each vow be duly paid in Jerusalem.* We make our vows here, and it is right that we should fulfill them there. But do any people make vows here, and not fulfill them? Yes, those who do not persevere to the end in what they have vowed. This is why another psalm admonishes us, *Make your vows to the Lord your God and carry them out* (Ps 75:12(76:11)).

To you will each vow be duly paid in Jerusalem, duly rendered there, because there we shall be whole, in perfect integrity, at the resurrection of the just. There our vowed offering will be rendered in its entirety: not our souls alone but our flesh itself, because it will be corruptible flesh no more. When we have left Babylon behind, the body of each of us will be a transfigured, heavenly body.

---

11. See Heb 6:19 for the image of the anchor.

Scripture's promise gives a hint of what this transformation will be like. *Though we shall all indeed rise again, we shall not all be changed,* says the apostle;[12] and he goes on to tell us who will be changed: *in the twinkling of an eye, at the last trumpet (for the trumpet will sound, and the dead will rise incorrupt), and we shall be changed.* We shall be whole, not subject to decay, he means, and he goes on to give us an inkling of what the transformation will be like: *This corruptible body must put on incorruptibility, and this mortal body be clothed in immortality. And when this corruptible body has put on incorruptibility, and this mortal body has been clothed in immortality, then the saying will come true: Death is swallowed up into victory. O death, where is your sting?* (1 Cor 15:51-55). The first-fruits of the re-creation of our minds are ours already, and they prompt us to long for Jerusalem, but many forces arise from our perishable nature to wage war against us still. When death has been swallowed up in victory they will contend against us no longer. Peace will be victorious, and warfare ended. But when peace is victorious, that city which is named Vision of Peace will be victorious too. Death will not have the strength to put up a fight then.

Yet at present, how unremitting is our warfare with death! It is the source of the carnal desires that prompt us to many unlawful acts. We do not consent to these urges, yet even the withholding of consent entails a struggle. At first carnal concupiscence led us, and we followed; then we resisted, and it dragged us along; then we were given grace and the desire weakened, and ceased to lead and drag us, yet it fought against us still. After this warfare there will be victory. Concupiscence attacks you now, but do not let it defeat you; when death is finally swallowed up in victory it will cease even to fight. What does scripture promise? *Death, the last enemy, will be destroyed* (1 Cor 15:26).

Then I will duly render my vow. What kind of vow is it? It is like a holocaust. A sacrifice is called a holocaust when fire consumes the whole of it, for *ὅλον* means "all" or "whole," and *ʹ~δεῖν* means "burning." So a holocaust is a wholly-burnt offering. Let the fire seize us, that divine fire that blazes in Jerusalem; let us begin now to burn with charity until all that is mortal in us is consumed and whatever has fought against us goes up to the Lord in sacrifice. This is the prayer made elsewhere: *In your good will, O Lord, deal kindly with Zion, and let the walls of Jerusalem be rebuilt. Then you will accept a sacrifice of righteousness, oblations and holocausts* (Ps 50:20-21(51:18-19)).

A hymn to you in Zion is fitting, O God, and to you will each vow be duly paid in Jerusalem. We may inquire whether there is a hint here of the King of that city, our Lord Jesus Christ; but we had better go on singing the psalm until we come to some clearer indication of this. I could tell you straightaway that it is he to whom these words are addressed, *a hymn to you in Zion is fitting, O God, and to you will*

---

12. Augustine's Latin version reflects a different understanding of the Pauline text.

each vow be duly paid in Jerusalem; but if I told you that, you would believe me rather than scripture. Or perhaps you would not believe me. So let us listen to the following verses.

Verse 3. All flesh will come to you

5. *Hearken to my prayer; to you all flesh will come*, so prays the psalm. And we find our Lord claiming that to him had been given power over all flesh.[13] So our King is beginning to appear in this verse, where it says, *To you all flesh will come*. It says, *To you*, notice: *to you all flesh will come*. Why to him? Because he assumed our flesh. By what right does all flesh come to him? By this right: that he took the first-fruits of it from a virginal womb, and once the first-fruits have been taken the rest will necessarily follow, so that the holocaust may be complete.

What does *all flesh* signify? It means every human being. But how can it be said that every human being will come? Was it foretold that all mankind would believe in Christ? No. Are there not many impious people, people even heading for damnation? Are there not many unbelievers dying in their infidelity every day? And if this is so, how are we to understand the declaration that *to you all flesh will come*?

When the psalm says, *all flesh*, it means "every kind of flesh"; it means that people will flock to you from flesh of every kind. And what does that mean—every kind of flesh? Well, we can hardly say, can we, that poor people have come, but not the rich? Or lowly folk, but not those of elevated station? Have the untaught come, without the educated? Or men, but no women? Or masters, but no servants? Have old men come to him, but no young men? Or have young men come, but no adolescents? Or adolescents, but no children? Or have children come, but no babies in arms? Finally, consider this: surely we cannot say that Jews have come to him (for they have, of course: the apostles were from Jewry, and so were many thousands who at first handed Christ over, but later believed in him), but Greeks have not come? Or that Greeks have come, but Romans not? Or that Romans have come, but no barbarians?[14] Who can count all the nations who are rallying to Christ, to whom these words are spoken? *Hearken to my prayer; to you all flesh will come*.

---

13. See Jn 17:2.
14. The ordinary term in antiquity for races outside the traditions of classical culture.

Verse 4. The lingering influence of pagan upbringing; Christ the sacrifice for sins; letter and spirit, the veiled hearts

6. *The words of sinners had power over us; but you will be propitiated over our impieties.* What is this about — *the words of sinners had power over us, but you will be propitiated over our impieties*? Since we were born on this earth, we inevitably fell in with bad people, and we listened as they talked. I ask you to help me now by your close attention, beloved ones,[15] while I try to explain my thoughts on this. Every human being, wherever he or she is born, learns the tongue of that country, or district, or civic community, and is imbued with the customs and way of life proper to the place. How, for instance, could a child born among pagans avoid paying cult to a stone idol, when his parents have trained him in that form of worship? In that milieu he heard his earliest words; he sucked in that falsehood with his mother's milk. And since those who spoke about such things were adults, and he but a child when he was learning to speak, what could the little one do, except be guided by the authority of his elders, and take it for granted that what they recommended was good for him?

Then later the Gentile nations are converted to Christ. They remember the impiety of their ancestors, and make their own the words spoken long ago by Jeremiah: *Truly our ancestors worshiped a lie, a futile thing that could not help them* (Jer 16:19). When they admit this, they renounce the beliefs and sacrilegious practices of their forebears. But those relatives were supposed to have enjoyed great authority in virtue of their more advanced age, and so their persuasion carried weight, and sowed erroneous opinions and impious attitudes in younger minds. Therefore each convert who now wants to return from Babylon to Jerusalem is bound to confess, "*The words of sinners had power over us.* They taught us bad lessons and led us astray; they made us into citizens of Babylon. We abandoned our Creator and worshiped a creature; we forsook him by whom we were made, and worshiped what we had made ourselves. *The words of sinners had power over us,* yet they have not stifled us completely." Why not? Because, Lord, *you will be propitiated over our impieties.*

Concentration is needed here, beloved.[16] The words, *you will be propitiated over our impieties,* can be used only with reference to a priest who is offering something whereby impiety may be expiated and God propitiated.[17] Propitiation

---

15. *Caritatis vestrae.*

16. *Caritas vestra.*

17. *Unde impietas expietur et propitietur.* Expiation means the atoning for an offense committed; propitiation means the appeasing of God who is offended by sin. Both notions have ancient roots in Israelite cult, and came to be prominent especially in the ritual of the Day of Atonement, as Augustine goes on to say. In the New Testament the sacrifice of Christ is alone seen as the expiation for sin and the means of atonement; and it is emphasized that this propitiatory act derives from God's reconciling love. See Rom 3:25; 2 Cor 5:19. 21; 1 Jn 2:2; 4:10; Heb 2:17.

for impiety can be said to have been made only when God is propitious toward that impiety. But what does this mean, that God becomes propitious? It means that he forgives, and grants pardon; but in order to obtain God's pardon, we must propitiate him by some kind of sacrifice.

Accordingly a priest was raised up for us, one sent by the Lord God. He assumed from us the humanity that he would offer to the Lord: this was the holy first-fruits of our flesh that he took from the Virgin's womb, as we have already explained. He offered it as a holocaust to God. He stretched out his hands on the cross, in such a way that he could say, *Let my prayer rise like incense before you, and the raising of my hands be an evening sacrifice* (Ps 140(141):2). It was in fact toward evening when our Lord hung on the cross, as you know. Propitiation was thereby offered for our impious acts, which otherwise would have ruined us. The words of sinners would have had decisive power over us; the preachers of Jove, and Saturn, and Mercury would have led us where they liked. *The words of sinners had power over us*; but what will you do about it, Lord? *You will be propitiated over our impieties.* You are the priest, and you are the victim; you are the one who offers, and you yourself are the offering.

He is the priest who has now made his entry through the veil. Out of all who have worn human flesh, he alone is there to intercede for us.[18] This mystery was foreshadowed among the earlier people, in the earlier temple, where one single priest was accustomed to enter the Holy of Holies while the whole congregation stood outside. He who alone penetrated beyond the veil offered sacrifice on behalf of the people who waited. If this ritual is rightly understood, the spirit gives life; but if it is not understood, the letter kills. When the apostle's letter was being read just now you heard him say, *The letter is death-dealing, but the spirit gives life.*[19] The Jews failed to understand what was being enacted among them; indeed they do not know even now, and of them scripture justly says, *Whenever the law of Moses is read, a veil is drawn over their hearts* (2 Cor 3:15). The veil here means the figurative representation; let the veil be removed, and the truth present in these mysterious things will appear plainly. When will the veil be removed? Listen to the apostle's answer: *When you cross over to the Lord, the veil will be lifted* (2 Cor 3:16). We conclude from this that as long as they do not cross over to the Lord, their hearts remain veiled, though they go on reading Moses. The radiance on the face of Moses pointed toward this mystery. So bright was it that *the Israelites could not bear to look at Moses' face* (2 Cor 3:7)—you heard about this when the passage was read. So a veil was interposed between

18. See Heb 6:19-20; 7:24-25; 9:11-12.
19. 2 Cor 3:6. Ambrose's application of this principle had been a source of enlightenment for Augustine in his early days in Milan, when the crudity of some Old Testament passages had seemed to him a barrier to the acceptance of Christianity: see *The Confessions* VI, 4, 6. In the present passage, following Paul, Augustine makes powerful use of it himself.

the face of Moses as he spoke, and the people who listened to what he said. They heard his words through the veil, but did not see his face. And what is the apostle's comment? *The Israelites could not look at Moses' face; even to the end they were unable to look upon it.*[20] What does *even to the end* suggest? Until they should come to acknowledge Christ; for, as the apostle says, *Christ is the end of the law, bringing justification to everyone who believes* (Rom 10:4). Glory there is on the face of Moses, but it is glory on a carnal, mortal face; can it be enduring or eternal? Death will come, and then it will assuredly vanish. But the glorious radiance of our blessed Lord Jesus Christ is everlasting. The radiance seen in Moses was a figure, and transient; but what the figure pointed to is the reality. The Jews read the law but fail to perceive Christ. Their gaze does not lead them right through to the end, because the veil gets in the way and blocks their view of the splendor within. But you, on the contrary, you must see Christ there. Our Lord Jesus Christ himself warned them, *If you believed Moses, you would believe in me as well; for he wrote about me* (Jn 5:46).

But as for us, our sins and our impiety have been atoned for by that evening sacrifice, and so we cross over to the Lord, and the veil is taken away. This is why the temple veil was torn in half when the Lord was crucified.[21] *Hearken to my prayer; to you all flesh will come. The words of sinners had power over us, but you will be propitiated over our impieties.*

Verses 5-6. The single chosen one

7. *Blessed is the one whom you have chosen and taken up.* Who has been chosen by him, and taken up? Is it some particular person who is referred to, someone chosen by our Savior Jesus Christ? Or is it perhaps Christ himself in his flesh, Christ in his humanity, who is meant: is he the one who is chosen and taken up? That could well be; and then we would be addressing this prayer to the Word of God who existed in the beginning, as the evangelist teaches: *in the beginning was the Word, and the Word was with God; he was God*; for he is the Son of God, the Word of God, of whom it is also said that *everything was made through him; nothing came to be without him* (Jn 1:1-3). It would mean that we should say to the Son of God, *Blessed is the one whom you have chosen and taken up* — say it, that is, because he is our priest, and it can be referred to him after he has taken up our flesh. We can say it of you, Lord, in the manhood in which you have clothed yourself, since as man you had a beginning in time, being born of a woman, so that your humanity is like a temple for him who lives eternally, and from eternity.

---

20. See 2 Cor 3:14-15.
21. See Mt 27:51.

But perhaps it is better to understand it of Christ himself having taken up someone. The singular is used for the one he has taken up, although this one comprises many; for he has taken up "one" in the sense that what he has taken up is a unity. He did not take up schisms, nor did he take up heresies; they have made themselves into a crowd, so they are not the one person who could be taken up. Very different are those who remain bonded into the structure of Christ and are members of him, for they in some sense form a single person, of whom the apostle speaks: *Until we all meet in knowing the Son of God, to form a perfect man, and attain to the mature stature of the fullness of Christ* (Eph 4:13). Hence it can be said that a single person is taken up, one whose head is Christ: as scripture affirms, *The head of a man is Christ* (1 Cor 11:3). This one person is pronounced blessed in another psalm: *Blessed is the person who has not gone astray in the council of the ungodly* (Ps 1:1). This is the one who is here said to be taken up. But this person is not someone apart from ourselves. We are among his members, we are ruled by the one head, we all live by the one Spirit,[22] and we all long for the one homeland.

We must examine what is said of Christ, therefore, to see what it has to do with us, and whether it is said of us. Let us question our consciences and scrutinize the love we find there. If it is still a weakly plant, only sprung up lately (as it may be in some persons), we must diligently root out any thorns that are growing round it—worldly cares, I mean—lest they grow rank and smother the holy shoot. *Blessed is the one whom you have chosen and taken up.* Let us abide in him, and allow ourselves to be taken up; let us abide in him, and be his chosen.

The beauty of God's house is righteousness

8. And then, what will he give us? The one you choose and take up *will dwell in your courts*, says the psalm, the courts of that Jerusalem to which are sung the songs of those who are beginning to leave Babylon. The chosen one *will dwell in your courts. We shall be filled with the good things of your house.* What are the good things of God's house?

Let us imagine some rich dwelling, brothers and sisters. It is a house cram-full of good things. How abundant everything is, how many gold vessels there are, but silver vessels too; what an ample staff of servants, how many cattle and other animals! How delightful it is, with its pictures, its marble, its paneled ceilings, its pillars, its spacious rooms and bed-chambers! All highly desirable—but all part of the confusion that is Babylon. Cut off all such desires, O citizen of Jerusalem, cut them off once and for all! If you want to make your way home, do not fall in love with your captivity. But you have begun to quit Babylon

---

22. Or "breath."

already, so do not look back, or loiter on the road. There is still no lack of enemies who will tempt you with the attractions of your captivity and your sojourn in that foreign land, but do not let the words of sinners have power over you now. Long for the house of God, and long for the good things in his house; but do not hanker for the kind of things you are accustomed to desire in your own house, or your neighbor's, or in the house of your patron. The good of God's house is something quite different. But is there any need for us to say what the good things of God's house are? Rather let the one who is leaving Babylon tell us. *We shall be filled with the good things of your house*, says our psalm. What are these good things? Perhaps we had lifted our longing hearts toward gold, or silver, or other precious objects? No, do not seek things like that: they only weigh you down, they cannot lift you up.

Let us give some thought now to the good things of Jerusalem, the good things of the Lord's house, the good things of the Lord's temple; for the Lord's house is also his temple. *We shall be filled with the good things of your house; holy is your temple, wonderful for righteousness*. These are the good things of his house. The psalm did not say, "Holy is your temple, wonderful for its pillars, wonderful for its marble, wonderful for its gold-encrusted roofs;" no, it said, *wonderful for righteousness*. You have external eyes with which to appreciate marble and gold, but within you is an eye which enables you to see the beauty of righteousness.

I repeat, the eye with the capacity to appreciate the beauty of righteousness is within you. If there were no beauty in righteousness, how could we love a righteous old man? What bodily charms has he to offer that could delight our eyes? All he has is a bent back, a wrinkled face, white hair, weakness, and bodily complaints throughout his frame. Nothing to please your eyes in this worn-out old man, then. But perhaps there is something to delight your ears? His speaking voice? His singing? What are they like? Even if he did sing well as a boy, all such talent has fallen away with age. Is even the sound of his speech pleasant to your ears, when he can scarcely get his words out, having lost his teeth? Yet all the same, if he is a righteous man, if he does not covet other people's property, if from his own possessions he is generous to the needy, if he gives good advice and is a man of sound judgment and honest faith, if he is prepared to sacrifice even shattered limbs in defense of the truth (for many martyrs were elderly)—then, isn't that why we love him? What good do our carnal eyes find in him? None at all. This proves that righteousness has a beauty of its own, which we perceive with the eyes of the heart, and love, and kindle to, a beauty which people have dearly loved in the martyrs, even when their limbs were being torn by wild beasts. Surely we might have supposed that when people were covered with reeking blood, when brutal bites were tearing out their entrails, the eyes of onlookers would see nothing but horror? What was there to attract them in such a scene, except the untarnished beauty of righteousness, which shone out amid the foulness of lacerated limbs?

Such are the good things of God's house. Prepare yourself to find your total satisfaction in them. But if you are to be satisfied by these things when you reach home, you must hunger and thirst while you are still on the journey. Thirst for righteousness, hunger for it, because the good things of God will consist in this. Listen to the King to whom these words are addressed, the King who came to lead you home and made himself the way for you.[23] What does he say? *Blessed are those who hunger and thirst for righteousness, for they shall be satisfied* (Mt 5:6). *Holy is your temple, wonderful for righteousness.*

One last thing, brothers and sisters. Do not think of this temple as something extraneous to yourselves. Love righteousness, and you yourselves are the temple of God.

The present world is a turbulent sea, full of varied fish

9. *Hearken to us, O God, our Savior.* The psalm now openly indicates whom it is calling "God," for our *Savior* is, properly speaking, the Lord Jesus Christ. It has also become clearer now who it was to whom the psalm said earlier, *To you all flesh will come.* Now it prays, *Hearken to us, O God, our Savior.* This one person who is taken up to become God's temple is both many people and one person. Speaking as one person, he prayed earlier, *Hearken to my prayer, O God*; but since this one person comprises many, he now prays, *Hearken to us, O God, our Savior.* And now listen to Christ being proclaimed yet more openly: *Hearken to us, O God, our Savior; you are the hope of all the ends of the earth, our hope too in the distant sea.* This clarifies the earlier profession, *to you all flesh will come*, by showing where people will come from: they will come from every part of the world. *You are the hope of all the ends of the earth*, not the hope of one little corner of it only, not the hope of Judea alone, nor of Africa alone, nor of Pannonia alone, not the hope of the East only, or of the West, but *the hope of all the ends of the earth, our hope too in the distant sea.* He is the hope of the very ends of the earth; the point is stressed.

And in the distant sea. It would have to be distant, if it is the sea, for the sea is used as a symbol of this world, harsh in its saltiness and battered by storms. In this sea the perverse and depraved lusts of human beings have made them like fishes devouring each other. Look at this terrible sea, this harsh sea with its rough waves, and observe what kind of people fill it. Does anyone hope to inherit property without at the same time desiring someone else's death? Or does anyone look to make money, except through someone else's loss? How many

---

23. See Jn 14:6.

people there are who aspire to high rank, but only through the downfall of others! And how many want other people to sell their possessions, in order that they themselves may buy them! How cruel they are to each other, how eager are the powerful to swallow others! No sooner has a big fish devoured a smaller one than it is devoured itself by one even bigger. You savage fish, you hunt a little one as your prey, but you will soon be the prey of a monster.

These things happen every day before our eyes. We observe them, but let us shrink from them. Let us not act like that ourselves, brothers and sisters, because Christ is *the hope of all the ends of the earth*. But if he were not also *our hope in the distant sea*, he would not have said to his disciples, *I will make you fishers of a human catch* (Mk 1:17; Mt 4:19). We are in this sea, but already caught in the nets of faith. Let us be happy that we are still swimming within those nets, for though the sea is still raging stormily around us, the nets in which we are enclosed will be safely brought ashore. As the shoreline marks the boundary of the sea, so does it symbolize our arrival at the end of the world.

Meanwhile, brothers and sisters, let us live good lives within the nets, and not break them in any attempt to escape. Many people have torn their way out of the nets: they caused schisms,[24] and departed, saying they were not prepared to put up with the bad fish caught in the nets; but in fact they became bad themselves by doing so, worse than those they declared themselves unable to tolerate.[25] The nets certainly have caught fish both good and bad. The Lord said this would be so: *The kingdom of heaven is like a dragnet cast into the sea, which collected all kinds of fish. When it was full they drew it in, sat down on the shore, and picked out the good fish, placing them in containers. But the bad fish they threw away. This is how it will be at the end of the world* (you see, he mentions the shore, the end-point of the sea). *The angels will go forth and pick out the wicked from among the righteous, and throw them into a burning furnace, where there will be weeping and gnashing of teeth* (Mt 13:47-50). So take heart, citizens of Jerusalem, who find yourselves in the nets—you, I mean, who are good fish. Put up with the bad ones, and do not burst the nets. You are swimming among the bad fish in the sea, but you will not be sharing the containers with them. Christ is *the hope of all the ends of the earth, our hope too in the distant sea*. Distant, because we are still in the sea.

---

24. The word derives from the Greek εἴῳἀἒ , to split or tear, which is used in Jn 21:11, "the net was not torn," in spite of the huge catch.
25. The Donatists primarily, who believed that the Church ought to be an assembly of the pure, not a net holding all kinds of fish. See note on section 2 above, and note at Exposition of Psalm 10, 1.

Verses 7-8. The mountains, steadfast in Christ's strength

10. *Preparing mountains in his strength*: not in their own strength. He prepared great preachers, and called them mountains; they were lowly in their own eyes, but towering in him. *Preparing mountains in his strength.* What did one of those mountains say? *In ourselves we found nothing but the token of death, to ensure that we should put our trust not in ourselves, but in God, who raises the dead* (2 Cor 1:9). Anyone who trusts in self, and not in Christ, is not one of those mountains he prepares in his strength.

Preparing mountains in his strength, he is girdled about with might. His might I understand; but why is he said to be *girdled about* with it? Because people who put Christ in the center of their lives are girding him about, as it were; they are encircling him on every side. We all possess him communally, and so he is in the middle. All of us who believe in him are like a girdle round him; but because our faith derives not from our own resources but from his power, he is said to be *girdled about with might.* With his own might, that is, not with any strength of ours.

11. *You stir up the depth of the sea.* He surely did this, for what he did is plain to see. He prepared the mountains in his strength; he sent them out to preach; he was girded about with might in the believers who surrounded him; and the consequence was a great disturbance in the sea. The world was disturbed, and began to persecute his saints. *Girdled about with might, you stir up the depth of the sea.* Notice that the psalm does not say, "You stir up the sea," but *the depth of the sea,* for the deep heart of wicked people is the depth of the sea. A movement that wells up from the deepest part is more violent than any other, for the deepest part controls everything else. So too in the case of persecution. Whatever proceeded against the Church through the agency of tongue, or hand, or the various powers, emanated from the depth; for if that root of iniquity had not existed in the persecutors' hearts, none of those proceedings against Christ would have occurred. But Christ stirred the depth. Perhaps indeed, he did so because he meant to drain those depths dry, for in the case of some bad people it did happen that he drained the very depth of the sea, and turned the sea into a desert. Another psalm speaks of this transformation: *He turns the sea into dry land* (Ps 65(66):6). All the impious and the pagans who came to believe had been a sea, but they became earth. Formerly they had been sterile with their salty waters, but later they became fertile, and produced a harvest of righteousness. *You stir up the depth of the sea, and who can bear the roaring of its waves?* Why does it ask, *Who can bear* this? Because there could scarcely be anyone able to withstand the roaring waves of the sea, which symbolize the orders of this world's rulers. How could anyone endure them? Only because Christ prepares the mountains in his strength. So by saying, *Who can bear it?* the psalm means, "We could not possibly endure those persecutions unaided, but we can if he

grants us fortitude." *You stir up the depth of the sea, and who can bear the roaring of its waves?*

Verses 8-9. The turbulent sea. Escape at morning and evening

12. *The nations will be troubled.* Initially, yes, they are troubled. But what of those mountains prepared in the strength of Christ? Were they troubled? Not at all. The sea was turbulent, and dashed itself against the mountains, but it was the sea that broke; the mountains stood unshaken. *The nations will be troubled, and they will all be afraid.* Yes, all of them are afraid now. At first they were merely troubled, but now they are thoroughly frightened. The Christians were not afraid, and today it is the Christians who are formidable. All who used to persecute them are afraid now, for he who is girded about with might has conquered. To him all flesh has come, and the persecutors on seeing it are terrified by the dwindling of their own numbers. *All who dwell throughout the earth will be filled with awe by your wonderful signs.* The apostles worked miracles, and on seeing them all the ends of the earth were filled with awe, and believed.

13. *The way out in the morning, and the way out in the evening—both will bring you joy.* You, O Christ, will make them joyful for us. What are we promised, even now, in this life? That our *way out in the morning, and the way out in the evening*, will be delightful.

There are morning escapes, you see, and evening escapes. Morning represents worldly prosperity; evening stands for trouble in this world. Close attention is needed here, beloved ones.[26] Both of these pose temptations to the souls of men and women, for we must neither be corrupted by prosperity nor crushed by adversity. Morning can fittingly stand for prosperity, because morning is a cheerful time, when the night, which has a sad feel about it, has passed away. The darkness that falls as evening approaches represents sadness. That is why it was at the world's evening[27] that Christ offered his evening sacrifice.[28] No one should either dread the evening or be bribed by the morning.[29] Suppose somebody has promised you a reward, to induce you to do something wrong: that is an example of morning temptation. The prospect of plentiful money beams upon you, and for you this is like the morning light. If you resist the bribe, you will have a morning exit, you will not be captured. The promise of reward is like the bait in a mousetrap. Take it, and you are confined, with no way out; you are caught in the trap. But the Lord your God has provided an exit for you so that you may not be caught by the prospect of gain: he says to you in your heart, "I am

---

26. *Caritas vestra.*
27. That is, the "last age."
28. See Ps 140(141):2, and section 6 above.
29. Variant: "Let each of us fear the evening, so as not to be bribed by the morning."

your wealth." Think not about what the world promises, but about what you are promised by the world's Creator. Have regard to what God has promised to give you if you act justly, and scorn what some human being promises you in order to seduce you from just action.[30] Keep your eyes not on what the world promises, but on the promises made to you by the world's Creator, and then you will have a morning exit through the Lord's warning, *What advantage is it to anyone to gain even the whole world, and suffer the ruin of his own soul?* (Mt 16:26).

Suppose, on the other hand, the person who unsuccessfully tried to corrupt you with the promise of money, and to lead you into sin, now changes his tactics and threatens to hurt you. Suppose he turns nasty and begins to say to you, "If you don't do it, I will show you something. I will deal with you. You will have to reckon with me as an enemy." In the former case when he was promising you a reward it was morning for you, but now evening is closing in, and you are shadowed by sadness. But God, who provided you with a morning escape, will give you a way out in the evening as well. Just as you scorned the world's morning by looking to the light of the Lord, so too scorn its evening in the strength of the Lord's sufferings. Say to your soul, "Can this fellow do anything worse to me than my Lord suffered for me? Let me hold fast to justice and not consent to iniquity. Let him wreak all the cruelty he can on my body: the mousetrap will simply break open, and I will fly away to my Lord, who bade me, *Do not be afraid of those who kill the body, but cannot kill the soul* (Mt 10:28). And he gave us reassurance even about the body's safety when he said, *Not a hair of your head will perish"* (Lk 21:18).

It is a splendid assertion that the psalm has made. *The way out in the morning, and the way out in the evening—both will bring you joy*, for if the way out does not itself seem to you a joyful thing, you will make no effort to escape. If our Savior's promise does not attract you, you will put your head into the trap to seize the promised bribe. Or, if you do not find your joy in him who suffered first, in order to forge a way out for you, you will yield to the person who after tempting you begins to terrify you. *The way out in the morning and the way out in the evening—both will bring you joy.*

Verses 10-11. God's brimming river

14. *You have visited the earth and inebriated it.* What did he do, to inebriate our earth? Another psalm tells us: *How excellent is your intoxicating chalice!* (Ps 22(23):5). *You have visited the earth and inebriated it*, for you sent your clouds, and they dropped the rain of truth, intoxicating the earth. *You enriched it with abundant increase.* How did you do that? Through your river: *the river of*

---

30. Variants: "You have regard . . ."; "You scorn . . . let this lead you to just action."

God is brimming with water. What is God's river? His people. The elder people was filled, so that the rest of the earth might be watered by it. Listen to the Lord's promise of this water: *Let anyone who is thirsty come to me and drink. If anyone believes in me, streams of living water shall flow from within that person* (Jn 7:37-38). If there are streams there is also a single river, because in the strength of this unity many form only one. There are many churches, but one Church; many believers, but one bride of Christ; so too there are many streams, but one river. Many Israelites believed, and were filled with the Holy Spirit. Then they were dispersed among the Gentiles; they began to preach the truth, and from this river of God which was brimming with water the entire earth has been irrigated.

You have prepared their food, indeed, that is how you prepared it. The people whose sins you forgave did not deserve you, for they had nothing to their account except bad deeds. But you, moved by your own mercy, *prepared their food*, for *that is how you prepared it.*

15. *Saturate its furrows.* But the furrows must be formed first, if they are to be drenched; our stony hearts must be opened up by the ploughshare of God's word. *Saturate its furrows, and multiply its growth* We can watch this process. People believe, and from these believers others come to believe, and from them others again believe; and no one is satisfied if, when he or she has become a believer, only one more is won over. It is like the sowing of seed: a few grains are sown, and whole cornfields spring up.

Saturate its furrows, and multiply its growth. The newly-sprung crop will rejoice under gentle drops. When the crop has only just come up, and is perhaps not yet ready for the full spate of the stream, it will flourish happily under *gentle drops*, that is, under an irrigation suited to it. Careful droplets are distilled from our mysteries to those who are still small and weak, for they cannot yet take in the fullness of truth. We have an example of this gentle dripping for the benefit of little ones newly emerging, those whose recent arrival means that their capacity is limited; listen to the apostle: *Not as spiritual persons could I speak to you, but only as carnal, as if to little children in Christ* (1 Cor 3:1). By calling them *little children in Christ* he suggests that they are people who have sprung up, certainly, but are not yet capable of receiving the rich wisdom of which he says, *We speak wisdom among the perfect* (1 Cor 2:6). Let the new crop rejoice in the gentle drops supplied to it while it is emerging and growing to maturity. Once he or she has become strong, the new believer will be open to that wisdom as well, just as a baby is nourished with milk at first, but later becomes capable of solid food. The baby could not take solids at the beginning; that is why milk was provided for him. *The newly-sprung crop will rejoice under gentle drops.*

Verse 12. The crop is still mixed

16. *Of your kindness you will bless the crown of the year.* Now is the time for sowing, and now is the growing-time for what is sown; the harvest will be reaped later. Yet an enemy has oversown the good seed with tares. Bad people have sprung up among the good, pseudo-Christians who have similar leaves but do not bear the same grain. Indeed, the weeds that are properly called tares are the ones that look like wheat, such as darnel, and barren oats, and others whose early shoots closely resemble those of the genuine crop. Of the sowing of the tares the Lord says, *An enemy came and oversowed the field with tares. And when the shoots had grown up and come into ear, then the tares became apparent.* So, the enemy has come and has introduced his tares, but what effect has this had on the wheat? The good ears are not smothered by the tares; rather does the wheat yield an ampler crop as a result of struggling against the tares. There were certain workers who wanted to eradicate the tares at once, but the master restrained them: *Let them both grow together until harvest time. In trying to uproot the tares, you may uproot the wheat as well. At harvest time I will instruct the harvesters, "Collect the tares first, and tie them up in bundles for burning; but store the wheat in the barn"* (Mt 13:29. 30). The harvest of the world is represented in this psalm by the end of the year.

Of your kindness you will bless the crown of the year. The word *crown* is used to evoke the glory of ultimate victory. Vanquish the devil, and you will receive the crown. *Of your kindness you will bless the crown of the year.* Once again we are reminded of God's kindness, lest any of us boast of our own achievements.

Verses 12-13. The first harvest and the second

17. *Your fields will be filled with rich produce. The desert regions will grow fertile, and the hills will be girdled with joy.* Fields, hills, and desert regions: all these are symbols of human beings. Fields[31] are so called because they are level; and so righteous people can be called fields because they are on the level, as it were. Hills are ground that has been lifted high, so just people can also be called hills, because when they humble themselves God exalts them in himself. The desert regions must be the Gentiles. Why should they be called desert regions? Because they had been deserted: no prophets had been sent to them; they were like tracts of wilderness, untrodden by anyone. No word of God was sent to the Gentiles, for the prophets preached only to the people of Israel.

But now we come to the Lord's time. Such of the Jews as were true wheat came to believe in him, for he said to his disciples, *You say that the harvest is a long way off; but no, look round and see that the fields are already white with*

---

31. *Campi.*

their harvest (Jn 4:35). There was a first harvest, then, but there will be a second at the end of the world. The first harvest was reaped from the Jews, because the prophets were sent to them to announce the Savior who was to come. This is why the Lord said to his disciples, *See that the fields are already white with their harvest*; he meant the regions of Judea. He continued, *Others have labored there, and you have come into their labors* (Jn 4:38). The prophets toiled over the sowing, and you have come in with your sickles to reap the results of their labors.

There was a first harvest, therefore, and from the grain winnowed from this preliminary harvest the whole world has been seeded, so that another crop may grow, to be reaped at the end. But this second crop has been oversown with tares, and consequently we have to work hard now. Just as the prophets labored over the first growth, until the coming of the Lord, so the apostles labored over the second crop, and all preachers of the truth still labor over it, until the end-time when the Lord sends his angels out to reap his harvest. The Gentile world was formerly a desert, but *the desert regions will grow fertile*. Where the prophetic trumpets never rang out, the Lord of the prophets has been accepted. *The desert regions will grow fertile, and the hills will be girdled with joy.*

Verse 14. Joyful shouting

18. *The rams in the flock are clothed* — are clothed with joy, evidently. The same joy that girdles the hills also clothes the rams of the flock. The rams are the same people as the hills: they are called hills because of their eminent grace, and rams because they are leaders of the flocks. The apostles are these rams clothed with joy, because they are delighted with the crops they reap, and know that they have neither labored pointlessly nor preached without profit. *The rams of the flock are clothed, and the deep valleys[32] will abound with grain.* This means that the humblest people will bear much fruit. *They will shout*; yes, and that is why they will abound with grain—because they will shout. What will they shout? *Indeed, they will sing a hymn.* It is one thing to shout against God, and quite another to lift your voice in a hymn; one thing to shout blasphemies, another to shout God's praise. Shout blasphemies and you have brought forth thorns, but if you shout out a hymn, you abound with grain.

---

32. *Convalles*, valleys enclosed on every side.

Exposition of Psalm 65

A Sermon to the People

Verse 1. The hope of resurrection: Jesus corrects the Sadducees

1. The title assigned to this psalm is, *Unto the end, a psalm to be sung about the resurrection.* Whenever the psalms are sung and you hear the phrase, *unto the end,* you must understand it to be a reference to Christ, for the apostle tells us, *Christ is the end of the law, bringing justification to everyone who believes* (Rom 10:4). With the grace that God grants us and in the measure that he opens our mind, we propose to explain to you how the resurrection is sung about in this psalm, and whose resurrection is celebrated. As Christians we know that the resurrection of our head has taken place already, and that it will take place in his members. Christ is the head of the Church, and the Church forms his members. What has occurred first in the head will follow in the body. This is our hope, and with this in view we believe, we hold out, and we persevere amid all the obstacles the world throws up against us; for until hope becomes reality, the hope itself is our consolation. But the reality will come when we too rise again and become equal to the angels, for we shall be transformed, to live the life of heaven.

Who would have dared hope for such a destiny, had Truth himself not promised it? Admittedly the Jews did hold some such hope, and believed that they had received the promise of it; and they took great pride in their so-called good and just actions. But they hoped that by living in accordance with the law they had received they would be rewarded with material goods in this world, and they expected to be given at the resurrection the same kind of good things that had afforded them pleasure in the present life. They were therefore unable to refute the Sadducees, who denied the possibility of resurrection, when these Sadducees posed a hard question to the Lord. We know that the Jews could not answer it themselves, because they were astonished when the Lord did so. This was the puzzle they set him: a certain woman had seven husbands (successively, of course, not simultaneously). There was an injunction in the law which was designed to ensure the increase of the people: if a man died childless his brother, if any, should marry the widow, and raise up offspring for his dead brother.[1] The Sadducees therefore put forward the hypothetical case of a woman who had

---

1. See Dt 25:5-6.

284

married seven times: all the brothers had married her in an attempt to do their duty, but all had died without issue. So, asked the Sadducees, *Whose wife will she be at the resurrection?* (Lk 20:33). It is quite obvious that the Jews were only toiling and moiling over the problem because they hoped to be doing in the risen life the same sort of things that they were doing at present. But what the Lord was promising was not the corruptible life of the flesh, but equality with the angels, so he said to them, *You are going wrong because you know neither the scriptures nor the power of God. In the resurrection men and women do not marry, for they will not be faced with death; but they will be equal to the angels of God* (Mt 22:29-30; Lk 20:36). He pointed out that replacements are necessary where there are displacements by death, but since in the resurrection there will be no deaths, there will be no need for births either. This is why he added, *For they will not be faced with death.* However, the Jews were delighted with this refutation of the Sadducees, with whom they had carried on a controversy over this undecided and obscure question—delighted because they did hold to a hope of the future resurrection, even though they conceived it in carnal terms.

In hoping for a resurrection from the dead, the Jews believed that they themselves would be the only ones to[2] rise to a blessed life, because of their observance of the law, and because they were justified by possession of the scriptures, a privilege reserved to the Jews and denied to the Gentiles. But Christ was crucified, and *blindness has fallen upon part of Israel, until the full tally of the Gentiles comes in* (Rom 11:25), as the apostle teaches. Resurrection from the dead thus began to be promised for the first time to the Gentiles, who believed that Jesus Christ had risen. Accordingly this psalm militates against the presumption and pride of the Jews, but supports the faith of the Gentiles who have been called to the hope of resurrection.

Catholic shouting

2. It could be said that you have heard the essence of this psalm now, brothers and sisters. Your undivided attention should be focused on what I have just said, on what I have proposed to you. Keep this before your minds, and do not let your thoughts wander from it: the psalm is directed against the self-satisfaction of the Jews, who hoped to attain resurrection for themselves through justification by the law. They crucified Christ, who was the first to rise again; and he meant to have as members of his body, destined also to rise again, not Jews alone but all who had believed in him. And that means all nations.

This is why the psalm opens with the words, *Shout with joy to God.* Who is to shout? *All the earth.* Not only Judea, then. Notice how the universal Church is

---

2. Variant: "they alone believed that they would."

hinted at here, brothers and sisters, the Church spread throughout the world. By all means commiserate with the Jews who envied the Gentiles this grace, but deplore the heretics even more; for if people who have never been gathered in are to be pitied, how much more so are those who, once gathered, have split off?

Shout with joy to God, all the earth. What does *shout with joy* suggest? Burst out into a joyful noise, if you cannot find words to express what you feel. Shouting does not necessarily imply words. We hear people rejoicing simply by making a noise, like the sound of a heart laboring to bring forth into its voice its happiness over what it has conceived, something that cannot be put into words. *Shout with joy to God, all the earth.* No one should be shouting in some exclusive part of it. No, I repeat, let the whole earth shout with joy, let the Church Catholic shout. This Church that is Catholic grasps the whole. Anyone who holds to a sect only, and is cut off from the whole, should be wailing, not shouting with joy. *Shout with joy to God, all the earth.*

Verse 2. Praise and glory are for God alone

3. *Play the psaltery to his name.* What is the psalmist recommending here? "May God's name be blessed when you play psalms." Now I explained yesterday what playing the psaltery is, and I am sure you remember, beloved friends.[3] To play psalms means to take up the instrument called a psaltery, to strike it and play it manually as an accompaniment to the voices of singers. So just as you shout with joy in a way that God hears, so too you must play psalms in such a way that men and women may see and hear you. But beware of doing this in your own name. *Be careful not to do your good works in the sight of other people, to attract their attention* (Mt 6:1). "But," you will say, "in whose name am I to play psalms, so that my deeds may not be seen[4] by other people?" Well, consider another of the Lord's sayings: *Let your deeds shine before men and women in such a way that they see the good you do, and glorify your Father who is in heaven* (Mt 5:16). Notice that you are told to work so that people *may see the good you do, and glorify* not you, but God. If you perform your good works with the aim of glorifying yourselves, you will deserve the censure the Lord pronounces against people who seek the credit for their deeds, *I tell you truly, they have had their reward.* You must hide them, he says, *otherwise you will have no reward from your Father, who is in heaven* (Mt 6:2.1). "So," you will say, "I had better hide my good deeds, hadn't I, so as not to perform them where other people can see?" No. What does the Lord tell you? *Let your deeds shine before men and women.* "But that leaves me thoroughly confused. On the one hand you tell me, *Be careful not to do your good works in the*

---

3. *Caritatem vestram.* Augustine meditates on the psaltery in his Exposition 2 of Psalm 32, 5; Exp. of Psalm 42, 5; Exp. of Ps 56, 16; Exp. 2 of Psalm 70, 11; Exp. of Psalm 80, 5.
4. Variant: "may be seen."

sight of other people, and on the other, *Let your deeds shine before men and women*. How can I do both? Which am I to obey, and which leave aside? Just as no one can serve two masters who issue different orders, no more can we serve one master who orders contrary things." But I am not giving you contrary orders, says the Lord. Look to the end, keep your eye on the end as you sing. Consider what your objective is in what you do. If you do your good deeds to win glory for yourself, I forbid it; but if you do them so that God may be glorified, you are acting as I have commanded.

Play and sing the psalms not to your own name, then, but to the name of the Lord your God. You offer the psalmody, but let him be praised; you live good lives, but let the glory be his. Anyway, who gives you the power to live as you should? If that power had been yours from eternity, you would never have done wrong; and if you had had it as from yourselves, you would never have done otherwise than live well.[5] *Play the psaltery to his name*.

4. *Give glory to him, praise him.*[6] The psalm focuses our whole intention on the praise of God, leaving us no ground on which we may claim praise for ourselves. Let us rather glory in him, and rejoice to do so; let us cleave to him, and be praised only in him. When the apostle's letter was being read you heard this: *Look at your own vocation, brethren; not many of you are wise in a worldly way, not many are powerful, not many noble. But it is the foolish things of this world that God has chosen to confound the wise, and the weak things of this world to confound the strong; it is the lowly and contemptible things of the world that God has chosen, even the nonentities, to bring to nothing things that are* (1 Cor 1:26-28). What was Paul saying? What was he trying to show us? Jesus Christ, our Lord and God, came down to renew the human race, and to give his grace to all who understand that this restoration is the work of his grace and not due to their merits. In order, therefore, to ensure that no one should glory in any natural advantages, he chose the weak.

Now, observe that even Nathanael was not among the weak from whom the Lord drew his chosen ones. Why do you suppose that the Lord chose Matthew, who was sitting in the tax office,[7] but not Nathanael, the man to whom the Lord himself gave testimony by saying, *Look, there is a true Israelite, in whom there is no guile* (Jn 1:47)?[8] We may suspect that Nathanael was well versed in the law.

---

5. Reading *si a vobis haberetis, numquam non bene vixissetis*. Some codices, followed by the CCL editors, omit *non*: ". . . as from yourselves, you would never have lived well." Augustine seems to be thinking of the human race as a whole, not only the immediate hearers.

6. Literally, "give glory to his praise."

7. See Mt 9:9.

8. It is generally assumed that John's Nathanael is the same person as the Synoptics' Bartholomew, but Augustine apparently does not think so. He implies here, and more definitely asserts in his *Homilies on the Gospel of John* 7, 17, that Nathanael was not one of the Twelve. It is implied that his expertise in the law was a disqualification, for the reasons Augustine goes on to explain.

I do not mean that Christ did not intend to choose any learned people; but if he had chosen them first, they might have thought that their election was based on the excellence of their teaching, and then their knowledge would have won praise, while the praise of Christ's grace would have been diminished. Christ commended Nathanael as a good and faithful man, in whom there was no guile; yet he did not include him among the disciples he chose first, all of whom were uneducated.

But how do we know that Nathanael was conversant with the law? Like this: when he was told by one of those who had followed the Lord, *We have found the Messiah, that is, the Christ* (Jn 1:41), Nathanael inquired where he came from, and the answer was, *from Nazareth*. Nathanael replied, *From Nazareth something good may come* (Jn 1:46). Clearly, anyone who knew that something good could come from Nazareth must have been an expert on the law and have studied the prophets carefully. I am aware that another interpretation can be put on his words, though it is not approved by reputable scholars: Nathanael could be thought to have replied dismissively when he heard the place mentioned, *Nazareth? Can anything worthwhile come from there?* In other words, "Surely not from Nazareth?" He would be suggesting that it was a hopeless sort of place. Now the reply he received was, *Come and see* (Jn 1:47), and this reply would fit either interpretation of Nathanael's words. If you understand his reaction to be incredulity: *Nazareth? Can anything worthwhile come from there?* the other's response would mean, "*Come and see* what you do not believe." Alternatively, if you take Nathanael's response to be an endorsement of what he had just been told — *From Nazareth something good may come* — then the reply he received means, "*Come and see* how good it is indeed, what I am announcing to you from Nazareth, and how right you are to believe. Come and experience it for yourself."

However, in spite of the accolade, *Look, there is a true Israelite, in whom there is no guile*, he was not chosen among the disciples by the Lord, who gave preference to the foolish things of the world. From this fact we can infer that Nathanael was learned in the law. The Lord did choose orators as well, but only later on, for they would have been proud about their election if he had not chosen fishermen first; he chose rich folk, but they would have attributed their election to their riches if he had not chosen the poor before them. Later he even chose emperors, but it is better that when an emperor comes to Rome he should lay aside his crown and repent at the tomb of the fisherman, than that a fisherman should repent at the tomb of an emperor. True it is that *the weak things of this world has God chosen to confound the strong; the lowly and contemptible things of the world has God chosen, even the nonentities, to bring to nothing things that are.*

And how does the apostle conclude these remarks? *That no flesh may glory in the presence of God* (1 Cor 1:29). See how he has stripped us of glory in order to give us glory; he has taken away what was ours to give us his own; he has taken what was empty away from us in order to give us his fullness; he has taken our rickety glory, to give us the glory that stands firm. How much stronger, how much more stable is our glory, for being in God! You may not glory in yourself, for Truth has forbidden it; but Truth has commanded what the apostle enjoins on us: *Let anyone who glories glory in the Lord.*

Give glory to him, then, *and praise him.* Do not be like the Jews, who tried to win justification by their own merits, and were jealous of the Gentiles who flocked to the grace of the gospel, so that all their sins might be forgiven. As though the Jews did not have sins themselves that needed forgiveness, as though they only needed to wait for their wages, like good workers! They were sick, but thought themselves healthy, and their illness was all the more dangerous for that. If they had been even a little less ill, they would not have killed the doctor in their delirium. *Give glory to him, and praise him.*

Verse 3. Rejoicing and awe at God's dealings with Jews and Gentiles

5. *Say to God, How awesome are your works!* Why are they regarded as awesome, rather than simply lovable? The answer comes from another psalm: *Serve the Lord in reverence, and rejoice before him with awe* (Ps 2:11). But what does that mean? Listen to the apostle's advice: *Work out your own salvation in fear and trembling.* Why *in fear and trembling*? Paul gives the reason: *for it is God who is at work in you, inspiring both will and work, for his own good purpose* (Phil 2:12.13). If God is at work in you, it is by God's grace that you act rightly, not by any powers of your own. Rejoice, then, by all means, but fear too, lest the gift bestowed on a humble person be withdrawn when the recipient becomes proud. This was what happened to the Jews on account of their pride, as you know. They behaved as though they could justify themselves by observing the law, and in consequence they fell. As another psalm puts it, *Some find joy in chariots and some in horses*; they thought they could raise themselves by their own swiftness or their vehicles. But, continued that psalm, *as for us, we will exult in the name of the Lord our God* (Ps 19:8(20:7)). Notice how the one group were high and mighty in themselves, while the other gloried in God. And what was the outcome? *They were shackled and they fell, but we have arisen and we stand upright* (Ps 19:9(20:8)).

Our Lord himself taught the same lesson. Listen to him. *I came so that they who do not see may see, and those who see may become blind* (Jn 9:39). One half of his declaration bespeaks goodness, the other seems cruel. Yet could any policy be better, more merciful, more just? Why does he say, *that they who do not see may see?* Because of his goodness. And why, *that they who see may become blind?* Because of their arrogance. Does it mean that they truly did see, but were struck blind? No, they did not see, but they thought they did. This is quite clear, brothers and sisters, from the exchange that followed. The Jews asked, *Are we blind? And the Lord said to them, If you were blind, you would be without sin; but because you say, "We see," your sin remains in you* (Jn 9:40-41). And what about you? Have you come to visit the doctor, claiming to have good sight? Then the supply of eye-salve will be stopped, and you will be permanently blind. Confess that you are blind, and then you will deserve to receive the light.

Consider the Jews on the one hand, and the Gentiles on the other. *That they who do not see may see* says the Lord. But *I came that they who see may become blind.* The Jews saw our Lord Jesus Christ himself in the flesh. The Gentiles did not see him. But what happened? Those who saw him crucified him, while those who had not seen him believed in him. What did you do, then, O Christ, to defeat the proud? What did you do? Through your merciful condescension we see, and we are your members. We see, though you hid your godhead and exposed only your humanity to the eyes of men and women. Why did you do that? *So that blindness might fall upon part of Israel, until the full tally of the Gentiles should come in.*[9] That was why you hid your divinity, and presented only your humanity to the eyes of men and women. They saw, yet did not see: they saw what you had taken upon yourself, but did not see what you were. They saw the form of a servant, but did not see the form of God;[10] they saw the form of a servant, whereby the Father was greater than he,[11] but did not see that form of God, in virtue of which, brothers and sisters, you heard him claim that *I and the Father are one* (Jn 10:30). What they saw they laid hands on, what they saw they crucified; they jeered at him whom they saw, and failed to recognize him who lay hidden. That is what the apostle states: *If they had known him, they would never have crucified the Lord of glory* (1 Cor 2:8).

You Gentiles, who have been called, must consider those branches that have been lopped off by the Lord's severity, and consider how you yourselves have been grafted in by the Lord's kindness to become participants in the richness of the olive tree. You must not on that account think too highly of yourselves, or be proud; scripture warns you to *remember that it is not you who support the root, but the root you* (Rom 11:18). You should rather be filled with fear at the sight of natural branches lopped off, for the Jews were descended from the patriarchs and born of Abraham's stock. Moreover, what was the apostle's warning? *You maintain, Those branches have been broken off so that I could be grafted in. Yes,*

9. See Rom 11:25.
10. See Phil 2:6-7.
11. See Jn 14:28.

but they were broken off because of their unbelief. You, for your part, you stand only through faith, so be not high-minded, but wary. If God did not spare the natural branches, he may not spare you either (Rom 11:19-21). Contemplate those amputated branches, and your own insertion; do not vaunt yourself over them, but rather say to God, *How awesome are your works!*

And how much less should we adopt an arrogant attitude toward the fresh wounds of more recent amputations! Long ago the Jews were cut off and the Gentiles grafted in; but then from this engrafted shoot itself the heretics were lopped off. But we must not be high and mighty in their regard either, because any of us who enjoy laughing at excised branches may perhaps deserve to be excised ourselves. We beg you—however unworthy the bishop you are listening to, brothers and sisters—we beg you to be on your guard about this: whoever you are who are in the Church, do not mock those who are not, but rather pray that they may be inside it, *for God is powerful enough to insert them once more* (Rom 11:23).

The apostle was referring to the Jews when he said that, and of the Jews it was verified. The Lord rose from the dead, and many of them believed. They had not understood when they crucified him, but afterward they believed in him; and then their crime was forgiven them, heinous though it was. These homicides—not to say deicides—were forgiven for spilling the Lord's blood, because *if they had known, they would never have crucified the Lord of glory.* Now the shed blood of the innocent victim has been given[12] to those who killed him, and the very blood that they spilled in their fury they have drunk through his grace. Say then to God, *How awesome are your works!* Why so awesome? Because *blindness has fallen upon part of Israel, until the full tally of the Gentiles comes in* (Rom 11:25). O you full tally of the Gentiles, say to God, *How awesome are your works*, and rejoice with an undercurrent of fear. Do not gloat over the lopped-off branches, but say to God, *How awesome are your works!*

Christ's resurrection, the unique miracle

6. *Your enemies will lie to you over your greatest act of power.* It seems to be saying that your enemies' lying serves this very purpose: to magnify your power. What can this mean? Please be extra-attentive, brothers and sisters. The power of our Lord Jesus Christ was manifested above all in the resurrection, to which the title of this psalm alludes. When he rose, he appeared to his disciples. He did not appear to his enemies, but to his disciples only.[13] At his crucifixion he was seen by everyone, but in his resurrection only by believers, so that later

---

12. There is a play on the two notions of "give" and "forgive" in the preceding lines, the same verb *donare* being used for both.
13. See Acts 10:41.

anyone who was willing might believe too, and so a like resurrection might be promised to every believer. Now many holy people worked many miracles, but none of them rose to life again after being dead; and even those whom the saints raised to life were raised only to die again later. Think hard about this, beloved friends.[14] The Lord drew his hearers' attention to his works, saying, *If you will not believe me, believe in my works* (Jn 10:38). The deeds of the prophets of old certainly merit consideration, and if not all of them are the same as our Lord's works, some at least are the same, and all were worked by his power. The Lord walked on the sea, and he commanded Peter to do the same.[15] And was the Lord himself not there when the sea split in half, so that Moses might cross with the people of Israel?[16] Of course he was; it was the same Lord who was at work there. His own miracles he worked through his own flesh, and the others he worked through the flesh of his servants. But there was one thing that he did not do through his servants. He never empowered any of them to die and then rise again to eternal life.

So when the Lord worked miracles the Jews were able to say, "Moses did that too," or "Elijah did that, or Elisha." Yes, they could tell themselves that after all the prophets raised the dead and performed many wonders; but when they asked the Lord for a sign, the one he gave them was a unique sign, one proper to himself, something that would take place in himself alone. He said, *This depraved, provocative[17] generation is seeking a sign, but no sign will be given it except the sign of the prophet Jonah; for as Jonah was in the belly of the whale for three days and three nights, so also will the Son of Man be in the heart of the earth* (Mt 12:39-40). What was Jonah's sojourn in the whale's belly all about? It was a prelude to his being vomited up alive, wasn't it? What the whale was for Jonah, the underworld was for the Lord; and so he drew their attention to this unique sign, this sign proper to himself, this most powerful of all signs. It is a mightier deed to come to life after being dead than not to have died. The magnificence of our Lord's power in his incarnate state shines forth in his mighty resurrection. The apostle emphasizes this when he writes, *Not having any righteousness of my own, derived from the law, but that which comes through faith in Christ, the righteousness that is from God, through faith, that I may know him, and the power of his resurrection* (Phil 3:9-10). The same assertion is made in another place: *though he died in weakness, he is alive by the power of God* (2 Cor 13:4).

Clearly, then, the Lord's almighty power is manifested in his resurrection, to which our psalm alludes in its title. And when the present verse says, *Your*

---

14. *Caritas vestra.*
15. See Mt 14:25-29.
16. See Ex 14:21.
17. Variant: "evil and adulterous."

enemies will lie to you over your greatest act of power, what else can it mean, except "Your enemies will lie to you, to bring you to the cross, but you will be crucified in order to rise again; and so their lying will serve only to demonstrate the magnitude of your power"? Why do enemies usually lie? To diminish the power of the person they are lying about. But the opposite happened in your case. Your power would be less obvious if they had not lied about you.

The destruction of the temple: witnesses falsify the Lord's words

7. Now turn your attention to the lies of false witnesses as recorded in the gospel, and see how they relate to the resurrection. They demanded of the Lord, *What sign can you show us, to justify what you are doing?* (Jn 2:18). Over and above the sign he had already given them, the sign of Jonah, he made the same point again through a new parable, to make sure that this, his greatest sign, was abundantly clear. *Destroy this temple*, he said, *and in three days I will raise it up again. They objected, This temple was forty-six years a-building; will you raise it up in three days?* Then the evangelist adds an explanation: *Jesus was speaking of the temple of his body* (Jn 2:19-21). By this simile he declared that he would manifest his power to men and women. He used the temple as a figure of his flesh, for his body was the temple of the godhead hidden within. The Jews were accustomed to see this material temple, but they did not see its indwelling divinity.

From these words of the Lord, in which he foretold his future resurrection under the image of a rebuilt temple, perjured witnesses concocted a lying charge to bring against him. When asked what they had heard him say, they alleged, *We heard him claim, "I will destroy this temple, and raise it up again after three days"* (Mk 15:58; Mt 26:61). They had certainly heard him say, *I will raise it up again after three days*. But they had not heard him say, *I will destroy it*; what they had heard was, *Destroy it*. They altered one word, or a few letters, to support their false evidence against him. But against whom are you changing a word, O human futility, human feebleness? You change a word against the unchangeable Word! You may well change your own word, but can you change the Word of God? In another psalm it is justly said of you, *Iniquity has lied to itself* (Ps 26(27):12). Why did your enemies tell lies against you, Lord, against you to whom all the earth shouts with joy? *Your enemies will lie to you over your greatest act of power*. They will allege, *He said, "I will destroy it,"* when what you really said was, *Destroy it*. Why did they alter your word like that? To make themselves appear innocent of the crime of destroying the temple,[18] but a vain attempt that was.

---

18. Of his body.

Christ died indeed because he willed to; all the same, you killed him. Well, all right, you liars, we grant you this much: that he did destroy the temple himself. The apostle says of Christ, *He loved me, and delivered himself up for me* (Gal 2:20); and of the Father he said, *He did not spare even his own Son, but delivered him up for us all* (Rom 8:32). If, then, the Father handed over his Son, and the Son handed over himself, what part did Judas play?

What the Father did in handing his Son over to death was a good thing; what Christ did in handing himself over for our sake was a good thing; but what Judas did in handing over his Master for gain was a very bad thing.[19] The blessings conferred on us through the passion of Christ are in no way to be ascribed to the malice of Judas. He will be requited for his treachery, but Christ praised for his grace. Assuredly Christ did destroy that temple; he destroyed it himself, he who said, *I have the power to lay down my life, and I have the power to take it up again. No one takes it away from me; but I lay it down of my own accord, and I take it up again* (Jn 10:18). He destroyed the temple by his own gracious will, but it was destroyed also by your ill-will.

Your enemies will lie to you over your greatest act of power. Yes, they lie; yes, they are believed; yes, you are roughly handled; yes, you are crucified; yes, people mock you, and shake their heads over you, saying, *If he is the Son of God, let him come down from the cross.*[20] Yes, you lay down your life when you choose. Your side is struck with a lance,[21] and the sacraments flow from your side.[22] You are taken down from the tree, wrapped in linen cloths, and laid in a tomb. Guards are posted there, in case your disciples steal you away. But the hour of your resurrection comes, the earth quakes, graves are torn open, you rise again secretly and appear manifestly. Where are those liars now? Where is the false testimony they devised in their malevolence? Have your enemies not lied to you over your greatest act of power?

The lying guards make their contribution

8. Now let us consider the guards at the sepulcher. Let them report what they saw, let them be paid for their story, and let them too tell their lies. Perverted themselves, let them be briefed by perverse mentors and say their piece; let these men speak, who have been corrupted by the Jews because they would not be sound and whole in Christ. Let them speak, let them too tell their lies. What are they to say? Go on, say it, and let us see how you too will lie in the presence of the

---

19. The verb *trado* which is used in the foregoing lines means both "hand over/on" and "betray."
20. See Mt 27:40.
21. See Jn 19:34.
22. The blood and water flowing from Christ's side were seen from early times as symbols of baptism and eucharist, or as the giving of the Spirit. But we could translate more loosely here: "The Christian mysteries flow forth. . . ."

Lord's greatest act of power. What are you going to say? *While we were asleep, his disciples came and removed him from the tomb.*[23] You certainly have nodded off, you stupid men! Either you were awake, and then it was your duty to prevent them; or you were asleep, and cannot know what happened.

The guards made themselves accomplices in the lying of Christ's enemies; but the number of liars was increased only so that the reward of believers might also increase, for *your enemies will lie to you over your greatest act of power.* They lied indeed; they lied over your mightiest act. But you appeared to truthful people to refute the liars, and you even appeared to the liars once you had made them truthful.

Verses 4-5. The homage of the Gentiles

9. Let the Jews stick fast in their lies. But for you, Lord, over whose greatest work of power they told their lies, for you may the succeeding prayer be answered: *May all the earth adore you and sing psalms to you, let it sing psalms to your name, O Most High.* Not long since you were most deeply humbled, but now you are the *Most High*: most humbled in the hands of your lying enemies, but *Most High* above the pinnacle of angels singing your praise. *May all the earth adore you and sing psalms to you, let it sing psalms to your name, O Most High.*

10. *Come, all of you, and behold the works of the Lord.* Come, you Gentiles, you nations from the farthest lands, abandon the lying Jews and come yourselves, confessing Christ. *Come, all of you, and behold the works of the Lord; he is terrible in his designs for the sons of men.*[24] He was called a son of man himself, and truly that is what he became. Being in the form of God he was the true Son of God, but taking the form of a servant he became truly Son of Man.[25] But do not equate his servant's status with that of others who share the servant condition, for *he is terrible in his designs for the sons of men.* Sons of men devised a scheme to bring Christ to the cross, but the Crucified One struck his crucifiers with blindness. What have you done, you sons of men, by setting up your cruel plot against your Lord, who seemed so weak, but in whom majesty lay hidden? You plotted to do away with him, but his plan was to blind and to save: to blind the proud and save the humble. But even his design to blind the proud was to ensure that they would be humbled by their blindness, and being humbled would confess, and having confessed would be open to the light.

---

23. See Mt 28:13.
24. The rendering "sons of men" can scarcely be avoided here in favor of inclusive language, if Augustine's parallels are to be retained.
25. See Phil 2:6-7.

He is terrible in his designs for the sons of men. Terrible indeed, for see what has happened. Blindness has fallen upon part of Israel;[26] the Jews, from whose race Christ was born, are now outside; and the Gentiles who fought against Judah are now inside, because they are in Christ. *He is terrible in his designs for the sons of men.*

Verse 6. Crossing the river of mortality

11. What did he effect, then, by his awe-inspiring plan? He turned the sea into dry land, for this is how the psalm continues: *He turned the sea into dry land.* The world was a sea, harshly salty, whipped about by storms, raging with the breakers of persecution. But this sea was undeniably changed into dry land; for now the world, once full of salt, is thirsting for sweet water. Who has wrought this change? He who *turned the sea into dry land.* And what does the Gentiles' soul cry out now? *My soul is like waterless earth before you* (Ps 142(143):6). *He turned the sea into dry land.*

They will cross the river on foot. These same people who were formerly a sea[27] will cross the river on foot. What river is this? The river is the fluid, mortal condition of our world. See how much like a river it is: things come and go, other things take their place, and then pass on in the same way. A spring is born from the earth, and flows on away from its source; and likewise everyone who is born must give way to another who is born later. All this order of unstable beings rolls on like a river. The soul must not fling itself greedily into the river; no, it must not plunge in, but stand fast. And how will it make a safe crossing over the pleasures offered by things destined to perish? Let it believe in Christ, and it will be able to walk across. With Christ leading, it will cross over on foot. What does crossing on foot suggest? That it will be an easy passage. The believer seeks no horse to get across, nor is he or she proudly mounted to cross the river. The believer makes the crossing in humility, and all the more safely for that.

12. *There we shall be joyful in him.* You boast of your good works, you Jews. But give up this proud boasting about yourselves, and accept the grace of being joyful in Christ. There we shall be made joyful, but not in ourselves: *there we shall be joyful in him.* When shall we be made joyful? When we have crossed the river on foot. Eternal life is promised to us, resurrection is promised. Our flesh is like a river now, in this condition of mortality, but hereafter it will be a river no more. Reflect on its transience now: does any stage of life stand still? Children want to grow up, but they do not realize that as the years pass their span of life is shrinking. As children grow, years are not being added, but subtracted, as the water of a river flows onward, but in doing so is distancing itself progressively

---

26. See Rom 11:25.
27. Variant: "salty."

from its source. So too children want to grow up in order to escape from the domination of their elders; they grow—and how quickly it happens! They leave childhood behind and arrive at youth; but let them hang onto their youth if they can. It too passes. Old age succeeds youth, and even though old age seems to go on for ever, it comes to an end with death. All flesh that comes to birth is like a river rolling on.

Those who approach this river of mortality in a humble spirit, so that concupiscence with regard to mortal goods may not sweep them off their feet and carry them away, cross it easily. Or, as the psalm says, they cross it on foot, for their Leader is he who crossed it first, he who drank from the wayside torrent even to death, and therefore has lifted up his head.[28]

When we have crossed this river on foot, when we have made our easy passage over this flood of mortality, *there we shall be joyful in him*. But what is the source of our joy now? Surely even now it is in him, or at least in hoping for him? We are given joy now, certainly, but it is a joy in hope; one day we shall be joyful in him. Even now he is our joy, though still in hope; then we shall enjoy him face to face.[29]

Verse 7. The law does not justify; only grace justifies. There is no place for jealousy

13. *There we shall be joyful in him.* Who is he? None other than he who *rules for ever in his might*. What might have we? And is what little we have eternal? If our might were eternal, we would not have fallen, we would not have plunged into sin, we would not have earned the punishment of mortality. But he voluntarily accepted the mortality into which our conduct had justly cast us, he who *rules for ever in his might*. Let us share in him, and so become strong by sharing his strength, though he is strong in a strength all his own. We are the illuminated, he the light that illumines us. We grow dark if we have turned away from him, but he cannot turn away from himself. We are set on fire by his heat, and set on fire anew as we draw near to him; for we had grown cold as we moved away. Let us ask him, then, to keep us safe in his strength, for we want to be joyful in him who *rules for ever in his might*.

14. This grace he grants to Jews who believe in him; for there have been many Jews who initially prided themselves on their own virtue,[30] but later came to realize whose strength it was that empowered them to reach salvation, and some of them became believers. But winning them was not enough for Christ. He paid a heavy price, an enormous price, and he was not satisfied that what he paid

---

28. See Ps 109(110):7.
29. See 1 Cor 13:12.
30. Or "strength/might." The same word *virtus* is used for them and for God.

should purchase Jews only. *His eyes are on the nations.* Yes, there it is plainly stated: *his eyes are on the nations.* "But what about us?" the Jews will complain. They will protest, "What we have is bestowed on the Gentiles equally. We received the gospel, and they are receiving the gospel; we were given the grace of the resurrection, and they are given the grace of the resurrection. No allowance is made for our prerogatives: we received the law, and lived according to its justifying ordinances, and held fast to the commands of our forebears. Yet all this now seems irrelevant, since the Gentiles are getting as much as we are!"

But they must not quarrel or dispute the justice of God's bounty. *Let not the resentful be lifted high in their own esteem.* O miserable, fragile flesh, are you not sinful? Let your tongue cease its clamor, and your conscience speak instead. All of us have sinned, and all have been stripped of God's glory.[31] See yourselves for what you are, weak humans. You received the law, but only so that you could be shown up as a transgressor of the law, for you did not keep the law you received. What accrued to you from the law was not the righteousness that the law requires, but only your own transgression of it. If sin flowed so abundantly, why are you jealous because grace has flowed more abundantly still?[32] Do not be resentful, then, for the psalm warns, *Let not the resentful be lifted high in their own esteem.* At first sight that looks like a condemnation: *let not the resentful be lifted high in their own esteem*; in fact it means that they are to be lifted high, but not in themselves. Let them be humbled in themselves, and lifted high in Christ, for all those who humble themselves will be exalted, while those who exalt themselves will be brought low.[33]

Verses 8-9. Life in the Lord

15. *You Gentiles, bless our God.* The resentful grumblers have been silenced; they were given their answer. Some of them were converted, others remained stubborn in their pride. Those who are jealous of the grace of the gospel being granted to the Gentiles must not intimidate you, for we are the posterity of Abraham, in whom all nations are blessed.[34] Bless God, in whom you are blessed: *you Gentiles, bless our God, and hearken to the voice of his praise.* Do not praise yourselves, but praise him. What voice is it that praises him? A voice confessing that insofar as we are good, we are so by his grace. *He established my soul in life.* A voice of praise it is that proclaims this: *he established my soul in life.* Your soul must have been in death before; it was dead within you. That is why you had no business to be lifted high in your own esteem. Your soul was in a

---

31. See Rom 3:23.
32. See Rom 5:20.
33. See Mt 23:12; Lk 14:11; 18:14.
34. See Gn 12:3.

state of death within yourself, and where will it be in life, if not in him who said, *I am the Way, the Truth and the Life* (Jn 14:6)? The apostle was teaching the same lesson when he said, *You were darkness once, but now you are light in the Lord* (Eph 5:8). So you are darkness in yourself, but light in the Lord, just as you are death in yourself, but life in the Lord.

He established my soul in life. He set it down in its new place, in life, because we came to believe in him. He set it down there, but what do we need now? To persevere even to the end. And who will enable us to do that? He alone, of whom the psalm goes on to say, *He did not allow my feet to slip.* He established our souls in life; he guides our feet lest they deviate or slip or stumble; he makes us live, and makes us persevere to the end so that we may live for ever. *He did not allow my feet to slip.*

Verses 10-12. Trial and correction

16. On what grounds did you say, *He did not allow my feet to slip*? What have you suffered, what indeed could you possibly have suffered, that could have caused your feet to slip?[35]

"What have I suffered? Listen, and I will tell you. Why did I thank him for not letting my feet slip? Because we have endured a great many troubles that might have swept our feet from under us, if he had not been guiding them and saving them from slipping." What were these troubles? *You put us to the test, O God, you proved us by fire, as silver is proved.* You threw us into the fire, but like silver, not like straw, for you did not reduce us to ashes but purged us of dross. *You proved us by fire, as silver is proved.*

Think how fiercely God tries those whose souls he has established in life. *You led us into a snare*, not that we should be trapped and killed, but that we might know from our own experience who is our liberator. *You laid tribulations on our backs.* We stood up straight, proudly and wrongly; then our wrongly straightened backs were bent down, so that after being rightly bent we might be straightened up again. *You laid tribulations on our backs, and set human oppressors over our heads.* All these things the whole Church suffered throughout many and varied persecutions; individual churches have also had to endure them, and still do today. No one can claim to be immune to such trials while in this life. Other human beings are set over our heads; we do not choose them, but have to put up with them as our betters, though sometimes we know them to be worse than ourselves. If a person is free from sins, he or she is truly superior, but one who has many sins is in that measure inferior. It is good for us to consider our own sinfulness, and tolerate those set over us, confessing to God that we deserve

---

35. He is putting the question to the Church, whose voice he habitually hears in the psalms.

to suffer. How could any suffering be unjust, if imposed on you by him who is just?

You laid tribulations on our backs, and set human oppressors over our heads. God seems to be acting very severely when he does these things; but do not be afraid. He is our Father, and his severity never destroys us. You behave badly, and if he spared you then, it would be a sign of greater anger. Nothing is more certain than this: all these tribulations are the whips wielded by the One who corrects us, to ensure that they will not be needed as the sentence of One who punishes. *You laid tribulations on our backs, and set human oppressors over our heads.*

Through fire and water

17. *We passed through fire and water.* Fire and water—both are dangerous to us in this life, though of course water puts out fire and fire dries up water. The same dangers beset us through the temptations of which our life is full. Fire burns things and water rots things; and both of these are perils we must fear: being scorched by troubles and being wet with decay. When we are in straitened circumstances, and something this world calls misfortune falls upon us, we are as though in the fire. But when our enterprises prosper, and the world's abundance laps all round us, we are as though in the water. But take care that the fire does not devour you, or the water cause you to decay. Stand firm against the fire. You need to be cooked. You are placed in the fiery kiln like a piece of pottery, so that what has been shaped may be hardened. Once fired, the pot has no fear of water; but an unfired pot, when put into water, dissolves back into mud. So don't be in too much of a hurry to get into the water. Pass through the fire to reach the water, and then you will be able to pass through the water too.

This is why in our sacramental rites fire is applied first, through the catechumenate and the exorcisms. If these are not like fire in their action, why is it that the evil spirits often scream, "It's burning me"? After this fire of exorcism the candidate comes to baptism, as one passing from fire to water, and from water to a place of cool relief.[36]

The sequence observed in the sacraments is found also in the trials of our present life. Stress and fear come first, acting upon us like fire. When the fear is taken away, we are in new danger, for worldly prosperity may corrupt us. But if the fire has not cracked you, and you have not drowned in the water but managed to escape by swimming, you cross over through this discipline to a place of cool relief. By passing through fire and water you will be led into cool relief; for as these things are represented by signs in our sacraments, so do the realities behind

---

36. *In refrigerium.* Coolness, typically thought of as a relief by Mediterranean nations.

the signs await us in the perfect life of eternity. When we have crossed over to that place of cool relief, my dearest brothers and sisters, we shall have there no enemy to fear, no tempter, no ill-disposed person, no fire, no water. There will be relief, cool and everlasting. It is called "cool relief"[37] because it is a state of peace; for if you call it warmth, you will be right, and if you call it coolness, that will be right too. If you were to take the word "cool relief" in a bad sense, you might think that we shall be in a state of frozen lethargy there. No, we shall not become lethargic, but there we shall rest. Nor should we expect to suffer from heat in that place, because it can just as well be called "warmth." No, we shall not suffer from the heat, but our spirits will be aflame. Remember how another psalm spoke of heat like this: *no one can hide from his heat* (Ps 18:7(19:6)). And what does the apostle tell us? *Be ardent in spirit* (Rom 12:11). *We passed through fire and water, but you brought us through to a place of cool relief.*

Verses 13-15. The final holocaust of the Church

18. Notice, however, that the psalm was not satisfied with speaking about cool relief; it also had something to say about a fire, and this we must long for just as much. *I will enter your house with holocausts.* What is a holocaust? An offering wholly burnt, but by divine fire. A sacrifice is called a holocaust when it is burnt entirely.[38] Partial sacrifices are one thing, holocausts another. When the entire offering is burnt, wholly consumed by the divine fire, that is a holocaust; when only part is burnt, it is simply called a sacrifice. So every holocaust is a sacrifice, but not every sacrifice is a holocaust. Here the psalm promises holocausts. It is the body of Christ, the unity of Christ, speaking now: *I will enter your house with holocausts.* May your fire consume everything in me; let nothing of mine remain mine, but let it all be for you. This prayer will be answered at the resurrection of the just, *when this corruptible body has put on incorruptibility, and this mortal body has been clothed in immortality. Then the saying will come true: Death is swallowed up into victory* (1 Cor 15:54). This victory is like a divine fire; when it absorbs even our death, then there will be a holocaust. Nothing mortal will remain in our flesh, and nothing capable of sin in our spirit. Everything belonging to mortal life will be consumed, so that in eternal life it may be consummated. Then those holocausts will be truly offered.

19. And what will it mean, to approach him with holocausts? *I will pay my vows to you, the vows my lips have uttered with discernment.* This is what the discernment entails: that you accuse yourself, and praise him; that you know yourself to be a creature, and him the Creator; that you confess that you are dark-

---

37. *Refrigerium.*
38. He explains the etymology in his Exposition of Psalm 49, 5, and Exposition of Psalm 64, 4.

ness, but he is the light-bringer, he to whom you pray, *You, Lord, will light my lamp; my God, you will enlighten my darkness* (Ps 17:29(18:28)). When you boast, human soul, that your light derives from yourself, you are failing to make the essential distinction; and if you do not make it, you will not be able to render your vows with discernment. Draw the distinction and pay him your discerning vows. Confess that you are subject to change, but he unchangeable; that you are nothing without him, but he is perfect without you; that you need him, but he does not need you. Cry out to him as another psalm does: *I said to the Lord, You are my God, because you have no need of any good things from me* (Ps 15(16):2). God does not grow greater by accepting you as a holocaust; he is not enhanced thereby, or enriched, or better equipped. What he does with you for your benefit brings you to a better state, but improves him not a whit. If you discern all this you will be paying your vows to God, making good the distinct utterance of your lips. *I will pay my vows to you, the vows my lips have uttered with discernment.*

20. *As my mouth spoke amid my tribulation.* Tribulation is often very welcome, and very necessary. What did this person say amid tribulation? *I will offer you holocausts with marrow.* Why *with marrow*? Because, he says, I want to hold your charity deep within me. It will not be something superficial. The love I have for you will be in the innermost part of me.[39] There is nothing more inward than our marrow; for while the bones are more interior than the flesh, the marrow is more interior than the bones themselves. Anyone who worships God on the outside, where it shows, is more concerned with impressing other people; such a person has different sentiments inside, and so does not offer holocausts with marrow. But when God looks into the very marrow of a person, he accepts the offerer whole and entire.

I will offer you holocausts with marrow, along with incense and rams. Rams are the leaders in the Church. It is the whole body of Christ that speaks here, stating what it is offering to God. What does incense represent? Prayer. So what is the implication of *along with incense and rams*? It means that the rams, above all, pray for the flocks. *I will offer you oxen, with goats.* We found a reference to oxen threshing, and they too are to be offered to God, for the apostle shows that we should understand a certain provision in the law as an allusion to those who preach the gospel: *You shall not muzzle an ox while it is threshing. Now, does God care about oxen?* (1 Cor 9:9).

We have important rams, then, and powerful oxen. What about the rest of us, those who are perhaps conscious of serious sins, and those who may have fallen even while they were on the way, and those who have sustained injuries but are being healed through repentance? Will they be left out, and have no place in the

---

39. *In medullis.* The *medulla* is the marrow in the bones, or the kernel of the wheat, or the quintessence of anything.

holocausts? Surely not. Even these must not be anxious, because the psalmist added *goats* at the end of his list. *I will offer you holocausts with marrow*, he said, *along with incense and rams. I will offer you oxen, with goats.* This addition is the saving of the goats. They cannot be saved by themselves, but in the company of the oxen they are accepted. They have made friends for themselves through iniquitous mammon, so that those friends may welcome them into the tents of eternity.[40] These particular goats will not find themselves at the Lord's left hand, because through their dealings with mammon they won themselves friends. Which goats will be at the Lord's left? Those to whom it must be said, *I was hungry, and you did not feed me* (Mt 25:42), for they did not atone for their sins by almsgiving.

Verses 16-17. What God has done in my soul: prayer and sincerity

21. *Come and hear, all you who fear God, and I will relate....* Let us answer this call and come, and hear what he has to relate. *Come and hear, and I will relate....* But to whom is this call addressed; who are being invited to come and hear? *All you who fear God.* "If you do not fear God," he implies, "I shall not tell my story. If no fear of God is present, there is no one to listen. Let the fear of God open ears, so that something may find its way in, and there may be a pathway for what I am about to relate."

But what is the speaker about to tell? *What great things God has done for my soul.* He wants to tell us a story, but what will it be concerned with? With how vast is the extent of the earth, perhaps, how far the heavens stretch, how many are the stars, and what are the changing faces of sun and moon? All this created order continues in its appointed way, and those who have investigated it with avid curiosity have generally failed to recognize its Creator.[41] But no, he says. "This is what you must hear from me, this is what you must take to heart, *you who fear God: what great things he has done for my soul*, and how much he will do for yours as well, if you are willing. *What great things he has done for my soul! To him I cried with my voice.*" So this is what he says has been done for his soul! The fact that he cried to God with his voice—this is the sum of what happened to his soul! But we can concur, brothers and sisters, can't we? We were pagans—or if we personally were not, at least our ancestors were. And what does the apostle say to people like us? *You know how you were led along and climbed up*[42] *to dumb idols, when you were pagans* (1 Cor 12:2). But now let the Church declare,

---

40. See Lk 16:9.
41. Compare Wis 13:9.
42. *Ascendebatis.* The idea of climbing/mounting is not present in the Greek original, which uses the ordinary verbs for taking or leading someone in both occurrences. Possibly the climbing idea in Augustine's Latin version was suggested by the "high places" favored by pagan cults.

What great things he has done for my soul! To him I cried with my voice. As unregenerate humanity I was wont to cry to a deaf post; I was accustomed to cry out to idols both deaf and dumb. But now the image of God has turned to its Creator. I used to *say to a tree, You are my father, and to a stone, You begot me* (Jer 2:27); but now I say, *Our Father, who are in heaven. To him I cried with my voice,* because it is my own voice now; I am not mouthing the words of others. When I used to cry to stone deities in the idle chatter of my ancestral traditions[43] I was mouthing the words of other people; but now when I cry to the Lord in words he has given me and he has inspired, I am crying out with a voice of my own.

And I have exalted him beneath my tongue.[44] What is implied here, when the psalm claims, *To him I cried with my voice, and I have exalted him beneath my tongue*? It means, "I preached him publicly, and confessed him in secret." It is not enough to exalt God with your tongue; you must do so just as much beneath your tongue, so that what you speak when others are listening tallies with what you silently think. *To him I cried with my voice, and I have exalted him beneath my tongue.* You can see how this person who offers holocausts full of marrow longs to be whole and entire within. You must do the same, brothers and sisters. Imitate this integrity, so that you too may say, *Come and hear what great things he has done for my soul,* for whatever the psalm has to relate comes about in our soul too, by the grace of God. Now see what else he has to tell.

Verse 18. Different ways of looking at iniquity

22. *If I have looked at iniquity in my heart, may the Lord not hear me.* Reflect how easily, and even daily, people accuse others of iniquities, brothers and sisters, feigning shame as they do so. "That fellow has behaved badly, he is an abandoned character, a crook," so they say, and perhaps they say it only to justify themselves in the eyes of others. See if you cannot observe iniquity in your own heart, consider whether what you are censuring in another is not what you are thinking of doing yourself. And if so, ask yourself whether you are raising the hue and cry against that other person not because he did whatever it was, but because he was found out. Return to yourself, and be your own judge within. In your private, secret room, in your inmost heart of hearts, where you are alone with God who sees you, let that iniquity be unacceptable to you, so that you may be acceptable to God. Do not eye it with affection; no, look down on it, despise it, turn away from it. Whatever the pleasant results it may have promised, to allure you to sin, or whatever the calamity it may have threatened, to drive you toward

---

43. Compare 1 Pt 1:18.
44. This last phrase, *exaltavi sub lingua mea,* is the Old Latin's literal reproduction of the Septuagint. The meaning is "inwardly, in my thoughts," as opposed to what is outwardly professed.

wrongdoing, all that is nothing, for it will pass away altogether. Iniquity deserves to be looked down on, so that you may trample on it, not eyed with a view to acceptance.[45]

Iniquity sometimes makes its suggestions through our thoughts, or through words spoken in conversations between bad people, for *evil conversations corrupt good morals*,[46] so you must have no regard for these. But it is not enough to shun the sin in outward appearance, and by restraining your tongue; you must not look favorably on it in your heart: you must neither love it nor accept it. Our common idiom associates the favorable glance with love, doesn't it? We say of God in the first place, "He has looked favorably upon me."[47] How can you say, "He has looked upon me"? Did he not see you before now? Or was he waiting up there, until he was alerted by your prayers to turn his eyes in your direction? Of course he was looking upon you before this; yet you say, "He has looked upon me." He has loved me.

Then again, there is some human being who can see you well enough, but you want him to be kind to you, so you beg him, "Look upon me." He sees you already, yet you say, "Look upon me." What does it mean? It means, "Be kind to me, take heed of me, have mercy on me."

The psalm did not use the words, *if I have looked at iniquity in my heart*, to mean that no iniquity whatever is even hinted at in the human heart. It is hinted there, undoubtedly. The suggestions never cease, but let them be given no favorable consideration.[48] If you give sin an approving look you are casting a backward look,[49] and then you incur the condemnation spoken by the Lord in the gospel: *No one who lays a hand on the plow and then looks back is fit for the kingdom of God* (Lk 9:62). What am I to do, then? Take the apostle's advice: *Forget what lies behind and strain to what lies ahead* (Phil 3:13). No one comes to God from a starting-point of goodness; all have sinned, and are justified through believing.[50] There will be no perfect righteousness except in the life beyond. All the same, we can make progress toward it, because good conduct is inspired by God and made possible by his gift. Do not try to reckon your merits; do not even think of doing so. And if iniquity whispers suggestions, do not consent. What does the psalm say? *If I have looked at iniquity in my heart, may the Lord not hear me.*

---

45. Many reliable manuscripts omit all the rest of this section 22, except the final repetition of verse 18.
46. Quoted by Paul from Menander in 1 Cor 15:33.
47. *Respexit me*. Throughout this section Augustine is playing on three similar verbs of looking: *conspicio* (translated above by "look at"); *despicio* ("look down on"); and *respicio* ("look favorably upon, have regard for, respect").
48. *Respectio*.
49. *Si . . . respicis iniquitatem, retro adspicis*. The pun is not easily reproduced in translation.
50. See Rom 3:22-23.

Verses 19-20. Persevering prayer

23. *Therefore God has heard me*, because I have not looked at iniquity in my heart. *And he hearkened to my voice as I prayed.*

24. *Blessed be my God, who has taken away neither my prayer nor his mercy from me.* To understand this we must refer to the earlier verse where he said, *Come and hear, all you who fear God, and I will relate what great things he has done for my soul.* He then went on with the narrative you have heard, and now he rounds it off by saying, *Blessed be my God, who has taken away neither my prayer nor his mercy from me.* The speaker has attained to the resurrection, where we already are in hope. Or, rather, we are there, and the voice that speaks is our voice. But as long as we are in this world we must entreat God not to take away from us either our prayer or his mercy; that is, we must ask that we may perseveringly pray and he may perseveringly have mercy on us.

Many people grow weary of prayer. In their first fervor after conversion they pray ardently, then later more lazily, then rather coldly, and at last quite negligently: they think themselves secure. The enemy is on the watch, and you are asleep. But the Lord commanded in the gospel *that we must pray always, and not give up* (Lk 18:1). And he put before us the parable of the unjust judge, who neither reverenced God nor had any respect for men and women. A widow went on appealing to him every day to hear her case, and the wicked judge said to himself, *Perhaps I do not fear God, or respect men and women. But since this widow plagues me every day, I will hear her case, and see justice done for her.* And the Lord added, *If the wicked judge did that, will not your Father see justice done for his elect, who cry to him day and night? I tell you, he will vindicate them very speedily* (Lk 18:4-8). We must not grow weary, then, in our prayer. God may delay, but he will not disappoint us[51] over what he means to grant. Fully confident in his promise, we must not get tired of praying; and if we persevere, this too is by his good gift. This is what the psalmist gave thanks about: *Blessed be my God, who has taken away neither my prayer nor his mercy from me.* When you see that your prayer has not been taken away from you, be of good cheer, because his mercy has not been taken away from you either.

---

51. *Etsi differt, non aufert.*

Exposition of Psalm 66

A Sermon to the People

Verse 2. God is the true farmer

1. Dearly beloved,[1] you will remember that in two psalms which we have expounded already, we addressed our own soul, exhorting it to bless God. We sang devoutly, *Bless the Lord, O my soul.*[2] If in those other two psalms we urged our soul to bless the Lord, it is only right that in the present psalm we should pray, *May God have mercy on us and bless us.* May our soul bless the Lord, and may God bless us. When God blesses us, we grow, and when we bless the Lord, we grow; so in either case the gain is ours. He is not increased in any way by our blessing, or diminished by our curse. On the contrary, those who curse the Lord are themselves diminished, while any who bless the Lord grow in the process. The Lord's blessing of us has the priority, and our blessing of the Lord is its consequence. His blessing is the rain, and our response in blessing him is the fruit.[3]

Our blessing is offered like a harvest to God, for he is the farmer who sends rain on us and cultivates us. We must sing to him, therefore, not with sterile devotion, nor with fallow protests, but with truth in our hearts; for God the Father is quite plainly said to be a farmer in our regard. The apostle tells us, *You are God's cultivated field, and God's building* (1 Cor 3:9). In the work of this visible world a vine is not a building, and a building is not a vineyard. Yet we are the Lord's vineyard, because he tends us and encourages us to bear fruit, and we are also God's building, because he who cultivates us also dwells within us. Moreover the same apostle spells it out: *I planted, Apollos watered, but God gave the growth. So the planter is nothing, and the one who waters is nothing; only God matters, who grants the increase* (1 Cor 3:6-7). So the increase is due to God. "Perhaps we should also call the apostles farmers, though?" someone may ask. No, I don't think so. "But one who plants and waters deserves the name of farmer, surely? And the apostle said, *I planted, Apollos watered.*" Ah yes, but

---

1. *Caritas vestra.*
2. Pss 102(103):1; 103(104):1. Augustine must have preached on these two psalms to the same congregation, perhaps at Carthage, not long before delivering the present sermon, which some commentators assign to the later months of either 411 or 412.
3. These themes of blessing and fruitfulness, together with that of divine providence, run through the sermon, possibly suggesting late summer or autumn as its setting.

what if we ask the apostle whence he derived the power to do it? He will reply, *It was not I, but the grace of God with me* (1 Cor 15:10). Whichever way you turn, you will always find that God is your farmer. If he works through his angels, he is your farmer; if through the prophets, he is your farmer; if through the apostles, still you must recognize him and no other as your farmer.

What of ourselves, then?[4] Well, perhaps we can be called workmen employed by the farmer. We labor only with the strength he has conferred on us, and by the grace he has given. He cultivates the crop himself, and gives the increase. An ordinary human farmer cultivates a vineyard to this extent, that he weeds, and prunes, and carries out all the other procedures required of diligent vine-dressers; but he has no power to send rain on his vineyard. Even if he has the ability to irrigate it, where does he get that power? He channels water into the conduit, but it is God who fills the spring. And in the end he cannot induce growth in the young branches, or form the fruit, or cause the seeds to germinate, or change their time of sprouting. God can do all these things. He is our farmer, and we are safe.

Possibly someone may still be minded to argue. "You say that God is our farmer; but I insist: the apostles are farmers. They testified, *I planted, Apollos watered.*" All right: if I say it, no one need believe me. But if Christ says it, woe betide anyone who does not believe him. And what does he say, Christ, our Lord? *I am the vine, you are the branches. My Father is the vine-dresser.*[5] Let our earth feel its thirst, then, and cry out in its parched longing, for it is written, *My soul is like waterless earth before you* (Ps 142(143):6). Let our earth cry out, let us, who are this thirsty earth longing for God's rain, cry out, *May God have mercy on us and bless us.*

God is the source of all the good things we desire

2. *May he make his face shine upon us.* Perhaps you were keen to explore the meaning of the earlier phrase, *may he bless us.* People hope to be blessed by God in a variety of ways. One person wants to be blessed by having a home chock-full of all sorts of useful things; another longs for the blessing of health that never fails; another, who is ill, wants to be blessed by the recovery of health; another longs for children, and is grieved when they do not arrive, because he or she is longing to be blessed with posterity. Who could count all the varied yearnings of people who long to be blessed by the Lord God? And indeed, which of us would deny that it is a blessing from God if our crops yield heavily, or someone's home

---

4. The bishop and his priests, or other bishops. Or perhaps we should simply see the "episcopal plural" here, as often when Augustine is preaching, and translate "myself."

5. Jn 15:5.1. The word *agricola* used throughout this section can mean "farmer," "gardener," "vine-dresser," etc., according to the context.

is amply provisioned with temporal goods, or bodily health is preserved, or, if lost, is restored? Fertility in women, too, and the chaste longings of those who hope for children—do these not concern the Lord our God? He created our race when it did not exist, and he ensures that what he created will continue through recurrent generations. God does these things, God gives these things.

But it is not enough to say, God does these things, God gives these things; we must specify: God alone does them, God alone gives them. Otherwise it might be thought that God does them but someone else does too, someone other than God. No, God does these things, and he alone. It is pointless to beg them from other human beings, or from demons. Moreover, whatever good things come the way of God's enemies are given to them by God. If they beg them from other sources, and get what they want, they are still receiving good things from God, though they do not know it. It is the same when people are punished. They think they are being punished by others, and do not realize that they are punished by God. So too when they are invigorated, filled, saved, liberated: they may in their ignorance attribute their good fortune to other people, or to demons, or to angels;[6] but they receive these benefits only from God, who has power over all things.

We have mentioned this, brothers and sisters, to make sure that anyone who desires such earthly goods, either to meet some need or to heal some infirmity, may seek them from God alone, who is the source of all that is good—he, the creator and re-creator of all that exists.

Good things are given to the good and the wicked, and taken away from both. The example set by the ant

3. But there is a difference between the gifts God gives to his enemies as well as his friends, and those he keeps for his friends alone. What are the gifts he bestows on his enemies? Those I have enumerated already. It is not good people only who have houses well stocked with necessary commodities; it is not the good only who either stay well, or recover from illness; not the good only who have children, or money, or all the other things which are useful to us in this temporal, transient life. The wicked too have these things, and the good sometimes lack them; but then the wicked sometimes lack them too, and perhaps more often than do good people. Moreover, when good people have them, they may be more plentifully supplied than the wrongdoers. God has willed that these temporal commodities be distributed randomly, because if he were to give them to good people alone, bad people would think it worthwhile to worship God for

---

6. Not only was demon-worship widespread in the Roman Empire of Augustine's day; there were also numerous cults of divinized human beings, who in some cases were former local heroes. To them people would appeal in material need. Devotion to local martyrs was lively in Christian Africa, and it is probable that in the minds of the unsophisticated these played the same role as had the demi-gods and demons of pagan days, and were appealed to similarly.

the sake of them. On the other hand, if he were to give them only to the wicked, some there would be—well-meaning, but weak—who would hang back from conversion because they were afraid of being deprived.

You see, this can happen. A soul still weak is not yet capable of receiving God's kingdom; and so God, our farmer, must take special care of it. Even a tree strong enough to withstand storms was once a little shoot, when it first emerged from the soil. The divine farmer knows how to trim and prune robust trees; but he also knows how to put protective fencing round delicate young saplings.

So, as I was saying, dearly beloved, if temporal benefits were bestowed on good people only, everyone would want to be converted to God on their account. Or, if such benefits were accorded only to bad people, weak souls would be afraid that after conversion they might lose what was reserved for the wicked. This is why they are distributed randomly to good and bad. Then think of it the other way round: if such advantages were taken away only from good people, there would be the same dread on the part of the weak, deterring them from conversion to God. But if the advantages were withdrawn from bad people only, others might suppose that this was the only punishment the wicked were destined to undergo. By conferring benefits on good people, God comforts those who are journeying onward;[7] but by conferring them on bad people as well he warns the good that they must desire quite different gifts, which they will not share with the wicked.

Then again, God takes his gifts away from the good people when he so chooses, to make them question themselves about how much staying-power they have, and to help them to know themselves more fully than perhaps they did previously. They are forced to ask themselves whether they have the strength to say, *The Lord gave, and the Lord has taken away. This has happened as the Lord willed: may the Lord's name be blessed.*[8] The soul that made that declaration blessed the Lord; it had been richly nourished by the rain of the Lord's blessing, and now it yielded him its fruit. *The Lord gave, and the Lord has taken away*; he has withdrawn the gifts, but not the Giver. Blessed is the soul that is entirely simple![9] It does not stick fast in earthly things; its wings are not glued or entangled. Gleaming with splendid virtues it soars on the twin wings of two-fold love, freely into the upper air. From there it sees that what has been taken from it are things it only trampled on,[10] not anything it needed for its support. Secure in this

---

7. *Itinerantes*, a favorite idea of Augustine's, and characteristic of his spirituality. It derived partly from the Platonic doctrine of the return of the soul to God, but was enriched by the biblical theme of journeying and the parable of the prodigal son.

8. Jb 1:21. Job is represented in the Old Testament as non-Hebrew, not of the chosen people, a "holy pagan." Though the point is not mentioned here, it suggested to Augustine the all-embracing character of salvation, the catholicity of the holy city. Compare *City of God* 18, 47.

9. See Prv 11:25 (LXX).

10. *Calcabat*: the verb was used of a Roman conqueror who trampled on the prostrate bodies of his enemies.

knowledge it repeats, *The Lord gave, and the Lord has taken away. This has happened as the Lord willed: may the Lord's name be blessed.* He gave, and he has taken away; he who gave stays with me, all that has gone is what he gave. May his name be blessed. This is why good things are taken away from good people.

But there may be some weak person who asks, "When can I ever be as strong, as virtuous, as holy Job?" You marvel at the mighty tree because you are no more than a newly-sprung plant yourself,[11] but this great tree that you admire, under whose shady boughs you could find coolness, was a little shoot once. So you are frightened, are you, that things you value may be taken away from you when you mature like that? But look around you: they are taken away from bad people too. So why dither about conversion? What you fear to lose once you are good, you will perhaps lose anyway while you are bad. If you are good when you lose them, he who takes them from you will be close at hand to comfort you. Your coffers may be empty of gold, but your heart is full of faith; you are outwardly poor, but inwardly rich, for the wealth you carry with you is wealth you could not lose even if you were to escape naked from shipwreck. So if you are perhaps going to lose these things in any case, bad as you are, would it not be preferable for the same ruin to overtake you when you are good, seeing that the wicked are ruined equally?

But not equally, in fact. Their loss is worse. Their house is desolate, but their conscience more desolate still. When a bad person suffers a loss like that, he has nothing to hold onto outside himself, nor anywhere to rest within. He shuns the place where he has been ruined, where he used to flaunt himself and his riches before the eyes of others. He cannot boast before other people anymore, but neither can he take refuge within himself, for nothing remains for him there.

Such a person has not imitated the ant,[12] by collecting seeds while it was still summer. What do I mean by that—while it was still summer? When his life was tranquil, while worldly prosperity was his lot, when he had leisure, when everyone deemed him fortunate, it was summertime for him. If he had listened then to the word of God, collecting grains and storing them within, he would have been following the example of the ant. Troubles might then have overtaken him to put him to the test, as though the frozen apathy of winter, or a storm of fear, or a cold snap of sadness, had overtaken him: it could have been through some loss of fortune, or a threat to his health, or the death of his dear ones, or some disgrace or humiliation. Then it would have been winter for him. But the

---

11. *Quia modo nata es.* The feminine evidently worried one copyist, who substituted a masculine, *natus.*But the feminine could be correct if a young tree (*arbor*, feminine) is being addressed. The CCL editors dispose of the difficulty by amending *es* to *est*: "because it [the mighty tree] has only now sprung up," which makes little sense.

12. See Prv 6:6; 30:25. The image of the ant was probably also familiar to Augustine from Virgil (*Georgics* 1,186; 1, 380; *Aen.* 4, 402-407) and Horace (*Sat.* 1, 32-35).

ant falls back on what it collected in the summer; and there within, in its private place where no one sees it, the ant is refreshed by the fruits of its summer toil. While it was collecting these items during the summer, it was obvious to the onlookers; but when it feeds on them in winter, no one sees.

Now how are we to apply this? Think of God's ants. They rise daily and hurry to church, pray, listen to the reading, sing the hymn, ruminate on what they have heard, think it over at home, and store within themselves whatever grains they have collected from the threshing-floor. Any of you who are listening prudently to what I am telling you now will act likewise. Everyone sees them making their way to church, coming home from church, listening to the readings, finding a book,[13] opening it and reading. They can be observed by all when they do these things. They are like the ant scurrying along, carrying its spoils and stowing them away, seen by everyone who cares to look. Sooner or later, winter arrives. Is there anyone who never goes through a winter? Some loss befalls them, or some bereavement. Perhaps other people are compassionate, pitying the one they regard as afflicted, because they have no notion of what supplies of food he or she, ant-like, has stored within. They say, "How dreadful for the man to whom that happened!" or "Poor woman, what an appalling thing!" and "What must he feel like? How upset she must be!" They are judging by their own standards, and their compassion is in proportion to the little strength they would themselves command in like circumstances. They are mistaken, therefore, because they are applying a criterion that fits themselves to someone they do not know. You see that other person financially ruined, or humiliated, or crushed by bereavement, and what do you make of it? You think, "That fellow must have done something bad to bring this on himself. Let a heart in that state, a mind so troubled, be the fate of my enemies!"[14] You don't know what you are talking about. You are truly your own enemy, since you are not gathering supplies for yourself in summer, as that other person did. That ant is eating its summer store now, but within. You could have seen it collecting its food, but you cannot see it eating.

Well, brothers and sisters, now we have told you why God gives all these temporal benefits randomly to both good and bad people, and why he takes them away from both the good and the wicked. We have told you why, insofar as God has graciously indicated the truth to us and instructed us in our weakness; and in the measure of our small capacity we have explained it to you. If he has given you good fortune, do not be puffed up; if he has taken it away from you, do not be brokenhearted. Are you afraid that he may take such things away from you if you begin to live a good life? He may take them just as easily while you are bad. It is

---

13. Or, more probably, *the* book.
14. This last sentence could be understood not as part of the onlooker's judgment but as part of Augustine's comment, in which case we might translate, "Let a heart like that, an attitude like that, be found only in my enemies!"

better for you to be good, and lose God's gifts, but hold onto God. But the same is true for that bad fellow over there. We entreat him: you are bound to suffer some kind of loss (does anyone avoid the pain of bereavement, for example?). Some accident will befall you, some calamity will catch you on the wrong foot. The world is full of such disasters; we hear about them every day. Now, while you are enjoying summer, I tell you, while there are plenty of grains you can collect, study the ant, you sluggard.[15] Gather them now, in summer, while you have the chance. Winter will not permit you to forage, but then you will be able to eat what you have collected. How many people there are who are overtaken by misfortune in circumstances where they have no leisure to read or to hear anything useful, and perhaps have no access to persons who might console them! The ant has loitered in its lair; let it see whether it has anything from its summer store that will stand it in good stead now that winter has come.

The image, radiant and restored

4. But if God blesses us, why does he bless us? And what kind of blessing does the psalm have in view when it prays, *May God bless us*? It asks for the blessing God reserves for his friends, the blessing he gives only to good people. Do not value too highly the things that bad people receive just as often. Because God is good, he creates these things; because he is good he causes his sun to rise over the good and the wicked, and sends his rain on just and unjust alike.[16] What special privilege do the good have, then? What is the prerogative of the just? *May he make his face shine on us.* You make the face of the sun up there shine over both the good and the wicked; but make your own face shine on us. Both good and wicked behold the daylight, and they do so along with the cattle; but the clean of heart are blessed, because they will see God.[17]

May he make his face shine on us. This can be understood in two different ways, and we need to look at both. Here is the first: when the psalm asks God to make his face shine on us, it is praying, "Show us your face." This does not mean, of course, that God just decides at a given moment to light up his countenance, as though he had been in the dark until then. No, but we ask that he should make his face shine for us, so that what was hidden from us may be seen openly. Let what was light already, but concealed from our sight, be revealed for us; let it be lit up for us.

The other way of understanding the verse is to take it like this: "Illumine your own image in us." The psalm would then be praying, "Bring out the light of your face in us. You have stamped your features upon us, you have made us in your

---

15. See Prv 6:6.
16. See Mt 5:45.
17. See Mt 5:8.

own image and likeness;[18] you have made us your coin.[19] But your image ought not to remain obscured. So send forth a ray of your wisdom to scatter our darkness, and let your image in us shine forth in all its splendor. Let us recognize ourselves as your image, and hear for ourselves that word in the Song of Songs, *Do you not know yourself, most beautiful of women?"* (Sg 1:7). This question is put to the Church: *Do you not know yourself?* What does it mean? Do you not know that you have been made in the image of God, O precious soul of the Church redeemed by the blood of the[20] stainless Lamb? Consider how valuable you are, reflect on the immense price paid for you. As we say this verse, let us hope as the psalm hopes: *may he make his face shine on us*, for we carry God's face upon us. Even as the faces of emperors are said to be present,[21] so it is with us, because the sacred countenance of God is truly present in his image, though the wicked fail to see the image of God in themselves. What should they say, then, if the face of God is to shine in them too? *"You, Lord, will light my lamp; my God, you will enlighten my darkness* (Ps 17:29(18:28)). I am engulfed in the darkness of my sins, but may my darkness be dispelled by a ray of your wisdom. May your countenance shine forth, and if there appears in me some degree of deformity, may what was formed by you be reformed by you." So then, *may he make his face shine on us*.

Verse 3. Christ, our way on earth

5. *That we may know your way upon earth*. It says, *on earth*, so it must mean here, in this life, *may we know your way*. What is *your way*? The way that leads us to you. Enable us to recognize both where we are going and the way by which we must travel; but in darkness we cannot discern either. We are travelers, and you are far distant, so you have stretched out before us a way whereby we can return to you. Help us to discern *your way upon earth*. What can this way be, since we are prompted to pray *that we may know your way upon earth*? We are the people who must seek it, but we cannot learn where it is by ourselves. We can learn it from the gospel, though, for the Lord says, *I am the way*. Yes, Christ told us, *I am the way*. But are you worried that you may take a wrong turning? Don't worry, because he continued, *I am the truth*. How could anyone go astray while walking in the truth? Only a person who withdraws from the truth goes astray. Christ is the truth, and Christ is the way; walk, then. Or are you fearful that you may die before you reach your journey's end? Don't worry, for he said, *I am the*

---

18. See Gn 1:26.

19. Compare Mk 12:17 and parallels.

20. Variant: ". . . O soul of the Church, redeemed by the precious blood of the. . . ."

21. The official likeness stamped upon coins was thought of as making the emperor present in all the provinces.

life. Christ tells us, *I am the way, the truth, and the life* (Jn 14:6). He seems to be reassuring you: "Why are you afraid? You walk by me, you walk in me, and you find rest in me."

What else is the psalm asking when it prays, *that we may know your way upon earth*, what else but "let us know your Christ upon earth"? But it is better to let the psalm make the point for itself; otherwise you might think that evidence, lacking here, is being imported from other scriptural passages. And it does make the point, by clarifying through repetition what it has just said. *That we may know your way upon earth*, it prayed; and then, as though to respond to your query, "What earth, what way?" it continues, *Your salvation among all nations*. Upon what earth, did you ask? I will tell you: the earth populated by *all nations*. And what way, you inquired? Again I will tell you: *your salvation*.

Do you doubt, perhaps, that God's salvation is Christ himself? What do you make of the words of old Simeon, then? I mean that old man who appears in the gospel, preserved to extreme old age, even to the unspeaking age of the Word. That old man took the unspeaking Word of God[22] into his arms. If Christ graciously willed to rest in the Virgin's womb, would he ungraciously refuse an old man's embrace? The same Christ lay in both the Virgin's womb and the old man's arms; he was weak, he spoke not, either in the womb or in those aged hands. He was weak in order to give us strength, he through whom all things were made—and if all things, then his mother too. He came humbly, he came in weakness, but he meant to transform his garment of weakness, for *though he died in weakness, he is alive by the power of God* (2 Cor 13:4), as the apostle says. So Christ was held in the arms of the old man, and what did that old man say? What did he say as he gave thanks, now that the time had come for him to be released from this life? What did he say, as he saw safely held within his hands the one by whom and in whom his salvation was held safe? *You give your servant his discharge in peace, now, Lord, for my eyes have seen your salvation* (Lk 2:29-30).

To sum up, then: we pray, *May God bless us and have mercy on us, may he make his face shine upon us, that we may know your way upon earth*. And if we ask, "What earth would that be?" the answer is *among all nations*. If we further ask, "What way?" the psalm tells us: *your salvation*.

Verse 4. Singing the new song along the way

6. What is the consequence? If God's way is recognized on earth, if his salvation is recognized among all nations, what follows? *Let the peoples confess to you, O God, let all peoples confess to you*. Then some heretic pops up and says,

---

22. *Infantem Verbum Dei*. Augustine uses *infans* precisely: an "infant" is one who cannot speak.

"I have such peoples, here in Africa." And someone else chimes in, "And I have peoples like that in Galatia." You have them in Africa, and he in Galatia; very well, but I want him who has his people everywhere. No doubt you had the effrontery to crow when you heard the psalm say, *Let the peoples confess to you, O God*; but listen to the next line. It is not talking about some restricted area: *Let all peoples confess to you.*[23]

Walk in the way with all nations, walk in the way with all peoples, O you children of grace, children of the one Catholic Church; walk in the way, and sing as you go. This is what wayfarers do to lighten their fatigue. You do the same. Sing along the road. Through the way himself I beg you, sing in this way, and sing a new song. Let no one still sing the old song there; sing love-songs about your homeland, and let the old songs be heard on no one's lips anymore. A new way, a new wayfarer, and a new song. Listen to the apostle urging this new song upon you: *if anyone is in Christ, there is a new creation. The old things have passed away, and lo, everything is made new!* (2 Cor 5:17). Sing the new song in this way you have come to know *on earth*. And where is this earth? *Among all nations*. Obviously the new song is not the property of a sect.[24] Anyone who sings in a sect is singing the old song. Whatever he or she sings, it is the stale, old self singing the stale, old song, the old self that is divided, and carnal. To the degree that we are carnal we are old and stale, and to the degree that we are spiritual, we are new. See what the apostle has to say about this: *Not as spiritual persons could I speak to you, but only as carnal*. And how does he prove that they are carnal? By pointing to the partisanship among them: *When one says, "I belong to Paul," and another, "I belong to Apollos," does that not show you up as carnal?* (1 Cor 3:1.4).

As for you, sing the new song in the Spirit[25] as you walk along the safe way. This is how travelers sing, and often they sing at night. Dreadful things rattle all round them, or, worse still, surround them silently, all the more terrifying for being unheard. But still the travelers sing, even those who fear robbers. How much more securely will you sing in Christ! This way has no robbers infesting it; you will fall in with a robber only if you leave the way. Sing then, sing, I say, with complete confidence in this way that you have come to know *upon earth*, that is, *among all nations*. Listen to the apostle's reproach: *not as spiritual persons could I speak to you*, he complains, though that was what he wanted them to be. *Sing a new song to the Lord*, another psalm exhorts us; and it continues, *Sing to the Lord, all the earth* (Ps 95(96):1).

Let the peoples confess to you, O God. They have discovered your way, so let them confess. When you break into song, brothers and sisters, your singing is

---

23. These paragraphs seem to indicate that Donatism was still a live issue.
24. Or "region"; either way, something provincial and restricted.
25. Or "spiritually."

itself a confession: a confession of your sins and of God's power. Confess your iniquity, confess God's grace; accuse yourself and glorify him; censure yourself and praise him, so that when he comes he may find you your own severe judge, and reveal himself as your Savior.[26] Why are you afraid, all of you, afraid to confess, when you have found this way among all nations? Why are you afraid to confess, and in your confession to sing the new song with all the earth, in all the earth, in Catholic peace? Do you[27] fear to confess in case you are damned for what you confess? If you do not confess it, but conceal it, you will be damned when you are forced to confess it. By refusing to confess out of fear you cannot be hidden; you will be condemned for your silence, when you could have been set free by confession. *Let the peoples confess to you, O God, let all peoples confess to you.*

Verses 5-6. The joy of confession

7. This kind of confession does not lead to your punishment, so the psalm continues, *Let the Gentiles be glad and exult.* Robbers who have confessed their guilt wail before a human judge, but let believers who have confessed be glad before God. In a human tribunal, there is a collaboration between a torturer and fear to elicit a confession from a criminal; or, again, fear sometimes suppresses the confession which pain is trying to extort, for the accused person, though screaming in torments, is afraid that he will be killed if he confesses. He therefore bears the torments as best he can; but if the pain is too much for him, he blurts out his confession, and in so doing pronounces his own death-sentence. For the criminal there is no gladness, no exultation, either way. Before he confesses, he is lacerated with hooks; when he has confessed, he is condemned and led away by the executioner. There is nothing but misery for him on every side. But *let the Gentiles be glad and exult.* Over what? Their confession itself. Why? Because he to whom they confess is good. He demands confession only so that he may free the humble; he condemns the one who refuses to confess only because he must punish the proud. You must therefore be sad before you confess; but once you have confessed, dance for joy, because now you have the prospect of healing. Your conscience had accumulated morbid matter, and a boil swelled up. It caused you agony and allowed you no rest. The physician applies the poultice of his words, and eventually lances it. He uses a medicinal knife to correct the trouble, and you must acknowledge the doctor's hand. Confess. Let all the pus come out and flow away in your confession; then dance for joy and be

---

26. The preceding admonitions are in the singular. At this point Augustine switches to the plural, addressing the sectarians.
27. Singular again.

glad. Any residual sore will heal easily. *Let the peoples confess to you, O God, let all peoples confess to you.*

And because they do confess, *let the Gentiles be glad and exult, for you judge the peoples in fairness.* Make no mistake about this: the person who rejoices at the prospect of being judged is the one who has reverenced the judge. Such a person has made prudent provision and has forestalled the judge by coming into his presence confessing.[28] But he, the Lord, will judge the peoples in fairness when he comes. What will the accuser's cunning avail there? The witness will be your own conscience; you will be there alone, with your case; the judge will look for no further evidence. He has sent you an advocate: make your confession out of love for him, and relying on his mediation. Plead your case with him, and you will find in him a defender of the penitent, a petitioner for pardon on behalf of one who confesses, and a judge who finds you innocent. Do you really think you need be anxious about the outcome of your case, where your advocate will be your judge?

Let the Gentiles be glad and exult, for you judge the peoples in fairness. But if they do indeed fear that the judgment may go against them, let them hand themselves over to him to be corrected; let them hand themselves over to him who will be their judge. Let them be corrected here, and then they will have no need to be afraid in the future when their case comes up. Look at the prayer spoken in another psalm: *O God, save me by your name, and judge me in your power* (Ps 53:3(54:1)). What does that suggest? "Unless you first save me by your name, I must needs be afraid when later you judge me in your power; but if you first save me by your name, why should I be afraid of your judging me in your power, seeing that salvation in your name has seized the initiative?" The same confidence underlies our present psalm: *let the peoples confess to you.* And in case anyone still thinks that there is something to be afraid of in confession, it adds, *Let the Gentiles be glad and exult.* Why should they *be glad and exult*? Because *you judge the peoples in fairness.* No one bribes you against us, no one can corrupt you, no one deceive you.

You, sinner, can therefore be quite secure. But what about your case? Obviously no one can bribe God. But perhaps he is all the more to be feared for being absolutely incorruptible? How can you be secure, then? In the same way as that other psalm indicated: *O God, save me by your name, and judge me in your power.* So too here: *let the Gentiles be glad and exult, for you judge the peoples in fairness.* But to ward off all fear from those whose conduct has not been at all fair, it adds, *You guide the nations on earth.*[29] The nations were depraved, the nations were twisted, the nations were perverted; and because of their depravity

---

28. See Ps 94(95):2.
29. Variant: "will guide."

and twisted lives and perversions they had good reason to dread the judge who was to come. But he came with his hand mercifully stretched out toward the peoples. They are guided and directed so that they can walk a straight path. Why should they now fear their future judge, when they already know him as the one who straightens them out? Let them surrender themselves into his hands, for he guides the nations on earth.

The nations have been corrected, and now they walk in faith, exulting in God and active in good works. They are still sailing through the sea of this world, of course, and it may happen that some water seeps in through tiny chinks, and makes its way through little cracks into the bilge. But they bale it out by good deeds, lest it accumulate and sink the ship; every day they bale it out by fasting, prayer, and almsgiving, and by saying with a pure heart, *Forgive us our debts, even as we forgive our debtors*. If you say this, walk securely, dance with joy along the way and sing as you go. Do not fear your judge. Even before you became a believer, you found him to be your savior. He sought you when you were an infidel in order to redeem you; will he desert you and let you perish now that he has redeemed you? *You will guide the nations on earth.*

Verses 6-7. The fruitfulness of the earth under God's rain

8. The psalmist dances with gladness, rejoices and exhorts us, repeating the same words as he makes his plea: *Let the peoples confess to you, O God, let all peoples confess to you. The earth has yielded its fruit.* What fruit is meant? *Let all peoples confess to you.* It was useless earth, choked with thorns; but the Lord's hand went to work on it, eradicating weeds; and his majestic, merciful vocation was addressed to it. The earth began to confess, and now the earth yields its fruit. Would it have yielded any fruit, if it had not been rained on first? Would it have produced anything, if God's mercy had not showered upon it from heaven?

"I can't accept that," you say. "Read me any text that proves it was rain that caused the earth to yield its fruit." Very well; listen to the Lord sending his abundant rain: *Repent, for the kingdom of heaven is near.*[30] He poured down his rain, but the rain was also thunder. Tremble before him who thunders, and gladly welcome him as he rains on you.

Let us see if there is any instance of this process later in the gospel, after God's voice has thundered and rained. Yes: there was a courtesan, a woman with a bad reputation in the city. She burst into someone else's house; she had not been invited by the host, but she was summoned by someone who had been invited—summoned not by his voice but by his grace. She was ill, and she knew

---

30. Mt 3:2, but the words are there attributed to John the Baptist. Compare a similar saying on the lips of Jesus at Mk 1:15.

there would be a place for her in the house where her doctor was at table. This sinful woman made her way in. She does not dare to come any nearer than his feet; she weeps over his feet, waters them with her tears, wipes them with her hair, and anoints them with ointment.[31] Why be surprised? *The earth has yielded its fruit.* There you have it. It happened in this instance because the Lord was giving rain through his own mouth; but, as we read in the gospel, the same happened when he poured out rain through the apostles whom he sent to preach the truth. Then *the earth yielded its fruit* in greater abundance still; and now the crop has filled the whole world.

Verse 8. God's blessing means fecundity

9. Now look at the next verse. *May God, our God, bless us; may God bless us.* It asks that he may not only bless us in the way I have explained already, but that he may bless us over and over again, multiplying his blessings. I would draw your attention, dearest friends,[32] to the fruitfulness of the earth in Jerusalem, from the very beginning. It was there that the Church was born: the Holy Spirit came upon it there, and filled the saints, who were gathered together. Wonders were wrought, and they spoke in the tongues of all nations.[33] Filled with the Spirit of God, many in Jerusalem were converted; awe-struck, they opened themselves to the divine shower. Through their confession they bore such plentiful fruit that they pooled all their goods and distributed them to the poor, so that no one could claim anything as private property, but all resources were held in common. There was but one soul and one heart among them, directed to God.[34] The blood of the Lord, which they had shed, had been given to them; it had been given[35] because the Lord forgave them, so that now they learned to drink the blood they had poured out. That was a magnificent yield. *The earth yielded its fruit*, and an abundant crop it was, of high quality.

But was that soil the only one required to yield a harvest? It was not. *May God, our God, bless us; may God bless us.* May he go on blessing us; for we generally think of blessing as the multiplication of things: that is the most proper meaning of blessing. This can be demonstrated from Genesis. Consider God's work in creation. God made the light, and God divided light from darkness. He

---

31. See Lk 7:37-38.
32. *Caritas vestra.*
33. See Acts 2:1-4.
34. See Acts 2:44-45; 4:32.
35. The word "given" is *donatus*. It may be a coincidence, or it may be a deliberate allusion to the name of the sectarian leader, in this context of the unity of the Church. If the sermon is to be assigned to 411 or 412, the great conference of June 411, where Catholic and Donatist bishops had debated in the presence of the emperor's representative, would have been a recent memory.

called the light "day," and the darkness "night." The text does not say, "He blessed the light." In fact it is the same light that comes and goes, marking the alternations between nights and days.[36] Then God named the firmament between upper and lower waters "sky," and we are not told that he blessed the sky. He separated sea from dry land, and gave names to each, calling the dry part "earth" and the gathering of waters "sea." Again it is not said that God blessed them. But now we come to the creatures that were to contain fertile seed, and would live in the waters. These sea creatures have the richest fecundity of all; and over them God pronounced his blessing: *Increase and multiply, and fill the waters of the sea; and let flying creatures be multiplied over the earth* (Gn 1:22). So also when to human beings, made in his own image, God subjected all other creatures, it is written, *God blessed them, saying, Increase and multiply, and fill the surface of the earth* (Gn 1:28). Blessing, therefore, is properly understood as the conferring of the power to proliferate and fill the whole of earth's surface.

Now listen to the same statement in our psalm. *May God, our God, bless us; may God bless us.* What is the force of this blessing? *And may all the ends of the earth reverence him.* So abundantly has God blessed us in the name of Christ, my brothers and sisters, that he is filling all the face of the earth with his children, adopted as co-heirs to his kingdom with his only-begotten Son. God begot one only Son, but did not will him to remain alone. I repeat, God engendered a unique Son, but would not have him solitary. God created brothers and sisters for his Son, not by generation but by adoption, and by making them the Son's co-heirs. He first made that Son a sharer in our mortality, so that we might believe it possible for us to be sharers in his divinity.

Fulfillment of all the promises. Take scriptural similes in the sense in which they are meant. Augustine's humility amid plaudits

10. Let us reflect on how precious this makes us in God's sight. All these events were prophesied, and all those prophecies have come true. The gospel is making its way throughout the whole world; and all the activity of the human race in the present age bears witness to the fulfillment of the predictions in scripture. Just as the prophecies have been proved right down to the present day, so will those that are still outstanding be verified. Let us therefore fear judgment day, for truly the Lord will come. He who once came humbly will come in sublime majesty; he who came to submit to judgment will come to judge. Let us acknowledge our humble Lord, so that we need not be terrified by his majesty; let us embrace him in his humility, so that we may long for him in his sublimity; for he will come in merciful grace to those who long for him. Those who hold

---

36. That is, the light does not have children; the same light goes on and on.

fast in faith to him, and keep his commandments, are the ones who long for him. But be sure of this: come he will, even if we do not want him. Clearly, then, we should desire his coming, since he will come in any case, whether we like it or not.

How are we to desire his coming? By living God-fearing lives and doing good. Memories of the past must not trap us in pleasure, nor must present affairs hold us fast. Let us not block one ear with our tail, and press the other to the ground.[37] Let us not be deterred from hearing by anything in the past, nor become so absorbed in things present that we are prevented from meditating on what is to come; but let us forget the past and stretch forward to what lies ahead.[38] What we struggle with now, what we groan over now, what we sigh for now, what we speak about now, all that of which we now have some dim intuition but cannot grasp—that we shall grasp, and fully enjoy, at the resurrection of the just. Our youth will be renewed like the eagle's,[39] provided we dash our old self against the rock of Christ.[40] Now I do not know, brothers and sisters, whether the reports about the snake and the eagle are true, or are only old wives' tales; but it does not matter. The truth is in the scriptures, and scripture has its own good reason for putting them before us. Our job is to act on whatever is signified by these similes, not to spend too much time on debating whether they describe things that really happen. You must be the sort of person whose youth can be renewed like that of the eagle; and you must be quite sure that it cannot be renewed until your old nature has been smashed against the rock. What I mean is this: you cannot be renewed except by means of the rock, except through Christ. Neither must you be deafened against the word of God by the delights of your past life, nor again be so trapped and hindered by your present concerns that you make the excuse, "I have no time to read, no leisure to listen." That is to press your ear to the ground. No, you must not be that sort of person; what you must prove yourself to be is the opposite: you must forget the past and stretch forward to what lies ahead, and so break off your old self against the rock.

Whatever similes may have been proposed to you, believe them. If what you find there is no more than a reflection of popular belief, do not put too much faith

37. As the asp was reputed to do, in its effort to deafen itself against the charmer's lure; see Exposition of Psalm 57, 7-10. The tail, being behind, represents past things, and the ground symbolizes earthly concerns, as he explained in that place, and briefly mentions in the next sentence here.

38. See Phil 3:13.

39. See Ps 102(103):5.

40. The immediate verbal allusion is to Ps 136(137):9. A popular belief, traceable at least as far back as Aristotle, pictured the plight of an elderly eagle so hampered by the excessive growth of the hooked upper half of its beak that it could no longer open its mouth to eat. It would remedy the situation by hammering its beak against a rock, to chip away the excess. Then it would eat, and be restored to full vigor. Augustine refers to this belief in his Exposition of Psalm 102. There, as here, he understands the rock to be Christ, with reference to 1 Cor 10:4.

in that; it may accord with reality, or it may not. What matters is that you make progress, and this imagery is meant to help you along to salvation. You do not find this particular image helpful? Very well, take another; the point is that you must act on it. Await God's kingdom without perplexity, and do not allow your very prayer to quarrel with you. When you pray, O Christian, *Your kingdom come*, what do you mean? *Your kingdom come*? Awaken your heart, open your eyes, listen: *Your kingdom come*! Christ is shouting to you, "I'm coming!" Doesn't that fill you with awe? Dearly beloved,[41] we have often told you that preaching the truth is nothing, if our heart is at variance with our tongue. And hearing the truth is nothing, if no fruit follows from the hearing. We are addressing you from a raised place, as though we were more honorable than you, yet God knows how our fear puts us under your feet. He knows it, whose kindness readily forgives the humble, for what gives us joy is not the plaudits of those who praise us, but rather the devotion of those who confess and the deeds of those whose lives are upright. God knows that it is your progress, and nothing else, that delights us, and he knows how gravely we are imperiled by your praise. He knows it, and may he free us from all dangers, save us together with you from all temptation, graciously acknowledge us all, and crown us all together in his kingdom.

---

41. *Caritas vestra.*

Exposition of Psalm 67[1]

Verse 1. The difference between "canticle" and "psalm" in a title

1. The title of this psalm does not seem, at first sight, to require elaborate explanation, for it looks simple and free from difficulty. It runs, *To the end, a psalm of a canticle for David himself.* Now in many other psalms we have remarked on the meaning of *to the end*, pointing out that *Christ is the end of the law, bringing justification to everyone who believes* (Rom 10:4). He is the "end" as one who brings perfection, not an end in the sense of using up something or destroying it.

It is a different matter, however, when one attempts to find out the meaning of *a psalm of a canticle.* Why not call it either a *psalm* or a *canticle*; why both? And what is the difference between "a psalm of a canticle" and "a canticle of a psalm"? Since various psalms bear a title of this kind, an inquirer may perhaps discover some different shade of meaning; but we must leave it to those with sharper minds and more leisure. Some of our predecessors,[2] though, have made a distinction between canticle and psalm. They noted that since a canticle is sung with the mouth alone, whereas a psalm requires the accompaniment of some visible instrument, such as the psaltery, it seems that a canticle represents intelligence in the mind, and a psalm symbolizes bodily activity. Now, applying this distinction to Psalm 67, which we have undertaken to expound, these scholars have pointed to the verse which says, *Sing to God, play psalms to his name.*[3] They think that *sing to God* refers to the activity of the mind within itself, which is known to God but unseen by human eyes. But good deeds need to be visible to other people, so that they may glorify our Father in heaven;[4] and therefore the psalm rightly adds, *Play psalms to his name*, which means "Play psalms to make him publicly known," so that his name may be invoked with praise. If I remember rightly, I drew this distinction myself in another context. I think I also remember that we read elsewhere, *Sing psalms to God,*[5] because the good deeds we perform in a visible manner are pleasing not only to other people, but also to

---

1. Though strongly marked, as usual, by Christological interpretations, this Exposition is less pastoral and more academic in tone than those which precede and follow it. A written or dictated piece, not a preached sermon.
2. Notably Hilary of Poitiers, a pioneer of prosopological method.
3. Verse 5, below.
4. See Mt 5:16.
5. See Ps 46:7(47:6).

God. The converse is not true, however; not all of the things that please God can give pleasure to human beings, because some of them humans cannot see.

In the light of this distinction it is rather perplexing that we find not only the double invitation, *Sing to God* and *Sing psalms to God*, but also in some other places, *Sing to his name*. If such an expression is indeed to be found in the holy scriptures, the aforesaid distinction has been worked out to no purpose.[6] Moreover, I am impressed by the common usage which calls these sacred songs "psalms" rather than "canticles"—so much so that the Lord spoke of *all that is written about me in the law, and the prophets, and the psalms,*[7] and the book in question is called "The Book of Psalms," not "The Book of Canticles." It is always so referred to, for instance in the passage, *as it is written in the Book of Psalms* (Acts 1:20), although by the criterion discussed above they should rather have been called canticles. I say this because there can be canticles where there is no psalm, but there cannot be a psalm in the absence of a canticle. In other words, there can be thoughts in the mind which do not issue in any corporeal works, but there cannot be any good work that is not thought about in the mind. Thus there are canticles or songs in both instances, but not psalms in both. And yet, as I have said, these songs are called psalms without distinction, not canticles, and the book containing them is the Book of Psalms, not of canticles.

Furthermore, if it comes to discussing the meaning of titles, where we sometimes find *psalms* alone, sometimes *canticles* alone, sometimes *a psalm of a canticle* as in the present case, but at other times *a canticle of a psalm*, I do not see how this principle of differentiation can be maintained. We will therefore leave these matters to people with the ability and the time to draw the distinctions and define the rules. For our part, let us consider and expound the text of the psalm as well as we can with the Lord's help, as we have begun to do.

Verses 2-3. The dispersal of the risen Lord's enemies

2. *Let God arise, and let his enemies be scattered.*[8] This has already happened. Christ has arisen, he who is God, blessed above all for ever;[9] and his enemies, the Jews, have been scattered abroad among all nations. In the very place where their enmity was unleashed against him they have been defeated,

---

6. Because if "sing"—that is, *cantate*, related to canticle—is supposed to refer to inward thoughts, and "his name" to the publication of his praise, "sing to his name" would be a contradiction in terms.

7. Lk 24:44. The last phrase, "the psalms," was sometimes used by the Jews to designate the third great section of the Old Testament, containing all the wisdom writings, foremost among which was the Book of Psalms.

8. The psalm is not crystal clear, and the corrupt text of Augustine's Latin version makes it more obscure still, but the general theme is a celebration of the Lord's victories in his people's history, here presented as a triumphal procession.

9. See Rom 9:5.

and from that place they have been dispersed throughout the world. And now they hate him, yet fear him, and their very fear goads them to act as the psalm goes on to indicate: *and let those who hate him flee before his face.* Spiritual flight is fear; for where can anyone flee in bodily wise from the face of One whose presence is effective and unmistakable everywhere? *Whither shall I go from your spirit, and whither flee from your face?* asks another psalm (Ps 138(139):7). So they flee not corporeally but spiritually, by being afraid, not by going into hiding; and what they flee from is not that face of his that they cannot see, but the face they cannot help seeing. Now his presence is called his face, his presence through his Church. This is what he meant when he said to his overt enemies, *Henceforth you shall see the Son of Man coming in the clouds* (Mt 26:64). He comes in his Church, diffusing it throughout the whole wide world where his enemies have been scattered. But he comes in those special clouds of which he spoke when he declared, *I will forbid my clouds to send rain upon it* (Is 5:6). *Let those who hate him flee before his face*: let them quake with fear at the presence of his saints and his faithful people, those of whom he said, *When you did that for even the least of those who are mine, you did it for me* (Mt 25:40).

3. *Let them fade away as smoke fades away.* The fires of their hatred sent them puffing up proudly; their boastful talk was directed to the sky[10] as they shouted, *Crucify him! Crucify him!* (Jn 19:6). They mocked him as their prisoner, and laughed at him as he hung on the cross; in their victory they were puffed up, but very soon they were vanquished and blown away.

As wax flows liquid in the presence of fire, so may sinners perish before the face of God. This could refer to the hard-heartedness of sinners which melts into tears of repentance; but it could also be a warning about the judgment to come. In this world Christ's enemies have exalted themselves in pride, and so like rising smoke they have faded away; but at the end the final condemnation will come upon them, causing them to disappear before his face into eternal perdition. At the end he will be manifested in his fiery splendor, as torment for the godless and light for the just.

Verse 4. A different joy

4. It continues, *And let the righteous delight, and exult in the sight of God, let them be gladdened in joy*, for then they will hear the invitation, *Come, you who are blessed by my Father, take possession of the kingdom* (Mt 25:34). Let those who have toiled find their delight, and let them *exult in the sight of God.* There will be no vain boasting in that exultation, as there often is when people exult before their fellows, for the exultation of the righteous will be under the gaze of

---

10. See Ps 72(73):9.

him who sees to the depths of what he has given, and is in no way beguiled. *Let them be gladdened in joy*, no longer rejoicing with fear[11] as they did in this world, where their life on earth was one long temptation.[12]

Verses 5-6. Joy in God amid tribulations from the world

5. The psalm now turns toward those to whom it has proffered so great a hope. It addresses them, still living as they are in the world, and invites them, *Sing to God, play psalms to his name*. We spoke about this in the way that seemed appropriate while discussing the psalm's title. Anyone who lives for God sings to God; and anyone who works for his glory sings psalms to his name. By singing thus, by playing psalms thus—I mean by living so, and working so—you must *open a way for him who ascends above the sunset*, says our psalm. Make a pathway for Christ, so that through the beautiful feet of those who bring the good news[13] the hearts of believers may be for him an open way. Christ is the one who ascends above the sunset, either in the sense that the new life of one who is turning toward Christ can receive him only through the sunset of the old life, as the convert renounces the world, or else in the sense that Christ ascends above his own sunset, when by his resurrection he overcomes the decline of his body into death. *For his name is the Lord*. If they had known that, they would never have crucified the Lord of glory.[14]

6. *Exult in his presence*. O you who have just been exhorted, *Sing to God, play psalms to his name; open a way for him who ascends above the sunset*, to you a fresh invitation is offered: *Exult in his presence*, for though you seem sorrowful, in reality your life is unceasing joy.[15] While you are preparing a pathway for him, and opening for him a way through which he will advance to take possession of the Gentiles, you will suffer many grievous things as the world sees it. But you must not only stand firm throughout; you must even exult, not in the presence of other people but in the presence of God. Rejoice in hope, be patient in anguish.[16] *Exult in his presence*, for those who trouble you in the presence of human beings *will themselves be troubled in the presence of God, who is a father to orphans and a vindicator for the widowed*. The world thinks them desolate, those parents who are severed from their children, those husbands sheared away from their wives by the sword of God's word;[17] but the orphaned and the widowed have

---

11. See Ps 2:11.
12. See Jb 7:1.
13. See Is 52:7.
14. See 1 Cor 2:8.
15. See 2 Cor 6:10.
16. See Rom 12:12.
17. See Mt 10:34.35.

God for their consolation, God *who is a father to orphans and a vindicator for the widowed.* They have him for their consolation when they can say, *My father and mother have abandoned me, but the Lord has taken me up* (Ps 26(27):10), and when their hope in the Lord keeps them persevering in prayer night and day.[18] The trouble-makers will be troubled before him when they see that they are achieving nothing, because the whole world has gone after him.[19]

Verse 7. The Lord builds people of one mind and heart into a holy house

7. It is out of these orphans and widows, who no longer have any hope in the secular society that has abandoned them, that the Lord fashions a temple for himself. Accordingly the psalm continues, *The Lord is in his holy place*; and what this holy place of the Lord is, we are told when the psalm speaks of *God, who makes people of the same way of life dwell together in a house.* Those who are of a common mind, those who agree among themselves—these are the Lord's holy place. When the psalm stated that *the Lord is in his holy place*, we might have questioned where such a place could be, since God is entirely present everywhere, and no corporeal space can contain him; so the psalm immediately added the phrase to exclude any possibility of our looking for him anywhere else but in ourselves, and to ensure that by dwelling together in *the same way of life* in our house, we might deserve to be ourselves the place where he deigns to dwell. Nothing else but this is the Lord's holy place, the place so many people search for, a place where they can pray in the conviction that they will be heard. Such people need to become themselves the place they are seeking. What they say, they must say in their hearts, and in those secret rooms be smitten with compunction;[20] they must live together with other *people of the same way of life in a house*, in order to be themselves indwelt by the Master of that great house, and be heard within themselves when they pray. A great house it is, in which are to be found not only gold and silver vessels, but also others of wood and earthenware: some designed for honorable purposes and others for common use. People who have cleansed themselves from all that is dishonorable will share a common way of life with others in the house, and will form the Lord's holy place. Just as in a great house the owner does not take his rest in any unsuitable spot, but only in some place that is private and dignified, so does God dwell not in all those who are found within the house, not in the vessels destined for common use, but in his own holy place, constituted by those *people of the same way of life* whom he causes to *dwell together in the house.* Or we could translate, "He makes people of the same moral conduct dwell together in the house," for the Greek word

---

18. See 1 Tm 5:5.
19. See Jn 12:19.
20. See Ps 4:5(4).

ἔ"ἔ"ῑ can signify either "ways of life" or "moral conduct."[21] The Greek does not have *He who makes* but only *He makes* them dwell together in the house. *The Lord*, then, *is in his holy place*. What place is this? The place God makes for himself, for God *makes people of the same moral conduct dwell together in a house*, and they are his holy place.[22]

8. The next words intimate that he builds this place for himself by his own grace, irrespective of the merits of those from whom he builds it. Look what the psalm says: *He leads out the fettered in fortitude*. He loosens the heavy fetters of sin, which hindered the sinners from walking in the way of his commandments, and he leads them forth in a fortitude which they did not possess before his grace came to them. *And likewise those who provoke him, who dwell in the tombs*; this refers to those who are utterly dead, and are engaged in dead works. They provoke God by rebelling against the call to righteousness, unlike the fettered, who perhaps want to walk in his way, but are unable. These fettered folk pray to God for strength and beg him, *Lead me out from my grievous necessity* (Ps 24(25):17). And when he hears their prayer they thank him, exclaiming, *You have burst my bonds* (Ps 115(116):16). Quite different are the tomb-dwellers. They are of the type to which scripture draws attention elsewhere: *No confession can be made by a dead person: he is as though non-existent* (Sir 17:26). Another text suggests the same: *A person devoid of reverence goes deep into sin and is defiant* (Prv 18:3). It is one thing to long for righteousness, another to fight against it; one thing to want to be set free from wickedness, and another to defend one's wicked deeds rather than confessing them. Yet the grace of Christ *leads forth* both sorts *in fortitude*. What fortitude is meant here? Surely the grace to struggle even to blood against sin.[23] From both these groups are drawn persons fit to be used in the construction of God's holy place: the one because they have been set free, the other because they have been raised from the dead. The Lord with a word of command broke the fetters of a woman bound by Satan for eighteen years,[24] and defeated death in Lazarus with a shout.[25] The same Lord who worked these wonders in their bodies has the power to effect still more wonderful transformations in our conduct; he can *make people of the same way of life dwell together in a house, leading forth the fettered in fortitude, and likewise those who provoke him, who dwell in the tombs*.

---

21. In Latin *modi* or *mores*.
22. In his *Confessions* IX,8,17, Augustine refers to this verse in connection with the desire he shared with his companions, soon after their baptism, to set up house together.
23. See Heb 12:4.
24. See Lk 13:16.
25. See Jn 11:43.44.

Verses 8-10. Rain in the desert of the Gentiles

9. *When you go out ahead of your people, O God.* God is understood to go out when he appears through his works. He appears, not to everyone, but to those with eyes to see what he is doing. I do not mean now the works of God which are evident to all, such as the earth and the sea, and all the creatures in them, but those works whereby *he leads forth the fettered in fortitude, and likewise those who provoke him, who dwell in the tombs,* and that work in which *he makes people of the same moral conduct dwell together in a house.* That is how he goes out in the sight of this people, in full view of those who recognize his grace.

The psalm continues, *When you marched through the desert, the earth trembled.* The Gentiles were a desert, for they had no knowledge of God; where they lived was a desert, because none of the prophets had lived there, or foretold there that the Lord would come. That was why, *when you marched through the desert,* O God, when you were proclaimed among the Gentiles, *the earth trembled,* for earthly men and women were stirred to faith. But what moved the earth? *The skies poured down rain from the face of God.* On hearing this, someone may possibly think of the period when God was journeying through the desert in company with his people, the children of Israel, in a pillar of cloud by day, and a brilliant fire by night.[26] Such a person may then assume that the psalm is referring to the manna God rained down on his people[27] when it says, *The skies poured down rain from the face of God*; and, further, that the next phrase, *Mount Sinai, before the face of the God of Israel, when you allotted gratuitous rain to your inheritance, O God,* is again an allusion to the exodus. God did indeed speak to Moses on Mount Sinai when he gave them the law;[28] and the manna was like a gratuitous rain that God reserved for his inheritance, that is, for his own people, because he fed them only, not other nations. In this same line of interpretation the next phrase, *and it grew weak,* is predicated of God's inheritance because the people murmured and spurned the manna, hungering for the flesh meat they had been accustomed to eat in Egypt.[29]

But this cannot be right. Even if we look only for the precise literal meaning, and disregard the spiritual sense, we would have to show what fettered persons, and what tomb-dwellers, were led forth in fortitude at that time. Furthermore, if that ancient people, that inheritance of God, were being described as "weakened" through its distaste for and rejection of the manna, the psalm could not go on to say, as it does, *But you made it perfect.* It ought rather to say, "But you struck it." And in fact God was offended by their murmuring and finicky atti-

---

26. See Ex 13:21.
27. See Ex 16:13-16.
28. See Ex 19:18-25.
29. See Nm 11:4-6.

tude, so a terrible plague fell upon them.[30] Finally, all of them were laid low in the desert, so that none of them, except two, was found worthy to enter the promised land.[31] We could, perhaps, stretch it to the point of saying, "Well, at least in their descendants the inheritance was made perfect"; but we ought more readily to concentrate on the spiritual meaning, for everything that happened to them had figurative force,[32] until the day should breathe, and the shadows retire.[33]

10. As we knock at the door, then, may the Lord open to us, and may his secret mysteries be revealed to us in the measure that he graciously wills. Now, it is clear that when the gospel was propagated through the desert land of the Gentiles, the earth could be stirred to faith only because *the skies poured down rain from the face of God*. These skies are none other than the heavens of which another psalm said, *The heavens proclaim God's glory*, and of which it goes on to say, *There is no speech, no language, in which their voices are not heard; their sound went forth throughout the world, their words to the ends of the earth* (Ps 18:2.4-5(19:1.3-4)). However, this magnificent glory is not to be ascribed to the heavens, as though the grace that fell upon the desert of the Gentiles, the grace whereby the earth was stirred to faith, derived from human ministers. No, the heavens produced no rain as from themselves, but only *from the face of God*, though certainly he dwelt within them, and had made these men of like moral conduct live together in the same house. They are the preachers of whom it is said elsewhere, *I have lifted my eyes to the mountains, from where comes help for me*. Yet there too the psalm guards against any appearance of reliance on human agents by adding immediately, *My help is from the Lord, who made heaven and earth* (Ps 120(121):1-2). In another text the same point is made: *You send your wondrous light from the eternal mountains* (Ps 75:5(76:4))—from the eternal mountains, yes, but it is you who send it. So too in our present psalm: *the skies poured down rain*, but *from the face of God*. The preachers were themselves saved through faith, and not through any merits of their own: not through works, lest anyone should find grounds for boasting. We are the handiwork[34] of him who *makes people of the same way of life dwell together in a house*.

Fulfillment of the law by grace

11. But what do the next words mean? *Mount Sinai, before the face of the God of Israel*? Perhaps the words "poured down" are to be understood. In that case, what the psalm called *skies* are here referred to under the symbol of Mount Sinai,

---

30. See Nm 11:33.
31. See Nm 14:29-30.
32. See 1 Cor 10:11.
33. See Sg 2:17.
34. See Eph 2:8-10.

just as we have mentioned already that preachers called "heavens" in one psalm are called "mountains" in another. If this interpretation is accepted, it should not worry us that here we have *mount*, not "mountains," whereas the preceding clause spoke of *skies*, not "sky" in the singular. The same switch occurs in another psalm where, after saying, *The heavens proclaim God's glory*, scripture in its customary way repeats the same idea in different words by adding, *and the firmament tells of his handiwork* (Ps 18:2(19:1)). It spoke first of *heavens*, not "heaven," but followed it with *firmament*, not "firmaments." In Genesis it is written that *God called the firmament sky* (Gn 1:8). Obviously, then, heavens and heaven mean the same thing, and so too do mountains and mountain; and similarly we can speak of many churches but one Church, and mean the same thing.

Well now, why does the apostle speak of *Mount Sinai, which bears children into slavery* (Gal 4:24)? Perhaps because by Mount Sinai we are meant to understand the law, which the skies poured down from the face of God, causing the earth to quake. Is this quaking of the earth not an apt symbol of the terror of human beings who find themselves powerless to fulfill the law? And if this is correct, the law is also referred to in the following words about the freely-given rain: *you allotted gratuitous rain to your inheritance, O God.* Gratuitous it was, for God did not deal thus with any other nation, nor did he reveal his judgments to them.[35] He allotted freely-given rain to his inheritance by giving them the law. *And it grew weak*, the psalm continues; this could refer either to the law itself, or to God's inheritance. If the weakening of the law is meant, we could understand it to be saying that the law proved weak because it could not be fulfilled: not that the law was weak in itself, but that it weakened those who should have kept it, by threatening them with punishment but not helping them through grace. The apostle uses the same figure of speech when he says, *God accomplished what the law was powerless to do, weakened as it was by the flesh* (Rom 8:3). He was explaining that the law can be fulfilled only through the Spirit,[36] yet he called the law itself weak, since it cannot be implemented by weak people. Alternatively, we could take the psalm to mean that God's inheritance, that is, his people, became weak when the law was given to it. This is evident and undeniable. *The law stealthily entered, that sin might abound* (Rom 5:20), says scripture.

The next words, *but you made it perfect*, are a statement about the law, which was made perfect, or fulfilled, in the way our Lord indicated in the gospel: *I came not to annul the law, but to bring it to its fullness* (Mt 5:17). The apostle said the same. He had described the law as weakened through the flesh, because flesh is impotent to fulfill what can only be fulfilled spiritually: through spiritual grace,

---

35. See Ps 147:20.
36. Or "in a spiritual way."

that is. Then he explained that this had been allowed *so that the righteousness of the law might be realized in us, who walk not according to the flesh, but according to the spirit* (Rom 8:4). The statement that *you made it perfect* is true because *the fullness of the law is charity* (Rom 13:10), and *the charity of God has been poured out into our hearts*, not by our own doing, but *through the Holy Spirit who has been given us* (Rom 5:5).

The phrase, *but you made it perfect*, is thus satisfactorily explained, if it refers to the perfecting of the law. If, however, it is God's inheritance that is said to be made perfect, the interpretation is easier. If God's inheritance, God's people, is spoken of as having been weakened when the law was given, since *the law stealthily entered, that sin might abound*, then the statement that *you made it perfect* is readily intelligible in the light of the apostle's next words: *but where sin abounded, grace abounded all the more* (Rom 5:20). As sin abounded, their infirmities were multiplied, and thereafter they made haste,[37] because they groaned and called upon God, so that the law, not fulfilled at his command, might be fulfilled by his help.

The "gratuitous rain" is grace. Mount Sinai could represent Paul

12. There is another way of interpreting these words, one that seems to me more probable. It is much more fitting to understand the gratuitous rain as grace, because grace is given freely, where there are no antecedent meritorious works. *If it is grace, it is not a reward for work done, for then grace would not be grace* (Rom 11:6). *I am not worthy to be called an apostle*, said Paul, *because I persecuted God's Church; but by God's grace I am what I am* (1 Cor 15:9-10). This is the gratuitous rain. *Indeed, of his own free will he begot us, by the word of truth* (Jas 1:18). This is the gratuitous rain. The same idea is expressed elsewhere: *you have encompassed us as with the shield of your good will* (Ps 5:13(12)). When God marched through the desert—that is, when he was preached among the Gentiles — *the skies poured down* this rain, not as from their own resources, but *from the face of God*, because they too are what they are only by God's grace. Paul could be thought of as Mount Sinai, inasmuch as he worked harder than any of the others (though it was not he himself, but God's grace with him)[38] to the end that grace might be the more abundantly distilled among the Gentiles. Gentile territory was a desert, where Christ had not been proclaimed, and Paul had no desire to build on anyone else's foundations.[39] Paul, I say, was an Israelite, sprung from the race of Israel and the tribe of Benjamin;[40] and he had been born into slavery, since he belonged to that earthly Jerusalem which even now is in

---

37. See Ps 15:4(16:3-4). When expounding that psalm Augustine explained that their infirmities were multiplied not to destroy them, but to make them cry out for a doctor.
38. See 1 Cor 15:10.
39. See Rom 15:20.
40. See Phil 3:5.

servitude along with her children.[41] This is why he persecuted the Church, for, as he warned us himself, *as at that time the son begotten according to the flesh persecuted the one begotten according to the spirit, so it is today* (Gal 4:29). But Paul obtained mercy, because he acted as he did in ignorance and unbelief.[42] If, then, we marvel that *the skies poured down rain from the face of God*, let us marvel all the more that Mount Sinai poured it down: marvel, I mean, that one who had been a persecutor did this, a Hebrew of Hebrew stock, and a Pharisee with regard to the law.[43] Yet why marvel? He did not send the rain down as from himself, but *from the face of the God of Israel*, and the Israel meant here is that of which Paul himself spoke: *the Israel of God* (Gal 6:16), the Israel to which the Lord was referring when he said, *Look, there is a true Israelite, in whom there is no guile* (Jn 1:47). This, then, is the gratuitous rain which God reserved for his own inheritance, irrespective of any antecedent merits on their part.

And it grew weak, because it knew that it was nothing of itself, and that whatever it was must be ascribed not to its own powers but to the grace of God. It experienced the truth of that saying, *Of nothing but my weaknesses will I boast* (2 Cor 12:9). It experienced also the truth of another saying, *Be not high-minded, but wary* (Rom 11:20). It experienced the truth of the promise, *To the humble God gives grace* (Jas 4:6; 1 Pt 5:5). *It grew weak, but you made it perfect*, for *God's power finds complete scope in our weakness*.[44]

A few codices, both Latin and Greek, have not *Mount Sinai*, but *from the face of the God of Sinai, from the face of the God of Israel*. The psalm has said, *The skies poured down rain from the face of God*, but then, if someone asked, "Of whose God?" it would be adding the precision, *from the face of the God of Sinai, from the face of the God of Israel*, which is to say, "From the face of that God who gave the law to the people of Israel." Why, then, did the skies pour down rain from the face of this God? Because in this way was the prophecy fulfilled: *He who gave the law will give a blessing too* (Ps 83:8(84:6)). He gives the law, and by it terrifies anyone who would rely on human ability to keep it, but he also gives a *blessing*, to set free anyone who hopes in God. Thus have you made your inheritance perfect, O God; for it was weakened in itself in order to be perfected by you.

Verses 11-12. Sweet provision for the poor

13. *Your living creatures will dwell therein*. It says, *Your creatures*, not creatures that are their own property; creatures subject to you, not free for themselves; creatures turned toward you in their need, not toward themselves in

----

41. See Gal 4:25.
42. See 1 Tm 1:13.
43. See Phil 3:5.
44. See 2 Cor 12:9.

self-sufficiency. The psalm continues, *In your sweetness you made provision for the needy, O God.* It stresses, *in your sweetness*; provision was not made from the resources your people has of itself. It is needy, because it has been weakened with a view to its perfecting; it has acknowledged itself as indigent, that it may be filled. This is the sweetness of God, of which it is said elsewhere, *Truly the Lord will give sweetness, and then our earth will yield its fruit* (Ps 84:13(85:12)). It enables the faithful to perform good actions not out of fear but out of love, not through dread of punishment but through delight in righteousness. This is true and healthy freedom. But the Lord has prepared it for the needy, not for the rich to whom such poverty is abhorrent. Of these wealthy folk another text says that it is *a disgrace to the affluent, and contemptible to the proud* (Ps 122(123):4). Significantly, it identifies the affluent with the proud.

14. *The Lord will give his word*—evidently as food for those who dwell there, his own living creatures. But what kind of work will these living creatures do, the ones to whom he will give his word? The work indicated by the following, surely: *to those who preach the good news, with great power.* What power could be envisaged, if not that fortitude in which the Lord leads forth the fettered? There could also be an allusion here to the power which the preachers of the good news demonstrated by the wonderful signs they wrought.

Verse 13. Christ, the beloved, is king of the powers; so too is the Father

15. Who, then, *will give his word to those who preach the good news, with great power?* The psalm tells us: *The King of the Beloved's powers.* The Father is king of the powers that belong to the Son; for when no different "beloved" is indicated, this title, "Beloved," means only the Son, by antonomasia. But is not the Son himself king of his own forces, of the powers that serve him? Surely, yes. Here it is said that the King of the powers will *give his word to those who preach the good news, with great power,* and he is identified elsewhere as the Lord of the powers: *The Lord of Hosts, he is the King of glory.* This interpretation stands even though the psalm did not call him "King of his own hosts," but *King of the Beloved's powers,* for anyone can see that this is a very common turn of speech in scripture. It is most clearly observed in the instances where, though there is a repetition of the proper name, there can be no doubt that the same person is meant. In the Pentateuch many examples are to be found of statements like *and Moses did* so-and-so, *as the Lord commanded Moses.*[45] It does not say, as we would, "Moses did as the Lord commanded him," but, *Moses did as the Lord commanded Moses,* as though the Moses who carried out the order, and the Moses who received it, were two different people, whereas they are, of course, the same. It is difficult to find examples of this idiom in the New Testament, but

---

45. See Nm 17:11, LXX.

there is one when the apostle says, *Concerning his Son, who was made for him from David's line, according to the flesh, but was designated Son of God in power according to the Spirit of holiness by the resurrection of Jesus Christ our Lord from the dead* (Rom 1:3-4). This almost sounds as though the Son of God who was descended from David's line according to the flesh, and our Lord Jesus Christ, were two different persons, whereas they are, of course, one and the same. However, in the books of the Old Testament this figure of speech is found frequently; and therefore when a particular instance of it renders the passage somewhat obscure, it can be understood from clear examples of the same usage elsewhere. It is somewhat obscure in the passage we are dealing with in the present psalm. If it had said, "Jesus Christ, the king of the hosts of Jesus Christ," the meaning would have been as unmistakable as it is in the text, *Moses did as the Lord commanded Moses*. But instead it says, *The king of the Beloved's powers*, so it is not immediately obvious that the one who is king of the powers is the same as he who is the Beloved. Thus *king of the Beloved's powers* is to be understood in the way it would be if the psalm had called him "king of his own powers," because Christ is the king of the powers, the Lord of hosts, and he is also the Beloved.

This interpretation does not, however, so inescapably impose itself as to exclude another, because the Father can be understood to be the king of the hosts of his beloved Son, since that beloved Son himself proclaimed, *All my things are yours, and yours are mine* (Jn 17:10). And if anyone doubts that God, the Father of our Lord Jesus Christ, can be called a king, I would say that it is unthinkable that anyone should deny him that title, in view of the apostle's words, *to the King of ages, immortal, invisible, the only God* (1 Tm 1:17). It is true that this prayer is offered to the whole Trinity, but where the Trinity is, there is God the Father. Furthermore, there is a psalm-verse which prays, *O God, commit your judgment to the king, and your justice to the king's son* (Ps 71:2(72:1)), and provided we do not take this in a carnal sense, I do not see how else it can be understood but as "Give it to your Son." The Father is therefore a king, and accordingly this fragment of our psalm, *king of the Beloved's powers*, can be taken either way.

To sum up: the psalm stated that *the Lord will give his word to those who preach the good news, with great power*. But since this great power is regulated by him who gives it, he who is *the Lord*, who *with great power will give his word to those who preach the good news*, he is rightly said to be *king of the Beloved's powers*.

Having despoiled the devil, Christ distributes his gifts to beautify the Church

16. The psalm proceeds: *It is the Beloved's part also to divide the spoils for the beauty of the house*. The word *Beloved* is repeated for emphasis. But in fact it

is not all the codices that have this repetition, and the more exact among them prefix a star to it. Such signs are called asterisks, and they inform us that the passages so marked are present in the Hebrew, but not in the interpretation by the Septuagint.[46] But whether we think *Beloved* was repeated, or was written once only, I think we must take the words that follow it, *to divide the spoils for the beauty of the house*, in the sense, *it is the Beloved's part also to divide the spoils for the beauty of the house*; that is, he was *chosen*[47] also for the division of the spoils. Undoubtedly the Church which Christ has created is a beautiful house, and he has adorned it by distributing his spoils to it, as a body is made beautiful by the due distribution of its limbs.

Now the word "spoils" is used of goods seized from vanquished enemies, and the gospel throws light on this passage by saying, *No one can get into a strong man's house and carry off his implements, unless he has tied up the strong man first* (Mt 12:29). Christ tied up the devil with spiritual chains by overcoming death and ascending from the underworld to heaven; he bound the devil by the sacrament[48] of his incarnation, because although the devil found nothing in Christ that deserved death, he was nonetheless allowed to kill him. The consequence was that Christ tied up the devil and took away his belongings as booty. These were the unbelievers through whom the devil worked his will.[49] But the Lord cleansed these tools by forgiving their sins; he left the enemy felled and chained, and sanctified the spoils he had seized. He then assigned them to their due places for the adornment of his own house, appointing some to be apostles, some prophets, some pastors and teachers for the work of ministry, for the building up of the body of Christ.[50] *As the body is a unit and has many members, and yet all the members of the body, many though they be, are one body, so too is Christ. Are all of them apostles? Are all prophets? Do all work miracles? Do all have healing gifts? Do all speak in tongues? Do all interpret them? But the one same Spirit is at work in all these operations, distributing appropriate gifts to each one as he wills* (1 Cor 12:12.29-30.11). And all these make for the beauty of the house in which the spoils are distributed. One of its lovers, fired by such beauty, cried out, *Lord, I have loved the beauty of your house!* (Ps 25(26):8).

---

46. An interesting comment: Augustine was aware that the Septuagint (3rd century B.C.) is not always an exact rendering of the Hebrew, but sometimes reflects an advance in understanding.

47. The word translated "Beloved" in this and the preceding section is the genitive of *Dilectus*, signifying the love of choice.

48. *Sacramento.* Originally denoting a sacred oath, especially that taken by soldiers, the word *sacramentum* was used by the Latin New Testament as equivalent to the Greek *ἔεεῶ ῑ* (mystery). Christian writers tended to use it for any visible, tangible reality which mediated or contained something sacred and sanctifying, the outward sign of the redemptive mystery. It is thus applicable above all to the incarnation, as here, or the passion of the Lord.

49. See Eph 2:2.

50. See Eph 4:11-12.

Verses 14-15. The silvery dove

17. In the words that follow, the psalm turns to the members by whom the beautiful house is constituted, and addresses them thus: *If you sleep in the middle of your allotted inheritances,*[51] *the silvery wings of the dove, and between its shoulders in the fresh sheen of gold.*[52] The first problem that confronts us is how to determine the correct order of the words. A sentence begins, *If you sleep,* but how does it end? It is obviously left hanging. Then, what about *the silvery wings of the dove?*[53] It is unclear whether "wings" is nominative, or vocative as though the wings were being addressed. Now, are we to understand the sentence to be completed by the words which preceded this phrase, or by those which follow? I mean, should we take it like this: *The Lord will give his word to those who preach the good news, with great power, if you sleep in the middle of your allotted inheritances,* O you *silvery wings of the dove?* Or like this: *If you sleep in the middle of your allotted inheritances, the silvery wings of the dove will be made white by the snow on Zalmon?* In the latter case it is saying that these wings will be made white if you sleep in the middle of your allotted inheritances; and it seems to be addressing those who are distributed like spoils to enhance the beauty of the house. The sense is: "O you who are distributed for the adornment of the house, through the diverse manifestations of the Spirit for the profit of all, so that to one is given wise utterance through the Spirit, to another knowledgeable speech through the Spirit, to another faith, to another gifts of healing in the same Spirit,[54] and so forth—if you sleep in the middle of your allotted inheritances, the silvery wings of the dove will be made white on Mount Zalmon." Alternatively, the sense could be: "If you, O you silvery wings of the dove, sleep in the middle of your allotted inheritances, they" (here we must understand people who through grace receive forgiveness for their sins) "will be made white on Mount Zalmon." In the Song of Songs the Church is spoken of in similar terms: *Who is this, who comes up washed white?*[55] And we hold God's promise that *though your sins be brilliant scarlet,*[56] *I will make you as white as snow* (Is 1:18).

---

51. *Inter medios cleros.* The Latin *clerus* (derived from the Greek Γ̔ φ̔""ῖ) meant an allotted portion of land, an inheritance; then by extension an appointment or office in the Church; hence "clergy," as Augustine explains in section 19 below. In the psalm the original reference seems to have been to the Reubenites who stayed at home guarding their sheepfolds and flocks when other tribes went forth to battle; see Jgs 5:16.

52. The text as found in Augustine's Latin version is evidently very corrupt. He struggles to make sense of it.

53. He discusses whether *pennae* is to be taken as a genitive singular, or as a plural, and opts for the plural. A sentence has been omitted from the translation.

54. See 1 Cor 12:7-9.

55. See Sg 3:6; 4:2.

56. *Phoenicium,* so called from the Syrian origin of a purple-red dye.

Another possibility is to understand the verb "you will be" with the phrase *silvery wings of the dove*. The sense would then be: "O you who are distributed like spoils for the adornment of the house, if you sleep in the middle of your allotted inheritances you will be the silver wings of the dove." That is, you will be borne up to higher things, while still holding fast to the structure of the Church. Certainly I can think of no better way of identifying the silver-decked dove than to take it as the Church, of which God says in scripture, *One only is my dove* (Sg 6:8). The Church is decked with silver because it is instructed by the words of God, and in another place the Lord's words are said to be *silver tried by fire for the earth, purified seven times* (Ps 11:7(12:6)). It is therefore a wonderful privilege to sleep in the middle of one's allotted inheritances, which some commentators take to be the two Testaments. Thus to sleep in the middle of one's allotted inheritances would be to rest in the authority of the Old and New Testaments, and to acquiesce in the teachings of both, so that when any teaching is demonstrably established by them, all dispute may be terminated in peace and quiet.

If this last interpretation is the right one, what are they being told, those who preach the good news with great power? Surely that the Lord will give his word to them, and so enable them to preach the gospel, only if they sleep in the middle of their allotted inheritances. Only if they are careful not to desert the authority of the two Testaments is the word of truth given to them. If they hold to it, they themselves are the silver wings of the dove, and by their preaching the Church is gloriously borne up to heaven.

18. *Between its shoulders.* The shoulders are, of course, a part of the body, a part near the region of the heart, only at the back. The psalm says that this part of the silver-decked dove is in the fresh sheen of gold, which means the vigor of wisdom. I think we can hardly do better than understand this vigor to be charity.[57] But why is it located at the back, rather than at the breast? Admittedly I am rather puzzled by the way the word is used in another psalm, where we read, *He will overshadow you between his shoulders, and you will find security beneath his wings* (Ps 90(91):4); for only someone held against his breast could be overshadowed by his wings. Perhaps, though, the phrase which comes through in our translation as *between the shoulders* can really be understood as either front or back, so that "shoulders" simply suggests the two sides, between which the head is situated. The Hebrew may be ambiguous, and capable of bearing this sense; but the Greek has *ἰεōῖῖ ῖ˜* , which can only mean the back parts; and so we get *between its shoulders*.

Is the fresh sheen of gold—wisdom and charity, that is—said to be there between the shoulders because the roots of the wings are there? Or is it rather because that is where the light burden is carried? What else are the wings but the

---

57. Variant: "... which means the green freshness of wisdom. I think ... this green freshness to be charity."

twin commandments of charity, on which depend the entire law and the prophets?[58] What is the light burden, if not the charity which finds its perfect expression in these two commandments? Though the commandments seem hard, fulfilling them is a light matter to one who loves. The saying, *My burden is light* (Mt 11:30), can be rightly understood only as describing our experience of the gift of the Holy Spirit, through whom charity is poured abroad in our hearts,[59] enabling us to perform freely what anyone who obeys out of fear can do only like a slave. If someone does what is right, wishing all the time that the right course were not imposed by precept, that person is no friend of right conduct.

The unity of the two Testaments, and unity among ourselves

19. Another question arises now: why did the psalm say, *In the middle of your allotted inheritances*, rather than simply, "among your allotted inheritances"? What can *in the middle of your allotted inheritances* mean?[60] I will explain what this expression, "in the middle," means to me. Scripture often uses the word "middle" to express a conjunction or agreement between two parties that excludes any dissension between them. Thus the word is used when God establishes a covenant between himself and his people. Our version has *between me and you*,[61] but the Greek has *in the middle of me and you*.[62] Similarly when God speaks to Abraham about the sign of circumcision, he says in our version, *It shall be a covenant between me and you, and all your issue* (Gn 17:7); but the Greek has *In the middle of me and you, and in the middle of your issue*.[63] Again, when God spoke to Noah about the bow which he was putting in the sky as a sign,[64] the phrase is constantly repeated, and where our codices have *between me and you*, or *between me and every living soul*, and so on, we find in the Greek ὃ ν ᾀ ἠέ ''', which means *in the middle of me and you*. David and Jonathan likewise agreed on a sign, so that there would be no divergence of interests between them,[65] and where our version has *between the two of them*, the Greek again has this expression ὃ ν ᾀ ἠέ '''.

It is fortunate, therefore, that in the current verse of our psalm the translators did not put "among your allotted inheritances,"[66] which would have been our

---

58. See Mt 22:40.
59. See Rom 5:5.
60. A sentence is omitted here: he discusses a more literal rendering of the Greek into Latin, which would result in *inter medium clerorum* instead of what his Latin version gives him: *inter medios cleros*.
61. *Inter me et vos.*
62. In Augustine's Latin version *inter medium meum et vestrum.*
63. *Inter medium meum et tuum, et inter medium seminis tui.*
64. See Gn 9:12.
65. See 1 Sm 20:23.42.
66. *Inter cleros.*

ordinary idiom, but *in the middle of your allotted inheritances*,[67] which more literally renders the Greek and is the usual way of speaking about two terms which must agree, as I have explained. Scripture is admonishing us that those who either are already the silver-bedecked wings of the dove, or hope to become so, should sleep in the middle of their allotted inheritances. Well now, if these allotted inheritances symbolize the two Testaments, what we are being warned about is surely this: we must offer no resistance to these two Testaments which are in mutual accord, but rather peacefully consent to them through our understanding; and, further, that we should ourselves be a sign and example of their concord, realizing that neither of them has said anything to contradict the other. When we demonstrate this agreement between the two, we do so with a peaceful admiration which resembles the sleep of ecstasy.

But why should the two Testaments be called inheritances? The word[68] certainly derives from Greek, but it does not mean testament. The reason is that through a will or testament a person is awarded an inheritance; and in Greek inheritance is $\tilde{\iota}\tilde{\iota}^{\nu\nu\nu\nu\vartheta}\tilde{\alpha}\sim$, and an heir is $\tilde{\iota}\tilde{\iota}^{\nu\nu\epsilon\nu}\tilde{\iota}$. But $\tilde{\iota}\tilde{\omega}^{\nu\nu}\tilde{\iota}$ in Greek implies a lot, or allotted portion, and the territories allotted by God's promise are called the parts of the inheritance. These were distributed to the people. The tribe of Levi, however, was commanded to hold no lot among its brethren, because it was to be supported by their tithes.[69] I think that those who have been ordained within the ranks of the ecclesiastical hierarchy are called clergy or clerics because Matthias, whom we read to have been the first person ordained by the apostles, was chosen by lot.[70] To sum up, then: to inherit something as your lot is the result of a will or testament, and so the two Testaments are called "lots," the name of the effect being transferred to the cause.

Another interpretation of a difficult verse: the "sleep" is a Christian death

20. There is still another interpretation of the verse which occurs to me, and, unless I am mistaken, a preferable one. We can with greater probability understand the "lots" or "allotted portions" as the very stuff of the inheritances. The inheritance promised by the Old Testament is earthly happiness, though this was a foreshadowing of what was to come. But the inheritance promised by the New Testament is eternal immortality. To sleep between (or "in the middle of") the allotted inheritances means not passionately seeking the former, and patiently awaiting the latter. People who serve God for the sake of happiness in this life and on this earth, or, rather, are unwilling to serve him because that is what they

---

67. *Inter medios cleros.*
68. *Clerus.*
69. See Nb 18:20-24.
70. See Acts 1:26.

are pursuing, lose their sleep over it; they cannot drop off to sleep. They are fretted by greedy desires, and incited to sins and crimes. What with the desire to acquire it and the fear that they may lose it, they get no rest at all. How different is Wisdom's teaching: *Anyone who listens to me will dwell in hope, finding rest and not fearing any malicious attack* (Prv 1:33). As I see it, this is what sleeping between the lots, or between the inheritances, amounts to. We dwell in hope of our heavenly inheritance, though we do not yet possess it in reality; and we are completely untroubled by greed for earthly fortune. But when our hope is fulfilled we shall no longer rest between two inheritances, for we shall reign in the new inheritance, the true one of which the old was only a shadow.

This explanation holds good even if we want to take the phrase, *if you sleep in the middle of your allotted inheritances*, to mean, "if you die in the middle of your allotted inheritances." It can quite well be taken that way, if we assume that the psalm has used the common scriptural idiom and called death a falling asleep. It is an excellent death when someone perseveres to the end in restraining his or her desire from earthly things, and hoping for our heavenly inheritance, and closes the last day of life in that frame of mind. People who fall asleep like that will be the silver wings of the dove, so that at the time of their resurrection they may be snatched up into the air to meet Christ in the clouds, and live for ever with the Lord.[71] Or we could equally well say that through people who die in such dispositions the Church becomes widely known, enjoying a sublime and unassailable reputation and lifted upon the wings of noble praise. With good reason are we warned, *Praise no one before his death* (Sir 11:30).

God had his saints from the dawn of the human race until the time of the apostles, saints who had the insight to say, *I have never craved the human light of day, as you know* (Jer 17:16), and *One thing have I begged of the Lord, and that will I seek after* (Ps 26(27):4). From the time of the apostles, when the difference between the two Testaments was more clearly revealed, there have been many saints again: the apostles themselves, the blessed martyrs and all the other righteous men and women. All of these, the rams and the rest of the flock[72] down to our own day, have slept in the middle of their allotted inheritances, already spurning the prosperity offered by an earthly kingdom and hoping for the eternal kingdom of heaven, though they did not yet possess it. And because of their holy deaths the Church can take wing upon them; the Church, like a silvery dove, is lifted high upon humanity's praise. By their renown generations invited later are stirred to emulation, with the result that all these others too fall asleep in like manner, and acquire their wings. Thus the Church is manifested in its sublimity, even to the end of the world.

---

71. See 1 Th 4:16-17.
72. See Exposition of Psalm 64, 18. The rams are the apostles, leaders of the flock.

Verse 15. The Spirit overshadows the "kings"

21. *When he who is above the heavens distinguishes kings upon her, they will be made white by the snow on Zalmon.* Clearly he who is above the heavens is he who ascended on high, beyond the heavens, to fill all things.[73] He *distinguishes kings upon her*: that is, upon the silvery dove of which we have been hearing; for the apostle continues, *Some he gave to be apostles, some prophets, some evangelists, some pastors and teachers.* What can "distinguishing kings upon her" mean, except that he gave all these *for the work of service, for the building up of the body of Christ* (Eph 4:11-12)? This must be the meaning, because the dove is the body of Christ. They are called kings because they rule,[74] and nowhere do they rule more effectively than over the desires of the flesh, so that sin may not reign in their mortal bodies to induce them to obey its lusts, nor their members be put at the service of iniquity to fight in the cause of sin, but rather that they may hold themselves ready for God like people risen alive from the dead, with their members mobilized to fight for the righteous cause of God.[75] These kings are in the first place distinguished from foreigners because they do not bear the yoke with unbelievers; but then they are distinguished among themselves by the diversity of their personal gifts, which yet contribute to the harmony of the whole. *Are all of them apostles? Are all prophets? Are all teachers? Do all have healing gifts? Do all speak in tongues? Do all interpret them? But the one same Spirit is at work in all these operations, distributing appropriate gifts to each one as he wills* (1 Cor 12:29-30.11). By giving the Spirit, he who is above the heavens distinguishes kings upon the silvery dove.

Now, when an angel was sent to his grace-filled mother, the angel spoke about the Spirit. She asked how it was possible that she would give birth, when she was a virgin; and the angel replied, *The Holy Spirit will come upon you, and the power of the Most High will overshadow you* (Lk 1:35). But what does *he will overshadow* signify, if not "will create a shadow"? And from this we can see why the kings *will be made white with snow on Zalmon*, when by the grace of the Lord Christ's Spirit they are distinguished on the silver-decked dove; for Zalmon means "Shadow." They are not distinguished from other people by any merit or virtue of their own, for *Who distinguishes you? What have you that you did not receive?* (1 Cor 4:7). Their sins are forgiven, to distinguish them from the godless, forgiven by him who promises, *Though your sins be brilliant scarlet, I will make you as white as snow* (Is 1:18). So this is how *they will be made white on Zalmon*, by the grace of Christ's Spirit, through whom also their individual gifts are given, each distinct from each. As I have already mentioned, it was said

---

73. See Eph 4:10.
74. *Reges . . . a regendo.*
75. See Rom 6:12-13.

that because of the overshadowing of the Spirit, *The child that will be born of you will be called holy, the Son of God* (Lk 1:35). This shadow can be understood as a shelter against the raging heat of carnal concupiscence, and accordingly the Blessed Virgin conceived Christ not through carnal desire but through spiritual faith. But a shadow is cast by the combination of light and some kind of body. And so too the Word who was in the beginning, the true Light, was made flesh and dwelt among us[76] in order to be a shade for us against the midday heat. Humanity was brought into conjunction with God, like a body to the light, and he covered with his protective shadow all those who believed in him. The shadow I mean is not like that of which it is said, *All these things have passed away like a shadow* (Wis 5:9), nor like that of which the apostle speaks: *No one should take you to task in the matter of food or drink, or the observance of a festival day, or a new moon, or the Sabbath, for these are but a shadow of what was to come* (Col 2:16-17). Rather is it the same shadow of which a psalm prays, *Protect me under the shadow of your wings* (Ps 16(17):8). When, therefore, he who is above the heavens distinguishes kings upon the silvery dove, they neither parade their merits nor trust in their own strength; but *they will be made white on Zalmon.* Through grace they will be made brilliantly white, within the protective shadow of Christ's body.

Verse 16. The mountain of nourishment and strength

22. With this in mind the psalm calls this mountain *the mountain of God, a rich mountain, a mountain full of curds* or *a lush mountain*. What does *lush* suggest, if not *rich*? There is indeed a mountain that can be so called, and it is *Zalmon*. But what other mountain than Christ the Lord himself should we regard as *the mountain of God, a rich mountain, a mountain full of curds*? Of him another prophet says, *In the last days the mountain of the Lord's house shall be manifested above all other mountains* (Is 2:2). He is like a mountain curdled into cheese because he tends with the milk of his grace the little ones who need nourishment; he is also a rich mountain because he strengthens and enriches us with his most excellent gifts. I say this because milk, from which cheese is made, is a wonderful symbol of grace. It flows from the abundance in a mother's breast, and is poured into babies free of charge, as delicious and tender mercy.

The Greek is slightly ambiguous here, because the word for mountain is neuter in Greek, and therefore we cannot be sure whether it is nominative or accusative. Some Latin translators have taken it as nominative, others as accusative. I think the latter gives the better sense: *on* (or onto) *Zalmon, the mountain of God*, as we have done our best to explain.

---

76. See Jn 1:1-14.

Verse 17. Christ is the mountain in a unique sense

23. No one should dare to infer from the fact that Christ is called *the mountain of God, a mountain full of curds, a rich mountain*, that he is being compared with the saints, who are also referred to as God's mountains. This title is indeed used of them, for we read, *Your justice is like God's mountains* (Ps 35:7(36:6)), and the apostle says that God made Christ into sin *so that in him we might become the justice of God* (2 Cor 5:21). These mountains are mentioned again elsewhere, in the text, *You send your wondrous light from the eternal mountains* (Ps 75:5(76:4)), for eternal life was given to them, and through them the supreme, most eminent authority of the holy scriptures was established. But it is God who radiates from them; that is why the psalm says, *You send your light*. Again, another psalm says, *I have lifted my eyes to the mountains, from where comes help for me*, but it states clearly that these mountains are not the source of the expected help, by adding, *My help is from the Lord, who made heaven and earth* (Ps 120(121):1-2). One of those mountains, a very eminent one, told us that he had labored harder than any of the others, but he immediately added, *Only not I, but the grace of God with me* (1 Cor 15:10). There were some people who thought our Lord was John the Baptist, others that he was Elijah, or Jeremiah, or some other one of the prophets;[77] but to exclude the possibility that anyone might compare these mountains—mere children of men—to him who is fairer than any of the children of men,[78] the psalm turns to the proponents of rash views and demands, *Why do you surmise that those other mountains full of curds are the one mountain in which it has pleased God to make his home?*

Why do you surmise that? Those others were light, in a sense, for they were told, *You are the light of the world* (Mt 5:14), but very different is he who is called *the true Light, who enlightens every human person* (Jn 1:9). So too they were mountains, but vastly different is he who is the mountain established above all other mountains. Those other mountains are glorious only because they are beneath his feet; one of them who knew this prayed, *Far be it from me to glory, save in the cross of our Lord Jesus Christ, in whom the world has been crucified to me, and I to the world; let anyone who glories, glory not in self, but in the Lord* (Gal 6:14; 1 Cor 1:31).

Why, then, *do you surmise that those other mountains full of curds are the one mountain in which it has pleased God to make his home?* This is not to say that God dwells in no other, but he dwells in them through Christ. With Christ himself it is different: in him *all the fullness of the Godhead dwells in bodily wise* (Col 2:9), not in a shadowy way, as once he dwelt in the temple built by King Solomon, but *bodily*; that is to say, substantially and truly. Scripture says that

---

77. See Mt 16:14.
78. See Ps 44:3(45:2).

God was in Christ, reconciling the world to himself (2 Cor 5:19). We could take this in either of two ways. The subject could be the Father, and the saying would then accord with our Lord's own statement that *The Father, who abides in me, himself performs the works. I am in the Father, and the Father is in me* (Jn 14:10). Alternatively, *God was in Christ* could mean that the Word was in a man. The Word was present in his flesh in such a way that only the Word could strictly be said to have been made flesh; that is, humanity was united to the Word to become the one person of Christ.

Why, then, *do you surmise that those other mountains full of curds are the one mountain in which it has pleased God to make his home?* It pleased God to dwell in Christ quite otherwise than as he dwells in other mountains, to which you would assimilate him. True, they are children of God, but by the grace of adoption. The Only-Begotten is not to be compared with them; to him it could be said, *Sit at my right hand, until I make your enemies into your footstool* (Ps 109(110):1).

For there the Lord will dwell to the end. This indicates that our Lord himself will dwell in those mountains which are not to be equated with this one mountain established above the summits of all the others. He will dwell in them in order to lead them *to the end*, that is, to himself, that they may contemplate him as he is, as God; for *Christ is the end of the law, bringing justification to everyone who believes* (Rom 10:4). It has pleased God to dwell in this one mountain, set above all mountain-peaks, this mountain to whom he says, *You are my beloved Son, in whom I am well pleased* (Mk 1:11; Lk 3:22). This mountain is nothing other than the Lord himself, who will abide in the other mountains, above which he is set, to the end. *There is one God, and one mediator between God and humankind, the man Christ Jesus* (1 Tm 2:5), who is the mountain of mountains, as he is the holy one of all holy ones.[79] This is why he prays, *May I be in them, as you are in me* (Jn 17:23).

So then, *Why do you surmise that those other mountains full of curds are the one mountain in which it has pleased God to make his home?* The Lord himself is the mountain full of curds, and he will dwell to the end in those other mountains full of curds, that they may become the reality to whom he says, *Without me you can do nothing* (Jn 15:5).

Verse 18. God's triumphant, joyful chariot

24. The next verse confirms this interpretation. *God's chariots are ten thousands multiplied*, it says. Other codices have *tens of thousands multiplied* or *ten times a thousand.* Each Latin translator rendered the same Greek word as best he

---

79. Or "the holy of holies" or "the saint of saints," *sanctus sanctorum.*

could: the word is *ἐ ι οει* . It cannot be exactly represented in Latin, because the Greeks express a thousand by *χί~*, several tens of thousands by *ἐ ιοιι* , and once ten thousand by *ἐ ιοι* . However, the psalm indicates an enormous number of holy and faithful people, who by bearing God become, as it were, God's chariot. By abiding in them and guiding them he steers them to the end, as he would direct a chariot to its appointed goal. Scripture speaks of *Christ in the lead, then those who are his in attendance on him; and then comes the end* (1 Cor 15:23-24). This multitude is holy Church,[80] and the Church is *thousands of joyful people*, as the psalm goes on to say. They *rejoice in hope* as they are led forward toward that end which they now await with patience.[81] It is very striking that immediately after describing them as *thousands of joyful people* the psalm adds, *The Lord is in them*. It is true that *we have to enter God's kingdom by way of many tribulations* (Acts 14:21), but, all the same, *the Lord is in them*. This is why they are *as if sorrowful, but always with cause for joy* (2 Cor 6:10); they are not in possession of their end, for they have not arrived there yet, but they are *rejoicing in hope, and patient in anguish* (Rom 12:12), because *the Lord is in them, on Sinai, in the holy place*. In some interpretations of Hebrew names we find Sinai translated as "The Commandment"; there are other suggestions, but I think this is the interpretation that fits best here. The psalm is telling us why those thousands who form God's chariot are rejoicing, and it says, *The Lord is in them, on Sinai, in the holy place*. This means, therefore, "The Lord is in them, in the commandment"; and this commandment is holy, as the apostle says: *Beyond question the law is holy, and the commandment is holy, just and good* (Rom 7:12). Yet what could the commandment achieve, if the Lord were not there? Of him it is said, *It is God who is at work in you, inspiring both will and work, for his own good purpose* (Phil 2:13). A commandment imposed in the absence of any help from God is simply a letter that kills,[82] for *the law entered stealthily that sin might abound* (Rom 5:20). But since *the fullness of the law is charity* (Rom 13:10), the law can be observed only through charity, not through fear. But now *the charity of God has been poured out into our hearts through the Holy Spirit who has been given us* (Rom 5:5), and that is what makes these thousands joyful. They have achieved the righteousness demanded by the law in the measure that the Spirit of grace helps them, for *the Lord is in them, on Sinai, in the holy place*.

---

80. The imagery of God's triumphal procession through his people's history becomes explicit here.
81. See Rom 8:25.
82. See 2 Cor 3:6.

Verse 19. Christ takes captivity captive

25. The next words are addressed directly to our Lord. *You ascended on high, you took captivity captive, and you have received gifts among men and women,* says the psalm. The apostle quotes this verse, and expounds it with reference to Christ our Lord, in the following words: *To each of us is given grace in the measure of Christ's bounty, which is why scripture says, Ascending to the heights, he led captivity captive, he gave gifts to men and women. But what does it imply to say that he ascended, if not that he first descended to the lowest parts of the earth? But he who descended is also he who ascended above all the heavens, to fill all things* (Eph 4:7-10). It is unmistakably to Christ that these words are spoken, *You ascended on high, you took captivity captive, and you have received gifts among men and women.* It should not worry us that when the apostle quotes the text he says, *He gave gifts to men and women,* rather than *you have received gifts among men and women.* By his apostolic authority he spoke thus because the Son is God, together with the Father. Accordingly he *gave gifts to men and women* by sending them the Holy Spirit, who is the Spirit of the Father and of the Son. But Christ is acknowledged to be present also in his body, which is the Church, because his holy and faithful ones are his members, and they are reminded that *You are Christ's body, and his limbs* (1 Cor 12:27). Certainly Christ has ascended on high, and is seated at the Father's right hand,[83] but if he were not also here on earth, he could not have cried out, *Saul, Saul, why are you persecuting me?* (Acts 9:4). And since he himself assures us that *what you did for even the least of those who are mine, you did for me* (Mt 25:40), can we doubt that in the persons of his members he receives the gifts his members receive?

26. But what is the meaning of the statement, *you took captivity captive?* Does it say this because he defeated death, which held people captive and tyrannized over them? Or is it calling the prisoners themselves "captivity," because they were held captive under the devil's dominion? This mystery is alluded to in the title of another psalm: *When the house was being built after the captivity* (Ps 95(96):1), which suggests the Church after the influx of the Gentiles. Thus the psalm is calling the people who were held captive "captivity," much as we call men who do military service "militia." And it says that this captivity has been taken captive by Christ. After all, why should captivity not be a happy experience? People can be caught for good purposes, which is why Peter was told, *Henceforth it is people that you will be catching* (Lk 5:10). They are captives because they have been caught in this way, caught because they have been subjected to the yoke. Under that kindly yoke[84] they are free from the sin to

83. See Mk 16:19.
84. See Mt 11:30.

which they used to be enslaved, and are slaves of the righteousness from which they earlier were free.[85] He who *gave gifts to men and women* and *received gifts among men and women* is present in them. In this captivity, in this enslavement, in this chariot and under this yoke there are, therefore, *thousands of joyful people.* The Lord *is in them, on Sinai, in the holy place.*

A different interpretation of the name *Sinai* takes it to mean "Measure," and this fits in equally well with the foregoing exposition. When the apostle was speaking about the gifts that bring spiritual joy, in the passage already discussed, he said, *To each of us is given grace, in the measure of Christ's bounty,* and then went on to quote the words of our psalm: *ascending to the heights, he led captivity captive, he gave gifts to men and women,* though the psalm says, *You received gifts among men and women.* What better harmony could there be between these two statements of the truth? And what could be plainer?

27. But something more is added: *and indeed, those who did not believe that they would dwell* (or, as some codices have it, *the unbelievers;* but unbelievers, and those who do not believe, come to the same thing). It is not easy to say who these are. It seems that the psalm adds the phrase to explain the words that precede it; so, after saying, *You took captivity captive, and you have received gifts among men and women,* it continues, *And indeed, those who did not believe that they would dwell.* But what is this all about? To whom is it referring?

Possibly the psalm is giving a more precise indication of why their earlier captivity was bad, the one that preceded their passage to the good captivity, I mean. They were the property of the devil because they refused to believe, the devil *who is now at work through the children of unbelief.* And you, scripture continues, *you were among them once, when you lived so* (Eph 2:2-3). He who received gifts among men and women took that captivity captive by the gifts of his grace, and those he captured were people who did not believe that they would dwell in God's house. Faith set them free from this captivity, so that now as believers they dwell in God's house; in fact they have themselves become God's house, and God's chariot, made of thousands of joyful people.

Verses 20-21. Praise of God who heals, saves, and shares our death

28. The singer foresaw these events in spirit, and he was filled with joy himself. He burst into a hymn: *Blessed be the Lord God, blessed be the Lord God from day to day.* Some codices have *by day, and every day,*[86] following the Greek, ὡˢ ἡ˘ ˷"ῖ˷" Δὼˢ ἡ˷" ˷", which is better translated *by day, and every day.* But I think that expression means the same as *from day to day.* Every day, and even to

---

85. See Rom 6:18.
86. *Die quotidie.*

the end, the Lord continues to take captivity captive, and to receive gifts among men and women.

29. Now he is steering his chariot toward its destination, its end; and so the psalm continues, *The God who constantly heals us*[87] *will prosper our journey; he is our God, the God who saves*. There is great stress here on grace. Who would be saved,[88] if he did not heal us?

It may occur to us to wonder why, if we have been saved by his grace, we still have to die. The psalm answers our thought by immediately adding, *And the Lord owns our death*.[89] It seems to be challenging us: "You are born to the human condition; why do you resent having to make your exit through death? Your Lord himself made his exit in no other way than through death. You ought to find that a comfort, rather than being resentful, for *the Lord owns our death*." We are saved, yes, but in hope, and if we hope for what we do not yet see, we must wait for it with patience.[90] So let us bear even death itself patiently, inspired by the example of him who, though he had committed no sin and owed no debt to death, though he was the Lord whose life no one could snatch away, yet laid down his life of his own accord. He, even he, ended his life in death.

Verse 22. The enemies' proud heads will be shattered

30. *Yet God will dash to pieces the heads of his enemies, the hairy scalps of those who persistently walk in their offenses*; this means the heads of those who brag and boast, taking great pride in those offenses which at the very least ought to have humbled them and brought them to the point of praying, *Lord, be merciful to me, a sinner*. But he will shatter their heads, because *anyone who exalts himself will be humbled* (Lk 18:13.14). Although the Lord made our death his own, he died in his flesh not out of any necessity, but by his free choice, for this same Lord is God; and therefore *he will dash to pieces the heads of his enemies*, not only those who insulted him on the cross, wagging their heads and jeering, *Let him come down from the cross, if he is the Son of God*,[91] but all others who proudly rear up against his teaching, and make light of his death as that of a mere man, for he is the one of whom they said, *Others he saved; himself he cannot save* (Mk 15:31; Mt 27:42). But he is *the God who constantly heals us, the God who saves*, and in order to leave us an example of humility and patience,

---

87. *Sanitantium nostrarum*. Variants include *sanitatum nostrarum* and *salutarium nostrarum*.
88. Or "safe."
89. *Et Domini exitus mortis*. At the Old Testament level this must have meant something like "Our escape from death is the Lord's doing," but Augustine reads it as a prophecy that Christ the Lord would make our death his own.
90. See Rom 8:24.
91. See Mt 27:40.

and to blot out with his own blood the record of our sins,[92] he made our death his own, so that we henceforth should fear not the death of the body, but rather that other death from which his bodily death has set us free.

Mocked and killed he was, yet *he will dash to pieces the heads of his enemies.* In another psalm he says, *Raise me up; then I will requite them* (Ps 40:11(41:10)), and he will keep that promise in two ways: by rendering good for evil, as he subjects the heads of believers to himself, or by meting out just punishment to the unjust, when he crushes the heads of the proud. Either way, the heads of his enemies are dashed to pieces and shattered, for they are beaten down from their pride, to be either corrected by humility or snatched away to the depths of hell.

Verses 23-24. The Lord turns toward us, and turns us toward himself

31. *The Lord said, I will turn away from Bashan*, or, as some codices have it, *I will turn them away from Bashan.*[93] He does turn us round so that we may be saved, for, as was said of him in the preceding verse, he is *the God who constantly heals us, the God who saves.* Moreover the psalms elsewhere beg him, *Convert us, Lord God of hosts; show us your face, and we shall be saved* (Ps 79:20(80:19)), and again, *Convert us, O God our constant healer* (Ps 84:5(85:4)). He promises, *I will turn them away from Bashan.* Now *Bashan* is understood to mean "Confusion." What can turning them away from confusion mean—what else but that he will convert those who in their confusion over their sins pray for God's mercy to forgive them? This was the attitude of the tax collector who was so confused when he examined himself that he did not dare even to raise his eyes to heaven. But he went home justified because *the Lord said, I will turn them away from Bashan.*

Bashan is also interpreted "Drought," and this too makes good sense. The Lord turns us away from drought, which symbolizes destitution; but those who think themselves wealthy when in fact they are starving, or full when they are completely empty, are not converted, for *blessed are those who hunger and thirst for righteousness, for they shall be satisfied* (Mt 5:6). From drought like this the Lord turns us away; that is why a parched soul says to him, *To you have I stretched out my hands; my soul is like waterless earth before you* (Ps 142(143):6).

The reading found in other codices, *I will turn away from Bashan*, also yields good sense, for God himself does turn toward us. He tells us, *Turn to me, and I shall turn to you, says the Lord* (Zec 1:3), and this must mean beyond the confusion we are in when our sin is constantly confronting us,[94] and well away from

---

92. See Col 2:14.
93. *Convertar*, passive with reflexive sense, or *convertam*, active. Augustine considers both possibilities.
94. See Ps 50:5(51:3).

the drought-stricken land where we long for a shower from God, who has allotted gratuitous rain to his inheritance. His inheritance is faint with thirst, but he turns to it and makes it perfect, he to whom the acknowledgment is made, *You turned and put new life into me* (Ps 70(71):20).

So then, *I will turn them away from Bashan; I will turn them into the depth of the sea*. It is easy to understand *I will turn them*, but why *into the depth of the sea*? When the Lord turns us round for our salvation, he turns us toward himself, and he is certainly not the depth of the sea. It may be that our translation is mistaken here: it should have said, *to the very depth*.[95] It is not God who turns, but he does turn people who lie sunken in the depths of this world, weighed down by their sins. Someone who had been there prayed after being converted, *Out of the depths I have cried to you, Lord* (Ps 129(130):1).

If we take the other reading, however, *I will turn to the depth of the sea*, we can understand this as spoken by our Lord, who in his mercy turned even to the deep places of the sea to rescue the most abandoned of sinners. I must admit, however, that in one Greek text I found not *into the depth*, but *in the depth*, ἥ͂ ἰε͂͂ρῖ; and this supports the former interpretation, that even there God turns toward himself those who cry to him from the depths. But if we read the passive, and think of the Lord turning there himself to liberate such sinners, it still makes sense. He turns them, or himself turns to them to free them, in such a way that his foot is dipped in blood. This is what the prophet says to the Lord: *So that your foot is dipped in blood*. What it means is this: those who turn toward you, or those to whom you turn to set them free, even though they have been held down in the depth of the sea by the load of their iniquity, make such progress through your grace—for *where sin abounded, grace has abounded all the more* (Rom 5:20)—that they find a place among your members; they become your foot, swift to proclaim your gospel and endure a long-drawn martyrdom for your name, fighting even to the shedding of their blood. This, I consider, is the better way to understand the reference to his foot being dipped in blood.

The Lord's faithful dogs

32. Then it adds, *The tongues of your dogs, once enemies, his doing*. He calls them dogs, these same people who have been destined to fight even to blood for the faith of the gospel, because they bark for their Lord. They are not the kind of dogs the apostle meant when he said, *Beware of dogs!*[96] The dogs envisaged here are those who *eat from the crumbs that fall from their masters' tables*. The

---

95. *In profundum*, as some might say, "in depth."
96. Phil 3:2. The Jews referred to the Gentiles as "dogs"; Paul used it disparagingly of Jews who did not accept the gospel.

Canaanite woman used this comparison, and she deserved to hear the Lord's commendation, *Woman, your faith is great; may it be done for you as you desire* (Mt 15:27.28). These are the dogs that deserve to be praised, not cursed; they are loyal to their Master, and defend his house by barking at enemies.

Notice also that it says not simply *dogs*, but *your dogs*, and that it is not their teeth but their tongues that are favorably mentioned. It was not idly, but with profoundly mysterious meaning,[97] that Gideon was commanded to lead into action only those who lapped the river water like dogs, and that no more than three hundred were found to do so amid so great a crowd.[98] Now this number, three hundred, is represented in Greek by the letter θ, which is a sign of the cross.

Another psalm says of these dogs, *They will be converted in the evening, and feel hungry like dogs* (Ps 58:15(59:14-15). Certain dogs were rebuked by the prophet Isaiah, not because they were dogs, but because they did not know how to bark, and were fond of dozing.[99] The prophet showed clearly that if they stayed awake and barked in the service of their master they would be good dogs and earn praise, just as those of whom our present psalm speaks—*the tongue of your dogs*—deserve praise too. But our prophet foretold that even the Lord's enemies would turn into praiseworthy dogs of this type, by means of that conversion he had spoken about earlier. And this accords with the other psalm, which foretold that *they will be converted in the evening, and feel hungry like dogs*.

Finally the psalm imagines them inquiring how it had happened that they who had formerly been the Lord's enemies had now become his dogs, and what was the source of this great good that had come their way. The psalm answers. It is *his doing*. This is what the verse says, *the tongue of your dogs, once enemies, his doing*. It comes about through his elective love, his mercy, his grace. How could they ever have achieved it by themselves? When we were enemies, we were reconciled to God by the death of his Son;[100] this is why our Lord made our death his own.

Verses 25-27. The grace of the Old Testament manifested in the New; the melodious procession of the young churches

33. *Your steps were seen, O God*, the steps by which you have traveled through the world, as though encompassing the whole earth in your chariot. These steps symbolize his saints and faithful servants, who are also called "clouds" in the gospel, for Christ said, *Henceforth you shall see the Son of Man coming in the clouds* (Mt 26:64). This does not refer to his final coming as judge

---

97. *Nec sine magno sacramento*; see note at section 16 above.
98. See Jgs 7:5-6.
99. See Is 56:10.
100. See Rom 5:10.

of the living and the dead,[101] for he said, *Henceforth you shall see the Son of Man coming in the clouds.* These steps of his *were seen,* that is, they were manifested, when the grace of the New Testament was revealed. That is why it is said, *How beautiful are the feet of those who announce peace and bring good news!* (Rom 10:15). This grace, these steps, were hidden under the Old Testament, but when the fullness of time had come, and it pleased God to reveal his Son,[102] that he might be proclaimed among the Gentiles, then *your steps were seen, O God, the steps of my God, of the king who dwells in the holy place.* What *holy place* could this be, other than his own temple? *For his temple is holy, and that temple is yourselves* (1 Cor 3:17).

34. The steps needed to be seen, so *the princes led the way, accompanied by those who played the psalteries, and all around them were young maidens sounding their tambourines.* The princes are the apostles, who went ahead so that the peoples could follow; they *led the way,* announcing the New Covenant. They were *accompanied by those who played the psalteries,* by whose evident good works God was glorified as though on instruments resounding with his praise. The princes marched in the midst of *young maidens sounding their tambourines,* for the apostles exercised an honorable ministry as governors of the new churches. These young churches are called *young maidens* to signify that they praised God by their conquest of the flesh; and the phrase, *sounding their tambourines,* makes the same point, for tambourines are made from dried, stretched skin.

35. To make sure that no one takes the foregoing description in a carnal sense, or thinks of some kind of licentious singing and dancing, the psalm exhorts us, *Bless the Lord in the churches.* The psalm almost seems to be warning us, "When you hear about young maidens playing tambourines, how dare you think of lascivious entertainments? *Bless the Lord in the churches.* It is the churches that are brought before you under this mysterious imagery. The churches are the young maidens adorned with new grace; the churches are the players of tambourines, spiritually melodious because they have the flesh severely in check. So *bless the Lord in the churches, the Lord God from the springs of Israel.*" It was indeed from Israel that he chose the people he intended to make into springs for others; the apostles were chosen from Israel, and they were the first to hear the Lord's promise, *Anyone who drinks of the water I shall give will never be thirsty, for it will become in that person a fountain of water springing forth to eternal life* (Jn 4:13-14).

---

101. See 2 Tm 4:1.
102. See Gal 4:4.

Verse 28. The significance of the tribal names

36. *There is Benjamin, the youngest, in ecstasy.* There is Paul, the latest-born of the apostles, who claimed, *I too am an Israelite, from the seed of Abraham and the tribe of Benjamin* (Phil 3:5). But there is good reason to add, *in ecstasy*, for everyone was filled with awe at the great miracle that occurred at his calling. Ecstasy is a state of being "out of one's mind." It may be brought on by fear; but sometimes on the occasion of some revelation there is a disjunction between the mind and the bodily senses, so that the truth to be revealed can be shown to the spirit. Accordingly the phrase that we find here, *in ecstasy*, can be understood as follows: when Saul, still a persecutor, was questioned from heaven, *Saul, Saul, why are you persecuting me?* (Acts 9:4), he was deprived of his bodily sight, but responded to the Lord whom he saw in his spirit. His companions heard his voice as he replied, but could not see whom he was talking to. Our present text may also be compared with that other ecstasy experienced by Paul. He said that he knew someone who had been caught up in rapture to the third heaven, whether in the body or out of the body he did not know. He further said that the person thus caught up to paradise had heard words beyond utterance, which no human lips might speak.[103]

Their leaders are the princes of Judah, the princes of Zebulun, the princes of Naphtali. As we have seen, the word *princes* stands for the apostles, among whom is Paul, signified by the phrase, *Benjamin, the youngest, in ecstasy*. No one doubts this. But alternatively we could take the title *princes* to apply to all those in the churches who are most excellent and worthy of imitation. But what is the point of naming these other Israelite tribes? If Judah alone had been mentioned, we might have supposed that the princes of the New Covenant were symbolized by the princes of Judah because the kings came from that tribe, and from it Christ the Lord was descended according to the flesh.[104] But this will not do, because the psalm adds, *The princes of Zebulun, the princes of Naphtali.* Someone may allege that the apostles came from these tribes, and not from any others. I do not see how this theory can be proved, but I find no way to rebut it either; and since I see that this verse commends the princes of the churches, and the leaders of those who in the churches bless the Lord, I think it not unreasonable to favor[105] this opinion.

However, there is another explanation that appeals to me more strongly, one that emerges from the interpretation of the names themselves. The names are Hebrew. Judah means "Confession"; Zebulun means "A Habitation of Fortitude"; Naphtali is interpreted as "My Enlarging." All these suggest to us the

---

103. See 2 Cor 12:2-4.
104. See Rom 9:5.
105. Variant "to advance."

most authentic princes of the churches, the people worthy to lead, worthy of imitation, worthy of honors. I mean the martyrs, who hold the highest rank in the churches, and are pre-eminent on that pinnacle of holy dignity. In martyrdom there is first of all a confession. Then the martyr gathers the fortitude to endure whatever may ensue from that confession. Finally, when all the pain has been borne, and all the sore straits left behind, there is the large freedom of the reward.

Another way of applying the same interpretation is this: the apostle enjoins upon us three things especially—faith, hope, and charity.[106] The confession is made in faith, brave endurance is possible in hope, and wide freedom is experienced in charity. The essence of faith is that we believe in our hearts and so are justified, and confess with our lips to be saved.[107] In the endurance of suffering, present reality is a sad business, but hope[108] is strong, for *if we hope for what we do not see, we wait for it in patience* (Rom 9:25). But the spreading abroad of charity in our hearts brings us into unrestricted freedom, because *charity made perfect casts out fear* (1 Jn 4:18), whereas fear constricts the soul and tortures it. *The princes of Judah* are therefore those who lead the way in confession, fortitude, and wide freedom; they are the leaders in faith, hope, and charity.

Verse 29. Christ, the Power and the Wisdom of God

37. *Command your power, O God.* One only is our Lord Jesus Christ, through whom all things exist, and we in him,[109] and he, as we read, is the Power of God and the Wisdom of God.[110] How, then, can God command his Christ? Surely by commending him, for *God commends his love for us in that while we were still sinners Christ died for us; so how can he fail to give us everything else along with that gift?* (Rom 5:8; 8:32).

Command your power, O God; and confirm, O God, what you have wrought in us. Command by teaching us, and confirm by helping us.

Verses 30-31. Heretics distort scripture, but they are made to serve a good purpose

38. *From your holy temple in Jerusalem, kings will offer you gifts.* It is our mother, the mother who is free,[111] who is meant here, because she is your holy temple. From this temple *kings will offer you gifts.* Whoever these kings may

---

106. See 1 Cor 13:13.
107. See Rom 10:10.
108. The contrast, as often in Augustine, is between *res*, the [present] reality, and *spes*, the hope of what is to come.
109. See 1 Cor 8:6.
110. See 1 Cor 1:24.
111. See Gal 4:26.

be—whether earthly monarchs, or those kings distinguished upon the silvery dove by him who is above the heavens—they *will offer you gifts*. And what gifts find favor with you, if not sacrifices of praise? But people who bear the Christian name, yet foment discord, drown this sound of praise. We must pray, then, as the next verse prays, *Rebuke the wild animals of the reed*. They are wild because they wreak havoc uncomprehendingly, and they are wild animals of the reed because they distort scripture to suit their errors. We can take scripture to be signified by a reed just as well as speech is by the tongue. We are used to saying, "The Hebrew tongue," or "the Greek tongue" or "the Latin tongue," or any other, and when we do so we signify the effect by naming the instrument that produces it. A similar idiom calls writing "the pen" because a pen is used for it; and by extension we could call something written "a reed." The apostle Peter says that uneducated and unstable people distort the scriptures to their own ruin;[112] so these are the wild animals of the reed, against whom the psalm prays here, *Rebuke the wild animals of the reed*.

39. They are still the subject of the following phrase: *A batch of bulls is among the cows of the peoples, so that those who have been proved sound by silver may be pressed out*. The psalm calls them bulls because they are so proudly stiff-necked[113] and insubordinate, for it is heretics who are in view here. I think that the *cows of the peoples* must be taken as souls liable to be led astray, being all too willing to follow the bulls. It is not all the people who are seduced, for some among them are weighty, stable characters, which is why another psalm promises, *In a weighty people I will praise you* (Ps 34(35):18); only those who prove to be *cows* are at risk. As the apostle warns, *Some there are who make their way into people's homes, and entrap miserable women burdened with sins and swayed by conflicting desires, who are always avid to learn but never arrive at knowledge of the truth* (2 Tm 3:6-7).

Nonetheless, as the same apostle testifies, *Heresies there must be, so that those who have been proved sound may be clearly identified among you* (1 Cor 11:19), and that is why our psalm continues, *So that those who have been proved sound by silver may be pressed out*. Such persons are tested and proved by the utterances of the Lord, for *the words of the Lord are pure words, silver tried by fire for the earth* (Ps 11:7(12:6)). The verb *may be pressed out*[114] is used in the sense "that they may become visible" or "stand out clearly," or, as the apostle says, *may be clearly identified*. That is why silversmiths are called *exclusores*; they are adept in bringing forth from a shapeless lump the form required for utensils. There are many meanings in scripture that lie hidden, known only to a few people with keener perception than the rest; they are not declared in a form

---

112. See 2 Pt 3:16.
113. See Acts 7:51.
114. *Excludantur*; compare Exposition of Psalm 54, 22, and note there.

more useful and accessible to everyone until the duty of replying to heretics demands it. In such an emergency those who have neglected to study their faith shake off their drowsiness and rouse themselves to listen carefully to what they are taught, in order to rebut our opponents. Just think how many aspects of scriptural teaching on Christ's divinity were affirmed against Photinus![115] And how many others concerning Christ's humanity were asserted against Mani![116] How many on the Trinity against Sabellius![117] How many concerning the unity of the Trinity against the Arians,[118] Eunomians,[119] and Macedonians![120] And how many scriptural teachings have been brought clearly to light against the Donatists[121] and the Luciferians,[122] and others (if any others there are) who contradict the truth and share similar errors! Against them scriptural teachings have been exposed concerning the Catholic Church diffused throughout the world, and the presence within it of bad people until the end of the world, though this does no harm to the good, with whom they associate in the celebration of the mysteries. How many other scriptural meanings have been brought to the fore in controversy with other heretics—meanings which it would take too long to enumerate or mention here? A complete list is in any case unnecessary for present purposes. Yet the proven defenders of these scriptural teachings would have continued in obscurity, or at least would have been less prominent than they became through contesting the denials of the proud. The apostle referred to

---

115. Bishop of Sirmium, c. 344-351. Photinus apparently taught a variant of Sabellianism (see note later in this section), possibly denying the pre-existence of the person of Christ. He was deposed and exiled by the Council of Sirmium in 351, and his followers were condemned by the Council of Constantinople in 381.

116. Founder of a theosophy in the third century after Christ, in Persia. A mingling of Christian elements, Gnostic beliefs, and bizarre speculation, Manicheanism held that two aboriginal kingdoms were at war, the kingdom of light and the kingdom of darkness. During an attack on the former, the kingdom of darkness had swallowed certain particles of light, which were now trapped within the visible world and within human beings. This accounted for the tension between good and evil in our experience. Augustine had been a disciple of the sect for nine years in his youth. See also notes at Expositions of Psalms 10,3 and 80,14.

117. A theologian of the early third century. Sabellius and his associates, Noetus and Praxeas, were influential in the Modalist wing of the Monarchian heresy. This latter was imbued with the fully orthodox determination to safeguard the absolute unity of the Godhead (the "Monarchy"), but in grappling with the problem of how to state the relationship of the Son to the Father, Monarchians arrived at solutions later to be regarded as heretical. The Modalists or Sabellians apparently denied the real distinction of Persons within the Trinity, holding that the only differentiation within God is a series of "modes" or operations.

118. See notes on Expositions of Psalms 35,9 and 54,22.

119. Eunomius, Bishop of Cyzicus in the mid-fourth century, embraced the extreme form of Arianism known as Anomeanism, which asserted that the Son is unlike the Father; see also note at Exposition of Psalm 52,4.

120. Macedonius, Bishop of Constantinople, belonged to the Semi-Arian persuasion. He died c. 362.

121. See note at Exposition of Psalm 10,1.

122. Lucifer of Cagliari was an anti-Arian champion, who initiated a schism at Antioch in about 362. It is not clear that he was a heretic.

these proud adversaries, who like bulls are not submissive to the peaceful and kindly yoke of discipline. He stated that a candidate for episcopal office must be *capable of encouraging the people in sound teaching, and refuting those who speak against it* (Ti 1:9). There are many insubordinate persons; they are bulls who toss their heads and will not tolerate the plow or work in a team. They talk frivolously and lead the minds of others astray, the minds of those our psalm calls *cows*.

Divine Providence has permitted these bulls to congregate among the cows of the people for the profit of all, for by this means *those who have been proved sound by silver may be pressed out*, or become prominent. Heresies are allowed to spring up *so that those who have been proved sound may be clearly identified*.

Another possible interpretation of the phrase is this: *A batch of bulls is among the cows of the peoples, so that* by these cows *those who have been proved sound by silver may be pressed out*. Heretical teachers aim to keep sound teachers away from the ears of those they try to seduce. The teachers who have been proved sound by silver, who are truly fit to teach the words of the Lord, would thus be *excluded*, and unable to gain a hearing.

Whether we accept the latter interpretation or the former, however, the next phrase prays, *Scatter the warring nations*, for they bend their efforts not to correction but to contention. The psalm is predicting that those who refuse to be corrected, and scatter the flock of Christ, are destined to be scattered themselves. It calls them *nations* not to imply any blood-relationship between them, but to suggest the propagation of sects in a series that successively aggravates the original error.

Verses 32-34. Faith and works; the conversion of the Gentiles

40. *Ambassadors will come from Egypt; Ethiopia will forestall his*[123] *hands.* The psalm mentions a part to signify the whole: under the name of Egypt, or Ethiopia, the faith of all the Gentiles is foretold. Those it calls ambassadors are the preachers of reconciliation, a figure of speech the apostle also uses: *We function as Christ's ambassadors, for through us God makes his appeal. We beg you, be reconciled to God* (2 Cor 5:20). In this mysterious way the psalm prophesied that the preachers of Christian peace would come not only from Israel, whence the apostles were chosen, but from other races as well.

The words, *will forestall his hands*, mean that by conversion to God Ethiopia will forestall any intention on God's part to punish her, for at her conversion all her sins will be forgiven, and there will be no persistent sinners to deserve

---

123. In this section it is necessary to shift between "his" and "her" to represent Augustine's *eius*; see the note below.

punishment. The same thought is expressed in another psalm: *let us forestall him by coming before his face confessing* (Ps 94(95):2). As the psalm signifies punishment by God's hands, so too it signifies revelation and visible presence by his face, the manifest presence of God at the judgment.

Since, then, Egypt and Ethiopia represent the peoples of the whole world, the psalm immediately adds, *To God, kingdoms of the earth*. Not to Sabellius, not to Arius, not to Donatus, not to any of the other arrogant bulls, but *to God, kingdoms of the earth*.

41. However, many Latin and especially Greek codices divide the verse differently. Instead of attaching the phrase, *to God*, to what follows — *to God, kingdoms of the earth* — they attach it to the preceding words, to read, *Ethiopia will come before her hands to God*; and then continue with a new phrase: *kingdoms of the earth, sing to God, and play psalms to the Lord*. The agreement between many codices, and those the more reliable, makes this latter division preferable. It seems to me that if we accept it, we are reminded of the priority of faith over works. In the absence of good works a godless person is justified by faith, as the apostle says: *When someone believes in him who justifies the impious, that faith is reckoned as justice to the believer* (Rom 4:5), so that afterward faith may begin to work through the love of choice.[124] Indeed, only works performed through this love of God deserve the name of good works. But faith must precede them, so that the works spring from faith, not faith from the works, because no one performs good works out of such love of God unless he or she already believes in God. This is the faith of which it is written, *In Christ Jesus neither circumcision nor uncircumcision has any value, but only faith that works by choosing to love* (Gal 5:6). This faith is spoken of also in the promise addressed to the Church in the Song of Songs: *You will come and pass through, beginning from faith* (Sg 4:8, LXX). The Church *comes*, like God's chariot comprising thousands of joyful people, enjoying a favorable passage, running its course from this world to the Father, so that in the Church that prayer may be answered which the Bridegroom made as he himself left the world to go to the Father:[125] *I will that where I am, they too may be with me* (Jn 17:24). But this journey begins from faith.

Since, then, faith comes first in order that good works may follow, and there are no good works other than those consequent upon faith, it seems that when the psalm says, *Ethiopia will come before her hands to God*, it can mean nothing else but, "Let Ethiopia believe in God," for that is how she will *come before her*[126] *hands*, that is, her good works. Whose works can these be? Ethiopia's, obviously. There is no ambiguity in the Greek here, because the feminine pronoun is used. Clearly, then, what the psalm is saying is that *Ethiopia will*

---

124. *Per dilectionem.*
125. See Jn 13:1.

come before her hands to God, or, rather, she will believe in God before performing any good works; for, as the apostle says, *Our argument is that a person is justified by faith, apart from any works. Is God the God of the Jews alone? Surely he is also God of the Gentiles?* (Rom 3:28-29). Ethiopia, which seems like the remotest of the Gentile nations, is therefore justified by faith, independently of any works of the law; she does not give her merits pride of place before her faith, but lets her faith take precedence over her works.

It is true that some codices have not *hands* but *hand*, but it comes to the same thing; in either case works are meant. I would prefer the Latin translators to have rendered the verse *Aethiopia praeveniet manus suas* (or *manum suam*) *Deo*;[127] that would have been clearer than *eius*, which is what we have. Nor would it have falsified the true meaning, because the Greek pronoun ~ήέῳῖ can be understood not only as *eius*, but also as *suas*, or *suam* if "hand" is singular. The Greek reads ίίρ̈~ ~ήέῳῖ in most codices, which can be rendered either *manum eius*[128] or *manum suam*[129] in Latin. More rarely the Greek codices have ίῆὖῖ ~ήέῳῖ, which can be translated either *manus eius*[130] or *manus suas*.[131]

42. The prophecy has now completed its review of all these events which we, for our part, see realized, so it invites us to praise Christ, and then foretells his future coming. *Kingdoms of the earth, sing to God, and play psalms to the Lord; play psalms to God who ascends above the heavens of the heavens to the east*; or, as some codices have it, *who ascends above the heaven of heaven, to the east*. Only those who believe in Christ's resurrection will find him here. The addition, *to the east*, is surely a geographical indication; after all, was it not in the eastern regions that he rose from the dead and ascended? And so above the heaven of heaven he sits at the Father's right hand. The apostle indicated the same truth by saying, *He it is who ascended above all the heavens* (Eph 4:10), for what more of heaven could there be beyond the heaven of heaven?[132] It makes no difference whether we call it the heaven of heaven or the heavens of heavens; the same shift is found elsewhere. God called the firmament or sky "heaven," yet we also find it

---

126. Augustine's Latin text gave him *Aethiopia praeveniet manus eius Deo*, which should mean that the hands are those of God, not those of Ethiopia, which, as the subject of the sentence, would require *suas*. This properly grammatical understanding accorded with his first interpretation, in section 40, that hands = God's punishment. If hands are to mean works on the part of Ethiopia, he has to resort to the Greek, which could mean either *eius* or *suas*, as he goes on to explain.

127. Ethiopia will come before her own hands, or hand, to God.

128. In this context, "his hand."

129. "Her (own) hand."

130. "His hands."

131. "Her (own) hands."

132. In *The Confessions* XII,2,2 Augustine meditates on the words of Ps 113(115):16, which, according to the Septuagint, run "Heaven's heaven is for the Lord; but he has assigned the earth to humankind." He decides that "heaven's heaven" is the invisible, spiritual creation reserved for God. All the rest, including the sky (= "heaven") is for us, the material creation.

called "the heavens," as when scripture says, *And let the waters that are above the heavens praise the name of the Lord* (Ps 148:4-5).

From there he will come to judge the living and the dead, so take note of the next statement: *Lo, he will send forth his voice, a voice of strength.* He who *like a sheep, voiceless before its shearer, did not open his mouth* (Is 53:7) will *send forth his voice*, no longer a weak voice like that of one liable to judgment, but *a voice of strength*, the voice of one who is to judge. He will be no hidden God, as once he was, not opening his mouth before a human tribunal; no, *our God will come openly, our God will not keep silence* (Ps 49:3(50:2-3)). Why do you cast hope aside, you unbelievers? Why mock? What does the wicked servant say? *My master is a long time coming* (Lk 12:45). *Lo, he will send forth his voice, a voice of strength.*

Verses 35-36. The glorious consummation

43. *Give glory to God, for his majesty is over Israel.* This is the Israel of which the apostle says, *Over the Israel of God* (Gal 6:16). *For not all who spring from Israel are Israelites* (Rom 9:6); there is also an Israel according to the flesh. The apostle directs our attention to it: *Consider Israel according to the flesh* (1 Cor 10:18). *It is not the children of Abraham's flesh who are children of God; it is the children of the promise who are accounted Abraham's descendants* (Rom 9:8). One day there will no longer be any mingling of the wicked among his people, for his wheat will have been winnowed clean,[133] and made into an Israel in which no guile is to be found.[134] On that day his most splendid *majesty will be over Israel, and his strength will be in the clouds*, for he will come to judge not alone, but *with the elders of his people* (Is 3:14), to whom he made the promise that they will sit enthroned with him to judge;[135] and indeed, they will judge even angels.[136] These holy ones are the clouds.

44. The psalm adds another phrase to exclude any other interpretation of the clouds: *God is wonderful in his saints, he, the God of Israel.* On that day the name Israel will most truly and most fully correspond to the reality, for the name means "One who sees God,"[137] and then *we shall see him as he is* (1 Jn 3:2). His people are fragile and weak now, but then *he will give strength and power to his people. Blessed be God.* By a supremely glorious transfiguration of our bodies *he will give strength and power to his people*, for although *this body of ours is sown in weakness, it will rise in strength* (1 Cor 15:43). He will give us that

133. See Mt 3:12.
134. See Jn 1:47.
135. See Mt 19:28.
136. See 1 Cor 6:3.
137. A popular etymology; see notes at Exposition 1 of Psalm 21,4; Exposition of Psalm 24,22.

strength which he first displayed in his own flesh, the strength the apostle longed to know, *the power of his resurrection* (Phil 3:10), that same power by which *death, the last enemy, will be destroyed* (1 Cor 15:26). At last, with God's help, we have finished this psalm, so long and so difficult to understand. For that, *blessed be God.* Amen.

Exposition 1 of Psalm 68

First Sermon

Introduction: From an age when the Church is prosperous, think back to the hard, humble beginnings

1. We have been born into this world and united to the flock of God's people at a time when what was once like a tiny mustard seed has grown into a mighty plant and spread its branches widely, at a time when the yeast which once seemed so insignificant has already leavened a good three measures of flour.[1] These three measures represent the entire world, restored and made habitable again by the three sons of Noah;[2] for many are coming from east and west, from north and south, to sit at table with the patriarchs, now that the carnal descendants of the patriarchs have been excluded for failing to imitate their faith.[3] We opened our eyes to this glorious Church of Christ. When we first beheld her she was no longer the sterile woman who had been bidden to rejoice at the promise of bearing more children than one who had a husband.[4] No, when we found her she had already forgotten the shame and ignominy of her widowed state. This very fact may give rise to a feeling of strangeness on our part when we read in some prophecy words that proceed from Christ's lowly condition, or our own. It may also mean that we are less responsive to those cries, for we were not there in an age when they seemed very poignant to readers upon whom persecution was lying heavy.

We should think soberly about our own situation, however. How narrow is the way[5] in which we walk—if indeed we walk in it at all—and through what hardships and sufferings does it lead us to our eternal rest! We should remember that what passes for happiness in this life is more to be feared than wretchedness, since the experience of wretchedness often bears sound fruit later, when we have come through our trouble, whereas good fortune corrupts the soul, lulling it into false security and offering the devilish tempter a foothold. If we think straight and weigh these matters realistically, like a victim well seasoned with salt,[6] and

---

1. See Mt 13:31-33.
2. Who repopulated it after the flood; see Gn 9:19; 10:5.
3. See Mt 8:11-12.
4. See Is 54:1; Gal 4:27.
5. See Mt 7:14.
6. The reference is evidently to Mk 9:48; compare Lv 2:13. But some codices amend *sicut salita victima* to *psallit haec victima*, "as this victim sings in the psalm."

if we reflect that human life on earth is one long temptation;[7] if we realize that none of us are secure, or can ever be secure, until we arrive at our homeland, where no friend will leave us nor enemy gain access, then even now, in the Church's time of glory, we can make these anguished prayers our own. As members of Christ, subjected to our head by the strong bond of charity and supporting one another, we shall use the prayer of the psalms, as the martyrs used it before us; to own that tribulation is the lot of us all, from the earliest days to the end.

This psalm, which we have undertaken to expound, and about which we have resolved to speak to you in the Lord's name, beloved ones,[8] is nevertheless one where we find the mustard seed in its initial stages. We must for a little while turn our minds away from the tall plant, from the spreading branches, from the glorious luxuriance that affords roosting-places to the birds of the sky; we must hear how the magnificence that delights us in the mature plant sprang from a tiny seed. It is Christ who is speaking here (we need only remind you of this, for you know it already); and Christ is not the head alone, but the body too. We recognize him from the very words, and we can have no doubt whatever that he speaks in this psalm. Words are uttered here which find their full meaning in his passion: *they put gall into my food, and in my thirst gave me vinegar to drink* (verse 22). This is what literally happened. Just as such events were prophesied, exactly so did they take place. Hanging on the cross, Christ said, *I am thirsty*, and in response they offered him vinegar on a sponge. After taking it he said, *It is accomplished*, and bowing his head, he gave up his spirit.[9] In this way he declared that all the prophecies had been accomplished in himself. We have no right to understand it otherwise. The apostles too, when speaking about Christ, adduced evidence from this psalm.[10] Who would wish to disagree with their judgment? Would any lamb refuse to follow where the rams lead?[11] Unquestionably, Christ is speaking here. The challenge to us is not so much to prove this as to point out where his members are speaking, in order to show that the speaker is the whole Christ.

Verse 1. Christ's passover brings about the change in us

2. The psalm's title is, *To the end, for those who will be changed, for David himself.* You should understand this as a reference to change for the better. Change can, of course, go either way, for worse or for better. In the case of Adam

---

7. See Jb 7:1.
8. *Caritati vestrae.*
9. See Jn 19:28-30.
10. Compare verse 5 with Jn 15:25; verse 10 with Jn 2:17 and Rom 15:3; verse 26 with Acts 1:20.
11. See Exposition of Psalm 56, 18; the rams are the apostles.

and Eve there was change for the worse; but the descendants of Adam and Eve who have fastened themselves to Christ have changed for the better, for *as through one man came death, so too through one man has come the resurrection of the dead; and as in Adam all die, so in Christ shall all be made to live* (1 Cor 15:21-22). Adam was changed from the creature God had formed into something inferior fashioned by his own iniquity; but believers are changed from iniquity's handiwork into something better, through God's grace. Our change for the worse was the effect of our iniquity, but we change for the better thanks to God's grace, not to any righteousness of our own. Let us impute our deterioration to ourselves, therefore, but praise God for our improvement.

This psalm is sung *for those who will be changed.* How did this change come about? Through the passion of Christ. *Pascha* means "Passover" in our language. *Pascha* is not a Greek word, but Hebrew. It does sound like the Greek word for "suffer," which is *"ὄεἰῑῑ"* , but in Hebrew it means something different. *Pascha* means a crossing over, or passing. John the evangelist made the point: when the Lord was approaching his passion, he came to the supper at which he was to entrust to his disciples the sacrament of his body and blood; and the evangelist marked the moment thus: *When the hour had come, at which Jesus was to pass from this world to the Father . . .* (Jn 13:1). He expressly mentioned Christ's passover, his pasch. If Christ, who had come for our sake, had not made his passover from this world to the Father, how could we pass over from here? We did not come down to lift up anything; we simply fell. Christ did not fall; he came down to raise up fallen humanity. It is both his and ours, this passover from here to the Father, from this world to the kingdom of heaven, from mortal life to life eternal, from earthly life to the life of heaven, from decay to indestructible life, from the experience of tribulation to everlasting security. This is why the psalm is headed, *For those who will be changed.* Let us find in the text of the psalm the cause of this change in ourselves, which is nothing other than the Lord's passion; and as we find it let us also find the voice of our own suffering, and recognize it as ours, and unite our groaning with it. By listening, understanding, and groaning with the psalm, let us be changed, so that in us the title of the psalm may find valid application: *for those who will be changed.*[12]

Verse 2. The bitter passion to be endured in fear and hope

3. *Save me, O God, for the waters have flooded in even to my soul.* The seed is despised now, the seed which seems to be speaking from a place of humiliation. It is buried in a garden, but the garden is the world which will wonder at the stature of the grown plant, sprung from the seed which the Jews despised. Yes,

---

12. For Augustine's view of the therapeutic effects of psalmody, see the *Introduction* in Part III, Volume 15, of this series.

true it is: look carefully at this mustard seed; it is tiny, dark in color, contemptible even, but only so that the prophecy may be fulfilled: *there was no comeliness in him; we saw him, and he had no beauty to attract us* (Is 53:2). He says that the waters have flooded in even to his soul, because the crowds (who are here represented by the waters) were able to prevail over Christ even to the point of killing him. They proved powerful enough to treat him with contempt, to arrest him, bind him, insult him, strike him and spit on him. How far did their power prevail? Even to his death. This is why he says, *The waters have flooded in even to my soul*. By his soul he means his mortal life, for their savagery engulfed even that. Yet would they have had such power, if he had not himself allowed it to them? No. And so we must ask, Why does he cry out, as though he were suffering involuntarily? Because the head was prefiguring his members. The truth is that though he suffered because he willed to, the martyrs suffered even if they did not will it. The Lord foretold Peter's passion by saying to him, *When you have grown old, someone else will fasten your belt for you, and take you where you do not want to go* (Jn 21:18). Although we long to keep close to Christ, we do not want to die. We suffer willingly—or at least patiently—only because there is no other way for us to make our passover and cleave to Christ. If some other way were open to us whereby we could come to him and to eternal life, who would be prepared to die? The apostle gives us some teaching on our nature as a partnership of body and soul, and on our familiar experience of how strongly the two are glued together and built into our very structure. He reminds us that we have an eternal home in heaven not built with hands. This is the immortal nature prepared for us, with which we are to be invested at the end, when we have risen from the dead.[13] *We who are still in this earthly dwelling groan under our burden; not that we want to be stripped of it, but wishing to be invested with the other one on top, so that what is mortal may be swallowed up by life* (2 Cor 5:4). If only it were possible, he says, we would opt to make the transition to immortality in such a way that our immortal nature might come upon us immediately, and change us as we are now, so that what is mortal in us might be absorbed by life, rather than our body having to be buried and restored to us only at the end. Clearly, then, although we are destined to pass from bad conditions to good, our passover itself is in some degree a bitter thing; there is gall in it, like that which the Jews gave to the Lord in his passion. We have to endure something sour in our passing, as they gave him vinegar to drink.[14]

The Lord both prefigured us, and took us over into himself,[15] and so he cries, *Save me, O God, for the waters have flooded in even to my soul*. His persecutors

---

13. See 2 Cor 5:1.
14. See Mk 15:36; Mt 27:48.
15. *Praefigurans . . . et transformans in se nos ipsos.* A key phrase for Augustine's Christological reading of the psalms; see the *Introduction* in Volume 1.

were able to go as far as killing him, but after that there was nothing more that they could do. The Lord had instructed us earlier, *Do not be afraid of those who kill the body, but after that can do no more. Fear him rather who has the power to kill both soul and body in hell* (Mt 10:28). That mightier fear drives us to set little store by lesser things, and a more passionate desire for eternity fills us with distaste for all that passes away. In this life temporal pleasures are certainly sweet to us, and temporal troubles bitter; but will any of us refuse to drain the cup of temporal tribulation if we fear hellfire, and not spurn the world's delights when we yearn for the delights of eternal life? Let us cry out to be delivered, lest when anguish is heavy upon us we consent to iniquity, and be sucked under without hope of recovery. Let us beg, *Save me, O God, for the waters have flooded in even to my soul.*

Verse 3. What does "substance" mean? Riches, perhaps?

4. *I am stuck fast in the mud of the deep, and there is no substance.* What does he mean by "mud"? Those who persecuted him, perhaps? This could be so, for human beings were made from mud;[16] but by falling away from righteousness persecutors became the mud of the depths. Whoever refuses to yield to them when they persecute us and try to drag us toward iniquity, turns our human mud into gold. Any such person's mud will be found worthy of being converted into the condition proper to heaven, and he or she will have deserved fellowship with those mentioned in the title of this psalm: *those who will be changed.*

But the persecutors were mud of the depths, and I stuck fast in them, says the psalm; that is to say, they seized me, overpowered me, and killed me. *I am stuck fast in the mud of the deep, and there is no substance.* What does this last phrase suggest—*there is no substance*?[17] Surely mud itself is a substance? Or should we take it this way: By sticking fast there, I ceased to be a substance? Can *I am stuck fast* mean that? But Christ did not stick fast in that sense, did he? Should we perhaps understand it to mean that he did indeed stick fast, in the sense indicated in the Book of Job: *Earth has been given over into the hands of the ungodly* (Jb 9:24); he was fixed firmly in his body, since it was capable of being held prisoner, and even crucified? If he had not been stuck fast with nails, he could not have been crucified.

Or does the verse mean that the mud is not a substance? If we are going to make any attempt to grasp what is meant by *there is no substance*, we must first understand what substance is. One meaning of the word is "riches"; so we say,

---

16. See Gn 2:7.

17. The word is *substantia*, and in the context of the psalm obviously means "firm foothold," that which ought to "stand underneath" the speaker's sliding feet. But Augustine is too keenly aware of the philosophical background to let it go at that, and he plays with other meanings in the next few paragraphs.

"He is a man of substance," or "He has lost his substance." But we can hardly think, can we, that the phrase, *And there is no substance*, means here, "There are no riches"? There is no question of riches raised here, or any discussion of riches. Possibly, however, we should understand that the mud itself was poverty, and no riches will be ours until we have been made sharers in eternity. Then indeed there will be true riches for us, for then we shall lack nothing at all.

In line with this interpretation of the word, "substance," we could take the statement that *I am stuck fast in the mud of the deep, and there is no substance* to mean, "I have been reduced to poverty." The speaker declares later, *I am poor and sorrowful* (verse 30); and the apostle says of Christ, *Though he was rich, for your sake he became poor, so that by his poverty you might be enriched* (2 Cor 8:9). Perhaps, then, the psalm wished to remind us about the Lord's poverty when it said, *There is no substance.* He reached the very pinnacle of poverty when he clothed himself in the form of a servant. How rich is he? *Being in the form of God, he deemed it no robbery to be God's equal* (Phil 2:6). This is huge wealth, wealth beyond compare. But how, then, did he become poor? *He emptied himself and took on the form of a slave. Bearing the human likeness, sharing the human lot, he humbled himself and was made obedient to the point of death.* That gave him the right to say, *The waters have flooded in even to my soul.* And if you want to take it even further, and add something to "death," what are you going to say? That he died an ignominious death; so it continues, *Even to the death of the cross* (Phil 2:7-8). What profound poverty this is! But it will yield vast riches, for as his poverty was taken to the uttermost, so will our riches be utterly full, deriving from his poverty. How great must his wealth be, if he can make us rich by his poverty! And if he has enriched us by his poverty, what will he do for us by his riches?

Another idea: the philosophical meaning of substance. Iniquity is not a substance

5. *I am stuck fast in the mud of the deep, and there is no substance.* Substance can be understood in another way: it means what we are—whatever we are. This is rather difficult to understand, because although the matter itself is quite familiar to us, the word is not, so some little comment and explanation are needed. If you pay close attention, it will perhaps not be too laborious for us. We speak of a man, an animal, the earth, the sky, the sun, the moon, a stone, the sea, the air: all these things are substances, simply in virtue of the fact that they exist. Their natures are called substances. God too is a substance; for anything that is not a substance is not anything at all.[18] A substance is something that is. This is

---

18. Augustine had struggled hard in his youth to arrive at the notion that anything could be substantial yet immaterial; see his *Confessions*, VII, 1,1 — 2,3.

why within the Catholic Church we are built up in faith to speak of the Father, and the Son, and the Holy Spirit, as one substance, as against the poisonous teaching of certain heretics. What does that mean—one substance? Well, for example, if the Father is pure gold, the Son is pure gold as well, and the Holy Spirit is pure gold. Whatever the Father is as God, that the Son is, and that the Holy Spirit is. But as Father he is not that which is; for he is called Father not with reference to himself, but in relation to the Son, whereas he is called God with reference to himself. From the fact that he is God, he is a substance. And because the Son is of the same substance,[19] obviously the Son too is God. But the Father's name as Father is not the name of a substance, but indicates his relationship to the Son; and therefore we do not say that the Son is the Father, in the manner in which we say that the Son is God.

Now, if you ask, "What is the Father?" the answer is "God." If you ask, "What is the Son?" the answer is "God." If you further ask, "What are the Father and the Son?" the answer is "God." If you are questioned about the Father alone, you must answer, "God"; and if you are questioned about the Son alone, you must answer, "God"; but if you are asked about both, what you must answer is not "Gods" but "God." This is different from the way things are with human beings. If you ask what our father Abraham is, the answer comes, "A man"; the answer indicates his substance. If you then ask what his son Isaac is, the answer again is, "A man"; for Abraham and Isaac are of the same substance. But if you ask what Abraham and Isaac are, the answer will not be, "A man," but "Men."

Not so with God. The communion of substance in God is so great that it admits of equality, but not of plurality. Suppose, therefore, that someone says to you, "You tell me that the Son is what the Father is. That must mean that the Son is the Father, then?" You must reply, "When I told you that the Son is what the Father is, my statement concerned the substance of God, not a relationship with something or someone else." The Son is said to be God in himself, but Son in relation to the Father; and similarly the Father is said to be God in himself, but Father in relation to the Son. Since he is said to be Father in relation to the Son, he is not the Son; and since the Son is called Son in relation to the Father, he is not the Father. But what the Father is said to be in himself, and what the Son is said to be in himself, that both Father and Son are, and that is God.

Well then, what does *there is no substance* mean? In the light of our examination of substance, how can we interpret the cry of the psalm, *I am stuck fast in the mud of the deep, and there is no substance*? God made human beings, and in so doing he created a substance. If only they had remained that substance which God created! If they had, the Son whom God begot would not have become stuck in what God had made. But they fell away through sin from the substance in which

---

19. The affirmation of Nicea.

they were created; for iniquity is not a substance.[20] Iniquity is not a nature created by God, but a perversity which human beings brought about. The Son of God came to the depths of the mud, and there he stuck fast, but he was not stuck in any substance, because he was stuck in the iniquity of men and women. *I am stuck fast in the mud of the deep, and there is no substance.* All things were made through him; apart from him nothing whatever was made.[21] All natures were made through him, but iniquity was not made through him, because iniquity was not made.[22] The substances that praise him were made through him. The three young men in the fiery furnace sang of the entire creation as praising God; the hymn of all the beings that praise him resounds from earthly things to things of heaven, and back again from heavenly beings to those of earth.[23] It is not as though all these creatures have the intelligence to praise God, but all of them when rightly contemplated evoke our praise, for as we consider creation our hearts become full, and blurt out praise to the Creator. All things praise God—all things that God has made, that is. Did you find in that hymn any mention of avarice praising God? Even a snake praises God, but avarice does not. All crawling things are named there as participants in God's praise; yes, all crawling things are mentioned, but no vices, for vices are in us by our own doing and our own will, and vices are not substances. The Lord was stuck fast in them when he was subjected to persecution, but he was stuck in the vice of the Jews, not in the human substance that was made through him. *I am stuck fast in the mud of the deep, and there is no substance*, he says. I am stuck fast, and I cannot find what I made.

The deep and the storm

6. *I have sunk into the depth of the sea, and the storm has overwhelmed me.* Thanks be to the mercy of him who sank to the depth of the sea and consented to be swallowed by the sea monster. But he was vomited up on the third day.[24] He sank into the depth of the sea, right down to the depths where we had sunk, to the depths where our shipwreck had left us. He sank even to that deep place, and the storm overwhelmed him, because there he was exposed to the billows and storms of men, the voices of those who shouted, *Crucify him! Crucify him!* Pilate objected, *I find no crime in him that deserves death*,[25] but their voices grew

---

20. This again was a conclusion Augustine had reached after prolonged grappling with the problem of evil; compare the *Confessions* VII,11,17.
21. See Jn 1:3.
22. Variant: "because iniquity is not a substance."
23. The hymn of the Three is absent from the Hebrew text of the Book of Daniel, but is found in the Greek of Theodotion and (with some differences of order) in the Septuagint, between Dn 3:23 and 3:24.
24. See Jon 2:1.11 and Mt 12:40.
25. See Jn 19:6.

louder: *Crucify! Crucify!* The storm blew more and more fiercely, until he had reached the deepest places of the sea. At the hands of the Jews the Lord suffered a fate he had not suffered when he walked on the waters.[26] Indeed, not only had he not then suffered it himself; he had not even allowed Peter to suffer it. But now, *I have sunk into the depth of the sea, and the storm has overwhelmed me.*

Verse 4. Hoarse throat, weary eyes

7. *I put all my effort into shouting, until my throat was hoarse.* Where did that happen? And when? Let us put our questions to the gospel, for we certainly recognize the passion of the Lord in this psalm. We know well that he did suffer. And we read, we believe, that the waters flooded in as far as his very soul, because the people had their way even to the point of demanding his death. We acknowledge that he was overwhelmed by the storm, because the uproar was powerful enough to kill him. All this we know; but we read nothing about his having put all his effort into shouting, or about his throat becoming hoarse. Not only do we read nothing about this; we read the contrary: that he answered them not a word, so that the prophecy in another psalm might be fulfilled: *I was like a deaf man who heard nothing, and like a dumb man who does not open his mouth* (Ps 37:15(38:14)), and also that of Isaiah: *He was led like a sheep to the slaughter, and like a sheep voiceless before its shearer, he did not open his mouth* (Is 53:7). If he became like someone who hears nothing, and does not open his mouth, how can it be said that he put all his effort into shouting, until his throat was hoarse? Does it mean that he was silent then because he had been reduced to it, through shouting to no avail? We also know about a word he spoke from the cross, quoting from a psalm: *O God, my God, why have you forsaken me?* (Ps 21:2(22:1)). But did he shout that so loudly, and for such a long time, that his throat grew hoarse?

No; but we know what he did go on shouting for a long time, and that was *Woe to you, scribes and Pharisees!* (Mt 23:13-15). For a long time he shouted, *Woe to the world because of scandals* (Mt 18:7). Truly he must have been so hoarse from shouting as to be nearly unintelligible, for Jews began to object, *What is he saying? This is hard doctrine, who could listen to it? We don't know what he is talking about* (Jn 16:18; 6:61). He spoke all these words, but for those who did not understand them his throat might as well have been hoarse. *I put all my effort into shouting, until my throat was hoarse.*

8. *My eyes grew weary of hoping in my God.* There is no way in which this can be attributed to our head. It is out of the question that his eyes could have wearied of hoping in his God; for God was in him, reconciling the world to himself,[27] and

---

26. See Mt 14:25.
27. See 2 Cor 5:19.

he was the Word who had been made flesh and dwelt among us,[28] in such wise that not only was God in him, but he himself was God. This verse cannot apply to him, to our head, for his eyes never wearied of hoping in his God; but the eyes in his body did weary: that is to say, his eyes wearied in the persons of his members. It is the voice of his members that is speaking now, the voice of the body, not of the head.

So how can we find the truth of it in the body and the members? Need I spell it out? Do you need further reminders? When he suffered, and when he died, all his disciples lost their hope that he was the Christ. The apostles were worsted by a robber, who believed when they had fallen away.[29] You can get a glimpse of Christ's despairing members by considering the two whom he met on the road after his resurrection, talking together—Cleopas was one of them — the two whose eyes were hindered from recognizing him.[30] How could they know him with their eyes, when in their minds they had reeled away from him? What had happened to their eyes matched what had happened to their minds. They were conversing, and when he took them to task and asked them what they had been discussing, they replied, *Are you the only stranger in Jerusalem? Do you not know what has happened, and what the leaders and chief priests did to Jesus of Nazareth, who was so powerful in deed and word? How they killed him? And we had been hoping that he was the one to redeem Israel* (Lk 24:18-21). They had hoped, but they were hoping no longer. Their eyes were weary of hoping in their God. Christ identified them with himself[31] when he said, *My eyes grew weary of hoping in my God.*

But he gave that hope back to them when he offered his scars to be handled. As soon as Thomas had touched them he returned to the hope he had lost, and exclaimed, *My Lord and my God!* Your eyes had wearied of hoping in your God; you handled the scars and found your God; you felt the form of the servant, and knew your Lord. Yet to Thomas the Lord said, *Because you have seen, you have believed.* And then he looked ahead at us, and there spoke the voice of mercy: *Blessed are those who do not see, yet believe* (Jn 20:28.29). *My eyes grew weary of hoping in my God.*

Verse 5. Not the penalty, but the cause, determines martyrdom. Christ suffered innocently

9. *Those who hated me without reason were multiplied, to exceed in number even the hairs on my head.* How far did they multiply? Until they recruited even

---

28. See Jn 1:14.
29. See Lk 23:42.
30. See Lk 24:13-35.
31. *Ipsos . . . in se transfiguravit.*

one of the Twelve.[32] *Those who hated me without reason were multiplied, to exceed in number even the hairs on my head.* He likened his enemies to the hairs on his head, and they were justly shaven off when he was crucified at a place called Calvary.[33] Christ's members must take this complaint to heart, and learn how to be hated for no reason. Think of it this way, O Christian: if it is in any case inevitable that you should be hated by the world, why not make sure that the world's hatred of you is unjustified, so that you may recognize your own voice in the body of your Lord, and in this psalm which speaks prophetically in his name? How will it come about that the world hates you for no reason? If you do no harm to anyone, and are hated for that, the hatred will be undeserved, without justification. But do not be content simply to be hated without cause; go further and give, so that they will be repaying your goodness with evil.

The enemies who persecute me unjustly have increased in strength. His former lament, *They exceed in number even the hairs on my head*, is echoed here by another cry: *They have increased in strength*; and the earlier description of them as *those who hated me without reason* here becomes *those who persecute me unjustly.* The qualification, *without reason*, corresponds to *unjustly.* This is the cry of the martyrs; but it is warranted by the cause, not by the pain as such. What is praiseworthy is not suffering persecution, not being arrested, not being whipped, not being imprisoned, not being outlawed, not being killed. But to endure all these things because your cause is good—that merits praise. The commendable element is the goodness of the cause, not the intensity of the pain. However fierce the torments of the martyrs may have been, they scarcely equal the torments of all robbers, all violators of sacred shrines, and all criminals, do they?

Moreover, does the world not hate those people too? Certainly it does. By their wicked excesses they go beyond what the world will tolerate; they undermine even earthly peace, and are in some sense outcasts even from the society of worldly folk. Consequently they are subjected to many punishments, but not without reason. The point emerges most clearly from the words of the robber who hung beside the Lord on the cross. One of the robbers—the one on the other side of our crucified Lord—insulted him: *If you are the Son of God, free yourself.* But the other one restrained him: *Do you not fear God, even subject as you are to the same sentence? And rightly, for what we have done.*[34] His punishment was not undeserved, but he poured out the corrupt matter[35] from within him by his confession, and fitted himself to eat the Lord's food. He turned his iniquity out of doors, repudiated it, and was free of it. There were the two robbers, and

32. See Mk 14:10; Mt 26:14; Lk 22:3-4.
33. An allusion to the etymology of the word *Calvaria* which he often mentions: "a bald place."
34. See Lk 23:39-41.
35. Variant: "blood."

there was the Lord; they were crucified, and he was crucified; the world hated them, but not without reason; it hated him too, but without reason.

I was paying the price, though I had committed no robbery. This is gratuitous payment. I committed no robbery, yet I was making restitution; I committed no sin, yet I was paying the penalty. Christ alone could make that claim, for only he had not robbed at all. Not only had he never robbed; in order to come to us he even emptied himself of what he possessed without having stolen it; for *he deemed it no robbery to be God's equal*, yet *he emptied himself and took on the form of a slave* (Phil 2:6-7)[36] This was by no means robbery! Who was the robber, then? Adam. And the primordial robber? The being who seduced Adam. How, then, did the devil seize what did not belong to him? *I will set my throne in the north; I shall be like the Most High*, he said.[37] He grabbed for himself something not given to him; that was robbery. The devil tried to usurp what had not been granted to him, and thereby lost what he had been given. Then from the cup of his own pride he offered a drink to the humans he was trying to seduce, saying, *Taste it, and you will be like gods* (Gn 3:5). They too wanted to make a grab at divinity, and they lost their happiness. The devil robbed, and paid for it; but Christ declares, *I was discharging a debt, though I had committed no robbery.*

As the Lord approached his passion, he testified, *Now the prince of this world* (that is, the devil) *is coming, and he will find nothing in me* (that means, he will find no justification for killing me). *But so that the world may know that I am doing my Father's will, rise, let us leave here* (Jn 14:30-31). And he went out to his passion, to pay back where he had committed no robbery. What else does his statement mean—*he will find nothing in me*? He will find no fault. Had the devil found anything missing from his house? Let the devil pursue any robbers he may find;[38] *he will find nothing in me*. But notice this: when Christ avers that he has seized nothing, he means seized sinfully; he is referring to unjust seizure, iniquitous appropriation. But he did extort from the devil what that malefactor had stolen. *No one can get into a strong man's house and carry off his implements, unless he has tied up the strong man first*, he said (Mk 3:27; Mt 12:29). He did bind the strong one, and seized his equipment; but this was certainly no robbery. He will tell you why not: "Those vessels had been stolen from my great house; I was not stealing, only recovering what had been stolen from me."

Verse 6. The folly of the cross

10. *O God, you know my folly.* Again it is the body that speaks; for what folly was there in Christ? Is he not the Power of God and the Wisdom of God? But

---

36. The Philippians hymn implicitly contrasts Adam and Christ, as Augustine goes on to show.
37. Is 14:13-14; see note at Exposition of Psalm 59,10.
38. Variant: "Let him who is himself a robber pursue. . . ."

perhaps what he is calling "folly" here is what the apostle was referring to when he said, *The foolishness of God is wiser than mortals* (1 Cor 1:25). In that case, *my folly* means "the quality in me that was derided by those who think them-selves wise." You know why that happened, for *you know my folly*. What, indeed, could seem more like folly than that one who had it in his power to fell his persecutors with a single word should allow himself to be arrested, scourged, spat upon, punched, crowned with thorns, and nailed to a tree? It looks like folly, it seems to be foolishness; but this foolishness gets the better of all the wise. Yes, foolish it is; but to anyone who does not understand the methods of the farmer, dropping a seed into the earth looks foolish. The harvest was brought in with immense labor, carried to the threshing-floor, threshed and winnowed; at last, after all the perils of weather and storms, after all the hard work of the country people and the worries of their masters, the purified wheat was stored in the barn. And then, with the advent of winter, what was purified is brought out and thrown onto the ground! An apparently foolish procedure; but it is not the folly that it appears to be, because of the farmer's hope.

Christ did not spare himself because neither did the Father spare him, *but delivered him up for us all* (Rom 8:32). Of him the apostle says, *Christ loved me, and delivered himself up for me* (Gal 2:20), because *unless the seed falls into the earth to die there, it will bear no fruit* (Jn 12:24.25). This is the folly; but *you know it*. But as for the enemies, if they had understood, they would never have crucified the Lord of glory.[39]

O God, you know my folly, and my transgressions are not hidden from you. It is absolutely clear, evident and obvious, that this is to be understood as spoken by the body. Christ had no transgressions. Others transgressed against him, but he did not transgress. *My transgressions are not hidden from you*: this is a way of saying, "I have confessed all my transgressions to you, but even before I spoke you saw them all in my mind. You saw the wounds you meant to heal." But where does he see them? Undoubtedly in his body, in his members, in his faithful, among whom was this member who was confessing his sins and clinging to Christ. *My transgressions are not hidden from you*, he says.

Verse 7. *"Let them not blush over me"*

11. *Let not those who wait for you blush over me, O Lord, Lord of hosts.* Here is the voice of the head once more: *Let them not blush over me*; let no one taunt them, "Where is the one on whom you were pinning your hopes?" Let them not be challenged, "What has become of him who said to you, *Believe in God, believe in me as well?*" (Jn 14:1). *Let not those who wait for you blush over me, O*

---

39. See 1 Cor 2:8.

Lord, Lord of hosts. Let me not be a cause of dismay for those who seek you, God of Israel.

This verse could also be understood as spoken by the body, provided you do not think of the body as one man or woman alone. One such person is no more than a very small member, not the whole body; for the body consists of all the members. The body in its entirety is the whole Church. Well then, the Church certainly can say, *"Let not those who wait for you blush over me, O Lord, Lord of hosts.* Let me not be so afflicted by the persecutors who attack me, let me not be so trampled by my hate-filled enemies or by the heretics who bark at me (the heretics who went out from me because they had never been truly mine,[40] for if they had belonged to me, perhaps they would have stayed); let me not be so grievously upset by the stumbling-blocks they set for me, that those who wait for you are made to blush over me, *O Lord, Lord of hosts. Let me not be a cause of dismay for those who seek you, God of Israel."*

Verse 8. The right kind of shamelessness

12. *Since it was for your sake that I endured reproaches, my face was wholly shameless.* It is no great matter to say, *I endured*; the important thing is that *I endured for your sake*. If you have to endure hardship because you have sinned, you are enduring it for your deeds, not for the sake of God. *What credit is it to you*, asks Peter, *if you suffer punishment because you have sinned?* (1 Pt 2:20). But if you suffer because you have kept God's commandment, then you truly are enduring for God's sake; and your reward will be eternal, because you have been reproached on his account. He endured first, so that we might learn endurance. And if he, against whom no accusation could be made, held out bravely, how much more should we? Even if we are not guilty of the sin of which our enemy accuses us, we nonetheless have some other sin in us that deserves a whipping. Suppose someone calls you a thief, and you are not. You hear it as an insult. But you are not so far from being a thief that you are not anything at all that displeases God. Christ had committed no robbery whatever, and he could say with absolute truth, *Now the prince of this world is coming, and he will find nothing in me* (Jn 14:30). Yet he was called a sinner,[41] an unjust man, Beelzebub,[42] a madman. And do you, his slave, think yourself too grand to hear reproaches you deserve, when the Lord heard them quite undeservedly? He came to set an example for you. So you do not profit by it? Then he worked to no purpose.[43] Why did he listen to the insults? Only so that you might not weaken

---

40. See 1 Jn 2:19.
41. See Jn 9:24.
42. See Mt 10:25.
43. Reading *sic tu non proficis* with most codices. A variant is *si tu non proficis*, "if you do not profit, he worked. . . ."

when you hear them. But if you quail when you hear them, his hearing of them was pointless, for he did it only with you in mind.

Since it was for your sake that I endured reproaches, my face was wholly shameless. Shamelessness covered my entire face, he says. What does it mean, to be shameless? To be without embarrassment. But this almost seems to be a vicious trait. We say, "That fellow is utterly shameless," or "He is so shameless that he is incapable of blushing." Shamelessness is therefore a kind of impudence. But a Christian needs this shamelessness when in the company of people who do not love Christ. Any Christian who is ashamed of Christ in such circumstances will be blotted out from the book of the living. It is up to you to show this kind of shamelessness when you are derided for your allegiance to Christ, when people call you "devotee of a crucified man, worshiper of an executed criminal, lackey of someone who is dead." If you are ashamed then, you are dead yourself. Christ deceives no one, and his warning is clear: *If anyone is ashamed of me before men and women, I will be ashamed of that person before the angels of God* (Lk 9:26). You must watch yourself, then; be shameless, show plenty of effrontery when you are reproached on Christ's account. Do not let yourself be browbeaten. Why be timid about your brow, when you have armed it with the sign of the cross?[44] *Since it was for your sake that I endured reproaches, my face was wholly shameless.* Yes, it was for your sake, and because I did not blush about you when people mocked me on your account, I can say that *my face was wholly shameless.*

Verses 9-10. Christ's own people did not recognize him

13. *I became estranged from my brethren, an alien to the children of my mother.* He became an alien to the children of the synagogue, he means; for in his own country people were saying about him, *We know this is the son of Mary and Joseph, don't we?*[45] How then could they say, in a different place, *As for this man, we do not know where he comes from* (Jn 9:29)? He must have become *an alien to the children of his mother.* Did they not know where I come from, he asks, though my flesh was from the same stock as theirs? Were they persistently unaware that I was born from the loins of Abraham, my flesh already hidden in him when his servant put a hand under Abraham's thigh and swore by the God of heaven?[46] Yet *I became an alien to the children of my mother.* How did it

---

44. There is a play in the foregoing sentences between *frons* (the forehead), *frontosus* (one who behaves with effrontery) and the phenomenon of blushing, which the ancients seem to have connected mainly with the forehead.
45. See Jn 6:42; Mt 13:55; Mk 6:3; Lk 4:22.
46. See Gn 24:9.

happen? Why did they not know me? Why did they regard me as a stranger? How did they dare to say, *We do not know where he comes from?*

Because zeal for your house devoured me, I hunted down their iniquities, I did not patiently tolerate those who needed my correction, I wanted you to be glorified in your house, and I whipped the unjust traffickers out of the temple,[47] concerning which action the evangelist remembered this verse, *Zeal for your house devoured me.* This is why I was a stranger in their eyes, this is why I seemed alien, this is why they said, *We do not know where he comes from.* They would have acknowledged where I came from, if they had acknowledged your commandments; for if I had found them keeping those commandments of yours, there would have been no occasion for zeal for your house to devour me.

The reproaches of those who insulted you fell upon me. Paul also mentioned this testimony, in the passage we read just now. He reminded us that *whatever was written in earlier days was written for our instruction, so that through the consolation of the scriptures we might have hope* (Rom 15:4). Accordingly, when he cited the words, *the reproaches of those who insulted you fell upon me,* Paul indicated that they are spoken by Christ. But why *those who insulted you?* They were not insulting the Father, surely? Was it not Christ himself who was the butt of their insults? And if so, why does he say, *The reproaches of those who insulted you fell upon me?* Because, he told us, whoever knows me knows my Father too;[48] and, conversely, no one insults Christ without insulting God equally, as no one honors the Father except by honoring the Son.[49] *The reproaches of those who insulted you fell upon me,* because I was their target.

Verses 11-13. Fasting, sackcloth and derision

14. *I covered my soul with fasting, and it was made a pretext for insulting me.* We explained the meaning of Christ's fasting in a spiritual sense, when commenting on another psalm, beloved.[50] He fasted when all those who had believed in him abandoned him, because what he hungered for was that people should have faith in him. His experience of thirst was akin to this. When he said to a woman, *I am thirsty; give me a drink* (Jn 4:7), it was for her faith that he was thirsting, just as when he cried from the cross, *I am thirsty* (Jn 19:28) he was longing for the faith of those for whom he had prayed, *Father, forgive them, for they do not know what they are doing* (Lk 23:34). But what did they offer him in his thirst? Vinegar. Wine that has turned vinegary can also be called stale and old, and this is just what they would give him, from their old selves, because they

---

47. See Jn 2:15-17.
48. See Jn 14:9.
49. See Jn 5:23.
50. See Exposition 2 of Psalm 34, 4.

were unwilling to be made new. Why did they not want to be new? Because they had no kinship with the title of this psalm, where it is written, *For those who will be changed.* In this sense Christ could say, *I covered my soul with fasting.*

Notice, further, that he had refused the gall they offered to him, preferring to fast rather than accept bitterness. No one embittered by resentment enters his body, or any of the people alluded to in another psalm: *Let not the resentful be lifted high in their own esteem* (Ps 65(66):7). I therefore *covered my soul with fasting, and it was made a pretext for insulting me.* It was made a pretext because I did not acquiesce in their doings; that is to say, I fasted from them. Anyone who refuses consent to the persuasions of the wicked fasts from them, and by such fasting earns opprobrium, and that means that the righteous person's refusal becomes a pretext for insults.

15. *I made sackcloth my clothing.* We have already said something about sackcloth, in connection with the text, *When they were troublesome to me, I clothed myself in goat's hair and humbled my soul with fasting.*[51] He says, *I made sackcloth my clothing,* to imply, "I presented my flesh to those who raged against me, but my divinity I kept hidden." He calls his flesh *sackcloth* because it was mortal flesh; it had to be, so that God might condemn sin in the flesh.[52] *I made sackcloth my clothing, and so became a byword for them,* an example to be ridiculed. We speak of a byword[53] when a thing is cited as an example of something else that is being censured. So, for instance, if we say, "May he share the fate of So-and-So," the latter is being used as an illustration and a byword for the person being condemned. In this sense *I became a byword for them.*

16. *Those who were seated at the gate used to scoff at me.* The phrase, *at the gate,* simply means "in public places." *And the wine-drinkers would strike up their songs against me.* Do you suppose, brothers and sisters, that this happened only to Christ? By no means. It happens to him every day in the persons of his members. Whenever it happens to be necessary for a servant of God to forbid drunkenness and debauchery in some country place, or in a town, where God's word has not been heard, the drinkers will not merely sing; they will begin to make up songs disparaging the very person who tries to restrain their singing. A contrast is drawn here between Christ's fasting and their revelries. *The wine-drinkers would strike up their songs against me,* for they were drinking the wine of error, the wine of impiety, the wine of pride.

---

51. Ps 34(35):13. See Exposition 2 of Psalm 34, 3.
52. See Rom 8:3.
53. The basic meaning of the word he uses, *parabola,* is "something that is thrown alongside something else" to illustrate its meaning; but "parable" does not immediately suggest this in modern English. See also Exposition of Psalm 77,1, and note there.

Verse 14. Turn to God by prayer

17. *But I was turned toward you by my prayer, O Lord.* My orientation was toward you—but how did I manage that? By praying to you. When any of you are reviled, my brothers and sisters, and there is no way to avoid it, when reproaches are flung at you, and you can find no way of restraining the one who flings them, no recourse is left to you except prayer. But remember to pray also for the person who rails against you. *I was turned toward you by my prayer, O Lord.*

This is the time of grace, O God, for now the seed is being buried, and the crop will spring up. *This is the time of grace, O God.* The prophets spoke of this gracious time, as the apostle recalls: *See, now is the acceptable time, lo, this is the day of salvation.*[54] The psalm prays, *This is the time of grace, O God. In your manifold mercy*—this is where the time of grace is: *in your manifold mercy*; for if it were not for your manifold mercy, what would we do in the face of our manifold iniquity? *In your manifold mercy, hear me in the truth of your salvation.* He has spoken of *mercy*, and he adds *truth*, because all the Lord's ways are mercy and truth.[55] Mercy? How is he merciful? In forgiving sins. And truth? Yes, because he keeps his promises. *Hear me in the truth of your salvation.*

Verses 15-16. You may be mud-bound in body while free in spirit. Crying to God from the pit

18. *Keep me clear of the mire, so that I do not stay there.* He is harking back to what he said at the beginning: *I am stuck fast in the mud of the deep, and there is no substance.* You understood the exposition of that verse, so there is no need for lengthy development here. In the present verse he proclaims his need for rescue from that element where he formerly said he was stuck. *Keep me clear of the mire, so that I do not stay there*; and he explains the plea himself by adding, *May I be delivered from those who hate me*; they are the mire that holds me.

But there may be a hint of another meaning here. In the earlier verse he had said, *I am stuck fast*, whereas here he says, *Keep me clear of the mire, so that I do not stay there*. In view of his earlier description of his plight it seems that he ought to be praying, "Save me from the mire where I am already stuck; save me by pulling me out," not "Save me by preventing me from getting stuck." We must take it, then, that he was mired as to his flesh, but not in his spirit. And this he says with an eye to the weakness of his members. If you chance to be captured by someone who is putting you under pressure to commit sin, your body is certainly held fast. As far as your body is concerned you are stuck fast in the mud

---

54. 2 Cor 6:2, alluding to Is 49:8.
55. See Ps 24(25):10.

of the deep. But as long as you have not consented you are not mired for good; only if you consent will you stay there. In that situation you must pray that your spirit be not held fast, as your body already is; your prayer must be for freedom even in chains. *May I be delivered from those who hate me, and from the deepest waters.*

19. *Let not the stormy waters overwhelm me.* But he was already sunk, wasn't he? You said, psalmist, *I have sunk into the depth of the sea,* and you said, *The storm has overwhelmed me.* Evidently it had overwhelmed and sunk him as to his flesh, but not as to his spirit. When the Lord instructed his disciples, *If they have persecuted you in one city, flee to another* (Mt 10:23), he was warning them to keep clear of entanglements in both body and spirit. It is not a good idea for us to get stuck even physically; we should avoid it if we can. However, if we have become stuck by falling into the hands of sinners, then we are stuck as to our bodies, and we are held fast in the mud of the deep; but we can still turn to prayer for our souls, that we may not get stuck spiritually—may not consent, that is. Let the stormy water not sink us, so that we descend into the deepest mire. *Do not let the depths suck me under, nor the pit close its mouth over me.* What does that mean, brothers and sisters? What has he prayed for? The depths of human iniquity are a huge pit, and anyone who falls into it will fall very deep. But if a sinner confesses to God even from that deep place, the pit will not close its mouth over him; so another psalm pleads, *Out of the depths I have cried to you, Lord; O Lord, hear my voice* (Ps 129(130):1-2). The case is different if what has happened to the sinner is the disaster mentioned in another text of scripture: *A person devoid of reverence goes deep into sin and is defiant* (Prv 18:3). Then indeed the pit has closed its mouth upon him. Why has it closed its mouth? Because it has closed the sinner's mouth. The sinner who has lost the ability to confess is truly dead, and the verdict pronounced elsewhere has proved correct: *No confession can be made by a dead person: he is as though non-existent* (Sir 17:26). This is a fate of which we should be very much afraid, brothers and sisters. Suppose you see someone who has committed a sin. He or she is sunk in the pit. But if you point out that person's iniquity, and the sinner replies, "It is true, brother, I have sinned," the pit has not shut its mouth over him. But if you hear the sinner replying, "What's wrong with what I did?" then he has become a defender of his sin. The pit has closed its mouth over him and he has no way of escape. If confession is ruled out, there will be no room for mercy. If you have become a defender of your sin, how can God be your liberator? Make sure you are its accuser, so that he can be a liberator for you.

Exposition 2 of Psalm 68

Second Sermon

Verses 17-18. Yesterday's sermon recalled. Can we finish the psalm today? The sweetness of God's mercy

1. We spoke to you about this psalm yesterday, dearest friends,[1] but the last part of it was left over for us to expound today. I see that the time has come to give you what is still owing, though the length of the psalm may leave us still in debt to you even today. So before we begin, I want to say this: please do not expect any lengthy commentary on verses which are perfectly clear. If you do not, it will leave us free to spend more time on the obscure parts, if need be, and still complete the explanation we owe you. Then we may take on further debts on other days, and discharge those too.

Let us look, then, at the rest of this psalm. The last verse we read was, *Let not the pit close its mouth over me*; and we pointed out to you yesterday, dearly beloved, that we must take the utmost care, and strive by all the means our faith and devotion provide, that such an accursed fate may not befall us. The pit, which means the depth of iniquity, closes its mouth over someone when that person not only lies sunk in sins, but loses the way to confession. On the contrary, when someone says, "I am a sinner," some light is diffused through even the lowest region of the pit.

As the psalm continues our Lord Jesus Christ, both head and body, cries out amid his sufferings. We have already reminded you that in some places you must be alert to the words of the head; but when what is said is unsuitable for the head, you must understand it of the body. Christ speaks as a single person. Scripture says, *They will be two in one flesh* (Gn 2:24; Eph 5:31); and if there are two in one flesh, is it any wonder that there are two in one voice?

The psalm proceeds, then, *Hear me, O Lord, because your mercy is sweet.* He advances the fact that God's mercy is sweet as a reason why he ought to be heard. Would it not be more logical to say, "Hear me, O Lord, so that to me your mercy may be sweet"? Why does he rather choose to say, *Hear me, O Lord, because your mercy is sweet*? The reason becomes clear from other words he uses in his troubled state, different words which also suggest the sweetness of God's mercy. He says, *Hear me, O Lord, for I am in distress.* Obviously anyone who says, *Hear me, O Lord, for I am in distress*, is putting forward a reason why he is

---

1. *Caritati vestrae.*

asking to be heard; and to a petitioner in this distressed condition God's mercy must necessarily be sweet. Scripture speaks of the sweetness of God's mercy in another text. Listen: *Very lovely is the Lord's mercy in time of trouble, like a rainy cloud in drought* (Sir 35:26). That passage calls it *very lovely*; our psalm calls it *sweet.* Bread would not seem delicious if we had not been hungry beforehand. Similarly when God permits or causes us to be in some tribulation, even then he is being merciful; for he is not taking our food away from us, but just stimulating our appetite. What, then, is the psalm saying here: *Hear me, O Lord, because your mercy is sweet?* "Do not delay, but hear me swiftly. I am in such serious trouble that to me your mercy is very sweet. You were putting off the time for bringing me relief only so that the relief you brought would be sweet to me. But there is no reason to delay any longer. Surely my distress has reached the appointed measure? Let your mercy come to me now and do its beneficent work. *Hear me, O Lord, because your mercy is sweet. In accordance with the multitude of your mercies look upon me*, not in accordance with the multitude of my sins."

2. *Do not turn your face away from your child.* The word chosen suggests humility: "from your child,"[2] that is, from a little one; for through the discipline of tribulation I have by now learned to shed my pride. *Do not turn your face away from your child.* This is the very lovely mercy he has mentioned earlier, because the next line clarifies what he has said: *Hear me speedily, for I am in trouble.* What does *speedily* imply? There is no reason to delay: I am in trouble, my affliction has gone ahead, so let your mercy follow.

Verse 19. The deliverance of God's servants may be either secret or manifest

3. *Look upon my soul, and redeem it.* This needs no explanation, so let us go on to the next phrase: *Deliver me, on my enemies' account.* Well, that is a very remarkable petition! It is not one to be touched on only briefly, or skipped over swiftly, but rather one to surprise us. *Deliver me, on my enemies' account.* What does he mean — *deliver me, on my enemies' account?* So that my enemies may be confounded and racked with misery at my deliverance? Well, yes; but if there were no enemies to be tormented by my deliverance, would I have no motive for expecting help? What? Is deliverance only acceptable to you when it entails the condemnation of someone else? Suppose there are no enemies to be discomfited or tormented by your deliverance, will you be left forlorn? Will you not be rescued in that case?

Or are you, perhaps, thinking that it will be good for your enemies, because they may be converted on seeing you delivered? Even so, this is a curious

---

2. The Hebrew of this psalm has the ordinary word for servant, which in the Septuagint became "-ρῖ (child or servant), and in Augustine's Latin version *puer*, which again can mean either child or servant; but he chooses the former sense.

motive, if indeed it does prompt the petition. Is any one of God's servants rescued by the Lord his God in order that other people may profit? Would it mean that, in the absence of any who might benefit, God's servant would not be worth saving?

Whichever way I turn, whether to the punishment of the enemies or to their salvation, I do not see the motive for this request, *deliver me, on my enemies' account*, except for one way of understanding it which I will put before you, with the Lord's help. He who dwells in you will evaluate it in you.

Here it is, then. There is a hidden deliverance of the saints which is granted for their own sake; and there is also a public, manifest deliverance, which is effective for their enemies, either to punish them or to save them. Clearly, God did not rescue the Maccabean brothers from the fires of their persecutors. The cruel Antiochus even brought their mother to them, hoping that by her tender pleas they would be swayed toward love of this life, and so, by lusting to live in the sight of men, they would die to God. But this mother was not like Eve; she was more like Mother Church. She had borne her sons in pain in order to look upon them living, but now she joyfully watched them dying,[3] and begged them to choose death for the laws of the Lord their God, laws inherited from their ancestors, rather than live in defiance of them.[4] What are we to think, brothers and sisters? Surely we must believe that they were delivered? Yet their deliverance was a hidden one; in fact Antiochus, who killed them, believed that he had accomplished all that his cruelty dictated, or, rather, incited.

In the case of the three young men in the fiery furnace, deliverance was plain to see. Since not only their souls but even their bodies were rescued, their salvation was a public matter. So those in the one group were crowned, but in secret; those in the other were openly delivered; but all were saved. What good resulted from the deliverance of the three young men? To what purpose was their crowning deferred? Nebuchadnezzar himself was converted to their God. The king proclaimed the God who had rescued his servants, the very God he had scorned when he threw them into the furnace.[5]

We conclude, therefore, that there is a hidden deliverance, and a manifest deliverance. Hidden deliverance is a matter of the soul; manifest deliverance extends even to the body. The soul is delivered in secret, the body in full view of everyone. If this is how things stand, let us hear the Lord's voice in our psalm. When he said earlier, *Look upon my soul, and redeem it*, he obviously envisaged a hidden deliverance. But there remained the prospect of liberation for his body; for when he rose again, and ascended into heaven, and sent the Holy Spirit from

---

3. Or possibly, "She had borne her sons in pain in order to see them live for ever, and therefore joyfully watched. . . ."
4. See 2 Mac 7.
5. See Dn 3:19-29.

above, those who had raged against him at the time of his death were converted to belief in him. They were changed from enemies into friends, but by his grace, not through any righteousness of their own. This is why he continued his prayer by saying, *Deliver me, on my enemies' account.* For secret deliverance, he prayed, *Look upon my soul*; but he also pleaded, "*On my enemies' account* deliver my body as well. It will not help my enemies if you deliver only my soul, for they will believe that they have won and attained their objective. What is the use of my blood, if I sink down into corruption?[6] *Look upon my soul*, then, and *redeem it* in a way known to you alone; but also *deliver me, on my enemies' account*, that my flesh may not see corruption."

Verses 20-21. God knows all the Church's experience: insults, remorse, and shameful timidity

4. *For you well know the insults flung at me, and my remorse, and my shame.* Let us look at these three. What is an insult? What is remorse? What is shame? An insult is what an enemy flings at you. Remorse is something that gnaws at your conscience. Shame is something that brings a blush to an honorable brow even at a false imputation of guilt; it is no crime, or at any rate no crime on the part of the person accused; yet such is the weakness of our minds that we are often ashamed even when falsely charged, not because the accusation was made, but because such a thing could be believed of us.

Now in the Lord's body all these are experienced. There could be no remorse in him personally, for there was no fault in him. Against Christians a charge was brought: simply the charge of being Christians.[7] And indeed that was their glory, so the strong among them admitted the charge, and admitted it so willingly that they blushed not a whit at the name of their Lord. Shamelessness had covered the faces[8] of those who shared the effrontery of Paul. He had declared, *I am not ashamed of the gospel, for it is the power of God unto salvation for everyone who believes* (Rom 1:16). Come now, Paul, are you not a worshiper of a crucified criminal? "It is an understatement to say that I am not ashamed of it," he replies. "Rather do I boast of that very thing, and that alone, which my enemy thinks ought to shame me. *Far be it from me to boast, save in the cross of our Lord Jesus Christ, in whom the world has been crucified to me, and I to the world*" (Gal 6:14).

---

6. See Ps 29:10(30:9), and Augustine's application of the verse to Christ in his Exposition 2 of Psalm 29, 19.

7. Early in the second century A.D. Pliny the Younger wrote to the Emperor Trajan (A.D. 98-117) inquiring whether Christians were to be punished "for the name alone," or only for crimes associated with the name; see his Letter 96. See also Tertullian, for consolers *Ad Nationes* 1,7; *Apol.* 2-4 on the stigma of the name.

8. See Exposition 1 of this Psalm 68, 12, and note there.

At anyone so boldly confident insult could be flung, but no more. There could be no remorse in a conscience already healed, nor any blush of shame on so noble a brow. But others, charged with having put Christ to death, were deservedly stabbed by their bad consciences,[9] and they suffered a salutary remorse. So they were converted, and could well say, *You know my remorse.* Christ therefore prays in his body, "You, Lord, are well aware not only of the insults I endure, but of my remorse as well, and in certain of my members you also know my shame, because although they believe in me, they blush to confess me publicly in the presence of the impious. Human tongues influence them more powerfully than the divine promise." Take stock of people like this. We should commend them to God, asking him not to leave them as they are, but to perfect them by his help. Someone who did believe, but was wavering, said, *Lord, help my unbelief* (Mk 9:23).

All those who trouble me are present to your sight. Why I am insulted, you know; why I feel remorse, you know; why I am ashamed, you know; so rescue me on my enemies' account. You know all these things about me, but they do not. My enemies are present to your sight, but they are so ignorant. There is no possibility of their being confounded or corrected unless you rescue me quite openly, on my enemies' account.

Verse 21. Christ's loneliness in the passion

5. *My heart expected reproach and misery.* What is implied by the word, *expected*? He foresaw what was to happen, he foretold his future suffering. He had come for no other purpose. If he had been unwilling to die, he would not have willed to be born; and both his birth and his death were oriented to his resurrection. Two moments in human experience were already familiar to us, but one other was unknown. We knew that people are born, and that they die; but we did not know that they would rise and live for ever. In order to reveal to us the destiny of which we knew nothing, Christ embraced as his own the two we knew already. He came for this very reason, and so he could say, *My heart expected reproach and misery.* But misery for whom? Misery he certainly anticipated, but more truly in those who crucified him, in those who persecuted him; because if in them there was misery, in him there could be mercy. He was merciful to their misery even while hanging on the cross, for he prayed, *Father, forgive them, for they do not know what they are doing* (Lk 23:34).

My heart expected reproach and misery; and I looked for someone to grieve together with me, and there was no one. What comfort was it that I had expected it? Or that I had foretold it? How did it help that I said I had come on purpose for

---

9. See Acts 2:37.

this? The time came for what I had prophesied to be realized: *I looked for someone to grieve together with me, and there was no one, and for consolers, but I found none.* This last phrase echoes the preceding one. Where that had *I looked for someone to grieve together with me*, the latter has *for consolers*; and where one had *there was no one*, the following line has *I found none.* He is not introducing a new idea, but repeating the same one. Now, if we go back over it more carefully, a question arises. Surely his disciples did grieve together with him when he was led out to his passion, when he was hanged on the tree, when he died? So deeply did they grieve that Mary Magdalene, who was the first to see him risen, ran joyfully to announce what she had seen to men who were mourning.[10] It is the gospel that tells us so; this is no assumption on our part, or conjecture. Quite certainly the disciples were sorrowful, quite certainly they mourned. Moreover women who were not of his immediate circle wept as he was being led to his passion; he turned to them and said, *Weep not over me, but over yourselves* (Lk 23:28). How is it true, then, that he looked for someone to grieve together with him, and there was no one? We look attentively, and we find sad people, mourning and weeping people; and the statement puzzles us, that *I looked for someone to grieve together with me, and there was no one, and for consolers, but I found none.*

But if we concentrate more closely we shall see that he did look for someone to grieve together with him, and there was no one. The sorrow felt by his disciples was a carnal sorrow about his mortal life, the life that was destined to be transformed by death and restored in resurrection. This was the source of their sadness. Their pity would have been better spent on those blind people who killed their physician, on the wildly delirious patients who attacked the one who had come to bring them health. He willed to cure them, but they thrashed about savagely; and this was the source of sorrow to the doctor. Now ask yourselves whether he found any companion to share this sorrow of his. The psalm does not say, "I looked for someone to grieve, but there was no one"; it says, *For someone to grieve together with me* (that is, someone to grieve for the same reason that I grieve myself), *and I found no one.* Peter certainly loved him dearly. He had flung himself overboard without hesitation to walk on the waves, and was rescued by the Lord's voice.[11] Moreover, when the Lord was led to his passion, Peter followed him with an audacity born of love; but he lost his head and denied the Lord three times. Why did he do that? Because death seemed to him an evil. He therefore shied away from a fate he believed to be bad for himself, and grieved that the Lord should suffer what he himself was anxious to avoid. This was why he had protested on an earlier occasion, *Far be it from you, Lord, have*

10. See Jn 20:18; Mk 16:9.
11. See Mt 14:29-31.

some pity for yourself. This will not happen. It earned him the appellation *Satan,* and this when he had only just been told, *Blessed are you, Simon, son of Jonah* (Mt 16:22.17).

The Lord was saddened on account of those for whom he prayed, *Father, forgive them, for they do not know what they are doing* (Lk 23:34), and in this sorrow he found no companion. *I looked for someone to grieve together with me, and there was no one.* No one at all. *And for consolers, but I found none.* Who are his consolers? People who make progress. For those are the ones who console us; they are the consolation of all who preach the truth.

Verse 22. Gall and vinegar: literal and figurative senses

6. *They put gall into my food, and in my thirst they gave me vinegar to drink.* This happened literally; the gospel tells us about it. But we should also understand it this way, brothers and sisters: "The very fact that I found no consolers, that I could find no one to grieve together with me, this was gall to me, this was bitter, this was vinegar. It was bitter in the grief it caused me, and vinegar because they were like old, sour wine."

The reason for taking it this way is that although the gospel does tell us about gall being offered to him,[12] it was presented as a drink, not as food. Yet we must take the prophecy seriously and believe that the saying was verified: *they put gall into my food.* We therefore need to consider the reality, and not only the words; we must seek the mystery concealed here, knock at the door of the secret meaning, enter through the torn veil of the temple, and see the holy sign[13] hidden under both the spoken word and the event. *They put gall into my food,* he says. What they gave him was not food, but drink; yet they did put it into his food. The Lord had already eaten food, and the gall was thrown into it. He had partaken of sweet food when he ate the passover with his disciples; and there he revealed the sacrament of his body. This is sweet food indeed, the delicious food of our unity in Christ of which the apostle speaks: *Because there is but one bread, we, though many, are one body* (1 Cor 10:17). Who pours gall upon this sweet food? Who else, but anyone who contests the gospel, thereby imitating Christ's persecutors? The Jews crucified a man who walked the earth, but their sin is less than that of people who defy him now enthroned in heaven. The Jews gave Christ a bitter drink after the food he had eaten, but they do no less who bring the Church into disrepute by their sinful lives. The heretics do the same by their bitter jealousy, but let them not be lifted high in their own esteem.[14] All these pour gall over Christ's delicious food.

---

12. See Mt 27:34.
13. *Sacramentum.*
14. See Ps 65(66):7.

But what does the Lord do? He refuses them entry into his body. His action was a holy sign:[15] when they offered him gall he tasted it, but would not drink.[16] For our part, if we had no occasion to put up with them at all, we would not even taste them; but since they have to be endured, they also have to be tasted. All the same, such people cannot find a place among the members of Christ; and therefore though they may be tasted, they cannot be taken into the body. *They put gall into my food, and in my thirst they gave me vinegar to drink.* I was thirsty, and I accepted the vinegar; this means, "I longed for their faith, but all I found was stale, vinegary wine."

Verses 23-24. Open-eyed iniquity leads to merited blindness and bent backs

7. *May their table become a trap for them, before their very eyes.* As they set a trap for me in offering me such a drink, so may a like trap be set for them. But why does it add, *Before their very eyes*? It would have sufficed to say, *May their table be a trap for them.* The addition suggests that some people are well aware of their iniquity, and continue in it with immovable obstinacy; for such sinners the trap is set before their very eyes. Those who go down alive to the under-world[17] are particularly wicked. And what does scripture say about persecutors? *If the Lord had not been among us, perhaps they would have swallowed us alive* (Ps 123(124):2.3). What does *alive* imply? That we were consenting to their will, and knew that we should not consent. The trap is set in front of them, where they can see it, but they are not corrected. (Or it could mean that since the trap is set in front of them they have no excuse for falling into it.) But clearly they know the trap is there, yet step into it, and allow themselves to be caught by the neck. How much better it would have been to steer clear of the trap, recognize their sin, repudiate their error, shake off their bitterness, make their way over into the body of Christ, and seek the glory of the Lord! But so gross is their arrogance that they see the trap in front of them, and yet fall into it. *Let their eyes be dimmed so that they cannot see*, the psalm continues. Since they saw to no purpose, let their sight be taken away from them. *May their table become a trap for them, before their very eyes.*

When the psalm prays, *Let it become a trap for them, before their very eyes*, this is not a wish but a prophetic statement; it is not hoping that this fate may befall them, but predicting that it will. We have often remarked on this distinction, and you must remember it; otherwise what is uttered by a prescient mind in the Spirit of God would seem like a malevolent imprecation. "Let it happen" is equivalent to "Things cannot turn out otherwise than that this fate befall such

---

15. *Sacramentum.*
16. See Mt 27:34.
17. See Ps 54:16(55:15).

people." And when we see that it is prophesied under the influence of God's Spirit that these things will happen to bad people, our insight serves as a warning that we must avoid them ourselves. It is in our interest to understand the outcome, and so make our enemies do us a good turn.

Let their table be for them retribution and a stumbling-block. This is scarcely unjust, surely? No, indeed, it is just. Why? Because if it is a *retribution*, nothing will happen to them that was not owing. It becomes *a retribution and a stumbling-block*, because they trip up themselves.

8. *Let their eyes be dimmed so that they cannot see; bend their backs over permanently.* If their eyes have grown dim so that they cannot see, curvature of the spine is the inevitable consequence. Why is that? Because when they have lost the sense of heavenly things, they cannot but have their thoughts focused on things below. No one who has heard and heeded the invitation, "Lift up your hearts,"[18] can have a bent back. An erect stance characterizes one who looks to the hope laid up for us in heaven, especially if we have sent our treasure there ahead of us, whither our heart looks to follow.[19] Those who, by contrast, are already so blinded that they have no understanding of our hope in the life to come can think only of affairs here below; and this means that their backs are bent, like that of the woman whom the Lord set free from her infirmity.[20] Satan had kept her bound for eighteen years, but the Lord healed her and straightened her up; but because he did this on the Sabbath, the Jews were scandalized. And well they might be scandalized over a woman standing up straight, since they were bent themselves. *Bend their backs over permanently.*

Verses 25-26. Retribution, both hidden and manifest

9. *Pour out your anger upon them, and let your furious wrath catch them.* This is perfectly clear. The only phrase to require comment is *let it catch them*: we assume that they are running away. But where will they run to? Up to heaven? You are there. Down to hell? There too you are present.[21] They refuse to accept the wings that would allow them to fly straight forward. *Let your furious wrath catch them*, and not allow them to escape.

10. *Let their dwelling place be derelict.* That this has already happened is plain to all. Earlier the psalm had prayed not only for hidden deliverance—*Look upon my soul, and redeem it*—but also for a visible deliverance for the speaker's body, by continuing, *Deliver me, on my enemies' account.* Here too he foretells certain calamities that will befall them, those punishments of which he has just

---

18. See note at Exposition of Psalm 10, 3.
19. See Mt 6:21.
20. See Lk 13:11-16.
21. See Ps 138(139):8.

been speaking. But these are hidden; for how many people would be aware of the misfortune of someone whose heart had gone blind? If such a person lost his bodily sight, everyone would deem him wretched; but if he loses his spiritual eyes, yet continues to be surrounded by ample material goods, they think him fortunate—or, at any rate, those who have lost their own spiritual sight think him so.

So much for hidden punishment. But is there any punishment that works openly, manifesting to all that retribution has been visited upon malefactors? The blindness of the Jews is a hidden punishment; has any open vengeance overtaken them? *Let their dwelling place be derelict, and let there be no one to live in their tents.* This has happened in the very city of Jerusalem, where they thought them- selves so powerful as they shouted against the Son of God, *Crucify him! Crucify him!* and seemed to prove the stronger, since they were able to kill the man who had raised the dead. How powerful they thought themselves, how mighty! But the Lord's vengeance was on their trail. The city was destroyed, the Jews were defeated, and countless thousands of people were slain. No Jew is allowed access there now. Where their shouting prevailed against the Lord, they are not allowed by the Lord to live.[22] They have lost the place of their anger; but if only they could, at last, acknowledge the place of their peace! What good did Caiaphas do them by warning, *If we let him alone like this, the Romans will come, and sweep away our land and our nationhood* (Jn 11:48)? They did not let him live, but now he is alive; and the Romans did come, and took from them their land and their nationhood, A few minutes ago, when the gospel was read, we heard Christ's lament: *Jerusalem, Jerusalem, how often I wanted to gather your children to myself, as a hen gathers her chicks under her wings, but you would have none of it! See then, your house will be left to you derelict* (Mt 23:37.38). The psalm says the same: *Let their dwelling place be derelict, and let there be no one to live in their tents.* By saying, *Let there be no one to live there*, it means no one from their own number; for all those places are full of people, but empty of Jews.[23]

Verse 27. Christ speaks in the voice of wounded humanity

11. Why did this happen? *Because they persecuted someone whom you struck, and added to the pain of my wounds.* If they persecuted someone who had been struck by God, why was that sinful? What sort of evil intent is being imputed to them? Malice. What happened to Christ was what had to happen. He had come in order to suffer, certainly; but he punished the man who brought

---

22. The city was destroyed by the Roman legions under Titus in A.D. 70. It was rebuilt by the Emperor Hadrian and renamed Aelia Capitolina in A.D. 135. At this time Jews were banished from the area.
23. Compare Augustine's reflections in his Exposition 1 of Psalm 58, 21.

about the suffering. The traitor Judas was punished, and Christ was crucified; but he bought us with his blood, and punished Judas for the blood-money he had received. Judas threw away the silver for which he had sold the Lord, but failed to realize what price the Lord had paid to redeem him.[24] This is what happened to Judas. But when we consider the general principle that there is always due measure in retribution, and no one is allowed to inflict more cruelty than the power accorded to him extends, how could people have added anything further to the one who is praying here? And in what sense had the Lord struck him?

The Lord is undoubtedly speaking here in the name of those whose body he had made his own, whose flesh he had assumed—that is to say, in the name of the human race, and of Adam, who was the first to be struck by death for his sin. As a consequence of this human beings are born mortal and subject to the same punishment; but any who persecute their fellow-humans add to this penalty. This or that human person would not have been liable to death unless the Lord had struck him; but what business have you, human yourself, to make things worse by your cruelty? Is it not bad enough for anyone that he or she must die sometime? Each of us bears his or her own pain, but those who persecute us are adding to it. The pain itself is a blow struck by the Lord. We know that the Lord struck men and women in accordance with his sentence: *On the day that you touch it, you shall die the death* (Gn 2:17). From this *death* Christ had drawn his flesh, and our old humanity was crucified with him.[25] In Adam's voice, in the voice of our human race, he says now, *They persecuted one whom you struck, and added to the pain of my wounds*. What are these painful wounds? He means that they added to the pain of sins, for he calls his sins wounds. But you must not look to the head here: rather to the body, in whose name he prayed in another psalm, a psalm that is certainly his, since his cry from the cross was its opening verse: *O God, my God, why have you forsaken me?* And there he continues, *The tale of my sins leaves me far from salvation* (Ps 21:2(22:1)). These wounds are the ones inflicted by wayside robbers on the man whom a Samaritan lifted onto his own mount. A priest and a Levite had passed by, seen him and spurned him; he had no hope of care from them. But a passing Samaritan took pity on him, approached, and hoisted him onto his own beast.[26] Now the name "Samaritan" means "guardian" in our tongue; and who else is our guardian but our Lord and Savior Jesus Christ? He has risen from the dead and can never die again,[27] and so he does not sleep, nor ever slumber, he who guards Israel.[28] *They added to the pain of my wounds*.

---

24. See Mt 27:5.
25. See Rom 6:6.
26. See Lk 10:30-36.
27. See Rom 6:9.
28. See Ps 120(121):4.

Verse 28. God's permissive will and human malice

12. *Heap further iniquity upon their iniquity.* What kind of request is this? Who would dare ask such a thing? The speaker is begging God to *heap further iniquity upon* the iniquity they are already committing. How can God add iniquity? Is there any iniquity in God, that he could add to theirs? No, certainly not, for we know that the apostle Paul spoke truly, *What are to say, then? Is there iniquity in God? Absolutely not* (Rom 9:14). How, then, are we to understand this petition in the psalm, *heap further iniquity upon their iniquity?*

May the Lord give us his assistance in explaining it, and enable us to be brief, since you are tired. Their first iniquity was that they killed a just man, but to that was added a further iniquity: that he whom they crucified was the Son of God. As they saw it, their savagery was directed against a human being, for if they had known him, they would never have crucified the Lord of glory.[29] In the iniquity that was their own they meant to kill him as simply human; but to this iniquity of theirs a further iniquity was added: that of crucifying the Son of God. Who heaped this iniquity upon them? He who had said, *Perhaps they will respect my Son; I will send him.*[30] They were used to killing the servants sent to them to collect rent and revenue. But God sent his Son, his own Son, so that they could kill him too.[31] In this sense God added further iniquity to the iniquity that was theirs. But did he do so out of cruelty, or as a just retribution? The psalm gives us the answer: *Let it be for them a retribution, and a stumbling-block.* They had deserved to be so blinded that they could not recognize God's Son. And God was the agent of this; he heaped further iniquity upon their iniquity, not by wounding them, but by not curing them. If someone has a fever, you may intensify the fever and worsen the disease not by making the person ill but by not doing anything to help. Similarly the iniquity of Christ's persecutors was aggravated by the addition of further iniquity, and their malice intensified, because they were unworthy of healing. As scripture says, *People of ill-will and villains go from bad to worse* (2 Tm 3:13).

And let them have no part in your righteousness. This is self-explanatory.

Verse 29. Who is written in the book of life?

13. *Let them be blotted out of the book of the living.* But had they ever been inscribed there? We must not take this to mean that God writes someone's name in the book of life, and then deletes it. If a mere man could say, *What I have*

---

29. See 1 Cor 2:8.
30. See Mt 21:37.
31. A sharp expression of the truth. A modern preacher might wish to add qualifications: that they killed him by God's permissive will; and that God's overall intention was the glorification of Christ and the redemption of our race, within which plan the crucifixion was a necessary part.

written, I have written, in connection with a title already inscribed *The King of the Jews*,[32] is it likely that God would write a name and then erase it? He has complete foreknowledge;[33] and before the world was created he predestined all who are to reign with his Son in eternal life.[34] These he has written, and the book of life contains all their names.

Moreover, what does the Spirit of God say in Revelation, when foretelling the persecutions that will be stirred up in the future by the Antichrist? *All whose names are not written in the book of life will take his part* (Rv 13:8). From this it is perfectly clear that those whose names are there will not take his part. But as for the others, how can their names be blotted out, if they were never included? The expression "blotted out" must be used from the standpoint of their own expectations: they thought their names were written. So what does the petition, *let them be blotted out of the book of life,* imply? "Let it become plain to them that they are not there."

A similar idiom is used in another psalm: *A thousand shall fall at your side, and ten thousand at your right hand* (Ps 90(91):7). This means: many will be scandalized, even among those who hoped to sit enthroned beside you, even among the crowd who expected to stand at your right hand, marked off from the goats at your left.[35] This does not mean that anyone who has stood there will later fall away, or that anyone who has sat beside Christ will be unseated. It means that any who thought themselves already there will subsequently be scandalized and fall. In other words, many who hoped to sit with you, and many who hoped to stand at your right, will fall—yes, these very people.

It is the same in our psalm. Some hoped that on the strength of their own righteousness they were written in God's book. Such were they to whom Christ said, *You search the scriptures, thinking that in them you have eternal life* (Jn 5:39). But when their condemnation has reached the point where it is obvious even to themselves, they will be blotted out of the book of the living; that is to say, they will know that they are not there. This must be the meaning, for the following line clarifies what has just been said: *And let them not be written with the just.* The speaker in the psalm is being more explicit: "I said, *Let them be blotted out*, because I spoke from the standpoint of their expectations. But what should I say in accordance with your just judgment? *Let them not be written.*"

---

32. See Jn 19:21-22.
33. *Praescius est.* A variant is *praecisus est*: perhaps "his decree is absolute."
34. See Rom 8:29-30; Eph 1:4-5.
35. See Mt 25:33.

Verses 30-31. Poverty and sorrow; riches in the shelter of God's face

14. *I am poor and sorrowful.* Why does he say that? Is it so that we may understand that all the bad things the poor man has said were spoken out of the bitterness of his spirit? He has indeed spoken of many disasters that will overtake his enemies. Are we meant to say to him, "Why do you say such things? Don't be so hard on them." To which he would reply, "*I am poor and sorrowful.* They brought me to penury, they reduced me to this state of grief. That is why I speak so."

No, this is not the right interpretation. His words are not the irritable outburst of one who curses, but the predictions of a prophet. He means to recommend to us some of the things he intends to say later concerning his poverty and sorrow, so that we may learn to be poor and sorrowful too; for *blessed are the poor in spirit, for the kingdom of heaven is theirs*, and *blessed are those who mourn, for they shall be comforted* (Mt 5:3.5). He first set us an example, and this is why he says, *I am poor and sorrowful.* The whole body of Christ says the same. Christ's body on earth is poor and sorrowful. But surely Christians may be rich? Yes, but from the very fact that they are Christians they are necessarily poor, because in comparison with the heavenly riches they hope for, they deem all their gold no better than sand. *I am poor and sorrowful.*

15. *And the salvation of your countenance has become my support, O God.* Is this poor person left abandoned? By no means. How often do you invite a poor ragamuffin to your table? Yet the salvation of God's countenance has become this poor person's support, for in his needy condition God has hidden the pauper close to his own face. So does another psalm promise: *You will hide them in the hidden recess of your face* (Ps 30:21(31:20)). Do you seek to know what riches are to be found there? Your earthly riches give you the choice of dining on what you want, and when you want; but those other riches preserve you from ever being hungry again. *I am poor and sorrowful, and the salvation of your countenance has become my support, O God.* To what purpose? That I may not be poor or sorrowful any longer.

I will praise God's name with song, I will magnify him with praise. There you have it: this poor person is praising God's name in song, magnifying him with praise. How could he presume to sing, if he had not been relieved of his poverty? *I will praise God's name with song, I will magnify him with praise.* These are vast riches! From his inner treasury he has brought forth wonderful jewels of praise to offer to God. *I will magnify him with praise*: this is my wealth. *The Lord gave, and the Lord has taken away.* Was Job left wretched, then? Not at all. Look at his riches: *This has happened as the Lord willed: may the Lord's name be blessed* (Jb 1:21). *I will praise God's name with song, I will magnify him with praise.*

Verse 32. The pleasing sacrifice; praise with horns and hooves

16. My praise *will be pleasing to God, more acceptable than a new calf sprouting horns and hooves.* A sacrifice of praise is more pleasing to God than the sacrifice of a calf. *By a sacrifice of praise I shall be honored, and there is the way where I will show him the salvation of God,* says another psalm in God's name. *Offer to God a sacrifice of praise, and address your prayers to the Most High* (Ps 49(50):23.14). So I will praise God, and my offering will be more acceptable to him than that of a new calf sprouting horns and hooves. The praise that proceeds from my mouth will please God more than a choice victim led to his altar.

Do we need to stop over the horns and hooves? Well, anyone who is well instructed, and rich in the praises of God, also needs horns for tossing an opponent, and hooves to churn up the earth. You know how calves do this when they are growing up, and developing toward the aggressive habits of bulls. But this calf is called *new* because it is full of new life. So if some heretic contradicts us, I will toss him on my horns. Another may not contradict, but he is earthly-minded, with no sensitivity except for base things: let this one be stirred up by my hooves. Then my offering of praise will please you, O God; it will already be part of the praise rendered in the company of the holy angels when this time of poverty and sorrow is over, where no opponent will challenge us and need tossing, nor any sluggish person need to be aroused from the earth.

Verses 33-34. Joy for the poor, a hearing for the fettered

17. *Let the needy see it and be glad.* Let them believe, and rejoice in their hope. Let them become more needy still, that they may deserve to be fed full, lest while belching with their over-rich pride they be denied the health-giving bread. *Seek the Lord,* you needy ones, hunger and thirst for him, for he is the living bread that came down from heaven.[36] *Seek the Lord, and your soul will live.* You seek bread to maintain the life of your flesh; seek the Lord, that your soul may live.

18. *For the Lord has listened to the poor.* He has heard the poor, and he would not have heard them if they had not been poor. Do you want to be heard? Then be poor. Let the cry wrung from you be one of pain, not of repugnance! *For the Lord has listened to the poor, and has not spurned his servants in their shackles.* He was offended by his servants, so he shackled them; but he did not disdain them when from their shackles they entreated him. What are these shackles? Mortality, and the perishable nature of our flesh—these are the fetters that bind us. Do you want an indication of how heavy these shackles are? Scripture says,

---

36. See Jn 6:51.

The corruptible body weighs down the soul (Wis 9:15). When people long to be rich in this world, what they are seeking is something to pad their fetters with.[37] But let the padding be limited to what the shackles require; seek only so much of material wealth as will keep you free from want. If you seek more than you need, you are trying to make your shackles heavier. In our captive state it may be better to leave the shackles as they are. Let the day's own troubles be enough.[38] From these troubles we cry out to God, *for the Lord has listened to the poor, and has not spurned his servants in their shackles.*

Verses 35-37. Praise from creation; the building of Zion

19. *Let the heavens and the earth praise him, the sea and all the crawling things in them.* The real wealth of this poor person is to contemplate creation and praise the Creator. *Let the heavens and the earth praise him, the sea and all the crawling things in them.* And is this creation alone in praising God, if God is praised through our contemplation of it?

20. Now listen to something else: *For God will save Zion.* He is restoring his Church by incorporating the believing Gentiles into his only-begotten Son, for he does not cheat those who believe in him of what he has promised. *For God will save Zion, and the cities of Judea will be built up.* These are the churches. Let no one carp at this, asking, "When will that happen—that the cities of Judea will be rebuilt?" Ah, if only you could see what a building is in question; if only you were willing to be a living stone and find your place within it! Even now the cities of Judea are being built up, for Judah means "Confession." The cities of Judea are built up by humble confession, so that proud persons who are ashamed to confess remain outside. *For God will save Zion.* What Zion is meant? Listen to what comes next: *The offspring of his servants will possess her, and they who love his name will dwell within her.*

21. We have finished the psalm; but let us delay for a moment over the last two lines, for they have something to teach us, if we are tempted to despair of our prospects and therefore hesitate to take our place in the building. *The offspring of his servants will possess her*, the psalm says. Now, who are *the offspring of his servants*? You will answer, perhaps, "The Jews, who are born from Abraham's stock. But we are not descended from Abraham, so how can we come to possess that city?" But the Jews to whom the Lord said, *If you are Abraham's children, act as Abraham did* (Jn 8:39), were no offspring of Abraham, were they? No; *the offspring of his servants* are those who imitate the faith of his servants, and they will *possess her*. The final line clarifies this one that has preceded it, and it seems

---

37. Literally rags, to ease the abrasiveness.
38. See Mt 6:34.

to settle your doubts. You might be worried when you hear the promise, *the offspring of his servants will possess her*; you might think this concerned the Jews alone, and say, "We are the offspring of Gentiles who worshiped idols and paid cult to demons, so what hope is there for us with regard to that city?" But the psalm immediately added reassurance to give you expectation and hope: *and they who love his name will dwell within her*. These are the offspring of his servants: the people who *love his name*. Since his servants loved his name, it follows that those who do not love his name have no claim to be the offspring of his servants. And it also follows that those who do love his name should not disclaim to be his servants' offspring.

Exposition of Psalm 69

A Sermon[1]

Verse 2. Christ, leader and exemplar of martyrs. Danger threatens always

1. Thanks be to the grain of wheat that willed to die and so be multiplied;[2] thanks be to God's only-begotten Son, our Lord and Savior Jesus Christ, who deemed it no unworthy act to undergo our death, in order to make us worthy of his life. Think of it: he was alone until he made the crossing: as he said in a psalm: *I am all alone, until my passover,*[3] because the grain was indeed solitary, but in such a way that it held within it huge potential fecundity. How magnificent are the grains that imitate his passion, those over whom we exult as we celebrate the birthdays[4] of the martyrs! Christ's members are very numerous, and all are united by the bond of charity and peace under one head, our Savior himself; but as you have good cause to know, having heard it so often, they all form one person, and their voice is frequently heard as the voice of a single person in the psalms. One cries out, voicing the prayer of all, because all are one in this one person. Let us listen to it and hear how the martyrs struggled, and in what peril they lived amid the world's tempestuous hatred. They were threatened not only in their bodies, which they would in any case have had to lay aside sooner or later, but even in their faith; for if they had weakened, and yielded to the sometimes agonizing pains of persecution, or to the lure of the present life, they would have lost the reward God had promised. Not by word alone, but by his example too, Christ had relieved them of every fear: by word, in telling them, *Do not be afraid of those who kill the body, but cannot kill the soul* (Mt 10:28); but also by example, for he acted as he had taught. He refused to evade the hands that scourged him, the slaps of those who struck him, the saliva of those who spat at him, the thorny crown they pressed on him, and the cross on which they killed him. He chose to avoid none of these, though he was in no way liable; he made that choice for the sake of those who were liable, and made himself a medicine for the sick. The martyrs faced the struggle; but they would certainly have broken down had he not unfailingly stood by them—he who said, *Lo, I am with you even to the end of the ages* (Mt 28:20).

---

1. Augustine, unusually, ignores the title this time.
2. See Jn 12:25.
3. Ps 140(141):10. The use of the verb *transire* strikes a paschal note.
4. *Natalitia*; see note at Exposition of Psalm 63, 15.

2. In this psalm, then, we hear the voice of people gravely troubled; and we must undoubtedly hear it as that of martyrs exposed to danger amid their sufferings, but fully confident in their head. Let us listen to them and from sympathetic hearts join our voice to theirs, even if we do not compare with them in pain. They are already crowned, but we are still imperiled, not because the persecutions that bore so heavily on them bear on us, but because we are beset by even worse dangers arising from scandals of every kind. Our age qualifies far more truly for that "woe" about which the Lord gave warning: *Woe to the world because of scandals* (Mt 18:7). And he predicted, *With iniquity increasing mightily, the love of many will grow cold* (Mt 24:12). Lot was a holy man, and while he lived in Sodom he was not subjected to any bodily persecution, or told that he could not stay there; but he faced persecution all the same in the wicked conduct of the Sodomites.[5] Similarly today: Christ is now enthroned in heaven and glorified; the necks of kings are bowed under his yoke and his sign dominates their brows; there is no one left now who dares to insult Christians openly. Yet we groan amid musical instruments and singers! The enemies of the martyrs, no longer able to persecute Christians by denunciation and the sword, undermine them with licentious entertainments instead. And if only it were from pagans alone that we had to bewail such attacks! It would be some comfort to us to think that, since they have not yet been signed with Christ's cross, we may anticipate that when they are so signed, and bound by his authority, they will cease their attacks. But unfortunately we also see people bearing Christ's sign on their foreheads, and at the same time flaunting alongside it shameless sensuality, people who insult the festivals and solemnities of the martyrs instead of exulting in them.

Amid these scandals we groan. This is our persecution, as long as there is in us that charity which cries out, *Is anyone weak, and I am not weak too? Is anyone scandalized, without my being afire with indignation?* (2 Cor 11:29). So no servant of God can be free from persecution. The apostle's warning is apposite: *All who want to live devoted to God in Christ will suffer persecution* (2 Tm 3:12). I want you to be alert to where it comes from, and the form it takes. The devil is two-faced. He is a lion in open attack, a dragon in ambush. If the lion menaces, he is the enemy. If the dragon lies in ambush, he is the enemy. Can we ever be secure? Even supposing that everyone became Christian, would the devil be a Christian? He never ceases to tempt us, never ceases to lie in wait. In the hearts of the godless he is unleashed and unrestrained, but let him not wreak havoc on the Church, and do what he likes here. The dignity of the Church and the peace of Christians set the teeth of the godless on edge. There is nothing they can do by way of violence; but by dances, blasphemy and debauchery they tear Christian souls apart, instead of assaulting Christian bodies.

---

5. See Gn 19.

Let us, then, shout these words with one voice: *O God, give heed and help me*; for as long as we are in this world we need his constant help. Whenever shall we not? Yet now most of all,[6] when we are in distress, let us say it: *O God, give heed and help me.*[7]

Verse 3. Salutary confusion for our enemies

3. *Let them be confused and stand in awe, those who seek my life.* These are the words of Christ. We can take them as said by either the head or the body; for he is speaking who said, *Why are you persecuting me?* (Acts 9:4), and *When you did that for even the least of those who are mine, you did it for me* (Mt 25:40). You know the voice of this person, this whole person, head and body; I need not keep on reminding you, because you know it well. *Let them be confused and stand in awe, those who seek my life*, he says. In another psalm he laments, *I have been looking right and left, but there was no one who wanted to know me. No chance of flight is open to me, yet there is no one to seek my soul* (Ps 141:5(142:4)). In that psalm, with his persecutors in view, he lamented that not one of them wanted to seek his soul; but here he prays, *Let them be confused and stand in awe, those who seek my life.*[8] He was mourning that no one sought him for the purpose of imitating him, and groaning that they did seek him to harass him. You seek the life of a just person when you seek to imitate; you seek the life[9] of a just person when you plan murder. Since there are two senses in which the life of a just person can be sought, the two possibilities are expressed, one in each psalm. In the other psalm he is sorrowful at the absence of anyone prepared to seek his soul in order to imitate his passion; in our present psalm he prays, *Let them be confused and stand in awe, those who seek my life.* They are seeking his life, but not in order to have two lives for themselves. Their hunt is not like that of a robber who wants a wayfarer's tunic; he kills so that he may strip the traveler and have the tunic for himself. But anyone who pursues someone else to kill him destroys the victim's life; he does not clothe himself in it. And these enemies are seeking my life, they want to kill me.

So what do you hope for them? *Let them be confused and stand in awe.* But then what has become of your Lord's admonition? You heard him say, *Love your enemies, do good to people who hate you, and pray for those who persecute you* (Mt 5:44). But here you are, suffering persecution, and you are cursing those

---

6. By varying the punctuation some codices yield the following sense: "Whenever can we say, 'Not now'? Yet most of all. . . ."

7. Augustine omits the second half of this verse.

8. The word is *animam* in both quotations. It can mean either "soul" or "life"; hence the ambiguity on which Augustine is reflecting here.

9. Or "soul," in both occurrences.

who are the agents of it. How are you following the example of your suffering Lord who, while hanging on the cross, prayed, *Father, forgive them, for they do not know what they are doing* (Lk 23:34)?

A martyr who is thus challenged will reply, "You have reminded me of the Lord's plea, *Father, forgive them, for they do not know what they are doing.* Listen, and hear my voice pleading the same thing, so that your own voice may too. What did I say about my enemies? *Let them be confused, and stand in awe.* But this is precisely the vengeance that has been wreaked upon the enemies of the martyrs. Saul persecuted Stephen, and Saul was covered with confusion and awe. He had been breathing slaughter, and hunting any whom he might drag off and put to death. But on hearing a voice from above that demanded, *Saul, Saul why are you persecuting me?* he was confused and knocked to the ground. He stood up again to obey, this very man who had been afire to persecute."[10]

This is the martyrs' hope for their enemies: *Let them be confused, and stand in awe*; for as long as they are not confused, and do not stand in awe, they must inevitably defend their actions. They think themselves worthy of great respect because they arrest, bind, scourge and kill, and because they dance and mock. But grant that they, sooner or later, be confused over all these actions, and stand in awe; for if they are confused, they will be converted, but they will never be converted except through prior confusion and feelings of awe. Let us then hope that this fate will befall our enemies, and let us have no scruples about hoping for it. Listen: I will say it, and I want you to join me in saying it: May all those who are still dancing and singing and mocking the martyrs *be confused and stand in awe.* And eventually may they beat their breasts in confusion within these very walls.

Verse 4. Persecution by violence, by cunning, by flattery

4. *Let them be thrust back, and blush for shame, those who think evil against me.* First we had the onslaught of the persecutors, now only the malevolent thinkers are left. Clearly there are different phases of persecution in the Church, succeeding each other. An open attack was launched against the Church when kings were persecuting. But it had been foretold that kings would persecute, and later come to believe, so when one half of the prophecy had been fulfilled, it was obvious that the other would be. And so it was: the kings came to believe, and peace was given to the Church. Then the time came for the Church to enjoy the highest dignity, even on this earth, even in this life. But the rage of the persecutors is not quelled; they simply change their open attacks into malevolent thoughts. In these thoughts the devil is tied up, as in a deep pit;[11] he fumes, but cannot burst out. It has been said, with regard to this phase in the Church's life,

---

10. See Acts 7:60; 9:1-6.
11. See Rv 20:2-3.

The sinner will be enraged at the sight. And what will he do then? The same as before? Drag them off, bind them, strike them? No, he does not do this. What, then? *He will gnash his teeth and pine away* (Ps 111(112):10). And our martyr seems to get angry with such people. But our martyr prays for them, nonetheless. Just as he was willing a good outcome for the people for whom he prayed, *Let them be confused, and stand in awe, those who seek my life,* so now he begs, *Let them be thrust back and blush for shame, those who think evil against me.*

Why does he pray for that? So that they may stop trying to rush ahead, and follow. Anyone who finds fault with the Christian religion, and wants to live in accordance with his or her own ideas, is trying to walk ahead of Christ. Such a person is suggesting that Christ has got it wrong, that he was weak and feeble in wanting to suffer at the hands of the Jews, or at any rate in reducing himself to a condition in which he could do so. Our sagacious critic means to avoid such mistakes, steer clear of death, resort even to base lies to escape it, and kill his own soul in order to save his skin. And he considers himself extremely wise and prudent to adopt such a course. The fault-finder thinks himself better than Christ; he is, as it were, walking ahead of Christ.

What he needs is to believe in Christ, and follow him; for what the psalm requests for those who harbor evil intentions is what the Lord himself ordered Peter. There was an occasion when Peter wanted to get ahead of the Lord. Our Savior had been speaking about his passion; if he had not accepted it, we should not have been saved. Just before this Peter had confessed him to be the Son of God, and for that confession he was called the Rock, on which the Church was to be built. But immediately afterward, when the Lord was speaking about his forthcoming passion, Peter protested: *Far be it from you, Lord, have some pity for yourself. This will not happen.* Only a moment ago Peter had been told, *Blessed are you, Simon, son of Jonah, for it is not flesh and blood that revealed this to you, but my Father, who is in heaven*; but now, suddenly, he is commanded, *Get behind me, Satan* (Mt 16:22.17.23). What does *get behind me* mean? Follow me. You want to rush ahead of me, you want to give me advice. It would be much better for you to follow my advice. This is what "Go back, get behind me" implies. He curbs the man who rushes in front, and makes him take his place in the rear; he calls him Satan because he wants to go one better than the Lord. A minute ago Christ called him *blessed*; now he addresses him as *Satan*. Why did he deserve to be called blessed? Because *it is not flesh and blood that revealed this to you, but my Father, who is in heaven,* said Jesus. Then why does he now deserve the name Satan? Because *you have no taste for the things of God, but only for human things.*

How does this apply to us? If we wish to celebrate the birthdays of the martyrs as we should, let us aspire to imitate the martyrs. Let us beware of trying to get ahead of them, and of flattering ourselves that we are better advised than they were, because we avoid suffering for justice and faith, whereas they did not avoid it. May all those who think evil, and pamper their hearts with self-indulgence, *be thrust back and blush for shame.* May they hear the apostle challenging them, once this prayer has been fulfilled, *What fruit have you ever reaped from the things that now make you blush?* (Rom 6:21).

5. What is the next line? *May they be promptly repulsed and ashamed, those who say to me, Splendid! Well done!* There are two sorts of persecutors: those who revile us and those who flatter us. The flatterer's tongue is a more dangerous instrument of persecution than the killer's hand, and scripture even calls it a furnace. To be sure, it was in speaking about persecution, and about martyrs who had been put to death, that scripture said, *He proved them like gold in a furnace, and accepted them like the victim in a holocaust* (Wis 3:6); but according to another text that is exactly what the tongue of sycophants is like: *Fire is used to test silver and gold; but a man is tested by the mouths of those who praise him* (Prv 27:21). The one is fiery, and the other is fiery, and the important thing for you is to come out safe in either case. If the man who passes judgment on you has succeeded in breaking you, you are like a piece of pottery that has cracked[12] in the kiln. The word[13] shaped you, and now comes the testing time, the time of distress. What has been formed must now be fired. If it has been well formed, the fire works on it to harden it. This is why he said in his passion, *My strength is dried up like an earthenware pot* (Ps 21:16(22:15)), for his suffering, and the furnace of distress, had made him stronger. But if you are praised by flatterers and toadies, and you welcome their adulation, like the foolish virgins who had to buy oil because they had none with them,[14] the mouths of these obsequious persons will be the kiln that cracks you.

However, we cannot escape these trials. We have to enter them, and emerge from them. Let us enter into the abuse we receive from wicked, scurrilous people, and let us enter also into the adulation of those who fawn upon us; but we must come through both. Let us ask the help of him of whom it is written, *May the Lord guard your entering and your going out* (Ps 120(121):8), that you may go into it whole, and come out whole. The apostle assures us, *God is faithful, and he does not allow you to be tempted more fiercely than you can bear.* There you have our entrance. He did not say, "May you not be tempted," for one who is not tempted is not proved sound, and one who is not proved makes no progress.[15] What was the apostle's wish for us? *God is faithful, and he does not allow you to be tempted more fiercely than you can bear,* he says; and there is our way into it.

---

12. Variant: "has been made."
13. Or perhaps "the Word."
14. See Mt 25:3.
15. Or "is of no use."

But now observe the way out: *But along with the temptation he ordains the outcome, so that you may withstand it* (1 Cor 10:13).

Let those people *be promptly repulsed and ashamed, who say to me, Splendid! Well done!* Why praise me? Let them rather praise God. Who am I, that I should be lauded in myself? What have I done? What have I that I have not received? *And if you did receive it,* Paul demands, *why boast as though you had not?* (1 Cor 4:7). With oil like this the heads of heretics have grown sleek; for they proclaim, "I am, I am," and assenting voices reply, "Yes, so you are, Lord."[16] They accepted the "Splendid! Well done!" They became blind leaders of blind followers.[17] In the most public way possible this acclamation is sung in honor of Donatus: "Splendid! Well done! Noble leader!" But he did not say, *May they be promptly repulsed and ashamed, those who say to me, Splendid! Well done!* Nor did he try to put them right, or encourage them to keep their cry of "Good leader, noble leader!" for Christ. How differently did the apostle deal with the eulogies people tried to direct to him! He recoiled from them. Wishing to deserve true praise in Christ, he refused to be praised instead of Christ. When certain people were asserting, *I belong to Paul,* he demanded of them, with all the freedom he enjoyed in the Lord, *Was Paul crucified for you, or were you baptized in Paul's name?* (1 Cor 1:12-13). Let the martyrs likewise say under persecution, even if it comes from flatterers, *May they be promptly repulsed and ashamed, those who say to me, Splendid! Well done!*

Verse 5. In all circumstances may God be glorified

6. What happens next, when all of them are repulsed and ashamed: all who seek my life, all who think evil against me, and all who in perverted and insincere kindness try to soften up with their tongues the one they aim to hurt? When these too are repulsed and shamed, what next? *Let all who seek you exult and be glad in you.* Not in me, not in him, not in her, but in you, for they who once were darkness have become light in you.[18] *Let all who seek you exult and be glad in you.* It is one thing to seek the Lord, and something else to seek a fellow-mortal. *Let them be glad in you, those who seek you.* Those who seek themselves will not be glad in you, though you sought them before they sought you. That sheep was not seeking its shepherd; it had wandered away from the flock, but the shepherd came down and searched for it, and carried it back on his shoulders.[19] Will he

---

16. Presumably Augustine's hearers were familiar with some arrogant claim of this kind from sectarian leaders; but he seems to have made it into a parody of Ex 3:14 to suggest blasphemous overtones.

17. See Mt 15:14.

18. See Eph 5:8.

19. See Lk 15:4-5.

despise you now that you are seeking him, you sheep, if he took the initiative in seeking you while you still despised him and were not seeking him? At least begin to seek him now, since he first sought you, and brought you back on his shoulders.[20] Behave as he indicated: *The sheep that are mine hear my voice and follow me* (Jn 10:27). If you seek him who first sought you, you have become his sheep, hearing his voice and following him. Then see what he shows you concerning himself, and concerning his body, so that in him you may not stray again, and in his Church you may not be misled. Then you will not be lured away if anyone says to you, "That is Christ," when it is not; or "This is the Church," of something that is not the Church; for many have contended that Christ did not have real flesh, and did not rise again in his body.[21] Do not go after such voices. Listen to the voice of the true shepherd, who clothed himself in flesh to seek out the flesh that was lost. He rose again, and said, *Handle me and see: a ghost does not have flesh and bones, as you see I have* (Lk 24:39). He shows himself to you, so follow his voice. He also shows you his Church, lest anyone deceive you by claiming the Church's name falsely. *It was necessary for Christ to suffer, and to rise from the dead on the third day, and for repentance and forgiveness of sins to be preached in his name throughout all nations, beginning from Jerusalem* (Lk 24:46-47). There you hear the voice of your shepherd; do not go after the voice of strangers. You need fear no thief if you have followed the shepherd's voice. How will you know you are following it? If you say to no human being, "Splendid! Well done!" as though ascribing the achievements to his or her own merits, and if you do not yourself listen to similar things with pleasure, for fear the oil of sinners may soak into your head.[22]

Let all who seek you exult and be glad in you, and let them say. . . . What are they to say in their exultation? *May the Lord be magnified always.* Let them say that, all of them who exult and seek you. Say what? *Let them say, May the Lord be magnified always, those who love your salvation.* Not just, "May the Lord be magnified," but *May the Lord be magnified always.* Remember how you went astray, and were turned away from him. He called you, so *may the Lord be magnified.* Then remember how he inspired you to confess your sins. You confessed them, and he granted you pardon, so *may the Lord be magnified.* Now you have begun to live a good life, and I think it fitting that you should have some commendation yourself; for when he called you from your misguided ways, the Lord deserved to be magnified; when he forgave your sins on your confession, the Lord deserved to be magnified; but now that you are listening to his words and have begun to make progress, and have been justified, and have arrived at a

---

20. Most codices condense the last two sentences as follows: "Will he despise you now that you are seeking him? Now you will seek him who first sought you, and. . . ."
21. The Manicheans, and some Gnostics.
22. See Ps 140(141):5.

certain degree of virtuous excellence, surely it is right that you should some-times get a little credit yourself? But no: *let them say, May the Lord be magnified always.* Are you a sinner? *May the Lord be magnified* for pardoning you. Are you now living righteously? *May the Lord be magnified* for guiding you. Will you persevere to the end? *May the Lord be magnified* for bringing you to glory. So *may the Lord be magnified always.* Let the just proclaim this, let those who seek him proclaim it. Anyone who refuses to say it is not seeking him. Take it to heart: *May the Lord be magnified.*

Let all who seek him *exult and be glad, and let them say, May the Lord be magnified always, those who love* his *salvation.* Salvation comes from him, not from themselves. The salvation of our Lord God is our Lord and Savior Jesus Christ. All those who love our Savior confess that they have been healed, and all who confess that they have been healed necessarily confess that once they were sick. *Let them say,* then, *May the Lord be magnified always, those who love your salvation*: not their own salvation, as though they had the power to save them-selves; not salvation offered by any fellow human, as though they could be saved by him. Scripture warns, *Put not your trust in princes, or in mere mortals, for in them you will find no salvation* (Ps 145:2-3(146:3)). Why not? Because *salva-tion is from the Lord, and may your blessing be upon your people* (Ps 3:9(8)). *May the Lord be magnified always.* Who says this? All those *who love your salvation.*

Verse 6. I am still poor and needy

7. So *may the Lord be magnified.* What about you? Are you never to be magnified? In no respect? "If anything worthwhile has happened it is due to him," is the reply; "there is nothing in me. Even if I have acquitted myself well, it is only in him. He does it, not I." What have you to say for yourself, then? *"I am needy and poor.* He is rich, he is overflowing with wealth, he needs nothing. He is my light, he is the source of any illumination I have; for I cry out to him, *You, Lord, will light my lamp; my God, you will enlighten my darkness* (Ps 17:29(18:28)). *The Lord sets prisoners free; the Lord lifts up those who are bowed down, the Lord gives sight to the blind, the Lord protects the stranger"* (Ps 145(146):7-9).[23] But what of yourself? *"I am needy and poor.* I am like an orphan; my soul is like a widow, destitute and desolate. I am begging for help, and incessantly I confess my weakness. *I am needy and poor.* My sins have been forgiven, and I have begun to keep God's commandments, yet still *I am needy*

---

23. In the original Hebrew of the psalm the last word in this quotation is the ordinary term for "stranger" or "sojourner," which could therefore mean a proselyte, one of Gentile origin who converted to Judaism. The Septuagint opted for this more restricted sense, which is reflected also in Augustine's Latin text, *proselytos.*

and poor." But why are you still *needy and poor?* "Because *I am aware of a different law in my members that opposes the law of my mind* (Rom 7:23). Why am I *needy and poor?* Because *blessed are those who hunger and thirst for righteousness* (Mt 5:6). I am still hungry, still thirsty, but the time for me to be satisfied is only deferred, not taken away for ever."

I am needy and poor; O God, come to my aid. The psalm began with the prayer, *O God, give heed and help me*; it ends with *O God, come to my aid.* It is very appropriate that the name Lazarus is interpreted "One who is helped," for he was needy and poor. He was carried off into Abraham's embrace,[24] and he is a type of God's Church, which is perpetually obliged to confess itself in need of help. This is true, and it puts us into the right filial attitude. *I said to the Lord, You are my God,* and why? *Because you have no need of any good things from me* (Ps 15(16):2). He does not need us, but we need him; that is why he is truly the Lord. But you, a human master, are not truly the lord and master of your slave, for both of you are human beings, and both need God. You may think that your slave needs you to give him his food, but you equally need him to help you with your work; so each of you needs the other. No one among you is really a master, and no one among you is really a slave. I will tell you who the real Lord is, the Master whose true slave you are; listen: *I said to the Lord, You are my God.* Why are you the Lord? *Because you have no need of any good things from me.*

So what about you? *I am needy and poor.* Well then, if you are needy and poor, may God feed you, may God lift you up, may God help you. So the psalm prays, *O God, come to my aid.*

8. *You are my helper and rescuer, O Lord; do not delay.* You are my helper and rescuer: I need your aid, so help me; I am entangled, so rescue me. No one except you can pluck me free of entanglements. The knotty problems of all our concerns surround us; on every side we are as though lacerated by thorny hedges; we are treading a narrow way, and perhaps the hedges catch at us. So let us say to God, *You are my rescuer.* He who pointed out the narrow way to us[25] has also enabled us to follow it.

Let us keep this prayer continually in our minds, brothers and sisters. However long we may have lived here, however much progress we may have made here, no one has the right to say, "That's enough now, I'm a righteous person." Anyone who says that is stuck on the road, and does not know how to reach journey's end. At the very point where someone says, "That's enough," there is he or she stuck. Listen to the apostle, who did not think anything was enough; see how he wanted to be helped until he arrived at the goal: *I do not suppose, brethren, that I have attained it,* he says (Phil 3:13); and to guard his

24. See Lk 16:22.
25. See Mt 7:14.

hearers against thinking that they have attained it themselves, he says elsewhere, *If anyone considers that he knows something, he does not yet know in the way he ought to know* (1 Cor 8:2). What is Paul telling us? *I do not suppose, brethren, that I have attained it.* Just before this he had said, *Not that I have gained it already, or am already perfect* (Phil 3:12), and then he went on with this statement, *I do not suppose, brethren, that I have attained it.* If he has not yet gained it, he is *poor and needy*; if he is not yet perfect, he is *poor and needy*. He has good reason to say, *O God come to my aid.* He had certainly understood something; indeed, he had understood to a sublime degree; nonetheless, listen to what he says, *To him who has power to do all things far more abundantly than we ask or understand . . .* (Eph 3:20). You can see that he has not yet arrived, not yet grasped the prize. So what does he say? *I do not suppose, brethren, that I have attained it; one thing only I do: forgetting what lies behind and straining to what lies ahead, I bend my whole effort to follow after the prize of God's heavenly call* (Phil 3:13-14). He is running, but you are stuck fast. If he admits that he is not yet perfect, can you boast that you are? May they recoil in shame, all those who say to you, "Splendid! Well done!" But may you be shamed along with them, for arrogating the same credit to yourself. Anyone who indulges in self-congratulation is saying, "Splendid! Well done!" to himself or herself. Anyone who is praised by others, and acquiesces, has forgotten to bring oil along; the torches are guttering out, and the Lord is about to close the door.[26]

9. Dearest friends, the solemnity of the martyrs has reminded us, and this psalm has briefly taught us, that as the martyrs underwent bodily suffering in this world, it is necessary for us to endure spiritual trials, however peaceful our times may be. It is necessary for the Church, like a mass of grain, to groan amid the troubles and weeds and straw until harvest time. The day for the final winnowing will come, when the winnowing-fork will do its work, separating straw from wheat until all the wheat is stored in the barn.[27] Until that happens, let us cry out, *I am needy and poor; O God, come to my aid. You are my helper and rescuer, O Lord; do not delay.* But what is the meaning of *do not delay*? Many people complain, "Christ is a long time coming." Does this suggest, then, that if we pray, *Do not delay*, he will come sooner than he had intended to? If not, what does the plea mean—*do not delay*? It means, "Let not your future coming seem to me too long delayed." It seems a long time to you, but not to God, for to him a thousand years are as a single day[28] or as the three hours of a night watch. But if you do not have the patience to hold out, it will seem slow to you; and if you think it slow you will be lured away from Christ. You will be like those people who grew weary in the desert, and were in too much of a hurry to beg from God deli-

---

26. See Mt 25:1-12.
27. See Mt 13:30; 3:12.
28. See Ps 89(90):4.

cacies he was reserving for them at their homecoming. When they were not given those dainties on their journey (which might have been bad for them) they murmured against God, and in their hearts went back to Egypt.[29] They had left Egypt corporeally, but returned there in their hearts. On no account must you be like them. Beware of the Lord's warning, *Remember Lot's wife* (Lk 17:32). She had already been plucked free from Sodom, and was on the road; but she looked back, and in the place where she cast that backward glance, she remained. She was turned into a pillar of salt,[30] to season you; for she was made an example for your sake, so that you may take courage and not linger tastelessly on the road. Look at the woman who did dally there, and pass by. Be mindful of her who looked back, and make sure that you are stretching out to what lies ahead, like Paul. What does it mean, to avoid looking back? *I forget what lies behind*, he says. You have been called, and you will follow, to seize the heavenly prize which will one day be your glory; for the same apostle affirms, *All that remains for me now is the crown of righteousness which the just judge will award me on that day* (2 Tm 4:8).

---

29. See Ex 16:2-3; Acts 7:39.
30. See Gn 19:26.

Exposition 1 of Psalm 70

First Sermon

Introduction: the psalm reminds us how gratuitous is grace

1. Every part of holy scripture commends to us the liberating grace of God, to the end that we may commend ourselves to grace. The present psalm sings about it, this psalm on which we have undertaken to speak with you, dearest friends.[1] The Lord will help me to conceive in my heart worthy ideas on the subject, and also to bring them forth in a way that will be useful to you. It is the love of God and the fear of God that chiefly bring the truth home to us: fear of God, because he is just, and love of God, because he is merciful. If he were to damn someone who is unjust, *who would have the right to demand of him, What have you done?* (Wis 12:12). How mighty, then, must be his mercy when he justifies an unjust person?[2]

It is for this reason that we had the passage from the apostle read beforehand,[3] for in it Paul most especially commends God's grace to us. By so commending it he inevitably incurred the enmity of the Jews, for they took their stand on the letter of the law, confident and boastful of their own righteousness. The apostle says of them, *I bear this witness against them: they have zeal for God, indeed, but it is not informed by knowledge* (Rom 10:2). Then, as though challenged, "What does it mean—to have a zeal for God that is not informed by knowledge?" he immediately explains, *They failed to recognize the righteousness that comes from God, and by seeking to set up a righteousness of their own, they did not submit to God's righteousness* (Rom 10:3). By priding themselves on their works, he says, they shut out grace, and, trusting in their supposed good health, they scorn the medicine they need. The Lord himself warned against people who took that line: *I did not come to call the righteous, but sinners to repentance. It is not the healthy who need the physician, but the sick* (Lk 5:32; Mt 9:12). The profoundest wisdom, the sum of wisdom for human beings, consists in this: to know that of themselves they are nothing, and that whatever they may be, they are only by God's gift and for his ultimate purposes. *What have you that you did not receive?* asks the apostle. *And if you did receive it, why boast as though you*

---

1. *Cum vestra caritate.*
2. The thought summarily expressed here is developed more fully in section 15 below.
3. 1 Cor 15, as appears shortly.

had not? (1 Cor 4:7). This, then, is the grace the apostle commends to us, and for teaching it he earned himself the hostility of the Jews, who boasted of the letter of the law and their own righteousness.

In the passage we have just read, the apostle speaks thus of grace: *I am not worthy to be called an apostle, because I persecuted God's Church* (1 Cor 15:9); *but,* he continues in another passage, *I received mercy, because I acted in ignorance.* And, a little further on, *It is a reliable saying, worthy of full acceptance, that Christ Jesus came into this world to save sinners, among whom I am foremost.* Surely he does not mean there were no sinners before him? If not, why does he claim, *I am the foremost?* He means he was the foremost not in time, but in malice. Yet he goes on, *I received mercy so that Christ Jesus might give proof in me of his long forbearance toward those who will believe in him unto eternal life* (1 Tm 1:13.15-16). The implication is that any and every sinner, every transgressor in a state of despair with an attitude as reckless as a gladiator's,[4] anyone who thought he might as well do what he liked because he would be damned in any event, could look to Paul's example. Reflecting that God had forgiven Paul for such cruelty and enormous malice, the sinner would be persuaded not to despair of his own case, and would turn back to God.

In our psalm God commends the same grace to us. Let us examine the psalm, and investigate whether this statement of mine is true, or whether I should draw some different inference. The fact is that I do judge this to be the gist of the psalm, the message that resounds from nearly every syllable in it. It reminds us that God's grace is entirely gratuitous, that it sets us free, unworthy as we are, and this not in response to any efforts we make, but by God's own act. So convinced am I that this is the teaching of the psalm that I think even if I had not pointed it out or given you this preamble, anyone of even mediocre ability would, on listening attentively to the words of the psalm, pick up the same message. If such a listener had some preconceived idea, he or she would probably be impelled to a change of mind by the very force of the words, and become a living instance of the truth here proclaimed. What truth is this? That all our hope must be in God; and that we must put no reliance whatever on our own strength, as though it derived from ourselves, lest by arrogating to ourselves what comes from him, we lose what we have received.

---

4. The gladiator knew he would be killed in any case, if not in this fight, then in another, so caution was misplaced.

*Verse 1. The title. The descendants of Jonadab, an example of obedience.
Adam and Christ*

2. This psalm has a title, and as usual it gives us on the threshold an indication
of what we shall find inside the house. *For David himself, of the sons of Jonadab,
and of those who were first taken captive.* Jonadab was a man who is favorably
mentioned in the prophecy of Jeremiah. He had commanded his children not to
drink wine, and to live not in houses but in tents. His descendants cherished and
observed their ancestor's instructions, and for doing so they deserved to be
blessed by the Lord.[5] Notice, however, that it was not the Lord himself who had
laid this command upon them, but their forefather. Yet they accepted it as though
it had been a precept of the Lord their God, because although the Lord had not
directly forbidden them to drink wine, or commanded them to live in tents, the
Lord had commanded children to obey their father. In this matter alone should
children not obey their father: if the father has ordered something in opposition
to the will of the Lord their God. In such a case the father has no right to be angry
because God is given preference. But when a father issues a command which is
not contrary to God's will, he must be heeded as God himself would be, because
God has commanded obedience to parents. Accordingly God blessed the
descendants of Jonadab for their obedience, and held them up as an example and
a rebuke to his disobedient people, because, while the family of Jonadab were
obeying their father, the Israelite people were not obeying their God.

Now at the time of Jeremiah's encounter with the children of Jonadab he was
trying to persuade the Israelites that they must prepare to be led away into
captivity in Babylon. They were not to resist God's will, nor hope for any other
destiny than that of being prisoners. It seems that the title of our psalm was
inspired by this situation, since after mentioning *the sons of Jonadab* it added,
and of those who were first taken captive. This does not suggest that the sons of
Jonadab were led away as captives, but that on account of their obedience to their
father they were contrasted with others who were to be taken captive, so that
these latter might understand that the reason for their captivity was their disobedience to God.

There is another point: the name Jonadab is interpreted "the Lord's Spontaneous One." What does that suggest—the Lord's Spontaneous One? It evokes a
person who serves God willingly and freely. What would it mean to be the
Lord's Spontaneous One? *The good things I have vowed to give you, and the
praise I will render you, are within me, O God* (Ps 55(56):12). What is it to be the
Lord's Spontaneous One? *Of my own free will I will offer sacrifice to you* (Ps
53:8(54:6)). If the apostolic teaching warns a slave to serve his human master
willingly and not under compulsion, and by this free service to make himself

---

5. See Jer 35:6-10.

free in his own heart, how much more must you serve God with your total, undivided, free will, knowing that your will is open to his gaze? If your slave is not serving you wholeheartedly, you can observe his hands, his face, and his manner; but you cannot see his heart. And yet it is to slaves that the apostle's admonition is addressed: *Serve not only where it shows.* What does he mean by *not only where it shows?* "What," the slave might ask, "is my master going to see the dispositions in which I serve him, that you say to me, *Not only where it shows?*" The apostle elaborates: *But like slaves of Christ.* The human master cannot see, but our Master Christ can. *From your hearts, and with good will* you must serve, the apostle emphasizes (Eph 6:6-7). Jonadab was this kind of person, as the interpretation of his name suggests.

Now who are the people *who were first taken captive?* The Israelites were taken captive a first, a second, and a third time; but this psalm, which is about those who were first taken captive, is not concerned with the Israelites. If we discuss the psalm minutely, examining it with the utmost care and questioning its every verse, what it tells us is something quite different. It tells us that it is not talking about those people, whoever they were, who at some time or other were overwhelmed by their enemies and hauled off from Jerusalem to Babylon as prisoners. What is the psalm teaching us, then? What else but the same lesson you have heard from the apostle? It commends God's grace to us; it reminds us that of ourselves we are nothing; it impresses on us that whatever we are, we are by the mercy of God, but that anything else we may be by our own actions makes us bad. But why, then, are we captives? And why is it in the guise of captives that we come to know grace, to know it as the grace of our liberator? The apostle makes it plain: *I take great delight in God's law as far as my inner self is concerned, but I am aware of a different law in my members that opposes the law of my mind, and imprisons me under the law of sin inherent in my members.* There you have someone who has been led into captivity. So what does this psalm propose to us? The same teaching that the apostle goes on to give: *Who will deliver me from this death-ridden body, wretch that I am? Only the grace of God, through Jesus Christ our Lord* (Rom 7:22-25).

But then, why *first?* We have seen why we are called captives. As I see it, the reason for calling us *first* is equally clear. The contrasting example of the children of Jonadab condemns all disobedience as sinful. But we were made captives through disobedience, for Adam sinned by disobeying. The same apostle told us, and with perfect truth, that *in Adam all die, as in him all have sinned.*[6] There is good reason to speak of those who *were first taken captive,* because *the first man was from the earth, earthly, but the second man is from*

---

6. 1 Cor 15:22; Rom 5:12. See a note at Exposition of Psalm 50, 10, on the interpretation of the second quotation.

heaven, heavenly. As the earthly man was, so are the earthlings; as the heavenly man is, so too are the heavenly ones. As we have borne the image of the man of earth, so too let us bear the image of him who is of heaven (1 Cor 15:47-49). The first man made us prisoners, the second man freed us from our captivity, *for as in Adam all die, so in Christ shall all be made to live* (1 Cor 15:22). But whereas they die in Adam through birth in the flesh, they are freed in Christ through faith in the heart. You had no power to avoid being born into the race of Adam, but you do have power to believe in Christ. In the measure in which you have chosen to throw in your lot with the first man, your lot will be captivity. But what does that mean? How do you choose to throw in your lot with him? And does it make sense to say, "Your lot will be captivity"? It is yours already! Cry out, then, *Who will deliver me from this death-ridden body?* Now let us listen to the psalm exclaiming precisely this.

3. *O God, I have hoped in you; O Lord, let me not be ashamed for ever.* I am ashamed now, but at least let it not last for ever! How could anyone not be ashamed when challenged, *What fruit did you reap then from things that now make you blush?* (Rom 6:21). What can we do, then, to make sure we are not put to shame for ever? *Draw near to him and receive his light, and your faces will not be put to the blush* (Ps 33:6(34:5)). In Adam you are shamed; distance yourselves from Adam and draw near to Christ, and you will be shamed no longer. *I have hoped in you, O Lord; let me not be ashamed for ever.*

Verse 2. Any righteousness you have is God's gift

4. *In your justice rescue me and deliver me.* Not in any justice of mine, but in yours; for if I relied on my own I would be ranking myself with those of whom it was said, *They failed to recognize the righteousness that comes from God, and by seeking to set up a righteousness of their own, they did not submit to God's righteousness* (Rom 10:3). Save me in your justice, not mine; for what does mine consist of? Unrighteousness preceded it. Even when I have been justified, it is by your justice, because I shall be just only by justice granted to me by you, and it will be mine only inasmuch as it is yours, and granted to me as your gift. I believe in him who justifies the ungodly, so that my faith may be imputed to me as righteousness.[7] Then the justice I have will truly belong to me, but not as something proper to me or having its source in myself, as those people supposed who gloried in literal observance and rejected grace. Certainly it is mine, for in another psalm the prayer is made, *Judge me, Lord, according to my righteousness* (Ps 7:9(8)); but there was no question of the speaker glorying in it as his own. Recall the apostle's question, *What have you that you did not receive?* (1

---

7. See Rom 4:5.

Cor 4:7), and speak of your justice only in such a way that you remember that you received it, and are not jealous of any others who receive it likewise. The Pharisee in the gospel did indeed speak of it as something he had received from God, for he said, O God, I thank you that I am not like other people. That's a good beginning: *O God, I thank you.* So far, so good. But *that I am not like other people?* Is that the motive for your thanks? Does your goodness afford you satisfaction only because the other fellow contrasts badly? And he went further, spelling it out: *Frauds, robbers, adulterers; or like that tax collector there.* Now you are insulting, not exulting. The other man was a captive, who dared not even raise his eyes to heaven, but beat his breast, saying, *Lord, be merciful to me, a sinner* (Lk 18:11.13).

Clearly it is not enough to acknowledge that any good there is in you comes from God; you must also refrain from exalting yourself above anyone else who does not yet have that gift. When the other person receives it, he or she may outstrip you. At the time when Saul was an accomplice in the stoning of Stephen[8] there were very many Christians to whom Saul was simply a persecutor; yet once he had been converted he surpassed all who had been Christians before him.

Say to God, then, the words you hear in this psalm: *I have hoped in you, O Lord; let me not be ashamed for ever. In your justice* (yours, not mine) *rescue me and deliver me. Bend down your ear to me.* This last plea is a humble confession. Anyone who says, *Bend down your ear to me,* is confessing that he or she is brought low, like a sick person prostrate before a physician who stands upright. Listen to what the patient says: *Bend down your ear to me, and grant me healing.*

Verse 3. God, our stronghold

5. *Be to me a protector-God.* Do not let the enemy's javelins find their mark in me, for I cannot protect myself. But simply to ask God to be his protector seemed insufficient, so the psalmist went on, *And a fortified place to keep me safe.* Be *a fortified place* for me; you are yourself my fortification. But, Adam, what has become of your flight from God, and your attempt to hide among the trees of paradise? What has become of your terror in that presence of God which had hitherto been your delight?[9] You ran away and you were lost; you knew yourself to be a prisoner. But he comes to look for you, and you are not abandoned; it is the ninety-nine sheep on the mountains who are left, while the one lost sheep is sought, and when it is found the cry is raised, *He was dead, but has come back to life, was lost but is found.*[10] God was once a terror to you, frightening you into

---

8. See Acts 7:60.
9. See Gn 3:8.
10. See Lk 15:4.24.32.

fleeing away; now he has become the refuge to which you flee. *Be to me a forti-fied place to keep me safe*, prays the psalm. I shall never be safe except in you. Unless I rest in you, my sickness will never be healed. Lift me up from the earth; let me lie in your arms so that I can reach up to that fortified place. Could any place be more securely fortified than this? Once you have taken refuge there, what adversaries need you fear? Can any stealthy attack reach you? There is a story that a man shouted from a mountain top when the emperor was passing by, "I don't care about you!" And the emperor looked round and replied, "Nor I about you!" That man had made light of an emperor with renowned weapons and a powerful army; but from where? From his fortified place. If he was secure in his lofty piece of earth, how much more should you be in the Creator of heaven and earth? *Be to me a protector-God, and a fortified place to keep me safe.* If I choose any other place for myself, I shall not be safe there. Go ahead, human creature, and find yourself a better defended one, if you can. Nowhere can you flee away from him, except to him. If you want to escape him in his anger, flee to him in his appeasement.

For you are my stronghold and my refuge. Why *my stronghold*? Because through you I am strong; from you I draw strength. *For you are my stronghold and my refuge*; let me flee to you, that I may grow strong in every respect where I have grown weak in myself. The grace of Christ makes you stand firm and immovable against all the enemy's temptations. But human fragility is still with us, our original captivity is still present, and we are still aware of that other law in our members in conflict with the law of our minds, attempting to lead us into captivity under the law of sin.[11] The perishable body still weighs down the soul.[12] However steady and strong you are by God's grace, you still need to fear for the fragile vessel, as long as you still carry God's treasure in an earthenware jar.[13]

So, then, *you are my stronghold*, enabling me to stand firm in this world against all temptations. But if they are many, and they harass me, *you are my refuge.* I will confess my weakness so as to become timid as a hare, for I am as full of spines as a hedgehog. But, as another psalm pointed out, *the rock is a refuge for hedgehogs and hares* (Ps 103(104):18); and the rock was Christ.[14]

Verse 4. All down the ages, this one person cries out for deliverance from sin

6. *O my God, rescue me from the hand of the sinner.* This means sinners in general, for among them the speaker is struggling, this person who looks to be freed from captivity, this person who is already crying out, *Who will deliver me*

---

11. See Rom 7:23.
12. See Wis 9:15.
13. See 2 Cor 4:7.
14. See 1 Cor 10:4.

from this death-ridden body, wretch that I am? Only the grace of God, through Jesus Christ our Lord (Rom 7:24-25). The enemy is within, the opposing law is in our members. But there are enemies outside as well, so where will you find help? In God, to whom another prayer was addressed: *Cleanse me from my secret sins, O Lord, and spare your servant from the faults of others* (Ps 18:13-14(19:12-13)). When you cry, *Save me!* the cry comes from the sickness within, from your own iniquity, under which you are held prisoner, from that which binds you to the first man. You cry out from the ranks of those who were first taken captive. But once saved from your own iniquity, have regard also to the iniquities of others, among whom you are obliged to live until this life comes to an end. And how long will that be? Your life is nearing its end, is it? But will the Church's life end? Only when the world itself ends. And this one person, this unity in Christ, cries out in the pleas we are hearing. Many people depart this bodily life as believers. This must be so; and may they find their place in that rest which God grants to the spirits of the faithful. But there are still members of Christ on earth, both among those alive today and those who will be born hereafter. Until the end of the world there will be this one person crying out to be set free from his sins, and from the law in our members that opposes the law of our minds. And in addition there are the sins of other people, among whom this one person must necessarily live until the very end. These sinners are of two different kinds: those who have received the law, and those who have not. Pagans have not received the law; all Jews and Christians have received it. The term, "sinner," is thus a general term, covering both a transgressor of the law (in the case of one who has received it) and one who is simply unrighteous irrespective of the law (in the case of one who has not received it). The apostle speaks of both types: *Those who have sinned without the law will perish without the law; and those who have sinned under the law will be judged by the law* (Rom 2:12).

But you, who are groaning amid both kinds, must offer to God the prayer you hear in the psalm: *O my God, rescue me from the hand of the sinner.* What sinner is this? *From the hand of the law-breaker and the wicked person.* One who breaks the law is also wicked, for it is not possible to transgress the law without wickedness; but though every law-breaker is wicked, not every wicked person is a law-breaker. *Where there is no law, there is no violation of it,* says the apostle (Rom 4:15). People who have not received the law may therefore be called wicked, but cannot be said to infringe it. Each type must be judged on its own merits.

But as for me, I long to be set free from captivity through your grace, and I cry to you, *Rescue me from the hand of the sinner.* What does "from the hand" mean? From the sinner's power; lest when the sinner rampages, he terrify me into consent, or when he attacks by stealth, he persuade me to iniquity. *From the hand of the law-breaker and the wicked person.* Challenge this speaker!

Demand of him, "Why do you seek to be freed from the hand of the law-breaker and the wicked person? All you have to do is withhold consent. If he rampages,[15] be patient, put up with it." But who can put up with it, if God, who has become our fortified place, deserts us? Why do I say, *Rescue me from the hand of the law-breaker and the wicked person*? Because the power to be patient is not in me, but in you, who grant me patience.

Verses 5-6. God, my hope since my youth and for ever

7. The reason why I said, *You are my patience*, will appear in a moment, says the psalmist. If God is my patience, I can rightly go on to say, *Lord, you are my hope since my youth*. Is he my patience because he is my hope, or is he my hope because he is my patience? The apostle tells us, *Suffering fosters endurance, and endurance constancy, and constancy hope; but hope does not disappoint us* (Rom 5:3-5). Let us question the psalmist.

You said earlier, and with good reason, *I have hoped in you, O Lord; let me not be ashamed for ever*. Now you say, *Lord, you are my hope since my youth*. Does that imply only since your youth? Would it not be true even from your childhood, even from your infancy? "Yes, of course," he responds. "Look at what comes next, then you will not think I said, *My hope since my youth*, to imply that God did nothing for me in my infancy or childhood. Listen to my next line: *Even from the womb I was strengthened in you*. And further, *From the belly of my mother you have been my protector*. Why did I first say, *From my youth*? Because I meant to indicate the time when I began to hope in you. Before that time I did not hope in you, even though you were my protector, and brought me safely to the age when I could learn to hope in you. From my youth onward I began to hope in you; and from that time you armed me against the devil, so that, equipped for battle in your army, and furnished with faith in you, charity, hope, and the rest of your gifts, I might contend against your invisible enemies, and hearken to the apostle's warning: *It is not against flesh and blood that you have to struggle, but against principalities and powers and the rulers of this world of darkness, against wicked spiritual beings* (Eph 6:12). It takes a young man to fight against such foes; but even a young man falls unless God is his hope, God to whom he prays, *Lord, you are my hope since my youth*."

8. *I will sing of you always*. Not merely from the time when I began to hope in you until the present, but *always*. What does this affirmation, *always*, evoke? Not only in the time of faith, but also in the time of vision; for now, as long as we are in the body, we are on pilgrimage and away from the Lord, and so we walk by

---

15. A few codices understand this as differently punctuated: "You who seek to be freed from the hand of the law-breaker and the wicked person, simply withhold consent." "But he is rampaging!"

faith, not by sight.[16] But the time will come for us to see what we now believe in without seeing. When we see what we have believed in, it will be joy for us; but when the wicked see what they did not believe in, they will be shamed. Then will come the reality; now there is simply hope;[17] because hope for something seen is not hope. But if we hope for what we do not see, we wait for it with patience.[18] At present we groan; at present you run for safety to your place of refuge; at present you are conscious of your weakness and you are entreating your physician. But what will you do when health, even perfect health, is yours? What will you do when you have been made equal to the angels of God?[19] Will you then forget the grace that set you free? Far from it: *I will sing of you always.*

Verses 7-9. Trusting God in the face of mockery, weakness and old age

9. *I have become a freak in the eyes of many.* But what about now, in this time of groaning, this time of weakness, this time of prayer offered by people in chains? What does the psalmist say now? *I have become a freak in the eyes of many.* Why *a freak*?[20] What reason have they to insult me, to think me a freak? They think me so because I believe in what I do not see. They are very different themselves: they find contentment in what they do see; they enjoy drink, wantonness, fornication, acquisitiveness, riches, robbery, worldly honors, and whitewashing a mud wall. With all these they are delighted. But I tread a different path, contemptuous of the good things of the present and even fearful of prosperity in this world, secure in nothing but God's promises. *Let us eat and drink, for tomorrow we shall die*, they say (1 Cor 15:32). What did you say? Tell me again? *Let us eat and drink*, says someone. Yes, but what was the next bit? *For tomorrow we shall die.* But that does not seduce me; it just scares me. With the motive you attached to your invitation you have struck fear into me. I dare not consent. *Tomorrow we shall die*, you say, and you give that as the reason for inviting me to eat and drink. First comes your invitation, *Let us eat and drink*, and you back it up with *for tomorrow we shall die*! Listen to me, and I will give you the opposite advice: let us fast and pray, for tomorrow we shall die.

As I hold to this strict and narrow way, *I have become a freak in the eyes of many; but you are my strong helper.* Keep close to me, Lord Jesus, and reassure me: "Do not flag on this narrow way. I walked it before you, and I am the Way.[21] I lead you, in myself I lead you, to myself I lead you home." Although *I have*

---

16. See 2 Cor 5:6-7.
17. The contrast is between *res* and *spes*, beloved of Augustine.
18. See Rom 8:24.
19. See Lk 20:36.
20. *Tamquam prodigium.*
21. See Jn 14:6.

become a freak in the eyes of many I will not fear, because *you are my strong helper.*

10. *May my mouth be filled with praise, to extol your glory in a hymn, your magnificence all day long.* What does he mean by *all day long*? Unceasingly. In prosperity, because then you are comforting me; in adversity, because then you are correcting me; before I existed, because you made me; after I came to be, because you saved me; after I had sinned, because you forgave me; after I had turned back to you, because you helped me; when I had persevered to the end, because you crowned me.[22] Indeed, then, *may my mouth be filled with praise, to extol your glory in a hymn, your magnificence all day long.*

11. *Do not cast me away in my old age.* You who are *my hope since my youth, do not cast me away in my old age.* Why this special mention of the period of old age? *When my strength fails, do not abandon me.* Here comes God's answer to your prayer: "Let your strength fail. All the better, as long as my strength abides in you, so that you can say with the apostle, *When I am weak, then I am strong*" (2 Cor 12:10). Do not be afraid of being cast aside in your time of weakness, when old age comes upon you. Was your Lord not reduced to weakness on the cross? Did the strong not strut before him, wagging their heads as at a helpless, captive, oppressed man? Did those fat bulls not taunt him, *If he is the Son of God, let him come down from the cross*?[23] And was he abandoned because he was so weak, he who preferred not to come down from the cross, lest it seem not a proof of power but a capitulation to his mockers? What did he teach you as he hung there, refusing to come down—what else but to be patient under insults and to be strong in your God? Perhaps it is even in the person of Christ himself that the lament is uttered, *I have become a freak in the eyes of many, but you are my strong helper*: in his person as weak, that is to say, not as powerful; in the identity of him who had taken us over into himself,[24] not in his identity as the one who had come down to us. He was indeed a freak in the eyes of many. And perhaps this was like old age for him, for the apostle says, *Our old humanity has been nailed to the cross with him* (Rom 6:6). If our old self was there, the weakness of old age was there.

Yet most truly was it promised, *Your youth will be renewed like an eagle's.*[25] Christ himself rose on the third day, and he promised us resurrection at the end of time. The head has preceded, and the members are to follow. Why be afraid that he may desert you, that he may toss you aside in your old age, when your strength

---

22. This litany of praise clearly transcends the limits of an individual life. As always in Augustine's perspective, it is the "one person" who speaks here, the whole Christ who spans the ages.

23. See Mt 27:39-40; Ps 21:13(22:12).

24. *Secundum id quod nos in se transfiguraverat.* See the Introduction in Volume 1 for comment on this profound truth.

25. Ps 102(103):5. On the myth of the eagle, see note at Exposition of Psalm 66, 10.

has failed? That is precisely the time when his strength will be in you, when your own is gone.

Verses 10-11. Was Christ abandoned?

12. **Why do I say this?** *Because my enemies threatened me, and those who spied against my life made common cause, saying, God has forsaken him; pursue him and seize him; there is no one to rescue him.* That was said about Christ; for though in the mighty power of his godhead, whereby he is equal to the Father, he had raised the dead, he had now suddenly become weak in the hands of his enemies, and was caught as though he had no power at all. How could he have been caught? Only because they had first told themselves in their hearts, *God has forsaken him.* And how could he have cried from the cross, *My God, my God, why have you forsaken me?* (Ps 21:2(22:1))? Did God abandon him, though God was in Christ, reconciling the world to himself?[26] Did God abandon Christ, Christ who was God, born indeed from the Jews according to the flesh, but God above all things, blessed for ever?[27] God forsook him? Of course not. But it was our voice that cried out then, the voice of our old nature; for our old self was crucified with him, and the body he had assumed was from this old humanity of ours, since Mary was descended from Adam. What Christ said on the cross articulated what his tormentors were thinking: *Why have you forsaken me?* Why do these people think in their wicked minds that I have been forsaken? But why can they be said to have thought so, in their wicked minds? Because if they had known the truth, they would never have crucified the Lord of glory.[28] *Pursue him and seize him.*

However, brothers and sisters, we can more naturally understand the reference to be to Christ's members, and recognize our own voice in this lament. Christ made the words his own inasmuch as he spoke in our name: not from his own power and majesty, not from what he was, he who made us, but from what he had become for our sake.

Verses 12-13. Don't be beguiled into fighting God, or the agents of your misfortune

13. *O Lord, my God, do not draw far away from me.* And so it is, for he certainly does not move far away. The Lord is close to those who have bruised their hearts.[29] *O my God, heed me and help me.*

---

26. See 2 Cor 5:19.
27. See Rom 9:5.
28. See 1 Cor 2:8.
29. See Ps 33:19(34:18).

14. *May they be shamed and enfeebled, those who provoke my soul.* What is he praying for? For them to be ashamed and enfeebled. Why? Because they *provoke my soul.* What does that mean—they *provoke*[30] *my soul?* They provoke it to some kind of quarrel. People who are egged on to fight each other are said to be provoked. Now if this is the right way to understand the expression, we should beware of people who try to provoke our soul. In what would such provocation consist? In the first place, they would provoke us to resist God, so that when things are going badly for us we would be annoyed with God. But when are you so upright that the God of Israel has a duty to be good to you, he who is good to the upright of heart?[31] When are you in the right? Listen, and I will tell you: when in the good you do, you are contented with God, and in the evil you suffer, you are not discontented with God. Think carefully about what I have just said, brothers and sisters, and be very wary of anyone who attempts to provoke your souls. When you are in grief or in trouble, people may work upon you, trying to make you weary of the struggle. Their real object is to persuade you to revolt against God over what you suffer, and to elicit from you resentful words like "What is the meaning of my trouble? What have I done?" Oh, so you have done nothing wrong? You are just, then, and God unjust? "Well, no," you say. "I admit it; I am not saying that I am just. I am a sinner, but so what? Am I as bad a sinner as that other fellow, whose affairs are going so well? What about old Gaius Seius?[32] I know all about his misdeeds. I know what his iniquities are like, and even though I am a sinner myself, I am a long way short of that. Yet I watch him enjoying success and all the good things of life, while I have to suffer so much! I am not saying, 'God, what have I done?' to mean that I have done nothing wrong at all. I mean that I have not done such bad things as to justify the woes I suffer." But there again, you are claiming to be just, aren't you, and accusing God of injustice? Wake up, you wretch, your soul has been provoked. "No," persists the objector. "I didn't say that I'm just." What are you saying, then? "That I am a sinner, yes, but I have not committed such great sins as to deserve what I have to suffer." All right; that means that you are not saying to God, "I am just, but you are unjust." But what you are saying is, "I am unjust, but you are more unjust still."

---

30. *Committentes.* The verb *committo* means to bring two things together, to establish a connection, bring into contact; and hence to engage (in battle) or to set two parties against each other. Augustine understands it in this last sense.

31. See Ps 72(73):1.

32. Perhaps an unidentified person known to the hearers. But the name "Seius" (in either masculine or feminine form) was used as a fictitious name in legal examples by the influential Roman lawyer Ulpian (third century A.D.); see, for instance, *Dig.* 27.5.9.10. Augustine may be using it similarly, as Tertullian also seems to have done in *Apol.* 3; see note at Exposition of Psalm 39, 26.

Look where you have landed yourself. Your soul has been provoked, and now your soul is at war. What is fighting? And against whom? Your soul, and against God—a created thing, against him who made it. Even by shouting against him you are already ungrateful. Get back to confessing your infirmity, entreat your physician. Stop regarding people who flourish for a brief spell as happy. You are being chastised, while they are spared; but perhaps an inheritance is being held in reserve for you as a punished and corrected child. Return then, return to your heart, you transgressor,[33] and do not allow your soul to be provoked. The one against whom you have declared war is a great deal more powerful than you are. The bigger the stones you hurl up to heaven against him, the more crushing will be the weight that falls back onto you. Return, and take an honest look at yourself. You are discontented with God; blush for it, and be discontented with yourself instead. You would effect nothing good, if he were not good, and you would suffer nothing bad, if he were not just. Wake up and listen to this: *The Lord gave, and the Lord has taken away. This has happened as the Lord willed: may the Lord's name be blessed* (Jb 1:21). While Job was oozing pus some unjust people were sitting beside him;[34] but Job was being whipped to get him ready for acceptance by God, whereas they were spared for the time being because they were due for punishment later.

Whatever trouble befalls you, whatever insults come your way, do not let your soul be provoked. Not only must it not be provoked against God; you must not let it be provoked against those who wrong you either. Even if you hate only them, your soul has been provoked into fighting against them. No; give thanks to God, and pray for the aggressors. Perhaps the psalm verse you heard is in fact a prayer for them: *may they be shamed and enfeebled, those who provoke my soul.* The psalm asks, *May they be shamed and enfeebled*: since they are so confident of their own righteousness, it will do them good to be shamed. It is to their advantage that they recognize their sins, and be ashamed, and that they become enfeebled, because they were mistakenly confident in their strength. Once enfeebled, let them acknowledge, *When I am weak, then I am strong* (2 Cor 12:10), and in their feebleness pray, *Do not cast me away in my old age.* So the psalm's prayer was for good to come to them, a prayer that they might feel the shame of their wrongdoing and lose their perverted strength. Enfeebled and shamed, let them seek God, who will shed his light on their blushing faces, and restore them after their debility.

Now look at the next petition: *May they be covered with shame and embarrassment, those who think evil against me.* He asks for *shame and embarrassment* to be their clothing: shame because of their bad consciences, and embarrassment to instill a sense of what is fitting. Let this happen to them, and

---

33. See Is 46:8.
34. See Jb 2:13.

they will be good. You must not think the psalmist is being vindictive; no, let his prayer for them be heard! It might have seemed that Stephen was being vindictive when with fiery speech he hurled at his opponents the accusation, *You stiff-necked people, uncircumcised in heart and ears, you are for ever resisting the Holy Spirit!* (Acts 7:51). What burning anger this was, how vehement was he against his enemies! It sounds as though his soul had been provoked into fighting. But no, by no means. He was seeking to heal them. He treated them like dangerously delirious patients, and tried to restrain them with his words. You can find proof that his soul was not provoked—not against God, but not against them either. He prayed, *Lord Jesus, receive my spirit* (Acts 7:59); evidently he did not blame Jesus for letting him be stoned as a result of preaching his word. His soul was not provoked against God. But again he prayed, *Lord, do not hold this sin against them* (Acts 7:60); so his soul was not provoked in that respect either, not even against his enemies. *May they be covered with shame and embarrassment, those who think evil against me*; for this is what all of them who trouble me are seeking: they want to do me harm. Job's wife was seeking to harm him when she suggested, *Curse God, and die* (Jb 2:9). So was Tobit's wife, who challenged her husband, *What good have all your righteous deeds done you?*[35] She said it to stir him to discontent with God for making him blind. Once discontented, his soul would readily be provoked.

Verse 14. Is it possible to add anything to God's praise?

15. If no one has led you astray by annoying you, if no one has elicited from you any word of resentment against God over what you suffer, or of hatred against people who cause the suffering, your soul is not provoked; and then you can peacefully pray the next verse: *But as for me, I will always hope in you, and add something extra to all your praise.* What can that mean? The promise that *I will add something extra to all your praise* ought to give us food for thought. Do you think you can make God's praise more perfect? Is there anything further that can be added? If it is all praise already, what are you going to add? God has been praised from of old by all the good things he has made, by the whole of his creation, by his disposition of all things, by his governance and rule of all the worlds, by his ordering of times and seasons, by the loftiness of the sky, by the fecundity of diverse lands, by the sea spread all around them, and by all the most excellent endowments of every creature born there. He has been praised by his human creatures, for giving them the law, for freeing them from captivity in Egypt, and for all the rest of his wonderful exploits.

---

35. See Tb 2:22.

But there was one thing for which he had not yet been praised: for raising flesh from death to eternal life. Let this special song of praise now be added through the resurrection of our Lord Jesus Christ. If we understand the verse in this way, we do well, and we rightly hear the voice of Christ above all the chorus of praise that went before.

But you, you are perhaps a sinner, one who needed to be careful lest your soul was provoked into resistance. You are a sinner who hoped in God alone to set you free from that first captivity, a sinner who had no righteousness of your own to count on, whose only reliance was the grace of God celebrated in this psalm. So what more are you going to add to all this praise of God? Ah, says the psalmist, but I will indeed add something. Let us see what he has to add. Your praise might have seemed complete, Lord; it might have seemed that nothing was lacking; and indeed nothing would be missing if you damned all wrongdoers. The divine justice, whereby God could damn all of them, would be no derogation of his praise; rather such justice would redound to his praise most highly. You created human beings, gave them free will, established them in paradise, imposed a command on them, and threatened them with justly deserved death if they should violate it. There was nothing that you failed to do for them, no one who could demand more of you. Yet they sinned. The human race became a solid mass of sinners, deriving from the original sinners. If, then, you were to damn this entire mass of iniquity, would anyone have the right to say to you, "You have acted unjustly"? Even in such an action you would unquestionably be just, and all of it would be to your praise. But because you chose instead to free sinners by justifying the ungodly, *I will add something extra to all your praise.*

Verse 15. *Singing praise in daylight and in darkness*

16. *My mouth will proclaim your justice,* not mine. This is how I will add something further to all your praise: the fact that I am just (if I am) is due to your justice in me, not my own; for you justify the ungodly.[36] *My mouth will proclaim your justice, and your salvation all day long.* Why *your salvation*? Because salvation is the Lord's.[37] No one may falsely claim the credit for saving himself or herself; salvation is the Lord's. None of us saves ourselves: salvation is the Lord's, and human aid is useless.[38] *I will proclaim your salvation all day long*: that means, all the time. If things are going badly with you, preach the Lord's salvation; if things are prospering, preach the Lord's salvation. You must not preach it in prosperity and keep your mouth shut in adversity, or you will not be

---

36. See Rom 4:5.
37. See Ps 3:9(8).
38. See Ps 59:13(60:11).

making good the pledge, *all day long*. A "day" includes its attendant night. When we say, for example, "Thirty days elapsed," we don't need to add, "And nights," do we? Obviously we include the nights in the number of days mentioned. What did Genesis say? *There was evening, and then morning, one day* (Gn 1:5). A whole day includes its own night, for the night is the servant of the day, not vice versa. Whatever you do in your mortal flesh must be done in the service of justice. Whatever you do must be done in obedience to God's command, not for the benefit of the flesh; for that would be to make the day the servant of the night. Sing God's praise all day long, then; that is, in prosperity and in adversity: in prosperity, as though in the hours of daylight, and in adversity as though at night. Sing God's praise, one way or another, all day long, so that you will not be making an empty claim when you sing in another psalm, *I will bless the Lord at all times; his praise shall be in my mouth always* (Ps 33:2(34:1)).

While Job's children were safe, along with his cattle, his household, and all his property, Job habitually praised God. This was like praise offered in the daytime. But then came the calamities. Bereavement fell upon him suddenly, what he had been saving was lost, and those for whom he had been saving it were dead. This was like nightfall. But listen to the way he kept on praising God all day long. After those daylight hours when he had been happy, did he give up praising God because the sun had set on his good fortune? Not at all. Was it not still broad daylight within his heart? And did the light not stream out from him as he said, *The Lord gave, and the Lord has taken away. This has happened as the Lord willed: may the Lord's name be blessed*? Yet so far it was only twilight. Blacker night was coming, and deeper darkness, in the shape of bodily pain, decay and maggots; but even amid decomposition this man did not tire of offering night-time praise to God, for within himself he was rejoicing in daylight. When his wife tried to persuade him to blaspheme, provoking his soul, he responded to the sinful suggestions of the unhappy woman as though to the shadows of night. *You have spoken like the silly woman you are*, he said; truly she was a daughter of night. *If we have received good things from the Lord's hands, should we not endure the bad too?* (Jb 2:10). We have praised him in daylight; are we to fall silent at night? *All day long*, throughout each day with its attendant night, *I will proclaim your salvation*.

Is fraud unavoidable in trade? A lively denial from a trader

17. *Because I have known nothing of trade*. He seems to be saying, "This is why I can proclaim your salvation all day long, *because I have known nothing of trade*." What kind of trading does he have in mind? Any traders present had better listen, and change their lives. If they have been traders, let them be so no

longer; let them not engage in their former pursuits, but forget them. And let them not approve or commend trade, but disapprove, condemn, and be weaned away from it, if trading is sinful. From your pursuits arises a kind of greed to make more and more money, you trader; and when you suffer some loss, the same greed tempts you to blaspheme. Consequently the psalm verse will not be true in your case: *I will proclaim your praise all day long.* When you not only lie about the price you paid for the goods you sell, but even perjure yourself over it, how can the praise of God be in your mouth all day long? Moreover, if you are a Christian, God's name is inevitably blasphemed as a result of what you say, for outsiders will exclaim, "That's what Christians are like!" We must conclude that if the speaker in our psalm tells God's praise all day long because he has not engaged in trading, Christians must correct themselves and keep clear of it.[39]

A trader replies to me, "But look, I bring merchandise from far away to places where the goods I supply are not available. I make my living by selling them more dearly than I bought them; the margin is my recompense for the work I have put into it. How else can I live? Scripture says, *The laborer deserves his pay*" (Lk 10:7). Yes, but it is lying that is in question here, and perjury. "Very well, but that is a vice in me, not in my trade. It is untrue to say that I could not carry on my business without it, so I am not going to shift the blame for the fault I commit onto my trade. If I tell lies, I am the liar, not my trade. I could quite well say to the customer, 'I paid so much for this, and I am selling it for so much. Buy it if you want it.' The customer would not be driven away by being told the truth. More likely lots of others would come running, because they like honesty even better than the goods." So, continues the trader, "Admonish me against lying and perjury, but don't tell me to wind up my business or disengage myself from it. Anyway, what are you going to steer me toward, if you forbid me to trade? Some craft? Suppose I become a shoemaker. All right, I'll make sandals for people. Do you imagine that shoemakers aren't liars too? Aren't they perjurers as well? You know what happens: they accept an order to make someone a pair of sandals, and they are paid to do it. Then someone else comes along and they take the money from the new customer, abandon the first job, and let down the person to whom they promised that they would make the sandals quickly. Don't they often say, 'I'll do it today; I'll have your order ready before the day is out'? What is more,

---

39. These extreme statements, surprising in their absoluteness and lack of balance, cannot represent Augustine's real thought on the matter of Christians engaged in trade. They are promptly demolished in the rest of this section, which argues that dishonesty in any trade or craft derives from the sinful practitioner, not the work. *Abusus non tollit usum.* It is unclear whether Augustine deliberately stated an impossible position first in order to arouse the indignation, and therefore the interest, of his congregation; or whether he put forward an unbalanced view because he had not thought through the consequences, and was brought up short by an outraged reaction. The former explanation seems the more likely, though the length and liveliness of the argument may catch echoes of a real protest. In any case, Augustine goes on to refine his interpretation of trading in the following section.

they cheat badly by shoddy sewing, don't they? They do all this, they say all this; but it is they themselves who are wicked, not the craft they practice. All bad craftsmen who do not fear God tell lies and perjure themselves, either for the sake of profiteering or through fear of loss or poverty. Incessant praise of God is obviously not forthcoming from them. So why dissuade me from my trade? Do you want to persuade me to become a farmer—and then grumble against God for sending thunderstorms, and consult a soothsayer when I am worried about hail, trying to find a way of defeating the weather? Do you want me to hope for a famine to afflict the poor, so that I can sell what I have left over? Is that where you are leading me? But, you say, good farmers don't do things like that. No, and neither do good traders. On your showing, it's even a bad thing to have children, because when the children have headaches, naughty unbelieving mothers go looking for sacrilegious charms to tie onto them, and try incantations! These things are the sins of human beings, not of the things they deal in."

The trader can say to me, "Make sure, Bishop, that you understand what kind of trading is meant in the passage you have read in the psalter. Make sure you do not misinterpret the text, and forbid me to trade. Admonish me as to how I should live: if I live in the right way, it will be well with me. But one thing I know: if I am bad, it is not the trading that makes me so, but my own iniquity." When the case is so truthfully argued, there is no gainsaying it.

*A different interpretation: trading means self-reliant activity,
as opposed to grace*

18. We had better inquire what kind of trading is envisaged, if it is true that no one who engages in it can praise God all day long. The word for trading in Greek is connected with the ordinary word for activity;[40] but in Latin *negotiatio*[41] is derived from *negato otio*.[42] But whether we think of it as activity, or as the negation of leisure, we need to discuss what it is. Traders who are very busily engaged are like those who rely on what they achieve themselves, and so praise their own work and never attain to the grace of God. In this sense "traders" are the enemies of that grace which the psalm commends to us; for it commends grace to warn us that none of us must glory in our own works.

But surely the text in scripture which states that *doctors shall not raise the dead* (Ps 87:11(88:10)) does not imply that everyone ought to give up medical care? No; so what is it warning us against? Under the term, "doctors," we are to understand those proud people who promise salvation to others, whereas salva-

---

40. ᵃ ~*r*~*éí@*~I from ᵃᵃᵗᵖᵖ~*úi*~I activity, undertaking, occupation.
41. Translated above as "trading," but also carrying similar meanings of "business, affairs."
42. "Leisure denied."

tion is the Lord's.[43] And just as the verse in our present psalm, *I will proclaim your salvation all day long*, cautions us against proud "doctors" promising salvation, so too does the line, *my mouth will proclaim your justice* (that is, not my own), put us on our guard against "traders" who find their satisfaction in their own activity and their works.

Who are these traders, those who flatter themselves about their activity? Those who know nothing of God's righteousness, but seek to set up their own, and have not been submissive to God's righteousness.[44] Their activity is justly called *negotium*, because it is the negation of *otium*.[45] How serious an evil that is can be inferred from the Lord's expulsion of traders from the temple. He said to them, *It is written, My house will be called a house of prayer; but you have turned it into a place of trafficking*.[46] This means, "You make your works a matter for boasting, instead of seeking holy leisure." You are deaf to scripture's censure of your restlessness and busyness: *Be still and see that I am the Lord* (Ps 45:11(46:10)). What is the implication of this command, *Be still and see that I am the Lord*, if not "Keep still, so that you may know that it is God who works in you, and may be pretentious no longer about your own works"? Can you not hear the voice that invites you, *Come to me, all you who labor and are heavily burdened, and I will give you relief. Shoulder my yoke, and learn from me, for I am meek and humble of heart*, and you will find rest for your souls (Mt 11:28-29)? This rest is proclaimed as a rebuke to busy traders; this rest is preached as a corrective to those who hate holy leisure, busily flaunting their works and unable to rest in God. The more they exalt themselves about their achievements, the further do they recoil from grace.

An alternative reading: should it be "writing" rather than "trading"? The same message comes through

19. Some witnesses to the text of the psalm have *Because I have known nothing of written texts*. Where other codices have *trade*, these have *written texts*;[47] and it is difficult to see how these readings can be harmonized. Neverthe-

---

43. *Salus* can mean either "salvation" or "healing." Augustine implies that Ps 87:11 seems to disparage doctors. But since it cannot mean that all medical care should be abandoned, we must look for a better interpretation. The term, "doctors," he suggests, must be used in a restricted or metaphorical sense, denoting those pompous persons who promise health/healing/salvation they cannot give. Against these, Psalm 70 warns. This reflection provides him with a useful parallel for his problem about "traders;" they too are to be taken as symbolic of the self-sufficiency condemned in the psalm.

44. See Rom 10:3.

45. Leisure, but with richer overtones of culture or contemplation than our word carries; see note at Exposition 1 of Psalm 36, 2.

46. See Mt 21:13; Jn 2:16.

47. The original Hebrew is uncertain at this point. The Greek yields two different readings: "٠٠-*î*°-*ėïą̃-î* (trade, business) and *î*°-°°-*ėïą̃-î* (literature, written texts, related to *î*°-°°-*ėïη̃î*, a scribe). The Vulgate *litteraturam* reflects the latter.

less the divergence may bring out the true meaning, rather than lead us into error. Let us consider, then, how best to understand *written texts* so as not to offend literary experts,[48] as we just now offended the traders;[49] for it is quite possible for an expert on literature to make an honest living from his profession, and keep clear of perjury and lies. We need to find out what kind of literature it was that the psalmist declined to know, in order to keep God's praise in his mouth all day long.

Now the Jews have written texts, and if we refer this passage to them, we shall find the answer. When we were investigating the allusion to traders, we found that scripture viewed trading as something to be abhorred because it symbolized activism and reliance on works; this was an attitude the apostle remarked on: *They failed to recognize the righteousness that comes from God, and by seeking to set up a righteousness of their own, they did not submit to God's righteousness* (Rom 10:3). He speaks against it elsewhere: salvation *does not come from works, lest anyone boast.* How are we to live, then? Are we not to do good? Yes, certainly, but we must work with God working in us, for *we are his own handiwork, created in Christ Jesus for good works* (Eph 2:9-10). We found scripture warning us against "traders"; that is, people who boast of their actions, exalting themselves in respect of that *negotium* which is the negation of *otium*, holy leisure, people who are restless rather than good workers; for good workers are those in whom God is working. In a parallel way we find written texts in the keeping of the Jews. The Lord has graciously granted me some insight into this parallel in my heart; may he now help me to put it into words.

The Jews were proud, taking their stand upon their own strength and the righteousness of their works; and they boasted too about the law: they prided themselves that they had received the law, and other nations had not. But in their pride about the law what they were boasting about was not grace but the letter. Now the law minus grace is simply the letter alone; it is a standing condemnation of iniquity, not a means of salvation. What does the apostle say of it? *If a law capable of giving life had been granted to us, then of course righteousness would have been obtainable through the law; but scripture has included all things under sin, so that through faith in Jesus Christ the promise might be given to believers* (Gal 3:21-22). And in another passage he says of the letter of the law, *The letter is death-dealing, but the spirit gives life* (2 Cor 3:6). Since you have the law, you are a law-breaker if you offend: *You will be judged as a transgressor of the law, for all your written code and circumcision* (Rom 2:27). Was the psalm not right to sing, *Rescue me from the hand of the law-breaker and the wicked*? You have the letter of the law, but you do not abide by it. In what sense

---

48. The *grammaticus* was more than a grammarian; the word could also cover experts on literature, or scholars more generally.
49. Possibly an indication that the argument in section 17 was a real outburst? See note there.

do you not observe even the letter? *You preach against theft, yet you steal; you preach that adultery is forbidden, yet you commit adultery; you loathe idols, but do you not violate their shrines? Through your fault the name of God is profaned among the nations, as scripture says* (Rom 2:21-22.24). What advantage to you is a written code you do not keep? But why do you not keep it? Because you rely on yourself. Why can you not fulfill it? Because you are a trader: you flaunt your own achievements and fail to realize that God's enabling grace is absolutely necessary if you are to carry out what he commands. God has given you his orders; now carry them out. You begin to do so by your own strength; then you fall down, and your written code stays there looming over you as a sentence of punishment, not a means of salvation. Truly is it said, *The law was given through Moses, grace and truth came through Jesus Christ* (Jn 1:17).

Moses wrote five books; yes, but in five porticoes which ringed a certain pool, sick persons used to lie, unable to find healing.[50] This is an image of the letter which convicted the guilty but could not save the sinner. In those five porticoes, which represented the five books of the law, sick people were exposed, rather than healed. What was it that could cure a sick person there? The movement of the water. When the pool was disturbed a sick person would go down into it, and one—just one—would be healed; this is a symbol of unity. Anyone else who went down at the time of the disturbance of the water was not healed. What a wonderful image this is of the unity of the body that cries from the ends of the earth![51] No one else would be cured until the pool had been stirred again. The movement of water in the pool thus signified the disturbance caused among the Jewish people by the coming of our Lord Jesus Christ; for it was believed that the water was stirred by the arrival of an angel. The pool surrounded by five porticoes was therefore a figure of the Jewish race encircled by the law. They lay there, helpless, in their porches; only when the water was disturbed and moved would they be healed. The Lord came, the water was troubled, he was crucified. Now let the sick man go down, and be healed! What does "go down" mean? Let him humble himself. But all of you, whoever you may be who are attached to the letter barren of grace, you will remain in your porticoes; you will be ill, lying there and never regaining your strength, for you presume on the letter. *If a law capable of giving life had been granted to us, then of course righteousness would have been obtainable through the law* (Gal 3:21). But the law was given to show you up as guilty, so that being guilty you would be afraid, and being afraid you would beg forgiveness, no longer presuming on your own strength or priding yourself on the letter.

There is another representation of the same truth: Elisha's action in first dispatching his servant with his staff to raise a dead child. The son of the woman

---

50. See Jn 5:2-4.
51. See Ps 60:3(61:2).

who had given Elisha hospitality had died; the news was brought to Elisha, and he sent his servant with the staff. *Go*, he told him, *lay the staff on the dead child* (2 Kgs 4:29). Was the prophet unsure what to do? The servant went on ahead, and placed the staff on the corpse; but the dead child did not revive. *If a law capable of giving life had been granted to us, then of course righteousness would have been obtainable through the law*. The law sent through a servant did not bring life. But Elisha, who had sent his staff with his servant, was to follow later himself, and bring the child to life. After hearing that the child had not revived, Elisha came in person; he was a type of our Lord who had sent his servant ahead of him with a staff that represents the law. He came to the dead child lying there, and placed his body over him. But the dead person was an infant, and Elisha a grown man, so he contracted his adult stature and somehow curtailed it, making himself like a child so that he matched the corpse in size. The dead child arose when the living man had fitted himself to him; the Lord accomplished what the staff had failed to do; grace achieved what the law could not.

Those who have continued with the staff make their boast of the law, and that is why they do not come to life. But for my part, I want to boast of your grace; as the apostle says, *Far be it from me to boast, save in the cross of our Lord Jesus Christ* (Gal 6:14), save in him who, when I was dead, reduced his living self to my small stature so that I might live—and live, no longer I, but Christ in me.[52] Boasting solely of this grace, *I have known nothing of written texts*. With my whole heart I have repudiated people who place their reliance on the letter of the law, and shy away from grace.

Verse 16. Reaffirmation of all that the preceding verses have said

20. It is fitting that the next line should be, *I will make my way into the power of the Lord*: not my own power, but the Lord's. Those others trust in their own power and boast of the letter of the law, but know nothing of the grace that has been joined to the letter; for *the law was given through Moses, grace and truth came through Jesus Christ*. Christ came to bring the law to perfection by giving us charity, through which we were empowered to fulfill the law, since *the fullness of the law is charity* (Rom 13:10). Those who lack charity persist in boasting of the letter: they do not have the Spirit of grace, who is *the charity of God poured out into our hearts*, the *Holy Spirit who has been given to us* (Rom 5:5). The *letter is death-dealing, but the spirit gives life*, and I have chosen, therefore, to *know nothing of written texts* alone; I will rather *make my way into the power of the Lord*. This verse confirms and completes the teaching of the previous ones, so as to fix it in people's hearts and exclude any possibility whatever

---

52. See Gal 2:20.

of a different interpretation creeping in. *Lord, I will be mindful of your righteousness alone.* What a precious word that is—*alone!* Why was it added? I am asking you. It would have been sufficient to say, *I will be mindful of your righteousness.* But no, the psalm insists, *your righteousness alone;* I will have no thought of mine. *What have you that you did not receive? And if you did receive it, why boast as though you had not?* (1 Cor 4:7). Your righteousness alone sets me free; nothing truly belongs to me except my sins. Let me not glory in my own strength; let me not stick at the letter. Let me reject mere written texts; that is, people who make their boast of the letter of the law, and against all reason trust in their strength like delirious patients. Let me repudiate all such, and make my way into the power of the Lord, so that when I am weak, I may be strong;[53] or, rather, that you may be strong in me, for *I will be mindful of your righteousness alone.*

---

53. See 2 Cor 12:10.

Exposition 2 of Psalm 70

Second Sermon[1]

Recapitulation of yesterday's sermon. Captivity, redemption, and grace

1. We pointed out to you yesterday, beloved friends,[2] that this psalm commends to us the grace of God by which salvation has come to us gratis. No antecedent merits on our part earned us salvation, for all that was owing to us was punishment. We did not manage to finish the psalm yesterday, but postponed the last verses until today, promising you in the Lord's name that we would discharge the remainder of our debt later. The time for doing so has arrived, so I ask you to be attentive, with your minds expectant like a fertile field, ready to multiply the seed and welcome the rain.

We drew your attention to the title yesterday, but to refresh the memories of those who heard it then, and to inform those of you who were not here, we shall briefly recapitulate, so that those who heard about it may be reminded, and those who do not know may learn. The psalm is about the sons of Jonadab, a man whose name is interpreted, "The Lord's Spontaneous One." This is a reminder that we must serve the Lord not with duplicity in our hearts but with a good, pure, sincere, and perfect will, as is suggested also in another psalm where it is said, *Of my own free will I will offer sacrifice to you* (Ps 53:8(54:6)). The present psalm is sung for the children of this man; that is to say, for the children of obedience, and for those *who were first taken captive*. We must therefore recognize our own voices groaning here, and certainly each day sees enough bad things to groan over.[3] If in our pride we have abandoned God, let us at least return to him in our weariness. But there is no returning except by grace. And grace is bestowed gratis; if it were not given gratis it would not be grace. But if it is grace only because given gratis, it is quite obvious that no merit on your part came first to entitle you to receive it. If any good works on your side did take precedence, you were getting your wages; and wages are not given gratis. But the wage due to us was punishment. Our liberation is therefore not to be ascribed to our merits, but to God's grace. Let us praise him, then, for we owe him everything that we are, and the fact that we have been saved. With this in view, and after saying much

---

1. Preached on the day after the preceding sermon.
2. *Caritati vestrae.*
3. *Sufficiat diei malitia sua* (Mt 6:34). The relevance of this allusion to the context is not entirely clear; the translation here offered is conjectural.

else, the psalmist concluded, *I will be mindful of your righteousness alone.* And with that verse yesterday's exposition also concluded.

We also saw the meaning of another phrase in the title. Those *who were first taken captive* were called *first* because of their kinship with the first man; and *captives* because in that first man we all die. But *it is not the spiritual that comes first. The animal body comes first, and what is spiritual afterward* (1 Cor 15:46); and so we were originally captives because of the first man, but we are later redeemed because of the second man. The very fact of being redeemed proclaims our earlier captivity: why would we have needed redemption, if not because we were captives? We also pointed out that this captivity is more vividly described by the apostle in another text. We quoted to you certain words from another of his epistles, and we repeat them now: *I am aware of a different law in my members that opposes the law of my mind, and imprisons me under the law of sin inherent in my members* (Rom 7:23). This is our first and original captivity, in which the flesh lusts against the spirit.[4] It was part of the punishment meted out for sin that a human being should be divided against himself, since he had refused to be subject to the one undivided God. Obedience is very good for the human soul, better than anything else; and if it is good for the soul of a servant to obey a master, for a son to obey his father, and for a wife to obey her husband, how much more is it good for a human person to obey God!

But Adam chose to experience what was bad for him, and every one of us is Adam, just as every one of us who has believed is Christ, for we are members of Christ. Adam, however, chose to experiment with evil, which he had no business to do, and would not have done if he had heeded the prohibition, *Do not touch.*[5] Since every Adam now has experience of what is bad for him, and has fallen ill through disobeying the physician's instructions, let him at least obey them now in order to get well. A good, honest doctor gives orders to a healthy person so that his own services may not be necessary; for it is not when people are healthy that they need a doctor, but when they are ill.[6] Reliable, friendly doctors are not eager to sell their skills; they are happier about people's health than about their sickness. Accordingly they lay down rules to be observed by those who are well, with a view to avoiding illness. But if these people ignore the rules and fall ill, they look to the physician for aid. When well, they slight him, but when sick they seek his help. And vital it is that they should at least seek it, for if the fever mounts and they go insane they may kill the physician instead. You heard how this can happen in the gospel read just now; you understood the parable directed against such people. Were they sane, the workers who said to each other, *This is the heir. Come on, let's kill him, then the estate will be ours* (Mk 12:7)? Of

---

4. See Gal 5:17.
5. See Gn 2:17.
6. See Mt 9:12.

course they were not. Suppose they did kill the son: were they planning to kill the father too? This is crazy. In the end they did kill the Son; but the Son rose from the dead, and the stone cast away by the builders became the headstone of the corner.[7] They tripped over it and were shattered; it will fall upon them and crush them.

Of a different mind is the one who sings in this psalm, *I will make my way into the power of the Lord*; not mine, but the Lord's. *Lord, I will be mindful of your righteousness alone*. I know of no righteousness in myself, so I will be mindful of your righteousness only. Whatever good I have, I hold from you; whatever I have as from myself is only evil. You did not requite me with the punishment I deserved; you bestowed grace on me gratis. Therefore *I will be mindful of your righteousness alone*.

Verse 17. God raises the soul to life by grace, and stays with it

2. *O God, you have taught me from my youth*. What have you taught me? That I should be mindful of your righteousness alone. When I reflect on my past life, I see what was owing to me, and what I have been given in place of what was owing. Affliction was what I deserved, grace what was granted instead; hell was what I deserved, eternal life what has been given. *O God, you have taught me from my youth*. From the very beginning of the faith by which you made a new person of me, you have taught me that there was nothing at all in me beforehand that could give me reason to think I merited what you have given. Who is ever converted to God, except by being turned away from iniquity? Who is redeemed, unless from captivity? Who dare say that our captivity was unjust, when we betrayed our commander and rallied to the standard of a deserter? God is the commander, the devil a deserter. The commander issued an order to us, and the devil dropped his guileful hints. To which will you give ear—prescription or deception? Is the devil better than God? Is the defector better than your creator? Yet you believed in the devil's promise, and discovered the truth of God's threat.

The psalmist speaks as one freed from captivity, though still in hope, not yet in full reality; as one who walks by faith, not yet by sight.[8] *O God, you have taught me from my youth*, he says. I have been made new by you who made me, recreated by you who created me, formed afresh by you who first formed me; and from the first moment I turned to you, I have learned that all this came from no prior merits of mine. Your grace came to me gratis, that I might be mindful of your righteousness alone.

3. What happens after this period of youth? *You have taught me from my youth*, but what about the time when youth is past? At your initial conversion you learned

---

7. See Ps 117(118):22.
8. See 2 Cor 5:7.

that you had not been righteous before it. Your previous state had been one of iniquity, and this had to be expelled so that charity could take its place. Now you have been made into a new person, though so far only in hope, not yet in full reality; and what you have learned at this stage is that nothing good on your part took the initiative, for you were converted to God by God's grace. But now that you are converted, what about the present situation? You will have something of your own now, won't you? Should you not rely now on your own resources?

No. It is like something people often say: "All right, leave me now. I needed you to show me the way, but now I can manage alone. I will walk along it by myself." And the person who showed you the way asks, "Don't you want me to guide you?" But you, if you are a proud sort, reply, "No, of course not; I can manage. I'll go this way alone." So you are left to yourself, and because you are weak you will go astray once more. It would be much better for you if the person who first set you on the right way continued to guide you along it; if he does not, you will go wrong again. Pray to God, then, *Lead me in your way, Lord, and I will walk in your truth* (Ps 85(86):11). Your first steps along this way were like your youth, the time when you were made new, the time when your faith began to grow. Before that time you were just a vagabond, roaming as you pleased. You wandered through woods and stony tracks, lacerated in every limb, searching for your homeland, searching for a place where your spirit could find some stability, where you could say, "This is it." You wanted to be able to say it in security, safe against all attack and all temptation, and eventually freed from all traces of captivity. But you did not find that place. What shall I tell you? That he who showed you the way came to your help? Was that all? No, more than that: the Way himself came to you, and you were established in the Way without any previous deserving, for all you had been able to do was go astray. But now, since you have begun to walk there, are you your own guide? Does he who taught you now leave you to yourself? No, says the psalm. *You have taught me from my youth, and even now I will proclaim your wonderful deeds*, for what you are doing now is indeed wonderful: that you who set me on the right path should now steer me. These are some of your wonderful deeds.

What are these wonderful deeds of the Lord? How do you see them? Among all the wonderful deeds of the Lord, what is more wonderful than raising the dead? But, you ask, am I dead? Well, you were; for if you had not been dead, scripture would not have invited you, *Arise, sleeper, rise from the dead: Christ will enlighten you* (Eph 5:14). All unbelievers are dead, and all grave sinners; they are alive in their bodies but the light of life is extinguished in their hearts. Anyone who raises a corpse to life raises that person to a state where he can see this light again, and once more breathe this air; but the one who raises him up is not himself the light or the air. The resuscitated person begins to see again in the same way that he did formerly. When a soul is raised to life it is different. The soul is raised up by God. It is true, of course, that the body too is raised by God;

but when God resuscitates the body he restores it to this world; when he raises up the soul, he restores it to himself. If the air of this world is cut off, the body dies; if God withdraws, the soul dies. It follows, therefore, that if God does not remain present to a soul he has revived, the revived soul cannot continue to live. He does not raise it to life and then leave it to live by itself.

The situation is not like that of Lazarus, who after being dead for four days was restored to bodily life by the bodily presence of the Lord. Christ approached the grave in bodily wise, and shouted, *Lazarus, come out!* (Jn 11:43). Lazarus arose, and came out of the tomb with the grave-bands on him; then he was untied and he went away. He was raised from the dead by the presence of the Lord, but he went on living when the Lord was absent. As far as appearances went, the Lord's bodily actions had resuscitated Lazarus, but in fact it was the Lord's divine majesty that had worked the miracle, and from that majestic presence Lazarus never did depart. Still, the actual situation was that the Lord raised up Lazarus to resume his visible life; and the Lord then left that town or that region. Did that mean that Lazarus could not live on? Clearly not.

The raising of a soul is something different, however. God raises a soul, but it dies if God goes away. I will put it boldly but truly, brothers and sisters. There are two lives: one of the body, the other of the soul. As the soul is the life of the body, so is God the life of the soul. As the body dies if the soul leaves it, so does the soul die if God leaves it. What his grace does for us is to raise us up and stay with us. In response to his act of raising us from our previous dead state, and giving us new life, we say to him, *O God, you have taught me from my youth.* But he does not abandon those he has raised to life, lest they die at his departure, so we say to him, *Even now I will proclaim your wonderful deeds*, because when you are with me I am alive. You are the life of my soul, and it will die if left to itself.

So then, my life, my God, is with me *even now*. What of the future?

Verse 18. The successive ages of the Church

4. *Even until I am old and gray-headed.* These two words both indicate old age for us, but the Greeks distinguish: they have one word for the period of dignified maturity that succeeds youth, and a different word for the last stage, the stage that follows dignified maturity. "ἱέ!ῃèῑῑ means someone grave and elderly, but ῃ̈ε̈ means an aged person. We do not have this distinction, so both words, old and gray-headed,[9] suggest old age. You will just have to bear in mind that two different stages are meant here.

You have taught me the reality of your grace *from my youth; and even now*, when my youth is past, *I will proclaim your wonderful deeds*, because you, who came to me to raise me up, abide with me still that I may not die. *Even until I am*

---

9. *Senectam et senium.*

old and gray-headed, that is, even to my last days, there will be no merit at all in me unless you are with me. May your grace persevere with me to the very end. Any one of us could say this—you, he, she, I—but it is the voice of the one, single, great person, the voice of unity itself; for it is the Church's voice that speaks here. So let us think of the Church's youth. Christ came, he was crucified, he died, he rose from the dead, he called the Gentiles. They began to be converted; martyrs suffered in the strength of Christ; the blood of the faithful was poured out and the Church's crop sprang up.[10] That was the time of youth. But as time rolls on the Church must confess, *Even now I will proclaim your wonderful deeds*. Not only in my youth, when Paul, Peter and the first apostles announced the message, but even now, at this later stage of my life, I will proclaim them—I who am your unity, your members, your body: *I will proclaim your wonderful deeds*. But what next? *Even until I am old and grey-headed* I will proclaim your wonderful deeds, for the Church will be here until the end of the world. If this were not to be the case, to whom did the Lord promise, *Lo, I am with you throughout all days, even to the end of the ages* (Mt 28:20)?

Now why was it necessary for these things to be said in the scriptures? Because enemies of the Christian faith would arise and say, "Christians will last only for a short time. Then they will die out, the idols will come back, and everything will be as it was before."[11] But how long will there be Christians? Until old age, until the age of gray hair; that is, until the end of the world. You expect Christians to fade away, wretched unbeliever, but it is you who will fade away, not the Christians. They will abide until the end of time. As for you in your unbelieving state, when your brief life is over, how will you have the face to go and meet the judge whom you blasphemed in your lifetime?

From my youth, and even now, and until I am old and gray-headed, do not forsake me, Lord. Your grace will not be with me for a short time only, as my enemies allege. *Do not forsake me, but let me tell of your strong arm to every generation still to come*. And to whom has the arm of the Lord been revealed?[12] The arm of the Lord is Christ. Do not forsake me, let there be no triumph for those who say, "Christians will not last long." Let there always be preachers to tell of your strong arm. To whom? *To every generation still to come*. If Christ is to be proclaimed to every generation yet to come, he will be preached until the end of the world; once time is finished, no more generations will be born.

---

10. For the echo of Tertullian compare Exposition of Psalm 39, 1 and Exposition 1 of Psalm 58, 5, and notes there.
11. An extended reflection on this theme is to be found in Augustine's Exposition of Psalm 40, 1. See also note there.
12. See Is 53:1.

Verse 19. Every generation must hear the full truth about grace

5. *Your power and your righteousness.* This means the same thing as, "Let me proclaim your mighty arm to every generation still to come." And what has this strong arm done for us? It has brought about our gratuitous, unmerited liberation. This is what I want to proclaim to every generation in the future: this grace I will proclaim. To every human being who shall be born I will say, You are nothing of yourself, call upon God; your sins are your own, but your merits are from God; what you were owed was punishment, and when reward comes to you instead, what God will crown is not your merits but his own gifts.[13] To every successive generation I will say, You came from a captive people, you belonged to Adam's race. All this I will say to every generation yet to be born; what I will proclaim is not any strength of my own, not any righteousness of my own, but *your power and your righteousness, O God, even to the highest, most glorious creatures you have wrought.* I am to proclaim *your power and your righteousness*; but how far shall my proclamation reach? To flesh and blood, but no further? No, indeed, *even to the highest, most glorious creatures you have wrought.* In the high places are the heavens; on high are Angels, Thrones, Sovereignties, Principalities, and Powers.[14] Whatever they are, they owe to you. To you they are indebted for the fact that they are alive; they owe it to you that they live in righteousness; they owe it to you that they live in beatitude. *Your power and your righteousness* will I proclaim—but how far? *Even to the highest, most glorious creatures you have wrought.* We must not suppose that God's grace is confined to humanity. What was an angel, before he came to be? And what would an angel be if his creator forsook him? I will proclaim *your power and your righteousness*, then, *even to the highest, most glorious creatures you have wrought.*

Who is like God?

6. And human beings are self-important! To make sure of their place in the primordial captivity they lend their ear to the serpent's suggestion, *Taste it, and you will be like gods* (Gn 3:5). Human beings like God? *O God, who is like you?* Nothing in the underworld, nothing in hell, nothing on earth, nothing in heaven; for you made them all. How dare the work contend with its Maker? But as for me, says wretched Adam—and Adam is every one of us—look what became of me when I perversely tried to be like you! I am reduced to crying out to you from my captivity. I was happy under a good sovereign, but I have become a captive

---

13. This famous phrase, found also in Letter 194, 19, became classical.
14. See Col 1:16.

under my seducer, and now I cry to you because I have fallen away from you. And how did I fall away from you? By seeking in a perverted way to be like you.

But how can this be? Does God not call us to be like him? Has he not himself commanded us, *Love your enemies, pray for those who persecute you, and do good to people who hate you*? And in saying this he is exhorting us to act in a Godlike way. He clinches it by adding, *You must be like your Father in heaven*; for what does our Father do? He *causes his sun to rise over the good and the wicked, and sends rain upon just and unjust alike* (Mt 5:44-45). Anyone who wishes well to his or her enemy is therefore like God, and it is not pride, but obedience, to strive for this. Why so? Because we were made in the image of God: he said, *Let us make humans in our own image and likeness* (Gn 1:26). If we hold the image of God within us we are not harboring something to which we have no right; all we need to worry about is that we do not lose it through pride.

What does it mean, then, to aspire to be like God out of pride? What should we think it was that reduced Adam to the captive status whence he had to cry out to God, *Lord, who is like you?* What is the twisted, distorted likeness that is here in question? Listen, and understand if you can. We believe that he who has put us here to say these things to you will also empower you to comprehend them. God stands in need of no good thing; he is himself the supreme good, and all that is good derives from him. In order to be good ourselves, we need God; but for God to be good he does not need us. Not only does he not need us, he does not even need *the highest, most glorious creatures he has wrought*, or any heavenly beings, or the supercelestial creation, or that which is called the heaven of heavens.[15] None of these does God need in order to be better, or more powerful, or happier. As for anything else that exists, what would it be, if he had not made it? What, then, could he possibly need from you, he who existed before you and was so powerful that when you did not exist, he made you? This is nothing like the way in which parents procreate children, is it? They generate, rather than create, their offspring through the concupiscence of the flesh, and as they generate, God creates. If you think you can create children in the way that God does, tell me what your wife is going to bear you! I needn't even say, "You tell me;" let her tell me! She can't, because she doesn't even know what is in her womb. Furthermore, men and women do generate children, but as a solace for themselves and a support in their old age. Did God create everything from that motive—to ensure that he would have help when he was old?

God knows everything he creates; he knows what it is like from the goodness of its being, and what it will become through its own will. God knows and ordains all things. If a human being wants to become something, he or she must turn to God, our creator. We grow cold as we move away from him, warm as we

---

15. See Ps 113(115):16, and note at Exposition of Psalm 67, 42.

draw nearer to him. We move into darkness if we withdraw, but become light as we approach him. From God we have our being, and also our well-being. Think of the younger son who wished to have under his own control the property which was being saved for him in the best possible way by his father. Having gained his independence he set out for a distant country, associated himself with a bad employer, and ended up feeding pigs. This young man who had gone proudly away from affluence and luxury was put to rights by hunger.[16]

If any one of us wants to be so truly like God that we can stand fast in close union with God, and guard our strength for him, as another psalm has it,[17] we must not distance ourselves from him, but cling to him so closely that his likeness is stamped upon us as wax is stamped by a signet-ring. Inseparably cleaving to him we shall bear his image, and find out for ourselves the truth of a psalm's assertion, *It is good for me to cling tightly to God* (Ps 72(73):28). Such a person truly preserves the likeness and image of God according to which we were made.

The opposite is true of anyone who tries to imitate God in a perverted fashion. As God is formed by no one and ruled by no one other than himself, so the would-be imitator of God wants to be autonomous, doing what he wishes with no one to form him or rule him, like God. But what happens, brothers and sisters? The perverse imitator freezes into immobility as he moves away from God's heat, sinks into futility as he abandons God's truth, and changes for the worse as he distances himself from God, who exists in the fullness of being, supreme and unchangeable.

7. The devil behaved like that. He wanted to imitate God, but in a distorted fashion; he wanted not to be subject to God's power, but to have power against him. In the case of human beings, though, a precept was laid upon them: they heard the Lord God say, *Do not touch.* "Touch what?" That tree. "But what is that tree? If it's a good tree, why shouldn't I touch it? If it's a bad tree, what is it doing in paradise?" It is in paradise because it is good; but I do not want you to touch it. "Why shouldn't I touch it?" Because I want you to be obedient, not rebellious. You are my servant, so submit to my order. Do not misbehave, servant. First listen to your Master's order, servant, and then you will discover his reason for giving it. The tree is good, but I do not want you to touch it. "Why not?" Because I am the Lord, and you are my servant. That is the whole reason. You think it trivial, do you, and disdain to be a servant? What do you think is good for you, if not to be subject to the Lord? And how will you be subject to the Lord if you do not bow to his command? But if it is to your advantage to be subject to the Lord, and submissive to his command, ask yourself what kind of command he was laying upon you. Is he demanding some service from you? Is he going to say to you, "Offer me a sacrifice"? Did he not create all things, your-

---

16. See Lk 15:12-16.
17. See Ps 58:10(59:9).

self among them? Is he going to order you, "Follow me and wait on me, to my couch when I rest, to table when I take my meals, to the baths when I choose to wash"? No? So if God requires no such service of you, does that mean he had no right to command you? If, however, he did have that right, it was necessary that you should be forbidden something, and so acknowledge yourself to be under his authority, knowing that it is expedient for you to be so. You were forbidden not because the tree was bad, but because for you obedience was good.

God could not have found any more perfect way of demonstrating the high value of obedience than to forbid us something that was not evil in itself. In those circumstances obedience alone wins the victory, and disobedience alone earns punishment. The tree is good, but I do not want you to touch it. You will not die of refraining from it. He who forbade you that tree has not taken other things away from you, has he? Is paradise not full of fruit trees? Are you in need of anything? But I do not want you to touch this tree, or to taste its fruit. In itself it is good, but for you obedience is better. Does it follow that if you do touch it, that tree will become lethal for you? No; but disobedience will have made you liable to death, because you will have touched what was forbidden. This is why the tree was called the tree of knowledge, the tree that gave discernment between good and evil.[18] It was so called not because such things dangled from it like fruit, but because whatever species of tree it was, and whatever kind of fruit it bore, persons who refused to discern good from evil on the basis of God's commandment would find out the difference from experience, for by touching what had been forbidden them they would discover only their hurt.

But why did they touch it, my brothers and sisters? Did they lack anything? Tell me what else they wanted or needed, established as they were in paradise, amid rich abundance, surrounded by everything that was delightful. Above all they had for their supreme delight the vision of God—God, of whose presence they were afraid after their sin, as though he had become their enemy. What else was wanting to their happiness, that they should touch the tree? One thing only did they want: to be autonomous. They took pleasure in breaking the commandment. They wanted to be like God, under no one's dominion, for obviously no one exercises authority over God. Straying to their own harm, fatally presumptuous, doomed to die, they abandoned the path of righteousness, discarded the commandment, shook their necks free from the yoke of discipline, and snapped the controlling reins in their headstrong leap. And where are they now?

Adam cries out now—but as a captive he is shouting it—*O Lord, who is like you?* In my twisted fashion I wanted to be like you, and I ended like a beast. Under your dominion and submissive to your command I was truly like you, but human beings failed to understand how they were honored; they were no better

---

18. See Gn 2:17.

than foolish beasts, and so became like them.[19] Cry out now, late as it is, from your bestial likeness, *O God, who is like you?*

Verse 20. God, our supreme good

8. *What dreadful troubles you have made me undergo! How many they are and how grave!* But you deserved them, you proud servant. You were created in the image of your Lord, but you chose to caricature your Lord instead. Did you think to ensure your well-being by moving away from your good? How wrong you were! God says to you, "If you can distance yourself from me, and find your well-being in doing so, I am not your good." But if God is good, and supremely good, if he is good of himself and not by derivation from any other good, and if he is the supreme good for us, what will you be if you distance yourself from him? What else but bad? Similarly if he is our beatitude, what will you find but misery if you leave him? Come back then, after you have found your misery; come back and say to him, *O Lord, who is like you? What dreadful troubles you have made me undergo! How many they are and how grave!*

Verses 20-21. The double resurrection: now through faith in the risen Christ, later in our bodies

9. But that was to teach you a lesson; it was a warning only. God has not abandoned you. So Adam shouts his gratitude: *You have turned to me and given me life, and you have brought me back again from the depths of the earth.* But why does he say *again?* When was there a first time? You fell from the heights, human creature, disobedient slave, proud rebel against your Lord: you fell low! The prophecy was fulfilled in you that *anyone who exalts himself will be humbled*; now may the rest of it come true in your case, that *the one who humbles himself will be exalted* (Lk 14:11). Come back from the depths. I am coming back, says Adam. I am on my way back, and I admit the truth: *O God, who is like you? What dreadful troubles you have made me undergo! How many they are and how grave! But you have turned to me and given me life, and brought me back again from the depths of the earth.*

"We understand!" I hear you say. "You have brought us back from the depths of the earth—that means, you have brought us back from the depths of sin where we had sunk!"

Yes, that's right; but why does he say *again?* When had it been done before? Let us press on; it may be that the remainder of the psalm will explain to us what we have not yet understood: why he says *again*. Let us listen, then: *What*

---

19. See Ps 48:13(49:12).

dreadful troubles you have made me undergo! How many they are and how grave! But you have turned to me and given me life, and brought me back again from the depths of the earth. How does the psalm continue from there? *You have multiplied proofs of your righteousness, you have turned to me and comforted me, and brought me back again from the depths of the earth.* Look—there is another *again*! If the first *again* caused us such perplexity, what are we going to make of a second? But there it is, a double *again*: first one and then another![20] May he who grants us grace assist us; may his strong arm work for us, that strong arm which we will proclaim to every generation still to come. May the Lord himself be near us, and with the key of his cross unlock the mystery enclosed in this verse. Significantly, the veil of the temple was rent apart when Christ was crucified,[21] for through his passion the secret recesses of all mysteries were thrown open. May he be with us, then, as we make our passage to him, and may the veil be lifted.[22] May our Lord and Savior Jesus Christ explain to us why the prophet said, *What dreadful troubles you have made me undergo! How many they are and how grave! But you have turned to me and given me life, and brought me back again from the depths of the earth.* There we have the first *again*; let us try to see what it means, and then we shall find out why *again* was repeated.

10. What is Christ? *In the beginning was the Word, and the Word was with God; he was God. He was with God in the beginning. Everything was made through him; no part of created being was made without him* (Jn 1:1-3). This is something magnificent, something very great. And what about you, you captive? Where are you, where do you lie prone? In the flesh, flesh subject to death. Consider then: who is he, and who are you? What did he subsequently become? And for whose sake?

Who is he, if not the One called the Word? What kind of Word is this: a word that sounds briefly and then fades away, perhaps? No, indeed not: the Word is God with God, the Word through whom all things were made. And what did the Word become, for your sake? *The Word was made flesh, and dwelt among us* (Jn 1:14). And *if God did not spare even his own Son, but delivered him up for us all, how can he fail to give us everything else along with that gift?* (Rom 8:32). Think, then: what did he become, what was he, and on whose behalf was it done? The Son of God became flesh, for a sinner, for the unrighteous, for a deserter, for

---

20. The Hebrew idiom "turn/return and do" is equivalent to "do again" or "restore to an original condition." The Hebrew text of the psalm does not repeat the phrase about bringing back from the depths of the earth; but it is repeated in the Septuagint, and hence in Augustine's Latin version.

21. See Mt 27:51.

22. Two veils here: Augustine's mention of the torn temple veil in the previous sentence reminds him of the other veil, the one over Moses' face that for Paul symbolized the veil over the hearts of the Jews, to be taken away when one turns to the Lord; see 2 Cor 3:16.

a proud creature, for a perverted imitator of his God. He became what you are, son of man, so that we might become sons and daughters of God. He was made flesh, and whence came that flesh? From the Virgin Mary. Whence came the Virgin Mary? From Adam. She was descended from the original captive, then, and the flesh Christ bore was drawn from the mass of captivity. Why did he do it? To give us an example. From you he took the humanity in which he would be able to die for you; from you he took what he could offer for you; from you he took the humanity in which he could teach you by his example. What did he mean to teach you? That you are destined to rise again. How could you ever have believed that, if you had not first seen it happen in flesh assumed from your own death-ridden humanity? In him, as the pioneer and prime exemplar, we rose again, because when Christ rose from the dead, we rose too. It was not the Word who died and rose again, but in the Word our flesh died and rose. In that flesh Christ died, and you too will die; and in that same flesh Christ rose, and you too will rise. By his own example he taught you what you must not fear, and for what you must hope. You used to be afraid of death. He died. You used to despair of ever rising from death. He is risen.

But you say to me, "He rose; but does that mean I will?" Yes, because he rose in that flesh which for you he took from you. Your nature went on ahead of you in his person. What he took from you ascended before you; and therefore in that flesh you too ascended. He was the first to ascend, but we ascended in him, because his flesh was drawn from our human race. It follows, then, that at his resurrection we were brought back from earth's deepest places. When Christ arose, *you brought me back from the depths of the earth*. But when we believed in Christ, *you brought me back again from the depths of the earth*. Here is our first *again*. Listen to a confirmation of this from the apostle: *if you have risen with Christ, seek what is above, where Christ is seated at the right hand of God. Have a taste for the things that are above, not the things on earth* (Col 3:1-2).

He has gone ahead, and in him we too have already risen, but as yet only in hope. Listen to Paul teaching us this also: *We ourselves groan inwardly as we await our adoption as God's children, the redemption of our bodies*. You are still groaning, still waiting. What has Christ bestowed on you, then? Listen to Paul's next words: *In hope we have been saved. But if hope is seen, it is hope no longer, for when someone sees what he hopes for, why should he hope for it? But if we hope for what we do not see, we wait for it in patience* (Rom 8:23-25). But this means that we have been brought back *again* from the depths of the earth. In what sense *again*? In this sense: Christ went on ahead of us. We are now living in hope that we shall rise again in fact;[23] we walk in faith. We have therefore been brought back from the depths of the earth by believing in him who rose from the

---

23. The usual contrast between *spes* and *res*.

depths of the earth before us. Our souls have been brought to life from their wicked state of unbelief, and thus the first resurrection has come about in us through faith.

But if that is all there is, what becomes of the apostle's statement that we are *awaiting our adoption as God's children, the redemption of our bodies*? And what of his other affirmation in the same passage? *The body indeed is a dead thing by reason of sin*, he says, *but the spirit is life through righteousness. If he who raised Christ from the dead lives in you, he who raised Jesus Christ from the dead will bring life to your mortal bodies too, through his Spirit who dwells in you* (Rom 8:10-11). Spiritually we have risen already in faith, hope and charity; but resurrection awaits us for our bodies too.

So now you have heard about the first *again*, and you have heard too about the second *again*: the first *again* because of Christ who preceded us, and the second *again* to which we hold already in hope, but which awaits us in fact.

You have multiplied proofs of your righteousness in those who believe, those who have already risen in hope in this first resurrection. *You have multiplied proofs of your righteousness*. But this righteousness demands that we submit to chastisement, for *it is time for judgment to take place, beginning from the house of the Lord*, says Peter (1 Pt 4:17)—beginning, that is to say, from his holy ones. God whips every child whom he acknowledges as his.[24] *You have multiplied proofs of your righteousness*, because you have not spared even your own children; you have made sure that those for whom you were saving an inheritance should not go short of discipline. *You have multiplied proofs of your righteousness, you have turned to me and comforted me*; and with regard to this body of mine which is to rise again in the end, *you have brought me back again from the depths of the earth*.

Verse 22. The psaltery and the lyre signify our twofold resurrection

11. *I will confess to you and sing of your faithfulness on instruments of psalmody*. The instruments of psalmody must mean the psaltery. What is a psaltery?[25] A wooden stringed instrument. What does it symbolize? There is a difference between the psaltery and the lyre which is explained by knowledgeable persons as follows: the hollow, wooden sounding chamber, across which the strings are stretched to give them resonance, is found in the upper part in a psaltery, but in the lower part in a lyre. Now since our spirit is from above, and our flesh from the earth, it seems that the psaltery represents our spirit and the lyre

---

24. See Prv 3:12; Heb 12:6.
25. On this subject, to which Augustine returns several times, see Exposition 2 of Psalm 32, 5, and note there.

our flesh. And the psalm has spoken of our being brought back from the depths of the earth in two stages: the first concerns our spirit and is a resurrection in hope; the second concerns our flesh, which is destined to rise in fact. Accordingly you can hear both mentioned in this verse. First it promises, *I will confess to you and sing of your faithfulness on instruments of psalmody*. That looks to the spirit; but what about the flesh? *With the lyre I will sing psalms to you, the Holy One of Israel.*

Verses 23-24. The prospect of everlasting, triumphant praise offered to God

12. Now listen once more, because we still hear the echo of that double *again*, as we did before. *My lips will exult when I sing psalms to you.* But lips can be attributed to both the inner and the outer person, and we might be unsure which is meant; so the psalm clarifies it by continuing, *And my soul, which you have redeemed.* It must refer, then, to interior "lips"; we have been saved in hope, and brought back from the depths of the earth by faith and charity, but we still *await the redemption of our bodies*. What are we to say, then? The psalmist has already given an affirmation concerning his spirit—*and my soul, which you have redeemed.* But if he left it at that, you might think that our soul alone is redeemed, the soul you heard about in connection with the first *again*; so the psalmist takes it further: *But what is more*—what more does he mean? *But what is more, my tongue*—so this must be the bodily tongue—*my tongue shall mull over your righteousness all day long*; that is to say, for all eternity, without end. When will that become a reality? At the end of the world, when our bodies rise again and are transfigured into a state like that of the angels.

How can it be demonstrated that this final consummation is what is meant by the words, *what is more, my tongue shall mull over your righteousness all day long*? The next words prove it: *when those who seek to harm me have been confounded and put to shame.* When will they be confounded, when put to shame, if not at the end of the world? There are two different situations in which they could be confounded: either when they believe in Christ, or when Christ comes. As long as the Church is here on earth, as long as the wheat groans amid the straw,[26] as long as the ears of grain sigh amid the weeds,[27] as long as the vessels of mercy mourn amid the vessels of wrath made for lowly purposes,[28] as long as the lily grieves amid thorns,[29] there will always be enemies to say, *When will they die, and their name disappear?*[30] What they mean is, "The days are

---

26. See Mt 3:12.
27. See Mt 13:30.
28. See Rom 9:21-23.
29. See Sg 2:2.
30. See Ps 40:6(41:5).

coming when Christians will be done for; there won't be any of them left. They sprang up at a certain time, and they will last only for a certain time." But even as they say this they are dying all the time themselves,[31] while the Church abides, proclaiming the Lord's strong arm to every generation still to be born. And at the last he will come himself in his bright glory. All the dead will arise, each with his or her own record. The good will be separated from the rest and placed at the Lord's right hand, but the wicked will be at his left. Those who vilified us will be confounded, those who prated will be put to shame; and then, after the resurrection, my tongue will mull over your righteousness and sing your praise all day long, *when those who seek to harm me have been confounded and put to shame.*

---

31. Variant: "they are dying without faith."

Exposition of Psalm 71

Verse 1. Christ the true Solomon, the peacemaker

1. Prefixed to this psalm is the title, *For Solomon.* But the main text of the psalm cannot refer to the Solomon who was King of Israel in the literal, historical sense, for it does not correspond with what sacred scripture has to say about him. It can, however, be most appropriately understood of Christ the Lord. It is clear, therefore, that even the name *Solomon* is used in a figurative sense; we must take it to indicate Christ. This is entirely suitable, because the name *Solomon* is interpreted "Peacemaker"; hence it can most fittingly be used of the Mediator through whom we, who were formerly God's enemies, are reconciled to him and granted forgiveness for our sins. So scripture affirms, *While we were still enemies we were reconciled to God by the death of his Son* (Rom 5:10). He certainly is our Peacemaker, since *he united* Jews and Gentiles, *and has broken down the dividing wall of hostility by his own flesh, annulling the law with its rules and regulations, to create from the two of them one new man in himself, thus making peace. He came to bring the good news of peace to you who were far away, and peace to those who were near* (Eph 2:14-15.17). Christ himself declares in the gospel, *My peace I give to you, my peace I leave with you* (Jn 14:27). Many other scriptural passages reveal our Lord Jesus Christ as the peacemaker, though the peace he imparts is not that which this world knows and seeks, but that of which it is said in a prophetic text, *I will give them true comfort, peace upon peace* (Is 57:18-19, LXX). This suggests that to the peace of our reconciliation is added the peace of immortality. The same prophet shows that after all those good things which God has promised have been granted to us, we must still look forward to the final peace in which we may live with God for all eternity; for he says, *O Lord our God, give us peace; for you have given us everything* (Is 26:12, LXX). It is obvious that peace will be perfect only when *death, the last enemy, has been destroyed* (1 Cor 15:26); and through whom can that happen, if not through our peacemaker and reconciler, Christ? *For as in Adam all die, so in Christ shall all be made to live* (1 Cor 15:22).

Now that we have discovered who is the true Solomon—that is, the true peacemaker—let us concentrate on what the psalm has to teach us about him.

Verse 2. The significance of parallelism

2. *O God, commit your judgment to the king, and your justice to the king's son.* The Lord himself testifies in the gospel that *the Father judges no one, but has entrusted all judgment to the Son* (Jn 5:22), so this must be the meaning of the psalm's prayer, *O God, commit your judgment to the king.* This King is also a King's Son, because God the Father is undoubtedly a King. This is why scripture speaks of a king who gave a wedding feast for his son.[1]

Now it is customary in scripture for a statement to be repeated in a parallel statement. So here: the psalm says, *your judgment* and then echoes it with *your justice*; and after saying *to the king*, it gives the parallel *to the king's son.* There are other instances. Another psalm says, *He who lives in heaven will laugh them to scorn, and the Lord will mock them* (Ps 2:4). In that case *he who lives in heaven* is repeated as *the Lord*, and *he will laugh them to scorn* is repeated as *he will mock them.* Similarly in another psalm we find *The heavens proclaim God's glory, and the firmament tells of his handiwork* (Ps 18:2(19:1)). There *the heavens* recurs as *the firmament, God's glory* is repeated as *his handiwork*, and *proclaim* is echoed by *tells of.* Repetitions of this kind are frequently used to drive home the meaning of God's utterances. Sometimes the same words are repeated, sometimes the same idea in different words. Such repetitions are especially common in the psalms, and in any other type of discourse that aims to arouse the affections of the spirit.

The poor are God's people

3. Then the psalm continues, *To judge your people in justice, and your poor with righteous judgment.* These phrases plainly show for what purpose the royal Father gave his royal Son his own judgment and his own justice, for *to judge your people in justice* is equivalent to "for the purpose of judging your people in justice." The same idiom is found elsewhere under the name of Solomon: *The proverbs of Solomon, son of David, to know wisdom and discipline* (Prv 1:1-2), which means, "The proverbs of Solomon, designed to promote the knowledge of wisdom and discipline." So here: *Give your judgment . . . to judge your people* means "Give your judgment . . . with a view to the judging of your people."[2]

Notice that the verse at first says *your people*, and follows it with *your poor*, just as it at first says *in justice* and then *with righteous judgment*, repeating the thought in accordance with the custom of parallelism that we have discussed. But the repetition in this instance demonstrates that God's people ought to be

---

1. See Mt 22:2.
2. He is explaining that the infinitive used in his Latin version is equivalent to a final clause, though a subjunctive or gerundive might have been more usual.

poor, which is to say not proud but humble, for *blessed are the poor in spirit, for the kingdom of heaven is theirs* (Mt 5:3). Blessed Job was poor in this spiritual sense even before he had lost his enormous worldly wealth. I think it necessary to make this point because there are some people who are more willing to distribute all their goods to the poor than to become God's paupers themselves. They are so puffed up as to consider that their laudable way of life should be credited to themselves, rather than to the grace of God; and this means that their lives are not really laudable at all, however impressive their good works may seem. They think their virtue is of their own making, and boast as though they had not received it;[3] they are the wealthy owners of themselves, not the poor of God; they are richly self-sufficient, not needy before him. But the apostle warns, *If I distribute all my resources to feed the poor, and deliver my body to be burnt, yet have no love, it profits me nothing* (1 Cor 13:3). It is as though he were saying, "If I have distributed all I have to the poor, but have not become God's pauper myself, it profits me nothing." *Charity is not puffed up* (1 Cor 13:4), nor is the true charity of God present in anyone who is ungrateful to him for the gift of his Holy Spirit, through whom his charity is poured abroad in our hearts.[4] It follows that those who refuse to be God's poor do not belong to God's people. These paupers of God confess, *We have not received the spirit of this world, but the Spirit which is of God, that we may know what gifts have been bestowed on us by God* (1 Cor 2:12). In our psalm the petition is made to the King, God the Father, *Give your justice to the King's Son.* It is expressed thus because of the Son's humble acceptance of humanity, the sacrament whereby the Word was made flesh. Yet proud persons do not want justice to be given to them, because they are confident that they can produce it of themselves. Ignorant of God's justice, and keen to set up their own, they are not submissive to the justice of God.[5] Accordingly, as I have pointed out, they are not God's poor, but wealthy self-owners, because they are not humble. They are simply proud.

But Christ will come to judge God's people in justice, and God's poor with righteous judgment, and in the process he will sort out those self-sufficient rich folk from his own poor—the poor whom he has enriched by his own poverty.[6] This poor people cried out to him, *Judge me, O God, and distinguish my cause from that of an unholy people* (Ps 42(43):1).

---

3. See 1 Cor 4:7.
4. See Rom 5:5.
5. See Rom 10:3.
6. See 2 Cor 8:9.

"Judgment" automatically means just judgment where God is concerned

4. It is noteworthy that the word order is changed: the psalmist first said, *O God, commit your judgment to the king, and your justice to the king's son,* putting judgment first, then justice; but then he turned it round, saying, *To judge your people in justice, and your poor with righteous judgment,* with justice coming before judgment. This variation indicates that by "judgment" he also means "justice"; it does not matter in which order the words are put because in this instance they mean the same. In ordinary usage we can speak of judgment as crooked or unjust; but we do not speak of justice as unfair or unjust. If it were crooked, it would also be unjust, and if unjust it could not be called justice at all. But in this instance by putting "judgment" and then in the repetition calling it "justice," or by putting "justice" and then calling it "judgment" when repeating it, the psalmist is making it clear that he is using the term, "judgment," to denote what we ordinarily call "justice"; that is, a quality which cannot be found in any misjudgment. When the Lord says, *Do not judge by appearances, but form a right judgment* (Jn 7:24), he shows that there can be such a thing as deviant judgment; and so he needed to admonish them, *Form a right judgment.* He is forbidding the former and directing them to the latter. But when he speaks of judgment without further qualification he certainly means us to understand it of just judgment, as when he says, *You have neglected the weightier matters of the law—mercy and judgment* (Mt 23:23). Jeremiah reflects the same usage: *She amasses her riches, but not with judgment,*[7] he says. Notice that he does not say, "She amasses her riches with crooked or unjust judgment," or "She amasses her riches, but not with right or just judgment." He simply says, *Not with judgment,* because he will use the word, *judgment,* only for what is straightforward and just.

Verse 3. The mountains and the hills among God's people

5. *Let the mountains receive peace for the people, and the hills justice.* The mountains are higher, the hills lower. These two groups are those spoken of in another psalm as *the little along with the great.* These *mountains skipped like rams,* and these *hills like newborn lambs, when Israel went forth from Egypt* (Ps 113:13.4.1(115:13; 114:4.1)), that is to say, on seeing the liberation of God's people from enslavement to this world. Those who are pre-eminent in the Church by their radiant holiness are mountains because they are fit to teach others;[8] they speak in such a way that other people may be soundly instructed,

---

7. Jer 17:11. For another use of this text see Exposition of Psalm 54, 27, and note there.
8. See 2 Tm 2:2.

and live in a way that others may safely imitate. The hills are the people who by their obedience follow the shining example of the former.

Now why does it say, *Let the mountains receive peace, and the hills justice*? Would it have made any difference if the psalm had put it round the other way: "Let the mountains receive justice for the people, and the hills peace"? Both need justice, and both need peace. Moreover it could be argued that another name for peace is justice, for true peace demands justice; what the unjust concoct among themselves is not true peace. Or should we rather think that a significant distinction is intended when the psalm says, *Let the mountains receive peace, and the hills justice*? Those of high renown in the Church must be extremely vigilant in fostering peace, lest by acting arrogantly to promote their own prestige they foment schisms and tear apart the structure that binds us into unity. The hills, for their part, must follow their leaders by imitation and obedience, but in such a way that Christ always comes first. They must not be led astray by the spurious authority of bad mountains, however conspicuous, and so tear themselves away from Christ's unity. This is why the psalm prays, *Let the mountains receive peace for the people*. It is quite right for some of our leaders to say, *Be imitators of me, as I am of Christ* (1 Cor 11:1); but they must also say, *Even if we ourselves, or even an angel from heaven, preach to you anything other than what you have received, let such a messenger be anathema!* (Gal 1:8). Let them go on to demand, *Was Paul crucified for you, or were you baptized in Paul's name?* (1 Cor 1:13). This is how the leaders must *receive peace* for God's people, God's poor: they must aspire not to reign over them but to reign with them.[9] On their side the people must not say, *I belong to Paul; I belong to Apollos; I belong to Cephas*; but all of them must say, *I belong to Christ* (1 Cor 1:12). This is what justice entails: not putting the servants above their Lord, or making them his equals. It entails lifting one's eyes to the mountains to seek help, certainly, but hoping for that help not from the mountains themselves, but from the Lord who made heaven and earth.[10]

The ministry of reconciliation: evangelical peace

6. There is another sense in which we may most fittingly understand this petition, *Let the mountains receive peace for the people*. This peace may be interpreted as the reconciliation whereby we are made one again with God; for the mountains do receive this reconciliation for the benefit of the people. The apostle bears witness to it: *the old things have passed away, and lo, everything is made new! All these things are from God, who through Christ has reconciled us to himself, and has entrusted us with the ministry of reconciliation*. That is clearly a reference to the mountains that receive peace for God's people. Paul

---

9. Clearly a desire habitually in Augustine's own heart and a pattern for his ministry.
10. See Ps 120(121):1-2.

continues, *God was in Christ, reconciling the world to himself, not reckoning their sins against them, and commissioning us with the message of reconciliation.* Who are commissioned with it? Surely the mountains who receive peace for his people. They go on to declare, *We function as Christ's ambassadors, for through us God makes his appeal. We beg you in Christ's name, be reconciled to God* (2 Cor 5:17-20). It is the mountains who on behalf of God's people receive this peace, or rather the duty of preaching his peace and of acting as its ambassadors; but the hills receive justice, which means obedience; for in human beings and in every rational creature obedience is the source and the perfection of all justice. So true is this that obedience is singled out as the major difference between two individuals: Adam, who was the originator of our death, and Christ, who is the fountainhead of our salvation; for *as through one man's disobedience many were accounted sinners, so through the obedience of one man many shall be accounted righteous* (Rom 5:19). *Let the mountains,* then, *receive peace for the people, and the hills justice,* so that by working harmoniously together they may fulfill the prophecy, *Justice and peace have kissed* (Ps 84:11(85:10)).

Other codices have *Let the mountains receive peace for the people, and the hills likewise.* I think this should be understood to mean that both are preachers of the peace of the gospel, whether they lead or follow. These same codices go on to give as the next phrase, *He will judge the poor of the people with justice.* But we can regard the other codices as more reliable, the ones that give the text as we have expounded it: *Let the mountains receive peace for the people, and the hills justice.* Some have *for your people;* others omit *your,* and simply say, *the people.*

Verse 4. Discernment of the poor; humiliation of the devil

7. *He it is who will give judgment for the poor among the people; he will save the children of the poor.* The poor and the children of the poor seem to me to be the same, just as the same city is called both "Zion" and "Daughter of Zion." But if there is in fact a subtle distinction, we could take *the poor* to be *the mountains,* and *the children of the poor* to be *the hills.* Thus the prophets and the apostles would be *the poor,* and their children—that is, those who are making progress under their authority—would be *the children of the poor.*

Since this verse first says, *He will give judgment,* and then, *He will save,* the latter expression serves as a clarification of the former, explaining how he will judge. He will judge his elect in such a way as to save them, separating them from others destined to be lost and condemned. To his own he gives the salvation made ready to be revealed in the last days.[11] They pray to him, *Do not destroy my*

---

11. See 1 Pt 1:5.

soul with the ungodly (Ps 25(26):9), and *Judge me, O God, and distinguish my cause from that of an unholy people* (Ps 42(43):1).

It is also worth remarking that the psalm does not say, "He will judge a poor people," but *the poor among the people*. In the earlier verse where it said, *To judge your people in justice, and your poor with righteous judgment*, it identified God's people with his poor; his people seemed then to consist only of the good, whose place will be at Christ's right hand. But in this world those of the right and those of the left graze together. At the end they will be sorted out, like lambs from kids, but for the present God's people is a mixture, and so they all go under the name of his people. However, judgment can be exercised with a good purpose in view: that of saving people; and so in the present verse the psalm prophesies, *He will give judgment for the poor among the people*: he will discern who are the poor among the people, and mark them out for salvation. We have explained already who these poor people are; let us understand also that the needy are included.

And he will humiliate their accuser. No one has a better title than the devil to be called so. His accusation is implicit in the question, *Job hardly worships God gratis, does he?* (Jb 1:9). But the Lord Jesus humiliates him, for by his grace he helps his faithful ones to worship God gratis by finding their delight in the Lord.[12] Christ humiliated the devil in another way too: the prince of this world had found nothing in him[13] to deserve death, but killed him all the same through the charges brought by the Jews; for the prime accuser made use of them as his instruments, working through the children of unbelief.[14] But he was humiliated when the man they had killed rose from the dead and abolished the reign of death. Death was the devil's sphere of dominion, because by means of one man, Adam, whom he had seduced, he had been able to drag all the rest through death to condemnation. But now he was humiliated, because if on account of one man's transgression death reigned through one man, far more will those who receive abundant grace and justice reign in life through one man, Jesus Christ.[15] So did Christ humiliate the accuser who ranged against him false charges, corrupt judges, and perjured witnesses, with a view to destroying him.

Verse 5. The eternity of the Word, the transience of creatures

8. *He will abide to the sun*; or *he will abide with the sun*, which some of our scholars consider the better translation of the Greek verb, εἐ᾽᾽~᾽~᾽ῖ᾽ίϼ .[16] But

---

12. See Ps 36(37):4.
13. See Jn 14:30.
14. See Eph 2:2.
15. See Rom 5:17.
16. The next two sentences are omitted in the translation. Augustine remarks that there is no exactly equivalent compound verb available in Latin for this Greek verb, but that the sense is adequately conveyed by *permanebit cum sole*, "he will abide with the sun."

if we are speaking of him through whom all things are made, without whom no created thing came to be,[17] are we saying anything special if we say that he abides with the sun? Perhaps not; but it may be that this ancient prophecy was uttered to refute those who think that the Christian religion will survive in this world only for a limited time, after which it will cease to exist. The psalm contradicts them by saying that it *will abide with the sun*; which means that as long as the sun rises and sets, as long as the ages roll on, the Church of God, which is Christ's body on earth, will not fail.

The psalm's next words, *And before the moon, generations after generations*, could have been intended to include the idea, "and before the sun too"; or, in other words, "this permanence is both with the sun and before the sun," which is tantamount to "with time, and before time." Now what exists before time is eternal. We must regard as eternal that which suffers no variation with time; such is the Word which exists from the beginning. By contrast the psalmist chose the moon to represent the waxing and waning of mortal creatures. Thus after saying, *Before the moon*, he wanted to explain why he had preferred to use the moon as his symbol, so he added, *Generations after generations*: before the moon; that is, before any of those successive generations which come and go with the births and deaths of mortals, like the waxing and waning of the moon. To "abide before the moon" must therefore signify to have precedence by reason of immortality over all mortal creatures. How could we find any better interpretation than that?

There is another quite acceptable way to understand this verse. Now that the accuser has been brought low, Christ sits enthroned at the right hand of the Father, and this is to abide *with the sun*. The Son is known to be the splendor of eternal glory,[18] so we can say that the Father is like the sun's orb, and his Son is his radiance. But we must make such a statement only in the way that it can be made of the invisible substance of the Creator,[19] not in the way that we would make it about the visible creation, which includes the heavenly bodies and, pre-eminently bright among them, the sun. This created sun provides the comparison, just as various things on earth also provide it—the rock, for instance, the lion, the lamb, the man who had two sons, and so forth. With this proviso we can say that after humiliating the accuser Christ abides *with the sun*, because after defeating the devil by his resurrection he sits at the right hand of the Father, where he can never die again, for death will never again have dominion over him.[20]

---

17. See Jn 1:3.
18. See Heb 1:3.
19. Or, as later theology will say, in an analogical sense.
20. See Rom 6:9.

And in this victory he is *before the moon*, because as the first-born from the dead[21] he precedes the Church, which is variable in character by reason of the deaths and births of mortals. These are the *generations after generations*. Alternatively, we could take the first *generations* to mean the process of our mortal birth, and the phrase, *generations after generations*, to indicate our rebirth to immortal life. In any case the reference is to the Church which Christ preceded, to abide *before the moon*; for he is the first-born from the dead.

We should mention that the Greek *ιῖ' ιῦῖ   ιῖ' ῖ'   * is interpreted by some not as *generations after generations*,[22] but as "of the generation of the generations,"[23] because the case of *ιῖ' ῖ~ῖ   * is uncertain. It could be either genitive singular, *ἐῶῖ ιῖ' ιῦῖ   *, "of the generation," or accusative plural, *εὐῖ ιῖ' ιοῖ   *, as we took it to be. We cannot be sure, but the preferable interpretation is to take the phrase as explaining why the psalmist mentioned *the moon*.

Verse 6. *"Like shower upon the fleece"*

9. *He will come down like the shower upon the fleece, or like raindrops sprinkling the earth.* The psalm recalls the episode concerning Gideon, one of the judges, suggesting to us that it found its fulfillment in Christ. Gideon asked God that, as a sign, the fleece that he spread out on the threshing floor should alone be witted with rain, while the floor around remained dry; and then again that the fleece alone should be dry, while the ground was soaked with rain. And that was what happened.[24] The meaning of the incident was this: the fleece represented the elder people, Israel, placed on the threshing floor which symbolized the whole world. Israel was parched, but Christ came down upon it like rain on the fleece, though all the rest of the earth was still arid. As he said, *I was not sent except for the lost sheep of the house of Israel* (Mt 15:24). From Israel he chose his mother, from whom he would receive the form of a servant to appear among men and women; from there too he drew his disciples, to whom he would give the explicit instruction, *Do not go in the direction of the Gentiles, or enter Samaritan towns. Go first of all to the lost sheep of the house of Israel* (Mt 10:5-6). The words, *first of all*, indicate that later on, when the time should come for the whole threshing floor to receive the rain, they were to go also after other sheep who did not belong to the ancient people of Israel. Of these he said, *Other sheep I have, not counted in this fold; them too I must lead in, that there may be but one flock and one shepherd* (Jn 10:16). The apostle speaks similarly: *I maintain that Christ Jesus was a servant of the circumcised, to save the faithfulness of*

---

21. See Col 1:18; Rv 2:5.
22. His Latin is *generationes generationum*, which can hardly be reproduced in English.
23. *Generationis generationum.*
24. See Jgs 6:36-40.

God and confirm the promises made to our fathers. So the rain fell upon the fleece, while the surrounding area was still dry. *But,* continues Paul, *he gave the Gentiles cause to glorify God for his mercy* (Rom 15:8-9). When the time was right, the prophecy was to be fulfilled that *a people I never knew has come to serve me, and as soon as they heard me they obeyed me* (Ps 17:45(18:43-44)); and so we see that today the Jewish people has remained dry, untouched by the grace of Christ, while the whole earth with all its Gentile nations is being drenched from clouds laden with Christian grace. The psalm uses a different word to indicate this same rain when it speaks of *raindrops sprinkling*—not the fleece now, but *the earth.* It means the same thing, though, for what else are those sprinkling drops but rain?

I think the Jewish nation is symbolized by a fleece either because it was to be stripped of its authority to teach, as a sheep is stripped of its fleece, or because it concealed the rain and withheld it, not wishing it to be proclaimed to the uncircumcised by revelation to the Gentiles.[25]

Verse 7. Death will be destroyed, and the moon-Church will be exalted

10. *In his days righteousness will flourish, and plentiful peace, until such time as the moon shall be taken up.* The word here rendered *taken up*[26] is rendered by others *removed,*[27] and by others again *uplifted;*[28] for each translator rendered the Greek word *ὅ ἐ~″~ῖ″ῖέ″ῖ*   in the way he thought best. Those who put *taken up* and those who preferred *removed* do not differ all that much; for the expression *taken up*[29] is more often used in the sense of "taking something away so that it will no longer be there" than in the sense of "raising higher," and *remove* can mean nothing else but "do away with something so that it will no longer be there." But the phrase, *until the moon shall be uplifted,*[30] can mean nothing but being raised higher. When the word is used pejoratively it is an image of pride, as in the warning, *Do not be uplifted in your own wisdom* (Sir 32:6). Used in a favorable sense, however, it signifies enhanced honor, the raising up of something; so a psalm invites us, *Lift up your hands to the holy place*[31] *at night, and bless the Lord* (Ps 133(134):2).

---

25. Grammatically the subject of the verbs "concealed . . . withheld . . . not wishing" could be God, not the Jewish nation, in which case the reference is to the time before God willed to extend the gospel to the Gentiles, as Augustine mentioned earlier.
26. *Tollatur.*
27. *Auferatur.*
28. *Extollatur.*
29. *Tollatur.*
30. *Extollatur.*
31. Or "to holy things."

But if we take it that the reading here should be *removed*, what can it mean to say, *until such time as the moon shall be removed*, if not "until it is abolished"? Perhaps the sense intended is that God will bring it about that mortality will exist no more, when *death, the last enemy, is destroyed* (1 Cor 15:26). He will ensure that peace abounds to such a degree that no residual trace of the weakness of mortality shall mar the happiness of the blessed. This will come to pass in that other world concerning which we have God's faithful promise through Jesus Christ our Lord. Of him our psalm says, *In his days righteousness will flourish, and plentiful peace*, until with the total defeat and destruction of death, mortality is swallowed up for ever.

Alternatively, we could take the word, *moon*, to signify not the fleshly condition through which the Church is passing in the present age, but simply the Church itself. In that case the verse is a prophecy that the Church will abide to eternity, freed from its present mortal state. We must then take the verse this way: *In his days righteousness will flourish, and plentiful peace, until such time as the moon shall be uplifted*; or, in other words, in Christ's days righteousness will flourish and overcome the resistance and insubordination of the flesh. Then there will be peace, growing and abounding until the moon is uplifted. This means until the Church is exalted to reign with Christ in the glory of the resurrection, for as first-born from the dead he has gone ahead of the Church, to sit at the right hand of the Father. There he abides *with the sun* and *before the moon*, so that the moon too may eventually be raised up there.

Verse 8. Worldwide proclamation of Christ

11. *He will rule from sea to sea, from the river to the ends of the earth.* Obviously it is still referring to the person of whom it said in the preceding verse, *In his days righteousness will flourish, and plentiful peace, until such time as the moon shall be uplifted.* If we are correct in taking the word, *moon*, to signify the Church, this verse shows how widely he intends to diffuse the Church: *he will rule from sea to sea*. We know that the earth is wrapped around by a great sea called the Ocean, from which a small quantity leaks through into the earth to form the seas well known to us, where ships ply to and fro. Hence the expression, *from sea to sea*, would mean that he will have dominion from any point on earth to any other point; his name and his power are to be proclaimed throughout the whole world, and will achieve wonders. To make sure that we do not understand *from sea to sea* in any other way than this, the psalm immediately adds, *And from the river to the ends of the earth.* This last phrase means the same thing as *from sea to sea*. But in specifying *from the river* the psalmist obviously draws our attention to the place from which Christ wished to announce his power, the place where also he began to choose his disciples, namely the river Jordan. There the

Holy Spirit came down upon the Lord at his baptism, and there resounded the voice from heaven, *This is my beloved Son* (Mt 3:17). His teaching and his authoritative power as our Master took this as their point of departure and are spreading to the ends of the earth, as the gospel of the kingdom is preached all round the world as a testimony to all nations. When this is complete, the end will come.

Verse 9. The prophecy about Ethiopians indirectly convicts schismatics

12. *Ethiopians will fall prostrate before him, and his enemies will lick the earth.* The psalm indicates the whole by naming a part, so by Ethiopians it means all the nations. The Ethiopian people were chosen in particular because they live at the end of the earth.

They will fall prostrate before him is a way of saying that they will worship him. But there was a special reason for adding immediately after this, *And his enemies will lick the earth.* The reason is this: there would be schisms in various parts of the world, arising from hatred of the universally extended Catholic Church. These schisms would fight among themselves under the names of their leaders, and in their infatuation with the men who had initiated the schisms they would make themselves enemies of the glory of Christ, which shines in all lands. Thus the prophecy that *his enemies will lick the earth* means that they will be so enamored of human beings as to hate the glory of Christ, to whom another psalm cries out, *Be lifted up above the heavens, O God, and may your glory spread all over the earth* (Ps 107:6(108:5)), whereas on a mortal man the sentence was imposed, *Earth you are, and back to earth you shall go* (Gn 3:19). By licking this earth, which is to say by delighting in the empty eloquence of those who assume authority in the sects, by fawning upon them and making much of them, schismatics try to nullify the divine oracles in which the Catholic Church was prophesied; for scripture foretold that the Church would not be confined to one region, like this or that schism, but would spread throughout the world by its fruitfulness and its growth, and reach even the Ethiopians, who are regarded as the most alien and brutal of races.[32]

Verses 10-11. The gifts brought by kings

13. *The kings of Tarshish and the islands will offer him presents; the Arabian kings and those of Sheba will lead gifts to him. All the kings of the earth will*

---

32. The contrast between the universality of the Catholic Church and the provincial outlook of the Donatist sect, which scarcely reached beyond Africa, was a favorite point in Augustine's polemic against Donatism. On the Ethiopians as a byword for stupidity or coarseness, compare Cicero: *De Senectute* 6.

worship him, and all nations will serve him. This prediction calls not for an expositor, but for a reader disposed to contemplation; it is offered for the consideration both of rejoicing believers and of lamenting unbelievers. But there is, perhaps, one point that requires comment: why does the psalm say that they will *lead* gifts to him?[33] It is generally of things that can walk that this verb is used. Surely the reference was not to victims being led to slaughter? We can hardly think that compatible with the righteousness that will flourish in Christ's days. It seems to me preferable to understand it of human beings led along as gifts, men and women led into the fellowship of Christ's Church by the authority of their kings.[34] In another sense even persecuting kings can be thought of as having led gifts to Christ, not knowing what they did in making the holy martyrs into sacrificial victims.

Verses 12-13. Defeat for the powerful, salvation for the poor

14. The next verse explains something of the reason why so much honor should be paid to him, and why all nations should serve him: *He has delivered the needy from the tyrant, that poor person who had no other champion.* This needy and poor person is the people that believes in him, and within this people are kings who worship him. They are not too proud to be needy and poor, which means humbly acknowledging that they are sinners and in need of the glory of God,[35] so that the true King, the Son of the King, may free them from the powerful foe. Powerful indeed he is who has been called the accuser. Yet it was not his own strength that brought men and women into subjection to this powerful tyrant, and kept them there in captivity, but human sins. The powerful tyrant is also called in scripture "the strong man," but Christ, who humiliated the accuser, also broke into the strong man's domain to bind him and seize his possessions.[36] Christ is the one who *has delivered the needy from the tyrant, that poor person who had no other champion,* for no one else had the strength to accomplish that—no righteous person nor even any angel. There was no champion at all, therefore; but Christ came and saved them.

15. It might occur to someone to ask, "If it was on account of their sins that men and women were held as prisoners by the devil, does that mean that Christ came to rescue the needy and poor because he liked their sins?" Certainly not; but *he will be merciful to the needy and poor.* He forgives the sins of those who

---

33. *Dona adducent.*
34. A common event when a ruler was converted, not only in Augustine's day but for centuries afterward in the barbarian world.
35. See Rom 3:23.
36. See Mt 12:29.

are humble, who place no reliance on any merits of their own and do not hope in their own virtue for salvation, but know their need for the grace of their Savior.

The psalm draws our attention to two aspects of the help afforded by grace. It says, *He will be merciful to the needy and poor*, to indicate the forgiveness of sins; but it adds, *And the lives of the poor he will save*, to show that we are made to share in righteousness. No one is capable of attaining salvation without the help of God's grace, and this salvation is perfect righteousness, because the law is fulfilled only by charity. But the charity that is in us does not spring from ourselves; it is spread abroad in our hearts by the Holy Spirit who has been given to us.[37]

Verse 14. Debts and interest are written off

16. *He will redeem their lives from usurious debts and iniquity.* What are these usurious debts that they owe? Their sins, clearly, for sins are also called debts.[38] But I think they are stigmatized as usurious because the evil suffered in the penalty exacted for them is greater than the evil committed in the sins. A murderer, for instance, kills only the body of his victim and cannot harm the soul, but the murderer's own soul and body perish together in hell. To sinners who make light of God's commandment in the present life, and deride the possibility of future punishment, the words are addressed, *I could have recovered my money with interest on my return* (Mt 25:27). The souls of the poor are bought back from these interest-burdened debts by the blood of Christ, shed for the forgiveness of sins. He will redeem them from usurious debts by redeeming them from the sins to which greater punishments were due; and he will redeem them from *iniquity* by helping them with his grace, so that they are empowered to act justly.[39] The same two aspects of grace that we saw in the preceding verse are commemorated here too. There we read, *He will be merciful to the needy and poor*, and here is the same idea: *He will redeem them from usurious debts*. There it was said, *And the lives of the poor he will save*, to which corresponds in the present verse *from iniquity*. In both cases redemption is implied, for by his merciful dealings he will redeem them from the usurious debts, and by saving them he will redeem them from iniquity. Thus when he is *merciful to the needy and poor* and saves their lives, he will also *redeem them from usurious debts and iniquity*.

The verse proceeds, *And his name is held in honor by them.* They give glory to his name for such immense benefits by their response, that it is right and fitting to give thanks to the Lord their God.[40] Some codices, however, have it in this form:

---

37. See Rom 5:5.
38. See Mt 6:12.
39. The contrast is between the "in-equity" of iniquity and the "equity" of justice.
40. An echo from the liturgy of the Eucharist.

And their name is held in honor by him. In the eyes of this world Christians may appear contemptible, but the name they bear is held in honor by him who gave it to them. He no longer perpetuates their former names upon his lips,[41] the names they bore when entangled in pagan superstitions, the labels that celebrated their evil conduct.[42] Their present name is honorable in his sight, even though it seems contemptible to their enemies.

Verse 15. The gold of the wise is brought to Christ

17. *He shall live, and gifts shall be given him from the gold of Arabia.* It would not have said, *He shall live,* if ordinary life were meant, for this expression could be used of anyone who lived on earth, however briefly. Clearly a different life is envisaged, that of which it is said, *Christ will never die again, nor will death ever again have the mastery over him* (Rom 6:9). And this assertion, *he shall live,* was also made because he was despised while dying, for, as another prophet says, *His life will be swept away from the earth.*[43]

But what is the meaning of *and gifts shall be given him from the gold of Arabia?* Long ago King Solomon received gold from that region, and in this psalm the same is reported in a figurative sense of another Solomon, who is the true one—the true one because he is the real peacemaker, and because the earlier Solomon never had dominion *from the river to the ends of the earth.* But this prophecy concerning gold was made about Christ because even the wise of this world were destined to believe in him. By *Arabia* we understand the Gentiles, and by *gold,* wisdom, which shines out among all other forms of learning as gold among metals. This is why holy scripture advises, *Value prudence like silver, and wisdom like refined gold* (Prv 8:10).

They will pray about him always. The Greek here has "ἵᾶ ~ῆἕ῏ὅ , which some translate *about him,* others *for him.* What does *about him* suggest? Surely nothing else but what we pray for when we say, *Thy kingdom come;* for the coming of Christ will reveal God's kingdom to the faithful. It is more difficult to interpret *for him;* but this could be understood as prayer offered for the Church, since it is his body. A great mystery[44] was prophesied concerning Christ and the Church: *They will be two in one flesh* (Gn 2:24; Eph 5:31).

The next words, *all day long,* signify that this will continue throughout time. And *they will bless him* is clear enough.

---

41. See Ps 15(16):4.
42. Perhaps he is thinking of names like Epaphroditus; compare Phil 4:18.
43. Is 53:8; compare Acts 8:33.
44. *Sacramentum.*

Verse 16. Christ the firmament. The fruit that surpasses Lebanon

18. *There shall be a firmament on earth, on the peaks of the mountains,* for, as scripture says elsewhere, *All the promises of God find their "Yes" in him* (2 Cor 1:20). That means, they are consolidated and firm in Christ. Everything that was prophesied with a view to our salvation has been fulfilled in him. The peaks of the mountains are best understood as the authors of the divine scriptures, or, rather, those through whose ministry the scriptures were delivered to us. Upon them rests Christ, the firmament, because all those things which were written under divine inspiration refer to him. But God willed the firmament to be *on earth* because all scripture was written for the sake of people on earth; and for their sake Christ came to earth himself, to make all those prophecies firm by showing them to be fulfilled in himself. *All that is written about me in the law, and the prophets, and the psalms, had to be fulfilled,* he said (Lk 24:44); written, that is, on *the peaks of the mountains.* This was how *the mountain of the Lord's house* came to be *established above all other mountains in the last days* (Is 2:2), or, as the psalmist has it, *on the peaks of the mountains.*

His fruit shall be lifted high above Lebanon. We are accustomed to take Lebanon as a symbol of worldly rank, because Mount Lebanon has very lofty trees, and its name is said to mean "Making white or dazzling." Small wonder, then, if Christ's fruit is lifted above every highest, most exalted dignity this world has to offer. Those who love his fruit have made light of all temporal ascendancy. But if we take Lebanon in a favorable sense, thinking of the psalm which speaks of *the cedars* God *planted on Lebanon* (Ps 103(104):16), what fruit can we suppose is meant as overtopping Lebanon, other than that of which the apostle speaks when he is about to extol charity: *now I will point out to you a higher way* (1 Cor 12:31)? He gives charity the first place among God's gifts when he says, *The fruit of the Spirit is charity* (Gal 5:22), and with it are associated all the others he enumerates.

From the city they shall flourish like the grass of the earth. The word, *city,* is ambiguous here, because the psalm does not say, "His city," or "God's city," but only "the city" without further qualification. So it can be understood in a good sense, as a prayer that they may flourish from God's city—that is, from the Church—like grass; but this certainly must mean some fruitful kind of grass such as wheat. This is a reasonable assumption, because wheat is evidently called "grass" or "a herb" in holy scripture: in Genesis the earth was commanded to produce every species of tree and every kind of herb;[45] there is no mention of "all types of wheat," as there undoubtedly would have been if wheat had not

---

45. See Gn 1:11.

been included under the name, "herb." Similar usage is found in many other scriptural texts.

If, however, the prophecy, *they shall flourish like the grass of the earth*, is to be understood in the same sense as in another prophetic passage, *All flesh is but grass, and all its splendor like the flower of the field*, we must identify the "city" accordingly. In that case it must signify the society of this world. It is by no means insignificant that Cain was the first man to found a city.[46] Christ's fruit is therefore more exalted than Lebanon, nobler than those long-lived trees with their imperishable timber, because his fruit lasts for ever. All human renown, all that is reckoned lofty by this temporal world, is compared to grass. Believers, people who already hope for eternal life, spurn temporal success, knowing the truth of scripture's assessment: *All flesh is but grass, and human glory like the flower of grass. The grass is dried up and the flower is fallen, but the word of the Lord abides for ever* (Is 40:6.8).

This is Christ's fruit, the fruit nobler than Lebanon. Flesh has always been no better than grass, and its glory no more lasting than the bloom of grass; but as long as it had not been made clear to us what kind of happiness we should choose and prefer, the bloom on the grass was highly prized. Not only was it not scorned; people sought it above all else. But the psalmist seems to have spoken at a moment when things were beginning to change, when whatever flourished in this world was beginning to evoke distaste and contempt; and so he proclaimed, *His fruit shall be lifted high above Lebanon, and from the city they shall flourish like the grass of the earth*. What we are promised as lasting for ever will be esteemed above all earthly goods, while whatever is highly valued in this world will be reckoned no better than the grass of the earth.

Verses 17-19. Doxology

19. *May his name be blessed for ever, that name which abides since before the sun was made*. The sun represents time; so his name abides eternally. What is eternal exists before time, and does not end when time is finished.

All the tribes of the earth shall be blessed in him, for in him the promise made to Abraham is kept. *Scripture does not say, "To his descendants," as though indicating many, but as to one only: "And to your seed," which is Christ* (Gal 3:16). To Abraham the promise was given, *In your seed shall all the nations of the earth be blessed* (Gn 22:18), but *it is not the children of Abraham's flesh, but the children of the promise who are accounted his descendants* (Rom 9:8).

---

46. See Gn 4:17. Behind the scriptural text lies the ancient nomadic ambivalence about settled, city life, at once despised and alluring. Behind Augustine's remarks lies the concept of the city of this world, set over against the City of God.

All nations will magnify him. This seems to be a repetition and explanation of what has been said before. Because they will be blessed in him, they will magnify him—not in the sense of conferring greatness on him, for he is great of himself and not by their making him so, but in the sense of praising him and confessing his greatness. This is how we "magnify" God. It is like the way in which we pray, *Hallowed be thy name*, which of course is always holy.

20. *Blessed be the Lord, the God of Israel, for he alone works wonders.* After pondering all that has been said, the psalmist bursts into a hymn, blessing the Lord, the God of Israel. The prophecy once made to the barren wife is being realized: *the God of Israel who delivers you will be called the God of all the earth* (Is 54:5). He *alone works wonders*, because although other people also work wonders, he is working in them, he who *alone works wonders*.

21. *May his glorious name be blessed for evermore, and for ages unending.*[47] How else could the translators render it? They could not say, "For ever, and for the ever of ever."[48] Our translation seems to suggest that *in aeternum* is something different from *in saeculum*; but the Greek has *ἰαῖ ἐᾷ″ ~ᾷ″~I ῖ~ᾷ ἰᾷῖ ἐᾷ″ ~ᾷ″~ ἐ″ὸ ~ᾷ‴ῖ* , which might have been better translated, *in saeculum, et in saeculum saeculi.* That would have conveyed the idea that the first *saeculum* means "as long as this world shall endure," but *in saeculum saeculi* refers to that other world which is promised to us after this world ends. *All the earth shall be filled with his glory; may it be, may it be so!* You have issued your command, O Lord, and so it is. So will it continue to be until what began *from the river* reaches everywhere, even *to the ends of the earth.*

---

47. *In aeternum, et in saeculum saeculi.*
48. *In aeternum, et in aeternum aeterni.*

Exposition of Psalm 72

A Sermon[1]

The title: how have David's hymns failed?

1. Listen, oh listen, you tenderly beloved members of Christ's body, you whose hope is the Lord your God, who have no eyes for empty things and lying foolishness.[2] If any of you still do have eyes for such things, you too must listen, that you may regard them no longer. Over this psalm is inscribed a title that reads, *The hymns of David, son of Jesse, have failed.*[3] The title then continues, *A psalm for Asaph himself.* We have many psalms that bear David's name in their titles, but the extra designation, *son of Jesse,* is never added anywhere else. We must believe that this was not done capriciously or without purpose, for God drops hints for us everywhere, and summons careful, earnest minds to deeper understanding. What, then, is the significance of this phrase, *the hymns of David have failed*?

Hymns are praises offered to God with singing; hymns are songs, with God's praise as their theme. If there is praise, but not praise of God, there is no hymn. If there is praise, and the praise is offered to God, but not sung, again there is no hymn. For there to be a hymn, three elements are required: there must be praise, it must be for God, and it must be sung. In what sense, then, have *the hymns failed*? What? Praises sung to God have failed? That looks like a gloomy piece of news, an announcement of mourning; for anyone who sings praise is not only praising, but praising cheerfully. The singer of praise is not only performing musically but showing love for the one who is sung about. To confess God by praise is a way of preaching him; to pour out passion in song is the way of a lover.

The hymns of David have failed, says the psalm; and it adds, *David, the son of Jesse.* David, who was king of Israel and Jesse's son, lived at a certain time in the Old Testament, and at that time the New Testament was hidden within the Old, as fruit is in the root. If you look for fruit in a root you will not find it; yet you will not find any fruit on the branches either, unless it has sprung from the root. At

---

1. Delivered in the Basilica Restituta at Carthage, possibly in the night of 13-14 September 411.
2. See Ps 39:5(40:4).
3. These words occur as the last verse of the preceding psalm in the Septuagint and the Vulgate, but Augustine, like Ambrose, regarded them as part of the title to the present psalm. The word ἤ ἤ ἴ˘ʷʷ in the Septuagint means "have come to an end" as the Latin *defecerunt* can also; but Augustine reads more into it, as the succeeding paragraphs show.

470

that early time the prophets spoke to the first people, the people who were Abraham's descendants in the carnal sense (for of course the second people, the people who belong to the New Covenant, are Abraham's posterity too, but spiritually). The few prophets who were sent to the first people understood what God desired and when he willed it to be publicly proclaimed, so they spoke to that still carnal people, foretelling future events and the coming of our Lord Jesus Christ. Christ himself, inasmuch as he was to be born according to the flesh, was hidden in the root, that is to say, in the bloodline of the patriarchs. At the appointed time he was to be revealed, like fruit forming from the flower, and so scripture says, *A shoot has sprung from Jesse's stock, and a flower has opened* (Is 11:1). Similarly the entire New Covenant was hidden in Christ in those early days, and known only to the prophets and a few devout persons—not known, of course, as already manifest and present, but revealed as to come later. To take one simple example, brothers and sisters: what was the meaning of that gesture when Abraham, about to send his trusty servant to find a wife for his only son, required the servant to swear to him and, in administering the oath, ordered the servant, *Place your hand under my thigh, and so swear* (Gn 24:2)? What was present in Abraham's thigh, that the servant should have been ordered to place his hand there to take the oath? What else but that posterity promised to Abraham when God said, *In your seed shall all the nations of the earth be blessed* (Gn 22:18)? Now the thigh symbolizes the flesh; and from Abraham's flesh, through Isaac and Jacob and (to shorten the list) Mary, our Lord Jesus Christ was born.

Insertion of a Gentile graft into patriarchal stock

2. How are we to prove that the patriarchs constituted the root? Let us put our question to Paul. He rebuked the Gentiles who had come to believe in Christ, and imagined that their faith gave them the right to despise the Jews who had crucified him. They were forgetting that from the Jewish people proceeded one wall, and from the uncircumcised Gentiles the other wall, and that these two were destined to meet at the corner, that is, in Christ.[4] When these Gentiles behaved arrogantly, then, Paul took them to task: *If you were cut out of the wild olive and engrafted into the Jewish stock,* he says, *do not boast at the expense of the branches. If you are tempted to boast, remember that it is not you who support the root, but the root you* (Rom 11:24.18). He reminds them that some branches were broken from the patriarchal root on account of their unbelief, and that the shoot of wild olive, which is the Church called from the Gentiles, was grafted in to draw on the olive's richness. But who would ever graft a wild olive into the cultivated variety? We usually do it the other way round—the olive into the

---

4. See Eph 2:20.

stock of a wild plant. We never see a wild olive grafted into a cultivated one. Anybody who does that will find no fruit except the wild berries. It is the graft that grows, and the fruit of the graft that we pick; we gather no fruit from the root, only from the scion.

Yet the apostle demonstrates that this was exactly what God had by his almighty power caused to happen: that a wild olive should be inserted into the stock of the true olive, and the graft bear not wild fruit but real olives. The apostle reminds us of God's omnipotence, saying, *If you were cut out of the wild olive and unnaturally grafted into the true olive, do not boast at the expense of the branches. But you maintain, "Those branches have been broken off so that I could be grafted in." Yes, but they were broken off because of their unbelief. You, for your part, stand in faith; be not high-minded, but stand in awe* (Rom 11:24.18-20). What does he mean by *Be not high-minded*? Do not be proud because you were grafted in; rather beware lest you be broken off for unbelief, as they were broken off. *They were broken off because of their unbelief. You, for your part, stand in faith; be not high-minded, but stand in awe*, Paul warns them. *If God did not spare the natural branches, he may not spare you either* (Rom 11:21). Then follows a fine text, one eminently necessary and worthy of our attention: *Look at the kindness and the severity of God: severity indeed toward those who were broken off, but goodness toward you, who were grafted in. Be sure to abide in that goodness; for if you do not, you too will be cut out, whereas they, if they do not persist in their unbelief, will be grafted in again* (Rom 11:22-23).

3. During the period of the Old Covenant, brothers and sisters, the promises God made to that carnal people concerned earthly, temporal matters. They were promised an earthly kingdom; they were promised a land, and were led into it after their deliverance from Egypt; for Joshua, son of Nun,[5] led them into the land of promise, where the earthly Jerusalem was built and David reigned as king. They did indeed receive the land, for after being rescued from Egypt, and crossing the Red Sea, after tramping along all the winding ways[6] and wandering through the wilderness, they were given the land and the kingdom. But after they had been given their kingdom they sinned, because the good things bestowed on them were no more than earthly; and as punishment for their sins they began to suffer attacks, and defeats, and at last captivity. In the end their very city was overthrown.

Such were the provisional promises, promises that were not meant to last, but served as signs of other, future promises that would endure. This whole collapse of temporal promises was itself a sign, a prophecy of what was to come. The

---

5. In Augustine's version "Jesus, son of Nave."
6. Variant: "terrors."

kingdom failed, the kingdom where David ruled—David son of Jesse. When we call him by that title we remember that he was only a man, even if a prophet and a holy man, since he beheld Christ who would come one day, and would indeed be born according to the flesh from David's own line. Still, David was no more than a man; he was not yet the Messiah, not yet our King, the Son of God, but only King David, son of Jesse. His kingdom was doomed to fail, that kingdom for which a carnal people was wont to praise God, since all they cared about was that they had been granted temporal deliverance from their taskmasters, and had escaped from their pursuers through the Red Sea, and had been led through the wilderness, and had found their own country and their kingdom. Only for benefits of this order were they accustomed to praise God, for they did not yet understand what God was foreshadowing and promising through these gifts.

We can see, then, that when these good things failed—the gifts for which a carnal people, David's subjects, were wont to praise God—*the hymns of David failed*. Not those of David, Son of God, but those of David, son of Jesse. So now we have navigated through the title of this psalm, dangerous place though it was, in the way that the Lord willed us to; and you have been instructed as to why the title stated that *the hymns of David, son of Jesse, have failed*.

The title, continued: Asaph, the synagogue, represents believers under the Old Covenant

4. Whose voice is it that speaks in this psalm? Asaph's. But what is Asaph? Those who have translated the Hebrew into Greek and the Greek into Latin for us interpret *Asaph* as "the synagogue." So it is to the voice of the synagogue that we listen here. When you hear the name, "synagogue," do not immediately think of it as something detestable, the people that put the Lord to death. There was a synagogue that killed the Lord; no one doubts that. But remember also that it was from the synagogue that there came the rams, whose children we are. This is why another psalm says, *Bring the offspring of rams to the Lord* (Ps 28(29):1). Who are the rams that came from the synagogue?[7] Peter, John, James, Andrew, Bartholomew, and the rest of the apostles. From the synagogue too came the man who was at first Saul, then Paul; first a proud man, then a humble one. You remember that the earlier Saul, his namesake, had been a proud king, uncontrollable. It was not out of vanity that the apostle changed his name; on the contrary, his change from Saul to Paul was a transition from being proud to being cut down to size, for "Paul" means "small." Shall I remind you what he was like as Saul? Listen to Paul recalling what he had been through his own malice, and what he was now through God's grace; listen to how he had been Saul, and how he was

---

7. On the apostles as rams, leaders of the flock, see Augustine's Exposition of Psalm 64, 18.

now Paul. *I was originally a persecutor and a blasphemer, and harmed people* (1 Tm 1:13), he says. You have heard about Saul; now listen to Paul: *I am the least of the apostles*. What does he mean by saying that he is the least, if not, "I am just Paul"? He continues, *I am not worthy to be called an apostle*. Why not? "Because I was Saul." What does that mean—"I was Saul"? Let him tell us: *Because I persecuted God's Church*, he says. *But by God's grace I am what I am* (1 Cor 15:9-10). He has renounced all his towering stature. Now he is very small in himself, though great in Christ.

And what does Paul teach us? That *God has not cast off his people*, the people sprung from Jewish origins. *God has not cast off his own people, whom he foreknew. For I am myself sprung from the race of Israel, from the stock of Abraham, and the tribe of Benjamin* (Rom 11:2.1). So Paul came to us from the synagogue; Peter and the other apostles came from the synagogue. When you hear the name, "synagogue," think not of what it deserved, but of the children it brought to birth.

In this psalm, then, the synagogue is speaking. The hymns of David, son of Jesse, have failed, as the temporal goods for which a carnal people used to praise God have failed. But why did they fail? So that other blessings might be looked for. What other blessings? Blessings in no way present as yet? No: blessings present but hidden under prophetic types; blessings not entirely absent, but concealed there in the root under mysterious signs. What are they? These things are symbols for us, says the apostle.[8]

The prophetic value of Israel's experiences

5. Now consider briefly how these things have symbolic import for us. The Israelite people dominated by Pharaoh and the Egyptians represents the Christian people which, before it came to faith, was indeed predestined for God, but still served demons and the devil, prince of demons. It was a people under the Egyptian yoke and enslaved to its sins, for the devil has no way of gaining control over us other than through our sins. The Israelites are freed from the Egyptians through Moses; the Christian people is freed from its former life of sin through our Lord Jesus Christ. The one people makes its passover through the Red Sea, the other through baptism. All the enemies of the former people die in the Red Sea; all our sins die in baptism. But notice this point, brothers and sisters: after crossing the Red Sea the Israelites are not given their homeland immediately, nor are they allowed carefree triumph, as though all their foes had disappeared. They still have to face the loneliness of the desert, and enemies still lurk along their way; so too after baptism Christian life must still confront temp-

---

8. See 1 Cor 10:6.

tations. In that wilderness the Israelites sighed after their promised homeland; and what else do Christians sigh for, once washed clean in baptism? Do they already reign with Christ? No; we have not reached our homeland yet, but it will not vanish; the hymns of David will not fail there.

Let all the faithful listen and mark this; let them realize where they are. They are in the desert, sighing for their homeland. Our foes died when we were baptized, but those were the enemies who pursued us from the rear. What do I mean by that—enemies who pursued from the rear? I mean that what we have in front of us is the future; the past is behind. All our past sins were blotted out in baptism. The things that tempt us now are not pursuing from behind, but lying in ambush along our path. This is why the apostle, still on this desert trek himself, declared, *Forgetting what lies behind and straining to what lies ahead, I bend my whole effort to follow after the prize of God's heavenly call* (Phil 3:13-14), which is another way of saying, "The country of God's heavenly promise." Though it all happened so long ago, brothers and sisters, whatever that people endured in the wilderness, whatever God lavished upon it, whatever the chastisements and whatever the gifts, all of them were prophetic types of what we receive for our consolation or suffer for our probation as we walk in Christ through the desert of this life, seeking our homeland. Small wonder, then, that the type which foreshadowed the future should itself pass away. The former people were led all the way to the promised land; but was it a country that would be theirs for ever? If it had been, it would not have been a symbol, but the real thing. No, it was a figure only, for what the people were brought into was something temporal; and if they were led only to a temporal goal, that goal had to fail sooner or later. When it failed, they would be forced to seek another, one that would never fail.

If temporal blessings were all God gave and promised, the happiness of the wicked was scandalous

6. The synagogue consisted, then, of the people in Israel who faithfully worshiped God, but did so for the sake of temporal goods and immediate advantages. They were not like impious people who seek such present goods from demons; clearly the Israelites were in this respect better than the Gentiles, because they did at least seek the good things of the present life and temporal blessings from the one God, who is the creator of all things, both spiritual and corporeal. Devout persons among the Israelites were nonetheless preoccupied with carnal concerns, for the synagogue consisted of people who were good, but good only with regard to this temporal order of things, not of people who were good in a spiritual sense. There were a few of these latter, certainly: spiritual persons like the prophets, a few who understood about a heavenly kingdom that would last for all eternity. But for the most part the synagogue kept its thoughts

fixed on what it had received from God, and what God had promised to his people: namely, an amplitude of earthly goods, a homeland, peace, and happiness in this world. Yet all these things were fraught with symbolic meaning, and the people did not understand what lay hidden under these signs. They thought these were the greatest things God had to give, and could not imagine that he reserved better gifts for those who love him and serve him. So Israelites concentrated on immediate rewards, and observed that there were sinners, impious people, blasphemers, demon-worshipers, children of the devil, who lived in wickedness and pride, yet had plenty of worldly and temporal goods. And it was precisely with an eye to such benefits that the synagogue itself paid cult to God. So a very pernicious thought arose in the heart of the synagogue, one which sent its feet slithering and all but slipping off God's path.

Now that thought, understandably, occurred to people under the Old Covenant. But how I wish it were not found even today in our carnally-minded brothers and sisters—today, when the happiness brought us by the New Covenant is openly proclaimed! What did the synagogue say, long ago? What did the earlier people say? "We serve God, yet we are rebuked and chastised. The things we loved, the things we prized so highly as God's gifts, are taken away from us. Yet those wicked, guilt-laden folk, proud, blasphemous, turbulent people, are awash with all the good things for which we serve God! There does not seem to be any point in serving him."

These are the sentiments expressed in our psalm, which is the protest of a people fainting and staggering. When it considers that the goods for which it was accustomed to serve God are available in abundance to others who do not serve him, it totters and almost falls. It fails, along with the hymns we spoke about, because hymns were bound to fail in hearts so troubled. Why should that be so? Because while they were entertaining such thoughts, they were not praising God. How could they praise God when they believed that he was acting perversely, in giving so much prosperity to the faithless while refusing it to those who served him? To their way of thinking God did not seem good, and those who did not consider God to be good would certainly not praise him. And when they stopped praising God, hymns fell silent as far as they were concerned.

Later on, however, they came to understand. When God withdrew temporal goods from his servants, yet bestowed them on his enemies, on blasphemous and unbelieving sinners, he meant to teach his servants to seek something different. They came to understand that besides all those things that he gives to the good and the wicked, and sometimes takes away from both good and wicked, there is something else that he reserves for the good alone. What does he reserve for good people? What does he keep for them? Himself.

Now, as I see it, we have launched into the psalm: in the name of the Lord we have already grasped what it is about. Listen to the plaint of one who had gone astray by thinking that God cannot be good, because he gives earthly goods to bad people, and takes them away from his own servants. Listen to this speaker remembering his error and repenting. He came to understand what God was keeping for his faithful ones all the while; and so he changed his mind, he castigated himself, and burst out. . . .

Verse 1. Rectitude of heart and clarity of sight

7. *How good God is to Israel!* But to whom in Israel? *To those of straightforward hearts.* What is he to the perverse of heart? He seems perverse to them. A similar idea is expressed in another psalm: *With a holy person you will be holy, and with the innocent you will be innocent; but with the perverse you will deal perversely* (Ps 17:26-27(18:25-26)). What can it mean by saying, *You will deal perversely with the perverse?* It means that a crooked, perverse person will see God as perverse. Not that God can in any way be perverted: perish the thought! He is what he is. But it is like the effect of sunshine. The sun seems soothing to one whose eyes are clear, healthy, vigorous and strong, but on inflamed eyes sunlight strikes like sharp darts. Sunlight invigorates the one observer and tortures the other, yet the sun is unchanged; the change is in the beholder.[9] So when you begin to be crooked yourself, God will seem crooked to you; but it is you who have changed, not God. What brings joy to good people will be painful to you. This is what the psalmist experienced, what prompted him to exclaim, *How good God is to Israel, to those of straightforward hearts!*

Verses 2-3. The psalmist totters

8. But how is it with you? *My feet had all but slipped.* And when did your feet begin to slip? "When my heart was not straightforward." In what sense was it not straightforward? "Listen, and I will tell you: *my steps had very nearly slid out of control.*" He has repeated the thought: *all but* becomes *very nearly*; and *my feet had all but slipped* is echoed by *my steps nearly slid out of control.* So his feet were slipping, his steps slithering wide; but why? His feet slipped, causing him to miss the path, and his steps went out of control, not to the point where he fell headlong, but very nearly. What exactly did happen? "I was beginning to go astray, but had not fully done so; I was on the point of falling, but had not quite fallen."

9. Why was that? "*Because I envied sinners, seeing the peace that sinners enjoy.* I studied their situation, and I saw that sinners had peace. What kind of peace? A peace that is temporal, fleeting, transient and earthly; yes, but that was just what I too longed to get from God. I saw that people who were not serving

---

9. Variant: ". . . but it changes the beholder."

God enjoyed what I longed to have on condition that I served God, and so *my feet had all but slipped* and *my steps very nearly slid out of control."*

Verses 4-6. Temporal prosperity but eternal punishment for the wicked

10. He now tells us briefly why sinners enjoy peace at present: *There is for them no avoidance of death, and their scourging will be inexorable. But they have no part in the hardships of mortals, and will not be scourged as others are.* "Already I understand why they enjoy peace and flourish on earth," he says. For them death is unavoidable; that is to say, certain and eternal death awaits them. They will no more be able to dodge it than it will turn aside from them. *There is for them no avoidance of death, and their scourging will be inexorable.* Over the punishment reserved for them stands an immovable decree; their scourging is to be no temporal chastisement but one that will last for ever.

If such woes await them in the future, is there any compensation in the present? Yes, for *they have no part in the hardships of mortals, and will not be scourged as others are.* No indeed, for the devil himself is not chastised along with human beings, is he? Yet for him eternal punishment is being prepared.

11. How do they react, then, these people who are spared at present the afflictions and labors others undergo? *Therefore pride has taken possession of them,* says the psalm. Watch these proud, insubordinate folk, and see them as a bull marked out for sacrifice, allowed to wander freely and do as much damage as he likes until the day of slaughter. Yes, brothers and sisters, it is a good thing for us to hear in the prophet's words an evocation of the bull I have mentioned. Scripture uses the same image elsewhere, likening sinners to victims destined for slaughter, and permitted an ominous freedom meanwhile.[10] *Therefore pride has taken possession of them,* says the psalm. What does it mean when it says that *pride has taken possession of them? They are entirely enveloped in their iniquity and impiety.* It does not say they are covered, but that they are *entirely enveloped;* every inch of them is contaminated by their impiety. Small wonder that these wretched folk can neither see nor be properly seen. So enveloped are they that the character of their inner life cannot be discerned. If anyone were able to inspect the inmost character of these bad people who seem to be so fortunate in the present life, such an observer would see the grim state of their consciences; anyone who could see into their souls would see how fiercely those souls are buffeted by the storms of desire and fear. The discerning observer would therefore recognize that such people are miserable, even though they are reputed to be happy. But because they *are entirely enveloped in their iniquity and impiety* they neither see nor are seen. The Spirit who inspired these words had the measure of

10. Compare Prv 7:22.

such people; and we must regard them with the insight that is possible for us when the blindfold of impiety is lifted from our eyes. Let us look hard at them. When they are fortunate, let us steer clear of them; when they are fortunate, let us not imitate them. And let us not set our dearest hopes on getting from our God the kind of favors that people who do not serve him have deserved to receive. He is keeping something else in reserve, something that we must long for. Listen now to what this is.

Verse 7. Wealth, pride, and implicit denial of the human condition

12. First of all, let us have a description of them. *Their iniquity will leak out as though from folds of fat.* You can recognize the bull in that, can't you? Listen carefully, brothers and sisters; we certainly must not pass too hastily over these words, *their iniquity will leak out as though from folds of fat.* There are some people who are bad, but bad out of inadequacy. They are bad because they are deprived, because they are exiles, unimportant, laboring under some kind of need. Bad they are, yes, and reprehensible, for it is better to put up with any straitened circumstances than to commit iniquity. All the same, it is one thing to sin out of need, and quite another to sin amid abundance. A poor beggar steals: his iniquity proceeds from his penury. But what of a rich man, lapped in luxury: why does he seize other people's things? The iniquity of the former issues from his meager condition, that of the latter from his obesity. If you say to the destitute thief, "Why did you do it?" he replies, all humble and woebegone and abject, "I was forced into it by my need." But why did you not fear God? "Poverty drove me to it." You say to the rich person, "Why did you do that? Had you no fear of God?"—though in practice you may not be important enough to say anything of the kind. However, if the rich person does deign to listen, see whether the iniquity that oozes out of his folds of fat does not wash over you as well. Such people declare war on all who instruct or rebuke them. They become enemies to all who speak the truth, because they are used to being cosseted by the words of flatterers; they are tender of ear, because unsound of heart. So who dare say to a wealthy person, "You did wrong in seizing the property of others"? But even supposing that someone does say it, someone of such stature that the accused cannot reject the question, what will the answer be? A rich person's reply will be entirely contemptuous of God. Why? Because such a person is proud. Proud about what? About being plump and fat. Why so? Because that is the sleek condition of one destined for sacrifice. *Their iniquity will leak out as though from folds of fat.*

13. *They have crossed over into a certain attitude of heart.* Within themselves they have crossed a boundary. What does *they have crossed over* suggest? They have gone off the path. *Crossed over*—in what sense? They have gone beyond

the bounds assigned to the human race, they think they are not like other mortals. Yes, I tell you, they have violated the boundaries appointed to humans. You should say to a person of this type, "That poor beggar is your brother or sister. You both descend from the same ancestors, Adam and Eve. Forget your swollen status, forget your high and mighty pride. Although you are surrounded by a vast household, although your gold and silver are plentiful, although you live in a marble house and beneath a paneled roof, you[11] and the poor person are sheltered alike under the one roof of the sky. You are distinguished from the poor man by things that are not truly yours, but only added on from the outside; have regard to yourself, surrounded as you are by them, and not to them as though they were the reality of yourself. Turn your gaze on yourself, and on what you are in relation to that poor person—on yourself, not your possessions. How can you despise your brother? You and he were alike naked in the wombs of your mothers. And when both of you depart this life, when you have breathed forth your souls and your flesh has rotted, let anyone try then to tell the bones of rich and poor apart!"

What I am speaking of is the human condition common to all, the common lot of mortals into which all are born. Here on earth a person may be rich or poor, but it will not always be so. As the rich person did not come rich into the world, neither will he be rich when he leaves it. They both come into the world in the same way, and they will not be distinguished by their departure.

Don't forget that the two of you can change places. The gospel is preached everywhere today, so each of you wealthy folk can recall a certain poor, ulcer-ridden man who used to lie at a rich man's gate, longing to be filled with the crumbs that fell from the rich man's table.[12] Now remember someone else, someone like yourself,[13] who was habitually clothed in purple and fine linen, and accustomed to feast sumptuously every day. Eventually the poor man died, and was carried by angels to Abraham's embrace. The rich man also died, and was buried (perhaps no one had bothered to arrange a funeral for the poor man). When the rich man was in torments below, did he not lift his eyes and behold a man now in unlimited joy, the very man whom he had formerly scorned outside his gate? Did he not beg for a drop of water from the finger of someone who had begged for the crumbs that fell from that opulent table?

Think about it, brothers and sisters. How much hardship had the poor man endured? How long had the rich man's luxury lasted? Not long; but the fates that had befallen them were fixed for ever. In the one case the rich man had no means of avoiding death, and now he was to be scourged inexorably, for he had had no part in the hardships of mortals, nor had he been scourged as others are. The

---

11. Plural, but some witnesses have the singular.
12. See Lk 16:19-31.
13. *Parem tuum.* Some codices have *patrem tuum*: "Remember your own father, who. . . ."

other man had been scourged here, but found rest in the world beyond, for God whips every child whom he acknowledges as his.[14]

"To whom do you address this reminder?" you ask.[15] To anyone who feasts sumptuously and goes clad daily in purple and fine linen. "To whom are you speaking?" To one who has crossed over *into a certain attitude of heart.* Such a person may well say, *Send Lazarus; let him at least warn my brothers,*[16] but for himself it will be too late; the time accorded him for fruitful repentance has passed. Or, rather, it is not that space for repentance is denied him, but that there will be everlasting repentance and no salvation to follow it. These people *have crossed over into a certain attitude of heart.*[17]

Verses 8-9. Arrogant speech, lofty plans

14. *They thought and spoke maliciously.* Some people speak maliciously, though with cautious restraint; but how did these folk speak? *They shouted their iniquity.* They were not content with wicked talk; they proclaimed it at the top of their voices, proudly, in the hearing of all. "Look what I'm doing! I'll show you! You will find out whom you have to deal with. I won't leave you alive!" If only they would confine themselves to thinking like this, without blurting it out too! If only their baleful greed were penned within the confines of thought, if only such a person could rein it in within his mind! But why should he? Is he a poor, skinny little man? No; *their iniquity will leak out as though from folds of fat. They shouted their iniquity.*

15. *Their boastful talk is directed to the sky, and their tongues have soared above the earth.* What does *soared above the earth* mean? The same thing as *talk directed to the sky,* for to *soar above the earth* is to put oneself above earthly realities. How would anyone do such a thing? It happens when people speak without remembering that they are human and may die suddenly; they utter threats as though expecting to live for ever. Their lofty plans outstrip their earthly frailty, and they take no account of the mortality that clothes them. Failing to understand what scripture says elsewhere of people like themselves—*his spirit will go forth and return to its own country, and on that day all his plans will come to nothing* (Ps 145(146):4)—they do not remember their last day, and talk proudly. Their boastful words are flung up to the sky, and soar above the earth. If a robber held in prison were unmindful of his last day—the

---

14. See Heb 12:6.
15. This and the following question could be from members of the congregation who found Augustine's remarks disquieting.
16. See Lk 16:27-28.
17. As Augustine considered it earlier in this section, the "crossing over" was an interior event occurring in the present life; but now he seems to be thinking also of the "great gulf" separating Lazarus from the rich man in the world to come.

day, that is, which will see him judged—nothing would seem more monstrous than he. Yet he might still have the possibility of escape. Where will you flee to escape death? Your judgment day is absolutely certain. Why promise yourself a long life? Can anything that comes to an end truly be long? But in any case human life is not long, and even if reckoned long it is precarious. Why does a proud person not consider this? Because his boastful talk is directed to the sky, and his tongue has soared above the earth.

Verse 10. Glimmerings of truth: the passage to understanding begins

16. *Therefore shall my people come back here.* Already Asaph is coming back, after considering how wealthy are the wicked and the proud. He is coming back to God; he is beginning to inquire and argue. But when does this occur? When *full days will be found in them.* What are these *full days? When the fullness of time had come, God sent his Son* (Gal 4:4). The fullness of time it was when he came to teach us to make light of temporal things, not to rate over-highly what bad people crave, and to bear courageously what bad people fear. He became our Way. He recalled us to our deepest convictions, and advised us as to what we should seek from God. Look at the transition that this entails: a crossing over to preference for what is real, away from the attitude of mind that is constantly beating back on itself and calling back the flood of its own desires. *Therefore shall my people come back here, and full days will be found in them.*

Verses 11-14. Does God not know? Is innocence pointless?

17. *And they said, How does God know? Is there any knowledge in the Most High?* Now we get an example of the kind of thinking they pass through: "Look how well off the ungodly are! Obviously God does not care about human affairs. Is he really aware of what we do?" Consider what is being said, brothers and sisters; and, we beg you, do not let Christians ever ask, *How does God know? Is there any knowledge in the Most High?*

18. Why does it seem to you that God does not know, and that there is no knowledge on the part of the Most High? The doubter replies, "*Look, they are sinners, yet they have won abundant wealth in this world.*[18] They are sinners, yet they have gained ample wealth in this world!" So the speaker has confessed that he refrained from sin only because he hoped for riches. A carnal soul had traded its righteousness for visible, earthly things. What kind of righteousness is that, if

---

18. The Latin could equally well be translated, "Look how sinners, and those who abound in this world, have won their wealth"; both the Hebrew original and the Greek Septuagint have this sense. But Augustine seems to take *abundantes* as qualifying *divitias*, as his following sentence shows.

it is preserved only for the sake of money? He is almost rating gold above righ-teousness, or assuming that when someone swindles another, the person whose property is unlawfully withheld suffers more harm than the one who withholds it. Not so; for though the one loses a garment,[19] the other loses honesty and good faith. "*Look, they are sinners, yet they have won abundant wealth in this world.* So that proves that God knows nothing about it, and the Most High has no knowledge of the matter!"

19. "*So I said, To no purpose have I justified my heart.* If I serve God, and have to go without wealth, while those who do not serve him have plenty, it means that *to no purpose have I justified my heart, and washed my hands in inno-cence.*[20] What I did is pointless. Where is the reward for my good life? What wages do I get for my service? I live virtuously, and I am in need, while a godless person has plenty. *I have washed my hands in innocence.*"

20. "*All day long I have been chastised.* God's whips do not spare me, I give him good service, and I am whipped; that other fellow gives him no service at all, and is highly honored." This is a hard question that he has set himself. His soul is perplexed; but it is a soul destined to make the passage to a state where it will despise earthly things and long for those of eternity, and here we see something of that passover. The searching inquiry is itself the passage; the soul is tossed by storms but sure of reaching harbor. People who are seriously ill often seem calmer when their cure is very distant, but when they are nearly well their fever rises. Doctors call this the critical onset through which the patient progresses toward health;[21] the fever is more intense, but the direction is toward recovery; the patient's temperature is up, but cool refreshment is not far away. The psalmist too is in a fevered condition, for these are dangerous words, my brothers and sisters, almost blasphemous: *How does God know?* But the ques-tion has something tentative about it, like his earlier words, *all but.* He stops short of declaring, "God does not know," or "There is no knowledge in the Most High"; he is seeking the truth, hesitant and doubtful. It was the same earlier, when he said, *My feet had all but slipped.* Now he asks, *How does God know? Is there any knowledge in the Most High?* He does not give a negative answer, but his doubting is itself dangerous.

Yet through this peril he makes his passage to health. Listen now to the healing: *To no purpose have I justified my heart, and washed my hands among the innocent. All day long I have been chastised, and sharp reproof comes to me early in the morning.* Sharp reproof implies correction, for anyone subjected to it is put straight. What does *early in the morning* suggest? It is not long delayed.

---

19. Perhaps Ex 22:26-27 is in mind.
20. Variant: "among the innocent."
21. Augustine comments on this phenomenon in his own progress toward spiritual healing; compare his *Confessions* VI,1,1.

For the godless, correction is delayed. Mine is not; but for them correction comes late, if at all, whereas for me it comes *early in the morning. All day long I have been chastised, and sharp reproof comes to me early in the morning.*

Verse 15. The doubter confronts tradition

21. *When I kept saying, That will be my story. . . .* Or, in other words, "That is what I will teach. . . ." What are you going to teach? That there is no knowledge in the Most High? That God is unaware of what goes on? Will this be the position you adopt: that those who live righteously do so to no purpose, that the just have wasted their service, that God either favors the wicked or does not care about anyone? Will you say this, will this be your story?

No, he checks himself, because authority restrains him. What authority? Sometimes a person does feel inclined to burst out into such complaints, but is brought back to his senses by the scriptures, which teach us that we must always live in accordance with right reason, that God does concern himself with human affairs, and that he does distinguish between the devout and the godless. This is why the speaker here, tempted to take that skeptical line, recalls himself to a better mind. What does he say? "*When I kept saying, That will be my story, why, then, I condemned the long line of your children.* I shall have turned my back on the whole race of your children if I talk in that fashion; I shall be condemning the long line of the just. Some codices have the reading, *Why, then, with whom in the long line of your children will I have been in harmony?*[22] With which of your children have I been in tune? With whom have I agreed," he means, "to which of them have I adjusted myself? I am out of tune with all of them, if I teach in that way. Only someone who keeps the tune is in harmony with others; anyone who loses the tune is out of harmony. Am I to contradict what Abraham said, what Isaac said, what Jacob said, what the prophets said? All of them asserted that God does concern himself with human affairs; am I to say that he does not? Am I wiser than they were? Is my mind more penetrating than theirs? A very wholesome authority it is that has pulled my thoughts back from such impiety."

Verses 16-17. Understanding dawns

22. What comes next? *When I kept saying, That will be my story, why, then, I condemned the long line of your children.* What did he do, in order to avoid condemning them? *I tried to solve the problem.* He has begun to understand, and may God be with him, to enable him to understand more fully. Already, though, brothers and sisters, he is being plucked back from what would have been a grievous fall, because he no longer takes it for granted that he knows the answer;

---

22. *Ecce generationis filiorum tuorum cui concinui,* but there are variants.

he has begun to realize that he does not know. Until this moment he wanted to seem knowledgeable, and to proclaim that God took no interest in the affairs of human beings. A very wicked and impious doctrine of this kind has been propounded, as you know, brothers and sisters. You must recognize that many people do argue like this, saying that God takes no interest in what happens to mortals, because everything is ruled by chance, or because our wills are controlled by the stars, since each of us is prompted to action not by any merit in ourselves but by astral influences.[23] This is an evil doctrine, thoroughly impious. The psalmist was sliding toward it, he who confessed, *My feet had all but slipped. My steps had very nearly slid out of control.* He was on the brink of that error, but he began to perceive that he was out of tune with the tradition perpetuated among God's children, so he repudiated the knowledge that put him out of harmony with the righteous who belong to God.

Let us listen to what he says, because he began to understand, and received help, and learned something, and explained it to us. *I tried to solve the problem,* he says, *but it is too hard for me.* It is a mighty task indeed, to understand how God takes care of human destinies, why things go well for bad people and why the good have such a hard time. A daunting question, certainly! This is why he says, *"It is too hard for me.* I might as well be up against a brick wall!" But you have the assurance of another psalm, *In my God I shall leap over the wall* (Ps 17:30(18:29)). No, *it is too hard for me.*

23. You are right to say that it is too hard for you, but it is not too hard for God. Put yourself in the presence of God, for whom it is not too hard, and then it will not be too hard for you either. This is what he did, for he tells us how long the question continues to be too hard: *until I enter God's holy place, and understand what the final outcome must be.* This is all-important, sisters and brothers. "I have been struggling with the problem for a long time," he says. "In front of me I see what looks like an insoluble difficulty: I am trying to understand how God can be just, and concerned about human conditions, and how he is not unjust even though sinners and criminals enjoy prosperity on this earth, while loyal believers and people who serve God are so often worn out with trials and hardships. I find it extremely difficult to solve the problem, but only *until I enter God's holy place."* What is given you in God's sanctuary, then, to help you solve it? "What I understand there," he replies, "is not the present state of affairs, but *what the final outcome must be.* From God's holy place I turn my gaze towards the end, passing over the present." All this crowd that we call the human race, all this mass of mortal creatures, will come to judgment; it will be brought to the scales where all human deeds will be weighed. A cloud envelops everything

---

23. Augustine discusses the denial of providence by astrologers and others in his Exposition 2 of Psalm 31, 16.18.25. He alludes briefly to the Priscillianists as holding similar views in *Heresies* 70; and in Letter 166, 7.

now, but the merits of every single person are known to God. *"I understand what the final outcome must be,"* he says, "but not by my own efforts, for the problem is too hard for me. How can I understand *what the final outcome must be?* Let me go into God's sanctuary." In that place he understood the reason why malefactors are happy in the present life.

Verses 18-19. Fraudsters defrauded

24. *It is because of their guile that you conferred these things upon them.* Because they are full of guile—in other words, fraudulent—because they are full of guile, they are themselves beguiled. What do I mean when I say that because they are frauds, they are themselves defrauded? By all their wicked deeds they attempt to commit fraud against the human race, but they are defrauded themselves in that they choose earthly goods, leaving aside those which are eternal. So it can truly be said, brothers and sisters, that in their very trickery they are tricked. As I asked some time ago, my friends, what kind of heart must a person have who forfeits honesty[24] to gain a garment? Which party has been cheated—the person whose garment was taken, or the one who has lost integrity? If a garment is really more precious than good faith, the former has lost more heavily; but if good faith is worth incomparably more than the whole world, the case looks different. The one will be seen to have lost a cloak, but the other will be asked, *What advantage is it to anyone to gain even the whole world, and suffer the ruin of his own soul?* (Mt 16:26).

What happens to them? *It is because of their guile that you conferred these things upon them; you threw them down even as they were lifting themselves up.* The psalmist did not say, "You threw them down because they lifted themselves up," as though they had been lifted up first and thrown down afterward. It was in the very moment and by the very fact of lifting themselves up that they were cast down. To be lifted up like that[25] is already to fall. *You threw them down even as they were lifting themselves up.*

25. *How suddenly they have been desolated!* He can marvel at their fate, because he understands what the outcome must be. *They have faded away*: smoke fades as it rises higher, and so too have they faded. How can he declare that *they have faded away?* Because he speaks as one who understands what the final outcome must be. *They have faded away, they have perished because of their iniquity.*

---

24. *Fidem*, but wider in meaning than "faith" here.
25. *Sic efferri*. Probably as translated above; but the verb *effero* can also mean "to carry out," as a corpse is carried out for burial, so there could be an Augustinian pun here.

Verse 20. Worldly prosperity is only a dream

26. *Like the dream of one who awakens.* How did they fade away? As a dream fades when the dreamer wakes up. Take the case of a person who dreams that he has discovered some treasure. He is rich—but only until he wakes. So have the proud faded away, *like the dream of one who awakens.* The dreamer looks for his wealth, and it is not there: nothing in his hands, nothing in his bed. He had fallen asleep a poor man; in his dreams he became a rich man, and if he had not woken up he would still be rich. But he did wake up, and he found again the penury he had escaped from in his sleep. These arrogant folk too will find the misery they have earned for themselves. When they have awakened from this life everything they possessed here will be like dream-wealth; it will pass away *like the dream of one who awakens.*

The psalmist seems to think that someone may object, "What? Does their present status seem trifling to you, does their pomp seem a trivial thing? Do you think so dismissively of their titles, their images, the statues erected to them, the praise heaped on them, their queues of hangers-on?" He counters with the statement, *In your city, O Lord, you will reduce their image[26] to nothing.*

That being so, my brothers and sisters, let me speak plainly to you from this place of mine, or any other that gives me the right to speak so (for when we are mingling informally among you, to use such words would seem more like striking you than teaching you).[27] In the name of Christ, then, in the fear of Christ, I beg you: if you do not have these marks of distinction, do not covet them; but to any of you who do have them, I say, do not presume on them. Well, that is what I had to say to you. I am not saying, "You are heading for damnation because you have them." I am saying that you are heading for damnation if you presume on such advantages, if you are puffed up over them, if on account of such things you think yourself important, if because of them you disregard the poor, if you are so dazzled by your vain self-esteem that you forget the human condition common to all. In such a case God is bound to requite the proud at the end, and reduce their image to nothing in his city.

Anyone who is rich should be rich in the way the apostle commends: *Instruct the rich of this world not to be high-minded, nor to put their trust in unreliable wealth, but in the living God, who gives us everything to enjoy in abundance* (1 Tm 6:17). He has demolished the grounds for pride, but he goes on to give the

---

26. Variant: "images."
27. *Quia quando vobis miscemur, magis vos ferimus quam docemus.* It is not entirely clear what this parenthesis means, partly because *ferimus* could be either from *fero* (to carry, lift, support, bear, etc.) or from *ferio* (to strike, knock, smite). If the former, we might translate, "When we are mingling . . . we would rather support you than teach you." If the latter, the sense seems to be as in the translation above; he is saying, "I don't want to be getting at you when we are on friendly, informal terms; but I can properly say these things from my official position."

rich good advice. We might suppose that they object, "We are rich. You forbid us to be proud, and order us not to make ostentatious use of our wealth. What are we to do with it, then?" Is it really so hard for them to find good use for it? The apostle has some suggestions: *Let them be rich in good works, give readily, and share what they have*, he says. And how will that profit them? *Let them use their wealth to lay a good foundation for the future, and so attain true life* (1 Tm 6:18-19). Where are they to make these profitable transactions? In the same place where the psalmist fixed his gaze, as he entered the sanctuary of God.[28] All our rich brothers and sisters must shudder with fear; all who have ample money, gold, silver, household slaves and marks of rank must shudder at the warning we have just heard: *In your city, O Lord, you will reduce their image to nothing*. Is not this a just sentence? Is it not right that God should reduce their image to nothing in his city, when in their own earthly city they have reduced the image of God to nothing? *In your city, O Lord, you will reduce their image to nothing*.

Verses 21-23. The change begins

27. *Because my heart was delighted, my kidneys were changed*. Perhaps he is admitting what tempted him when he says, *Because my heart was delighted, my kidneys were changed*: when those temporal things brought me delight, my emotions[29] were stirred.

But the verse could also be interpreted in this way: *because my heart was delighted* with God, *my kidneys too were changed*; that is, my lustful feelings were transformed and I became chaste all through. *My kidneys were changed*. Listen to how this happened.

28. *"I was brought to nothing, and I knew it not*. I, who now say these things about the wealthy, once coveted similar riches myself. That is why I can say that, at the time when *my steps had very nearly slid out of control, I was brought to nothing*. Moreover, since I too *was brought to nothing, and knew it not*, there is no need to despair of them either, the people against whom I have been speaking."

29. What does he mean by *I knew it not*? He says to God, *I became like a beast in your presence, yet I was always with you*. There is a great difference between him and some others. He became like a beast in his craving for earthly things, and when he was brought to nothing he did not yet know the things of eternity; but he did not abandon his God, for he would not seek those worldly things from demons or from the devil. I have reminded you already that the synagogue is speaking here, the people that refused to offer worship to idols. "I became a

---

28. In other words, in the Church.
29. In the biblical understanding of human nature, the kidneys were regarded as the seat of emotions and affections, the heart as the principle of thought.

beast, surely, by desiring earthly goods from my God, yet from my God I never departed."

Verse 24. The grasp of God

30. "Reduced to beast-like state though I was, I did not abandon my God." And what was the consequence? *You grasped the hand of my right hand.* He does not say, "My right hand," but *the hand of my right hand.* If it is the hand of his right hand, it seems the hand must itself have a hand. *You grasped the hand of my right hand,* to lead me. Why did he speak of a hand? It signifies power. We say that someone has something in hand when we mean that it is within that person's power; so the devil said to God, concerning Job, *Stretch out your hand and touch all his belongings* (Jb 1:11). What did he mean by *stretch out your hand?* "Give me the power," he meant. He called God's power God's hand, as in another passage of scripture it is said that *death and life are in the hands of the tongue* (Prv 18:21). Surely the tongue does not have hands? Why, then, does scripture speak of *the hands of the tongue?* It means, "in the power of the tongue," for *out of your mouth you will be justified, and out of your mouth you will be condemned* (Mt 12:37).

Accordingly "*you grasped the hand of my right hand,* the power of my right hand. What was my right hand? My persistence in staying always with you. To my left hand must I attribute the fact that *I became like a beast in your presence* and that earthly concupiscence was in me; but my right hand was my continuance with you throughout. You grasped the hand of this right hand of mine, which is to say, you directed its power." What power would that be? *He gave them power to become children of God* (Jn 1:12). So the speaker had already begun to be numbered among the children of God, and already belonged to the New Covenant.

Now see how God's grasp of the hand of his right hand was maintained. *You led me by your will.* What is the meaning of *by your will?* Not by any merits of mine. *By your will*—what does it signify? Listen to the apostle answering: he was originally a beast in his desire for earthly goods, and lived in Old Covenant mode. What has he to say about that phase? *I was originally a persecutor and a blasphemer, and harmed people, but I received mercy* (1 Tm 1:13). And what about *by your will? By God's grace I am what I am* (1 Cor 15:10).

And you have taken me up in glory. Which of us can give any account of what that glory was? Who can say? But let us look forward to it, because at the resurrection it will be ours. At the final outcome we shall say, *You have taken me up in glory.*

Verse 25. Longing for God in heaven, purity of desire on earth

31. He began to think about the happiness of heaven, and to reproach himself because he had been a beast in his desire for earthly things, *for what is there for me in heaven, and what else but you have I desired on earth?* he asked. Ah, I know by your exclamations that you have understood! He compared his earthly objectives with the heavenly reward he was destined to receive; he saw what was being reserved for him there. As he pondered on it he caught fire from his contemplation of something beyond all description, something eye has not seen, nor ear heard, nor human heart conceived.[30] And so he did not say, "This happiness" or "that happiness" awaits me in heaven; but he put the question, "*What is there for me in heaven?* What is that Something which is mine in heaven? What is it? How great is it? What is it like? Moreover, since what there is for me in heaven does not pass away, *what else but you have I desired on earth?* You are keeping for me—forgive me; I will say it as best I can; accept my effort and my earnest striving, for I lack the skill to state it clearly—you are keeping for me in heaven imperishable riches, nothing other than yourself. Yet I aspired to get from you on earth what the godless also have, what the wicked have, what villains have: money, gold, silver, gems, servants; what many criminals have, and many disreputable women, and many ignoble men—these things I craved from my God on earth as though they were all that mattered, when all the time God is reserving himself for me in heaven! *What is there for me in heaven?*" He can only point to that ineffable Something. *And what else but you have I desired on earth?*

Verse 26. The chaste heart, at last

32. "*My heart and my flesh have failed; but he is the God of my heart.* This is what is kept for me in heaven: *he is the God of my heart, and God is my portion.*" Take note of this, brothers and sisters. Let us assess our riches, and let the rest of humanity choose the portions it wants. Observe how people are torn apart by their conflicting desires: let some choose to serve in the army, others to practice at law. Let some choose various specialist studies, others trading, others farming; let them claim these avocations for themselves as their own portions out of all human possibilities, but let God's people cry out, *God is my portion.* Nor is he my portion for a time only, but *God is my portion for eternity.* I may possess gold, but even were I to possess it for ever, what would I have? But if I possess God, then even were I not to possess him for ever, how great a good would I have meanwhile! But that is not all: he promises himself to me, and promises that I will have that treasure for eternity. I have so much, and never will

---

30. See 1 Cor 2:9.

there be a time when I have it no longer. What a tremendous happiness this is! *God is my portion.* For how long? *For eternity,* for you can see now how he has loved him and how he has purified his heart.[31] *He is the God of my heart, and God is my portion for eternity.* His heart has become chaste, for now God is loved disinterestedly; the psalmist asks no other reward from God except God. Anyone who begs a different reward from God, and aspires to serve him in order to get it, is rating what he wants to get more highly than the God who, he hopes, will give it. Does this mean that God gives us nothing? Nothing, save himself. God's award is simply God himself. This is what the psalmist loves, this he chooses as his love. If he chooses anything else, his will not be a chaste love. If you distance yourself from the eternal fire you will grow cold, and decay. Do not move away, for that would mean corruption for you; and it would be fornication. The psalmist is on his way back now, already penitent; he is embracing repentance, and saying, *God is my portion.* How intense is his delight in the God he has chosen!

Verses 27-28. Union with God; praise in the new Jerusalem

33. *Lo, those who go far from you will perish.* The one who speaks here did go away from God, but not far away, for though he confesses, *I became like a beast in your presence,* he can still say, *Yet I was always with you.* But others have indeed gone to a far-off place, because not only have they coveted earthly things; they have even begged them from demons or the devil himself. *Those who go far away from you will perish.* What does it mean, to go far away from God? *You have destroyed everyone who leaves you to go a-whoring.* The opposite to such whoring is chaste love. What is chaste love? Already the soul loves its bridegroom, but what does it ask of him, of this bridegroom it loves? Can we suppose that it chooses him in the way women choose sons-in-law, or husbands, for themselves, setting their hearts perhaps on the man's wealth, loving his gold, his estates, his silver treasures, his money and horses and servants, and all the rest? No, far from it. The speaker in our psalm loves the bridegroom alone, and loves him for himself, disinterestedly; for in him we have all things, since all were made through him.[32] *You have destroyed everyone who leaves you to go a-whoring.*

34. But what about you—what are you doing? *My good is to hold fast to God.* In this consists total goodness. Do you want more? I grieve for those who want more. What more can you want, brothers and sisters? When we see God face to face[33] there will be nothing whatever that can be better for us than to hold fast to

---

31. The subject of "has loved" and "has purified" could be either the psalmist or God.
32. See Jn 1:3.
33. See 1 Cor 13:12.

him. But what of the present life? The psalmist answers, "I am speaking as one still on pilgrimage. *My good is to hold fast to God*, certainly; but it is good for me while on my journey *to place in God all my hope*, because the full reality[34] has not come yet for me." As long as you have not held fast to him inseparably, it is in him that you must put your hope. Tossed about, are you? Throw your anchor out ahead and hold fast. If you are not yet clinging to him in face-to-face presence, hold fast through hope.

To place in God all my hope. If you are putting your hope in God, how will you act here? What will your occupation be? Surely to praise him whom you love, and bring others to love him together with you. If you were enamored of a charioteer, would you not pester other people to become your fellow-fans? A charioteer's fan talks about his hero wherever he goes, trying to persuade others to share his passion. Dissolute human beings are loved gratis, yet people expect some reward from God as an incentive to love him! No, love God gratis. And do not begrudge God to anyone. Grab someone else, as many people as you can, everyone you can get hold of. There is room for all of them in God; you cannot set any limits to him. Each of you individually will possess the whole of him, and all of you together will possess him whole and entire.

Do this while you are here on earth, while you are placing your hope in God; for what does the psalmist say next? *That I may proclaim all your praise in the courts of the daughter of Zion*. So you are to proclaim God's praise without restriction, but where will you do that? *In the courts of the daughter of Zion*, because any proclamation of God outside the Church is worthless. It is not enough to extol God and trumpet all his praises; you must proclaim him *in the courts of the daughter of Zion*. Stretch out toward unity. Do not divide God's people, but seize them, pull them together, and make a single whole. I was forgetting that I had talked so long. The psalm is finished now, and from the stench in the building I surmise that I have given you rather a long sermon. But I can never keep up with your eager demands; you are extremely violent with me. I only wish you would be just as violent in seizing the kingdom of heaven.[35]

---

34. *Res*.
35. See Mt 11:12.

Index of Scripture

(prepared by Michael Dolan)

(The numbers after the scriptural reference refer to the section of the work)

Old Testament

Genesis

1:5	I, 70, 16
1:8	67, 11
1:22	66, 9
1:26	II, 70, 6
1:28	66, 9
2:17	52, 4; II, 68, 11
2:24	II, 68, 1; 71, 17
3:4	52, 4
3:5	I, 68, 9; II, 70, 6
3:19	71, 12
12:3	54, 21
17:7	67, 19
22:12	I, 58, 9
22:18	71, 19; 72, 1
24:2	72, 1
25:23	57, 5; 61, 7
26:4	54, 21
49:8	59, 10

Deuteronomy

13:3	52, 5
21:23	II, 58, 5

1 Samuel

23:19	53, 1

2 Kings

4:29	I, 70, 19

Tobit

4:16	57, 1

Job

1:9	55, 20; 71, 7
1:11	72, 30
1:21	53, 3; 55, 19; II, 68, 15; I, 70, 14
2:9	I, 70, 14
2:10	55, 20; I, 70, 16
9:24	I, 68, 4
34:30	51, 1

Psalms

1:1	64, 7
1:3	53, 4
2:1	57, 14
2:4	71, 2
2:6-9	I, 58, 1
2:7	60, 8
2:8	60, 2
2:11	51, 13; 65, 5
3:6(5)	56, 11
3:9(8)	69, 6
4:3(2)	61, 23
4:6-7	53, 8
5:5(3)	II, 58, 10
5:13(12)	67, 12
6:8(7)	54, 5; 54, 7
7:9(8)	I, 70, 4
10:6(11:5)	61, 22
11:7(12:6)	54, 22; 67, 17; 67, 39
12:4(13:3)	62, 4
13:5(14:4-5)	55, 17
13(14):6	52, 7
15(16):2	65, 19; 69, 7
15:4(16:3)	II, 58, 8
16(17):8	67, 21
17(18):1	51, 2
17:26-27 (18:25-26)	72, 7
17:29(18:28)	52, 5; 65, 19; 66, 4; 69, 7

1:25	59, 9; I, 68, 10
1:26-28	65, 4
1:29	65, 4
1:31	51, 7; 67, 23
2:6	64, 15
2:8	65, 5
2:10	52, 5
2:12	52, 5; 71, 3
3:1	64, 15
3:1.4	66, 6
3:6-7	66, 1
3:9	66, 1
3:17	67, 33
4:5	55, 9
4:7	51, 17; 55, 7; II, 58, 11; 67, 21; 69, 5; I, 70, 1; I, 70, 4; I, 70, 20
8:2	69, 8
9:9	65, 20
9:25	57, 7
9:26	57, 7
10:4	55, 1; 60, 3
10:11	61, 8; 64, 1
10:12	51, 13
10:13	61, 20; 69, 5
10:17	II, 68, 6
10:18	67, 43
11:1	71, 5
11:3	57, 10; 64, 7
11:19	54, 22; 67, 39
12:2	65, 21
12:12.29-30.11	67, 16
12:27	I, 58, 2; 67, 25
12:29-30.11	67, 21
12:31	71, 18
13:1-3	54, 19
13:3	59, 9; 71, 3
13:4	71, 3
15:9	I, 70, 1
15:9-10	67, 12; 72, 4
15:10	66, 1; 67, 23; 72, 30
15:19	57, 10
15:21-22	I, 68, 2
15:22	61, 7; I, 70, 2; 71, 1
15:23-24	67, 24
15:26	64, 4; 67, 44; 71, 1; 71, 10
15:32	52, 3; I, 70, 9
15:43	67, 44
15:46	61, 7; II, 70, 1
15:47-49	I, 70, 2
15:51	57, 20
15:51-55	64, 4
15:54	65, 18
15:55	51, 1

2 Corinthians

1:9	64, 10
1:12	53, 8
1:20	71, 18
3:6	I, 70, 19
3:7	64, 6
3:15	64, 6
3:16	64, 6
4:18	57, 10
5:4	I, 68, 3
5:6	64, 1
5:15	55, 14
5:17	66, 6
5:17-20	71, 6
5:19	59, 8; 67, 23
5:20	67, 40
5:21	67, 23
6:10	67, 24
7:5	55, 6
8:9	I, 68, 4
9:7	62, 14
10:3	64, 3
11:26	55, 9
11:29	54, 8; 55, 6; 69, 2
12:7-10	II, 58, 5
12:8-9	53, 5
12:9	57, 16; 67, 12
12:10	57, 16; I, 58, 7; I, 70, 11; I, 70, 14
13:4	53, 4; 65, 6; 66, 5

Galatians

1:8	71, 5
2:20	65, 7; I, 68, 10
3:13	II, 58, 5
3:15-16	54, 21
3:16	71, 19
3:21	I, 70, 19
3:21-22	I, 70, 19
4:4	72, 16
4:9	62, 9
4:19	52, 1; 57, 5
4:24	67, 11
4:29	67, 12
5:6	67, 41
5:22	71, 18
6:1	51, 13
6:14	67, 23; II, 68, 4; I, 70, 19
6:16	67, 12; 67, 43
6:17	54, 8

Ephesians

2:2-3	67, 27
2:3	57, 20
2:6	55, 3
2:9-10	I, 70, 19
2:14-15.17	71, 1
3:14.17.18-19	51, 12
3:20	69, 8
4:7-10	67, 25
4:10	67, 42

Index

(prepared by Joseph Sprug)

The first number in the Index is the Psalm number.
More than one Exposition is cited by the number in parentheses, for example (2)
The number after the colon is a paragraph number.
Different expositions in the same heading are separated by a semi-colon.
Biblical texts/words are in italics.